D1603520

THE
Commedia dell'Arte
IN PARIS

THE

Commedia dell'Arte

IN PARIS

1644  1697

VIRGINIA SCOTT

UNIVERSITY PRESS OF VIRGINIA
Charlottesville

THE UNIVERSITY PRESS OF VIRGINIA
Copyright 1990 by the Rector and Visitors
of the University of Virginia

First published 1990

Library of Congress Cataloging-in-Publication Data

Scott, Virginia, 1934–
The Commedia dell'arte in Paris, 1644–1697 / Virginia Scott.
p.   cm.
Includes bibliographical references.
ISBN 0-8139-1255-5
1. Comédie-Italienne (Paris, France)—History. 2. Commedia
dell'arte—History. 3. Theater—France—Paris—History—17th
century. I. Title.
PN2636.P4C937   1990   *67835*   89-22520
792'.09443'61—dc20   CIP

Printed in the United States of America

To Peter, Kate, and Sarah

◆◆◆◆◆◆◆◆◆◆◆◆◆◆◆◆◆◆

Contents

	Illustrations	IX
	Acknowledgments	XI
	Introduction	3

Part I: 1644–1659

1.	Debuts in Paris	15
2.	Actors of the 1640s and 1650s	31
3.	The Magician of Fano	52

Part II: 1661–1668

4.	Establishment at Palais-Royal	81
5.	The Second Arlequin	101
6.	The Old Italian Repertory	122

Part III: 1668–1680

7.	From Palais-Royal to the Guénégaud	155
8.	The Stable Company	180
9.	The New Repertory	192

Part IV: 1680–1688

10.	The Hôtel de Bourgogne	223
11.	A Company Rejuvenated	252
12.	The Transitional French Repertory	275

Part V: 1688–1697

13.	Struggle and Expulsion	311

14.   The Terrible Costantinis   332

15.   The Gherardi Repertory   353

        Appendix   391

        Notes   407

        Bibliography   437

        Index   449

Illustrations

1.	Grande Salle of the Petit-Bourbon, 1614	24
2.	Tiberio Fiorilli as Scaramouche, 1700	33
3.	Torelli's design for *La finta pazza*	58
4.	Title page, *Explication des décorations*	62
5.	Auditorium and stage, Grande Salle at Palais-Royal, 1641	88
6.	Plan and section, Grande Salle at Palais-Royal, c. 1673	90
7.	Domenico Biancolelli as Arlequin, c. 1700	106
8.	Girolamo Cei as Capitan Spezzafer	184
9.	Domenico Locatelli as Trivelin	186
10.	Prologue of *Arlequin Protée,* 1683	231
11.	Frontispiece to *Arlequin Protée*	232
12.	The cascades, finale of *Arlequin Jason,* 1684	234
13.	Fracansani as Polichinelle, Turri as Pantalon	259
14.	Final scene of *Arlequin Protée*	261
15.	Guiseppe Tortoriti as Pasquariel	263
16.	Angelo Costantini invested as Arlequin, 1689	312
17.	Evaristo Gherardi as Arlequin	339
18.	Angelo Costantini, second Paris debut, 1729	349
19.	Frontispiece to *Arlequin Phaeton*	368

◇◇◇◇◇◇◇◇◇◇◇◇◇◇◇◇

Acknowledgments

THE SEEDS FOR THIS STUDY were planted many years ago at the University of Iowa, when I undertook a paper on the origins of English pantomime for a seminar in theatre history conducted by Oscar Brownstein, now at Yale. Margaret Hall, then the costume designer for the University Theatre, suggested that I have a look at the frontispieces in Gherardi's *Le théâtre italien,* my first encounter with the commedia dell'arte in Paris. That Gherardi's original edition of 1700 was on the library shelf—in the open stacks—I think was due to Oscar Brockett, who had recently decamped to Indiana, but who had been studying the fair theatres and may have prompted the University Library to do some acquisitions in French popular theatre. So my thanks to all three, and especially to Oscar Brownstein, who said my organization was horrendous but that I might make a historian one day.

My deepest thanks, too, to David Mayer of the University of Manchester, Laurence Senelick of Tufts University, Brooks McNamara of New York University, and Don Wilmeth of Brown University, all of whom have been very helpful and supportive. And to the late Marian Hannah Winter, who wrote notes to French *conservateurs* for me for my first trip to Paris and encouraged me to apply for funding. And to my colleagues in the Department of Theater at the University of Massachusetts: Richard Trousdell, who took time out of a busy week in Milan to look at a painting for me, and June Gaeke, who is happy to go along to France any time.

I learned, with some difficulty, to appreciate the great national libraries and archives of France, where *almost* nothing is ever missing, and especially the Bibliothèque de l'Arsenal, the library around the corner, where I eventually felt at home. I also greatly appreciate the efficiency of the Interlibrary Loan Office of the University of Massachusetts Library, which found every book or article I asked them for—except one. My thanks to Alan Woods of the Ohio State University Theatre Research Institute who had it and sent it.

I owe a deep debt of gratitude to the John Simon Guggenheim Foundation, whose generous support sent me to Paris for eight months, and to the National Endowment for the Humanities, who helped me get back there when I needed to.

Finally, I want to express my appreciation to three Italian women whom I have never met but whose work made it much easier for me to do mine: Stefania Spade, who transcribed and published the manuscript of Gueullette's translation of the zibaldone of Domenico Biancolelli; Guiliana Colajanni, who transcribed and published B. N. Ms. 9329; and Anna Migliori, who transcribed and published a number of very important documents from the Minutier Central relating to the Comédie-Italienne. Without them, I would still be peering at xeroxed copies and microfilms instead of writing these acknowledgments.

The

Commedia dell'Arte

in Paris

1644–1697

◆◇◆◇◆◇◆◇◆◇◆◇◆◇◆◇◆

Introduction

ALTHOUGH THE commedia dell'arte was a theatrical form that originated in Italy, it played an important and often overlooked role in the popular cultural life of France. Beginning in 1571, when the first troupe crossed the Alps to entertain the king of France, his court, and his subjects, the skill, energy, and comic imagination of the Italian improvisers enchanted the French.

Known in its own day as the "commedia degli zanni" (theatre of the buffoons) or the "commedia all'improvviso" (improvised theatre), commedia dell'arte held the stage in Italy and throughout Europe for more than two hundred years. In France, after some ninety years of intermittent performances, a troupe established itself in Paris in 1662 and played there for thirty-five years. A second troupe arrived in 1716 and performed until it was merged with the Opéra-Comique in 1780. The first troupe is the subject of the present study.

This Comédie-Italienne, as the Parisians called it, came to France a conventional troupe playing a traditional repertory. Thirty-five years later, its original members nearly all dead or retired, it also played a French repertory characterized by satire, burlesque, and spectacle. At its beginning a creature of patronage, wholly dependent on the whims of the monarch, it ended a cog in the glory machine of the ancien régime. Yet institutionalization did not save it from that same monarch, who sent "his Italian actors" back to Italy in April 1697.

The troupe that came to France in 1662 was composed in the usual way of lovers, old men, and zanni. This particular company included two male and two female lovers: the First and Second Amoureux and Amoureuses. The old men, or "vieillards," were a Docteur, or pompous pedant, and—possibly—a Pantalon, the Venetian magnifico who left few traces in Paris. The original troupe also included a Capitan, a character derived from the classical miles gloriosus but transformed in late Renaissance Italy to a burlesque of the Spanish conqueror. The zanni, or clowns, were Trivelin, Scaramouche, and Arlequin. First Zanni, the "fourbe intrigant," or clever rascal, was usually Trivelin, sometimes Scaramouche. Second Zanni, the "fourbe balourd," or slow-witted rascal, was always Arlequin.

Arlequin was usually in love with Diamantine, the "servante," who joined enthusiastically in the intrigues of the zanni.

Each of these personages was characterized by a set of fixed verbal and physical behaviors. Lovers courted each other in the rhetorical ruffles and flourishes of the Renaissance. Capitans uttered rodomontades, elaborate tirades in which they boasted of their extraordinary exploits in war and love. Docteurs pronounced pseudolearned harangues in dog Latin. First Zanni explained and Second Zanni misunderstood. First Zanni beat and Second Zanni got beaten. Second Zanni were gluttons and servantes were wonderful cooks, especially of macaroni and Parmesan cheese.

The vieillards and the zanni, often referred to as the "masques," wore traditional costumes and masks, instantly recognizeable and infinitely functional. Most are known to us from the works of Callot, Gillot, and Watteau, as well as from the vast popular iconography of the commedia dell'arte. Pantalon in his tight red doublet and hose, pointed nose and beard thrust out; the Docteur in black, his gown flying, his huge floppy hat nearly hiding his nose mask; the Capitan with his Spanish breeches, sword, and plumed hat—they are still familiar images. Even more familiar are the zanni. First Zanni is in white, with braid down the front and on the seams; he wears a sinister olive brown mask. And Second Zanni—Arlequin—wears patches transformed into diamonds and a black mask with a tightly curled beard and at least one enormous wen. First Zanni carries his guitar, Arlequin his bat, a slapstick with a phallic handle. As for Scaramouche, the "man in black" appears in a tight black doublet and breeches, baggy black beret, white ruff, and above the ruff not a mask but a face painted white, *enfariné,* ornamented with a descending handlebar moustache and a tiny chin whisker. Other zanni joined the troupe later: a Polichinelle with humps before and behind; a Pierrot all in white, his round face gleaming beneath his little round hat; a tiny Mezzetin in red with white stripes.

The amoureux and amoureuses, like all young lovers of the baroque comic stage, wore fabulous, fashionable, expensive clothes. They and the servante played without masks, creating the verisimilar against which the fantastic displayed itself. In the early years of the commedia dell'arte, Pantalon and the Docteur wore costumes appropriate to their conditions or professions, and the zanni, though masked, wore loosely fitted white tunics and trousers, peasant clothes. The three groups—lovers, fathers, and clowns—were less visually disassociated than they were to become later, when the vieillard's clothes were a hundred years out of style and the zanni's costumes colorful abstractions. The lack of visual coherence by the mid-seventeenth century is especially striking and a sign of how conventionalized the commedia dell'arte had become.

The origins of commedia dell'arte are obscure. Although the general course of development of the Italian theater in the Renaissance is known, the commedia, which must be the heir of an oral tradition, seems simply to have come to life or to consciousness in the mid-sixteenth century. It is distinguished from the regular, or legitimate, Italian theatre by several characteristics. It was a theatre of professional actors, whereas the literary Italian theatre, the "commedia erudita," was performed by court functionaries or members of academies. Furthermore, it employed the "tipi fissi" (fixed character types), and it was engendered without written texts, improvised by the performers.

Improvisation was at the heart of the enterprise, although we must not assume that everything said or done onstage each day was spontaneous. What the actors of the commedia dell'arte achieved was the generation of plays without the use of a playwright. The plays were constructed, for the most part, from known elements, verbal and physical. Actors retained a store of amorous arias and dialogues, tirades and harangues, rodomontades, imbroglios, and puns, often recorded in "zibaldoni," or actors' notebooks, while the zanni also hoarded lazzi, standard comic routines featuring beatings, chases, pratfalls, scatology, obscenity, and roguery of all sorts. Like all theatrical companies of the period, commedia dell'arte troupes played a repertory, an accumulation of entertainments, and there is every reason to believe that once a particular piece had been worked out to the satisfaction of all through improvisation, it joined the repertory to be played as finished work. On the other hand, the possibility of improvisation always must have been present in the consciousness of the actors, who no doubt continued to improve on their work with a new joke, an unexpected punch line, or a reference to a local scandal picked up that morning in a tavern. It was improvisation that created the acting style that made the commedia dell'arte famous at home and welcome throughout Europe, a style characterized by energy, concentration, and ensemble play. But it was the use of the tipi fissi that made improvisation possible. The actors brought to the creation of the piece characters whose behavior was known and predictable, characters "accumulated" over the years both by those actors and by their predecessors and contemporaries. Circumstances, events, and relationships could differ from play to play, but the essential personalities of the characters provided a stable foundation.

The tipi fissi, combined with the use of conventional plots, also created an ideal relationship between play and audience. The popular theatre depends on irony, on the probability that the audience is thinking ahead of the characters, able to predict with accuracy the outcome of whatever action is in progress. The play can both fulfill the expectations thus evoked and confound them, in certain agreed-upon and delightful ways.

In Italy most commedia dell'arte troupes were relatively evanescent; that is, although a troupe's name and key personnel might survive for many years, the membership could change yearly. And although a troupe was normally attached to a particular Italian court, it toured for much of the year, returning to home base for carnival. In France, with a more or less fixed company established in Paris for thirty-five years, the relationship of play to audience was even more clearly ironic. The Arlequin of Domenico Biancolelli and the Scaramouche of Tiberio Fiorilli were, like the clowns of the twentieth-century silent film, utterly known quantities; and Biancolelli and Fiorilli, like those clowns, became stars because their characters entered into complicity with the audience, allowing the spectators to become in some sense makers as well as perceivers.

Establishment was at the root of many of the changes that took place in the repertory and production style of the commedia dell'arte in Paris, changes that have been often labeled signs of decadence by those who have written about them. Critics like Allardyce Nicoll and Gustave Attinger have called attention not only to the rise of the star zanni but to the declining importance of the romance plot and the increased use of scenes and machines. For Attinger the end result was "a very curious kind of theatre . . . composed of anomalous elements assembled for the needs of the moment, some the antipodes of the others: a mélange and not a fusion," and he concludes that "the *comédie italienne,* despoiled of its principal literary ornaments and turned completely toward visual expression, loses . . . all hope of taking its place in the world of letters." Nicoll assumes that because the audience in France could not understand the dialogues and dialects of the actors, the troupe turned to scenic spectacle and special effects, disastrously violating the perfect balance achieved in the "classical" commedia dell'arte.

This notion of the commedia dell'arte as a harmonious balance of the serious and the comic, the romantic and the ridiculous, the lovers and the masques seems to arise from the repertory of scenarios published in 1611 by Flaminio Scala and from various eighteenth-century efforts to preserve the form. Scala's collection of scenarios, the oldest and only published collection available, has been granted special authority because

Scala himself was an actor and deviser of entertainments. It consists almost exclusively of neo-Plautine comedies with romance intrigues, similar in structure to the commedia erudita, and it has served as the primary source for our understanding of commedia dell'arte from at least the eighteenth century. It was in that century as well that the writings of Goldoni, Gozzi, and especially Luigi Riccoboni created an idea of the commedia dell'arte that was essentially literary and theoretical, one in which primary value was placed upon the implicit literary text created by the improvising performers.

Out of these eighteenth-century elements has grown a normative definition that has reduced a set of complex and fluid theatrical activities to "an abstraction and a set of norms," as Cesare Molinari suggests in his excellent essay "L'idea di commedia": "An abstraction which seeks to unite different phenomena in one category . . . and a set of norms tending to define the pertinent features and impose them as necessary." Once such a definition is established, it becomes the criterion against which everything is to be judged. Molinari points out that between the middle of the sixteenth century, when the first records of what we now call the commedia dell'arte appear, and the end of the seventeenth century the features we associate with the form were present but not immutable. There could be no commedia degli zanni without zanni, but sometimes there were four or six or only one. Sometimes there were three old men. Or one set of lovers. Troupes played neo-Latin love intrigues but they also played tragicomedies, farces, pastorals, fantasies, and plays based on Spanish models. One play may require only the conventional setting of a street with houses and can be played anywhere; the next needs a mountain that opens and a fire effect. It was in the eighteenth century, argues Molinari, that the commedia dell'arte becomes fixed and "all seems to function perfectly. The masques, reduced to four (Pantalon, Docteur, First and Second Zanni) are counterpointed . . . to the four lovers, the balance is even numerical." The effects of this mode of thought can be seen in statements like Constant Mic's that Evaristo Gherardi's *Le théâtre italien,* a collection of scenes and plays performed in Paris in the late seventeenth century, must be used by historians with extreme prudence, since it can "only give a very false idea of the commedia dell'arte."

Normative definitions are by their nature destined to exclude; the round hole is the original normative definition. The commedia dell'arte in France was, in the view of many critics, a square peg. If the commedia dell'arte must be distinguished not only by its professionalism, its use of masks, its tipi fissi, and its reliance on improvisation, but also by its neo-

Plautine comic structures and staging, its balanced casts and patterned alternation of romantic and farcical elements, and its membership in the literary canon, then the comédie italienne in France was only a remote descendant. If, however, we regard the commedia dell'arte as living and organic, not fixed under glass for eternity, than we will be less concerned with the extent to which any single instance fits a set of predetermined categories, more concerned with describing a phenomenon unimpeded by evaluative assumptions.

Like all living things, the commedia degli zanni changed with time and circumstance. What the Italians performed in Paris in 1662 was different from what they were performing in 1697, when they were dismissed, yet critics see their repertory and style of performance as all of a piece; another set of norms has been imposed. In general, our idea of the repertory has been derived from fairly superficial readings of the collections of materials performed in French after 1681 and published by Evaristo Gherardi, second Arlequin of the troupe, in 1694 and 1700. Like Scala's collection, they have the advantage of having appeared in print. But just as a study of the Italian manuscript sources corrects assumptions derived from Scala about the Italian repertory, so a careful look at French manuscript and other sources reveals that much of what has been said about the comédie italienne is subject to qualification.

It is true that many members of the Paris audience did not understand Italian and that over the span of thirty-five years the Italian improvisers—some of them—learned to memorize and began to perform scenes and some complete plays written in French. Tiberio Fiorelli and Domenico Biancolelli became extremely popular, in part because of the perfection of their physical play. And the troupe did occasionally indulge in spectacular scenes and machines when it had the money. But as late as 1696 the Italian actors continued to improvise complete entertainments in Italian, while throughout the 1690s some plays were set on the street or in a simple interior and required no special effects. The zanni dominated some actions, played a less conspicuous role in others. The tipi fissi changed—sometimes—to conform to French social and theatrical stereotypes; at other times, they remained themselves. Play structure continued to alternate plot scenes and ornamental scenes, although the kinds of ornament changed, while the French taste for satire encouraged the introduction of material ridiculing the bourgeois fathers, coquettes, and *petits marquis* of contemporary Paris. This complex course of development, which began with the company's efforts to appeal to French taste in 1668, cannot be reduced to a few simple assertions and a highly successful, highly theatrical form damned because it reacted with energy and imagination to changing times, tastes, and circumstances, because it de-emphasized the rhetorical ornaments so dear to the departed Renaissance and adopted the baroque flourishes of the age of the Sun King.

The time has come to apply theatrical rather than literary criteria to the study of the commedia dell'arte in Paris in the seventeenth century in order to describe the troupe, its theatres, its repertory, and its perform-ance style. My assumptions, unlike those of my predecessors, are that great performers are treasures, that flying dragons are delights, and that a valet transformed into a streetlight which is about to be shot out by his amorous master is the result of a comic imagination worth knowing about. Attinger's conclusion, that a theatre "despoiled of literary orna-ment and completely turned toward visual expression" loses all hope of respectability and risks descending to the level of the street entertainers reveals what has been for so long a problem for theatre studies: a pre-occupation with text at the expense of performance.

The comédie italienne was a genre, improvised as well as written; the Comédie-Italienne was the troupe itself, the institution. The troupe, like the genre, has been studied, but not recently, not extensively, and not carefully. The basic document for its history, the notes collected by the eighteenth-century magistrate and playwright Thomas-Simon Gueullette and attached to his translation of the zibaldone attributed to the Arlequin Domenico Biancolelli, has been published only in part, in François and Claude Parfaict's *L'histoire de l'ancien théâtre italien* in 1753. Other data are available in the works of Campardon, Jal, and Rasi, late nineteenth-century savants who combed the archives of Italy and France for traces of the Italian actors in their native and adopted lands, and in the two collections published by Madeleine Jurgens and her collaborators, who have searched the Archives Nationales and the files of the Minutier Cen-tral, that vast storehouse of Parisian legal documents, for anything per-taining to Molière and to the literary history of the last half of the seventeenth century. Since, however, no one has sorted through the avail-able information, drawing together what is coherent and discarding what is not, errors first created in the eighteenth century continue to haunt the twentieth.

My goal has been both to correct error and to add as much as pos-sible to what is known of the commedia dell'arte as played in Paris in the seventeenth century. I have collected and analyzed all the information I could find on the Italians and their repertory from 1644—when several of the actors who were later to be established first came to France—in order to construct an accurate historical chronicle of the troupe, its members, and its repertory. In addition to Gueullette's manuscript notes and the gleanings of Campardon, Rasi, and Jal, I have used legal documents of all kinds, from loan contracts to murder inquiries. I have sorted through available financial records of Louis XIV's court, and combed La Grange's *Registre* for any mention of the Italian troupe. The gazetteers of the day—Loret, Robinet, and Donneau de Visé—frequently mention the Italians, sometimes at length, and their accounts supplement the printed synopses, manuscripts, and published texts that serve as sources of information about the Italian repertory.

These sources include Gueullette's translation of the actor's notes attributed by him to Domenico Biancolelli, seventy-nine entries ranging from a paragraph to many pages, which give detailed information about action and dialogue used onstage by Arlequin and his colleagues between 1662 and 1680. Biancolelli's notes, the authorship of which is not seriously in question, can be elaborated by scenarios from various Italian collections, by several surviving "arguments"—plot synopses in French prepared for non-Italian-speaking audiences—and by the French scenarios in BN Ms. 9329, which probably reflect entertainments played for the most part after 1683.

The French repertory, which begins with ornaments in French in 1668 and includes nearly complete plays in French after 1685 or so, is known to us from the zibaldone, from the two editions of *Le théâtre italien* published by Evaristo Gherardi in 1694 and 1700, and from several pirated collections, especially the so-called *Supplément,* which appeared in Brussels in 1697. The repertory sources, both manuscript and printed, present problems of attribution, dating, and interpretation that will be taken up in the body of the study. Whatever their problems, they do permit detailed descriptions of the entertainments the Italians produced and can be used—with caution—to trace the course of developments.

Finally, of course, any scholar working on the history of the theatre in seventeenth-century France must be grateful for the industry of those predecessors and contemporaries who have left no file unopened, no document unexamined, in their search for the facts about the theatre in the age of Corneille, Molière, and Racine. Although many have excluded the Italians from their studies, as, for instance, does S. Wilma Deierkauf-Holsboer, who ends her two-volume work on the Hôtel de Bourgogne when the Italians took possession of it, their discoveries about company organization, theatre reconstructions, machines and decors, audience composition, and so forth, have been most useful.

Throughout the study I have been especially concerned with such matters as the relationship of the Italian troupe to the monarch, Louis XIV, and its role at his court, the theatres in which the troupe played, both royal and public, and the troupe's organization, staging practices, and performance style. I have constructed the fullest possible biographies of the actors, whose private lives often impinged upon their fictional ones. Finally, since this is a historical study and not a work of criticism, I have set out to describe the repertory, not to evaluate it. While I have been quick to observe the changes that took place in repertory, staging, use of the tipi fissi, and so forth, I have also been alert to what did not change, remembering that an entertainment all'improvviso, *La folie d'Octave,* was played at court as late as 1695.

It would finally be unreasonable to expect a theatre, especially a popular theatre devoted to entertainment, to remain static, to stand fast against the seductions of its own time and place. The commedia dell'arte troupe in Paris did maintain its traditions in some form, but it also sought new channels and avoided stagnation. Beset with the usual pressures of attracting an audience and making a living, and the unusual pressures of doing so in a foreign land and a foreign language, the Italian actors made choices that enabled them to survive as an established entity for thirty-five years. What follows is essentially a study of those actors and those choices.

Part I
1644-1659

Debuts in Paris

O N 16 JUNE 1644, a year after the ascension of five-year-old Louis XIV to the throne of France, Olivier d'Ormesson noted in his journal: "Thursday after dinner I went with M. de Breteuil to the Italian theatre which had begun three days before. Their troupe was good." [1] With this laconic notice d'Ormesson signaled the beginning of fifty-three years of nearly continuous efforts on the part of a troupe of Italian commedia dell'arte actors to amuse Parisian audiences. The first established theatrical company in Western Europe with the sole mission of entertainment, the Comédie-Italienne of seventeenth-century Paris stands in contrast to the French theatres of the classical period. Outside the pale, under no pressure from the academy, free to sing, to dance, to enchant the eye, to explore the farthest reaches of genre from farce to pastoral, from *féerie* to Spanish romance, the Italian actors—solidly supported by the queen regent and her Italian first minister, Mazarin—returned to Paris after a hiatus of nearly twenty years.

Italian theatrical troupes, from their first known performances in France in 1571, had always come at the invitation of the monarch, who traditionally paid traveling expenses, furnished a royal theatre, reimbursed the expenses of court performances, and added a royal subvention to whatever the actors made playing for the public. The Bourbon kings, in particular, enjoyed the Italians enough to make this substantial charge on the royal purse worthwhile; the Bourbons also made it possible for the Italians to play in Paris without harassment by the public authorities.

During the sixteenth century the Italian troupes—even though under the protection of the king—were not always welcome in Paris. When Alberto Naseli (known as Zan Ganassa) and his company opened in Paris in August 1571, the Parlement de Paris argued that they were charging excessive ticket prices, "a sort of exaction on the poor," and forbade them to play in public on pain of "prison and corporal punishment." The fact that the actors had letters patent from the king and permission from the prévôt des marchandes made no difference. The prévôt was told to give no more such permissions in the future, and the residents of Paris were forbidden to attend performances under pain of a ten-livre fine.[2] The actors apparently were unable to continue playing and returned to Italy.

The Parlement de Paris was responding to the complaints of the Confrérie de la Passion, a once-pious brotherhood originally organized for the purpose of producing religious plays, and the owners of the Hôtel de Bourgogne, the only public theatre in Paris. On 17 November 1548, in order to make up to the Confrérie for the prohibition of the religious drama just as the brotherhood had completed its new theatre, the Parlement published an act that granted the sole privilege of theatrical performance in Paris or its suburbs to the Confrérie "under its name and to its profit."[3] In practice, this privilege meant that theatrical troupes either played at the Hôtel de Bourgogne or paid a forfeit to the brotherhood in order to play elsewhere. Actors who performed at the Hôtel de Bourgogne in the sixteenth century were mere salaried employees of the brothers, in whom commercial instincts had long replaced religious obligations. The Confrérie set ticket prices, collected receipts, and approved or disapproved repertory. The Italians, secure in their royal protection, refused to submit to these conditions, and were thus subjected to the rulings of the Parlement.

When the Gelosi troupe played in Paris in 1577, even though it performed at a royal theatre, the Petit-Bourbon, it paid the Confrérie a forfeit of one ecu a performance. This sop to their sensitivities did not make up to the brothers for their anguish at the loss of what would have been very substantial receipts at the Hôtel de Bourgogne. The company was extremely popular; according to l'Estoile, it attracted a bigger crowd than the four best preachers in Paris all together.[4] Once again, the Parlement de Paris attacked; the actors defended themselves with their letters patent which the Parlement refused to recognize since the king was away. This time, however, the king returned and further armed the Italians with a *jussion expresse*. Parlement and the Confrérie folded their tents and stole away, and the power of the monarch in such a situation was confirmed.

Nonetheless, Henri IV, the first Bourbon king, renewed the privilege of the Confrérie in April 1597. Theatrical companies were absolutely obliged to receive permission from the masters of the brotherhood before setting up in any other theatre, and to pay the forfeit of one ecu a day. In 1599 the Confrérie took an Italian company to court for violating this privilege. The judgment of the Châtelet: it is forbidden for these "so-called Italian actors of the king" to play elsewhere than the Hôtel de Bourgogne without the permission of the Confrérie.[5]

Although he supported the rights of the Confrérie, Henri IV was particularly fond of the Italian actors. In order to be certain that a company would come to Lyon to entertain at the festivities during his marriage to Marie de Medici, he himself wrote to the Arlequin, Tristano Martinelli, assuring him that "you will be well treated to your advantage and profit."[6] What he meant by "advantage and profit" becomes clear a little later in the reign. Isabella Andreini, the most famous Italian actress of the day and a member of the Gelosi, wrote from the royal palace of Fontainebleau to the grand duke of Tuscany, her patron, on 7 December 1603. "I was with the troupe at Fontainebleau where I spent thirty-six days, the king and queen finding my services good and entertaining us at 200 ecus a month." The king also gave the actors 600 ecus at the end of 1603 for expenses incurred during the preceding five months.[7]

These royal subventions were especially welcome when the troupes played at the Hôtel de Bourgogne, where the demands of the Confrérie made it difficult for the actors to earn a decent living. Italian troupes in 1607, 1608, and later not only paid their one ecu or more a day in rent, they were forced to cede to the Confrérie the revenues of the majority of the theatre's twelve boxes. When Marie de Medici brought Tristano Martinelli's company to Paris in 1613, the queen herself arranged for the rental of the Hôtel de Bourgogne for their public performances.[8] The lease (which she did not, however, sign) was for six months, from 1 October to the end of March; the rent was 200 livres a month or 200 ecus for 183 days—a little more than the one ecu charged earlier. The Confrérie also reserved nine boxes to its own profit, leaving the Italians with the proceeds from only three.[9] These sparse receipts were augmented by a royal subvention of 600 livres a month, or 1,800 a quarter, the same paid to the Gelosi in 1604.[10]

Louis XIII was apparently just as fond of the Italian actors as his father had been, perhaps even fonder. When Tristano Martinelli returned with the Fedeli in 1621 and played at court, the young king saw twenty-three performances in January and February. At his express request the company stayed in Paris through carnival of 1622 and followed the court to Fontainebleau and back to Paris. The king was away from the end of April 1621 to the end of January 1622, but when he returned he immediately asked for an Italian play. And he saw fifteen more between the end of January and 20 March, when he left Paris again.[11]

The Fedeli continued to play in France and for Louis XIII, though not necessarily continuously, at least until the end of 1624. The royal accounts for that year include an order from the king on 17 December requesting payment to the Italian actors of 2,400 livres for the comedies played in his presence the preceding September and October.[12] This appears to be a payment for expenses, probably at Fontainebleau, and not a subvention, and is the last sure evidence of the presence of an Italian troupe for twenty years.

Several reasons explain the retreat of the Italian actors from Paris. Finding playing space began to be a real problem in the 1620s. Although the Fedeli rented the Hôtel de Bourgogne as late as the fall of 1621, after 1622 that theatre became the exclusive territory of rival French companies battling for supremacy in Paris. Royal theatres were not always available, and even if one was, at this period the extent to which a royal theatre could also be used as a public theatre is not clear. The Petit-Bourbon, apparently the theatre most often used by the Italians at court in early years, was not a good performance space; it was very large, difficult of access, and perhaps not always in usable condition. The stage with which it was equipped for a ballet in 1615 may have been cannibalized for succeeding ballets in the Grande Salle of the Louvre. Furthermore, in 1621, when the Fedeli were in France, two grand ballets were held in the Petit-Bourbon; one opened on 14 February, the other on 2 March.[13] The Italians, who we know played constantly for the king in January and February, must have played, as they had in 1614 and as they were to do in 1622, in the Salle des Gardes of the Louvre, which was not a public theatre. After they returned to Paris from Fontainebleau, however, they rented the Hôtel de Bourgogne, first from 1 May to 31 July, then from 16 October to 16 November with right of renewal. In January 1622 the company was back at court in the Salle des Gardes.[14] The lease of 16 October 1621 was the last an Italian troupe of this era signed for the Hôtel de Bourgogne; in 1629 that theatre became the official home of the French royal troupe by act of the Council, and Paris had no major public theatre available to traveling companies.

Another explanation for the departure of the Italians in 1624 and for their twenty years of exclusion may lie in the rising star of Armand-Jean du Plessis, duc de Richelieu. Allied to the party of the queen mother and exiled from court with her in 1617, Richelieu regained the king's favor after the death of the duc de Luynes in 1621, received his cardinal's hat from the hands of Louis XIII in 1622, and joined the king's Council in April 1624. In August of the same year he became principal minister. Louis XIII, whether because of the influence of his Italian mother or simply because of his own taste, adored the Italian actors, but Richelieu was both a nationalist and a neoclassicist. His ambition was to encourage an artistically pure and intellectually prestigious French drama. Surely the return of the Italians less than two years after Richelieu's death in December 1642 was not coincidental, though unfortunately too late for the king, who died in May 1643. Ironically, in Lyon on 10 December 1622, after bestowing the red hat on the new cardinal, Louis refreshed himself by attending an Italian comedy.[15]

When the Italians returned in 1644, it was at the request of the queen regent, Anne of Austria, and her principal minister, Cardinal Mazarin. The troupe played in Paris until at least 1647, and probably until the beginning of the Fronde in 1648. Some of the same actors returned after the Fronde in 1653 and stayed until 1659. There is little information about royal financial support during these two periods; what there is supports the continuance of the established principle that the French monarch would furnish round-trip expenses, establish a subvention to be paid quarterly, and reimburse the actors for lost profits when court performances interfered with public performances. In 1645 Giulia Gabrielli and her husband, Pietro Paolo Leoni, complained in a letter that Carlo Cantù had kept all their travel money for himself.[16] Thomas-Simon Gueullette, the eighteenth-century chronicler of the Comédie-Italienne, also offers information about travel: "It must be understood that before the year 1660 the troupes of Italian actors were not established in France. They were brought from Italy, their travels paid for. They stayed in Paris or followed the court, and after several years were sent back and given a sum for the expenses of their return. This is a fact which I was assured of by M. Riccoboni, who had it from some Italian actors whose fathers, mothers, and relatives had thus come to France."[17]

There is no specific evidence of royal subvention in the 1640s, but in 1659, a legal document refers to it: "28 June 1659. Promise by Tiberio Fiorilli, one of the Italian actors of His Majesty, living on the quai de l'Ecole, to Jacques Torelli, engineer in ordinary to His Majesty, to return before six months to Pierre-Paul Lion, nephew of the late Pierre-Paul Lion, the following sums: 455 livres received by the said Fiorilli from Zanotti, Italian actor, for the pension given to the actors, and 210 livres received from Marc-Antoine Biancki, Italian actor, of the said pension."[18] This curious document, of which more later, does not make it possible to discover the size of the subvention in the 1650s, but it does offer proof that royal support continued to exist.

Royal support went beyond financial support, moreover. Both Henri IV and Marie de Medici wrote directly to the Arlequin, Tristano Martinelli, and Martinelli responded in kind. In 1600, during the royal wedding festivities at Lyon, he presented the king with a little "book,"

Compositions de rhétorique de M. Don Arlequin, which included fifty-nine blank pages and a dedication "to the magnanimous gentleman, Henry de Bourbon, first bourgeois of Paris, chief of all the gentlemen of Lyon ... admiral of the sea of Marseille, master of one-half of the bridge at Avignon and good friend of the master of the other half, ... secret secretary of the most secret cabinet of Madame Maria di Medici, high treasurer of the Italian actors." [19] It was this same Madame Maria, during negotiations for a troupe to come to France in 1611, whom Martinelli addressed as "la Reine ma commère" (the Queen, my gossip), this same Madame Maria who answered "Arlequin mon compère." [20]

Later Bourbon rulers negotiated for the actors through intermediaries, but there are many anecdotes, some probably apocryphal, indicating personal relationships between the actors and their royal patrons. One of the best known and most doubtful is recorded by Gueullette as a tale told by the elder Riccoboni:

> Aurelia and Scaramouche ... played in France under Louis XIII, well before the year 1640. This woman, who had an infinity of wit, was very well thought of by the queen mother, who liked Scaramouche just as much. One day they were both in the dauphin's room (since Louis XIV), the queen present. This prince was in a very bad humor, crying and weeping without any reason. He was then a little more than two years old; nothing could appease him. Scaramouche took the liberty of asking if Her Majesty would permit him to take the dauphin in his arms. He thought he could put him in a good humor. The queen agreed. Scaramouche then (wearing his street clothes) made such funny faces that this excellent pantomime got the prince to cease crying and begin to laugh, and after the most comic scene, which infinitely pleased the queen, the dauphin voided on the hands and the clothes of Scaramouche, which redoubled the queen's bursts of laughter and those of all the ladies and gentlemen who were then in the apartments. Scaramouche was then about thirty-five, and every time he came to the court, he had orders to go to the dauphin's rooms who was infinitely amused by him and who liked him very much, so much so that he was always asked for when a troupe of actors was brought from Italy. [21]

There is, unfortunately, no evidence to support Gueullette's claim that Aurelia and Scaramouche were in France before 1640. Indeed, if Riccoboni was right about the age of Scaramouche, then the incident should have taken place in 1644 when Tiberio Fiorilli, who played the role, was thirty-five or thirty-six. Of course, by June 1644, when the Italians were certainly in Paris, the young Louis XIV was five years old and already king. It is certainly conceivable that a five-year-old might have laughed so hard at the famous actor that he lost control, but the tale is like many other commedia dell'arte legends that take a theatrical element—in this case, a bit of scatological humor—and transform it into biography. Whether or not the incident took place, there is no doubt that Louis XIV was fond of Fiorilli, so fond, in fact, that he may have supported the Comédie-Italienne long past the point when he was personally entertained so that the old Scaramouche could continue to receive his share of the royal subvention.

Other evidence indicates some personal relationship between Louis and Dominique, Domenico Biancolelli, Arlequin of the established troupe after 1662. Like Molière, Dominique spoke for his company during negotiations with the monarch, at least during the early days when the king took a personal hand in the management of the royal troupes. Louis served as godfather to one of Biancolelli's sons, as he did to one of Molière's, while Anne of Austria and Mazarin were godparents to an infant Fiorilli.[22]

Another indication of mutual admiration between court and comedy was the dedication by Aurelia (Brigida Fedele)[23] to the queen mother of a translation into Italian of a Spanish play in 1659. The gazetteer Loret remarks that the queen valued it highly and in recompense gave Aurelia a pair of diamond pendants for the ears worth 3,000 livres.[24]

These kinds of relatively formal relations between the royal family and actors brought across the mountains to entertain them are a far cry from the casual chumminess of Louis's grandparents with Tristano Martinelli. The young Louis XIV, like his father, was very fond of farce; his response to Molière's performance of *Le docteur amoureux* at the Louvre in 1658 tells us that. But Louis, whatever his personal tastes, was remarkably dignified, even at a very young age, and addicted to etiquette. His Italian actors were certainly less free of the court than their predecessors, but they continued to experience royal support, even royal bounty. They were honored guests of the Bourbon kings, and they were treated as such.

In 1644 the honored guests needed a theatre, the Hôtel de Bourgogne being no longer available. A second public theatre, the Théâtre du Marais, had opened in Paris by this time, but it too was occupied by a permanent French troupe. Four court theatres or performance spaces existed which the monarch could have put at the disposal of the Italian troupe: the Grande Salle of the Petit-Bourbon, the Salle des Gardes at the

Louvre, and two theatres in Palais-Royal. Olivier d'Ormesson does not say where he saw the Italian actors play on 16 June 1644, but the most likely venue was one of the theatres in Palais-Royal.

Cardinal Richelieu included, in his splendid new town house opposite the Louvre, not only the large theatre that was later to be the home of Molière's troupe and the established Comédie-Italienne, but a small theatre—holding perhaps five hundred spectators—used when His Eminence enjoyed a private performance. Richelieu left his Palais-Cardinal to his master, Louis XIII, and on the latter's death, his widow with her two young sons left the Louvre in October 1643 for what was now to be known as Palais-Royal. Even before her mourning was over, Anne of Austria apparently had returned to her favorite pastime. Early in 1644 Mazarin made a note to "have the shutters put in place so the queen can see the play."[25] According to the *Gazette de France,* an Italian play was performed in the Grande Salle of the Palais-Royal on 28 February 1645 before a ballet,[26] which permits the inference that the large theatre in Palais-Royal was used, although it seems likely that for normal private theatregoing, when there was no ballet to follow, the queen might have preferred the smaller space.

The Italians probably preferred the larger. The Grande Salle was large enough for a decent profit and had direct access to the street and a stage with machines that had cost the late cardinal 100,000 livres.[27] On the other hand, assuming that the theatre had undergone no modifications since the production there in February 1641 of the *Ballet de la prospérité des armes de France,* the entertainment shown in the famous engraving by Van Lochen, the auditorium furnishings consisted only of two narrow galleries along each side. There were no accommodations for the public. Modifications seem unlikely in view of the fact that Molière's company brought the interior fittings along from the Petit-Bourbon when it moved to Palais-Royal in 1660.[28] On the other hand, the Petite Salle did not open directly onto the street, was not large enough for a commercially viable theatrical operation, and may well not have been furnished as a public theatre either. Given those options, the Grande Salle seems the more probable choice.

With the royal family living elsewhere, the Salle des Gardes of the Louvre seems an unlikely venue, especially since there is no evidence of its ever being used as a public theatre. The Grand Salle of the Petit-Bourbon is an even less likely choice in early 1644, although it was to become the home of the troupe from 1645 to 1648. Last used for two ballets in 1621 and by the Italians in January 1623, this great, vaulted hall

was not even an alternative royal performance site in the late 1620s and
the 1630s. Ballets were held in the Grande Salle of the Louvre, at Hôtel
de Ville, and, after 1632, even in a remodeled tennis court, the jeu de
paume du Petit Louvre. Furthermore, Carlo Cantù, one of the Italian
actors who arrived in Paris in 1645, wrote home to his patron about the
actors' difficulty with the designer and machinist Giacomo Torelli:
"When Signor Torelli arrived in Paris with us, in the hope of earning
money, we offered him a share in our profits for building a stage with
machines."[29] This letter, dated 10 October 1645 during preparations at
the Petit-Bourbon for *La finta pazza*, an Italian machine play with music
and ballet, suggests that Torelli, in building the stage and installing the
machines, was also meeting the company's need for an adequate theatre.

The time when a commedia dell'arte troupe could set up a trestle
and entertain exclusively with pratfalls and wit was long gone. Troupes
like the one playing in France in 1644–45 had in their repertories not
only the traditional neo-Roman farces but pastorals, romances, and tragicomedies which relied on all kinds of machines and special effects. The
Grande Salle of the Petit-Bourbon—after Torelli's ministrations—had a
stage fully equipped for Italianate spectacle as well as auditorium fittings
suited to the needs of a public theatre. Torelli had some problems con-
verting the old hall. The original room, represented in several famous
engravings showing the assembly of the Etats Généraux in 1614 (fig. 1),
is described in the synopsis of the *Ballet de Madame*, 1615:

> The said room is 18 toises [114 feet] long and 8 toises [50 feet, 8
> inches] wide; at the high end [the St.-Germain l'Auxerrois end ac-
> cording to the *Gazette*, which reprinted the description] there is a
> hemicycle 7 toises [44 feet, 4 inches] deep and 8½ toises [53 feet, ten
> inches] wide, vaulted and with the vaults sprinkled with fleurs-de-
> lis. The periphery of the said room is ornamented with columns with
> their bases, capitals, architraves and cornices of the Doric order, and
> between these cornices, arcades and niches; the said cornice is up-
> held by brackets bearing a corridor all around the periphery of the
> said room, above which is another corridor borne on corbels.[30]

Torelli's stage in 1645 must have been built in front of the hemicycle in
order to take advantage of the height of the room for the flying machinery.[31] The vaulted area behind could have been used for the perspective
vistas, which required little height. Torelli's grumble, "such a little
stage,"[32] was probably a response to the difficulty of mounting a stage
and providing for a goodly number of paying customers in the space of
70 feet.[33] Olivier d'Ormesson, who was much impressed by Torelli's sce-

FIG. *1. The Etats-Généraux meeting in the Grande Salle of the Petit-Bourbon in 1614.* (Bibliothèque Nationale; phot. Bibl. Nat. Paris)

nery, reports that in all the different vistas "the perspective was so well observed that all the alleys appeared lost to view, although the stage has only four or five feet of depth."[34] Torelli's "little stage" was certainly not that shallow, though it could not have been as deep as the designer's own passion for self-promotion.

Size of stage notwithstanding, the machines installed for *La finta pazza* were complex. The arrangements for scenic changes, relatively new to France, worked with amazing speed and smoothness, if their inventor can be believed. Five scenes were employed: a garden; a city with a river, port, and a perspective of Paris; a palace with a vista of rooms diminishing into the distance; a city square with multiple vistas; and a royal garden with alleys and a fountain. The machinery included rigging for flying both individual performers and chariots, a water effect with moving ships, several glories, and a working fountain.

Nothing is known of the auditorium installed by Torelli in the Petit-Bourbon, except for the two rows of seventeen "loges," or boxes, which the king gave Molière's troupe permission to move to Palais-Royal in 1660. The typical interior of a seventeenth-century public theatre—although there were variations—included a "parterre," or standing pit, sometimes raked, with two or three rows of loges ranged along the side and rear walls. At the back of the parterre, between it and the first loges along the rear wall, there was usually an "amphithéâtre," a raised and raked area with seven or eight rows of benches for seated spectators. The Hôtel de Bourgogne, early in the century, also had galleries along the side walls above the second loges and a paradise at the rear, all later replaced by a third row of loges. When the stage itself became a popular location from which to watch the play and unruly spectators made performance difficult, the theatres added "bancs," benches along the sides of the downstage area, and "balcons," or stage boxes; and in the last decades of the seventeenth century, orchestra pits and "parquets," benches set up between the orchestra pit and the parterre, were also introduced.

The Petit-Bourbon must have lacked many of the fittings and amenities that were typical of later theatres. It also had one grave defect as a public theatre: it was difficult of access. In his 1622 novel *Francion,* Charles Sorel describes the vicissitudes his hero meets in attending a ballet there, probably the *Ballet de Madame* in 1615: "When I entered . . . that was not the end of my troubles; I had to pass through so many doors and cross so many rooms that I thought I would never get there. . . . What's more, the crowd was so great, it prevented my entry as much as the archers did. Finally, I found myself in the long Galerie de Bourbon

... where I had to stop."[35] When the doors were finally opened, he rushed in and found that all the seats had been taken by the courtiers. No doubt the ballet attracted a far greater crowd than the average play, but still there were rooms, corridors, and galleries to be crossed in order to reach the theatre.

Gomboust's map of Paris (1652) gives the best view of the Louvre and the Petit-Bourbon at this period. Situated along the quai between St.-Germain l'Auxerrois and the Old Louvre, a site now occupied by the Place du Louvre and Perrault's Colonnade, the Petit-Bourbon functioned as an extension of the royal residence. Louis XIII, for example, attended mass usually at the Bourbon chapel, and the Grande Salle, as we have seen, was used for entertainments from time to time. The Grand Salle is very clearly indicated on Gomboust's plan. It is a long, narrow structure with an elliptical end, a semidetached north wing of the palace, with the chapel to its north. Other plans show essentially the same configuration.[36] The palace appears to occupy a closed precinct with public access to the chapel from the rue du Petit Bourbon to the north. The plans show no similar easy direct access for the public from the street to the Grande Salle. Horn-Monval, also citing Sorel's novel, places the entry on the rue des Pouliés at the corner of the quai de l'Ecole,[37] and the Gomboust plan does show a gate into the precinct near that point. A plan of the remains of the palace, drawn late in the seventeenth century, clearly shows that same entry and also defines the convoluted path a spectator would have taken, down an L-shaped corridor, into the great Galerie d'Or in the west wing, and finally into the Grande Salle.[38] No evidence exists to suggest that this arrangement was ever modified when the Petit-Bourbon became a public theatre in the 1640s and 1650s.

The company that played there appears to have been a relatively conventional commedia dell'arte troupe. Known members include Brigida Fedele and her husband, Marc' Antonio Bianchi, who played Aurelia and Horace, an amoureuse and an amoureux. They were later replaced by Giulia Gabrielli, Diana, and her husband, Pietro Paolo Leoni. What character he played is unknown. A First Zanni, Briguelle, was later replaced by Carlo Cantù, Buffetto. The Second Zanni was Domenico Locatelli, Trivelin; his wife, Luisa Gabrielli, played Lucille, probably an amoureuse. Tiberio Fiorilli was Scaramouche, a mixture of zanni and capitan, and his wife, Lorenza Elisabetta del Campo, was Marinette, a servante.[39] In 1645 the troupe also included a singer, Marguerita Bertolotti, of whom nothing else is known. A Pantalon, a docteur and another amoureux must have also been there, and a capitan may have been as well, but their names do not seem to have survived.

Like all such troupes, this was a legal association of actors, formed especially to be sent into France as the result of a request from the French monarch. Like all such troupes, it was a sharing company, the actors paying whatever daily expenses they had incurred and dividing the remaining profits according to shares held. At this time it seems likely that each actor had one share; later, when the number of shares was fixed by royal mandate, newly entered actors often began with a half or even a quarter of a share. We have no information about expenses or profits during this early period.

The only production that we have evidence of between 1644 and 1647–48 is *La finta pazza,* which opened on 14 December 1645. Some of the actors who had performed in *La finta pazza* left France after carnival of 1646, but the queen requested replacements.[40] We know that the troupe was still in Paris in January of 1647 when the king, by royal brevet, granted to "Trivelin, His Majesty's Italian actor," the property of one Laurent, an Italian, who had died in Paris.[41] We know that Tiberio Fiorilli and his wife were preparing to leave Paris in September of 1647.[42] Fiorilli was, however, the most independent of the Italian actors, constantly on the move between Italy and France. It seems reasonable to assume, then, that the company probably stayed on until driven out by the beginning of the Fronde in late 1647 or early 1648.

The troupe that returned in the summer of 1653 included many of the same actors: Aurelia and Horace, Trivelin and Lucille, Scaramouche and Marinette. Joining them at some point between 1653 and 1658 were Angelo Agostino Lolli, Docteur Baloard; Giovan Andrea Zanotti, Octave, Second Amoureux; a Pantalon often misidentified as G. B. Turi (or Turri); a Flamine, a Mlle. Beatrix, and a capitan. Pietro Paolo Leone was apparently also a member of the company at some point since his nephew invoked the offices of Torelli to retrieve his share of the subvention in 1659.

Loret was delighted to have the Italians back. He wrote in *La muze historique* of 16 August 1653: "Although the Italian language might be the Armenian language to me, and my mind is so foolish that I can't understand a word, I am going to see this troupe anyway, preferring to eat less soup and drink a little less wine than not see Trivelin." This was the troupe in residence at the Petit-Bourbon in 1658 when Molière returned to Paris with his company and was granted the right to play in the same theatre. The Italians were playing the "jours ordinaires," or preferred days—Tuesday, Friday, and Sunday; the French were given the "jours extraordinaires."[43] According to Chappuzeau, the jours ordinaires were the better days because Wednesday and Saturday were market days, because the coaches for Germany, Italy, and the provinces left on Mondays, and because Thursdays were consecrated to promenades.[44] The Italians did not like to play on Friday; in Italy theatres were closed on Fridays in honor of the passion of Christ. Thus, when they returned and took up shared residence with the French at Palais-Royal in 1662, the Italians were probably not distressed to receive the extraordinary days.

Throughout their history of sharing theatres, the French and Italian companies also shared employees. Thus the Italians' daily expenses for the Petit-Bourbon toward the end of this visit can be estimated by assuming them to be the same as those of the French company. These the diligent La Grange, one of the French actors, includes in his *Registre,* or account book, for 1659–60.[45]

Germain, porter.	3 livres	10 sous
St. Michel, porter	3	
Brouart, usher, loges	1	10
Mle L'Estang & Me Gobert, for the reception and control	3	
La Genty, usher, loges	1	10
Brillart & wife, ushers, loges.	3	
Mathieu, décorateur.	2	10
M. Torelli's servant, as concierge	1	
Musicians.	4	10
Candles.	10	4
Posters, for 2 times, red and black	7	10
A Charle, dresser		15
Wine, tea, bread	1	
	42 livres	19 sous

This list is of no help in arriving at the income of the Italian actors, since we have no information about their box office receipts. What these expenses do tell us is a good deal about the organization of the theatre and the level of production. Two doorkeepers suggest two entries; the lack of expenditure for guards or soldiers indicates that entry without paying and violence in the theatre were not yet the problems they were later to become. That four ushers were needed to unlock the boxes, but no ushers were designated for the amphithéâtre, tells us that this was very likely a theatre without an amphithéâtre, an unsurprising conclusion, given what we already know about the Petit-Bourbon. It also suggests that two galleries shown along the side walls of the hall in the engravings of 1581 and 1614 had been transformed into loges, probably in 1645 when the hall was prepared for *La finta pazza.*

Each troupe had its own "décorateur," who was not usually a designer of new scenery but rather a forerunner of the modern stage carpenter, the one responsible for the smooth functioning of the backstage and the one who selected and put into place the standard scenery for each night's performance. For the most part these companies used simple settings, even though the stage was equipped with elaborate machines. When those machines were brought into play, extra machinists and stagehands were hired, and listed under extraordinary expenses. A concierge to run errands and keep the theatre clean and a dresser shared by all the actors completed a minimal backstage staff. The largest expenses were—and were to remain—music, light, and publicity.

The time of performance is hard to establish for this period; it may have changed somewhat with the seasons. Henri IV ordered that the plays end by 4:30 from St. Martin's Day to 15 February, but his son, Louis XIII, often went to the play in the evening (although probably at court). According to Despois, who gives no source, public performances in Paris during the reign of Louis XIII began at 3:00; during the reign of Louis the XIV they began later, especially after the curé of St.-Eustache, a church around the corner from the Hôtel de Bourgogne, requested that plays not begin until after vespers.[46] Common sense suggests that plays began early during the short winter days in Paris, later during the long days of summer. An afternoon or evening at the theatre was not in France, as it could be in other countries during this period, a protracted event. Most of Molière's plays can be performed in less than two hours, even allowing time to trim the candles, and the farce afterpieces, which were by no means always played, are very short. The Italians, from the very little information available about their early repertory, seem to have done single plays, perhaps with added songs or dances. In later years, when they began to play a French repertory, they too did some afterpieces.

Although Loret gave up his soup and wine to see the Italians perform in 1653, he does not tell us the name of the entertainment. Nor do we know what he saw on 2 March 1656 when, before the ballet, the Italians diverted the court with "many an agreeable folly ... with leaps and comic turns." Nor does an anonymous letter to the duc d'Aumele, written probably in 1655, give us information about the repertory, though it does tell us that the author saw, at Fontainebleau, something with Trivelin, Aurelia, Flamine, Lucille, and Marinette.[47] For the entire visit of 1653–59, we are certain of only two productions, one a spectacle piece, the other based on a well-known Spanish tragicomedy. The first,

La Rosaura imperatrice di Constantinopoli, was performed for carnival in 1658; the second, an enormously successful *Il convitato di pietra*, appeared sometime before the end of that same year. *La Rosaura*, although a machine play, requires relatively few performers, making it a better financial choice than the earlier *La finta pazza*. *Il convitato di pietra* could also be performed by a normally configured commedia troupe.

One final mention of the company describes a most unusual entertainment devised for the court by the united companies of the Petit-Bourbon. It was performed at Vincennes in late May 1659, and Loret devoted the lion's share of the 31 May *Muze historique* to it: "What's more, several actors, three French, three Italian, on a subject they had devised, all six got together to do wonders. There was the husband of Aurelia (Signor Horace), tall Scaramouche, Signor Trivelin Canaille, Jodelet, that subtle jester, also Gros-René, and Gratian, as wise as he is foolish. Horace, with a beautiful singing speech, played the eloquent amoureux for Trivelin and Scaramouche who set themselves to skirmishing." And Loret goes on to praise Gros-René, pearl of the white-faced clowns, Jodelet, who talks through his nose and makes everyone laugh with the excellence of his farce, and finally Docteur Gratian, "esteemed by many a courtier for his pedantic jargon." The joint effort, however, was not entirely successful; Loret reports that "according to several spectators, the French and Italian actors are worth more separately than together."

A little more than a month later, preceding his report of 11 July, La Grange notes in his *Registre:* "The Italian troupe returned at this time to Italy." The next day was Friday, a jour ordinaire. The French company played *Le Cid* to a small house.

Actors of the
1640s and 1650s

BECAUSE commedia dell'arte was an actors' theatre, historians have always been eager to identify these actors and reconstruct their biographies. This is not an easy task. The few documents that exist frequently refer to actors by the names of their characters, and these names are seldom unique. Furthermore, the actors lived nomadic lives, sometimes remaining in a troupe for only a year or two. In Paris, of course, after 1662 the Italian actors were established and their lives can be traced in legal documents, in marriage contracts and baptismal acts, in articles of association, in leases, loans, and investments, and, finally, in wills, burial records, and inventories.

The actors who played in Paris between 1644 and 1659 are more difficult to identify, and historians have, over the centuries, reached some questionable conclusions about them. Some actors were there only briefly and left few traces; others were important at the time but did not return as part of the established troupe. Still others,—especially Tiberio Fiorilli, Scaramouche; Brigida Fedele, Aurelia; Domenico Locatelli, Trivelin; Angelo Agostino Lolli, the Docteur; and Giovan Andrea Zanotti, Octave—were to come back and work in Paris for up to half a century, so it is important that the facts of their lives be determined as accurately as possible.

Tiberio Fiorilli was perhaps the best known of all the Italian actors who played in France in the seventeenth century, and one of the best-known commedia dell'arte actors of all time. A tall man, costumed in Spanish style in a black doublet and breeches from the early part of the century, with a short cape, a ruff, and a large, baglike hat, his *enfariné* punctuated by a large handlebar moustache and a tiny chin whisker, Scaramouche—half zanni, half capitan—was a court and public favorite throughout a career that lasted for fifty years.

An irritable, gluttonous, miserly fellow—according to his first biographer—Fiorilli was a magnificent mime, and this may account for the special favor in which he was held in France, where many members of his public audience, like the gazetteer Loret, understood not one word of

Italian. Although he is often referred to as famous in Italy, no record documents his company membership or performances there before his first certain appearance in France in 1644.

Gueullette gives Fiorilli's date of birth as 7 November 1608;[1] the source appears to be a print Gueullette owned and included with his historical notes (fig. 2). This print, though similar if not identical to earlier representations of the actor, is dated 1700, and the legend below it reads: "Tiberio Fiorilli known as Scaramouche, born at Naples the 7th of November 1608. This great original of the comic stage died at Paris the 8th of December 1696 at the age of 88 years and is buried in the Church of St.-Eustache." Unfortunately, the legend is wrong about the date of death (though it has the place of burial right), so its reliability is questionable. Fiorilli died 7 December 1694, not 8 December 1696. Neither his birth nor his baptismal record has ever been discovered, but 1608 seems to be a reasonable birth year for the actor, who was considered to be a very old man by the time of his death. The same year is given in a 1695 biography of Fiorilli, *La vie de Scaramouche,* written by Angelo Costantini, Mezzetin, First Zanni of the Italian troupe in Paris from 1686.[2]

Jal considers the question of Fiorilli's birthplace unsolved.[3] However, the actor's letters of naturalization clearly refer to him as "native of Naples,"[4] and he so describes himself in his son's marriage contract and his daughter's act of baptism.[5] Costantini says he was born there, and his probable connection with the Fiorillo family adds further support to the acceptance of Naples as his birthplace. Loret, however, reports on 3 June 1662 that Fiorilli is about to depart for Florence, "the place of his birth," and Rasi notes a reference in the *Storia del granducato di Toscana* to Fiorilli as a Florentine.[6] The solution to this minor mystery is to be found in the fact that Florence became Fiorilli's home, probably in the 1650s or early 1660s. His property there is referred to in both Costantini's book and in his son's marriage contract, and his first wife left Paris and lived there after 1664. In the same way his probable father, Silvio Fiorillo, though a native of Capua, was often referred to as a Neapolitan because Naples was the city to which he most often returned and where his wife was established.[7]

Fiorilli's parentage has long been at issue. In his biography of Scaramouche, Costantini writes: "His father, who was a Captain of Horse, desiring to marry a second time, wished to espouse one of his Cousins who resided in the town of *Capua,* but could never obtain the Bishop's permission on account of the nearness of kin." During an argument, this captain of horse killed the bishop's brother and, "being obliged to leave

FIG. 2. *Tiberio Fiorilli, Scaramouche. Engraving of 1700 by Hubert. This engraving and the others depicting actors of the Comédie-Italienne included in this volume were collected by Thomas-Simon Gueullette.* (Bibliothèque de l'Opéra, Ms. Rés. 625; phot. Bibl. Nat. Paris)

the Kingdom of *Naples* to escape the fruits of his action and finding himself in a strange Country with neither money nor any other employment than that of looking after his two Children, was forced, although a Nobleman, to play the Charlatan and sell quack Medicines. *Scaramouch,* his second son, was much more trouble to him than Trapolin, the elder one.... His Father ... beat him with a stick and drove him out of doors."[8] Without exactly saying so, Costantini clearly implies that Tiberio Fiorilli was the younger son of the famous Silvio Fiorillo, who played Capitan Matamoros, and the brother of Giovan Battista Fiorillo, who played Trappolino.

Gueullette takes from Costantini that Fiorilli's father was a cavalry officer but deletes the story of the bishop's brother and the flight from Naples. He adds a long tale of how Scaramouche, then twenty-five and a domestic servant in Naples, had to get married, a tale he heard from Mlle. Baletti (Flaminia in the eighteenth-century Italian troupe in Paris) who had heard it from her grandmother.[9] Campardon simply asserts that Fiorilli "belonged to a Neapolitan family of noble origins."[10] Later biographers, particularly Jal and Rasi, contend that Costantini was wrong, that Fiorilli was not connected to the Fiorillo family. Jal's chief argument is that Tiberio signed his name *Fiorilli* as did his son.[11] Rasi agrees, and adds to the argument various dates which demonstrate that Silvio Fiorillo was a famous actor long before the birth of Tiberio Fiorilli and thus could not have run off to become a "charlatan" after his son's birth.[12]

Rasi assumes, of course, that Costantini is either completely right or completely wrong, but *La vie de Scaramouche* is not unadulterated biography, nor is it meant to be. It is a "Life," a memorialization of Scaramouche, a compilation of legends that show the sort of fusion of actor and character to which all commedia dell'arte players, especially those who played a capitan, seem to have been prone. For the biography to tell us that Scaramouche was the son of a captain of horse who fell prey to misadventure seems perfectly reasonable if his real father played Capitan Matamoros. The captain's fatal quarrel with the bishop's brother could have come from any zibaldone, and is more than slightly reminiscent of the "Life" of Francesco Andreini, Capitan Spavento, said to be the scion of a noble family who fell into the hands of the Turks, was enslaved for eight years, and then became an actor. The "merry adventures of Scaramouche and Marinette" which fill Costantini's book are just as obviously stage adventures, many apparently taken from scenes of the zanni and the servante. Nonetheless, the book is not necessarily inaccurate when it is occasionally factual. Fiorilli's son's marriage contract also mentions the "fine piece of land" outside Florence that Costantini tells us Fiorilli bought before 1660. And, as Ulysse Prota-Giurleo points out, "no matter how many inaccuracies the biography contains, the assertion that Tiberio was the son of Silvio could not be entirely invented," given two such notable men.[13]

Another argument posed by Rasi to deny the relationship is that no evidence exists in Italy or France connecting Tiberio Fiorilli to either Silvio or Giovan Battista Fiorillo. Indeed, he argues, both Tiberio and Giovan Battista, along with their wives, were in Rome in July 1651; both were sought by the duke of Mantua for the next carnival, both responded negatively. The letter of Tiberio and his wife, Isabella, is dated the first of July, that of Giovan Battista and his wife, Beatrice, the last of July, and neither mentions the other couple.[14] According to Pandolfi, however, Tiberio wrote on 2 July 1651 to the duke of *Mantua,* while Beatrice wrote on 29 July 1651 to the duke of *Modena,*[15] so this argument hardly seems weighty.

Finally, agreeing with Jal about the value of signatures, Rasi says: "What strengthens my doubts [about the relationship] is that Tiberio and Isabella are always firmly Fiorilli, while Silvio and Giovan Battista are always firmly Fiorillo."[16] Jal claims that he saw four signatures, all *Tiberio Fiorilli.* However, although both forms exist in French legal documents, the majority are *Fiorillo.* These include signatures on the baptismal act of his daughter Anne Elisabeth, 29 July 1681, at St.-Eustache, and another baptismal act of October 1677 when Fiorilli was godfather,[17] one signature on the Accord et Transaction of 1680 with the French troupe sharing the Guénégaud,[18] one on a Déclaration of 1680,[19] two on the company's Convention of 1683;[20] one on a Déclaration of 1683,[21] one on a Constitution de rente of 1686.[22] Only the two last known signatures, 1691 and 1692, are different; the first of these is *Fiorilli,* the second *Fiorili.*[23] It seems justified to say, then, that *Fiorillo* was the actor's usual legal signature, even though the French normally spelled the name *Fiorilly* or *Fiorilli.*

Assuming that 1608 is more or less Tiberio Fiorilli's correct year of birth, and Naples his correct place of birth, then the known presence in Naples of Silvio Fiorillo in 1609 and his possible presence there in 1608[24] lend further weight to the presumption that the latter was father to the former.

Furthermore, the family character lines are connected. Not only did Silvio play Capitano, his son, Giovan Battista, first appeared in 1614 in Genoa as Scaramuccia,[25] the only actor other than Tiberio Fiorilli and his successors in France, Girolamo Cei and Guiseppe Tortoriti, known to have played the role. Scaramuccia was originally a capitan, as least if we are to believe Callot's image of him.[26] That Giovan Battista later changed roles and adopted the character of Trappolino suggests a family decision to turn Scaramuccia over to the younger brother. Not all commedia dell'arte character lines were "owned" by families, of course, but it was not unusual for them to be. The role of Colombine, for instance, was played, so far as I know, only by first the mother and then the daughter of Domenico Biancolelli.

The character Scaramuzza appears in one of Silvio Fiorillo's plays, *La Lucilla costante con le ridicolose disfide e prodezze di Policinella,* published in Milan in 1632. Rasi assigns the role to Giovan Battista, but by that time it could have belonged to the twenty-four-year-old Tiberio. Rasi is also disturbed by the fact that the list of actors published in Genoa in 1614 includes Silvio, his son Giovan Battista, and another "young son," Girolamo. Rasi wonders where Tiberio was (if Tiberio was, indeed, Silvio's son), or if Tiberio later changed his name from Girolamo; Prota-Giurleo points out that since Tiberio was six years old at the time, he was hardly old enough to figure on a company list. Silvio Fiorillo did have other children; in 1621 he wrote to the duke of Mantua that his wife had married off his daughter while he was in Lombardy, and he wanted to go home to Naples and meet his son-in-law.[27]

No document has come to light in France linking the famous Tiberio Fiorilli to the famous Silvio Fiorillo, and this is the final point that bothers Rasi. By the same token, however, nothing in France connects Domenico Biancolelli with his famous mother or even more famous stepfather, Carlo Cantù, although Cantù played in Paris in 1645 and his young stepson accompanied him. Silvio Fiorillo, on the other hand, almost certainly never played in France. He was never part of the Gelosi or the Fideli, never connected with Tristano Martinelli or Giovan Battista Andreini, who organized the companies for France during Silvio's years as an actor. In fact, in 1613 Martinelli wrote to the duke of Mantua that the company then being organized had rejected Fiorillo.[28] One final note that may help to tip the scales. Tiberio Fiorilli named one of his sons Silvio.

On balance, though there is no way to be certain, the probability is high that Tiberio Fiorilli was part of the Fiorillo family, that he was trained by a father and older brother already known for their skill, and did not simply spring, ready formed, from the forehead of some noble Neapolitan. Fiorilli's special skills as a musician and a mime are not the sorts of things that are simply innate; they require long years of study

and practice. There were reasons, especially in France, for actors to pretend to nobility of birth. With their civil and religious status often in
question, French actors adopted aristocratic-sounding names along with
the *de* indicating proprietorship. Italian actors, not at jeopardy in their
native country, may well have been ill at ease in a country that discrimi-
nated against members of their profession, so it is not surprising that
they too claimed membership in the upper classes.

Legend has it that Tiberio Fiorilli was with a troupe in Paris as early
as 1639,[29] but the first hard evidence of his presence is an act of baptism
for his son Louis, born August 1644 and baptised at St.-Germain
l'Auxerrois on 20 August.[30] The godparents were the queen mother and
Cardinal Mazarin, testifying to the favor in which Fiorilli was held. Little
Louis, who died in December 1646 in Paris, was the third known child of
Fiorilli and his first wife, Lorenza Elisabetta del Campo, who played the
servante Marinette. Other known sons of the marriage were Silvio Bernardo, born in Este, and old enough to be married in 1666,[31] and Charles-
Louis, date and place of birth unknown, but already a canon of Troyes
cathedral at the time of his brother's marriage.

Fiorilli is not mentioned at all in connection with the production of
La finta pazza in 1645, except in a peripheral way which hints that he may
have been out of France. Carlo Cantù, who was brought to Paris in the
spring of 1645 to replace the recently departed First Zanni, complained
in a letter of 10 October to the duke of Parma that his wife, Isabella
Franchini, who played Colombina, had written to him from Milan that
Scaramouche (acting in the interests of his wife, Marinette) had prevented her from coming to Paris, "believing that he has not had the order
to send her from the duke of Parma."[32] There is certainly no obvious role
for Fiorilli in *La finta pazza,* so he may well have left France during preparations for it. He was the most nomadic of all the Italian actors who
played in Paris; he seems frequently to have left after the Easter recess
and spent the summer in Italy, probably in Florence. During the 1660s,
court financial records show frequent payments to him for the cost of
traveling.

The family was in Paris in 1646, when young Louis died, and still
there in September 1647, when Fiorilli and his wife signed a contract
with the parents of a young Frenchwoman, Marguerite Charles, who was
to serve as personal maid during their impending trip to Italy.[33] The trip
probably marks the end of Fiorilli's first stay in Paris; the Fronde broke
out early in 1648, and the Italian actors were absent until its end.

Fiorilli and his wife were certainly in Rome in July 1651 and planning to be there through the following carnival. They may also have played in Florence, Naples, and possibly Palermo, but since the only source which describes these performances is Costantini, who gives no dates, the wise course seems to be to assume that Fiorilli engaged in the normal routines of the Italian actor in Italy between 1647 and 1653.

Scaramouche was definitely in the company that returned to France in August 1653; Loret welcomes him by name.[34] He was in Florence in May 1655, when the grand duke of Tuscany recommended to the duke of Modena "the actor Scaramuccia just returned from France."[35] He was in Paris during carnival of 1656; on 5 February Loret was an "eye witness," according to his marginal note, to a parody ballet arranged by the composer Lulli and the dancing master Beauchamps for Cardinal Mazarin and his guests. "Six Trivelins armed with wooden swords, by their naive monkeyshines, acrobatics, and comic routines, aroused happy laughter. And the inventor, Sieur Batiste, showed himself a perfect copyist of Trivelin and his turns." The Trivelins were followed by imitation Scaramouches, tutored by Beauchamps, who in "their figures, grimaces, and postures improved on the original." All was a riot of merriment until Fiorilli—to the extreme surprise of everyone, for he was not expected—happened in and, seeing himself parodied, took off his belt and lay about him, the crack of the belt "drilling through us like the wind."[36]

In 1658 Fiorilli performed "The Table of Scaramouche" in *La Rosaura imperatrice di Constantinopoli* at the Petit-Bourbon, and may also have played Don Juan's servant in *Il convitato di pietra*. On 31 May 1659, he was among the Italians performing with the French at Vincennes, and on 28 June of that year he signed, in Paris, a "Promise" to Torelli to pay back money owing the estate of Pietro Paolo Leoni.[38]

On 11 October 1659 Loret advised the courtiers and bourgeois of Paris, all lovers of the theatre like himself, to weep, sigh, cry out, beat their chests, pluck the hair from their heads and beards, rend their faces because—the famous Scaramouche is dead ... drowned by a sudden flood on the banks of the Rhône. Loret adds an "Epitaphe":

> Alas, it is not Lady Isabella
> Who sleeps under the cold tomb,
> Nor some other holy Touch-Me-Not:
> It is a comic without equal,
> As the heaven has but one sun,
> So the earth has but one Scaramouche.

A week later, Loret's gazette was filled with a joyful ode. "Don't pluck out your beards. ... Purge yourself of your unhappiness with no need for cassia or rhubarb." Someone had lied. Scaramouche was alive. He would return to France in late summer of 1661, to Paris in early 1662.

Brigida Fedele had a career in Paris almost as long and distinguished as that of her colleague Fiorilli, and although she ceased to play in 1682, she outlived him by several years. She is universally known as Brigida Bianchi, the name she signed to a book she published in 1659, but her legal signature, to the Convention of 1683 and the Constitutions de rente of 1686, was Brigida Fedele, and her son dedicated a poem to Brigida *Fedeli*, his mother.[39] The confusion engendered by early French theatre historians about this actress and her family is enormous and unchallenged and stands in need of correction.

On the word of Gueullette, she is without exception assumed by scholars to have been the wife of the actor "N. [Christian name unknown] Romagnesi," who played the amoureux in Paris under the name of Horace in the 1650s.[40] But in the company's Convention of 1683 she is clearly described as "the widow of Marcantoine Bianchy."[41] Gueullette was apparently never aware of the actor Marc' Antonio Bianchi, who was in Paris in 1659 according to the note signed by Tiberio Fiorilli: "28 June 1659. Promise by Tiberio Fiorilli ... to return before six months to Pierre-Paul Lion ... 210 livres received from Marc-Antoine Biancki, Italian actor, of the said pension."[42] Anna Migliori has found another notarial act of December 1657 that also mentions Bianchi.[43]

It seems beyond a doubt that in the late 1650s, in Paris, Brigida Fedele was married to Marc' Antonio Bianchi and that he was the "husband of Aurelia" referred to by Loret and identified in a marginal note as "the Signor Horace."[44] But what is also unimpeachable is that Brigida Fedele was the mother of the actor Marc' Antonio Romagnesi, who made his debut with the Italian company in France in 1668 as Cinthio, took over the role of the Docteur in 1694, and played it until the dissolution in 1697. Not only does Loret's successor, Robinet, refer to him as "Cinthio, son of Aurelia,"[45] but Gueullette knew and interviewed his daughter-in-law who was a Costantini, had grown up in the troupe, and remembered her husband's grandmother.[46] At some point, then, Brigida Fedele must have been married to a Romagnesi, although his first name and the role he played remain unknown. Her son's exact birthdate is also unknown, but he was married in 1653 according to his daughter-in-law, making 1633 a reasonable guess. Brigida Fedele's own birthdate was c. 1613; according to Gueullette's family informant, she was eighty-nine when she died in 1703. Probably, then, her first marriage took place in the early 1630s. Possibly this husband was the Marc' Antonio Romagnezi who played Cinzio and who is known from a letter he wrote to the duke of

Mantua in 1620.[47] Another candidate would be the Marc' Antonio Romagnesi who played Pantalone with the Confidenti in 1616.[48] Both of these actors would have been considerably older than Brigida Fedele, making her situation consistent with early widowhood and remarriage.

It is true that the actress's name on the title page of her translation *L'inganno fortunato* (Paris, 1659) is "Brigida Bianchi, actress known as Aurelia." However, for her second publication, *Rifiuti di pindo* (Paris, 1666) the author signs herself "Aurelia Fedeli, Italian actress." A number of interpretations are possible. By and large, the Italian actresses did not use their husbands' names. In fact, the only well-known actress who did so was Isabella Andreini, although she was usually referred to simply as "Isabella." In Paris all of the other actresses in the Italian troupe used their own, legal names: Orsola Cortesi, Patricia Adami, Catherine and Françoise Biancolelli, and Angela Toscana. All were married women; most were married to members of the company. All signed legal documents with their maiden names, although in one instance, in 1696, several used both maiden and married names. Furthermore, since Brigida Fedele was surely an established actress by the time she married Bianchi, and since she had not taken her first husband's name as her professional name, there seems little reason to assume she would have done so with her second. Why she used *Bianchi* on the title page of her translation is not apparent; perhaps she did so to remind those she wanted to impress with her erudition of the great Isabella, perhaps to distinguish herself as author from herself as actress. Orsola Cortesi, the Second Amoureuse of the Paris company and the wife of Domenico Biancolelli did the same thing. Her play *La bella bruta,* also taken from the Spanish, is signed Orsola Biancolelli.[49]

The use of *Aurelia Fedeli* is easier to interpret. The combination of a character name and an actor's real name is not unusual, and even appears in some legal documents. When the Italians signed their Accord et Transaction with the French actors of the Guénégaud in 1680, the two amoureux of the troupe wrote "Ottavio Zanotti" and "Cintio Romagnesy," although the two gentlemen were actually named Giovan Andrea and Marc' Antonio. Zanotti, a member of the older generation, did this with some consistency. On the other hand, no actor ever signed a legal document with other than his or her legal surname.[50]

Assuming, then, that the actress who played Aurelia in Paris was legally named Brigida Fedele, we face a whole new range of questions about her origins. It has been simply taken as a matter of course by scholars and biographers that Brigida Bianchi was the daughter of an actor named Giuseppe Bianchi who played Capitan Spezzafer and was head of the troupe in Paris in 1644–45. Unfortunately, a careful look at the available evidence suggests that Giuseppe Bianchi is as much a chimera as N. Romagnesi, or even more so, since Brigida Fedele was married at some point to a Romagnesi but was never the daughter of a Bianchi, especially Giuseppe.

Rasi devotes two pages to this actor who is known to him from the *Histoire de l'ancien théâtre italien* of François ʼand Claude Parfaict.[51] But Giuseppe Bianchi is simply not mentioned in that work, most of it taken from the notes of Gueullette, who also never mentions him.

A Giuseppe Bianchi was in Paris in 1645; he was not a capitan but a singer and, what is more, a castrato. He is first mentioned in 1643 when Cardinal Mazarin was planning the production of an opera, a plan cut short by the death of Louis XIII. Mazarin's agent in Rome, Elpidio Benedetti, wrote on 7 May: "As for the castrati, the best would be Giuseppi who serves D. Taddeo, but I believe he wouldn't come for less than twenty ecus a month in salary and a gift for the voyage." Henry Prunières identifies this Giuseppe as "Giuseppe Bianchi in the service of the prefect of Rome Don Taddeo Barberini."[52] He was a favorite of Queen Christina of Sweden, and a bone of contention between her and the duchess of Savoy.[53] Apparently Giuseppe allowed himself to be lured to Paris in late 1644 to cheer the mourning of Anne of Austria, but he was back in Rome on 29 May 1645, when Benedetti wrote to Mazarin: "Capitando Giuseppe Musico. Will administer to him the ten scudi owing him in conformity to your order,"[54] suggesting that Bianchi was being paid for services rendered during carnival in Paris. There was certainly no reason for Mazarin to pay him for services rendered in Rome.

Brigida Fedele, in any case, was not Giuseppe Bianchi's daughter. She may have been the daughter or granddaughter of an actor known as Lutio Fedele who was active in Naples between 1592 and 1615. Although his original name was Carlo Fredi, he is the exception that proves the rule, since he is referred to in various contracts as Lutio or Lutio Fedele. His first wife died in 1608, somewhat too soon to have been the mother of Aurelia, but he was remarried in 1614 to a young widow, Ippolita Laudisiello, who played the donna. If the two had a child, the child must have been born after Lutio's death, which happened some eighteen months after the marriage. His will includes a legacy to a stepdaughter, Angelica, to be used as her dowry, but has no mention of a child of the second marriage. Lutio also had a son, Flaminio, who married a serva, Camilla Positano, and died young, leaving two children, Marco and Diamante.[55]

Another Fedele or Fedeli active in the right period to have been the father of Brigida Fedele called himself Aurelio Fedeli and performed with Cecchini and with Silvio Fiorillo.[56] No connection can be proved between the actress who signed herself Brigida Fedele in Paris in the 1680s and the Fredi-Fedele clan in Italy in the first years of the century, but the name is that of a family long connected with the profession.

Of her husband, Marc' Antonio Bianchi, who played Horace in Paris in the late 1650s, little is known, unless he can be linked to the actor known as Orazio Carpiano (or Carpiani). The adoption of a complete professional name was rare but not unheard of; an earlier Orazio was known as Orazio Nobili.[57] Orazio Carpiano (or "il carpiano") was in the troupe of Jacopo Fidenzi in 1638 with Giovan Battista Fiorillo and his wife, Carlo Cantù, and Brigida Fedele. In a letter to the duke of Modena, Fidenzi refers to all of these actors by their character names: Trappolino, his wife Beatrice, Buffeto, Aurelia, and "il carpiano."[58] The actor himself wrote from Parma in 1641, describing himself as head of a large troupe and signing the letter "Horatio Carpiani Comico."[59] Rasi identifies the actor as Marc' Antonio Carpiani, but gives no source for the Christian name.[60]

We can thus connect Orazio Carpiano with many of the actors who were in France in the 1640s and 1650s, most importantly, with Brigida Fedele. Since he describes himself as a capocomico in 1641, there would be nothing surprising about finding him at the head of a troupe in Paris in 1644. He was definitely in Turin and Milan in 1645, both cities on the return route from Paris. And we know that Aurelia, a Briguelle, and someone identified by Henry Prunières as "Giulio Cesare Bianchi" left Paris in high dudgeon after carnival of 1645.[61]

Prunières found, in the Archives of Naples, a series of letters written to the Marquis Gaufredi, secretary to the duke of Parma, by various persons connected with the production of *La finta pazza* in 1645. Unfortunately, although he promises to "study elsewhere" these letters, he apparently never did.[62] Thus, though he tells us that "Maurice Sand and Campardon are absolutely wrong about the composition of the Italian troupe in 1645," he is not entirely accurate himself, especially about the person he identifies first as Giulio Cesare Bianchi, then as Giuseppe Bianchi.

According to Prunières, the queen mother became enamoured of several Italian singers who had been brought to France in the winter of 1645, most especially of "the divine Leonora," and, believing herself to be out of favor, Aurelia left Paris in early spring of 1645, before the end of the agreed-upon visit, in the company of Briguelle, the First Zanni, and "Giulio Cesare Bianchi." The queen mother wrote to the duke of Parma on 12 March 1645 requesting that he send her, to complete the troupe, Buffetto (to replace Briguelle) and "Anjuline, Ipolita, or Diana" to replace Aurelia. No mention is made of another actor, although the queen mother also wanted Balbi, the dancer, and Camillo, the designer. Buffetto (Carlo Cantù) came, along with Diana (Giulia Gabrielli) and her husband, Pietro Paolo Leoni. What role this last actor played is unknown, and the only other existing mention of him seems to be in the note Tiberio Fiorilli signed in 1659 agreeing to pay part of the pension of the now deceased Leoni to his nephew.

In Prunières's view, Leoni succeeded Giuseppe Bianchi, Capitan Spezzafer, who in the space of a few paragraphs, has replaced Giulio Cesare Bianchi among the returnees. But since there was no Capitan Spezzafer in the troupe, it seems reasonable that the letter referring to Aurelia's flight home, a letter from Cantù of 6 June, not reproduced by Prunières, mentions *a* Bianchi, our Marc' Antonio Bianchi, but does not distinguish him by Christian name, leading to Prunières's confusion. There *was* a Giulio Cesare Bianchi connected with *La finta pazzi;* he supposedly wrote a dedicatory letter in November 1645 that forms the preface to the *Explication des décorations du théâtre et les argumens de la pièce* published in Paris in advance of the production. This publication, though the synopsis, or "argument," was useful to the audience member who did not understand Italian, is a piece of skillful puffery on behalf of Giacomo Torelli, the great Italian designer-machinist who was out to make his name in France with the production. The *Explication* purports to be the work of Bianchi and demonstrates his astonishment at the wonders Torelli has wrought, but the privilege to print the piece was awarded to Torelli himself. There was a well-known Italian composer of the period named Giulio Cesare Bianchi. Though born in 1576–77, he is known to have been alive and living in Monteverdi's house in Cremona in 1637,[63] and he would not have been impossibly old in 1645. The Paris production of *La finta pazza* included a new prologue which was sung and which specifically praised the Bourbon monarchy. Someone must have composed the music for it, and the composer could have been Giulio Cesare Bianchi. On the other hand, Torelli could have simply borrowed his name for the *Explication.* It does seem unlikely, however, that a Giulio Cesare Bianchi was ever the husband of Brigida Fedele or acted in the Italian troupe in Paris. It is possible, of course, that all these Bianchis—Marc' Antonio, Guilio Cesare, and Giuseppe—were somehow connected, but nothing allows us to speculate about what the link might have been.

That Horatio Carpiano Comico was the professional name of Marc' Antonio Bianchi is also, finally, nothing but speculation. We know that Bianchi was an "eloquent amoureux" according to Loret.[64] What role was played by "il carpiano," described as "vainglorious and puffed up from too many honors,"[65] is not entirely clear. Horatio is generally a name used by the amoureux, and it is parodied as such in Molière's *L'école des femmes*. But Carpiano suggests words like *carpa,* the fish, *carpiono,* soused, or even a form of *carpire,* to snatch or get by trickery. Its overtones are definitely comic and not romantic. A few traces of Horatio remain in the zibaldone of Domenico Biancolelli, but they are too few to draw any conclusions about the character. In *Les engagemens du hazard,* Horatio is a character in a play that includes two other amoureux, Valerio and Octave. In one scene he enters to deliver a letter to Diamantine; in another he plays a scene of lazzi with Valerio and Arlequin.[66] In *Le triumvirat de l'amitiez* he is referred to as "a certain count Horatio Malade."[67] And in *Le baron allemand* Arlequin mentions the name, but there is no indication that the character appeared onstage.[68]

According to the Parfaict brothers, Brigida Fedele's husband died in Paris shortly after the troupe left for Italy in July 1659.[69] They assumed that his wife returned in 1660, "without doubt because of the news that she had received of the death of her husband." According to La Grange, however, Aurelia and Trivelin stayed in Paris when the others left on 8 or 9 July.[70] Where the Parfaicts heard the news of Bianchi's death remains a mystery. Their usual source is Gueullette, but Gueullette says nothing about it. Brigida Fedele was a widow in 1686, but the possibility exists that her husband was still living after the troupe's return to France in 1661. This possibility will be explored in chapter 5.

Brigida Fedele is first heard of in 1634 in Genoa;[71] she is mentioned in a burlesque *Infirmità, testamento e morte* of Scapino in 1638,[72] the same year she was in Fidenzi's company in Parma. She may have been in Paris as early as 1639; she is mentioned in the probably apocryphal tale of the infant Louis XIV soiling the hands and clothing of Tiberio Fiorilli.[73] She was certainly in Paris for carnival of 1645, though as we have seen, she left before the end of the season.

When she returned is unclear. She is not mentioned in any of Loret's letters before the end of May 1659, although when he announces the troupe's impending departure a month later, he remarks that he has loved her for more than two years.[74] That, combined with the document of December 1657 mentioning Bianchi, implies they were in Paris at least from before the carnival of 1657. Unfortunately, the small extant repertory from this period is of no help. Aurelia could have performed in *La Rosaura imperatrice di Constantinopoli* and in *Il convitato di pietra,* but so could any other amoureuse.

Domenico Locatelli, known as Trivelin, played First Zanni in the Paris troupe during the 1660s. However, Trivelin probably began as a Second Zanni, as his black mask, flat hat, patches, and bat would indicate. No mysteries present themselves about him or about his wife, Luisa Gabrielli, known as Lucille, although not very much is known about them, either.

There is no evidence linking Domenico Locatelli to Basileo Locatelli, the Roman who between 1618 and 1622, "as a recreation after my work . . . clothed and adorned" some eighty commedia dell'arte scenarios "so they may appear on the stage in any company without shame."[75] The Basileo Locatelli who prays that "God in his mercy" will allow him to make restitution for "the many days wasted in such occupations" does not sound like an actor. Luisa Gabrielli was however, probably a member of the family of the famous Scapino Francesco Gabrielli and a sister of Giulia Gabrielli, Diana, who also played in *La finta pazza*—though it should be noted that Scapino's *Infirmità, testamento e morte* mentions only his wife, Spinetta, and his daughter Diana.[76]

Often thought by scholars to have been the capocomico of the so-called Troupe of Locatelli, the Paris company of 1660–71, the actor was in Paris as early as 1644–45. His son Charles-François was baptised there on 9 January 1645; the godparents were "a marshal of France and the princesse de Condé."[77] He is not associated with the production of *La finta pazza,* although his wife was one of the three actresses mentioned in the *Explication des décorations.* Locatelli must have been playing Second Zanni at this point, since the letters of Carlo Cantù indicate that he came to Paris in 1645 to replace a Briguelle, or First Zanni. Locatelli was still there and very much in royal favor in 1647 when a brevet of the king granted him the inheritance of the property of "one Laurent dead in Paris."[78] During the Fronde, Locatelli was in Verona in 1651 and in Modena with his wife and Giovan Andrea Zanotti in 1652.[79] As we have seen, in 1653, on the troupe's return to Paris, Loret greeted him especially, writing that he would rather "eat less soup and drink a little less wine than not see Trivelin."[80] Over the next six years Loret continues to mention Trivelin occasionally, perhaps because the name is easily rhymed, no small consideration to a man writing hundreds of lines of jingles a week.

In 1658 Locatelli was granted a privilege to publish the synopsis of

La Rosaura imperatrice di Constantinopoli, "which he has composed in French prose." The zanni role in *La Rosaura* was clearly played not by Trivelin but by Scaramouche, as probably was the role of Don Juan's valet in *Il convitato di pietra.*[81]

Locatelli was a prominent member of the company, although whether it should be called "the troupe of Locatelli," either in the 1650s or later, is open to question. True, Locatelli did receive the privilege of publication for the Argument of *La Rosaura,* but Torelli received the same privilege for *La finta pazza* and he was hardly the capocomico. Financial records show that Locatelli signed for quarterly pension payments, but so did Fiorilli, Zanotti, Bianchi, and later Biancolelli, Lolli, Cei, and Romagnesi. In the later years of the troupe, Lolli was its "man of business," though not its leader, while first Zanotti and then Romagnesi were the ones to travel to Italy to find new company members. The whole notion of capocomico arises in commedia dell'arte largely from the system of patronage, the need to have someone who would represent the interests of the actors to whatever Este or Medici or Gonzaga was sponsoring them at the time. In Paris, especially in the early years, the need was for someone to represent the actors to the court, either to the queen mother and Mazarin or, later, to Louis XIV. In 1645, when the Italians quarreled with Torelli, it was Carlo Cantù who went to Anne of Austria and wrote the actors' side of the story home to Parma, suggesting that the original capocomico was among those who had returned to Italy, either the Briguelle whom Cantù was replacing, or the husband of Aurelia, Marc' Antonio Bianchi. In any case, it would not have been Locatelli, who stayed on in France.

Locatelli could have been the one to maneuver the troupe through the choppy waters of the post-Fronde court, but Tiberio Fiorilli appears to have been better placed to do so. On the other hand, Fiorilli was continually returning to Italy, while Locatelli seems to have been more consistently in Paris. The role of the capocomico in France should not be overvalued. The Italians never had a single charismatic leader like Molière; even Domenico Biancolelli—though an extremely popular actor and an effective advocate for the troupe—was not its capo, or head, in any legal or even de facto way.

Angelo Agostino Lolli played the Docteur in the established troupe from 1661 to 1694. Known as Monsieur Ange, he was also the business manager and in charge of devising the spectacle. He may have been in Paris as early as 1653; he was certainly there in 1659, when he took part in the entertainment at Vincennes. A native of Bologna, according to his papers of naturalization,[82] Lolli was probably born around 1620. According to Jal, he was eighty when he died in 1702.[83] He gave his own age as fifty-eight in a deposition he made in 1692,[84] but since he retired two years later "because of his age and infirmities,"[85] that seems unlikely. His signature was very shaky in 1691.[86]

Few records exist of his appearances in Italy, nor has his relationship to two other actors named Lolli been established. One, Giovanni Antonio Lolli, also played the Docteur, and in the same period. Rasi has collected letters from him and references to him from 1661 to 1692. The other, Eustachio Lolli, played a zanni, Fichetto, and was in the Modena troupe in 1651.

Campardon and others have assumed that Angelo Agostino Lolli was in France from 1653 because of an odd incident recorded by Loret. According to *La muze historique* of 14 February 1654, "Baloardo the actor, who though Italian is a melancholy fellow, dared the other day to boldly attack the Pantalon Bisognoza in a public place." Pantalon fought back, and the aggressor found himself on the ground. Lolli did play as Docteur Gratian Baloard, but the problem with the evidence is that the Parfaicts miscopied Loret,[88] and succeeding scholars have not looked back at the original. The name appears three times, once as *Baloardo,* twice as *Odouardo.* And there was an actor working in Italy around that time who used the name Odoardo. He is proposed for Second Amoureux in a company sponsored by the duke of Parma in 1664.[89] Of course, Lolli could have been in Paris at the time; no other actor is known to have played the role of Docteur there at any time before his retirement in 1694. But Lolli was playing in Rome, not Paris, in 1658,[90] and the behavior attributed to Baloardo-Odouardo hardly fits the image of Monsieur Ange, who in later years was neither aggressive nor melancholy.

Lolli married Patricia Adami, who played the servante Diamantine, supposedly after the troupe's return in 1661. He had no known children.[91]

Giovan Andrea Zanotti joined the troupe sometime before 1659 as Second Amoureux. He played under the name Octave. He was born Giovan Andrea Cavazzoni in 1622 at Caselle near Bologna; Zanotti was his mother's name. According to Rasi, Zanotti took the name in 1640 after the death of a maternal uncle whose will obliged him to do so if he wanted to inherit. Zanotti is first heard of with Carlo Cantù in service to the duke of Modena in 1647. The troupe played in Parma, Rome, and Naples. In 1651 he was in the company of the duke of Bologna. In 1652 he was with Domenico Locatelli in Modena; in 1655 he was in Genoa.[92]

Zanotti probably did not arrive with Locatelli and the others in Paris in 1653, but he was certainly there in June 1659, when he is mentioned as one of the actors who had received pension money and turned part of the share owing Pietro Paolo Leoni over to Tiberio Fiorilli. Zanotti was married at that time to Teodora Blasi, who was not, so far as is known, ever an actress.

Giovan Battista Turri (or Turi) played the role of Pantalon in Paris, but probably not in the 1650s. That the company had a Pantalon is clear from Loret's anecdote describing the battle between Pantalon Bisognoza and Baloardo-Odouardo. Gueullette identifies this early Pantalon as N. Turi; Rasi, thanks to a letter he found of March 1671, identifies him as Giovan Battista Turri.[93]

Turri had a son who played under the name Virginio. In the letter Rasi found, his father recommends him as ready for employment as a second amoroso. Gueullette believes this son appeared in Paris in 1653 as Third Amoureux, but if he did, and if he was applying for a promotion nearly twenty years later, then he was a remarkably slow learner.

In fact, the only proof that Turri played Pantalon in Paris at all is his signature on two loan contracts in 1686.[94] Although it is possible that Turri was the Pantalon of 1653–59 or the new Pantalon announced by Robinet in 1670, the evidence as it stands permits only the conclusion that Turri was the Pantalon who made his debut at court in December 1684. The Turris will be considered in greater detail in chapter 11.

Several other actors who played in France between 1643 and 1648 and from 1652 to 1659 have never been confirmed as part of the later established company. These include Carlo Cantù, Giulia Gabrielli and her husband, Pietro Paolo Leoni, Marguerita Bertalotti, a Mlle. Beatrix, a Flamine, the wives of Tiberio Fiorilli and Domenico Locatelli, and the husband of Brigida Fedele, who has already been discussed.

Carlo Cantù was only briefly in Paris to replace the First Zanni who got angry and went home after carnival of 1644. Cantù was the second husband of Isabella Franchini (the mother of Domenico Biancolelli) and played under the name of Buffetto. He was accompanied by Diana, Giulia Gabrielli, and her husband, the latter two complaining that Cantù had not shared out the travel money.[95] Both Buffetto and Diana were specifically requested by the queen mother, although Diana was third on the list. She, her sister Luisa (the wife of Locatelli), and an unknown singer, Marguerita Bertalotti, are all mentioned in the *Explication des décorations* of *La finta pazza*. By the end of March 1645, Cantù and Giulia Gabrielli had returned to Italy, and the queen mother was once again requesting a Briguelle and several other actors to replace the ones who had just left.[96]

No further report is found of them in France, except for Torelli's effort to get the deceased Pietro Paolo Leoni's share of the royal pension back from Tiberio Fiorilli.[97] The involvement of Zanotti in that business makes it unlikely that the pension in question was left over from 1645, and implies that Leoni, at least, was in France in the late 1650s. Aside from this document and the letters Prunières found and never published, there seem to be no references to Leoni in any of the materials published or studied by scholars of the commedia dell'arte.

Leoni might have been the actor who played Flamine, mentioned in the extract of a letter in verse to the duc d'Aumele relating a visit of the king and court to Fontainebleau c. 1655 and copied into his manuscript by Gueullette.[98] The Italians were with the court performing, and the writer of the letter describes "diverse divertissements . . . where one sees Flamine fight, Aurelia promenade, and Trivelin *triveliner*." Gueullette has made a marginal note, "Flaminia," but "fighting" (the French is *se battre*) hardly seems like decorous stage behavior for an amoureuse, so the more likely reading is "Flaminio." The most probable candidate for the actor playing the role is Marco Napolioni, in the company of the duke of Modena midcentury and linked to many of the actors who played in France.[99] Were *Pietro Paolo* Leoni not clearly mentioned in the notarial document of 1659 in France, or were Marco Napolioni less well known, the temptation might be to wonder whether some slip of the pen had created either Leoni or Napolioni.

Mlle. Beatrix is mentioned once, by Loret, when he welcomes the troupe in 1653, and although he was delighted to see Trivelin and Scaramouche, it was "Mlle. Beatrix" who "enchanted the ears, swooned, wept, did marvels," and clearly "carried off the prize of the day."[100] Without doubt an amoureuse, Beatrix was Beatrice Vitelli, the wife of Giovan Battista Fiorillo and—very likely—the sister-in-law of Tiberio Fiorilli. Popular in Italy, she was once kidnapped by a Count Bonoparte Ghislieri; a letter from Cardinal Sacchetti to the grand duke of Tuscany asks that she be recovered and returned to her husband.[101] Her presence in Paris in 1653–54 is confirmed by a letter written from Paris, 5 June 1654, to Cardinal d'Este by his affectionate uncle Tomaso. According to Uncle Tomaso, "La Signora Beatrice Vitelli Comica, in the course of her labors, has moved here from the Piedmont."[102] She was anxious to avoid the effects of not having procured the protection of the duke of Modena for herself and her family.

Since Loret says clearly in 1659 that he has "loved Aurelia" for more than two years, the probability exists that Beatrice Vitelli played the

First Amoureuse in Paris from 1653 to at least the middle of the decade. Her husband may have been with her as well, since the letter to Cardinal d'Este does mention a family. However, there seems to have been no place for Trappolino in a company that included Trivelin.

Luisa Gabrielli, Lucille, accompanied her husband, Domenico Locatelli, to Paris, where she played—as has been seen—in *La finta pazza* and may well have served as Second Amoureuse until 1659. The same is true of Lorenza Elisabetta del Campo, wife of Tiberio Fiorilli, who played the servante under the name Marinette. Both are mentioned in the *Epistre* to the duc d'Aumele.[103]

We cannot, of course, perfectly reconstruct these early Italian troupes; a thorough search of printed sources and Paris archives has filled some gaps, opened others. The company rosters now look as follows with dates included only when known, but with a few attributions as yet unproved. These are marked with an asterisk.

Troupe of 1644–48

First Amoureuse	Brigida Fedele (Aurelia)	1644–45
	Giulia Gabrielli (Diana)	1645
Second Amoureuse	Luisa Gabrielli (Lucille)	1644
Servante	Lorenza Elisabetta del Campo (Marinette)	1645
First Amoureux	Marc' Antonio Bianchi (Horace)	1644–45
	*Pietro Paolo Leoni	1645
Second Amoureux	unknown	
Pantalon	unknown	
Docteur	unknown	
Capitan	unknown	
First Zanni	unknown (played as Briguelle)	1644–45
	Carlo Cantù (Buffetto)	1645
Second Zanni	Domenico Locatelli (Trivelin)	1644–47
Scaramouche	Tiberio Fiorilli	1644–47

Troupe of 1653–59

First Amoureuse	Beatrice Vitelli (Beatrice)	1653–54
	Brigida Fedele (Aurelia)	1657–59
Second Amoureuse	Luisa Gabrielli (Lucille)	c. 1655

Servante	Lorenza Elisabetta del Campo (Marinette)	c. 1655
First Amoureux	Marc' Antonio Bianchi (Horace)	1657–59
Second Amoureux	*Pietro-Paolo Leoni	dead in 1659
	Giovan Andrea Zanotti (Octave)	1659
Pantalon	unknown (played as Bisognaza)	1654
Docteur	Angelo Agostino Lolli (Gratian Baloard)	1654(?), 1659
Capitan	unknown	
First Zanni	unknown	
Second Zanni	Domenico Locatelli (Trivelin)	1653–59
Scaramouche	Tiberio Fiorilli	1653–59

The Magician
of Fano

T HE ITALIAN TROUPES that visited France in the 1640s and 1650s must have performed, for the most part, the standard repertory of a mid-seventeenth-century commedia dell'arte company. This repertory, which has been described in detail by Kathleen M. Lea,[1] was no longer limited to the neo-Latin plays or the imitations of the Renaissance commedia erudita, which are often the only pieces attributed to the commedia dell'-arte. Though the traditional plots of domineering fathers, distressed lovers, and clever servants were still an important part of the repertory, other kinds of entertainments were offered as well. Many seventeenth-century scenarios are borrowed from Spanish plays (and many seventeenth-century amoureuses, like Brigida Fedele looking for literary respectabil-ity, published translations of Spanish plays). Company repertories also included tragicomedy, pastoral, and romance, all three often requiring elaborate spectacle, music, and dance.

Only three plays can be identified as having been performed by the Italians in Paris in the 1640s and 1650s, and none of those were from the standard neo-Roman repertory. The zibaldone of Domenico Bianco-lelli—notes on dialogue and physical play made by the troupe's Arlequin after 1662—very probably includes information about pieces first per-formed in the earlier period. But since it is impossible to tell which of the plays included by Biancolelli might have been done earlier—with the one exception of *Il convitato di pietra*—the zibaldone will be considered in chapter 6, and the three known plays discussed here with no attempt to generalize about the repertory.

The three known productions were of *La finta pazza* in 1645 and *La Rosaura imperatrice di Constantinopoli* and *Il convitato di pietra* in 1658. The first two are machine plays that were produced in elaborate settings de-signed by Giacomo Torelli; the last is a second-generation descendant of the Spanish *El burlador de Sevilla* by Tirso de Molina and the first Don Juan play performed in Paris. Although not a machine play, its popularity was certainly enhanced by the statue of the Commander who came to dinner.

La finta pazza, with text by Giulio Strozzi and music, now lost, by Francesco Sacrati, is not a typical commedia dell'arte play and is usually treated as an opera. First produced in Venice in 1641 to open the Teatro Novissimo, it is a play with music designed to feature the latest machines of the great Giacomo Torelli, the "Magician of Fano," as well as interludes of comic dance choreographed by Giovan Battista Balbi. The production was repeated in Florence for carnival of 1645, with "all the intermezzi and changes of scene as had been done in Venice."[2] Both Torelli and Balbi were brought to Paris for the production there in December 1645. Both made sure that their contributions to *La finta pazza* would be recognized. Torelli published the *Explication des décorations du théâtre et les Argumens de la pièce* together with engravings by Cochin of the settings.[3] Balbi also had a series of engravings published of his dances, which he accompanied by a preface. Both try hard to leave the impression that their work in Paris was original; Balbi excuses himself "for having dared to undertake to perform these ballets in Paris," which he had to imagine in order to give pleasure to the king, who was only six. However, the same bears, apes, and ostriches that appeared in Paris had already appeared in Florence and in Venice.

Nevertheless, it was the penchant of the designer and the choreographer for self-aggrandizement that generated the materials which enable us to describe the production. Unfortunately, Balbi was concerned only with the intermezzi, and Torelli was displeased by having to work with a troupe of common actors, so neither has much to say about the Italian company.

Either the queen mother or the actors themselves had a machine play in mind as early as March of 1645 when she wrote to the duke of Parma that she needed a First Zanni and a First Amoureuse to complete the troupe in Paris. Brigida Fedele and an actor who played Briguelle had returned early to Italy, possibly because they felt threatened by the presence at court of several Italian singers, especially the diva Leonora.[4] At the same time, the queen mother asked for Giovan Battista Balbi, the dancer, "and a décorateur of the theatre called Camillo." This was, she said, a thing she "passionately desired."[5] Balbi, who was in Florence, was ordered to Paris post haste, but instead of "Camillo" the duke sent the great Torelli himself. Torelli's arrival in June 1645 did nothing to further the project. Discovering that he was expected to construct a stage and design scenery for the Italian troupe, Torelli wrote a furious letter on 11 June to the duke of Parma, announcing that "to serve the actors is a thing contrary to my genius and my custom," and that it was impossible for a man "exercising a profession as high and honorable as mine to be the hireling of a troupe of actors."[6]

Torelli sulked for months while the queen mother ordered the scenery for court ballets from others. On 11 September he wrote to the duke's secretary, the Marquis Gaufredi, that no one was answering his letters and that he had heard "from a good source that there is going to be given in the queen's rooms a ballet with stage and machines and that the work will be executed by their workers and not by me. I will be so mortified by such an attack, not on my self-interest, for which I care little, but on my honor, that without a doubt I would return right now to Italy, since such a great affront is offered me, despite the promise that I was to serve Her Majesty, on the grounds of which I decided to leave Venice and, what's more, told everyone about it as I was leaving." The heart of the issue is bared next: "It cannot be denied that I have acted with great care for my reputation since I have no share in the subvention nor in the receipts of their ridiculous plays, but only in the works which will be celebrated and will include music, as for example, *La finta pazza*."[7]

The actors' side of the story is told by Carlo Cantù, writing also to the Marquis Gaufredi on 10 October:

> When Signor Torelli arrived in Paris with us in the expectation of earning some money, we gave him his share in our performances if he set up a stage with machines, which we have done, and he was not at all averse to it. But when we understood that he blushed to be associated with the actors, all the while taking his share in our labors, and that he intrigued with Cardinal Mazarin and M. de Lionne, his devoted friend, in the plan to make a new theatre for the musicians, we were disgusted with him and our resentment grew when we heard that M. de Lionne was bringing some singers and had advanced to them from his own pocket 10,000 ecus which were to be reimbursed from their first labors. We went to find the queen who, after having heard our explanations and how Torelli had been brought especially for us, wanted to see in what terms the secretary Agra had written on the subject to Torelli, and, observing that he had called him an engineer of machines and Balbi a ballet dancer and that both were brought for us . . . Her Majesty asked Torelli why he didn't want to work for us. Torelli answered that he was a gentleman and ready to execute no matter what work, but he wanted an order from Her Majesty to associate himself with the actors and that he is

obliged by his honor to work his wonders in other circumstances
than with the actors. We answered him all together: "We had you
brought here for us and the proof that you are our associate is that
you take your share of our labors every day that we play." The *gentle-*
man replied that he would pay back his share. The queen began to
laugh and went into her room, out of which soon came Commander
de Souvré, who said as follows: Signor Torelli, Her Majesty the
Queen says that you are here for the Italian troupe as a result of the
request it made to Her Majesty and that you must work for it or not
work at all.[8]

A new accommodation was reached. Torelli would no longer receive a
daily share of the profits, but would get two shares for each performance
of the machine play under preparation. Lionne and the dreaded troupe of
singers would be beaten at the gate.

Torelli went to work, built the stage the actors required in the Petit-
Bourbon, and fitted it with intricate machines and splendid decorations.[9]
On 4 October he told the duke of Parma that he was sending a book
describing the magnificent scenery he had invented. Two days earlier
Balbi wrote that they hoped to have the opera ready by the end of the
month. "Curiosity is great," he added, and we count on good receipts."[10]

La finta pazza (in French *La folle supposée*) was not performed until
December, nor was it really an opera as produced in Paris, whatever it
may have been in Italy. Although some scenes were sung, many were
not. The *Gazette* describes the event as follows:

> The 14th of this month, the queen with a great part of the court was
> at the play which the Italian Company performed under the title of
> the *Finta pazza* of Jullio Strozzi, in the Grande Salle of the Petit-
> Bourbon, all the audience being no less charmed by the poetry and
> the music, than by the decoration of the stage, the artifice of the
> machines, and the admirable changes of the scenes, until now un-
> known in France, which transported the eyes of the spirit as well as
> the eyes of the body by their movements, which were too quick to
> be seen: invention of the sieur Jacques Torelli of the same nation.[11]

Olivier d'Ormesson saw it and recorded his impressions in his journal:

> Wednesday, 27 December, I went, after dinner, with M. de Fourcy to
> the Italian Comedy, where I saw five different faces of the stage, the
> one representing three cypress alleys, so long as to be lost to view;
> the other, the port of Chio where the Pont Neuf and the Place Dau-
> phine were admirably represented; the third, a city; the fourth, a
> palace where you see an infinity of rooms, the fifth, a garden with

beautiful pilasters. In all these different faces, the perspective was so well observed that all the alleys appeared lost to view, although the stage has only four or five feet of depth. With the play, which is *The Discovery of Achilles by the Greeks,* they danced a ballet of bears and monkeys, a ballet of ostriches and dwarfs, and a ballet of Ethiopians and parrots. At the beginning, Aurora rose imperceptibly from the earth in a chariot and then crossed the stage with marvelous speed. Four zephyrs were raised to the heavens in the same way, four descended from heaven and remounted with the same speed. The machines are worth seeing.[12]

The production can be recreated, although without perfect authority, from the *Explication des décorations* which, if not written by Torelli, certainly reflects both his intentions and his interests, and the French synopsis provided for the audience members who did not understand Italian. Since both the *Explication,* written in the future tense, and the synopsis, written in the present, were published in advance of the opening, they cannot be taken as exact descriptions of what happened on the stage. D'Ormesson's brief journal entry does confirm some details, however, and the fact that the pamphlet was apparently used both for publicity before the fact and as a sort of program for the performance suggests that it cannot have been too far off the mark. The *Explication* begins:

> After the great curtain is raised with very great speed, there will be represented the beautiful and delicious gardens of Flora. . . . Three cypress alleys will stretch into the distance [which d'Ormesson confirms] leading to a palace. . . . On the left will be seen a chariot. . . . pulled by two "forerunners of the day" with torches in their hands, in which will be seated Aurora, the dawn. . . . As the chariot rises and moves from east to west, the stage, which was dark, will little by little become light . . . and Flora will be seen, gathering flowers to present to the Goddess of the Light. Aurora will then command marvels to appear in the air, gardens and flowers that will show how the fields of Heaven surpass the fertility of the Earth. Then five winged spirits will appear, two of them supporting a royal crown and three the golden lillies. . . . The chariot . . . will fly out to the right, gradually rising until lost to view while the two winged spirits rise and . . . return for Flora, whom they will take by the arms and legs and lift to Heaven.

The whole scene then disappears in one imperceptible movement, thanks to "a very ingenious wheel invented solely by the one responsible for the decoration of the stage." Thus, Torelli introduced himself to the court and theatre audience of Paris.

The prologue, newly devised for Paris and the French monarch, was sung principally by Marguerita Bertalotti, who had no other known connection with the Italian actors and was probably a singer hired for the occasion. It combined a maximum of spectacle with a maximum of flattery. Both poet and composer are unknown. Prunières suggests that it may have been the work of Giovan Battista Andreini, who had been in Paris first with Martinelli and then as leader of the Fedeli and who wrote several spectacular musical pieces.[13] Andreini may have been in Paris in the 1640s as Prunières believes, but he was old—nearly seventy—and had not led a company since the mid 1630s. There is certainly no evidence to suggest he was actively involved with this company. In any case, Torelli was pleased with Bertalotti who, he writes, has a "such a ravishing voice that I cannot praise it highly enough." Louise Gabrielli Locatelli, known as Lucille, was Flora. Torelli calls her "nice and pretty . . . a true luminary of harmony," so apparently she also sang.

The second setting (1.1–2), according to its creator, "will represent the port and city of Scyrus," although not with any historical accuracy, since the center of the scene was the Ile de la Cité with the spire of Ste.-Chapelle, the towers of Notre-Dame, the Pont Neuf, and even the equestrian statue of Henri IV. To one side was a fort along the banks of a river; to the other, a seaport with ships. The view of the Cité was taken from the quai along the side of the Louvre (fig. 3). Not only is this a somewhat astonishing anachronism, but the setting is not original with Torelli. In 1638, in Rome, the French ambassador, in honor of the birth of the dauphin, had mounted a production of *La sincerita triomfante* by Ottaviano Castelli da Spoleti with music by Angelo Cecchini. The settings, of which there were eight, were designed by Joannes Andreas Potestas. A copy of the opera and watercolors of the designs were sent to Cardinal Richelieu in Paris, who was considering a similar operatic celebration. Submitted to Chapelain for approval, the libretto was severely criticized and the project dropped. The watercolors remain, however, and the eighth scene shows the Pont Neuf, Henri IV on his horse, and a rough approximation of the spire of Ste.-Chapelle. The Pont Neuf features a large fleur-de-lis, and a gondola with a scalloped awning floats on the Seine, suggesting that the designer had probably never seen Paris but was copying from something of the same genre representing Venice.[14] Torelli's design is both more elegant and slightly more accurate, at least insofar as the background is concerned. The foreground, with fort to the left and port to the right, is impressive, though oddly out of scale, while the Pont Neuf absolutely looms over the river thanks to a low point of view.[25] The design

FIG. *3. Torelli's design for act 1, scenes 1 and 2, of* La finta
pazza. (Bibliothèque Nationale; phot. Bibl. Nat. Paris)

looks as if the backscene has been added to an already existing setting, and perhaps it has, since we know Torelli used the same setting in Florence that he had used in Venice. The original scene may well have shown Venice, just as Potestas's original may have done. The combination of cityscape, bridge, and seaport seems more likely if Venice is the city represented. Torelli had done such a setting in 1642 for *Bellerofonte*.[16]

Into this Greco-Parisian fantasy sails a ship. The gangplank is thrust forth, and Ulysses and Diomedes with eight soldiers are met by eight Armed Inhabitants, their Captain, and six pages. At first the Greek ambassadors are prevented from landing, but once recognized as friends, they are led off to King Licomedes. The ship is put in its place "according to the usage of ports." This scene, says Torelli, is to be played without music, "but so well that the past harmony will almost be forgotten."

The plot now begins to interfere with the scenery. Ulysses and Diomedes have come to Scyros to find Achilles, whose mother, Thetis, has hidden him there among the daughters of Licomedes so that he will not be killed in the Trojan War. Minerva and Juno, the enemies of Troy who have led the Greek ambassadors to Achilles, now descend from the sky on a cloud while Thetis enters from the sea, riding in a shell pulled by two dolphins. The three dispute—in song—and Thetis is convinced by the powerful arguments of the goddesses who then reascend, their cloud splitting in two with each half becoming as large as the original. Thetis is played by Giulia Gabrielli, known as Diana, who "will marvelously reveal the anger and love" of the character.

The third setting (1.3–5) is the palace of Licomedes, in Doric architecture, richly ornamented, with statues in niches and a double order of gilded columns supporting vases of orange trees. At the rear is an arch or passageway, above it a second story. The passageway is covered by a curtain of gold cloth, "seeming to enclose something very precious within." Achilles, in women's clothing, hears of the arrival of the ambassadors as he secretly enjoys the embraces of Deidamia, the king's daughter, his mistress by whom he has had a child and whom he has promised to marry. King Licomedes, accompanied by his court and guards and the ambassadors, "to the number of forty persons," enters. When the ambassadors beg for the honor of seeing the King's daughters, the King has the curtain raised, and a sort of paradise appears where Deidamia, Achilles, and eight other ladies with four pages embroider while they try to persuade a Eunuch to sing. He, "bizarre like those of his kind," refuses, then agrees if the Daughters will sing with him. Licomedes summons his Daughters, and as they leave to join the Greeks, the Eunuch sings.

Achilles is recognized by a ruse and decides to follow his destiny. As the characters exit, a vista is revealed of rooms leading to a far-distant garden, "where the rule of perspective will be so well observed that the eye will fool itself and will believe the distance to be a true thing." The act ends with a divertissement for the ambassadors. Four eunuchs sweep the courtyard for a dance of four bears and four monkeys. The monkeys, as well as the parrots in the third divertissement, were danced by children, according to Balbi, who complained that they did not speak Italian and he did not speak French, so he had difficulty making them understand what he wanted them to do.[17]

By the end of act 1, Torelli has used three of his five settings along with two flying effects, two moving boats, a scene of local color, a paradise, and a vista. Act 2 begins a sequence of alternation. "In the first scene will appear a great square with several perspectives" leading to the city gates. Downstage to one side are Egyptian pyramids, to the other, tombs of heroes. Act 2, scenes 1–3, take place here; then the scene reverts to the palace. Scene 5 is in the square, scenes 6 and 7 in the palace. During these scenes Vulcan brings Achilles a new lance, so heavy that only Achilles can bear it. Deidamia complains to her Nurse of Achilles' neglect. Achilles sustains in combat (offstage) against the Captain the proposition that a man can change his mistress, and Deidamia, in despair, decides to pretend to be mad. In scene 8, the Magician of Fano once again takes the reins. "The Heavens will visibly move, then the Horizon will rise in an instant, and the Clouds which shadow the Heaven will dissipate and there will be discovered the glory of a paradise full of rays of light in which will be seen with majesty a seated Iris, Jupiter the thunderer with the Eagle armed with thunderbolts and all around, on various levels, the Gods of antiquity. On one side, will be seen Victory in a cloud, and on the other Cupid." Victory, on Jupiter's orders, flies to Deidamia to ensure her triumph, and as she flies down, Cupid rises and "the Heavens will close." Deidamia plays her mad scene to end the act. The divertissement between the acts is a ballet of six ostriches which, by means of an ingenious mechanism, stretch out their necks to drink at a fountain.

Act 3, scenes 1–3, are in the city square. Deidamia tries to tell her father that she has had a son by Achilles, but Licomedes will not believe her, thinks she is indeed mad, and has her bound. In scene 4 the stage changes to a royal garden with palisades of roses and myrtles and a perspective vista to be revealed for the final divertissement. Achilles finds Deidamia tied up in the garden and takes pity on her. She confesses her pretense, and he confirms his promise to marry her. In the final scene,

Licomedes recognizes Pirrus as his grandson, the vista is revealed, a fountain begins to play, and five American Indians enter with five parrots for the final ballet, at the end of which the parrots fly away, and the gentlemen embark for the Trojan War.

Acts 2 and 3 are less spectacular than the prologue and act 1, but Torelli has still managed two new settings, the obligatory glory, still another revealed perspective vista, and a final flying effect. Alternation of settings results from the newly invented "ingenious wheel," Torelli's winch system, which made it possible to return a set of wings and back-scene to the stage as easily as remove it. The settings clearly demonstrate the way in which the baroque stage was divided into three zones: a narrow acting area usually well lighted by chandeliers, a front scene using painted flat wings, and a backscene, sometimes closed off by a shutter, sometimes open to reveal a forced-perspective vista. Torelli's flying effects operated in front of the backscene. When there was flying to be done, the designer used no borders closing off the top of the set. Since actors appeared in the glories and flew in just in front of the backscene, heavily forced perspective was unlikely in the downstage zones. The dividing line is often referred to in France as the "optique"—"behind the optique" meaning "in the zone of perspective vistas."

Torelli certainly made an effective debut in France with *La finta pazza*. His role is clear, but the role of the Italian actors is not. Nothing is known for certain about which actor played which character (with the exception of the three women mentioned in the *Explication*), nor is it known whether they played as commedia dell'arte masques. One clue which suggests that they did is a print by Stefano della Bella (before 1664) which shows Carlo Cantù, Buffetto, fingering his guitar against a background almost identical to the view of the Ile de la Cité shown in the engraving of Torelli's act 1 setting.[18] The point of view is higher, but the equestrian statue of Henri IV, the spire of Ste.-Chapelle, and the towers of Notre-Dame are in precisely the same relationship. Not only are the backgrounds the same, the round tower at the left of the Cantù print is the Tour de Bois of the Old Louvre, similar to the tower on the first wing of the stage design, although in general the foregrounds are not the same. The same images appear, though separated, on the frontispiece of an Italian edition of the *Explication et Argumens* in the collection of the Bibliothèque de l'Arsenal. The frontispiece shows a rather vexed looking Victory leaning on a pedestal that holds a mask, some papers, and a guitar (fig. 4). Above her head, two winged putti support the crown and arms of France. At her feet are draftsman's tools. To her right are the Pont

FIG. *4. Title page of an Italian version of the* Explication des décorations
. . . pour La folle supposée *dedicated to Anne of*
Austria. (Bibliothèque de l'Arsenal; phot. Bibl. Nat. Paris)

Neuf, Henri IV, and the spire of Ste.-Chapelle, to her left the Tour de Bois. She herself is located on the Left Bank, making the scene geographically possible.[19]

Taken all together, the images in the prints imply that Cantù appeared in *La finta pazza,* which the Paris scene appears to symbolize, in his character of Buffetto. If he did, then probably he appeared as the Eunuch, who "shares in the bizarre behavior of those like him," refuses to sing unless the Daughters sing with him, and continues to sing as the Daughters tidy themselves and slip away to meet the Greeks. This scene is the only one which includes any traditional zanni play.

Giulia Gabrielli was the First Amoureuse of the troupe, the one sent for by name by the queen mother herself. She presumably played Deidamia as well as Thetis; we know from her participation in the musical dispute in act 1 that she could sing. Luisa Locatelli and Marguerita Bertalotti, who appeared first as Aurora and Flora, very likely reappeared as Minerva and Juno, although one could have appeared as Victory in act 2, scene 8. Neither the *Explication* nor the *Argumens* indicates any other musical scenes beyond those already noted, but it seems reasonable that any scene containing gods and goddesses, with the possible exception of Vulcan's scene, would include song.

The *Explication* strongly implies that Ulysses and Diomedes as well as the Captain of the Armed Inhabitants were not singers. The Capitan, if there was one in the company, probably played the Captain; act 2, scene 7, sounds like a typical scene for the character. "The Captain of the Armed Inhabitants is angry at having been defeated by Achilles in the presence of his Mistress; having become a mocker of women, he comes to the court to declare the hatred of Achilles for the Royal Daughters." Diomedes falls in love with Deidamia, suggesting the role was played by a young man, perhaps the Second Amoureux. The Docteur seems a possibility for the wily Ulysses, while Pantalon could have played Licomedes, who does have one rather comic scene when he tries to make excuses to the ambassadors who want to see his daughters. Lorenza Elisabetta del Campo, Marinette, was available for the Nurse, and the First Amoureux of the troupe for Achilles. Vulcan, the limping blacksmith of the gods, could have been a comic role filled by the Second Zanni. The characters actually do fit reasonably well the roster of a standard commedia dell'arte troupe.

In addition to the speaking-singing actors, *La finta pazza* requires at least sixteen male extras for the ambassador's guards and the Armed Inhabitants, eight female extras for the Royal Daughters, and five children

to play winged zephyrs, pages, monkeys, and parrots. Children were pe-
rennially useful in elaborate flying effects because of their lack of weight.
Also needed were at least six adult dancers for eunuchs, bears, ostriches,
and Indians. Torelli boasts that in act 1, scene 2, "Licomedes will enter
with the ambassadors, his court and his guards to the number of forty
persons." But since this same Torelli complained of the "little stage,"
thirty-seven additional extras seem unlikely. Actually, a combination of
Licomedes, the Captain and the Armed Inhabitants, the ambassadors and
their guards, Deidamia, Achilles, the Daughters, the pages and the Eunuch would add up to thirty-five actors on stage—quite a presentable
crowd in itself.

As for the deities, if Flora and Aurora doubled as Minerva and Juno,
(and various guards and daughters appeared as extras in the glory), then
only Jupiter and Victory remain as probable speaking-singing roles yet
unfilled. Since the only character on stage during the glory scene is Deidamia, any other members of the troupe could have filled in as Jupiter
and Victory.

Clearly this was an expensive production, though one from which
both Torelli and Balbi expected to make money. Although there exists no
evidence from the royal accounts to support it, the inference that the
court paid the cost of stage and machines, sets and costumes seems justified; the troupe could not possibly have borne such a large expense. On
the other hand, the inference that the troupe did bear the daily expenses
also seems justified, since a wholly court-supported event would not have
paid the daily shares Torelli was to receive. This means the troupe paid
orchestra, dancers, extras, and additional backstage workers. Torelli was
given two shares in the profits; we must assume Balbi had at least one.
Even with prices doubled and full houses, the actors could not have made
a great deal of money. They did, of course, get a fully equipped modern
stage with state-of-the-art machines to use for the rest of their stay in
Paris.

La finta pazza may have remained in their repertory for some time.
In the fall of 1646, the Swedish ambassador paid the Italians 400 ecus for
a special performance of an "Italian machine play."[20] The size of the
payment suggests something as spectacular as *La finta pazza*. Though
Cantù and Giulia Gabrielli had returned to Italy at the end of carnival,
they were replaced, presumably by others who played their roles. It was
not unusual in the seventeenth century for a company to retain a spectacle piece for several months, although the production was often simplified as audience and receipts fell off.

La Rosaura imperatrice di Constantinopoli, another spectacle play, was performed by the Italian troupe at the Petit-Bourbon for carnival of 1658. Although the production was in some ways even more spectacular than *La finta pazza*, the play itself conforms more closely to the exotic genre common in the commedia dell'arte baroque repertory. No longer based on mythology, *La Rosaura* unites *turquerie* with a female magician for a small-cast fairy tale. Easily performed by a company of ten, with a few extras and the dancers for the divertissements, this is the extravaganza of a professional theatre company, not of the court itself.

The gazetteer Loret was there the night the court attended: the king, the queen mother, the king's brother, Monsieur, with his bride-to-be, Princess Henrietta of England, and their cousin the Grande Mademoiselle. Loret lists the attractions: four ballets; twelve changes of scene; hydras, dragons, and demons; seas, forests, and mountains; brilliant decors; the most charming music; superb costumes; incredible perspective vistas; fire, lightning, and thunder; Hymen, Love, Peace, War; and the most enchanting actresses. Best of all, according to Loret, was a comic scene played by Scaramouche.[21]

Once again the company prepared a synopsis for the use of the French-speaking audience. This *Argument*, "in French prose," was composed by Domenico Locatelli, who received the royal privilege to print it.[22] The play is described as "an Italian play," which usually means in France that it was improvised by the actors, However, the title page promises "the most agreeable and magnificent verse," a promise which, when seen in connection with Locatelli's "French prose," might suggest that this play was written. On the other hand, no author is indicated, no script exists in Italian, and no other performances are known to have occurred, so "verse" may refer solely to the lyrical passages, especially to the prologue, which Locatelli specifically describes as "composed in verse and sung." Improvisation was at the heart of the Italian actor's craft; the Italians thought of actors who could not improvise as mere speaking apes. In 1645 *La finta pazza* was not improvised; an actor cannot, of course, improvise to music. But it was also not at all the kind of play the Italians usually performed. The troupe was either following the instructions of Anne of Austria or trying to fend off the importation of an Italian opera company. In 1658, however, the company, back in France for five years and well-established, could perform their own kind of spectacle play, one that showed to the best advantage their mode of acting. At the very least it can be assumed with certainty that the comic invention of Scaramouche was not confined by a written script.

The plot is purest fairy tale. Rosaura, the empress of Constantinople, refuses to marry because an oracle promises sinister events if she
does. Pressed by the principal lords of the court, she asks for a year's
grace. Her cousin Aldora, a magician, promises to help her find a way to
marry while preserving the empire and herself. She conjures up four
possible suitors: the princes of Poland, Scotland, and Transylvania and
the Count Partinopolis. Rosaura is attracted only to the last of these, but
he is promised to Isabella, only daughter of the King of France.

The Count, while hunting with the King of France and his daughter,
is given a casket taken from the sea by two fishermen. It contains a portrait of Rosaura. The Count is immediately struck by the tender passion,
and he and Scaramouche, his valet, go in search of the beautiful lady.
They are shipwrecked and land on a deserted island where Rosaura,
made invisible by magic, sings to the Count and sends him back to France
to deliver Paris from a siege. Rosaura then returns to Constantinople, is
courted by the three princes, and promises to consider them. The Count
returns victorious to the island, meets Rosaura in the darkness, and they
kiss. When she falls asleep, he has a light brought and recognizes her.
Furious, she orders Aldora to shut him up in the tower.

Isabella arrives to rescue the Count, but Aldora appears and spirits
him away so he can take part in a tournament for the hand of Rosaura.
The final scene is the tournament. Isabella enters and pleads for the freedom of the Count. The contestants enter; the Count is victorious. He
marries Rosaura, while the other three princes marry Isabella, Aldora,
and a hitherto unmentioned sister of the Count who arrives in the nick of
time.

This pleasant romance was served in a production highly spiced
with Torelli's best brand of spectacle. Eight different settings were used
for thirteen different scenes, and some of them were extraordinary. The
prologue featured a forest surrounding a mountain, upon which was situated a temple to Victory. At the end of the scene the temple was transformed into rocks and sank into the mountain while the mountain sank
into the earth. Nothing like this took place in *La finta pazza,* which has no
transformation scenes. The other settings that may have been special
were the "superb golden palace, made by enchantment" in act 3 and the
final scene of "an amphitheatre filled with a great assembly." The "courtyard of a palace," "wood with perspective alleys," "seashore," "wood
with castle and tower," and "delicious garden" were standard decors.
Loret mentions "incredible perspective vistas," but the synopsis, this time
not written on behalf of Torelli, mentions only one, a view of Constantinople seen through the great gate of Rosaura's palace.

What makes this entertainment spectacular is not the settings per se but the special effects, which are truly prodigious. There are several transformation effects: the temple and mountain mentioned above is one; another is a lion that turns into Rosaura and then into a clump of trees. Isabella and her army arrive by sea, much as the Greek ambassadors do in *La finta pazza,* but *La Rosaura* includes as well a storm at sea and a shipwreck. Another storm scene includes thunder and lightning. As for flying effects, the God of Valour ascends in the prologue, but much more exciting are the dragon and hydra that descend from the sky to take the Count and Scaramouche back to France and the Cloud of Fire in which Aldora travels.

Music plays an important role, especially in the prologue, "composed in verse, sung to music, accompanied by the most exquisite instruments." In it, France, sent by Fate, welcomes Valor. The temple opens discovering a statue of Louis XIV triumphant over the monsters of envy and sedition, that is, the Fronde. France bows with profound respect and sings the praises of the one who gave birth to such a glorious monarch as well as a brother "so worthy of his origins" and a minister (Mazarin) granted them "for the preservation of the crown and the growth of the empire." The flattery is so fulsome as to make the prologue to *La finta pazza* seem perfectly restrained. Music returns at the end of the play when Valor once more descends on an eagle to congratulate the Count and deliver one last encomium to Louis XIV, "to whom, one day, all the kingdoms of the East must submit." This was done in "three stanzas of poetry set to music." Rosaura also sings, once after she has been turned into a clump of trees, once while invisible, once with Aldora to celebrate her beauty. Finally, after she has ordered Aldora to lock up the Count, she sings "a little air about the cruel necessity which has forced her to condemn to prison the one she calls 'her heart and her love.'"

A ballet concludes each act. After act 2 (the first act of the play itself), and following the shipwreck, the audience is suitably entertained by a dance of tritons. After act 3, still in the enchanted golden palace, there is a ballet of phantoms and "extravagant dreams." Act 4 ends as the Count rises with Aldora on the Cloud of Fire while two magicians and six spirits dance, and the play concludes with a ballet of French and Greek pages, symbolizing the Greek Count Partinopolis, hero of the siege of Paris.

According to Loret, however, "among a hundred exquisite things which cause happy surprises, among a quantity of happenings, what makes us laugh until our teeth ache, what would give delight to a stump, is the *table de Scaramouche.*" Part special effect but mostly an extended lazzi by a master of mime, the "table of Scaramouche" is the first extant example in France of the kind of comic action that made stars of the zanni. The scene is described in the *Argument:*

> The scene changes into a superb golden palace, made by enchantment, in which Rosaura appears with Aldora singing about the conquests of her beauty. But having perceived in the distance the Count coming toward them, they begin to sing a little air while fleeing in order to rob him of the sight of Rosaura. Finding themselves alone in this marvelous habitation, Scaramouche, pressed by hunger, cannot hold back his complaints to his master, but barely has he made his feeble accents heard than he sees a great table, which is invisibly revealed and appears to be filled with all sorts of dishes, without his seeing who has prepared it and who is going to serve. Scaramouche, without ceremony, approaches the table, invited by his master, and sets about satisfying himself with the food; he is hindered by so many ridiculous accidents which follow and by so many invisible tricks that anger and hunger grow in him equally. The table is removed, Scaramouche follows it, in despair at not having eaten.

Scaramouche has several other major scenes in the piece, including the shipwreck at the end of act 2. Just before he embarks with the Count earlier in the act, he plays a scene of fright during a thunderstorm. The scene of fright was one of Fiorilli's most famous, according to a long appreciation of it by Evaristo Gherardi.[23] Perhaps this was why he played a second scene of fright in act 4 when he was expected to fly to Paris by dragon.

The character of Scaramouche in *La Rosaura* is not exactly what we might expect Fiorilli to play. Fiorilli's costume suggests the sort of Spanish capitan which his father played, and he was associated in France with irascibility, but the character here is clearly a Second Zanni, the cowardly glutton usually played by an Arlequin. With Trivelin (whose costume was that of an Arlequin) in the company, there seems to be no reason why Scaramouche should be a Second Zanni—unless by this time Locatelli had already made the transition to First Zanni that is so clearly evident in Biancolelli's zibaldone, where the "two Arlequins," one a First Zanni, the other a Second, add a bizarre note of fantasy to the entertainments.

Fiorilli's Scaramouche is always difficult to define and seems to have changed depending on the needs of the company. In the 1660s he must have been playing a form of capitan, for he was replaced by Girolamo Cei, who reverted to Capitan Spezzafer when Scaramouche rejoined the company. In later years Scaramouche was doubled by Guiseppe Tortoriti, who played Pasquariel, a capitan role, until he adopted the masque of Scaramouche when Fiorilli stopped acting in 1690. Yet Scaramouche was famous for several Second Zanni lazzi, and the roles he played in 1658 are Second Zanni roles. What is even more confusing is that Angelo Costantini's biography of 1695 makes the character into a wily, rascally First Zanni, but perhaps that was because Costantini himself played First Zanni and knew best the tricks associated with that character.

In 1658, however, the one certain casting in *La Rosaura* is Scaramouche as the Count's valet. The distribution of the other roles offers no insurmountable difficulties, assuming that two of the women in the troupe could sing reasonably well and play Rosaura and Aldora. The possibility exists that Giulia Gabrielli may have returned to play Rosaura. This would explain why her husband, Pietro Paolo Leoni, was owed a share of the subvention in 1659; he could have played one of Rosaura's suitors. A nonsinging amoureuse would have played Isabella, the First Amoureux the Count, Pantalon the king of France, and the Docteur a Turkish Lord. The Second Amoureux and the Capitan would have played the other two suitors. The troupe needed to hire actors only for the third suitor, if not played by Leoni, and perhaps for another Turkish lord. The play requires very few extras—the fishermen, a French soldier or two— since the "great assembly" in act 5 is painted on the scenery. Two singers were probably hired for Valor and France; eight dancers are called for at the end of act 4—a male and female magician and six spirits—and the same eight could manage the other divertissements.

The troupe could well have made money this time with large crowds, doubled prices, and only two singers, eight dancers, and two or three extra actors to pay along with the increased backstage crew. The actors' profits depended, of course, on their costs, which were heavily affected by the extent to which the crown subsidized the settings and special effects. The fact that the settings remained in the theatre until it was destroyed in 1660 implies that the court owned them and not the company, which left Paris in 1659. The actors' profits could also have been affected by their arrangement with Torelli, but he—though still a magician, as he was to demonstrate when he designed the magnificent outdoor setting for Molière's *Les fâcheux* at the ill-fated fête at Vaux-le-Vicomte in 1661—was losing favor at court and was no longer a novelty to the public after thirteen years and six or more spectacular productions in France. So perhaps Torelli was also no longer mortified at having to work with the "common actors" and no longer had enough leverage to pry two shares out of the company. Two years later, when the theatre of the Petit-Bourbon was razed to make way for the new East Front of the Louvre, the new Italian miracle maker, Carlo Vigarani, who had been selected instead of Torelli to build and equip the opera theatre at the Tuileries, refused to allow Molière and his actors to move Torelli's settings to Palais-Royal "under the pretext that he was going to use them." In fact, La Grange tells us that Vigarani "had them burned to the last scrap, so that there would remain nothing of his predecessor, Signor Torelli, whose memory he wanted to bury."[24] A pity, since many of the settings from *La Rosaura* were stock scenes, useful for everyday productions.

La Rosaura was, itself, a stock pastoral-romance, "fantasy smothered in magic," in the words of Kathleen Lea. "Every now and then," she says, "the commedia dell'arte is swept out on the receding waves of a fairy tale." The magician, the shipwreck, the food magically provided and then snatched away are common elements of the pastoral, while the exotic princess and her international band of suitors are among the most familiar ingredients of romance. Both forms rely heavily on spectacle. The property list for one Neapolitan romance includes a cloud machine, a subterranean cave, a dragon who flies away with one of the characters, an apparatus to transform a character into a fountain and back again, and an apparatus which enables Polichinella to fly through the air and leave a dog hanging in his place.[25] There was thus nothing unusual about the production of *La Rosaura,* the first of many such plays the Italians would perform in Paris to the end of the century.

Il convitato di pietra (*Le festin de pierre*) followed hard on the heels of *La Rosaura,* perhaps in more ways than one. Slipping into some of its predecessor's settings, but with a special effect all its own, this earliest of the Don Juan plays in France was, according to its imitators, a prodigious success. Two of the three French companies in Paris copied it, as did one provincial company. Performed, according to Guellette, in 1658 after *La Rosaura* but in any case before the appearance of Villiers's version at the Hôtel de Bourgogne in 1659, *Il convitato di pietra* was at best a grandchild, illegitimate at that, of Tirso de Molina's *El burlador de Sevilla,* the play that introduced Don Juan to the world sometime before 1630.

The scenario of the version done by the Italians in France is not a scenario at all but notes of his own scenes written out by Domenico Biancolelli, Arlequin, who first played the role of Don Juan's valet in a reprise the company introduced between 1662 and 1668. While that production undoubtedly had a strong likeness to the earlier production, it may also have changed in important ways, especially since it is probable that neither the Don nor his servant was played by the same actor in both productions. On the other hand, the notes seem to be relatively close to the Italian version regarded as the ancestor of the various commedia dell'arte scenarios, an adaptation of Tirso usually attributed to Jacinto Andrea Cicognini.[26] Cicognini introduces many of the comic elements that became traditional: the valet's gluttony, the test of his loyalty, the list of his master's women which he unrolls into the audience, and his concern about his wages after his master's departure to hell.

Dominique's scenario is clearly an accretion, with additions and variants both in the middle and at the end. In his zibaldone Dominique placed it twenty-third of the thirty-five largely undated scripts preceding *Le regal des dames,* which we know was performed in 1668. The play was still in the repertory of the Italian troupe in February 1668 when the duke of Monmouth saw it with Monsieur, the king's brother, and his wife Madame, and in November 1669, when, according to Robinet, King Casimir was in the audience. Perhaps the version without additions was performed before 1668, while the additions reflect changes made later. The Italians may have remounted their play in 1665 to take advantage of whatever furor was aroused by Molière's briefly seen *Dom Juan,* or Molière may have been imitating a recent production of the Italians. Dominique does note that a final scene—in which Arlequin tells the court, "My master is with the devils *where you other great lords will also go some day*"—was suppressed. Perhaps that piece of gratuitous moralizing had been acceptable in the post-Fronde 1650s, but it was a little too personal for the glorious "personal reign."

With all appropriate caveats, then, here is Dominique's "scenario" without the additions, the first detailed description which documents the zanni play seen in Paris at midcentury.

Characters

Arlequin	Don Juan
The King	Pantalon
The Duke Octavio	A fisher girl
The Commander	The amoureuses

In the first scene I arrive with the King who speaks to me of the libertine ways of Don Juan. I say to him, "We must be patient. When young men become a little older, they change their ways. Let's hope that happens to Don Juan." The King orders me to tell him an amusing story. I take a chair, sit down beside him, and tell the story of Queen Joan. A tumult outside. I escape.[27]

This scene is at night. I enter alone and talk to myself about the debauchery of my master who thinks of nothing but dishonoring whatever women or girls come to hand. Don Juan, who hears me, takes his sword in his hand and asks: "Who goes there?" I say, "Arlequin, valet of Don Juan." He says some bad things about himself; I agree that he is right, then I repent of having spoken thus, and I say that I want to support the honor of my master. He answers me that, that being so, he will challenge me. After several lazzi of fright, I agree, but I throw myself on the ground on my back holding my sword in two hands and I stir it around so that he finds it everywhere. Finally I collapse and say I am dead. Don Juan, very vexed at having wounded me, calls me by my name and asks if I am really dead. I answer that if it truly is Don Juan who asks, then I am alive, but if it's not, I am departed. Finally, I get up from the ground and we do the lazzi of the archers who are chasing him and of the purse that they offer me to reveal Don Juan, etc.

[When my master is at table, I tell him that I used to serve a doctor who taught me that such a dish was hard to digest. He gives it to me; I eat gluttonishly. He reminds me of what my doctor told me; I answer that it's the dish that's hard to digest and not what's in it.][28]

In the scene of the shipwreck, I am in my shirt in the water with ten or twelve bladders. I raise and lower myself as if swimming and I enter the stage saying: "too much water, too much water, let's have some wine." I perceive Don Juan in the arms of a young fisher girl. I say, "Well, if I ever fall in the sea, I'd like to be saved by a boat like that," and then I wring out my shirt and cry "Ohimé. There's a pike attached to my belly." I thank Neptune for having saved me from the sea, and looking at the bosom of the fisher girl, I say: "If I had had two gourds like that, I would not have been afraid of drowning." My master wakes from his faint, and while he talks to her, I do the lazzi of breaking one of the bladders by falling on it. That makes a noise which I say is from a cannon I've fired, rejoicing that we have been saved. When my master exits with the fisher girl I complain, saying "My master is such a libertine that if he ever goes to Hell, which he certainly will, he'll want to debauch Proserpine."

The fisher girl in this scene says to Don Juan that she counts on his keeping his word to marry her. He answers that he cannot, and that I can tell her the reason. He exits, the girl despairs. Then I show her that she is not the hundredth that he has promised to marry. "Look at this" I say. "Here is the list of all those who are in the same boat as you, and I'm going to add your name." I throw the rolled-up list to the parterre and I hold one end of it, saying, "Look, gentlemen, see if you don't find one of your relations there."

We enter, my master and I, and we find the Duke Octavio and Pantalon. After we exchange greetings, I move alongside of Pantalon and each time he looks at me, I make a deep bow. This lazzi, repeated several times, makes him impatient. He crosses to the other side of the stage. I cross also and begin the lazzi again. As I have my cloak, I take it off and play with it as one would a flag, I give Pantalon a blow in the stomach from which we both fall down. Finally, I blow my nose in Pantalon's handkerchief. He notices and hits me; I return the blows. Don Juan proposes to the Duke to change cloaks with him for good luck. He accepts. I do the same with Pantalon. They exit; I remain with Don Juan who tells me that he wants to go to the house of Donna Anna, the mistress of Octave. I oppose this and speak to him of heaven. He hits me and I say, "Oh, well, go if you must," and we exit.[29]

Don Juan introduces himself into the house of the Commander, Don Pierre, father of Donna Anna, the mistress of Octave, whom he tries to dishonor. At her cries, the Commander arrives, pursues Don Juan, who kills him. I do then some scenes of fright, I try to escape, I fall over the body, I get up and run away.

In this scene the borrowed cloaks are returned with several lazzi on my part of tearing Pantalon's robe.

In this scene I reflect on the public cry which promises 10,000 ecus [30,000 livres] and the property of four bandits to whoever discovers the author of the Commander's death. While I talk to myself about this business, Don Juan enters. I learn from him what has been published on behalf of the King; after several lazzi of fright on the subject of the archers, Don Juan, who is angry with me, takes his sword in his hand and threatens me with death if I speak. I swear to him that I will not say a word. "But," he says, "if someone asks you?" "That will not make me speak." "We'll see about that." He pretends then to ask me the question and to be the chief of police. I admit to everything. He becomes furious and redoubles his menaces, wants to change clothes with me and leads me away to do that. I promise him. He claims that the archers are at our heels. I am frightened and escape; he runs after me.

In this scene, which takes place in the country, I joke with the village women and I say to the husband of one of them that if he is not Seigneur Cornelio, he will be soon. And when they dance, I say, "My master will soon have them dancing to another tune." Finally we leave them.

In this scene where appears the tomb of the commander, he

reads the inscription which is on the pedestal and pretends to be afraid of what is threatened there. Finally laughs at the vanity of men on the subject of epitaphs. I read in my turn what is written, and remember that I have had a share, so to speak, in the debauches of my master, I begin to fear just punishment for that. My master, to cheer me up, orders me to go invite the statue of the commander to dinner that evening. I laugh at his madness, but I go issue the invitation. The statue answers me with an inclination of the head. I fall down with fright and tell my master what I have seen. He doesn't believe me. Ask him yourself. It makes the same inclination to him. He is astonished. We exit.

Pantalon in this scene comes to interrogate me and tell me that the 10,000 ecus will be given to whoever names the murderer of the Commander. As he presses me on the subject, I tell him that if I were sure of the recompense, I would name him. After several lazzi, I say that I don't know him. "Imagine," he says to me, "that I am the King and that I am questioning you. Bonjour, Arlequin." "Your Majesty's servant," I answer. "Do you know who is the murderer in question?" "Yes, Sire." "Name him, and you will have the sum promised." "Well, Sire, it's . . . it's . . . it's Pantalon." Pantalon sends me to the devil, threatens to have me hanged, and exits furious with me. I also exit.

In this one I want to reprimand Don Juan for his faults; I tell him the fable of the ass loaded with salt and then with sponges. [The ass can go in the water with the salt because it melts; when he goes in with the sponges, he drowns.] I apply it to him. He pretends to be sensitive to my reprimands, I throw myself on my knees, he pretends to begin to implore Jupiter, I render thanks to Heaven for his conversion, he rises, kicks me in the backside, and laughs at me. Then I get up and say, "Let's go to the brothel." He asks for supper. After all the lazzi of setting the table: to sneak several bits off the table, that of the fly that I try to kill on his face, I steal a morsel from the table, one of the servants snatches it from me, I give a blow to another who I believe to be the thief, I wipe a plate on my rear end then present it to Don Juan, finally I speak to him of a very pretty young widow who spoke to me about him in very flattering terms. Then he orders me to sit down at the table with him, I obey eagerly. "Let's go, rabble," I say. "Bring me a plate." I say to my master, "Don't eat so fast." I wash my hands and dry them on the tablecloth. Embarrassed by my hat, I put it on his head, I toss the salad with my bat, I cut a chicken, I turn over the lamp, I blow my nose on the tablecloth. Someone knocks at the door. A servant returns from it very frightened and knocks me over. I get up, take a chicken in one hand, a candlestick in the other and I go to the door. I return very horrified and knocking down three or four valets, I tell Don Juan that the one who did this (I nod my head) is at the door. He takes a candlestick and goes to receive him while I hide under the table. As I stick my head out to see the statue, Don Juan calls me and threatens to knock me senseless if I don't come back to the table. I answer that I'm fasting, finally obeying his repeated orders, I sit at the table and cover my head with the tablecloth. My master orders me to eat. I take a bite and as I am conveying it to my mouth, the statue looks at me and makes a movement of the head which frightens me. Don Juan orders me to sing. I tell him I have lost my voice. Finally I sing and, following the orders of my master, I drink the statue's health, who answers me with a sign of the head. I do a somersault, glass in hand and get up. Finally, after the statue has invited Don Juan to supper in turn and he has accepted, the statue exits. Don Juan sees him to the door while I eat gluttonishly. He reenters. I try to dissuade him from going to supper with the statue. We exit.

In the last scene I say that the washerwoman of the house must be dead for everything here is dead black. He approaches the table where the statue is and takes a snake on his plate, saying, "I would eat it if it were the Devil; (he even bites it) I want to give him horns." The statue counsels him to repent. I say *Amen*. He won't listen; he disappears under the ground. I cry, "My wages, my wages. I'll have to send a bailiff to hell to get my wages."

In the last scene (it is suppressed) when the King comes on the stage I fall on my knees and I say to him, "Oh, King you should know that my master is with the devils *where you other great lords will also go some day,* reflect then on what has just happened to him."[30]

Although *Il convitato di pietra* is not a machine play, it does require a rather large number of settings. Many scenes take place on the street, but others are in the court of the King of Naples, the court of the King of Castille, Duke Octavio's residence in Naples, at the seashore, at the tomb of the Commander, and in Don Juan's rooms. Because Cicognini, the principal source of the commedia dell'arte versions, copied Tirso and because Tirso wrote for a stage that, like Shakespeare's, did not use illusionistic scenery, the scenes are often short and follow quickly one upon the other. Although it seems unlikely that the scenery was changed for every change of location, the conventions of the baroque stage do not allow for generalized stage space. Plays produced in the baroque period either require the classical single setting—the *palais à volonté* of tragedy or the *scène à quatre portes* of comedy—or multiple settings for multiple locales. Most of the locations required by *Il convitato* are standard, and the settings likely to be in stock. Torelli had done a new seascape with shipwreck machinery for *La Rosaura;* his settings for the Turkish court with view of Constantinople and the golden palace could also have been reused. Only one setting is unique to the play: the tomb of the Commander. This tomb apparently featured an equestrian statue. Villiers, in the preface to his Don Juan play, published in 1659, explains how he came to write it, and mentions the importance of the statue: "My comrades, infatuated with this *Festin de pierre* after having seen all Paris rush in crowds to see the production the Italian actors had done, were persuaded that if this subject were put in French . . . it would attract a great number of those . . . little attached to that so-sought-after regularity so little to be found here, and, provided the figure of D. Pierre and his horse be well made and well proportioned, the play will answer to the rules they require."[31]

Villiers's predecessors do not mention a horse. Tirso sets the scene in a church, while Cicognini calls for "an open temple." Dorimon's version, played in the provinces, asks only for a "tomb in the woods." Dominique merely mentions the "tomb of the Commander," but at least in 1658 the statue surmounting the tomb must have been equestrian.

The horse presumably remained stationary. Villiers's Statue enters Don Juan's rooms and sits down, which would be difficult on a horse. So the effect of the speaking and moving statue, presumably the lure that brought the crowds of people unlettered in neoclassic theory to the theatre, was not so much the kind of effect Torelli specialized in but rather an effect achieved by costume and actor.

The distribution of parts for *Il convitato di pietra* would have been relatively normal. Dominique's cast list mentions only one king; perhaps one actor doubled as King of Naples and King of Castille. The Docteur was available for mature roles. The First Amoureux would have played Don Juan; the Second, Duke Octavio. Pantalon should have played the Commander, but the use of Pantalon as Octavio's servant in Dominique's version indicates that some other actor, perhaps the Capitan, played Anna's father. If the troupe was aiming at a terrifying and not a comic effect with the statue, then it should not have been played by one of the easily recognized masques. There are four women in the play, assuming it follows Tirso and Cicognini, although Dominique mentions only Anna, the fisher girl, and "the village women." If Giulia Gabrielli and her husband were in Paris at this period, perhaps she would have played the fisher girl, who sings in most versions, leaving Isabella and Anna to the two other amoureuses, Brigida Fedele and Luisa Gabrielli, and the peasant girl to the Servante, Lorenza Elisabetta del Campo.

As for the zanni: though it is normally assumed that Domenico Locatelli played Don Juan's valet in 1658, a more likely assumption is that the role was played by Tiberio Fiorilli. This valet is similar to the one Scaramouche played in *La Rosaura*. Both characters perform extensive lazzi of fright and of gluttony. Also, according to Angelo Costantini, Fiorilli made his debut in Italy in *Il convitato*, "which he esteemed above all other [plays] on account of the eating there is in it." [32] Both Fiorilli's Scaramouche and Biancolelli's Arlequin are characterized by extreme gluttony and a special fondness for macaroni, while Locatelli's Trivelin is not, so far as the rather limited evidence indicates. Octavio's valet, who tries to bully Don Juan's servant into betraying his master, seems a more suitable role for Trivelin who, at least in the 1660s, played First Zanni.

The two survivals of the repertory played by the Italians in 1658 may suggest the reason why the troupe returned to Italy the following year. Both the spectacle play *La Rosaura* and the Spanish tragicomedy *Il convitato di pietra* were special events, outside the limits of the standard commedia dell'arte repertory. The actors had been in Paris for six years, and their repertory was not infinite. Nor was there, apparently, anyone among them able to devise new scenarios, as Marc' Antonio Romagnesi was to do in 1668 when, once again, after six years the standard repertory may have ceased to attract audiences to the Comédie-Italienne.

The Italians may have tried to get new material from French authors before 1660 as they were to do after 1668. According to Donneau de Visé, Molière's *Les précieuses ridicules* was indebted to a play first produced by the Italians, who had left Paris before Molière's play was performed. Donneau de Visé is, of course, hostile to Molière, but his hostility does not necessarily invalidate what he says: "Our Author [Molière] reflected on what was happening in the world and especially among the people of quality, in order to recognize defects; but since he was not yet bold enough to undertake a satire, nor capable of bringing it to an end, he had recourse to his good friends the Italians and accommodated to the French stage the *Précieuses* which had been played on theirs and which had been given them by one of the most gallant abbés." [33] The Parfaicts identify the celibate socialite as the abbé de Pure, a literary and theatrical hanger-on, just the sort of mediocre man of letters whom Molière so often parodied. Nonetheless, he could well have furnished the Italians with a scenario, as, for instance, Girardin was to do in 1672.

Competition among the four troupes playing in Paris at midcentury was rabid; the available audience was not large. [34] Clearly, when one company had a success, the other companies imitated it, on the grounds that it was impossible to have too much of a good thing. But it must have been considerably easier for the French to imitate the Italians than for the Italians to imitate the French, given the limitations implicit in the conventional forms of commedia dell'arte. Nor would it have been easy for the troupe to find many French authors to devise new scenarios for it. Without new material, however, the Italians may have had difficulty successfully competing with the Hôtel de Bourgogne, the Marais, and the French troupe of their own Petit-Bourbon. It makes sense, then, that in 1659 the Italians took a sabbatical leave and returned to Italy to refurbish their repertory.

Part II
1661-1668

Establishment at Palais-Royal

O N 1 JANUARY 1661 Loret published in *La muze historique* a summary of the theatrical troupes then playing in Paris: the troupe of the Hôtel de Bourgogne, the troupe of Monsieur, the troupe at the Marais, the new troupe of Mademoiselle, the king's cousin, and the Spanish troupe at court. He then announced that "in the time of the next campaign, that is, in April or May, when the weather is mild and gay, we will have [the troupe] from Italy with Scaramouche and Aurelia." In his gazette of 7 May he noted that the actors of the Hôtel de Bourgogne had just left Fontainebleau (after earning large sums of money), and the court was now awaiting the new Italian troupe, "whose facetious zanni will provoke infinite laughter."

The next time Loret mentions the Italians the actors had arrived in Paris, possibly delayed by the terrible earthquake that struck the north of Italy in early May. Another near tragedy certainly affected the troupe in June or July when Domenico Locatelli, who played Trivelin, became seriously ill. Loret reported on 27 July that the fever had finally moderated and Locatelli was better. Still, the company did not open in Paris until 8 January 1662.

According to La Grange, the chronicler of Molière's company, who noted their opening in his *Registre,* the Italians had been five months at Fontainebleau, August through December, before coming to Paris. These various references suggest that the troupe never reached Fontainebleau in the spring, when it was expected, but arrived in Paris, remained there, unable to play because of Locatelli's illness, and traveled to Fontainebleau to perform for the court after he recovered. The possibility that he might not recover must have existed, since Louis XIV wrote to the duke of Parma on 5 July 1661 asking that a replacement be sent to Paris.[1] The duke sent the stepson of his favorite, Carlo Cantù, the young Domenico Biancolelli, who, legend has it, was in Vienna at the time. Biancolelli—known in France as Dominique—played Arlequin, a Second Zanni, similar to the traditional Second Zanni Locatelli played or had played as

Trivelin. Locatelli did, of course, recover, leaving the troupe in the odd position of having two patchwork Second Zanni.

The company of ten that made its debut on 8 January 1662 included a number of actors who had played in France before: Locatelli; Tiberio Fiorilli as Scaramouche; Brigida Fedele as Aurelia, the First Amoureuse; Giovan Andrea Zanotti as Octave, the Second Amoureux; and Angelo Agostino Lolli as the Docteur. New members of the company besides Biancolelli included Orsola Cortesi as Eularia, the Second Amoureuse; Giacinto Bendinelli as Valerio, the First Amoureux; Patricia Adami as Diamantine, the servante; and Francesco Manzani as Capitan Terremoto.[2] A Pantalon, name unknown, may also have been part of the troupe at the beginning, although the royal subvention paid to the actors implies otherwise.

The king awarded his Italian troupe 15,000 livres a year, or 1,500 livres per actor. The first recorded payment of this subvention was made in 1664 for the first quarter of 1663. "To Domenico Locatelli and Domenico Biancolelli, Italian musicians, for themselves and the other actors for their appointment during the quarter of January."[3] Subventions were always figured at so much per full share and were treated as income to the individual actors, not as support for the company. Molière's actors, for instance, were originally awarded 300 livres each by Monsieur (although this subvention was never paid) and later—in 1665—were granted 6,000 livres by the king, 500 livres to each of the twelve sharers. The royal troupe at the Hôtel de Bourgogne was receiving 12,000 livres a year in 1658 when it was comprised of twelve actors.[4] Expenses and gifts were also paid according to the number of sharers in a troupe. Molière's troupe received 14,000 livres in expenses for a long stay at St. Germain-en-Laye in 1662, and La Grange writes: "The king has given the troupe fourteen thousand livres, believing that it had only fourteen shares. However, the troupe has fifteen."

Fifteen hundred livres remained the annual award for a full share in the Italian troupe until at least 1683, when a document was signed agreeing that 2,250 livres were owed the widow of Giovanni Gherardi for six quarters of pension.[5] The total subvention remained 15,000 as well. After 1683, when the troupe increased in size, full shares were undoubtedly—in this company as in others—divided and subdivided. When a *Règlement* of c. 1684 allotted twelve shares to the Italians, the subvention did not increase although the number of actors did. New members entered on half or quarter shares. Not all troupes were supported by the crown; the actors at the Marais never received a subvention, nor did the troupe at the Hôtel Guénégaud. After 1680, however, and the establishment of the Comédie-Française, all legitimate theatrical activity in Paris was subsidized and regulated by the monarchy.

The Italians received the largest subvention of any of the Parisian public troupes. The Italians were, of course, invited guests of the court. Italian actors had always received subventions in France, part of the package designed to lure them from Italy. The size of the award was probably related to two factors: the number of public performances the company missed because of court appearances and the likelihood of a lower box-office income.

Since no registre has survived for the Italians, there is no way of knowing exactly how often they played at court in the early years. (In later years, the regularity of the royal year and the financial records kept by the court make it possible to see a pattern of court performances.) We do know the troupe spent many months at Fontainebleau in 1661 and that it was at St.-Germain-en-Laye for All Saints in 1666.[6] We know that the Italians, along with Molière's troupe, participated in the *Ballet des muses* in December of 1666.[7] Some information can also be extrapolated from La Grange's *Registre*. The two companies shared a theatre as they had done in the late 1650s, although now the French had the jours ordinaires, Tuesday, Friday, and Sunday, and the Italians the jours extraordinaires. At times, however, the French played on the days when the theatre normally belonged to the Italians, leading to the assumption that the Italians were playing at court. In 1666, for instance, the French played on Thursday 28 October, Thursday 11 November, and Thursday 25 November. This suggests that the Italians were away for a substantial period with the court, perhaps at St.-Germain-en-Laye, and indeed they were, as other evidence confirms.[8]

The subvention not only made up for lost revenues during attendance at court, it also supplemented box office receipts consistently lower than those of the French companies, at least until after 1680. The Italians, after all, played in a language not understood by most Parisians, no matter how fluent the monarch and his family were. Unfortunately, we have almost no information about the profits of the Italian actors. One much later note does suggest that the Italians made somewhat less than the French actors with whom they shared theatres. Gueullette includes, in his translation of Biancolelli's manuscript, the latter's note referring to the run of *La magie naturelle* in December 1678: "This play in twenty-four performances furnished to each of those who hold a full share 1,064 livres."[9] That Biancolelli took note of a profit of slightly more than 44 livres per playing day suggests that the amount was quite extraordinary for the Italians, although it would have been only good for the French. Molière's troupe, for instance, averaged just over 100 livres per share per playing day for the first twenty-four performances of *Tartuffe.*

A comparison of the various pensions reveals the beginnings of a bureaucratic ordering of theatrical activity in Paris under the aegis of the monarch. Pension figures indicate that an income of approximately 3,000 livres a year was considered appropriate for an actor with a full share in the 1660s. A Spanish troupe that played only at court received an annual subvention of 3,000 livres a month, 36,000 a year; it was probably a company of twelve each getting 3,000.[10] The ten Italians—with 1,500 livres each—were expected to receive half their income from the court, half from the box office. The royal troupe of the Hôtel de Bourgogne got a subvention of 12,000 livres, or 1,000 livres per actor, leaving them to earn two-thirds of their own income, while Molière's troupe, undeniably good at making money, got only 500 livres per actor, or one-sixth of the anticipated figure. In 1665, the first year the pension was paid to the French company at Palais-Royal, La Grange reports that a full share was worth exactly 3,011 livres and 11 sous. Lack of box-office records for the other companies makes it impossible to prove that the widely differing pensions were not awarded to show favoritism but rather to impose uniformity, but the continuing history of the relationship between the court and the theatres demonstrates precisely that kind of thinking.

Subventions probably saved the monarchy money in the long run. Molière's company received a gift of 14,000 livres from the king for a long stay at St.-Germain-en-Laye in 1662 and 10,000 in 1664 for three weeks at Versailles in May, three weeks at Fontainebleau in July and August, and two more weeks at Versailles in October. Beginning in 1665, the company got the 6,000-livre pension plus 6 livres per actor for "fire and nourishment" each playing day at court. Transportation was also provided and lodging if necessary. Standardization and organization are the likely motives for this new system, however, rather than thrift. As *pensionnaires,* the actors—French as well as foreign—were less independent of the court, more specifically "on call," and no longer in a position to negotiate. The earlier arrangement was one of simple patronage— gifts and protection in return for periodic service—based on the monarch's personal tastes and on his private relationships with the actors. The system coming into being of subvention and fees made the theatres part of Louis XIV's overall scheme to enroll the arts in his campaign of glorification.

In the 1660s the king still had a direct relationship with the Italians, especially with Fiorilli and Biancolelli. Fiorilli received sums of money over and above his share of the subvention throughout the 1660s: 1,330 in 1662, 2,400 in 1664, 1,000 in 1666, and 600 in 1668.[11] Some of this was travel money, "to give him the means to return to his country"; some was awarded "in consideration of his services." Biancolelli received no gifts, but the queen arranged his marriage to her favorite, Eularia, according to Sebastiano Locatelli, a Bolognese traveler in France. Locatelli claims to have known Orsola Cortesi Biancolelli well, and says that the queen "lent" her the royal obstetrician on the occasion of the birth of her first child.[12]

Royal gifts or no, that the Italians eventually made a good deal of money, especially after the troupe moved into its own theatre in 1680, can be inferred from various legal documents related to Biancolelli, Fiorilli, and Marc' Antonio Romagnesi. In the early years, however, the Italian actors, with the probable exception of Fiorilli, were not well-to-do. They were not impoverished, of course, at a time when a theatrical company paid its own employees between one livre and three livres a day. Records relating to two deaths in the company in the 1660s give a view of the finances of a working actor in the first decade of the company's establishment.

On 19 May 1662, only a few months after the troupe had opened in Paris, its Capitan, Francesco Manzani, was murdered on a Paris street. Presumably a fully sharing member of the company, he was living at the time of his death with Giuseppe Giaratoni, a "gagiste," or actor employed by the troupe, and Annibal Barbieri, the troupe's décorateur, in a room Barbieri had leased from the sieur Morice on the rue des Boucheries-St.-Honoré. Police investigators found 5 ecus, one 15-sou coin, and 4 double and 17 single sous on the body along with two letters and an etui containing a pair of scissors and a key. The key opened a square, leather-covered trunk that contained 42 ecus and 2 ecus d'or. The police took the money "to give . . . to whomever it will be ordered by the court," folded Manzani's wardrobe, and put it in the trunk which they locked and sealed.[13] The actor had accumulated 155 livres in France, although he was living in bachelor quarters and had few possessions. The sum of money is substantial, half a year's wages for a worker, and the way of life normal for an actor on the road.

When Giacinto Bendinelli, the troupe's First Amoureux, died of natural causes six years later, his life was no longer that of a touring actor. Married to a French woman and the father of two young daughters, Bendinelli made his will on 11 March 1668, requesting that an inventory be made of his goods in Paris so that they could be sold and "the half of the profits belonging to his children be invested with some notable bourgeois at interest ... for the nourishment and education of his children." The inventory was made on 13 April, and the goods were valued at 1,189 livres, but Bendinelli's debts amounted to 1,986 livres. The Bendinelli family had lived reasonably well in a lodging with a main room, ante-room, and kitchen. The rooms were well furnished and hung with coarse tapestries for color and warmth. Bendinelli owned twenty-five books, all in Italian. He owed a quarter's rent. He did not owe the butcher or the baker, but he did owe the candle maker—a quite astonishing 58 livres. He owed his wine merchant 60. It cost him 52 livres to die and 113 to be buried.[14]

Most of what Bendinelli owned (and owed) involved his profession as a First Amoureux, since dressing well for the stage was extremely expensive. His major costume pieces were valued at 706 livres, 60 percent of his estate. His debts included 1,232 livres to the sieur Francisque for costumes, 308 livres to the sieur Durant also for costumes, and smaller sums for ribbons, laces, cloth, and so forth. Bendinelli did not accumulate a great deal of property in his six years in France, but his inventory does not suggest an impoverished way of life for a young married man. In any case, we can be sure his life was full of light and wine and that he was conscious of his obligation as jeune premier to look absolutely wonderful on stage.

When the troupe arrived in Paris in 1662, having presumably ne-gotiated its subvention with the monarch, it did not return to the theatre that had been reconstructed by Torelli for its predecessor in 1645. The Grande Salle of the Petit-Bourbon, home of ballet and spectacle from 1615, remodeled as a modern theater for *La finta pazza* in 1645, had been marked for demolition in 1660 to make way for the present east front of the Louvre. Molière's company, which was playing at the Petit-Bourbon at the time, was astonished and outraged to find itself unexpectedly on 11 October without a theater. Complaints were filed immediately with the king, who had been told by his superintendent of buildings that the site was needed and that since the building belonged to His Majesty there was no reason to take the actors into consideration. "The bad will of M. de Ratabon was apparent," writes La Grange, but the troupe was "grati-fied" to receive instead from His Majesty permission to play in the Grande Salle of the Palais-Royal. It was, thus, to the Palais-Royal that the Italian actors repaired in 1662. In 1658 Molière's company had paid the earlier Italian company 1,500 livres to use the Petit-Bourbon; now the Italians were directed by the monarch to pay the French 2,000 livres for use of the extraordinary days at the Palais-Royal, one half of the cost of repair and redecoration.[15]

The large theatre at the Palais-Royal, the so-called Grande Salle, had been built by Le Mercier for Cardinal Richelieu as the crowning touch to his Palais-Cardinal and inaugurated on 14 January 1641, with a production of *Mirame,* composed for the occasion. The theatre, a separate wing to the east of the main structure, cost Richelieu 300,000 livres, according to contemporary chronicler Henry Arnauld, a third of which went for the machines.[16] Sauval describes the stage as fully modern, raised at one end of a rectangular room. The rest of the room was occupied by twenty-seven stone degrees "which rise gradually and imperceptibly and which are finished by a sort of portico or three large arcades." The room was "disfigured by two gilded balconies set one above the other on each side which begin near the portico and end near the stage" and "crowned by a ceiling in perspective where Le Maire has made a long order of Corinthian columns which carry a very high vault."[17] The theatre in its original state is familiar to us from an often reproduced engraving by Van Lochen of an anonymous grisaille showing the cardinal entertaining Louis XIII, his queen, and the young dauphin at a machine play, probably the ballet *La prospérité des armes de France* (fig. 5).[18]

Although *Mirame* itself requires only a single set, machines were brought into play for the inaugural performance since the *Gazette de France* of 19 January reports not only on the beauty of the Grande Salle but on the "majestic ornaments of this superb stage upon which, with a transport difficult to express and which was followed by a universal exclamation of astonishment, appeared delicious gardens with grottoes, statues, fountains, and great terraces above the sea, the agitations of which seemed natural to that great element." The stage was also equipped with the latest in lighting devices: "The sky was lit by the moon . . . night was imperceptibly succeeded by day, the dawn, and the sun." A second setting was introduced when the play, "circumscribed by the laws of poetry," was followed by a ball on stage. The curtain fell, a golden "bridge" was rolled out from the stage to the foot of the royal scaffold, and the curtain rose on a great room painted in perspective, gilded and enriched by magnificent ornaments, and lit by sixteen chandeliers. Her Majesty crossed the "bridge" to the stage followed by her ladies and the ball began. A month later, on 7 February, *La prosperité des armes de France* was produced with eight settings and machines for flying.[19]

LE SOIR, LE ROI, ET LES PERSONNES DE LA COUR VONT A LA COMEDIE

FIG. 5. *Engraving by Van Lochen of an anonymous grisaille that shows Cardinal Richelieu entertaining the royal family in his new theatre at Palais-Royal for a performance of the ballet of* La prospérité des armes de France. (Bibliothèque Nationale; phot. Bibl. Nat. Paris)

Cardinal Richelieu died in 1642 and left his palace to his royal master; after Louis XIII's death five months later, the queen mother and the young Louis XIV moved into what was now known as Palais-Royal and resided there until the Fronde forced them out of Paris. The Grande Salle was often used as a court performance space. Torelli redid the stage and machines for *Orfée* in 1647, which was also followed by a ball on the stage in a room made "*à machine,* put in place in a moment ... an agreeable sight to those who occupied the amphiteâtre." [20]

But when Molière and the troupe of Monsieur took possession of their new theatre in 1660, the cardinal's magnificent gift to the monarchy was in sad disrepair. The perspective ceiling, a *trompe l'oeil* colonnade, had been devised originally because this theatre, unlike the Petit-Bourbon, was not very high. The roof, "a mansard covered with lead," rested on "eight oak beams each of 2 square feet by 10 toises long." (The length of the beams was just over 63 feet; a toise is 76 inches and is divided into 6 pieds.) According to Sauval, "Never was seen nor read about nor heard of beams of such an extraordinary length and so prodigious. It cost 8,000 livres to bring the trees from the royal forest at Moulins." [21] The beams, unfortunately, were probably too long since La Grange tells us that by 1661 three had "decayed" and were "propped up leaving half the room uncovered." Sauval writes that the problem was caused by covering the beams with planking and adding several apartments above the theatre.

Ratabon had been instructed to make gross repairs to the building, but the rest of the work was done at the charge of the actors. The king permitted them to bring from the Petit-Bourbon the loges and "other things necessary for the new establishment" with the exception of Torelli's settings, which Vigarani kept on the pretext of needing them for the Tuileries but which, as we have seen, he actually had burned.

We are able to reconstruct this theatre as it was in the time of Molière and the Italians with some degree of accuracy thanks to Sauval's description, to two builders' contracts from November 1660,[22] and to a set of plans discovered by Agne Beijer which he dates to the remodeling done by Vigarani when Lulli took over the theater for the Opéra in 1673 (fig. 6). [23] Sauval reports that the interior width of the Grande Salle of the Palais-Royal was 9 toises [57 feet], which accords with the beams of 10 toises, and that the room was *quarré-longue*—which I take to mean that Le Mercier had used the double square and provided a length of 18 toises, or 114 feet. The plan discovered by Beijer shows 17 toises, 3 pieds. In general most available information, including several later plans and sec-

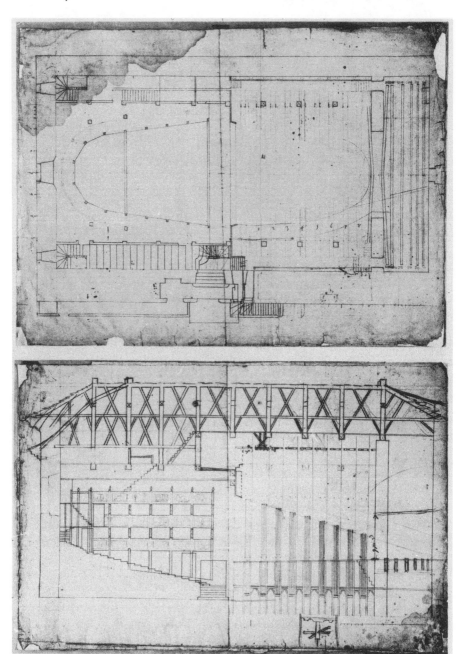

FIG. 6. *Plan and section identified by Agne Beijer as the Grande Salle at Palais-Royal c. 1673.* (Statens konstmuseer, Stockholm)

tions, confirms a length of about 18 toises and a width of about 9. What follows is based on the dimensions of the plan discovered by Beijer.

Sauval gives no dimensions for the stage, only for the audience area; the 27 degrees rising in the parterre were, according to him, each 23 pouces [a pouce equals 1.06 inches] wide and 5.5 pouces high. The degrees would thus have taken up 8 toises, 4 pieds, of the length of the room, leaving 8 toises, 5 pieds, for the stage, the area in front of the stage with steps—clearly shown in Van Lochen's engraving—and the rear arcade.

The original stage was not especially high. The engraving shows five fairly shallow steps leading from the stage to the floor of the auditorium. The Vigarani section (fig. 6, bottom) shows what appears to be the original stage below the new stage built when the theatre was converted to a public theatre with a standing parterre. On the section the original stage is approximately four feet above the base level of the auditorium. Four feet also agrees with the relationship shown between the height of the stage and the height of the performers standing on it in Van Lochen's engraving.

The auditorium rose from the baseline fairly steeply. If each of the 27 stone degrees rose 5½ pouces, than the total rise must have been just over 2 toises, or approximately 13 feet. Sauval's description of it suggests that Le Mercier was basing his design on the classical amphitheatre but adjusting it to conform to the space available and providing for the comfort of the seventeenth-century court audience. The degrees were not curved but placed "in a straight line across the entire width" of the room. Since they were too low to be used as seating, wooden forms or benches were put in place when a play was performed. Each form covered two-thirds of the depth of a degree. If the degree was, as Sauval says, 23 pouces, or just over 2 feet deep, then each form was 16 inches deep, leaving 8 inches for knee room. Decidedly tight quarters by modern standards, but people in the seventeenth century were smaller. The result, says Sauval, was that "when the auditorium is full one sees only heads arranged in rows, one above the other, rising imperceptibly." Oddly enough, Van Lochen's engraving does not show the degrees or the royal "scaffold" also mentioned by Sauval. The floor appears to be flat, and the royal party is seated in comfortable armchairs. Other evidence, however, supports the unquestionable existence of the raked auditorium.

The degrees furnished a view of the stage similar to that in a modern theatre; they did not provide for that staple of Renaissance and baroque public theatres, a standing pit. Exactly what Molière's troupe did to rectify the problem is not clear, in spite of two documents of November 1660 describing the work of reconstruction and renovation. Their first of these, which includes the specifications agreed to by the troupe and Paul Charpentier, master carpenter, calls for the construction of a parterre 9 toises wide (obviously the width of the room) and approximately 4½ toises (28¾ feet) deep. The original plan for this parterre was to build walls around the area and fill it with rubble, "the walls to incline to the rear and to be covered with good plaster." This plan was apparently not carried out, because the paragraph describing it in the specifications is crossed over and in the margin is written "approved the cancellation of the recommendation at this place as useless." The marginal note is initialed by Philbert Gassot, sieur du Croisy, who was the company member charged with overseeing the reconstruction.

The second document, a contract between the troupe and Denis Buret, master builder, signed on 24 November, calls for a different solution. Buret agreed to build a grooved floor 4 toises deep and 6 toises wide (25½ feet by 38⅓ feet) for the parterre. No information is given about how this floor is to be supported or what is to be done with the extra space on the sides. The Charpentier contract also calls for partitions to create a separate passage to the parterre ending at the foot of the degrees, by which must be meant the remaining degrees, which will now serve as an amphithéâtre. This new parterre floor, assuming it to be flat and not raked, would have covered the first thirteen of the old degrees, intersecting them at approximately 6 feet of rise, provided that the front of the stage was not moved forward during this first reconstruction. The original plan of building walls and filling in the degrees with rubble certainly seems to indicate that a flat parterre was wanted. Later views of the theatre appear to show a raked parterre area, however, although the rake is less than that of the original degrees.

The theoretical existence of a raked parterre is strengthened by the specifications for the new stage. Buret was to "put supports both under the stage which is presently in the room and under the [new stage] floor with a partition to close the frame of the front of the stage of the height of 6 feet and the width of 30 feet." A stage height of 6 feet at the front is normal for the convenience of a standing pit. The problem with this height in this instance is, once again, the problem of placing a flat parterre floor over the stepped degrees of the old auditorium. The contract clearly calls for a partition 6 feet high to close the front of the stage; we must thus assume that the stage front was visible to that height. The Vigarani section also shows a 6-foot stage on top of a 4-foot stage.

Furthermore, it makes sense to assume that the joists for the new parterre floor were supported at the stage end by the old stage floor. But a floor level from this point, 4 feet above the auditorium baseline, would intersect the degrees at approximately 18 feet from the stage, not at the 25½ feet called for in the contract for the parterre floor. One solution to this dilemma: a lightly raked parterre.

Other new dispositions of the auditorium in 1661 are clear in outline though somewhat obscure in detail. The loges brought from the Petit-Bourbon were to be arranged in two rows of seventeen each. "The old gallery" was to be used for access to the new loges, meaning that the auditorium would be significantly narrower than it had been and explaining the contraction of the parterre to 6 toises. The lower of the original galleries, judging from Van Lochen's engraving, was approximately level with—perhaps a foot higher than—the top degree of the parterre; the second gallery was just above it. The new first loges, installed to take advantage of the gallery as a passage, would thus be 4 feet above the level of the new stage, 14 feet above the auditorium baseline. The loges were 6 feet wide from center to center of the decorative posts between them, but dimensions of depth or height are not given in the contracts. The Vigarani plan shows a new arrangement of what are probably the same loges; not only are they 6 feet from center to center, they are also 6 feet from the bottom of the first row to the bottom of the second. Various partitions are also called for in the documents, designed to separate the audience upon entry into the theatre. A new stairway was needed for access into the loges across the old gallery "from the door end" of the building, and a box office at the top of the stairway would collect money from those who wanted to sit in the expensive seats. Presumably the sides of the old parterre were walled off below the loges; the Vigarani section shows the area being used on one side for access into the amphithéâtre; on the other, entry into the parterre is shown through a passage along the outside of the building past what appears to be a box office, then up five steps to a landing and down four curving steps into the pit.

The theatre, already thought to be lacking in height, would now, with the installation of the standing pit, seem even lower, especially since the marvelous perspective ceiling was gone, replaced only by a "great blue cloth" suspended from the roof.[24] Ratabon's "gross repairs" were clearly makeshift, and it was not until 1671 that a proper ceiling was installed. The troupe did, however, replace the decorative railing that finished the top of the room and originally joined it to the trompe l'oeil ceiling.

The depth of the new stage floor presents a problem. The contract with Buret calls for a floor 8½ toises wide—a perfectly reasonable dimension from all the evidence—and 5 toises, or 32 feet, deep. The original floor was at the very least 48 feet deep, assuming Sauval's dimensions to be right. In the Vigarani plan and section the stage is 60 feet deep. The question naturally arises why the troupe ordered a floor 32 feet deep to cover a floor at least 48 feet deep. The answer probably involves the *poutre,* or beam.

All available plans and sections of the Grande Salle at Palais-Royal show two massive supports intruding on the stage 14 feet in front of the back wall. In the Vigarani section they bear the weight of the roof at the north end of the building; the "eight oak beams" rest on smaller supports. Nothing is known of the construction of these enormous supports, each nearly 16 feet wide by 4 feet deep, but they may have served to bear the weight of the flying machinery. They definitely became a kind of inner proscenium that separated the main part of the stage from the part used for perspective vistas. It seems likely that during this first remodeling Molière's troupe installed its new stage floor only as far back as the beam. The dimensions are roughly accurate: a 32-foot stage floor added to a 4-foot support and a 14-foot area for vistas gives a total stage depth of 50 feet, or 7 toises and 5 pieds. This leaves 9 toises, 4 pieds, for the auditorium: 4 toises for the parterre, the rest for the amphithéâtre and entry area. This accords reasonably well with the dimensions that can be derived from Sauval: 8 toises, 4 pieds, for the auditorium, 1 toise for the arcades and the step area, the same 7 toises, 5 pieds, for the stage.

By December 1664 the rest of the stage had assuredly been floored. A contract for the decors for *Dom Juan* dated 3 December 1664 describes a palace setting "consisting of five wings on each side and a facade against the beam through which will be seen two garden wings and the backscene, the first wing of which will be 18 feet high and all the others diminishing in perspective."[25] In other words, the set implies five downstage wing positions, a false proscenium to hide the beam, and a perspective vista with two wings and a backscene. The second decor, a country hamlet, requires a grotto to hide the beam and a perspective of two wings and a backscene of the sea. And so on through six decors, three requiring vistas, three shutters closing off the stage. Two of the latter scenes call for three sets of wings and a shutter, one for five sets of wings and a shutter.

Dom Juan was the first play done by the French troupe at Palais-Royal for which La Grange notes expenses for decors. The Italian repertory of 1662–68, insofar as it can be established, calls for only the most ordinary of settings—though changeable scenery may have been occasionally used—and for no spectacle requiring special machines. Beginning in 1668 the Italians used changeable scenery, shipwrecks, transformations, magic, traps, and fire effects, but not flying machines. The first mention made of flight is in a piece entitled *Arlequin vallet enchanté, singe et Margot la pie* in which Arlequin, disguised as a magpie, ends the play by flying out. This play is not dated in the Biancolelli zibaldone, but it comes just before one dated June 1671. A refit of the theatre at Palais-Royal was begun 15 March 1671 and completed 15 April. According to La Grange, one reason for the work was to "render the stage suitable for machines." What all of this suggests is that from 1661 to 1671 Palais-Royal was not equipped with flying machines, but that it was equipped with the machines necessary for changeable scenery, at least after 1664.

The proscenium opening of Palais-Royal in the 1660s was 30 feet wide according to the Buret contract; it was probably about 18 feet high judging by the order for scenery. No available evidence indicates that the top of the proscenium opening was raised along with the stage. However, Van Lochen's engraving shows the dimensions of the proscenium opening exactly in the proportion of 30 to 18, and so do the Vigarani plan and section. At some point, then, the proscenium arch was raised by 6 feet to restore its original proportions after the addition of the second stage. This may have taken place in 1671, when a third row of loges was added to the theatre and the "great blue cloth" replaced by a ceiling, or it may have been done in 1661. A 30 by 12 proscenium would have looked out of proportion, would not have needed 18-foot flats, and certainly would not have permitted the addition of a third row of loges.

Although it is impossible to solve all the problems raised by the evidence available, what is clear is that the 1661 reconstruction was complex and expensive. The contract with Charpentier was for 1,100 livres, the one with Buret for 350 livres. The total cost of the work was, however, much higher. In January 1661, when the company moved into the refurbished theatre, La Grange records expenses of 2,115 livres incidental to the move; between then and the end of the season he makes ten marginal notes that various sums, amounting to some 1,800 livres, were taken from daily profits "for the carpenters," "for the painters," or merely for the "expenses of Palais-Royal." The total cost was probably on the order of 4,000 livres, since the Italians paid 2,000 a year later "for half the establishment of the theatre."

The French had been residents of what La Grange later referred to as this theatre that had been repaired "carelessly" and "with haste" for just under a year when the Italians returned to share it with them. As before, the theatre's employees were also shared; La Grange's breakdown of daily expenses—this time for 1661–62—once again will serve to define the organization and operation of the theatre.

St. Germain, porter	3 livres	15 sous
Gillot, porter	3	15
Their valet, brother of St. Germain	1	10
A sergeant and 12 soldiers of the guards	15	
Mme. de l'Estang, receiver	3	
Mme. Provost or Nanon Brillard	3	
4 ushers for the loges	6	
Ushers for the stage and amphithéâtre	3	
Décorateurs Crosniers	4	10
Sr. Chrestien, concierge	1	10
4 musicians	6	
Candles	11	
Red & black posters and billstickers	8	4
Refreshments for the troupe	1	
Charity	1	
Common valets (dressers)	1	
	73 livres	4 sous

The expenses have risen 30 livres, 5 sous, in two years, in part because of the change of theatre, in part because wages are higher, in part because of the addition of guards to prevent both entry without payment and violent behavior in the theatre.

Two doorkeepers and two women for the box office still suffice, although the doorkeepers have had a raise and now have a servant. But where four ushers were enough for the Petit-Bourbon, six are required for Palais-Royal, including one for the amphithéâtre and one for the stage. Backstage the troupes have added a candle trimmer. Costs are up for music, candles, and advertising, and a daily livre for charity has been added. But the major additional expense is for the soldiers and their sergeant.

The Italians had been back in Paris for less than two months when they called on 25 February for a *commissaire* to come from the Châtelet to take testimony about a scuffle outside the theatre which ended in death.[26] According to the porter, Germain, on duty at the entry into the parterre at 4:00 in the afternoon, seven or eight "fellows," known to him only because he had refused to admit them before, tried to force their way past him into the theatre. When he insisted they pay, they drew their swords, forcing him to run for his life into the courtyard of a nearby house. They followed him, swords in hand; two shots rang out, two of the "fellows" fell, the others ran away, and Germain was able to get back to Palais-Royal and complain to his masters. Fiorilli and Zanotti signed the complaint in which they were joined by Molière and Du Croisy of the French troupe. A number of neighbors also testified. No one admitted firing the shots, no one saw a gun. The assailants were identified as lackeys, liveried servants; the two who were wounded both died. Germain may have been wounded as well; La Grange added a marginal note to his *Registre* for 20 March 1661: "Given to St. Germain, porter, for his wound, 55 livres." Either the note belonged to 1662, or Germain was singularly unlucky.

Two months later the Italian troupe's Capitan Terremoto, Francesco Manzani, was murdered outside the theatre, stabbed and shot. Whether the two events were linked in any way is unknown, but the need to hire guards for the theatres seems clear. Violence both outside and inside seventeenth-century theatres was not unusual—a number of similar incidents are recorded—and guards became a normal part of the theatrical landscape.

The lackeys who tried to bully their way past the doorkeeper were trying to save themselves 15 sous, the usual price charged for standing in the parterre, unless, of course, a new play was on the boards that Saturday in March. An English traveler, Philip Skippon, saw two Italian pieces in 1666, one entitled *Il maritaggion d'una statua,* which cost 30 sous, the other entitled *Quattre Scaramuccie* which cost 15.[27] All the theatres appear to have charged the same price for the parterre, but not for other areas of the theatre. Molière's troupe, for instance, charged 44 livres for a first loge, eight seats, at the Petit-Bourbon in 1660;[28] the price was the same at the Palais-Royal in 1672–73, where we know that a loge cost 44 livres, an individual seat 5 livres, 10 sous.[29] The Italians, on the other hand, at a much later date—1688—charged 33 livres for a first loge, 3 livres for an individual seat in a first loge.[30] This was the same amount charged at the Comédie-Française after 1680.[31]

Exact ticket prices for the Italians at Palais-Royal in the 1660s cannot be determined. What is apparent is that the ratio of most expensive to least expensive was somewhere between 7:1 and 4:1, and even the least expensive places were not truly cheap. In the early seventeenth century in England—in the public theatres—the standing pit cost only a penny, one-twelfth of the daily income of a laborer. In France, most of the theatre's own minor employees—its ushers and valets—could not have afforded to stand in the parterre, where 15 sous represented one-half to three-fourths of their daily income.

The young king's support of the Italian troupe underscores the fact that this company of farceurs and acrobats appealed to much the same audience that enjoyed the works of Corneille and Molière. Critics of the day derided the Italians, but nothing suggests that they played to an audience significantly different from that of their French colleagues. Paris was the largest city in Europe in the mid-seventeenth century, but the theatre audience was small, supporting four companies at most, each playing three or four days a week to an estimated average attendance of four hundred. Liveried servants went to the theatre until laws were passed forbidding them to, and others of the lower classes, shop assistants and artisans, may have attended—perhaps on a Sunday or holiday—but most audience members, even in the parterre, were from the aristocracy and the bourgeoisie.[32] We meet two bourgeois members of that audience in Dorimond's *La comédie de la comédie,* printed in Paris in 1662. Lucindor tells his friend Léandre that he plans to take his wife and children to the theatre the next day, that they will profit since at the theatre virtue always triumphs, vice never. Léandre warns him that the Italians take more license than the French and may give offense. Lucindor agrees that the French theatre is more serious, says that he admires it more, but still, "one can without sin taste the foolishness" of the Italians. Chances are Lucindor continued to admire the morality of the French tragedies while entertaining himself and the family with the agility, mild licentiousness, and remarkable acting of the Italians, and this in spite of the fact that a foreign language was spoken.

Commedia dell'arte is a theatre of the actor. Sandro D'Amico well expresses what many scholars have said of it, that the reason for its amazing success throughout Europe was "the novelty of perfectly executed action and the total identification of the actor with his character—the first time this miracle took place."[33] Actor, clown, acrobat, dancer, and musician—possessed, according to Luigi Riccoboni, of a "lively and fertile imagination and a great facility for self-expression"[34]—the Italian actor of the mid-seventeenth century was an ingenious improviser as well. And improvisation was the key to the new style of acting which Fiorilli, Biancolelli, and the others now established in France. The classical French actor had a presence, a memory, and a voice; the Italian actor had as well a body, an active mind, and—most especially—a consciousness, what a modern actor would call concentration. Improvisation demands attention. The actor cannot function as a solo performer, a speaker of arias, but must be immediately aware of everything around him, imminently ready for whatever another actor chooses to do. Even though the extent to which commedia dell'arte actors improvised has been overstated, the potential for improvisation was always there. No doubt plays became fixed as they were successfully performed over and over, but fixed only until a new actor was added to the mix or the money found for a new transformation or a better machine. Add to the concentration required by improvisation the demands of chases, leaps, pratfalls, beatings, and physical action of all sorts, where a second's lapse of attention can mean injury and even death, and the result is an actor who is alive on the stage, natural, ready to "play the moment."

Granted that the Italians faced certain limitations in France. In Italy the comic action was balanced with romantic action, the donne and the amorosi as valued as the zanni. In France, the verbal elements of the plays were not so important; many members of the audience, after all, were unable to understand the dialogue. When Sebastiano Locatelli visited Paris in 1664–65, he was unhappy with his experience at the Italian theatre: "I swear I am little amused by actors playing in Italian for spectators who don't understand it, being obliged to gesture, find inventions, change the scenery, and other things of that sort to make the audience happy. The excellent Zanotti could not, in his dialogue with his Eularia, enchant the public with the finesse of his language, the subtlety of his repartee, the piquancy of his words and his puns. . . . The same is true of the other actors, all excellent."[35] But Locatelli's expectations, based as they were upon his experience of the commedia dell'arte in Italy, were not relevant to the experience of a French-speaking audience member in Paris. Scholars have taken Locatelli's statement to imply the beginning of the decadence of the commedia dell'arte in France as romanesque literary elements were transcended by zanni play and spectacle. But from the theatrical standpoint, accentuation of action and production values and de-emphasis of language are not necessarily decadent, especially in a form designed to entertain.

Locatelli's report does confirm that in 1664–65 the troupe was still playing a standard repertory, with some modifications to appeal to French taste. We know the titles of many of the pieces done between 1662 and 1668; they are included in Biancolelli's zibaldone (which will be considered in detail in chapter 6). We do not know performance dates; the gazetteer Loret, who provided so many details of their earlier seasons, says almost nothing about the Italians between their establishment in

1662 and his death in 1665. His "continuers," Mayolas and Robinet, mention one or two titles, most of which Biancolelli includes, and a very few other titles are known from other sources, but the lack of a confirmed chronology makes it difficult to draw inferences about any way in which the troupe may have selected or changed its repertory in response to audience preferences. One production suggests that the Italians did participate in the game of imitation in the 1660s. Molière mentions, in his preface to the 1669 edition of *Tartuffe,* an Italian play clearly devised to take advantage of the scandal:

> A week after [*Tartuffe*] had been forbidden [in 1664], a play entitled *Scaramouche ermite* was performed before the court; and the king, as he was leaving, said to the great prince [the Grande Condé]: "I would really like to know why the gentlemen who are so scandalized by the play of Molière do not say a word about that of Scaramouche." To which the prince answered: "The reason for that is the play of Scaramouche laughs at heaven and religion, which these gentlemen care nothing about, but that of Molière laughs at them, and that is what they cannot bear.

Or perhaps the *dévots* did not understand Italian.

No theatrical troupe had an easy time of it in Paris in the seventeenth century, but this company of foreign actors, playing in a language that much of its audience could not understand, cut off from personal and professional roots—and for reasons that finally can only be guessed at— decided to settle in, and in doing so became the first commedia dell'arte troupe to establish itself in a single city, to come in off the road. When the actors made their decision to stay is not known. Perhaps there never was a decision, just an achieved fact. Perhaps Louis XIV simply decided that his court would have a troupe of Italian actors appended and never permitted them to go. Perhaps they were so inordinately successful that they never wanted to go. But, finally, the fact is that Paris changed them and they could not go.

The Second Arlequin

T HE ITALIAN TROUPE in Paris, as it was constituted in January 1662, had
close ties to Modena. The earlier dominance of the commedia
dell'arte by the Gonzaga court of Mantua ended in the 1630s during the
war of the Mantuan succession, and the center shifted to Parma and Modena. The company of the duke of Modena in 1651 included Domenico
Locatelli, Giovan Andrea Zanotti, and Giacinto Bendinelli, all of whom
were to become established in Paris, along with Bernardo Coris, father
(or stepfather) of Orsola Coris (or Cortesi),[1] and Isabella Franchini, the
mother of Domenico Biancolelli.[2]

Domenico Biancolelli, Arlequin of the Comédie-Italianne, was born
in Bologna in 1636. Stefania Spada found his act of baptism in the register of the Baptistry:

> Die p   Mensis Septembris 1636
> Dom—Joseph filus D. Fran Jancolelli et D. Isabellae de
> Franchinis eius ux—natus die 30 Augusti—hora 6—sub Cap S
> Proculi—Comp Dom Mazzei et D Dom Baliana.[3]

Spada fills in and interprets the document as follows: "Baptised the first
of September 1636—Domenico Giuseppe, son of Francesco Biancolelli
and Isabella Franchini his wife, born 30 August at 6:00 o'clock." Both
parents were actors. Francesco Biancolelli, whose name and role are unknown, died sometime before 1645, the year by which his wife was remarried to Carlo Cantù. Isabella Franchini was the daughter of a
Pantalone, Francesco Franchini; she played Columbina, a serva. As Rasi
notes, the name Colombina seems to have belonged to the Franchini-
Biancolelli family. First employed by Isabella, it later was adopted and
made famous in France by her granddaughter, Catherine Biancolelli.[4]

Domenico Biancolelli was celebrated in his day for his extreme
youth at the time of his debut. Gueullette thought he had arrived in Paris
at twenty, already regarded as a very good actor. In fact, he was twenty-
five when the company opened at Palais-Royal. The Italian actors had a
habit of losing years from their life as they aged, a habit not unknown

among actors even today, which may have misled Gueullette. Dominique, as he was known in France, was trained as a zanni by his stepfather, Carlo Cantù, famous as Buffetto, a First Zanni. Cantù had, of course, come to Paris in 1645 at the time of *La finta pazza,* perhaps with his wife, but certainly with his young stepson, Menghino. Cantù describes the trip in his *Cicalamento in canzonette ridicolose,* a verse and prose account of the love story of Colombina and Buffetto.[5] According to Cantù, on their arrival in Paris he received three suits of clothing of "not ordinary beauty"; Menghino got some cash and an even more beautiful suit.

Gueullette seems to have believed that Biancolelli was part of the original troupe called to Paris in 1661; Jal, on the other hand, found a letter from Louis XIV to the duke of Parma dated 5 July 1661—after the arrival of the troupe—asking for Arlequin.[6] As we have seen, Domenico Locatelli, who played the Arlequin role as Trivelin, had fallen seriously ill. Biancolelli was brought to understudy, perhaps to replace Locatelli, who did, however, recover. Gueullette also reports that Biancolelli was in Vienna when the command came from the French court, playing in the troupe of a mountebank named Favarini. Spada has found no trace of Dominique in the archives of Vienna, and no trace of a Favarini. She did discover, however, that the emperor Leopold I had invited an Italian troupe from Venice to play in Vienna at carnival of 1660,[7] so perhaps the legend that Dominique came to Paris from Vienna is accurate.

Just over a year after his arrival, on 2 April 1663, Biancolelli was married at St.-Germain L'Auxerrois to the Second Amoureuse, Orsola Cortesi, Eularia.[8] According to their marriage contract, her mother, Barbara Minuti Coris, agreed to pay a dowry of 2,000 ducatoni.[9] The dowry could not be paid at the time, since Signora Barbara did not have such a sum with her in Paris, but she promised to pay it after her return to Bologna. Twenty-four years later, her daughter, Orsola Biancolelli, signed a "quittance", or receipt, in the margin of the contract for the money promised as a dowry.

The marriage was apparently a great success. Although Sebastiano Locatelli writes that it had been arranged by the queen, this seems un-likely. The two had probably known each other for years, since their families were in the same company in 1651. But if the queen did marry them off, she must have known what she was doing. The Biancolelli household was a model of respectability. Jean Nicolas de Tralage made two lists late in the century, when the moral value of the theatre was in question, of "honest" (i.e. decent) actors and debauched ones. He in-cluded "the late Arlequin, his wife Eularia, and his two daughters" on the first list along with Angelo Lolli, Michelangelo Fracansani (Polichinelle), and Sr. Pierrot (Giuseppe Giaratoni). None of the Italians were on his second list, which included the wife of Molière, and the Champmeslé couple, "the wife pregnant by her lover and her servant pregnant by the sieur Champmeslé at the same time."[10] An eighteenth-century lawyer, representing the children of Biancolelli's daughter, Françoise, character-ized their grandfather as one who "did not engage in domestic disorders in a profession which is not disreputable in Italy, and attracted even in France the esteem of everyone as much by the variety and depth of his knowledge as by the regularity of his manners."[11]

Dominique and his Eularia were a team onstage as well as off, even though in the traditional commedia dell'arte plot an amoureuse was not normally the love interest for a zanni. Although many of Dominique's comic routines were played with the servante Diamantine, others in-volved Eularia, usually pretending an attraction to Arlequin as part of a trick devised to bring her together with her amoureux. The plots were arranged to give the two the opportunity to play together as much as possible.

In 1679, in *Arlequin dogue d'Angleterre et médecin du temps,* Arlequin in disguise as a physician diagnoses the illness of Eularia, the supposedly virginal daughter of the Docteur. "Your illness, madame, is that you make a baby every month. In your pregnancies you are very indisposed and your husband gets the benefit of it since you complain all night, you wake him up, and the poor man can't get back to sleep! You have eight children, all living, which much perplexes your husband. You gave birth to one four months ago, and you are already three and a half months pregnant."[12] The actor was clearly speaking though the character.

According to Gueullette, there were twelve Biancolelli children in all. No wonder the abbé de Pure complained in 1668 that the actresses were too often pregnant.[13] Jal found records of birth or baptism of eleven children, eight of whom survived to adulthood. Dominique himself, in the self-referential scene quoted above, speaks of eight living children in June 1679, which agrees with the records Jal found. The children were: Françoise-Marie, baptised 1 December 1664; Catherine, baptised 26 Oc-tober 1665; Louis, baptised 9 November 1666 with the king as godfather; Anne-Caietan, baptised 22 October 1669; Marie-Apolline, baptised 25 January 1671; Elisabeth-Charlotte, born 13 April 1673, privately baptised 23 April 1673, formally baptised 18 October 1673, her godmother the second Madame, died 12 October 1674; Charlotte-Marie, baptised 15 July 1674, her godfather Colbert; a second Louis, born 24 December 1675, privately baptised 29 December, died 7 September 1677; Philippe, baptised 29 May 1677; Charles, baptised 10 February 1679, died before January 1690, when he is not listed among his father's surviving minor children; and Pierre-François, baptised 25 September 1680. Charles was the baby referred to by Arlequin in June as having been born four months before.[14]

Of the eight children who survived childhood, three—Françoise, Catherine, and Pierre-François—had careers in the theatre. Anne-Caietan married an Italian living in France named Jean-Thomas Bucelini; Charlotte-Marie married a Frenchman, Jacques Thurin de Bourneuf, and was still living at La Rochelle in 1650; Marie-Apolline became a Visitation nun at Ste.-Marie de Montargis, the convent to which her mother retired in 1704. The first Louis, godson of the king, became a captain, director of fortifications for Provence, and chevalier of the Ordre Militaire de Saint Louis. He married twice, had several children, and wrote a number of plays in the 1690s for the Comédie-Italienne. Philippe, councillor of the king, dean of the Council of St. Dominique, commissioner of the navy, and sieur de Boismoran, never married. He died in November of 1761 at the age of 84. He told Gueullette that he had made his debut as Arlequin when very young but gave it up at the request of his sister, Françoise, during her marital tribulations, which will be recounted below.[15]

Both Catherine and Françoise joined the Italian company in 1683. The youngest child, Pierre-François, who was only seventeen when the troupe was dismissed, joined a company organized by Giuseppe Tortoriti to play in the provinces and married Tortoriti's daughter. He made his debut as Arlequin in 1710 at the Paris fairs and was admitted into the new Comédie-Italienne in 1717 by an act of the regent. Although he began acting with that company as Pierrot, he finally played Trivelin. He married a second time, to Marie-Thérèse Lalande, in 1722 and had two children with her. One of them, Marie-Thérèse Biancolelli, made her debut at the new Comédie-Italienne in 1738 as an amoureuse and remained in the company until 1762. Pierre-François, also known as Dominique, acted in and wrote a number of plays for the new Italian troupe until his death in 1734.[16] It was he who gave his father's manuscript to the magistrate Gueullette.

Like the other Italian actors in Paris, Biancolelli and his wife were apparently meticulous in their religious observances. Unlike the French actors, the Italians were not in danger of excommunication nor were they required to recant their profession before death in order to receive last

rites and be permitted burial, although some did so. When Luigi Riccoboni was negotiating, with the duke of Parma, the conditions for the
establishment of the new troupe in Paris in 1716, one of his requests was
that the duke "make strong entreaties to the court that the troupe be
accorded the free usage of the holy sacraments, as it has in Italy."[17] The
new troupe did not, however, receive this indulgence from a French court
still aware of the power of the *dévots* and mindful of the "scandalous"
behavior of the Italian actors in the 1690s.

Much of that behavior can be attributed to the Costantini family, not
to the Biancolellis. A description of their family life was found by Spada
in a manuscript journal kept by three young Bolognese noblemen who
were in France in 1681–82.[18] On 9 January 1681 the Italian visitors were
invited to supper by "Monsieur Domenico and Madame Eularia who
have many children and especially two dashing girls, rather pretty, one
named Francesca and the other Caterina, and spent the evening in conversation with these girls who have very lively wits and speak both
French and Italian very well, having been born in France." The supper
party spent part of the evening listening to "a grand serenade in the street
offered by Monsieur de Gontur [or Gontour] who professed to be in love
with Mlle. Catto, and wanted to marry her." The serenade was grand,
indeed, consisting of violins, violas, trumpets, and other French instruments with five singers, and ended with the gentleman presenting Mlle.
Catto a bouquet of fresh flowers in the Parisian fashion, "in a great basket
all beflowered and garlanded with ribbon." The young men were told by
everyone that the suitor must have spent at least fifty louis d'or on the
event. The suitor was a rich merchant, but not very handsome and not
very well mannered, so in spite of his money, Mlle. Catto was not interested. The young Italian visitors were entertained again on 25 January,
when all the Bolognese then living in Paris came as well, and on many
other occasions.

The father who presided over this hospitable household was a
small, handsome man who apparently became a little too fat for an Arlequin in the last ten years or so of his life (fig. 7).[19] In *Le voyage de Scaramouche et d'Arlequin aux Indes* (1675) Arlequin makes jokes about his
height and weight. "Oh cruel fate," he says. "Why should such a little
man have such a big appetite?"[20] At the finale of act 1, Arlequin describes
his tour of the underworld where Pluto wanted to boil him, but Proserpine would rather eat "a little suckling pig à la broche." Arlequin escapes
from the spit by promising to bring their demonic majesties someone
even fatter than he: Crosnier, the candle trimmer of the Comédie. In *Le*

>

FIG. 7. *Domenico Biancolelli, Arlequin. Engraving by Hubert c. 1700.* (Bibliothèque de l'Opéra, Ms. Rés. 625; phot. Bibl. Nat. Paris)

baron de Foeneste (January 1674) Arlequin hides behind this same Crosnier; a good joke was never used only once.

Biancolelli could not, however, have become terribly fat since as late
as 1679 he was doing complex acrobatic lazzi. In *Arlequin dogue d'Angleterre
et médecin du temps,* he enters disguised as a legless beggar. "I carry before
me two false legs that I wave around saying one serves me as a bolster,
the other as a fan. . . . I persecute Spezzafer so that he will give me something, and I give him some great blows on the back with my false legs;
he gives me a great blow on the back and makes me fall on my nose so
that my real legs can be seen."[21] His notes call for less rough and tumble
in the later plays, to be sure, but the entertainments, as they adjusted to
French taste, were also less reliant on knockabout farce.

A portrait in the Museo La Scala in Milan is identified as Biancolelli
and included in nearly every available book dealing with the commedia
dell'arte. It shows a truly fat man in the costume of a dottore with a mask
dangling from his belt. Robert Erenstein remarks that he knows of no
appearance by Domenico Biancolelli as a dottore,[22] and there seems to
be no earthly reason why Dominique, the most famous Arlequin of his
day, would have had himself painted in a costume other than his own.
Perhaps the various scholars who have accepted the attribution simply
want the portrait—which is wonderful—to be Dominique and confirm
their assumption with the subject's obesity.[23] But Dominique, in spite of
"suckling pig" jokes, was surely not that fat.

He was both an acrobat and a dancer of note. He danced not only
on the stage of the Italian theatre but in court ballets as well.[24] Dancing
was responsible for his death in 1688, according to Gueullette. While
imitating Beauchamps to amuse the king, he became overheated, caught
a chill, and died a week later, probably of pneumonia.[25]

Gueullette also tells us that "the celebrated Dominique . . . had a
vocal defect to which he had so accustomed the public—as had his imitators since his death   that it was unimaginable that an Arlequin could
be tolerated unless he spoke from his throat and affected the voice of a
parrot."[26] The issue was the Arlequin of the new Comédie-Italienne,
Thomassin, who spoke in his natural voice. Arlequin's parrot voice was
not the result of a defect, however, but was a characteristic of the mask.
Even today, Punch and Judy men use an appliance in the mouth to produce the squawking voice of Punch. That Dominique *chose* to adopt a
raucous tone is supported by this note in *Le régal des dames*: "I take the
music from my pocket and put it in front of the blind man. I call the rest
of the musicians and I say to the singers to give us a drinking song; at
the end of the first couplet I sing the refrain *in a clear voice.*"[27]

Two books printed after Biancolelli's death, *Arlequiniana* and *Livre sans nom,* both attributed to Charles Cotolendi, give a picture of Biancolelli as an able courtier, gossip, and wit. Gherardi finds the *Arlequiniana,* like the *Vie de Scaramouche,* full of things never said nor done,[28] and, indeed, Cotolendi's two volumes are simply collections of anecdotes, many scandalous, some facetious, with a few glimpses of Arlequin on stage. In the introduction to *Arlequiniana,* however, Cotolendi has the ghost of Arlequin say: "I would not complain if you printed the good things we have said . . . the reflections that we have made on several things; our thoughts on the various schools of philosophy; the interpretations we have given to . . . the ancient poets; the rules of conduct that one must follow to live among illustrious persons . . . but you tell nothing but jokes."[29] Gueullette argues that this image of Dominique developed after his death was fraudulent. St. Simon writes that Biancolelli was "naturally serious and studious, and became learned by his own efforts,"[30] but Gueullette maintains he was "not a scholar or man of superior intelligence. . . . [He was] born with a natural wit, suitable to his estate . . . but was not a man of belles lettres." How could he have been, asks Gueullette, when "he must have acted in Italy from the age of fourteen or sixteen? Moreover I see by his manuscript that he did almost all the leaps, flips, falls, slight of hand tricks, tricks of strength and of the ladder that acrobats do . . . but it is not possible that a man who must begin such exercises in his bib should be instructed and know belles lettres."[31] In contrast, the dour duke confides that "the president d'Harlay [president of the Parlement de Paris] . . . met [Dominique] at the Bibliothèque de Ste.-Victoire, got into conversation with him without knowing who he was . . . and found him very well-versed and very modest at the same time." D'Harlay was surprised to discover that this pleasant gentleman was the actor Dominique, but was so charmed by him that "he embraced him and asked to be his friend . . . and always received him with esteem and special distinction." Perhaps Gueullette, who had, after all, translated hundreds of pages of Dominique's puns and ribaldry deserves the last word on this subject: "If one can judge by the original Italian manuscript of which I have made the translation, I see nothing which does not confirm that this was an excellent actor."

Orsola Cortesi, Biancolelli's wife, was an amoureuse in the Italian tradition. Like the great Isabella Andreini and like her own Paris colleague Brigida Fedele, she was a woman of letters. Her play *La bella brutta,* translated from the Spanish, was published in Paris in 1665 and Bologna in 1669. An amoureuse, unlike a zanni, was expected to evidence skill with language as part of the aura of humanistic learning that settled on the romantic characters of the commedia dell'arte in the late sixteenth century. In reality, if Domenico Biancolelli had no time for an education, then neither had Orsola Cortesi, who was also born into a family that had long practiced "the art." Although exactly which family she was born into is, once again, not wholly clear.

She herself used two names: Orsola Coris and Orsola Cortesi. According to her marriage contract, signed 29 March 1663, her name was Orsola Cortesi, and she was the daughter of the late Antonio Cortesi of Bologna. Her mother was Barbara Minuti, who "affirmed and promised" as Barbara Coris.[32] Barbara Minuti Coris was also the wife of Bernardo (or Bernardino) Coris and, according to Rasi, played the donna under the name Florinda.[33] The only confirmation that Barbara Minuti did play as Florinda is an entry Jal found in the *Registre du trésor royal* for 1661; "one Florinda by name of the Italian theatre received the sum of 600 livres for gratification."[34] Jal has no idea who this Florinda might have been, but Barbara Minuti did have some legal connection with the troop; she signed an agreement with the French company on the conditions of sharing the Guénégaud when the Italian company was away playing in England. According to Gueulette, she came to Paris with her two daughters by her *first* husband.[35] Her other daughter, Alessandra "Corisse," died unmarried "in the house of M. Biancolelly" on 2 May 1672.[36] Gueullette says that neither Barbara Minuti nor her husband played in France; nevertheless, she witnessed her granddaughter's marriage contract on 2 November 1685 as "Barbara Minutty widow of Bernardin Coris comédien du Roy."[37] Bernardo played as Silvio, but there is no record of a Silvio in the Biancolelli manuscript or any of the French documents related to the troupe.

Barbara Minuti's daughter, Orsola, usually but not always signed herself Cortesi in France. All the legal documents from the Minutier Centrale that I have seen are signed "Orsola Cortesi" in a clear, legible hand. However, the baptismal act for her sixth child, Elisabeth-Charlotte, is signed "Coris,"[38] as is the lease of a house the family rented on the rue St. Honoré.[39] Even more puzzling is the title page of *La bella brutta*, which reads: "da Orsola Coris Biancolelli, fra comici italiani de S. M. C.ma detta Eularia." Gueullette believes this actress-translator was Domenico Biancolelli's aunt;[40] Spada thinks she was his sister.[41] Either possibility seems beyond the bounds of logic. Surely there were not two actresses named Orsola playing the role of Eularia in Paris in 1665.

Her occasional use of the name Coris in Paris makes it incontrovertible that this was the same Eularia Coris who played the title role in Giovan Battista Andreini's *Maddalena* in Milan in 1652.[42] The published edition of this play contains several adulatory poems addressed to Signora Eularia, Signora Eularia Coris, and Signora Eularia Comica Celebre. The young actress was probably about twenty at the time. Gueullette says that she was eighty-six when she died in 1718; if so, she was born in 1632. She would have been thirty when she made her debut in Paris, thirty-one when she married, and forty-eight when her last child was born in 1680.

In 1658 she was with a company under the protection of the duke of Mantua to whom she wrote a series of chatty letters signed "Orsola Coris." Her familiar tone—"speaking in the interests of the company, complaining of her colleagues, demanding reprimands, giving intimate and delicate commissions, and revealing matters that would make a married woman blush"[43]—suggests to Rasi that she was the de facto head of the company and must have been an older, more experienced woman. But one of the letters ends with "my father and mother and Alessandrina join me in humbly bowing to Your Most Serene Highness."

The father was certainly Bernardo Coris, married to Florinda at least as early as 1643, when they were mentioned in a letter to the duke of Modena from his uncle Tomaso.[44] On the basis of available information, there seems to be no way finally to sort out the Coris-Cortesi question. The two names are close enough phonetically to be variants, but Orsola Cortesi would hardly have confused Antonio and Bernardo in her marriage contract. Gueullette says that Barbara Minuti claimed that her daughter's father was descended from the great Cortés who conquered Mexico; there was an Alfonso Cortese, a Neapolitan actor, who signed a compact in Naples in 1575.[45] The connection with Naples makes Spanish ancestry possible. There was also a "Flaminio" Curtesse who was granted £10 in London in August 1602 "for his Chardges and paynes of himself and certen other Italian Comedians who were comended hither out of Fraunce."[46] Cortesi (or Cortese) was not, then, an unknown family name among the Italian actors. Perhaps Barbara Minuti was married twice to two men with similar last names; perhaps she had one husband named Antonio Bernardo Coris who liked to think his name was a variant of Cortesi. What finally matters, however, is that there was only one actress, Orsola Coris or Cortesi, Eularia, who made her debut in Paris in 1662 as Second Amoureuse.

Gueullette, who saw her on stage late in her career, says she was "tall, well made, and very attractive without being beautiful."[47] She played Second Amoureuse until the retirement of Brigida Fidele, Aurelia; however, analysis of the repertory shows that many of the plays require only one amoureuse and that sometimes Aurelia is indicated and sometimes Eularia. As the romance plots become less important in France, the distinction between First and Second Amoureuse becomes one of seniority in the company rather than importance of role.

Because he saw her play a mute role in *La foire Saint-Germain* in 1695, and because she played in Italian in *La matrone d'Ephèse* and other plays of the 1680s and 1690s that included scenes in French, Gueullette implies that Eularia was essentially limited by language as the repertory changed.[48] But Gueullette also included with his manuscript a letter he had received from superior of the convent where she died in 1718. According to Soeur Geneviève Angélique du Cerceau, Orsola Cortesi "knew the French language which she spoke very well, nearly without accent." After a stroke she lived for six weeks, but then spoke only in Italian.[49]

Spada and Campardon believe Eularia retired from the stage in 1691; Gueullette, however, saw her in 1695 and she signed a Règlement et Convention regulating the conditions of admission into the company in 1696.[50] Chances are that she never officially retired; in fact, the only member of the company who seems to have done so was Angelo Lolli. Her daughter Françoise took over the major burden of the amoureuse in 1683, however, especially in the French repertory, leaving the old repertory and various minor roles in the new repertory to her mother.

Dominique Biancolelli and Orsola Cortesi became naturalized French citizens in April 1680, the first members of the troupe to do so.[51] Probably they chose French citizenship to protect their property in France, which was becoming considerable. Under French law the property of a foreigner resident in France could, upon death, revert to the crown. Domenico Biancolelli left a substantial estate, but the family had expensive legal problems in later years; his widow may have been grateful for the 300 livres a year in pension the king granted her after the dissolution of the company.[52]

Giacinto Bendinelli, Valerio, played an amoureux in the Italian company. According to his Act of Marriage registered at St.-Eustache, his parents were Luca Bendinelli and Francesca Sennasoni (or Scavasoni). In his will and his marriage contract he described himself as a native of Bologna; his date of birth is unknown.[53] The earliest record of him is in the company of the duke of Modena in 1651 with Zanotti, Locatelli, Isabella Franchini, and Bernardo Coris. In 1658 he was in Rome with Angelo Agostino Lolli according to the register of strangers in the district of the parish of S. Pietro.[54]

Although most scholars have followed the Parfaict brothers in naming Bendinelli First Amoureux, there is no way of knowing whether he or Zanotti played that role. Zanotti seems a likelier candidate for the senior line: we hear of him first in 1647; we know he was in Paris before 1659; and he was singled out by Sebastiano Locatelli as "the excellent Zanotti who cannot enchant the [French-speaking Parisian] public by the finesse of his expressions, the subtlety of his repartée, the piquancy of his words and his puns." On the other hand, Locatelli also speaks of Zanotti's "dialogues with his Eularia," and Eularia was the Second Amoureuse. The existing repertory does not permit us to discover whether the conventional pairings were consistently maintained in the early 1660s. Later they were not.

Only a few traces remain of Valerio in the Biancolelli zibaldone, but although little is known of him professionally, his personal life in Paris is better known than those of most of his colleagues. He was married on 1 September 1665 at St.-Eustache to a French woman, Jeanne-Marie Poulain. They had two daughters, one born 2 July 1665, the other 1 August 1667. On 5 April 1667 Bendinelli swore to the following complaint:

> That having had affection for and complete confidence in all matters spiritual and temporal in the person of Dom Pierre Gazotti, priest, native of the city of Modena, his compatriot, whom he has known for six years here and who lived with M. the abbé de Cyris [Vittorio Siri], historiographer of His Majesty at the Galleries of the Louvre, the said complainant found himself very surprised that the said Gazotti used him very badly, without considering the entry that he had in his house, participation at his table where he drank and ate very often, and the contribution of 30 sous a week to say masses for his intention, up to that time when his brutality carried him away during the absence of the complainant, who was at St.-Germain-en-Laye during the last Feast of All Saints, having gone to pay a visit to his wife and mother-in-law, only to hold a very lively discourse on her character with Jeanne-Marie Poulain, the said wife: And to better succeed, having arranged to meet on the street the said mother-in-law and solicited her . . . to win the mind of her daughter, wife of the complainant, in order to satisfy himself with her and in such terms which are not with honor and propriety to be expressed without causing embarrassment. The which attentions have always, since the time mentioned above, continued with such great assiduousness and heat toward the said lady . . . who always hid as much as possible

from the bad intention of the said Gazotti. That she found herself finally obliged to declare to him [Bendinelli] in what fashion things had happened, not wanting to suffer the vicious passions of Gazotti. At which the said complainant, his esteem for this man, whom he had known for his sanctity of life and good manner, entirely wounded, could not refrain from declaring to him his thoughts on this subject; but, instead of profiting from his remonstrances, he showed himself to be more obstinate and still disposed to put what he had conceived into execution. And out of spite, seeing that he could not bring it to a conclusion, practiced all things to harm the complainant, as for instance yesterday, near six or seven in the evening, sent two Swiss to the neighborhood of his house where they insulted him and one put a hand on the guard of his sword to give offense to him, the said Gazotti being then in the shop of a mercer, a near neighbor, who observed all that was happening. And . . . a few days previously he threatened to kill him.[55]

If Gazotti, the Italian Tartuffe, had hatched his nefarious schemes against the innocent Bendinelli earlier, we might have here the most important source of Molière's play. However, since Molière wrote *Tartuffe* in 1664, this version must be life imitating art.

A year later Bendinelli was dead, apparently of natural causes. He made his will on 11 March 1668, hoping to provide for his family. He requested that an inventory be taken of his goods, that they be sold, and that the half of the proceeds belonging to his children be put in the "hands of some notable bourgeois as an investment for their security."[56] Since he believed that his wife and children could not subsist in Paris or, indeed, in France with the little revenue they would have, and since they could live more comfortably in Italy, he asked that his wife take up residence there where his property was and where she could raise his children. For advice, Bendinelli suggested she consult his good friends Zanotti and Lolli. Finally, he asked for at least forty masses for the repose of his soul.

Bendinelli's goods were valued, unfortunately, at considerably less than his debts. His wife did not move to Italy, and the two daughters died in Paris, one after the other, in February and October 1669.

Bendinelli's inventory after death (discussed in Chapter 4) gives a picture of the way a working actor lived in Paris in the 1660s; it also permits a comparison of the Italian company with Molière's very successful French company. The jeune premier of that troupe, Charles Varlet de La Grange, had his property inventoried at the time of his marriage in

1672. His professional wardrobe was valued at 5,235 livres and included fifteen costumes, two of which—a "habit à l'anticque" embroidered in fine silver and a "suit in greenish brown cut velvet embroidered in fine silver"—were each worth 900 livres, almost exactly the value of Bendinelli's entire wardrobe.[57] The Italian actor's most expensive costume was valued at 165 livres and consisted of a suit in gray silk moire with silver and gold lace and a vest in gold brocade trimmed in all silver lace. Other costumes included a coat of blue holland cloth decorated with gold and silver lace, a suit of brown holland cloth embroidered in gold and silver, and a suit of patterned black velvet. There were ten suits in all in the inventory, though some were street clothes.

The requirement that he provide his own costumes was no light matter for an actor who adorned the stage of the Sun King. It was one thing to play Arlequin or Pantalon; even Molière, whose characters were usually either bourgeois or servants, did not spend a great deal on his costumes.[58] It was quite another to play a young lover, supposed son of a rich family. Bendinelli owed two tailors and various sellers of ribbons and lace a total of 1,500 livres at the time of his death. La Grange, totaling things up after Molière's death in 1673, noted that although he had received 2,000 livres over the years in special grants from the king for costumes to be worn at court, he had spent more than twice that on those particular costumes.

Unlike his colleague who played for six years in Paris before dying of natural causes, the Capitan of the troupe, who was known in France as François Mansac but was very probably an Italian actor named Francesco Manzani, played for just over four months. On 19 May 1662 he was murdered on a Paris street. The documents relative to his death tell us little about Manzani, privately or professionally, but do illuminate life in mid-seventeenth-century Paris.[59]

> At about midnight on 19 May a priest named Simon Dupont, living in the cloister of St.-Roch, came to an officer of Châtelet to report that while he was visiting the sculptor Hulot in his lodging on the rue de Richelieu he heard cries and the voice of a man saying "Help me! They're killing me! A confessor! Thieves!" Father Dupont went out with Hulot and Antoine Lefébure toward the house of M. Molière which was across the street.[60] Before the door they saw stretched on the ground a young man who asked for help and who seemed close to his end. The priest asked him if he repented his faults and wanted absolution. He was unable to answer in words but gave his hand and pressing the hand of the priest testified to being

contrite and wanting absolution. The priest gave him absolution and came to find the officer who returned with him to the rue de Richelieu where they found the body of the young man. Another young man was standing above him with a sword at his side, who said his name was Joseph Jératon [Giuseppe Giaratoni], an Italian actor, and that the young man found dead was also an Italian actor who played the character of Capitan. Giaratoni, who had heard of the death from two chairmen and come immediately to find out if it was true, asked the others to help him transport the body to the room on the rue des Boucheries-St.-Honoré where the two of them were living with Annibal Barbieri, the troupe's décorateur. When Mansac's corpse was undressed, the officer discovered the young man had been both shot and stabbed through both arms and thighs and especially above the left thigh just below the abdomen.

On 17 June Giuseppe Giaratoni testified to the events leading up to the murder. According to Giaratoni:

He was in the room they shared on the rue des Boucheries when Mansac's valet came to find him with a message to come and meet the Capitan on the Grand Place opposite Palais-Royal where he was waiting for him. Giaratoni immediately went to Palais-Royal where he found the Capitan with a woman called Mlle. Catherine, the niece of Mlle. du Parc who was then playing in Molière's company. Giaratoni stayed with the two until eleven, drinking beer in the house of a lemonade seller on the corner of the rue Fromenteau. The two young men then saw Mlle. Catherine to her aunt's home at the entry to the rue St.-Thomas-du-Louvre, and while Mansac was inside, Giaratoni, waiting on the doorstep, saw a tall fellow, whom he did not recognize for the night was dark, come up to him, look him in the face, and go into the court of the building where Mlle. du Parc lived. Giaratoni followed to find out what he wanted, and having seen him in the court, he went back to warn the Capitan to come out since he was suspicious of this fellow. On the step he met another fellow, short, armed with a sword, and with a plume of black feathers on his hat. A little later the Capitan left du Parc's niece and joined Giaratoni. They started back to their room, but were astonished when the man from the court came after them, as did the one who was on the step to the door and another who was in the middle of the Place. They followed Giaratoni and the Capitan to the entry into the rue de la Boucherie-St.-Honoré where the largest of the three, approaching the Capitan and looking him in the face, obliged him to ask what they wanted from him. Stepping back a step the fellow said to the Capitan: "Oh! God damn him! Rascally bugger! It's too much!" He put his naked sword in his hand and put two thrusts into the left thigh. The Capitan, resenting this, pulled a pistol from his pocket. Giaratoni tried to pull off the assailant, but was not strong enough. He followed the Capitan who fled toward the rue de Richelieu, caught up with him, and said to follow him toward the Quinze-Vingts. But Mansac continued to run up the rue de Richelieu. . . . Giaratoni got home and discovered the man he was looking for had fallen in the rue de Richelieu. Giaratoni added that since the time of the murder he had discovered that two of the three men were foot-men belonging to the queen and the other a trumpeter of the king's.

If the assassins were liveried servants of the king and queen, no record survives to tell us that they were arrested or punished. This murder may have been related to the difficulties the theatre at Palais-Royal had had in February with lackeys in livery trying to force their way into the parterre. Yet if that was the motive, the assassins should have been as interested in Giaratoni as they were in Manzani. So perhaps the quarrel was private; if it was, Giaratoni decided it should remain so.

Manzani's death is known; his life is not. He played as Capitan Terremoto. Like many of his colleagues, he published an Italian transla-tion from the Spanish, in his case a tragedy entitled *A gran danno gran rimedio,* which appeared in Turin in 1661.[61] The date and place of publi-cation support the identity of Manzani with Mansac. Turin was the regu-lar stopover for Italian troupes on their way to Paris, and this troupe must have been there in the spring of 1661.

What happened to the role of capitan after Manzani's death is un-clear. Eleven of the thirty-five plays in the first part of the Biancolelli repertory call for a capitan; these plays probably represent the old reper-tory still being played in 1668. Capitan Spezzafer does not appear until 1670, although the actor arrived in 1668 to replace Tiberio Fiorilli as Scaramouche. There is no record of any other actor playing capitan be-tween 1662 and 1668, but Biancolelli's zibaldone suggests that one was there. One possibility might be Guiseppe Antonio Fiala, who played Capitan Sbranaleoni from about mid-century. He had connections with the Paris troupe, having played with Zanotti, Bendinelli, and Locatelli in the Modena troupe in 1651.

The last of the new troupe members in Paris in 1662 may have been Patricia Adami (Diamantine) who played the servante. She probably be-gan playing slightly later, however, following the return to Italy of the wife of Tiberio Fiorilli, Lorenza Elisabetta del Campo, who had played Marinette before 1659 and was definitely in Paris and mentioned in the royal accounts of 1664. Almost nothing is known of Patricia Adami's life. She was married to Angelo Agostino Lolli, who played the Docteur. Gueullete claims that she was a widow of forty when she joined the troupe and was married to Lolli in France, but no documents have been found to support this. In her letters of naturalization of June 1683, she is referred to as a native of Rome.[62] There are no published references to her work in Italy.

Gueullette describes her as "small, dark, and quite pretty . . . a very good actress."[63] Her character of Diamantine is very much an Italian serva, cleverer than the zanni but willing to engage with them in all kinds of horseplay. Unlike Colombine, who replaces her, Diamantine participates in the physical lazzi; she is not only smarter than Arlequin, she is stronger as well. She is also the best cook in Paris for macaroni and cheese.

Although she did not play the French repertory introduced in the 1680s, Patricia Adami did not leave the company when Catherine Biancolelli joined it. She signed the Convention of 1683 and the loan contracts of 1686.[64] And she is still listed as a member of the troupe in a receipt issued in February 1692 testifying that a loan has been repaid. Like Orsola Cortesi, she probably continued to play the old Italian repertory into the 1690s, especially at court, while the debutante, Catherine Biancolelli, developed the French-style suivante, or lady's companion, in the new French repertory. Exactly when Adami quit playing cannot be determined. She died on 5 September 1693.

The returning actors in 1661–62 included Tiberio Fiorilli, Domenico Locatelli, Brigida Fedele, Angelo Agostino Lolli, and Giovan Andrea Zanotti. Tiberio Fiorilli remained the favorite of the king. He is referred to as head of the troupe in the court accounts of 1664, although nothing exists to tell us what exactly that might mean at this time in France. Other members of the company also signed for the quarterly subvention payments. On the other hand, Fiorilli received several special grants for trips "that he must make by order of His Majesty from the city of Paris to Florence." The king also awarded him 730 livres in 1662, partly as a gift, partly "in consideration for his services." In 1664 he got 2,000 livres "in wages" for himself and his wife "for the year ending the last of June; in 1666 he got another 1,000.[65]

His wife was still in Paris in 1664. Although most scholars have followed Gueullette in identifying Patricia Adami as the servante from the time the troupe was established in France, no documentary evidence supports that claim. Lorenza Elisabetta del Campo, on the other hand, was mentioned in the royal accounts, and I know of no other instance where wages were paid to a spouse who was not a performer. She was definitely not in Paris in September 1666, however, when the marriage contract was drawn up between Silvio Bernardo Fiorilli, son of Tiberio and Elisabetta, and Marie Roussel. Tiberio Fiorilli spoke for her, having been granted that right by a letter from Florence dated 14 August and joined to the marriage contract in which she consented to the marriage and ratified the agreement.

Silvio was marrying into the French middle class. His father-in-law, Gilles de Roussel, sieur de Lamy and Cloyes, was a functionary concerned with the *gabelles,* the salt tax. His name suggests that he owned two estates; his daughter's dowry was a handsome 60,000 livres. Silvio Fiorilli brought to the marriage only 3,000 livres, but to that was joined a set of very interesting promises. His father and mother made him an irrevocable gift: all of their "personal property, houses, fields, lands, woods, vines, olive trees, their appurtenances and dependencies . . . and in general all that belongs to them at present and will be found to belong to them at their decease, without reserve, in Italy as well as in France." The parents reserved to themselves the use of everything during their lifetime and required that Silvio support, house, and feed his brother Charles-Louis, canon of the cathedral church of Troyes, and give him 10 livres a month. If Charles-Louis chose to live separately, his brother was enjoined to pay him a pension of 300 livres a year and provide a room for his lodging. In the interim between Silvio's marriage and the death of his parents, the latter agreed to support, house, and feed the former, his wife, "their children and their servants in their houses in Florence or in their country house and provide the necessary furnishing and food without their having to ask and according to their condition." Perhaps the most interesting information contained in the contract relates to the property owned by Fiorilli in Florence: "the house of Casagio, situated in the Val d'Erne [Valley of the Arno] near the city of Florence, consisting of field, lands, woods, vines, and olive trees, the said house being twenty miles from Florence, together with the revenue and interests of [*illegible*] of the theatre in the city of Florence." [66] In 1666 none of the parties would have believed that it would be 1694 before Silvio and his wife could enjoy their gift.

In 1668 Tiberio Fiorillo received his last royal grant, 600 livres "to give him the means to return to his country." Apparently he did not intend to return, for the troupe brought another actor to Paris to replace him. He played in Rome in 1669 for the queen of Sweden. In the same year a Florentine diarist recorded that on 17 July a great storm swept through the Val d'Arno, killing a son of "an actor and clown called Scaramuccia."[67]

Domenico Locatelli also remained in favor in the 1660s; he is listed in the *Registre du trésor royal* for 1665 as the holder of a royal pension of 1,200 livres—in addition to his share of the regular pension.[68] After his recovery in 1661 from the serious illness that delayed the troupe's debut and led to the king's sending for Biancolelli, Locatelli remained an active member of the company, playing First Zanni to Dominique's Second Zanni. The repertory reflects this rather bizarre coupling of two Arlequins with a number of lazzi that play off it.

Locatelli's first wife, Louise Gabrielli, who had played Lucille, was probably dead before 1661 when Orsola Cortesi came to France as Second Amoureuse. Locatelli was married a second time on 9 June 1665 to Marie de Creil with Giuseppe Giaratoni as witness.

Brigida Fedele, the favorite of the queen mother, was probably near fifty when the troupe returned to Paris, and judging by Biancolelli's zibaldone, not as active as the Second Amoureuse, Orsola Cortesi, who was the favorite of the young queen.

As a traditional amoureuse, Brigida Fedele specialized in romantic discourse, in the "subtle repartee and piquant puns" which, according to Sebastiano Locatelli, could not be appreciated by the French. In 1666 she published a book of poetry: *I rifiuti di pindo* by Aurelia Fedeli, comica Italiana. The queen mother—who had rewarded her last publication so handsomely—being dead at the beginning of 1666, this book was dedicated to the king. It consists of poems in honor of the royalty and higher nobility of France followed by a series of pastoral love verses. No record survives to tell us if His Majesty's gratitude was expressed in palpable form.

Giovan Andrea Zanotti and Angelo Agostino Lolli, Octave and the Docteur, were certainly important company members, but no documents record their activities between 1662 and 1668. Lolli may have been married during this time to Patricia Adami, as Gueullette reports, but Jal, who searched the registers of all the Paris churches in the vicinity of the theatres, found no record of the marriage. Octave appears in nearly all the pieces noted by Dominique, as does the Docteur, who took on, for the most part, the full burden of the vieillards since the troupe only rarely included a Pantalon.

The only actor certainly associated with the troupe in Paris from 1662 until its dismissal in 1697 was not a sharing member for most of that time. He was Giuseppe Giaratoni, a gagiste, who developed the role of Pierrot in the French repertory and was finally accepted into the troupe in 1691. According to Tralage, he was from Ferrara;[70] Rasi has him born c. 1639, the possible son of a Dottore named Giarattoni lent by the duke of Modena to Prince Alessandro Farnese in 1655.[71] Although a gagiste, Giaratoni was active in the life of the troupe, sharing a room with Manzani and witnessing Locatelli's second marriage. He is several times referred to in Dominique's notes as "Geraton"; the role of Pierrot is first mentioned in *La suite du festin de pierre* in 1673. Gueullette, who remembered having seen him play, tells us that he married an elderly virgin with an income of 1,500 livres a year and, after the dismissal, retired to a small property he bought in the suburbs of Paris.[72]

The only other employee of the troupe we have knowledge of at this time was Annibal Barbieri, the décorateur. He was, of course, the original tenant of the room on the rue des Boucheries-St.-Honoré where Giaratoni and Manzani also lived. According to Campardon, he died in March 1665 and was buried at St.-Germain-l'Auxerrois. His death certificate, taken by Campardon from Piot's *Etat civil de quelques artistes* (Paris, 1873), reads: "Saturday, 14th day of March 1665. Funeral procession of Annibal Barbier, décorateur of the royal troupe of Italian actors, next to and in front of the Palais-Royal. Received 9 livres."[73] The problem with this is that "Annibal" appears with "Geraton" and "Crogne" (Gilles Crosnier, the Palais-Royal candle trimmer) as a gagiste in *Le collier de perle*, which was produced for the first time in 1672.

A number of characters occur in Biancolelli's zibaldone that cannot be easily matched with any actor known to be in Paris between 1662 and 1668. The most important of these is Pantalon, who appears in twenty-three of the thirty-five plays predating May 1668. Traditionally, following Gueullette, scholars have identified the actor as [N.] Turi of Modena or Giovan Battista Turri *detto* Pantalone, author of a letter of 30 March 1671 from Venice, recommending his son as a Second Amoureux. Turri did play Pantalon in Paris, but not until the mid 1680s. He might have been the Pantalon of nearly twenty-five years earlier, but it seems unlikely.

Another possibility, although a highly speculative one, is the actor discussed in chapter 2 known as Orazio Carpiano ("il Carpiano") whose first name, according to Rasi, was Marc' Antonio. Although his primary role was probably amoroso, he is described by Jacopo Fidenzi in 1638 as one who "does a marvelous Pantalone."[74] Assuming, as we have above, that Carpiano was a professional name and not a legal surname, and that this Orazio could have been the Paris Horace of 1659 and the husband of

Brigida Fedele whose legal name was Marc' Antonio Bianchi—a great many assumptions built on less than firm foundations—then we can also entertain the possibility that—with age—Carpiano gave up the role of First Amoureux and continued with his second role of Pantalon. It is true that Gueullette and especially the Parfaicts think that Horace died around 1660, but they have no evidence for it. Brigida Fedele refers to herself as the widow of Marc' Antonio Bianchi, but not until the 1680s. If Horace was still in the troupe in the 1660s he may also have continued to play an amoureux occasionally, since the character does occur in Dominique's zibaldone.

Whoever this Pantalon was, he either died or returned to Italy before May 1668, when the new repertory begins in the zibaldone. Pantalon is mentioned only twice in that new repertory, and although Loret welcomes a new Pantalon in March 1670, the repertory seems to indicate that he did not stay.

Capitan, who appears in thirteen of the first thirty-five plays in the zibaldone, is another problem, one for which I can offer no potential solution. Even if Manzani originally played in those thirteen, the scenarios would have been changed to reflect his death long before Biancolelli wrote down his own roles. The next actor we know of who played the capitan was Girolamo Cei, who arrived to take over Scaramouche in 1668 and who reverted to the capitan on Fiorilli's return in 1670. But Cei is always referred to in the zibaldone as Spezzafer, not Capitan. A few other names—Mario, Lelio, Fabritio, Angiola, Isabella—appear once or twice in the zibaldone, but nothing connects these character names with any actors known to have been in Paris between 1662 and 1668.

The troupe was very strong, a salutary mixture of seasoned stars and exceptionally talented young actors. Balanced between romantic characters and zanni, it was a company destined to play brilliantly the improvised repertory of the Italian theatre for the next six years, and then to adapt that repertory in the years following to the expectations of the Paris audience.

CHAPTER 6

The Old Italian Repertory

I N ORDER TO UNDERSTAND the shift that took place in seventeenth-century France from traditional commedia dell'arte to comédie italienne, a new form born of Italian conventions and French taste, we must first define the repertory and mode of performance the Italians brought to France in 1662.

Our understanding of the nature of commedia dell'arte is distorted, based as it is—according to Cesare Molinari—on eighteenth-century treatises, especially those of Riccoboni and Perrucci, which reduced a fluid and complex theatrical activity to a normative schema.[1] Most scholarly energy since the eighteenth century has been devoted to analyses arising from the definition of commedia dell'arte as improvised performance by professional actors playing fixed type characters, the tipi fissi, or masques. The problem with this formulation, as Molinari points out, is that we have evidence of performance of written texts by amateurs—and by professionals. And we have evidence of improvised performance by professionals—and by amateurs. Only the use of fixed type characters is a constant.

The evidence available about commedia dell'arte, the hundreds of scenarios and the vast iconography, is finally an embarrassment of riches. Molinari declares that "one would wish for less of it in order to 'know' more," since it is easier to reduce a few characteristics to a united and comfortably coherent schema than to find a synthesis for a large, diverse, and contradictory pool of evidence.[2] This is not to suggest that we discard our generally accepted definition of commedia dell'arte, but rather that we recognize that this definition represents a typically eighteenth-century effort to clarify and classify. In this case, a late Renaissance phenomenon, which to the Enlightenment eye had been embellished beyond recognition by baroque flourishes, was rescued and divided into such categories as "pure" and "decadent." The "pure" was then schematized.

For example, the commedia dell'arte play of the sixteenth century required lovers, old men, and zanni, but not in any particular numbers or combinations. It was the eighteenth century that formulated the rule: two lovers, two old men, two zanni. It was the eighteenth century—and especially Luigi Riccoboni—which also set the pattern of scholarship that made the study of commedia dell'arte essentially literary and theoretical. The sixteenth-century commedia scenario, in plot indistinguishable from the neo-Roman commedia erudita, became the model by which all commedia dell'arte plays were to be judged, and those deviating from the model were excluded as decadent.

The very term "commedia dell'arte" was invented as a label for this abstract, theoretical genre defined when the living genre had almost run its course. In its own day, what we now call commedia dell'arte was usually known as commedia degli zanni in Italy and simply as the Italian theatre outside of Italy. In Italy a troupe could play both a literary and an improvised repertory, but abroad, when the audience understood no Italian, the improvised repertory with its emphasis on the zanni dominated. Thus, the commedia degli zanni came to represent the Italian professional theatre, the commedia dell'arte.

The improvised repertory of the Italian troupes in their earliest years remains essentially unknown. The oldest surviving scenarios date from 1611, many years after the union of traveling entertainers and neo-Roman comedies that gave birth to the professional improvised theatre and sixty-six years after the first known contract of association of a theatrical troupe in Italy. These scenarios were published in 1611 in Venice by Flaminio Scala, an actor and "capitando," or troupe leader, active from about 1575. Scala's *Il teatro delle favole rappresentative* is also the first and last printed collection of scenarios and the only collection unquestionably connected to actual professional performance.[3] No wonder, then, that Scala's scenarios have become the model of the "pure," or literary, commedia dell'arte. Of the forty-eight plays in the volume, thirty-nine are neo-Roman love intrigues with oppressive fathers and clever servants. These Plautine plots are essentially similar to plots of the commedia erudita; Riccoboni calls them "traditional pieces going back at least a century."[4]

The neo-Roman comedies are characterized by a three-part structure that scholars like to believe is perfectly balanced. Plot scenes are alternated with two types of ornamental scenes. The plots are all basically the same: a young man loves a young woman; an obstacle—his father, her father, another lover—prevents his obtaining her; the obstacle is overcome, usually by means of a scheme devised by a clever servant. The plot may be complicated by the addition of a second set of lovers, a second heavy father, a second servant—this one stupid—and a female servant so that a parody love plot can be introduced, and a bravo, or capitan. Typically, each plot scene—that is, each scene in which an action is either planned or carried out—is followed by an ornamental scene. Two types of ornamental scenes—the sentimental and the comic—alternate as well. In the "pure" commedia, the sentimental scene is usually a duet on themes of romantic love while the comic scenes include the quibbles of the old men, the bravuras of the capitan, and the lazzi of the zanni.[5]

Scala's comedies follow this pattern, but not all of his plays are comedies. His repertory also includes a tragicomedy, a tragedy, a pastoral, and several fantasy plays. Other collections show the same mixture and also include comedies that do not display the "pure," balanced structure. The Locatelli manuscript (1618, 1622) includes in its 103 scenarios, collected by a Roman gentleman, 20 farces (where the comic outweighs the romantic), 12 tragicomedies, 8 pastorals, 2 tragedies, and 1 heroic romance.[6] In the manuscript held at the Museo Correr in Venice (before 1637), "farce runs riot," according to Kathleen Lea,[7] while most of the scenarios in the "Ciro Monarca" collection (after 1643) are clearly based on Spanish sources and are classified as tragedies, tragicomedies, romances, and melodramas.[8]

The "pure" commedia repertory, with its balance of elements and its reliance on humanistic rhetorical devices, may never have been other than one kind of play performed by the Italian actors, but it was the kind destined to appeal to later literary historians. Certainly, the ornamental romantic dialogues were a popular component of many commedia dell'arte pieces, and the actors and actresses who performed the lovers were favored, especially in the late sixteenth century and the first half of the seventeenth century. But it is equally certain that by the early seventeenth century—the first period for which we have evidence of repertory—the actors were also performing other genres, especially farces, pastorals, and fantasies, which featured the zanni or which abandoned the typical street with houses of the neo-Roman scenarios for fountains, magic mountains, lightning, and flames. The pastorals and fantasies also featured music, dance, and the exotic.

Twentieth-century scholars looking at the Italian theatre in Paris in the last half of the seventeenth century, seeing nothing but decline and decadence, have proposed that the pure Renaissance form, with its Roman conventions, its Plautine plots, and its courtly discourse—improvised by well-bred and learned actors—gave way before the pressures of commerce and a foreign audience.[9] But the available evidence suggests that the Italians brought with them in 1662 a repertory which was already a mixture of genres and which already included plays where farce and the zanni dominate.

Aside from some very general descriptions in the Paris gazettes, most of the information we have about the Italian repertory in France between 1662 and 1680 must be derived from a French translation made in the eighteenth century of a zibaldone, attributed by the translator to Domenico Biancolelli, Arlequin of the Italian troupe. There is no reason to doubt that translator, Thomas-Simon Gueullette, who reports that he received the Italian manuscript from Biancolelli's son:"After the death of Pierre-François Biancolelelli, known as Dominique at the spectacles of the Opéra Comique, who made his debut at the Comédie-Italienne 11 October 1717, I was given an Italian manuscript in-40 written in the hand of the sieur Dominique, his father. The manuscript is the collection that he had made of his own improvised scenes in the plays which were performed in his day by the troupe in which he wore the mask of Arlequin."[10] Yet even if Gueullette's statement is absolutely true, the manuscript presents the historian with a number of problems. First, it is a translation, and though French and Italian have similar structures and vocabularies, a translation is always a compromise. Gueullette is conscious of some of the traps to which translation is prey; he is careful, for instance, to indicate in some verbal routines that a joke cannot be expressed in French. What is also helpful is that Biancolelli's notes are utilitarian, not literary, and written in a working vocabulary that is simple and repetitive.

A more serious problem is that Gueullette admits to changing some character names. According to Gueullette's notes, Dominique used First Zanni instead of Trivelin throughout, except for one mention in *Les tapis,* and First and Second Donna, First and Second Amoroso and Serva at times, though not always.[11] Gueullette changed these generalized designations to the specific character names used by the actors he believed to have belonged to the Italian company in Paris, but his substitutions are not necessarily accurate. He has, for instance, substituted "Cinthio" for Second Amoureux, but Cinthio, Marc' Antonio Romagnesi, did not join the troupe until 1668. Gueullette's alterations make it impossible to date performances of the early plays in Biancolelli's zibaldone by reference to the specific actors who played in them.

Dating in general is a problem. The French manuscript contains notes describing some or all of Arlequin's scenes in seventy-nine plays. The last forty-five, beginning with *Le régal des dames,* first performed 2 May 1668, appear to be in chronological order; at least, those that can be dated from external evidence—normally mentions in the gazettes—are in chronological order. Of the first thirty-four, however, only two can be dated exactly, *La fille désobéissante*, which Robinet mentions on 28 October 1667, without telling us if the performance is a debut or a reprise, and *Le festin de pierre* definitely a reprise, mentioned by Robinet on 11 February 1668. The others cannot be dated from external or internal evidence; they contain no references to current events and include no obvious parodies. We do know, since Gueullette copied the original folio numbers into his translation, that the order is Biancolelli's.

My hypothesis is that the first thirty-four entries in the zibaldone represent part of the repertory brought to France and first played before May 1668. They are, in other words, examples of the conventional Italian repertory of the mid-seventeenth century. Eighteen of these first thirty-four correspond in some way to scenarios included in the various Italian collections, especially the Casamarciano manuscripts held in the National Library of Naples, whereas of the forty-five titles that follow, only four, two of which are too fragmentary for comparison, can be matched to titles of extant Italian scenarios. Unfortunately, the Naples manuscripts are late—1700—but many are analogous, at least in title, to other earlier scenarios. Spada has carefully indicated the relationship between each of Biancolelli's entries and its possible predecessors and descendants and added in an appendix to her published transcription of Gueullette's manuscript the relevant material from the Neapolitan manuscript collections.[12]

These correspondences help to address another problem: the fragmentary nature of the zibaldone. Although full of unusually specific descriptions of what the commedia dell'arte actor did onstage, the entries are not scenarios, even though some scholars have thought of them as such. The danger of treating the notes of a single actor as scenarios is that the actor's character appears to dominate the plays. Especially as edited by the Parfaict brothers, Dominique's zibaldone has been used to justify the conclusion that zanni play dominated the commedia dell'arte in Paris to the exclusion of other elements, a sign, of course, of baroque decadence.[13] While it is true that Biancolelli was a very popular actor and also true that physical comedy was more easily communicated to a French audience than verbal comedy, the comparison of the zibaldone to the Italian scenarios helps to establish the extent of Arlequin's stage time. In general, Biancolelli's notes show that Arlequin played six to eight scenes in the early scenarios; most commedia dell'arte scenarios have thirty to thirty-five scenes, but some have as many as fifty. While these numbers help us see that Arlequin did not dominate the plays before 1668, they also indicate how difficult it is to analyze the repertory from such fragmentary jottings.

It would also be easier for us to use Biancolelli's notes if we knew what he used them for. This kind of record keeping was not common in actors who played zanni. Most extant zibaldones are collections of rhetorical set speeches and romantic dialogues for the lovers or bravuras for the Capitan. They are not connected to particular plays but are materials for use in any appropriate play. Dominique, on the other hand, wrote out blueprints for performance: "In this scene I call Diamantine and beg her pardon, I say that someone wants to kill me, that she must hide me and that I will tell her all, she says she will shut me in the flour bin, I agree then I tell her that I don't want to get in there because if the old cook finds me covered with flour she will take me for a sole and try to fry me."[14] Dominique includes his own action as well as that of the other characters on stage. Sometimes he suggests dialogue with narrative; occasionally he includes dialogue. He pays little or no attention to plot, yet only once does he indicate that a scene can be used elsewhere. He often puts addenda at the end of an entry, sometimes as if he has forgotten something, at other times as if a bit has been added at a successive performance. Once he indicates that certain lazzi have replaced others that were unsuccessful.

The circumstances of the troupe's establishment in Paris may be the reason for the existence of this unusual document. Italian troupes were touring companies that played for a few months at most in any given city. Troupes were often brought together for the carnival season in a particular city, that is, for a period that began before Christmas and lasted until two weeks before Easter. A troupe playing for three months would need a substantial but not enormous repertory. An established troupe, however, would eventually use up its repertory; that is, its audience would get tired of the same thirty or forty plays, even if they were rearranged. The established troupe would require a changing repertory, one to which new pieces would periodically be added. One possibility, then, is that Biancolelli's repertory got too extensive for his memory and he began to write his action down. As his roles got larger after 1668, and especially as they began to include some set speeches in French, the aide-mémoire would have become even more useful.

Another possibility is that Biancolelli wrote down his repertory for someone else. According to Gueullette, in 1682 Angelo Costantini joined the company to double Dominique in the role of Arlequin.[15] If this was the case—and Costantini was interviewed by Gueullette many years later—we might argue that Dominique wrote out his repertory for his new understudy. The problem with this idea is that the documentary evidence indicates that Costantini probably came much later to replace Giovanni Gherardi as First Zanni. The fact that Costantini did replace Biancolelli briefly when the latter died in 1688 does not make an Arlequin of him, but only tells us that the company could not wait to play until a new Arlequin was found.

It also seems unlikely that the zibaldone was begun as late as the 1680s. On the other hand, it must date from at least 1668 since, with one exception, none of the cast lists or texts mention Scaramouche until *La folie d'Eularia,* played in September 1670. Tiberio Fiorilli was with the troupe until 1668, however, when he received 600 livres to return home.

The year 1668 was a watershed year for the troupe, and its production of *Le régal des dames* in May was obviously a watershed production: its first effort—and a very successful one—to devise a new entertainment determined by French taste. It coincides with the entry into the troupe of Marc' Antonio Romagnesi, who was to devise a number of new entertainments. It might be that Biancolelli's early notes represent that portion of the original repertory the troupe decided to retain in 1668. They do not include Scaramouche, perhaps because Fiorilli had decided to withdraw from the company rather than adapt to a new repertory.

Another oddity of the notes, however, is that they only mention Trivelin, Domenico Locatelli, by name once; instead they refer simply to First Zanni or Zanni. Locatelli, so far as we know, was active in the troupe until his death in 1671; furthermore, a number of lazzi described in the zibaldone require two Arlequins, something made possible by Locatelli's presence. We might conclude from Trivelin's absence from the notes that they were written down after Locatelli's death in 1671, but by that time Fiorilli had returned, so the absence of Scaramouche is unaccountable.

The organization of the notes for the first thirty-four entries may be chronological, but since almost no external evidence of dates exists, it is impossible to be sure. *La fille désobéissante,* which we know was performed in October 1667, is No. 4 in the zibaldone, while *Le festin de pierre,* performed as a reprise in February 1668, is No. 23. Possibly the zibaldone is organized topically, at least in part. For instance, the last three entries before *Le régal des dames*—*Les engagemens du hazard, Le maistre vallet,* and *Ma maîtresse est préférable à tout autre chose*—are the only ones in the repertory to be derived from Spanish sources. Another possible principle of organization is putting related materials together. *Le suite du festin de pierre,* for instance, played in 1673, was included in the zibaldone twice, once chronologically, and once following the notes of the earlier version. *Les morts vivans* and *L'hospital des fous* are grouped together, possibly because both include false deaths, as are *La hotte* and *Le médecin vollant,* which include Arlequin disguised as a doctor. For the most part, however, there seems to be no logic to the arrangement. The simplest conjecture, once again, seems to be that the entries before *Le régal des dames* record selected plays from the Italian repertory that continued to be played after the new repertory was introduced.

Even with all the problems they raise, Dominique's notes are a precious resource. No other extant material gives as clear an idea of the actual play of the commedia dell'arte, especially of the zanni. And by using some of the analogous scenarios—always with caution—to help create the necessary frame for Biancolelli's verbal and physical lazzi, we can obtain a reasonably clear notion of some of the plays performed by the troupe in the 1660s.

One particularly interesting comedy can serve as an introduction and also show how distant this repertory already was from the balanced structure of the sixteenth century. *Le dragon de Moscovie (Il basilisco del Bernagasso)* exists in five versions, all from after mid-seventeenth century: Biancolelli's, two from the Naples manuscript, one from Placido Adriano's *Zibaldone di Perugia,*[16] and one from the French Ms. 9329 of the Bibliothéque Nationale.[17] It was played well into the eighteenth century. Dominique's version has been of interest to students of Molière who find it in some analogies to *Tartuffe.* The fuller versions also echo *L'école des femmes* and *L'avare.* The distribution of roles is odd, since Arlequin's role seems more like that of a vieillard than a zanni. In the Naples manuscript the same central role is filled by Policinella; neither cast contains a Pantalon or Docteur. In other ways, however, the play seems fairly standard with a romance plot and subplot and the other characters performing their accustomed routines.

The most complete scenario is found in the Naples manuscript.[18] The cast of characters is as follows:

Policinella, merchant
Flaminia under the name of Spinetta, servant
Angela
Fiametta
Tartaglia, father of
Odoardo
Covello, servant

Lelio under the name of Basalisco
Capitano
The invalid notary
The chatterbox notary
Bravos

The Naples manuscript also calls for the following properties:

2 small pieces of metal (for coins) and 2 pilgrim's staffs
A beggar's costume for Basilisco, with clothing to dress Policinella
A wrapped up noose
Purses and money of various sorts
Letters, documents for the deed of gift
Bunch of flowers
Stick
Costumes for the notaries and the bravos
Two tobacco pouches

The scene is a standard street with houses, one belonging to Policinella, one to Tartaglia. In the first scene, Policinella and Spinetta enter quarreling. After Policinella exits, Spinetta complains of having become a servant in order to find her lover Lelio. In the second Naples version the amoureuse explains that while eloping with her lover they were attacked by thieves and separated. In Dominique's version, Arlequin's wife has just died and he has taken a housekeeper. Judging by the cast list, however, the housekeeper is played by Diamantine, which is at odds with the Italian version where the housekeeper is an amoureuse in disguise. Biancolelli includes a long and very specific description of the scene:

> I say that I am happy with her service; in speaking of my wife who is dead I begin to cry. She consoles me, I say heaven keep the poor departed in joy and good health; when I remember what good macaroni dishes she made I begin to cry again, I then console myself saying that when I came home she met me and took me to my room and gave me a thousand caresses, I begin to cry again. My housekeeper asks me what she died of, I answer *de parto*. In childbirth! she answers, I heard she was eighty-seven years old, how could she have had a child at that age, it's not possible.
>
> That's not what I meant, I answer. *Departo:* that is to say by parting, by leaving me, she has not come back, my dear wife, the most dishonest woman ever. You mean honest and not dishonest answers my housekeeper. Not just honest, it's as if I said ten times honest [i.e., *dix* honest], and what bothers me the most since her

death is that she gave me all her property and her relatives are suing me, saying that isn't so, but I want to get a summons for the dead woman to appear in court to assure them of the truth of the gift. Finally I say to my housekeeper that I regard her almost as a wife, that if I am happy with her, I'll make her fortune and that she will be pleased to have such a good master, then I tell her that I'm going to the post for my letters which ought to announce the arrival of a niece who was sister of the father of Perette Barbe, who was cousin of the mother of my father, and I thus finish my scene.[19]

In the first Naples version, the next scene introduces Tartaglia, who wants to marry Angela. Tartaglia tells his servant, Covello, to fetch the bride and her servant and bring them to his house. Covello agrees and exits followed by Tartaglia. Capitano enters, speaks of his love for Spinetta, and declares he will ask Policinella for her. He does, Policinella says no, Capitano threatens him and exits. Policinella decides to find a bravo to protect him from Capitano; he exits to the postoffice. Dominique does not include this scene, probably because the troupe did not include a capitan at the time he wrote out the scenario. The threat to Diamantine does not appear until the second act.

In the following scene in the first Naples scenario the First Amoureux, Lelio, enters disguised as a bravo, a "soldier of fortune," calling himself Basalisco del Bernagasso. The name echoes the kinds of names which the commedia dell'arte gave to capitanos to satirize the Spanish military presence in Italy. Lelio is not, however, a capitano, but a lover, searching for his lost Flaminia. Policinella enters with his letters, Lelio does the "usual lazzi" of the stick and the money. Policinella invites him to stay on, to be his servant and protect him from Capitano. Lelio agrees, does the lazzi of dressing Policinella, and they leave to inform Spinetta. Dominique describes the scene more fully:

> In this scene when Bernagasso has done his monologue, I come out and say that I have received the letter from my niece; Bernagasso approaches, salutes me, I open my letter, and return his greeting, I go to the corner of the stage to read it and I say: *to get back to our business* ... Bernagasso approaches and asks for charity, I answer that heaven will help you and I continue reading, then he hits me with his stick on the head and I say there's a strange way of asking for alms, I say then if I refuse he will beat me up, I give him a quarter of an ecu [a little less than a livre], He takes it and cries that he is very unhappy and gives signs of despair; I ask him why, he answers

that a sou would suffice him, and that an ecu might lead him astray, that with so much money the Devil could inspire him to go to lewd women and to gamble when he should sleep, and he forces me to take back the quarter ecu that I gave him; I say then, Well, here's an honest man and I give him a sou, he receives it humbly and thanks me and adds may heaven rain prosperity on you. I give him another sou; he says, may the earth open and share its precious treasures with you. I add a sou to those I have already given him, then he says may the waters . . . I interrupt to say that I never drink it, that I'd rather he spoke of wine; he says, Well, the fire . . . And forget the fire, my friend; and let's talk of other things, I ask him his name, he answers *Bazilisco del Bernagasso d'Ethiopia*. I am frightened of the name and I repeat: *Basilisco del brodo grasso* [fat broth] *d'Ethiopia;* I call him, he runs to me, he frightens me, I say it appears to me from the physiognomy of his face that he has some resemblance to the ancient German gentlemen. I ask him if he would like to work for me, and on that he says to me that would be for him a great honor, I tell him that I will keep him in my house, he shows great joy, takes his comb and combs me, at that I do my lazzi of laughter, he puts on my tie, powders my wig, I straighten up, walk, have him walk behind me, finally I call my housekeeper and tell her all and say to her that I have taken into my service this Ethiopian valet, and I go into my house, but before entering I say to Bernagasso that this is my house-keeper and that I have a taste for her.

The correspondence to *Tartuffe* is obvious here. Arlequin and Bernagasso enact Orgon's report of Tartuffe: "I made him gifts; but with modesty he always tried to give back a part. 'It's too much,' he would say to me, 'too much by half.'"[20] Whether this represents what the Naples manuscript calls "the usual lazzi of money" cannot be verified, nor is there any way of knowing whether this scene is a source or a derivative of Molière. But the scene does rather precisely clothe the skeleton of the Naples scenario.

That scenario continues with Lelio and Spinetta reproaching each other and Policinella trying to quiet them. After they all exit, Angela, her servant Fiametta, and Covello enter. Angela does not want to marry Tartaglia. Odoardo, Tartaglia's son, enters and Covello tells him that his father wants to marry Angela. Odoardo and Angela are, of course, in love. Tartaglia sees them embrace and flies into a fury, but Covello persuades him it was a ceremony. After they exit Capitano enters with his bravos. He wants to see Spinetta and knocks. Policinella, feeling menaced, brags about *his* bravo; Capitano abuses him, so he calls Basilisco.

Basilisco enters and does the lazzi of "that's nothing to me" and the lazzi of taking tobacco while Capitano manhandles Policinella; the situation is then reversed; finally, Basilisco beats everyone with his stick, and Capitano and his men run away. Policinella takes Basilisco in his arms, embraces him, says "Viva Basilisco," and the act ends.

Dominique does not include the preceding scene at this point, since in his version the housekeeper is not yet threatened by an outside force. In his second act, however, the amoureux comes with his band of bravos to kidnap Diamantine, Arlequin calls out "To me, *Bazilisco del Bernagasso d'Ethiopia*, to me, my hero." Bernagasso enters "with a great slapstick and chases them all away." Nothing is said of the lazzi of the tobacco and the "it's nothing to do with me"; however, in the version found in Ms. 9329 and probably played by the Paris company before 1683, a similar scene is included, also in act 2. Basilisco, now known as Dragon, is armed with a big stick which he calls Hierome. When Arlequin is threatened by Floridor (Cinthio) who wants Colombine, Arlequin calls Dragon: "Dragon tells him to say he does not want to give her up . . . while Arlequin speaks Dragon plays the flute and Floridor hits Arlequin; Arlequin says to Dragon this is no time to play the flute and it's time to talk to these clowns who want to kidnap Colombine. Dragon speaks to Floridor who treats him very badly and while he does so Arlequin plays the flute and Dragon says it's not time to play when it's a question of business." Dragon eventually beats them all off with Hierome.

In act 2, scene 1, of the first Naples scenario, Basilisco enters dressed as a nobleman with Policinella, who wants to give him everything he owns. Basilisco wants nothing. Spinetta enters and they do the "lazzi of the cape, the sword, and so forth." They continue with the "lazzi of sweeping the house, taking up wood, and so forth." At the end Policinella goes off to find the Notary. In Biancolelli's version, the scene is reminiscent of act 1 of Molière's *L'école des femmes* with the servants off-stage quarreling:

I enter from the house to congratulate myself for the acquisition I have just made, barely have I done so when I hear some noise inside. I call my housekeeper and Bernagasso and ask them what is going on, the housekeeper says, Monsieur our Master I told him he had to carry some wood up the stairs. He answered that he wouldn't do it. Oh well, I say to the housekeeper, I'll carry it myself; they go back in for a moment; new quarrel. Bernagasso returns with Diamantine, he says, Monsieur, she does not want to wash the dishes, I say, fine,

I'll wash them. They return to the house and as I still hear them quarreling I call to them to know why. My housekeeper says to me, Monsieur, he does not want to empty the tub; well, I say, I will empty it.

In the Naples version, the servants, actually lovers in disguise, are quarreling because each believes that the story of the robbers who separated them is an excuse the other is making. In the versions played in France, however, the housekeeper is apparently the *servante*—first Diamantine, then Colombine—while Basilisco-Dragon is probably First Zanni. In Biancolelli's notes Basilisco is from Ethiopia, strongly suggesting the role was played in black mask and probably by Trivelin. In Ms. 9329 Dragon plays the flute, indicating that the role may have been played by Giovanni Gherardi, Flautin, First Zanni from 1674 to 1683, who both played the flute and imitated it with his voice. Since Biancolelli's version does not include the original romance plot, the scenes of the bravo and Arlequin are zanni play, Arlequin himself is in love with the housekeeper, and the *amoureux*, not the Capitan, plays the "other man." In the Ms. 9329 version, Dragon is searching for his mistress, Colombine, but the third act of this version is totally different from the others; the romance plot gives way to magicians and a deus ex machina.

After the "housekeeping" lazzi at the beginning of act 2 in the first Naples scenario, Capitano returns and is chased away by Basilisco, who Policinella begins to think is "too furious." Then Odoardo tells Covello that he wants Angela; Covello knocks, she comes out, agrees to marry Odoardo. Tartaglia enters, scolds the women, and sends them in; Odoardo tells his father that he's too old for Angela, but Tartaglia will have her. Odoardo faints, Covello calls out, the women carry Odoardo into the house. Covello advises Tartaglia to give Angela to his son; Tartaglia can't decide. Odoardo pretends to be ill and says that if he can't have Angela he will die. Tartaglia knocks, the women come out, Tartaglia tells Angela that he wants to give her to his son. Angela pretends to refuse, then agrees; Covello takes Fiammetta, and the subplot ends.

Act 2 ends with a return to the main plot. Policinella wants to make a deed of gift of all his property in favor of Basilisco. He goes to the Invalid Notary ("lazzi and usual scene"), then to the Chatterbox Notary ("lazzi and usual scene.") The Notaries fight over Policinella and the act ends.

In act 3 Policinella gives Basilisco the deed of gift. Basilisco doesn't want it, but Policinella does the "lazzi of singing" and Basilisco takes it.

When Policinella goes to pay the notary, Basilisco grabs the money away, saying "This is excessive, give him two carlini." Basilisco then bullies Policinella, goes inside, and drives Spinetta out of the house. They beg him to let them in; he comes out with a package and gives it to her. Thinking it is something good, they unwrap it and unwrap it and unwrap it and finally come upon a noose. They decide to become pilgrims and wander the earth. Spinetta, however, knows a woman who will give her an opium poppy. She goes to get it and comes back. They leave it on the ground, knock, and run. Basilisco comes out—without his sword—sees the flower, picks it up, sniffs it, and is overcome by sleep. Policinella and Spinetta pick his pocket, take the deed of gift, go in the house and lock the door. When Basilisco wakes up and tries to get in, they reenter and Policinella tears up the deed of gift. Basilisco apologizes and says he did it only to teach the too generous Policinella a lesson and also from jealousy, fearing that Policinella had enjoyed his mistress. The lovers reveal themselves, embrace, and the play ends with the wedding.

Dominique's notes offer a much reduced version, heavily dependent on physical play:

> In this scene I come out with Bernagasso, and I tell him that for having saved my life, I want him to be master of my house . . . and the husband of my niece and I give him the deed that I have just signed at the notary. He takes it and begins to hit me, I begin to laugh thinking it's a joke, but as he continues I ask him in virtue of what does he strike me, he answers in virtue of the deed that I have just given him, that he is the master of the house and is free to hit me and chase me away; I beg him to let me see where it says that in the deed, he presents it to me, I snatch it and tear it up, then I grab the stick and beat him in turn; I call my housekeeper and my neighbors, they come, Bernagasso throws himself at my feet, I take away his hat and put it on my head, I do the same with his wig, his clothing; and I chase him away as a miserable wretch, and thus ends the comedy.

This version also seems closer to *Tartuffe,* although all the versions share the action of the protégé turning on his benefactor. But only in this one does the phrase "master of the house" appear and only in this one does Arlequin propose a marriage with a member of his family.

The second scenario in the Naples manuscript is very much like the first, although some of the character names are different. The main plot is essentially the same, without the complication of two notaries. The subplot is entirely different: two zanni—Covello and Giangurgolo—

fight for the favors of the serva Fravoletta. These same zanni serve as the bravos-servants to Capitano—and the lazzi among these three, Policinella, and Basilisco are more specifically indicated.

The Ms. 9329 scenario reflects the baroque taste for *féerie* and the marvelous, but unlike its predecessor in the repertory of the Italian troupe in Paris, it contains at least the remnants of the romance plot. Arlequin's servant, now Colombine, is being pursued by Floridor (Cinthio). Dragon enters and says that he has left his country and beggared himself searching for his mistress. Arlequin enters and the scene is played as before, with Arlequin offering and the Dragon refusing money. Dragon introduces his big stick, Heirome, and Arlequin hires him for protection. The scene ends with the lazzi of dressing. So far, with minor changes, the main plot is the same as in the other versions.

Colombine enters, meets Dragon, and they recognize each other. They quarrel and disguise their quarrel with the lazzi of the wood and so forth. Floridor comes to take Colombine, beats Arlequin, leaves and returns with his bravos. Arlequin and Dragon do the scene of playing the flute, Dragon brings out Hierome, Floridor and the bravos run away, ending act 2. Again, the plot remains the same in essence although different in detail from the other versions.

Act 3 begins with a new character, Isabelle, who is in love with Cinthio (apparently Floridor), but then continues in the usual fashion with the deed of gift and the turning of the worm. The denouement, however, is the sort of elaboration that is typical of the Italians' post-1668 repertory. Arlequin and Colombine are out on the street, looking for a way to get Arlequin's property back or at least get some money out of Dragon. Arlequin first pretends to be dead, assuming Dragon will pay something to get him buried. Dragon says, "Throw him on the rubbish heap." Arlequin then dresses up *en espagnole,* that is, as a capitan, to "strike terror in Dragon's heart." Dragon responds with Hierome. Floridor-Cinthio, who has sworn revenge on Arlequin, enters and says he wants to get rid of Isabelle, who torments him night and day. Arlequin returns with a new scheme; he will disguise himself as a girl, get taken on by Dragon, who now needs a servant, and steal back the document. Colombine dresses him up with assorted lazzi, but Dragon recognizes him and responds once again with Hierome. Having backed itself into a corner, the plot now gives birth to a magician who gives Arlequin a magical sword. All he has to do to enchant someone is touch them with the sword and say "berlique"; to lift the enchantment, he must touch them again and say "berloque."

Floridor enters with Isabelle, sees Arlequin, and draws his sword to take his revenge. Arlequin does his magic and while he is at it has Cinthio fall in love with Isabelle. Then Dragon enters and the inevitable happens; Arlequin enchants Dragon, takes back the deed of gift, and tears it up. The others enter, Dragon and Colombine reveal themselves, Cinthio-Floridor recognizes Dragon as his son, Arlequin recognizes Cinthio as his uncle, the lovers get married, and Arlequin agrees to pay for the wedding.

In principle, there is no great difference between the instantly acting Neapolitan poppy and the magic sword, but in practice the poppy is part of an action—however improbable—devised and carried out by the characters, while the magician with the magic sword is a simpleminded fairy godfather who casts "the glorious messenger" of *Tartuffe* quite into the shade. Dominique's slapstick ending, on the other hand, is uncomplicated and flat, very unlike the baroque garnish of the other French version.

If nothing else, these versions with their similarities and variants give a picture of the ways in which a commedia dell'arte piece shifted with time and circumstance. Probably at first a role for Pantalon, the master of the house was at some point taken over by Arlequin, who added to it a few of the standard Arlequin characteristics: cowardice, quibbles, and love of macaroni. Other standard characteristics are not present; this Arlequin, for instance, unlike Biancolelli's usual character, is not illiterate. The Naples scenarios—even though the collection is dated 1700—seem, with their emphasis on romance plot, to be closer to conventional commedia dell'arte structure than do the apparently earlier French versions. Dominique's notes are especially baffling since they not only ignore, but even contradict, the romance plot by making a zanni role of Basilisco. We cannot, as a result, simply "plug in" Arlequin, although Biancolelli indicates only five entries for his character in a piece which has thirty-one scenes in the Ms. 9329 version.

A more conventional play is *Le capricieux,* in which Arlequin plays the expected role of valet. This play (in Italian *Il lunatico*) corresponds with some variations to *L'amante lunatico* in the Naples collection.[21] Once again, Policinella is the equivalent to Arlequin. The plot in the Naples version is as follows: Cintio is meant to marry Prudenza, the daughter of Dr. Gratiano, who is coming from Bologna and whom he does not know. He is in love with Delia, the ward of Pasquarello; she gives him a letter, saying "read and make your choice." It seems that Pasquarello also wants to marry her. In the next scene Cintio intimidates Pasquarello, and he and Delia play a love scene.

When the Dottore enters from Bologna, Cintio pretends to be Policinella and introduces Policinella as Cintio's brother, Narciso, who looks
just like him. When the Dottore goes to bring his daughter from the inn,
Cintio tells Policinella to dress up in his clothes and pretend to be him.

Delia's second lover, Oratio, does a monologue on his love for her;
she enters, tells him she loves only Cintio, and goes in. Oratio wants to
kill Cintio, but doesn't know him. Pespica, Pasquarello's servant, says he
will introduce them.

When the Dottore and his daughter arrive, Cintio pretends to be
his majordomo Policinella and introduces Policinella as himself. Policinella does all the lazzi of pretending to be a gentleman and then proposes
to Prudenza. The proposal is overheard by Diana, Delia's servant who is
betrothed to Policinella. She is furious, scolds him and beats him. While
he is still licking his wounds, Pespica brings in Oratio and points out the
man he presumes to be Cintio. Oratio challenges Policinella, saying he
must give up Delia. They fight and are separated by Cintio who asks the
cause of the fight. Oratio says, "this rogue is in love with Delia." Cintio
believes him and beats Policinella. The Dottore arrives, gets involved,
and the act ends with Policinella grabbing the Dottore's stick and beating
everyone.

Act 2 begins with Oratio, desperate for Delia. Prudenza overhears
him and thinks he is in love with her. Oratio drives her off and exits.
Pasquarello tells Delia he is resolved to marry her. The Dottore comes
in with Prudenza, who complains of her treatment. Delia overhears her,
and when the Dottore leaves the two women play a scene in which Delia
discovers that Prudenza is meant to marry Cintio. Policinella returns in
his own clothes and explains to Cintio that rich clothes apparently lead
to beatings. Delia reproaches Cintio, then turns aside to say "I will love
you forever, my soul," and exits. Cintio thinks these words were meant
for Policinella and beats him again and exits. The Dottore enters, takes
him for Narciso, and negotiates a marriage with his niece. Policinella is
about to agree when Diana, who has been eavesdropping, storms in and
says "This man cannot take another wife; I am his wife." The Dottore
goes off to seek justice. Before Policinella can leave, Oratio enters, takes
him for Cintio in disguise, and beats him again. Delia enters and tells
him to tell Cintio, for her, that she will never think of him again. Cintio,
seeing the encounter, beats Policinella again, half kills him, but then they
clear up the misunderstanding and plot "the trick of the lunatic" where
Cintio will pretend to be a madman. After Cintio leaves the Dottore
enters with the officers to arrest Narciso for bigamy, but he is saved by

Pespica who swears he is Policinella. Policinella tells the Dottore that Cintio has gone mad. Cintio enters and plays the lunatic, threatening Prudenza and tricking the Dottore with a cup of flour. This scene ends act 2.

In act 3 all the plot strands are brought together. The Dottore and Prudenza are resolved to leave for Bologna. Cintio and Delia play a love scene at the window. The Dottore thinks Cintio is speaking to his daughter and doesn't notice Delia. Cintio, instead of embracing Prudenza, embraces Delia, who has come down, and goes inside with her, while the Dottore pulls Prudenza offstage by the hand, saying "To Bologna, to Bologna." Pasquarello, seeing that the madman Cintio is in his house, goes off to get the madhouse keepers. This is the final complication. Diana and Policinella are the first to make up. Delia chooses Cintio over Oratio, Oratio takes Prudenza, whose departure has been delayed by bad weather, and Pasquarello gets what he deserves.

Dominique's notes fit rather well into this scenario, although some scenes appear to be out of order. The first scenes of act 1 are the same. Arlequin opens the play with Diamantine, saying that she is his mistress, that he has already received "favors" from her, and that she will be his wife. In the second scene he dresses his master. What in the Naples manuscript is covered in a phrase—"From the house, dressing with the usual lazzi"—is in Dominique's notes a fully developed comic interlude: "I enter with the master. He scolds me and asks where I spent the night. I answer 'in a place where he would have been happy to find himself,' but every time I try to tell him, I begin to laugh. Finally I tell him I have been at the B . . . In a place where there were some willing girls; he says he wants to get dressed and I should get his clothes, I run off, bring his hat, he says, 'and my cloak,' I run to get it and take away the hat." And so forth. These "usual lazzi" of dressing appear in more than one scenario; this is a routine that can be inserted into any convenient spot. In this play, however, it establishes a kind of thematic structural principal: a man is identified largely by what he wears.

The dressing scene is followed by the arrival of the Capitan, "who says he is the brother of the woman I love." This scene takes place after Arlequin has disguised himself as his master, Octave. Before Arlequin can answer, Eularia enters and gives him a letter, saying "Read it and make your choice." Eularia is, then, analogous to Delia, but in this version she gives the letter to Arlequin believing him to be Octave (Cintio). Arlequin, who in this play *cannot* read, gives it to the Capitan, who begins: "My dear soul, my very sweet love . . ." Arlequin takes the letter and licks it for its sweet words. Eularia enters with Pantalon; Arlequin makes his compliment: "Madame, the naturalists say that terrestrial animals are not aquatic; apropos of animals, what sort is that with you?" And hearing this is the lady's father, he says, "Seeing him dressed in red and black, I took him for a half-peeled beet." These lazzi do not fit into the Naples scenario, the letter having become nonconsequential since Eularia is not threatened with marriage to her guardian.

In another scene with Eularia and Pantalon, Arlequin puts his hat on the end of his bat and rests it on Pantalon's head. When Pantalon hits the hat to the ground, Arlequin gives him a swift smack on the rear and then does the lazzi of the dwarf with a hat and cloak and hides behind Eularia. When Pantalon spots him, Arlequin rises to his full height and smacks him again. This scene also has no obvious connection to the Naples scenario.

The central comic event for Arlequin is his travesty as a gentleman. This was a favorite comic turn of Biancolelli's who gradually came to specialize in disguises. Later entertainments include multiple travesties for Arlequin, everything from nobleman to clock and table pedestal. In *Le capricieux* the disguise is clearly related to the plot, although the plot does not finally seem to be quite the same plot as in the Naples version. Dominique's description of his scene *en gentilhomme,* while displaying some of the characteristic features of this travesty, also does not seem to fit precisely into Policinella's role in the scenario. In Dominique's notes Arlequin

> comes dressed ridiculously as a gentleman with gloves. My cloak falls over my bat; I do some lazzi to put it back . . . Cinthio banters with me, my answers are not to the point, at the same time he holds a romantic conversation with Eularia to whom I say, Oh madame, I am this unhappy Octave whom fate persecutes and I do a nonsense routine. Eularia says that my servant, who is Cinthio, speaks more sensibly than me, I say that that is not astonishing since I have given him my wits to hold and he is using them on this occasion. I say to him, Hola, M. le Majordomo, make a few pretty compliments to this young lady.

The lovers go inside, leaving Arlequin. The scene has been overheard by Diamantine, who takes a stick and beats her faithless lover. Exactly where this scene fits into the scenario is hard to say. The problems are (1) that Arlequin seems to have disguised himself as Octave, his master, but is playing the scene with the other amoureux, Cinthio, who has disguised *himself* as a servant and (2) that there is only one amoureuse,

Eularia, mentioned in the notes. Spada, in analyzing the relationship between the two versions, thinks that Cinthio in Dominique's notes is the Oratio of the Naples version, but Oratio does not change identity with the zanni.

> Cinthio reenters in his ordinary costume and says I must stop loving Eularia, we scuffle, my hat falls, I tell him to pick up my hat, he draws his sword and answers, pick it up yourself. I say, oh, all right, I'll pick it up. I ask him, who are you who claim Eularia? He says, I am a gentleman, I answer, What is a gentleman? He says, I am going to teach you that, puts his sword in his hand . . . Finally my master Octave enters who defends me. I play the bravo and say, Come on, coward. He approaches, I hide behind Octave. He says, I will come back and find you, I answer, You lie in your throat, you'll never find me because I won't leave the house. Finally he says that he loves Eularia and will marry her and leaves, threatening me. Octave reproves me for my cowardice and hits me with a stick. Docteur enters, saying the future awaits me. I answer that I am going to come in, Octave begins to beat me again. Docteur, impatient, comes back to say that I am waited for, after several lazzi I say Please M. the Docteur, don't go in without me, Octave threatens me, I take the stick, beat him in my turn, and thus we finish the first act.

In act 2 Arlequin enters in his own costume, wanting nothing more to do with the trick. Octave, his master, asks why Arlequin has taken off his gentleman's outfit, then Eularia comes and reproaches Octave saying, just as Delia says in the Naples manuscript: "I will love you all my life, my dear heart." The scene does not, however, continue as it does in the Naples version, with Octave thinking Eularia's words are meant for Arlequin. Octave exits, Capitan enters and says he wants Arlequin to marry his cousin (in Italian, *cugina*). Arlequin will willingly take the *cucina*, that is, the kitchen, along with the dining room and the wine cellar. Diamantine overhears, and *she* goes off to seek justice.

Cinthio enters and offers to have the Docteur advise Arlequin. The Docteur asks how he can be useful; Arlequin answers that he does not want to abandon Eularia. Then Octave enters, the Docteur tells him what Arlequin has said, and Octave threatens him and exits. Diamantine returns and insists that Arlequin keep his promise to her. Eularia enters and says to Arlequin "Go tell your master to think of me no more." The Capitan, who has overheard all this, kicks Arlequin in the rear, so Arlequin confides in him that his master is crazy, a lunatic, "who has forced me to take his place and call myself the Marquis de Blanchefleur." Capitan exits, Arlequin remains, then Octave enters and plays the scene of the lunatic. Sword in hand, he chases Arlequin who falls down and says he is dead, or at least wounded, showing the red patches in his costume. After Octave leaves, Pantalon enters and Arlequin tells him "all the caprices of my master, Cinthio." Again, Arlequin seems unclear about which of the amoureux is his master. The reason for the confusion is probably Gueullette's translation, since Gueullette has tried to clarify the action by giving specific character names when Biancolelli merely noted donna or amoroso.

In act 3 Arlequin begs Diamantine's pardon and asks her to hide him since someone wants to beat him to death. He rejects the flour bin as a hiding place for fear the cook will take him for a fish and fry him. She proposes to shut him in a little hut in the garden next to a pond, but Arlequin is afraid that when the archers come to arrest him, the frogs will say "qua, qua, qua" and give him away. He also rejects the pigpen for fear the pigs will say "hon, hon, hon," meaning "yes, yes, yes," when asked if he is there.

Biancolelli adds notes for four other scenes, perhaps later additions. In one, Cinthio threatens to kill Arlequin who runs inside, shouting "lock the door, lock the door," then plays the bravo to Octave when Cinthio leaves. Cinthio returns, however, and Arlequin—finding the door now locked—scrambles back inside through a window. The other addenda include two verbal bits and a lazzi with a wig.

The differences between the Naples version and the Paris version seem to result by and large from differences in the companies. Arlequin's action, which largely consists of being beaten up because someone takes him for someone else, is the same as Policinella's. The romance plots are not exactly analogous because Dominique's amoureuse must evade her father rather than a guardian who wants to marry her. Whether there is a second romance plot in the Paris version is not clear since a second amoureuse is not mentioned. The Docteur, father of the second donna in the Naples manuscript, is a character in Dominique's version, but not enough is said about him to be able to ascertain his function. The Docteur does not suggest a marriage for Arlequin in this version; Capitan does. And Diamantine has to make her own complaint to justice.

The Paris and Naples versions are both standard commedia dell'arte entertainments of the seventeenth century. They rely on the conventional neo-Roman characters in the usual relationships. The setting is the traditional street with houses. The scenes alternate—although not in any absolute pattern—between plot scenes and ornamental scenes, and the play contains several romantic monologues or duologues, although not in the proportion to be found in earlier scenarios.

Arlequin disguised, or *en travesti*, is a common feature of the Biancolelli repertory, usually as part of a trick being played to bring the lovers together. In the earlier entries Arlequin sticks to simple disguises, usually as another character or perhaps as a merchant—achieved by using a false beard. In *Le coeur me fait mal* First Zanni disguises himself as Capitan, while Arlequin pretends to be First Zanni.[22] In *Les dédains* Arlequin himself is disguised as Capitan, speaking garbled Spanish, that is, jargon.[23] In *Le baron allemand*[24] Arlequin plays the ex-servant of a magician and does a long travesty scene as a German gentleman, again with the comic emphasis on jargon. The travesty is still part of the plot, however, as it is in *La hotte*[25] and *Le mèdecin vollant*,[26] where Arlequin pretends to be a physician in order to get access to the amoureuse. In *L'amour ne veut point de rivaux*,[27] however, when Arlequin appears as a painter and as a necromancer, he is still a trickster, but on his own account.

As Arlequin's travesties become more exotic or eccentric they tend to become less relevant to the romance plot. Turkish or Moorish travesties satisfy the contemporary taste for the exotic and give the opportunity for jargon and other kinds of ethnic humor. In some cases, the travesties become plot devices in themselves. One of the most interesting examples is *Arlequin cru prince*, which is analogous to *Il finto principe* in the Naples manuscript. It is also similar to *Il girello*, a "burlesque play with music," and a comedy, *Il finto principe*, published by Bartoli.[28] It is, thus, a standard of the repertory, although not by any means typical of the so-called balanced structure.

Policinella (Arlequin) is married to a flighty woman. The two vieillards, Pantalone and Pasquariello (Pantalon and the Docteur), take advantage of the absence of the Prince to have Policinella (Arlequin) arrested so that they can cultivate the wife.

In Dominique's notes, Arlequin is a kind of "merry prankster," tying the vieillards together and squirting them with a syringe, moving the judge's desk so that he falls on his nose when he leans over to write, and then moving his chair so that he falls on his rear when he tries to sit down.

After the interrogation is finished, the zanni is exiled, and while wandering through a forest he meets a magician. Dominique describes the scene as follows: "I am in the country, I climb a tree on which grows some beautiful fruit, when I go to pick it, a devil comes out of the trunk and frightens me, I want to get down, but another devil at the foot of the tree begins to climb. I climb up again and descend again several times, then the magician appears who touches me and leaves me in a ridiculous pose, then he gives me his wand and tells me marvels, etc."

Policinella (Arlequin) then returns to his country. When the vieillards threaten him, he "transforms" himself, through the power of magic, into the Prince. Biancolelli's Arlequin orders an arm chair brought, does various lazzi of falling while trying to sit down, and then commands a plate of macaroni followed by a small roast: a cow stuffed with a veal which is stuffed with a lamb which is stuffed with a chicken which is stuffed with a lark which is seasoned with salt and pepper. While waiting for his dinner, Arlequin decides to take a walk through the city. He has the Docteur get down on all fours, mounts him, takes Pantalon by the beard, and starts to stroll. The vieillards believe their prince has lost his wits, a conclusion confirmed by the following scene when Arlequin enters with a pot on his head which he breaks on the floor. He will have the potters hanged, he says, if they do not make their pots larger so they will hold more soup. The vieillards tell him it is time to hear the petitions of his subjects.

Most of the rest of Biancolelli's notes concern these petitions, which are not necessarily the same as in the other versions. In the version published by Bartoli, the following petitions are indicated: the ass, the pregnant lady, the creditor, and the dead piazza. Dominique's notes call for petitions which are related to the plot, but also for petitions which may be satirical, a very unusual quality in the early repertory of the Italians in Paris.

The first petitioner is a poor soldier who has lost an arm in the service of the Prince and asks for compensation. Arlequin's response: "Have it published that whoever finds this man's arm must return it under pain of the galleys." During a time when warfare at the whim of the monarch was in fashion, this might have been read as satirical, as might the following, an addendum: "A woman comes and tells me that one of my horses has killed her husband with a kick, and that she and her children have nothing to live on. I order the horse to pay her a pension, and if he hasn't the means to do so, to be hanged as an example to the other horses." There is a certain bite to these lazzi that is unusual in Biancolelli's material, but the prince whose royal purse was open to the troupe was not noted for his enjoyment of criticism, so one should not try to make too much of the possibly satirical cast of these petitions.

The other petitioners include a man whose chickens have been stolen and one whose purse has been snatched and who wants it back. Arlequin takes the purse, empties it, keeps the money, and returns the purse to the victim. When the latter complains, Arlequin says: "You only asked for the purse, you said nothing about the money." Arlequin's wife then enters and begs for justice. The Docteur and Pantalon have banished her poor Arlequin. Arlequin the Prince pardons Arlequin the husband, and orders him recalled from exile. He then calls the bailiff and the officers and orders them to put Pantalon in prison. The Docteur protests that Pantalon is the first counselor of state. "I answer that I know it, but that he is a scoundrel to have banished the gracious Arlequin, my best friend." This bit may also have certain echoes of reality, reminding the audience of the events of 1661, when Louis XIV imprisoned *his* first counselor of state, Fouquet.

When the real prince enters, Arlequin touches him with the magic wand, turning him into Arlequin. In the Naples manuscript, the real prince returns in act 2, and much of the plot confusion arises from the presence of two princes, not two Arlequins. In Paris, however, the troupe searched for opportunities for multiple Arlequins, playing off the similarities of Locatelli and Biancolelli. Biancolelli's notes end with the magician entering and restoring normalcy.

This play seems to have no place for a romance plot. The two amoureuses are employed as the Princess and her cousin, but nothing in either version suggests they are anyone's love interests. The only role for an amoureux, assuming the Prince is Trivelin, is the Magician. Presumably the various petitioners were played by gagistes as well as by company members.

The forest scene with its magical tree and its demons is unique in the pre-1668 repertory in Paris, but is the sort of spectacle scene often found in the pastorals and plays with music of the seventeenth-century Italian repertory. The spectacle is minor compared to that of the great machine plays done at court and to that featured in the public theatres during the spectacle wars of the 1670s and 1690s. The use of a magician or sorceress to account for transformations also permits disguises and travesties that are not devices of romance plotting.

A final type of play included in the zibaldone's early entries is the play based on a Spanish source. Spada has identified three of them, two based on plays by Calderón, one on a play by Zorilla.[29] Although they are Nos. 32 to 34 in the zibaldone, they may not have been performed in succession. The character list for *Les engagemens du hazard* includes Horatio along with Valerio and Octavio, suggesting an early production date. On the other hand, all three include various anomalies in casting.

Les engagemens lists Isabelle as well as Horatio, but this surely does not refer to Françoise Biancolelli, who did not play until 1683. The cast list of *Le maistre vallet* also includes Valerio, rarely mentioned, along with Lélio, who is totally unknown. The text, on the other hand, refers to Valerio and Octave, but because of Gueullette's meddling there is no way to be sure of what Biancolelli wrote. The third Spanish-based play, *Ma mâitresse est préférable à tout autre chose,* lists Cinthio in the cast list for the first time, according to Gueullette's note, which suggests that this piece was played in 1668 after Bendinelli's death and after Romagnesi had joined the troupe. The note also means that we must assume that Gueullette has changed Biancolelli's amoureux to Cinthio throughout the preceding entries.

Arlequin plays a traditional valet in all three; in *Le maistre vallet,* as the title indicates, he once again, as in *Le capricieux,* is disguised as his master and does the travesty of the gentleman. In *Ma maitresse* the servants appear to play very minor roles; Dominique's scenes are all with First Zanni and neither seems involved in the intrigue. The plays themselves are conventional seventeenth-century commedia dell'arte pieces; imitation of the Spanish repertory began about 1620 and continued through the century. As we have seen, many of the actors and actresses, including Brigida Fedele and Orsola Cortesi, demonstrated their humanistic learning by translating plays from Spanish to Italian.

Little can be said about the structure of those entries in Biancolelli's zibaldone for which no analogous plays or scenarios have been located. Nonetheless, the likelihood is fairly great that the plays from which only fragments survive are similar to the ones that can be reconstructed. What is even more certain is that the zibaldone offers an unparalleled opportunity to study the characteristics and actions of the masque of Second Zanni as conceived by Biancolelli.

In general, and with noticeable exceptions, Arlequin's participation in the plots consists of disguises and tricks—often unsuccessful—devised by the amoureux or the First Zanni. The role is also characterized by a number of recurring lazzi and comic attributes. Arlequin is usually illiterate, always naive, a coward and a glutton. His comic routines— increasingly *en travesti*—are based as well on misuse of language, jargon and imbroglio, and on Biancolelli's acrobatic ability. Several other kinds of comic routines also stand out as typical of the traditional commedia dell'arte played in Paris in the 1660s: equivocation, scatology, and violence.

The équivoque, or sexual innuendo, usually requires that the audience understand Italian; this may explain why it occurs less frequently in the later repertory. An example from *La double jalouzie* includes both a characteristic verbal blunder and a sexual innuendo. Arlequin is comforting his master, Octave: "My dear master you are melancholy, you have no confidence in me. You know, however, that just as one fishes for coral on the highest plains or finds diamond mines in the deepest sea, so the best swords are often in the plainest scabbards. Imagine that I am this scabbard where there is a good blade at your service. . . . Remember, I tell him, that the good valet is the principal member of his master."[30]

Another moment from the same play illustrates a use of obscenity as well as the kind of violence common in these pieces. Arlequin arrives on stage dressed "as a husband" with a cravat, paper cuffs, and a paper plume. After a scene with the amoureuse during which she tears up his ornaments, he knocks on the door of his wife, Diamantine. She comes out, scolds him, beats him, throws him on the ground, and taking his head between her legs, boxes his ears and goes back in to the house. Arlequin's response: "Pew, pew, I'd as soon have my head in a barrel of sardines."

Not all the word play is obscene. In *Les morts vivans* Arlequin plugs up his ears with his fingers so he will feel nothing when he is beaten. This naive routine rests on the fact that the verb *sentire* in Italian means both "to hear" and "to feel." This lazzi exemplifies a kind of comic play that is both physical and verbal and would work in French as well if Arlequin held his nose.

Scatology includes farting and fart jokes, accompanied by the slapstick, a repeated lazzi of the "perfumed letter" taken from under the back of the zanni's belt, and the use of laxatives both on purpose and by accident. In *Le baron allemand,* for instance, the greedy Arlequin drinks a laxative thinking it is soup and eats a cake of soap, thinking it is cheese. Scatology is also central to the doctor travesties since urine is the principal means of diagnosis. In his version of *Le médecin vollant,* Biancolelli includes a long section of dialogue that gives an excellent idea of the verbal play commonly used at this period. Arlequin enters dressed as a physician, accompanied by his master disguised as a student. Pantalon greets him:

PANT.   And what is your name?

ARL.   Doctor Olivastre, surnamed Asshead.

PANT.   My daughter is ill, Monsieur, and I believe you can cure her.

ARL.   Without a doubt. Have you ever read this aphorism of Hippocrates which says, *gutta cavat lapidem etc.,* which is to say that the water which falls drop by drop will pierce the hardest rock; I will fall drop by drop on your daughter, and by means of this anodyne remedy I will procure a certain cure.

PANT.   Oh, Monsieur, that won't work, I think that my daughter is obstructed (*opilata*).

ARL.   Pilate or Caiphus, no matter, I will cure her, I tell you. (Arlequin takes Pantalon's pulse.) But, Monsieur, you appear to me to be very ill.

PANT.   You are wrong, M. the Doctor, it is my daughter who is ill and not me.

ARL.   Have you never read Scotia's law on paternal power which says, *as the father, so the children?* Is your daughter not your flesh, your blood?

PANT.   Yes, monsieur.

ARL.   Well, your daughter's blood being hot, yours must be the same.

PANT.   This reasoning is specious, but . . .

ARL.   Signor Pantalon, is your daughter legitimate or a bastard?
Eularia enters. Arlequin says, I kiss the feet of this beautiful flower who blooms all year, you call her . . . ?

EUL.   Eularia.

ARL.   My student, go to my office etc.

EUL.   My stomach feels full.

ARL.   I wish I could say the same. How is your appetite?

EUL.   I have very little.

ARL.   And I have very much.

EUL.   I tell you, Monsieur, that I have a full feeling.

ARL.   Well, for that take a piece of assroot, rub it briskly under your nose while pressing hard. Galen says that for your malady this is a very good exercise and will return you to health. How do you sleep?

EUL.   I don't understand your question.

ARL.   When you sleep on the left side which is that of the heart, the lungs suffer. When you sleep on the right, the liver heats up. You must then sleep *à la Florentine,* the nose down and resting on your chest. Following that, you will eat a little roasted onion, turn it very slowly, very gently, and when you see it begin to render its juice, you must very quickly, quickly [Gueullette: "There is here an equivocation on the word *menare* in Italian which is very obscene, and I do not understand how Dominique, who was said to be such a virtuous man, could have dared to use this phrase, either in Italy or in Paris."].

EUL.   I feel an extreme melancholy.

ARL.   That will pass, but how are your bowels? Is the matter hard or liquid? Hippocrates says that when one has a looseness of the bowels, one has diarrhea. Is your heart beating?

EUL.   Yes, Monsieur.

ARL.   Then you have a gangrenous heart, but that's nothing, to cure that you must take six ounces of rose water in a powder and three ounces of filings from a unicorn's horn; make an unguent and rub yourself with it.

EUL.   Where?

ARL.   Where you like.

Arlequin finally sends her inside to produce some urine, which is brought to him. After smelling it, he says that if the meat tastes as good as the bouillon smells, he'd certainly like a slice. He takes a swallow and spits it out in Pantalon's face.[31]

Violence and beatings are even more common than ribaldry; almost every entry includes some physical abuse. In *Le capricieux,* as we have seen above, beating Arlequin no matter what his disguise is a structural device. The zanni beat as often as they are beaten, although in general First Zanni is the aggressor and Arlequin a victim. Even the women threaten and beat poor Arlequin. He rarely gets his own back (as he does in *Le dragon de Moscovie*), but he does occasionally manage a sneaky poke with his bat. This is all, of course, the violence of farce which is painless and comic largely because of the acrobatics that accompany it. When Arlequin is hit, what makes the audience laugh are the pratfalls, the somersaults, and the other acrobatic responses to violent or unexpected propulsion.

Not all of Dominique's comic action is obscene, indecorous, or violent. One of the most delightful of his routines, described in the notes for *Le baron allemand,* embroils all the other characters in a mimed fantasy:

When I arrive as the mailman . . . I pretend to be on horseback, to gallop in, to get off, and to attach my horse to the wings. I cross into the midst of the actors who are on the stage and say to them: Ask me who I am. They ask me, I answer Ah, Ah, you want to know my business? Well, I am a mailman watch out for my horse, it kicks. They get out of the way. I say that . . . I am looking for a certain gentleman . . . Is it Horatio? No, I have it on the tip of my tongue, look and see if it is there, watch out for my horse, it kicks. They back off, frightened, and say, the devil take your horse, etc. Then I search my letters . . . I look for a letter I pretend to have forgotten in

Bologna, finally I give [Pantalon] a well-wrapped package in which he finds a piece of cheese; I give him another, it's sausage, I say, I've made a mistake, that's for my soup, I am taken into the house, I pretend to remount my horse and I gallop in.[32]

Dominique's notes for a previous scene in the same play will serve as a final example of the kinds of things that were performed in the first years of the Italian troupe's establishment in Paris. *Le baron allemand* has a complicated Plautine twin plot according to the version found in the Naples manuscript. Biancolelli's version has nothing to say of the twins, but does include many of the comic devices discussed above: travesty, naïveté, phallic jokes, "jargoning," and violent physical action. It also offers an excellent example of First and Second Zanni play.

Octave has offered the zanni fifty ecus if they will play a trick for him. Arlequin enters, dressed ridiculously as a German gentleman, but when Trivelin explains the trick, Arlequin takes off the disguise and runs away.

He runs after me and brings me back, I say, You will send me to the galleys with this trick. He encourages me, tells me that I must play the character of a German baron. He asks me if I know any other tongues but my own, I answer that I have a pickled one some one gave me. He asks me if I know how to speak German. . . . I answer that all he has to do is take me to the tavern and get me drunk and I'll speak German, Swiss, Latin, Spanish. Then he teaches me to say *got morghen, mayer* [*gut morgen, mein herr*]. I do the lazzi of not being able to pronounce these words and taking off my disguise, I garble the words three or four times and finally pronounce them correctly, then he teaches me to say *bige*̧, *bige*̧, *bige*̧ [*wie gehts*]. Oh, that's too tiring, I tell him. Do it, my friend, says Trivelin, you'll get 500 ecus. I ask him how much for myself, 50 ecus he answers. I start to take off my clothes. He despairs, forces me to play this character, makes me repeat again *got morghen meyer bige*̧, *bige*̧, *bige*̧ and goes to knock. I repeat the words, he says it's not time yet, wait until Pantalon appears. As soon as I see him I say the words, repeating them. Trivelin signals me to be quiet. Pantalon notices me, my figure frightens him, I frighten myself, and I try again to undress. Trivelin despairs, Pantalon reenters, Trivelin gets behind me and pushes me forward, I retreat behind him, I repeat this lazzi, I turn so that my sword is between my legs, I do several pirouettes to get it back in place, I take the pommel in my hand and raise one of my legs very high, then the other without success, then I lie down on my belly and my sword is to the rear, I cry that someone has taken my sword,

I find it between my legs, my cloak falls ... it remains embarrassed on my sword, finally Trivelin puts it back on my shoulders and calls Eularia. I say that I have come to marry her, that I am in love with her beauty, I pretend to sneeze and take the servante's apron to blow my nose, she goes back in , I say to Trivelin ask for money, I want to go to the tavern, Trivelin goes to find me a bottle of wine and a glass, I present it to Pantalon, then to Trivelin, I carry the bottle to my mouth and pretend to empty it, I ask for a second saying *Estar bona vin* to each bottle they bring me. I sing a verse of a song, imitating the Swiss language, the refrain of which is *I Love Good Wine*. I give some to Eularia who reenters, and try to make her drink by force; I get drunk, I pirouette, and a valet of the theatre with an iron helmet under his wig tries to take my bottle, I break it over his head, then pull my sword to kill him for breaking my bottle of wine, I pursue him, I fall, and I end the act.[33]

Biancolelli's description of this scene—carefully devised and complete—confirms that by the mid-seventeenth century pure improvisation was no longer a definitive characteristic of the commedia dell'arte, if, indeed, it ever had been. Our modern understanding of improvisation as dialogue and action invented by the actor on stage during performance is not the same as the Italian *al'improvviso,* meaning a play invented by the actors, not written by a playwright. Constant Mic's *La commedia dell'arte* includes an excellent evaluation of the evidence relating to the kind and degree of improvisation used by the Italians;[34] much of the evidence is late, however, and related to the normative theorizing about commedia dell'arte discussed by Molinari.

What seems clear to Mic—and to other scholars of the commedia dell'arte—is that many verbal scenes and monologues were worked out by actors in advance and memorized, and that some were taken from printed and manuscript collections of materials. The lovers' dialogue, the pedant's declamation, the capitan's rodomantade were set pieces. As to the comic routines, Mic does not challenge Perrucci's statement that the zanni did not prepare their roles in advance but improvised them during performance. Dominique's notes would seem to deny that claim, however, especially since he carefully distinguishes certain improvised scenes which he titles *scènes de fantaisie.* These scenes are often played with the Capitan. In *La double jalouzie,* for example, Biancolelli notes: "In this scene I come with the Capitan, he makes me tell all I know about the mistress of my master, this scene is all *de fantaizie.*"[35] In *Les trois volleurs descouverts* the improvised scene again features the Capitan "telling me of his brave actions," which suggests that Biancolelli was improvising but Capitan was reciting a set speech.³⁶ Another *scène de fantasie* occurs in *La hotte;* this time Arlequin improvises with Octave, his master. In Act 2 he enters in a *déguisement de fantaisie,* or improvised disguise.³⁷ There are actually only a few scenes in the first thirty-four entries identified as improvised and even fewer in the later entries.

Other scenes may have originated from improvisation, but as Mic points out, "when a company of actors has played together for a long time and performs a popular scenario for the hundredth time," every element will be well ordered in advance.³⁸ What matters about improvisation in the commedia dell'arte is not the presence of unique moments at every performance but the creation of a play by a company using improvisation as its means. The performance style that emerged from this method of creation was the principal reason for the widespread popularity of the form. Le président des Brosses, writing during his travels in Italy in the eighteenth century, nicely summarizes why the Italians survived and prospered for so long in France. "This manner of playing *à l'impromptu,* which renders the [literary] style weak, at the same time leads to action which is very lively and very truthful. . . . the actors enter and exit, talk and act as if they are at home. This action is totally natural, totally real, in comparison to the French where four or five actors arranged in a row, like a bas-relief, at the front of the stage, declaim their dialogue one at a time."³⁹

Part III
1668-1680

CHAPTER 7

From Palais-Royal to the Guénégaud

At the beginning of the 1668 season, the Italian troupe in Paris, now stable and well established, introduced a new repertory. Largely devised by Marc' Antonio Romagnesi, who had replaced Giacinto Bendinelli as an amoureux, these entertainments were, according to Donneau de Visé, the first produced in France designed to appeal to French taste.[1] Why the new repertory was introduced at this point cannot be established with certainty, but a likely explanation is that, as in the late 1650s, the troupe had exhausted its standard repertory after six years in Paris. The presence of Romagnesi, who was capable of devising a new style of entertainment, may also have been a factor. The decision of Tiberio Fiorilli to leave the troupe at this juncture suggests that the new repertory was not fortuitous, and that the troupe had deliberated and decided to introduce novelties during the next season, perhaps against Fiorilli's wishes.

The first play of the new repertory, *Le régal des dames,* which opened in May 1668, featured Arlequin in a variety of travesties, including a marquis, a chimney sweep, a dentist-surgeon, a policeman, a judge, and Brioché, the famous mountebank and slight-of-hand artist who played the Paris fairs in the mid-seventeenth century. The play's intrigue is Italianate. Scaramouche (played by a new actor) is the guardian of the two amoureuses, Aurelia and Eularia. Intending to seize their property and marry the latter, he keeps them securely confined. Cinthio and Octave, aided by the zanni, try by means of various stratagems to see the women, and finally—thanks to Arlequin's disguise as a judge—Scaramouche is forced to renounce his intentions and the lovers prepare to be married.[2] What makes this play different from the thirty-four that precede it in Biancolelli's zibaldone is the use of changeable scenery, magic, and elements that are specifically French.

The scene of the action is not Italy but Paris. Arlequin enters, having just come from the Palais where he has spent 200 pistoles on baubles. He runs into Trivelin's arms, then—in a moment reminiscent of *Le misanthrope*—asks who the fellow is. Scaramouche is from Normandy, not

Naples. The women take a turn before supper at the foire St.-Germain where Arlequin, disguised as Brioché, does magic tricks with some goblets, under which he finds two little birds, two little dogs, and two little Scaramouches. When the women get hungry, he produces boxes of dried fruits from under the goblets, while a fountain of orange flower water rises from the middle of the table. The play also includes music and dance, with at least one song, "La chanson du ramoneur," sung in French.

For the first time since their establishment in 1662, the Italians were the subject of a long and laudatory notice in a gazette. Robinet gave them 122 lines in his letter of 5 May 1688, calling *Le régal des dames* "an enchanted spectacle, full of little miracles." Although Dominique says nothing about them, Robinet reports there were perspective views of woods and gardens as well as of the fair. The magic goblets receive a full accounting, as do the fruit and the fountain, the orchestra, and the little drinking song written by a "celebrated author." Robinet was especially taken by one of the miniature Scaramouches who danced "by rule and compass," and "turned his body and his steps in so many different ways that from here to Persia there is no little mountebank so pretty and so smart." The Italians were well launched on their new course.

If the repertory was changing, the troupe was remaining relatively stable. When Bendinelli died in the spring of 1668, Marc' Antonio Romagnesi, who replaced him, was already in Paris; his son Pierre was born there on 23 September 1667. Tiberio Fiorilli returned to Italy—apparently proposing to stay—the same year, even before the end of the season on 12 May. Robinet first mentions "Le Scaramouche Nouveau" on 21 April 1668, when he describes him as a little shorter but otherwise the living picture of his predecessor. The new Scaramouche was Girolamo Cei, who also played Capitan Spezzafer, the role he performed exclusively after Fiorilli's return to Paris in September 1670.

The company, still receiving its pension of 15,000 livres a year, had only nine members at the beginning of the 1668–69 season: Locatelli, Biancolelli, Cei, Lolli, Zanotti, Romagnesi, and the three women, Brigida Fedele, Orsola Cortesi, and Patricia Adami. It still lacked a Pantalon. Robinet mentions "a new Pantalon" on 8 March 1670 during his report on *Arlequin esprit follet;* the character also appears twice in Biancolelli's zibaldone, once in the entry immediately preceding *Arlequin esprit follet,* once in *Arlequin roy par hazard,* undated but after February 1673. Whoever the "new Pantalon" of 1670 was, it seems clear he did not stay in Paris for more than two or three years.

When Domenico Locatelli died in April 1671, the troupe replaced

him with an actor who played First Zanni as Briguelle. He was announced by Robinet on 13 June and appears in three entries in the Biancolelli zibáldone as well as in the printed scenario of *Le collier de perle,*
which was performed in July 1672. According to Gueullette, this actor
died and the king sent for "Giuseppe" Cimadori, but he also died en
route to Paris.[3] The search for the First Zanni to replace Locatelli was not
finally concluded until late 1674, when Giovanni Gherardi made his
debut.

The increasing attention paid by the Italians to the Paris audience
may have resulted from the decreasing attention paid them by the monarch. Robinet felt obliged to mention, on 2 June 1668, that His Majesty
had gone to St.-Germain-en-Laye without seeing *Le régal des dames.* The
queen mother, under whose aegis Fiorilli, Locatelli, and Brigida Fedele
had first come to France, died in April 1667. The queen, Anne of Austria,
had her own Spanish troupe which played at court. The Italians were
now of special interest only to the king, and the king was losing interest
in the theatre.

From the beginning of his personal reign in 1661, Louis XIV turned
away from Paris and toward what was to be his seat of government and
his lasting monument, Versailles. During its construction he spent as
much time as possible at the palace of St.-Germain-en-Laye. After 1682,
when the court was fully established at the former hunting lodge, the
Paris actors appeared there and at Fontainebleau on a regular basis and
were paid six livres a day in expenses in addition to their regular pensions. Before that time, however, the companies were summoned more
or less at whim.

In the 1670s, the first signs appear of the monarch's scheme to in-
stitutionalize the theatres. When the French actors resisted His Majesty's
plan to merge the existing troupes into a single Théâtre-Français, Louis
appears to have retaliated by withholding support from the troupe at the
Hôtel Guénégaud, which had refused to merge with the actors of the
Hôtel de Bourgogne.

With the exception of a single performance of *Le malade imaginaire*
at Versailles in July 1674, the former troupe of Molière ceased to play at
court. Nor is there any evidence of Italian performances there for some
years. Only near the end of the decade does La Grange's *Registre* show a
change in the pattern of playing days which indicates that the Italians
were not in Paris. La Grange also notes in the margin in September 1678
and August 1679 that the Italians had gone to Fontainebleau.

Perhaps the best indication that the king's interest in his Italians had declined in the early 1670s is the company's flirtation with the English court, which began in 1673. Molière's death in February of that year and the loss of the Palais-Royal to Jean-Baptiste Lulli made problems for the Italian company as well as for the remnants of Molière's. While La Grange and his colleagues doggedly traveled back and forth from Paris to St.-Germain, trying to avoid a forced merger with the Hôtel de Bourgogne, their fellow tenants packed up and sailed across the Channel at the invitation of His Majesty Charles II.

In 1673 the Italian company was in England from April to September. An order to admit their "clothes, vestments, scenes, ornaments, necessaries, and materials" was issued on 21 April; the export of their goods was approved on 12 September.[4] The actors were there at the invitation of and under the protection of the king, and orders were issued forbidding anyone to interfere with their liberty to act.[5] A stage was built for them at court costing £52. Scaramouche, Arlequin, and four others received chains and gold medals weighing 6½ ounces, and Scaramouche also received 20 ounces of "white plate."[6]

A letter from James Vernon to Sir Joseph Williamson reports that on 22 August 1673 "Senior Scaramouchio and his band have begged his Majesty's leave to returne, their affaires requiring their presence at home."[7] These affairs had to do with the fact that La Grange and the others had managed to find their new theatre, the remodeled tennis court on the rue Mazarine known as the Hôtel Guénégaud, and the king had ordered them, via Colbert, once again to share their stage with his Italians.[8]

The French company, still a royal troupe though without a royal subvention, began to play at the Guénégaud on 9 July. The French took very limited opportunity of the Italian's absence to perform on the jours extraordinaires; there was probably insufficient demand. They did, however, use the theatre on 21 September and 9 October, which may mean that the Italians, back from England in mid-September, were playing a fall season at Fontainebleau.

The Italian troupe apparently did not return to England in 1674, although a stage was built in St. George's Hall, Windsor, for "Scaramouchi."[9] But the *Registre* of the French troupe shows no breaks in its regular pattern of play, and English records include no notice of the import or export of the Italian's goods. In 1675, however, the pattern of play is broken on Monday, 24 June, and does not recur until Monday, 4 November. The treasury warrants for import and export of the Italians' belongings are dated 20 June and 4 October.

On 20 July 1675 Richard Bulstrode wrote: "There is arrived Scaramouche, Ye famous Italian Comedian with his crew, to act againe, and are to have ye King's Theatre in Whitehall for their use during their stay, and all people are allowed to come there and see them, paying as they do at other houses, so yt now a Papist may come to court for half a crowne. This is not much liked by our other players."[10] Not only were the Italians allowed to use Webb's Hall theatre and charge admission, the theatre was altered for them. The king's dais was turned into three boxes with four benches in each box and a twelve-penny gallery was added "for the convenience of his majesty's poor subjects."[11]

John Evelyn wrote on 26 September: "I saw the Italian Scaramucchio act before the King at White-hall . . . having seen him act before in Italy many years past, I was not averse from seeing the most excellent of that kind of folly."[12] John Dryden was less kind. In the Epilogue he wrote in 1673 to the University of Oxford for a performance there of *The Silent Woman,* he explains why the English actors have removed to Oxford:

No poor *Dutch* Peasant, wing'd with all his Fear,
Flies with more haste, when the *French* arms draw near,
Than We with our Poetique train come down
For refuge hither, from th'infected Town;
Heaven for our Sins this Summer has thought fit
To visit us with all the Plagues of Wit.

A *French* Troop first swept all things in its way,
But those Hot *Monsieurs* were too quick to stay;
Yet to our Cost in that short time, we find
They left the itch of novelty behind.

Th' *Italian* Merry-Andrews took their place,
And quite Debauch'd the Stage with lewd Grimace;
Instead of Wit, and Humours, your Delight
Was there to see two Hobby-horses Fight,
Stout Scaramoucha with a Rush Lance rode in,
And ran a Tilt at Centaure *Arlequin.*
For Love you heard how amorous Asses bray'd,
And Cats in Gutters gave their Serenade.
Nature was out of Countenance, and each Day
Some new born Monster shewn you for a Play.[13]

The play Dryden is referring to may have been *Les jugemens du duc d'Ossone* by Cinthio, first performed in Paris in June 1671, which includes the following: "In the joust on horseback after all the lazzi that I do, the duke says he wants to compensate me for having jousted the best. I thank him and I get my horse to kiss him, the duke exits. Scaramouche, who fell to the ground, gets up and we fight again, he knocks me to the ground, I fall in a heap with my horse on top of Briguelle."[14]

In 1678 Scaramouche apparently went alone to England. The troupe returned from Fontainebleau in October and settled into its usual winter season—at least there are no breaks in the pattern of playing days for the French troupe after 9 October. But English records show that Scaramouche arrived in England in early November with "6 portmanteaus, 2 great baskets, and 22 trunks."[15] Confirmation for this voyage is found in the final scene of *L'auberge d'Arlequin juge partie avocat et temoin,* undated but following *Arlequin dogue d'Angleterre* (June 1679) in Dominque's zibaldone. Arlequin, with the aid of several figures made of willow, plays the judge, two lawyers, a lady witness, and the brother of the victim. As the first lawyer, Arlequin begins: "The eighth of the month of October last, Scaramouche finding himself at Dover, an English seaport . . ."[16] The dates are congruent, but what Scaramouche was doing in England with a great deal of baggage and without the rest of the company is simply not deducible.

Charles II tried at least one more time to bring the Italians back. In April 1683 he instructed his ambassador to Paris to arrange for the company's return. Scaramouche said first that there were old debts—a hundred pounds' worth—to be paid. And they would need an advance in France, or some of the company would be unable to get away. The king issued a warrant on 20 April for the construction of a theatre for them at Windsor and the prince of Denmark wrote on 1 May that they were expected about the twentieth of the month. In August, still without word, the king wrote again to Paris, asking hopefully if the queen's death meant that the theatres were closed and, if so, might the Italians come.[17] But the theatres were not closed, and the Italians, busy with remodeling, reorganization, and a substantial change in the composition of the company, stayed home.

To a troupe without a theatre, no longer the recipients of the king's personal favor, the English invitation in 1673 must have seemed heaven sent. By 1683 matters were very different. Although Louis XIV was no longer an ardent partisan of the theatre, he expected his French and Italian actors, now regarded as functionaries, to be available on a regular basis for the entertainment of the court.

When the new repertory was introduced in 1668, these difficulties and changes were still in the future. The Italians were sharing the theatre at Palais-Royal with Molière and his colleagues, as they had been since 1662. The French played Tuesday, Friday, and Sunday, the Italians the rest of the week. The theatre had been reconstructed in 1662, but "hastily," as La Grange points out. It was serviceable and equipped for changeable scenery, at least after the mounting of Molière's *Dom Juan* in February 1665. The Italians were able to employ changeable scenery and to produce the sort of "minor" spectacle that was so successful in *Le régal des dames,* but the theatre was apparently not equipped with machines until later.

On 17 January 1671 at the Salle des Machines in the Tuileries, a musical play entitled *Psyché,* with text by Molière with Corneille and Quinault and others, was given an almost unbelievably spectacular production that cost the king more than 250,000 livres. The candles and oil alone cost more than 15,000 livres.[18] Molière's troupe not unreasonably wanted to capitalize on the immense curiosity aroused in all of those unlucky enough not to have been present on 17 January. The theatre at Palais-Royal, however, was not equipped for machine plays like *Psyché.* The French deliberated and decided to begin remodeling as soon as the theatre was closed for Easter. The Italians concurred and agreed to pay for half of the work. La Grange reports as follows:

> It should be remarked that Sunday 15 March of this year 1671, before closing the theatre, the troupe resolved to have the interior of the theatre repaired, which had been done in haste and carelessly at the time of the establishment, and that through deliberation it was concluded to remake the stage, especially the structure, and render it fit for machines; to repair all the loges and amphithéâtre, bancs and balcons both in what regards their structure and in the upholstery and ornaments and comforts, then to make a great ceiling to reign over the whole auditorium which up to this day 15 March has been covered only with a great blue cloth suspended on ropes. What is more, it was resolved to have painted the said ceiling, loges, amphithéâtre and generally all that concerns the decoration of the auditorium where will also be added a third row of loges which were not there before. And more, to have henceforth at all performances, whether simple or with machines, an orchestra of twelve instruments; this was not done until after the performance of *Psyché.*
>
> Upon this deliberation of the troupe, the work began on the repair and decoration of the auditorium on 18 March which was a Wednesday, and finished on Wednesday, April 15 of the same year. The general expense in wood, carpentry, joining, metalwork, paint-

ing, cloths, nails, ropes, tools, wages for workers and generally all necessary things rose to 1,989 livres 10 sous.

It should be noted that this expense, shared by the Italians, included "making the stage fit for machines" but did not include the machines themselves. These were paid for by the French as part of the cost of *Psyché*. And whereas the work on the theatre cost just under 2,000 livres, the production cost for "carpentry, joining, wood, metalwork, painting, cloths, ropes, counterweights, machines, tools, silk stockings for the dancers, wine for rehearsals ... and in general all things, the sum of 4,359 livres, 1 sou." The Italians did not share in the cost, and the Italians did not use the machines. Nothing in their repertory between 1668 and the mid 1670s calls for machine spectacle. When they did begin to use it, in 1677 and 1678, warfare erupted between the two troupes.

The remodeling of the theatre did not, then, have a substantial effect on the repertory of the Italians, nor did the move to the Théâtre Guéné-gaud in 1673, at least immediately. Dispossessed from Palais-Royal by Lulli along with their French colleagues, the Italians waited in England until the French had—with some difficulty—managed to preserve their company and find a new home. On 10 June 1673, according to an Accord et Transaction drawn up in 1680, the French company agreed to the king's request, transmitted by Colbert, that they permit the Italians to use their stage. The circumstances were, however, now altered. At the Petit-Bourbon and the Palais-Royal the troupes shared theatres located in royal palaces; neither paid any rent. Now the French were being asked to share a theatre for which they had paid 14,000 livres, along with a building rental of 2,400 livres a year. The king had them at a disadvantage because the theatre—which had been built to house the Opéra—was under a royal interdiction protecting Lulli's privilege. The date 10 June, just in the middle of negotiations for the theatre, suggests that the monarch and Colbert may have traded a space for the Italians for remission of the interdiction. Another part of the deal was that Lulli would pay the dispos-sessed Italians' share of the annual rent of the building, 1,200 livres. The French may have been not unreasonably aggrieved by the king's unwill-ingness to do the same for them, but the French had interfered with Louis's plan for a merger of the French companies and were not in high favor.

All of this goes some distance to explain why the French drew up a set of conditions to govern the Italians' use of the Guénégaud. Signed on 2 August 1673 by Barbara Minuti Coris, the mother of Orsola Cortesi, and Marie Marguerite Enguerans, the wife of Giovan Andrea Zanotti, neither of whom had gone with the actors to England, the agreement specified that the Italians would pay half of the rent, would play only on the jours extraordinaires, would *not* "use the decors, machines, or other things belonging to the French or make any opening in the stage, or touch any machinery, or displace or break anything." They were to have the use only of the stage, loges, amphithéâtre and parterre; they were even to stay out of the dressing rooms.[19]

The chandeliers symbolize the degree of amity existing between the troupes at various times. In 1660, while the Italians were out of Paris, the French troupe bought a set of crystal chandeliers for the Petit-Bourbon for 318 livres. These were moved to Palais-Royal and then to the Guénégaud. Because the Italians had not shared in the original cost—and possibly out of jealousy over Lulli's arrangement with them—the French began to charge 3 livres a day for the use of the chandeliers. In 1677, however, the two troupes shared the cost of some new chandeliers, very expensive ones, for the French paid 1,000 livres in addition to the trade-in of their old set. Perhaps relations between the two troupes were not as strained in 1677 as they had been in 1673, but any harmony that existed was the calm before the storm. Dominque's zibaldone makes it clear that from 1675 on, the Italians were not performing simple plays in single sets on the stage of the Hôtel Guénégaud, regardless of what they had promised in 1673, and it seems likely that *La magie naturelle,* a machine play produced in late November 1678, exacerbated the situation and led to a quarrel and legal actions at the end of the decade.

The theatre usually known to modern historians as the Hôtel Guénégaud (although it was not a hôtel, was not situated on the rue Guénégaud, and was often referred to in its day as the theatre on the rue Mazarine) is the least studied and least known of the seventeenth-century Paris theatres, perhaps because it was used for relatively few years and destroyed in 1688. Originally a tennis court, it was rented from its proprietor, Maximilien de Laffemas, by Pierre Perrin for the exercise of his opera patent; then its lease was taken over by the marquis de Sourdéac and his colleague, Laurent Bersac, self-styled sieur de Camperon. This doubtful duo meddled in various theatrical affairs in seventeenth-century Paris. The marquis, whose principal interest was in theatrical machines, gained some fame for his private production of Corneille's *La toison d'or* at his castle of Neufbourg in Normandy. He was an eccentric man, described by Tallemant des Réaux as taking exercise by "having his peasants hunt him as one hunts a deer."[20] Champeron had begun life as the son of a minor court officer and served, among other things, as a tax farmer. The two managed, through various maneuvers, to lay claim to the privilege to produce operas, granted by the king to Perrin on 28 June 1669.

Sourdéac and Champeron signed the lease for the Jeu de Paume de la Bouteille on the rue Mazarine on 8 October 1670, explaining that they intended to build there a theatre "for the musical productions called operas, in consequence of the permission and privilege that they had obtained by letter patent from His Majesty in the name of Sieur Perrin." They then had to, according to a later statement, "construct an auditorium, a stage, amphithéâtres, loges, raze some buildings, construct some new ones, dig more than twenty feet into the earth for the machinery, and adjust everything for the decors."[21]

No plan of this theatre survives, nor does any graphic representation of it. The only surviving document relating to its construction is a receipt for 400 livres owed for painting, and from it we derive only the information that Charles Hérault, painter of the king and member of the Royal Academy, was responsible for some of the decoration. Robinet describes the theatre as having a deep and wide auditorium with a superb ceiling, three rows of loges, and, "what is more, from end to end, in order that no one should stand, a very commodious amphithéâtre from which the whole stage can be seen."[22] Once again the professional actors were faced with a theatre without a parterre, a problem they quickly solved, although by what architectural means there is no way of knowing.

If the lack of parterre was a nuisance, this was somewhat made up for by the fact that the width of the proscenium opening was the same as at Palais-Royal, a fact we derive from a design for a 1684 reprise of *Psyché* found in the archives of the Comédie-Française.[23] The decors, at least, could be saved. According to Samuel Chappuzeau, the theatre on the rue Mazarine was the only one in Paris where machine plays could be given after the demise of the Marais, thanks to its wide, deep stage.

The auditorium could hold nearly 1,500 spectators with another 200 on the stage, although an audience of this size would be rare indeed. These figures have been extrapolated by Lancaster from the largest receipts of the French company. He estimates a maximum audience of 677 in the parterre, 222 in the amphithéâtre, 160 in the first loges, 281 in the second loges, 111 in the third loges, for a total of 1,451.[24] Estimates of the auditorium at Palais-Royal vary, but Sylvie Chevalley, in her analysis of Hubert's *Registre* for the season 1672–73, believes that it probably held about 1,450.[25] The two theatres were, then, similar in size of auditorium and stage.

Luckily, both stages were large, since both also included seating for spectators. The use of the stage for audience seating was not new, having begun in 1637 at the Marais, when the exceptional success of Corneille's *Le Cid* made the niches at the side of the stage, once the lurking place of pages, desirable seats for noblemen and gentlemen.[26] At Palais-Royal in 1672–73, Moliére's company charged 5 livres, 10 sous, for seats on the stage, a significant addition to the daily profits, even though the average number of spectators on stage was ten.[27] Moliére's company kept these spectators under control, never permitting more than thirty-six and providing *bancs* and *balcons*, that is, benches and stage boxes, for them at the sides just behind the curtain. Barbara Mittman, in her recent book *Spectators on the Paris Stage*, believes that Palais-Royal had only benches, but La Grange's memorandum on the reconstruction and refurbishment of audience seating in 1671 mentions *balcons* as well. The Guénégaud, on the other hand, appears to have had only benches at first. Mittman suggests that the *balcons* were added just before the season of 1676–77, when they are mentioned for the first time in the company's accounts. Also in that season, the average number of stage tickets sold jumps from the forty to forty-four of the preceding three seasons to eighty.

Nothing is more emblematic of the differences between the baroque theatre and the theatre of our day than the stage audience, present to be seen and heard, entering late, leaving early, blocking entrances and exits, flirting with the actresses. The abbé de Pure, among other highly desirable stage reforms for which he yearns in 1668, maintains that "the stage should be kept empty, except for actors. The people who are on it, or who arrive on it during the performance, cause intolerable disorder and confusion. How often, on hearing bits of verse such as: 'But here he is, I see him,' has one taken for an actor, for the expected character, some good-looking, well-dressed gentleman entering the stage and looking for a seat."[28] But as Mittman points out, the confusion of life and theatre was a dominant characteristic of the baroque.[29] "For the *petit marquis* who night after night made the rounds of the Paris stages, who lived illuminated by stage lights, life remained theatre and theatre remained life." The *bancs* and *balcons* did confine the spectators to specific places on the stage, alleviating the confusion noted by the abbé de Pure, and the *balcons* also made it possible to seat spectators on stage during machine plays when the stage floor had to be clear for special effects. The onstage audience continued to grow throughout the seventeenth century, rising to a maximum of over 200 at the Guénégaud during the last years of its occupation.

There is no reason why the Italians should not have benefited from the sale of seats on stage, at least during the years before they began to invest heavily in spectacle, and so long as the audience did not grow to the point of interfering with the realism of the Italians' stage action. The French, especially in tragedy, required little stage space, since most of what they did involved lining up and declaiming. The Italians needed room for pratfalls, acrobatics, mock battles, and chases. But apparently the stage of the Guénégaud was wide enough for this kind of action and some spectators; in *Arlequin berger de Lemnos* (November 1674). Arlequin, during a parody of a pastoral tirade spoken in French, in which he expresses his envy of the mushrooms crushed by the step of his beloved, turns "to those who are on the stage" and addresses them:

> You amorous stallions of Arcadia, you who by your tender and energetic accents make these woods resound, you to whom nature has refused the use of words, who of all the letters of your name can only pronounce the *O*, express my passion to my adorable Lizette, that the *A* signifies that Arlequin sighs for her. The *S*, that Sbroufadel languishes in her absence. The *I* and the *N* reproach her for her ingratitude and her nonchalance, and the *O*, that last letter of your name, accompanied by these soft trills so familiar to you will paint for her a true picture of my complaint, by going O O O O O.[30]

In other words, Arlequin invites the *petit marquis*—the *asino,* or amorous ass—to bray for him.

The theatre on the rue Mazarine had a short life as an opera house. It opened with *Pomone,* text by Perrin and music by Cambert, on 3 March 1671. The piece had a considerable success, in spite of Perrin's libretto, which St.-Evremond heard "with disgust." Robinet devoted 150 lines of his gazette for 18 April to it, following two visits by Monsieur, the king's brother. Louis himself did not go. A second opera, *La pastorale héroique des peines et des plaisirs de l'amour* by Gilbert and Cambert, was performed at the Guénégaud in late 1671 or early 1672 and considered a distinct improvement over the first by St.-Evremond.[31] Sourdéac's machines played a major role in both productions. But when the privilege of the opera was transferred to Jean-Baptise Lulli in March, the king ordered La Reynie, the lieutenant of the police, to see to it that performances ceased at Sourdéac and Champeron's theatre on 1 April.[32] The theatre, so magnificently equipped and decorated, stood empty for just over a year until it was bought by the remnants of Molière's company.

Another issue relevant both to Lulli's assumption of the opera privilege and the new repertory of the Italians is the use of music. While we assume that music always played a role in the Italian theatre, little mention is made of it in Biancolelli's zibaldone before *Le régal des dames.* After *Le régal,* with its French drinking song and its dancing Scaramouche, music is mentioned with some frequency, especially around 1672, when it became an issue of consequence in the Paris theatres.

As Donneau de Visé writes, in the introduction to his libretto for *Les amours de Bacchus et d'Ariane* (1672), "Music and dance have charms for everyone, and the productions which are full of them are much more popular than the others." Molière, who adapted his court entertainments for the public stage beginning with *Les fâcheux* in 1661 and *Le mariage forcé* in 1664, had achieved an enormous success in Paris with *Psyché,* a musical machine play, in 1671. Romagnesi's scenarios regularly included ballets after 1668, but in July 1672 the Italians opened in Paris a most peculiar entertainment entitled *Le collier de perle.* Based on an incident reported by Donneau de Visé in the first issue of his *Mercure galant* (January-March 1672), the story concerns a young man who stole a pearl necklace, swallowed the thirty-two pearls and the ribbon, "cut into imperceptible pieces," but was caught and forced—by means of a series of enemas—to yield up his booty. This somewhat sordid tale was turned into a play for the Italians by Girardin, probably Joseph Girardin, a court functionary, who although very young according to Tralage, was the author of some verses included on an engraving made of the ballroom at Versailles during the fete of 1668.[33] Later, Girardin was governor and tutor to the pages of the household of the dauphin, still later ambassador of France to the Grand Turk, and finally councillor and secretary of state of the duc de Savoy.[34] In his graver years he must have wondered at the appropriateness of his earlier literary activity—especially since he not only invented the silly scenario, he had a synopsis of it in French printed up for the audience.[35]

Girardin was not alone in the venture. The play is "agreeably ornamented" by three ballet entries, the last of which is a full pastoral divertissement with songs (in French), dances, a magician, demons, sorcerers, and so forth. According to Girardin's preface, the airs and ballet music are by a nameless but admirable genius, an "illustrious person [who] has employed only the few moments which the diversions that he prepares for the king leave him." Although it is hard to believe that Lulli would write for the Italians, he had ceased by this time to compose for Molière, and perhaps it amused him to collaborate with Molière's competition. On the other hand, Lulli seems to have been busily employed in 1672 making sure that the other Paris theatres would not compete musically with the Opéra for which he now held the privilege.

Lulli's war with Molière began in March 1672, when—according to testimony offered in several of the various legal actions surrounding the founding of the Opéra—the king was persuaded to order the other Paris theatres to accompany their performances with no more than two songs and two instruments.[36] Molière is said to have used his influence to persuade the king against this near total interdiction, and Lulli's patent was issued only with the statement that no other theatre could produce a play entirely in music.[37] But the sly Sieur Baptiste was not through, and on 12 August, the same day Lulli signed a lease for the Jeu de Paume de Béquet on the rue Vaugirard, the king issued a new order limiting all the other theatres to no more than six singers and twelve instrumentalists, with restrictions on which musicians and dancers could be employed.[38] Perhaps not coincidentally, Molière had reintroduced into his repertory on 8 July his old comedy ballet *Le mariage forcé,* without Lulli's music. The new version had musical ornaments by Charpentier, who was also to do the music for *Le malade imaginaire.*

At the same time, the Italians were preparing and then performing their musical cathartic, and, according to its author, Lulli himself, in his few spare moments, was composing the music for it. One imagines some tight lips backstage at Palais-Royal. Of course, the whole thing may have been prepared for performance at court. Girardin and Lulli were both involved in court festivities, and the king—still a relatively young man—appears not to have been averse to a little vulgarity. But Girardin's statement about Lulli seems to imply that this work was extracurricular.

The relatively liberal order of August made it possible for Molière to perform his own musical plays in his own theatre, but shortly after his death in February of the following year, a final order of 30 April reduced the number of singers allowed to two and the number of instrumentalists to six, without the express written permission of Lulli. It seems likely that the Italians abided by these limits during their sojourn at the Guénégaud, but Riccoboni, when negotiating the Italian return to Paris in 1716, asked "very humbly that the dances and music in the divertissements be granted to them as their predecessors had played them,"[39] which rather sounds like the Italians had some special dispensation.

The most elaborate musical play performed before 1680 by the company was *Le voyage de Scaramouche et d'Arlequin aux Indes,* produced in 1676. This play, like *Le collier de perle,* was accompanied by a printed synopsis of the action with the French lyrics of the songs. The printed sheets have not survived, but Gueullette made a handwritten transcription of them. The cast includes sixteen speaking roles, six singing roles, and eight mute roles, as well as dancers and extras, a large order. But the six singing roles can be played without difficulty by two singers. There are never more than two on stage at a time, one male and one female. Furthermore, the Italians often sang themselves; presumably they did not have to count company members as musicians.

The composer of the music for *Le voyage aux Indes* was Oudot; earlier Cambert composed the music for the *Suite de festin de pierre,* the refurbished reprise of their old warhorse which the Italians opposed to *Le malade imaginaire* in the winter of 1673.[40] A number of other entries in Dominque's zibaldone have characteristics that suggest they also relied on music and dance. *Arlequin roy par hazard* (probably 1673) includes lions and Turks and takes place on an island, *Arlequin berger de Lemnos* (November 1674) is a pastoral parody with "sweet concerts . . . and pretty songs in Italian and French,"[41] while titles such as *Arlequin roy de Tripoli* and *Arlequin et Scaramouche juifs errans de Babilonne* immediately hint at music, spectacle, and the exotic. A likely pattern would be the introduction of a new piece with ornaments each winter to take advantage of the carnival season.

Along with music and dance, the Italians judiciously spiced their performances with spectacle, but not of the sort they had introduced with Torelli in the 1640s and 1650s. There were no glories, no dawns or sunsets, no chariots crossing the sky, no thunder-and-lightning storms. The Italians between 1668 and 1680 provided minor spectacle: magic tricks, slight-of-hand, and exotic and eccentric transformations and travesties along with changeable scenery, the occasional perspective vista, the odd wave machine, the rare dragon. The spectacle became more elaborate toward the end of the period, and finally was a source of contention and legal action between the two troupes playing at the Guénégaud in 1680. *Le régal des dames,* with magic goblets and a fountain, brought audiences rushing to the theatre, but by 1675 the spectacle wars were underway and the Italians—though outclassed—were trying hard to dazzle the spectators.

From the beginning, a most important stage device seems to have been the trap. The magic goblets were followed up in *Le théâtre sans comédie* by a bottomless pot out of which Arlequin and Trivelin drew a number of ridiculous things until, reaching for a gold chain, they were driven back by a great flame. Small fire effects were also used in *Le remède à tous maux, Le monde renversé,* and *Arlequin esprit follet.* Traps were still important in 1680 when one of the issues between the two troupes was the Italian's desire to open new traps in the stage.

Travesties—increasingly bizarre—were a feature of Biancolelli's routines, and he began to enhance them with transformations. In *Les métamorphoses d'Arlequin* he appeared as a clock, a bass violin, and an armchair, in *Arlequin berger de Lemnos* he was Bacchus and Jupiter, but Jupiter disguised as a swan and a bull. In the notes for *Arlequin vallet enchanté, singe et Margot la pie*, Biancolelli explains how his travesties became transformations. Diamantine, a magician, was responsible for transforming him with her magic wand into a Docteur, a devil, a monkey, and a magpie. For the first change, he slipped into a column and emerged transformed, then—as the Docteur—crossed to the trap. Diamantine touched him, he descended under the stage, and a gagiste dressed as a devil took his place. To change into a monkey on stage, Arlequin wore his ordinary costume over his disguise with a long cloak over all. He took off his clothes without being seen under cover of the cloak, then emerged as the monkey at the touch of the wand. In the last scene, Diamantine transformed him into a magpie, but the notes do not describe how the effect was achieved.[42]

The most elaborate travesty is described in *L'auberge d'Arlequin juge partie avocat et temoin,* where Arlequin, by means of willow frames costumed on the front and open in the rear, plays the judge, prosecutor, defense attorney, witness, and brother of the victim all at once.[43]

Several years after the move to the Guénégaud, the Italians began to introduce some machine spectacle. *Le voyage aux Indes,* the musical extravaganza performed in 1676, also included scenes and machines. The printed scenario lists six settings: hell, the mountains north of Rome, the country of Cockaigne, the court of the Great Turk, the moon, and the shore of the "mer des Indes," which someone seems to have believed to be near Lima, Peru, The principal machines indicated are a fountain, which spouts wine and liqueurs until Arlequin and Scaramouche try to drink, at which point the wine turns to water and the liqueurs to fire, and a dragon, which Arlequin mounts to escape the Turks at the end of act 2.[44] In *Arlequin et Scaramouche juifs errans de Babilonne* the zanni enter swimming, Arlequin advancing over the waves, crying.[45] Apparently, a wave machine was available. And *La magie naturelle,* perhaps the most successful production the Italians did before 1680, calls in act 1 for a bed that rises and falls by magic, in act 2 for a windmill that turns, and in act 3 for the return of the dragon.[46]

The dragon, mentioned in plays performed in 1676 and 1678, is the first indication of the Italians' using a flying machine. Some simpler kind of flight may have taken place earlier, at Palais-Royal. According to Robinet, *Arlequin esprit follet* (1670) included machines and flight, but since this performance took place before the reconstruction at Palais Royal that made the stage fit for machines, any aerial work by Arlequin must have been done by means of a simple harness and line system. The same technique may have been used in *Arlequin vallet enchanté, singe et Margot la pie.*

The Italians used spectacle inventively and imaginatively, but not to the extent that justifies scholars concluding that, from its establishment, the Italian theatre in Paris relied on the "decadent" or "distressing" use of scenes and machines to attract an audience.[47] Only after 1690, when the troupe reconstructed the Hôtel de Bourgogne, was there dependence on Italianate spectacle, and that seems to have arisen in response to the need to compete with the French in their new theatre and with the Opéra. The Italian repertory always included many plays that did not employ any spectacle, and many other that employed it only in the finale. The Italians did use changeable scenery with some frequency, but that in itself hardly validates the antitheatrical criticisms that have been leveled at them.

Scenes and machines were expensive, and the Italians, although some of them were well-to-do in later years, probably did not have the resources to invest in them in the first decades of their establishment. Nor, of course, did they have a theatre of their own in which to install machines or to store decors. Almost no information exists about the finances of the Italian company, but one comparison is possible thanks to Biancolelli's marginal comment on the profits of *La magie naturelle* (1678): "This play, in twenty-four performances, provided each of those who hold a full share 1,064 livres." Their French colleagues did significantly better with their greatest success, *Circé* (1675), accumulating 1,404 livres each for the first twenty-four performances in spite of having to pay enormous daily expenses of 331 livres, 5 sous, and split the profits in seventeen shares rather than in ten. According to La Grange, the French troupe at the Guénégaud spent nearly 11,000 livres preparing *Circé,* an example of just how costly a machine play could be. Nothing in Biancolelli's zibaldone hints at expenses of this magnitude, and his marginal note implies that the Italians' receipts were, in general, modest.

A relatively economical visual delight, Arcadie the ass, was introduced as a member of the troupe by Robinet on 15 September 1668. Arlequin entered on Arcadie in *Le remède à tous maux* to do a mountebank discourse, the ass standing in for the mule normally associated with doctors. This ass is mentioned again in *La folie d'Eularia* (1670), and when

Arlequin refers in *Arlequin berger de Lemnos* to the *petits marquis* on stage as "amorous stallions of Arcadie," he may be punning, alluding both to Arcadia, the pastoral utopia, and to Arcadie, the progenitor of the *asini* to whom he speaks. In *La maladie de Scaramouche* (1676) there is a lazzi which uses what might be a real ass or might be a pantomime ass, but which, if real, may no longer be Arcadie. In *La dot par la metempsicoʒe* (1677 or 1678) Arlequin delivers an "Elegy for a Dead Ass," although that ass is named Margot and is a hermophrodite. Of course, Arcadie too may have been a pantomime ass, an awkward juxtaposition of a couple of gagistes in a donkey suit. But there is something rather agreeable about the thought of a real ass in a company so devoted to the asinine.

A final and very important change in the repertory of the Italians after 1668 was verbal, not visual, and involved the increasing use of French. Beginning with the "Panégiric de Scaramouche" in *Le théâtre sans comédie*, the Italians increasingly introduced French material into their repertory. Because of the nature of the available evidence, the most common use of French seems to be in Arlequin's comic discourse, or set speech. But, of course, other characters may have begun to use the language of their adopted country as well in other ways. (This innovation will be discussed fully in chapter 9.)

Thanks to two French writers, Samuel Chappuzeau and the abbé de Pure, who published books on theatre in France in 1674 and 1668, respectively, we know a good deal in general about the theatrical operations of the day, although we continue to know very little about the specific operations of the Italians. La Grange's useful listing of the theatre staff is discontinued after 1662, but Hubert's *Registre* for 1672–73 at Palais Royal shows daily expenses of 54 livres, 2 sous, a little less than La Grange's 73 livres, 4 sous, for 1663 minus the 15 livres for soldiers. In 1675 La Grange includes ordinary daily expenses of 51 livres, 16 sous, in the accounts for *Circé*. The trend seems to be either to have slightly fewer employees or pay them a little less.

Chappuzeau in 1674 describes the theatre staff and explains the duties of its members in some detail; his list is essentially the same as La Grange's. He mentions the concierge who keeps the theatre clean, the receiver who sells the tickets and the controllers who take them, the ushers who assign people to their seats and the porters who guard the doors to keep out ruffians and those who want to come in without paying. The modern custom of tipping the ushers in France may arise from the *douceurs,* or sweeteners, they were permitted to take from patrons who wanted the best available seats. Backstage is the domain of the décorateur and his assistant, who are in charge of "everything regarding the embellishment of the stage and its functioning." The décorateur also oversees the candle snuffers who must move quickly and "not leave the audience languishing between the acts" nor choking in the fumes of the guttering candles. The "mouchoirs" also serve as the theatre firemen, making sure that the hogsheads are full of water and the buckets are ready so that no one must run to the river for water in case of fire. When the theatre performs a machine play, the backstage crew swells according to the needs of the piece.[48] At Palais-Royal and the Guénégaud the décorateurs and candle snuffers served also as extras, some of them like Crosnier developing into running gags, if not polished performers.

One employee not listed by La Grange is the copyist, who serves the company also as archivist and prompter. For some reason Molière's troupe did not employ this important functionary, and we can assume that neither did the Italians, having no need of prompting or archive. Chappuzeau also details the various officers of the company: the treasurer who keeps the company's funds and distributes them for repairs, rentals, or new machines; the secretary who keeps the *registre* and enters the receipts and expenses; and the controller who testifies to the accuracy of the accounts. There is no reason to suppose the Italians organized their company differently, and certainly after the king established a bureaucracy overseeing the theatres in 1683, the Italians followed the same procedures as the other troupes.

A final officer of the company was the orator, whose function it was to make the harangue, or speech describing the next performance, and compose the poster. As Chappuzeau describes it, "The discourse at the end of the play has for its purpose to capture the goodwill of the assembly. He thanks them for their favorable attention, announces the play which is to follow, and invites them to see it." Usually the speech was short, unless the king or Monsieur was present, in which case the orator had to be prepared to make a well-wrought compliment. New plays and spectacle pieces got longer eulogies. The end of the season was the occasion for a formal farewell in the name of the troupe, while the beginning of the new season, two weeks later, required that the orator whet appetites for the pleasure to come. The posters, which went up at certain carefully selected sites in the aristocratic and bourgeois quarters—in the Marais, around the Louvre and Palais-Royal, and in the Faubourg St.-Germain—identified each theatre by color. Red was used by the Hôtel de Bourgogne, green by the Guénégaud, and yellow by the Opéra.[49] The posters, according to Loret in 1661, were meant to give the place, the time, the price, and the day. According to Chappuzeau twelve years later, the posters could also inform "the reader of the numerous assemblage of the preceding day, of the merit of the play, of the necessity to provide oneself with seats in good time," but fashion having changed in both posters and harangues, "the orator no longer makes long speeches but simply names the play to be performed."

The orator was also a de facto capocomico, who was responsible for convoking assemblies, calling rehearsals, and organizing the reading of new plays. In an addendum Chappuzeau lists the celebrated orators of the French troupes: Bellerose, Floridor, and Hauteroche at the Hôtel de Bourgogne; Mondory, Dorgemont, Floridor, and Laroque at the Marais; Molière and La Grange at Palais-Royal; and the latter at the Guénégaud. He does not include the Italians, but it seems likely that Dominique was the orator there. In the prologue to Regnard's *Le divorce* (1688), Arlequin comes out to tell the audience there will be no play that day since the porter is ill and Pantalon indisposed.[50] A successful confusion of reality and theatricality seems to depend on the literal verisimilitude of the event—that is, that Dominque was the one expected to make announcements to the audience, which would, at first, believe his news. Biancolelli was also the first member of the troupe to speak French on stage. Locatelli may have served earlier as the orator; his composition of the scenario in French of *Le Rosaura* would indicate the possibility that he did. Fiorilli probably did not. He was back and forth too much, and he was notably a man of action and not of words. In the last decade of the troupe's existence, Giovan Battista Costantini served as its orator, and in a very late play, *Arlequin misantrope* by Louis Biancolelli, Arlequin agrees to play the misanthrope only if Colombine will agree to announce the play.

Chappuzeau says nothing of the relationship between the theatres and the gazetteers, but the possibility certainly exists that the *Lettres en vers* of Loret, Robinet, and the others as well as the *Mecure galant* of Donneau de Visé, along with the various foreign gazettes printed abroad and eagerly bought in Paris, were all accessible to theatrical troupes in need of publicity. Coverage of the theatre by the gazettes was inconsistent. Loret, for instance, devoted hundreds of lines to the Italian troupe in the 1650s but almost never mentioned the troupe that established itself in 1662. Only after 1668, when Robinet devoted nearly an entire "letter" to *Le régal des dames,* were the Italians once more part of the small and recurring set of people and institutions followed by the gazetteers. Between 1668 and the end of Robinet's publication in 1675, he mentioned most of the new plays in Biancolelli's zibaldone, some of them as many as three times. Donneau de Visé, whose *Mercure galant* began publication in 1672, was also a devoted chronicler of the Italian theatre. No evidence exists to support a claim that these notices were paid puffery, even though they are uniformly laudatory, but it is interesting that the French actors at the Guénégaud paid Donneau de Visé 486 livres in September 1673, just as their new theatre was opening, and gave 55 livres to Samuel Chappuzeau whose 1674 book has only the most favorable things to say of them.[51] Perhaps the word *bribe* is too strong for what may have gone on; maybe *douceur* would be more appropriate.

In spite of the honeyed words of the gazetteers, the French theatre of the mid-seventeenth century had its problems; it was not Elysium. And while Chappuzeau might be described as an apologist for it, the abbé de Pure, a very minor man of letters, was rather more its critic. In his *Idée des spectacles anciens et nouveaux* he had a number of suggestions for improvement which add a note of reality to Chappuzeau's Panglossian views.

The play, says the abbé de Pure, needs four qualities if it is to assure the pleasure of everyone or most people or at least the best people: first, an action of great importance; second, a great novelty; third, a great passion; and four, something applicable to the times. But the play alone is not enough. "It is also to be wished that the actresses be young and beautiful and if not always virgins at least not always pregnant."[52]

The abbé also thought it would be nice if the plays were to start on time, in the winter at 3:30 and in the summer at 4:30. He wanted the stage to be empty of everyone but the actors to avoid the "insupportable disorders and confusions" caused by the gentlemen spectators. He believed that in general the theatre would be better off if long runs were avoided. Long runs, he says, are bad for the actors' memories and "furiously boring" for the habitual spectator. Take a new play off after nine or ten nights, he suggests.

Finally, and most important, something needed to be done about the disorder and lack of security in the theatre. In 1669, for instance, Robinet reported another major riot at the Italians, this time inside the theatre. Seven or eight "new actors" made "bellicose by Bacchus" chose the stage for a display of swordplay and fighting, much to the displeasure of the audience. The stage had never been so bloody, either from love or hatred, according to Robinet, but the bourgeois in the *parterre*, furious at not hearing the play and fearing to waste their fifteen sous, attacked the bullies and drove them from the theatre.[53] According to the abbé, these "bravos" who flock in "without interest, without knowledge, and without money, these despoilers who are only brave with bourgeois and women, should be absolutely forbidden to enter with arms and without paying." The number of guards and musketeers, who make noise "endlessly" must also be cut, and the theatre left to the "truly interested and the good bourgeois."

The poor abbé was not to get all his wishes. The actresses continued to be pregnant more often than not, especially at the Italians, where Eularia and later Marinette set records. Starting times got later, and more and more people sat on the stage. But the disturbances did lessen as the king and La Reynie issued ordinances against disorder and entry without payment in the theatres, as the wars with Spain and the Netherlands gave other employment to the bravos and musketeers, and as the court moved away from Paris.

The abbé de Pure would not have agreed, but the improvement most devoutly wished for by His Majesty was the merger of the two remaining French troupes into one, followed by the institutionalization of all theatrical activity under the aegis of the First Gentlemen of the Chamber. This wish was granted in 1680 when the French companies of the Hôtels de Bourgogne and Guénégaud were merged and in 1683 when the French troupe—along with the Italians and the Opéra—was placed directly under the supervision of the court. The merger of 1680, which resulted in the establishment of the Comédie-Française, may have in part grown out of the quarrel between the French troupe of the Guénégaud and the Italians sharing their facilities. The quarrel was over the Italians' increasing use of spectacle.

According to La Grange, legal action began on 14 December 1679 when the French sued the Italians over the use of machines and the innovations the latter wanted to make to the stage. The French had drawn up and delivered to the Italian actors, at the domicile of Signors Cinthio and Ange, by a sergeant of the Châtelet the following:

> Be it signified and declared to the Italian actors . . . that according to the information which has been given to them [the French] that the said Italian actors want to make changes and enterprises in the stage which belongs to the said French actors, they declare to them that they formally forbid them to make any changes or undertakings either on the said stage or on the machines and decoration belonging to it, considering that they all belong, as it is said, to the said French actors, who bought it from the sieurs Sourdéac and Champeron.[54]

The probable cause of this action was the growing use of spectacle by the Italians at a time when the French company was also heavily involved in scenic artifice. The French had opened, on 19 November 1679, a play entitled *La devineresse*, designed to take advantage of the trial of the notorious Voisin, the sorceress and poisoner, who was arrested on 12 March 1679 and burned on the Grève on 22 February 1680. *La devineress* by Thomas Corneille and Donneau de Visé, which had a success second only to that of *Circé*, owed a great deal to the kind of imaginative spectacle the Italians had introduced during their stay in Paris. Rather than the usual scenes and machines, it employed Italian gadgetry: a zigzag, a talking head, a mirror scene, and assorted body parts that flew through the air and joined together. What the Italians were doing at the same time cannot be deduced with any certainty. The most likely candidate, according to the chronology of the zibaldone, is *L'auberge d'Arlequin juge partie avocat et temoin*, but that should have posed no problems, since Biancolelli's notes suggest that no particular spectacle was required. A tempting fragment entitled "Dambreville" follows *Arlequin juge*, however, accompanied by a note of Gueullette's: "It has been thought up to the present that to have put Cartouche [put to death on the Grève, 20 October 1721] on the French and Italian stages was without a model; however, I find here on fol. 113 of the manuscript a very short note which proves incontestably that Dambreville who was burned was also put on the stage."[55]

The note seems to be a fragment of a tirade spoken by Arlequin in the person of Dambreville, who sounds like a male version of Corneille and Donneau de Visé's title character: "I earn my living honestly, I sell ointments for the spleen, I sell a water for the colic, I sell hooves for the feet, I have made a trip to Marseilles with twenty of my friends, we love each other passionately, we are chained together by inseparable friendship."

Whatever the specific play they were presenting, the Italians did something to aggrieve the French. On 20 January 1680 the lieutenant civil, Pierre Girardin, executed a judgment of the civil court which ordered the parties to the suit to continue on as they had been doing and permitted the Italians to have traps, and even machines, so long as they took away, after every performance, whatever inconvenienced the French. He also sent one Michel Richer to the theatre to examine "the beam" the French had complained of, and see whether it or the other machines placed by Italians could, in fact, interfere with the French or damage their machines.[56] Another judgment, issued on 31 January, was contested by the French who claimed that Richer had exceeded his power and favored the Italians.[57] On 6 February two expert architects were to meet at the theatre and inspect the machines under contention. The Italian's expert, Jean Herbert, arrived, but the architect d'Orbay, selected by the French, did not. He was, according to d'Auvilliers and Guérin, two of the French actors, "in the country." It was four o'clock, the French troupe began to play, and the inspection was not made.[58]

Girardin then ordered another inspection by Morestin, an expert named by the French, and the provost, but their conclusions being contradictory, the civil lieutenant decided to go and see for himself. He did so on February 15.

On 18 February Girardin issued, and the two companies signed, an Accord et Transaction that assigned with great specificity certain rights to the Italian troupe.[59] They were to be allowed to use the dressing rooms in spite of the French claim that the original agreement did not include access to them. They were to pay promptly half the rent and half of the "charges," that is, taxes for street lights and other civic services. They were permitted to install, below the galleries used by the French for their machines, two stone corbels protruding eight inches and mortised to accept the two joists which the Italians had been supporting on the galleries. The "joists" were the heart of the issue, the pieces of wood which "encumbered" the galleries, and put them in "imminent peril." The Italians were enjoined to have the joists taken down every day after the play was finished. The corbels were also to be installed under the rafters of the galleries in such a way as not to impede the operation of the French counterweights.

After various other admonitions—not to use the French scenes or machines, not to leave anything leaning against or on top of the French machines—the Italians were granted permission to use "whatever decors and machines they find apropos within the area of the stage up to the first of the two borders which are beyond the sea." But they were enjoined from making any openings between "the arbor of Circé" and the border. The "arbor of Circé" was a very complicated machine that rose from the floor, had ten bronze figures that moved, and a fountain with a jet. The French clearly wanted it in place and left alone so long as *Circé* was in the repertory. The Italians were also to avoid all machines in place under the stage and make sure that their own machines and decorations were taken out of the way immediately after each performance, so that the stage would be free for the French to use during all of the following day.

The Italians were to be permitted to have machines for changing decors beneath the stage, provided they made no new traps and placed their machinery in such a way as not to impinge upon, encumber, or displace the equipment belonging to the French.

La Grange hailed this as total victory. He wrote later in a note added to his *Registre* for 1673 that "the Italians were restrained to the simple use of the stage, loges and amphithéâtre without the right to innovate or use machines and obliged to take away each evening whatever they used for their performance, in order to leave the stage free to the French." In fact, the Italians were permitted some spectacle, but under conditions difficult to meet.

By August, the French victory was a hollow one. The two French troupes had been merged by royal fiat—"You will doubtless be surprised when I tell you . . . ," writes Donneau de Visé—and the Italians, for the first time since 1658, found themselves sole tenants of a Paris theatre, the Hôtel de Bourgogne. There is no way to prove that the founding of the Comédie-Française was in any way related to the plight of the Italians at the Guénégaud, but it certainly worked to their advantage, and one can easily imagine Dominique, who still had the king's ear, setting to work to free the troupe from its intolerable situation.

CHAPTER *8*

The Stable Company

THE ITALIAN TROUPE in Paris remained stable from 1668 to 1680. Although two important actors died and were replaced, the balance of the company remained the same: two amoureux, two amoureuses, two zanni, a servante, a vieillard, a capitan, and Scaramouche. This conventional cast of characters played a repertory increasingly weighted toward farce and fantasy, and both Capitan Spezzafer and Scaramouche usually functioned as zanni. Lacking a Pantalon, and with an aging First Amoureuse, the troupe employed single rather than double Plautine romance plots, which were often, in any case, pretexts for travesties and comic eccentric routines. As we have seen, this new repertory was largely devised by a newcomer to the company, Marc' Antonio Romagnesi.

When Giacinto Bendinelli died in March 1668, Marc' Antonio Romagnesi, Cinthio, who was to become a valuable member of the troupe as both actor and author, was already in Paris and ready to replace him. The son of Brigida Fedele and her first husband, an actor named Romagnesi, Marc' Antonio Romagnesi was born in Verona, according to his letters of naturalization, probably in 1633. He claimed to be fifty-three in 1692, but since he was married on 31 March 1653, that seems unlikely.[1] Actors then as now habitually pretended to be younger than they were.

The Romagnesi family's connection with the commedia dell'arte dates from at least 1612, when an earlier Marc' Antonio, who played Pantalone, was mentioned in a letter from Cecchini to the duke of Mantua. A second Romagnesi, also a Marc' Antonio, played the amoroso as Cinzio around 1620.[2] This Cinzio might well have been "Cinthio" Romagnesi's father. According to Rasi, the younger Marc' Antonio Romagnesi was educated in Italy at the Collegio Clementino in Rome and first heard of as an actor in 1655 when he was requested by the duke of Modena.[3]

In 1653, in Bologna, he married Elisabetta Giulia Della Chiesa, who was never an actress according to Gueullette.[4] Rasi was not impressed by the idea that she might have been the daughter of Girolamo Chiesa, who played Dottore, and his wife Isabella, who played a donna, although the dates are approximately right and the couple had connections to Bologna.[5] If Romagnesi's wife had been an actress in Italy, then she might be a candidate for the mysterious Isabella mentioned by Robinet on 15

September 1668 as a member of the cast of *Le remède à tous maux* and included in the cast list and notes of *Le monde reversé* in 1669. Isabella replaced Eularia in the first of the plays mentioned above (Robinet mentioned a week earlier that "Olaria" had no role in it) and Aurelia in the second. The two plays were produced a year apart, so "Isabelle" was not simply a tryout or someone travelling through Paris. Given Orsola Cortesi's string of pregnancies and Brigida Fedele's increasing age, the company—which had no room for another amoureuse—may, none the less, have been happy to have someone to stand in on occasion.

Elisabetta Giulia Della Chiesa was herself often pregnant. Jal found baptismal records of four Romagnesi children born in Paris: Pierre, born 23 September 1667, before his father was admitted to the troupe; Charlotte-Marguerite, baptised 30 April, 1669; Charles-Virgile, born 7 March 1670; and Marguerite-Mathilde, baptised 28 August 1671.[6] Other children, probably born in Italy, included Hipolite, Gaetan, Hierôme-Alexandre, and Auguste-Alexandre.

Romagnesi's son, Charles-Virgile, sieur de Belmont, who played an amoureux in the Italian troupe in the 1690s, married Elisabeth Costantini, the daughter of another troupe member. It was Romagnesi's daughter-in-law who was Gueullette's informant about the family. According to her, Hipolite became the provincial of the Dominican order in Rome; Gaetan, like his brother Charles-Virgile, became an actor, though not in Paris, and died in Brussels in 1700 leaving nine children; Hierôme-Alexandre was a professor of the Italian language in Paris who went insane and died in Charanton; and Auguste-Alexandre was in service to the duke of Mantua. Mlle. de Belmont offered no information on Pierre or the daughters, which suggests they may have died young.[7]

Romagnesi's wife died relatively young as well, in London when the Italians were performing there in 1675. Though the father of a large family of small children, he apparently did not remarry. In 1694, when Lolli retired, he took over the role of the Docteur and played it until the troupe was disbanded in 1697. After the death of Biancolelli in 1688, Romagnesi was one of the troupe members most responsible for its well-being; he was, for instance, the one entrusted with finding replacements for actors who died or left the company.

Cotelendi wrote that Romagnesi was a "good philosopher, learned in letters, a charming conversationalist, with polished manners and proper feelings."[8] Riccoboni, whose attitudes toward the baroque commedia dell'arte have influenced so many scholars, called him "the last of the amoureux with wit and learning."[9] Like most of those in his line of business, Romagnesi published a book to establish his credentials as a humanist scholar and artist. A book of verse, it was entitled *Poésies héroïques et amoureuses, sacrées et morales,* published in Paris in 1673.

Romagnesi served the company as "playwright," or deviser of scenarios, from at least 1668 to 1674. Robinet identifies seven of the entries in Biancolelli's zibaldone as by Cinthio, son of Aurelia, but it seems probable that most of the plays of the period are his unless otherwise identified by author. The plays performed after May 1668 cannot be matched with certainty to extant Italian scenarios.[10] They must, then, be the product either of members of the company or of people like Girardin, the inventor of *Le collier de perle,* and the unidentified Monsieur S. who was responsible for *Les trompeurs trompez* and *Arlequin et Scaramouche juifs errans de Babilonne.* According to Robinet, Angelo Agostino Lolli was the author of one scenario in 1670, but Cinthio, he says with questionable exaggeration, "furnishes [the troupe] a new one every week without any difficulty."[11] The seven attributed to Romagnesi by Robinet are *Le remède à tous maux* (September 1668), *Les métamorphoses d'Arlequin* (March 1669), *Le soldat par vengeance [La femme guerrière]* (June 1669), *Arlequin esprit follet* (March 1670), *Les jugemens du duc d'Ossone* (June 1671), *A fourbe, fourbe et demi* (October 1674), and *Arlequin berger de Lemnos* (November 1674.) Others that may well be his, judging by their structure and content, include *Le théâtre sans comédie* (July 1668), *Arlequin vallet enchanté, singe et Margot la pie* (1670 or 1671), *Arlequin roy par hazard* (1673), *Le voyage de Scaramouche et d'Arlequin aux Indes* (1676), *La propreté, ou Arlequin roy de Tripoli* (July 1677), and *La magie naturelle* (December 1678). It is tempting to assign him the authorship of *Le régal des dames,* since he had entered the company some six weeks before it was played. But according to Robinet it was written by "a clever anonymous gentleman, said to be of the quality."

Although Romagnesi was educated in Rome, it seems likely that he spent at least some of his childhood and youth in France. His mother was there for a year in the 1640s and for several years in the 1650s before becoming established in Paris in 1662. But whatever his background, Marc' Antonio Romagnesi's debut as actor and playwright marked the beginning of the adaptation to French taste that was to keep the company profitable and successful for the next thirty years.

This new repertory designed to appeal to the French public may have been what prompted Tiberio Fiorilli to return to Italy at the end of the 1667–68 season, apparently to stay. His replacement, Girolamo Cei, is first mentioned by Robinet on 21 April and appears in Biancolelli's notes for the first time in *Le régal.* Long unknown to scholars, in spite of the fact that La Grange mentions him in his *Registre,* the facts of Cei's life remain mysterious. Since neither Gueullette nor the Parfaict brothers knew his name, neither Jal in France nor Rasi in Italy looked for information about him. His birth, antecedents, marriage, children—all are unknown. Only his death was recorded, and that by a French actor: "Gieronimo Cey, known as Spezzafer, Italian actor and a good actor, died the beginning of April 1685."[12]

Robinet devoted a number of lines to Cei's debut, pointing out his similarities to and differences from Fiorilli:

> He played his role not so badly,
> And, by my faith, I found him droll.
> I never felt, in truth,
> My sense of humor more excited
> Than by his tricks
> And naive monkeyshines.
> Far from being tongue-tied,
> He has a glib chatter,
>
>   · · · · ·
>
> Talks enough for six,
> Or even for ten.
> For the rest, aside from a little less height,
> He's the living picture of his famous predecessor,
> It's him, the spitting image, face,
> Gesture, air, general appearance,
> Same tone of voice,
> Same beautiful ivory teeth.

According to Robinet, more than 2,000 spectators came to see him and stayed to laugh.[13]

When *Le régal des dames* opened, the "New Scaramouche" was featured, but in the role of an old man who wanted to marry his young ward. If the troupe had had a Pantalon, this would have been a Pantalon role. Robinet again praises him, saying that Arlequin, Trivelin, and Scaramouche would make a stump laugh. Two pedestals danced, he tells us, and so did Scaramouche, although "his body was not very slender." A very good Bonnart print shows Cei as Capitan Spezzafer, and although he was hardly fat, he did have a distinct belly (fig. 8).

Capitan Spezzafer was the role Cei adopted after Fiorilli returned to Paris in the fall of 1670. He appeared in almost all the plays included by

FIG. *8. Girolamo Cei, Capitan Spezzafer. Engraving by*
Bonnart. (Bibliothéque de l'Opéra, Ms. Rés. 625; phot. Bibl. Nat. Paris)

Biancolelli in his zibaldone, but rarely as a conventional capitan. He was rather a serviceable zanni, a kind of second banana to Arlequin and Scaramouche.

Several of his signatures exist on documents of the company. He may have served as secretary or treasurer in 1683 and 1684, when he signed receipts for payment of the royal pensions. Clearly not a star like some of his colleagues, he appears to have been a useful and faithful member of the troupe for seventeen years. The only anecdote about him to survive also is related to his death. Cotolendi writes: "When Capitan Spezzafer died, he was spoken of at Versailles. Monsieur M***, His Majesty's physician, remarked that he had been found to greatly resemble the actor. 'You are wrong,' replied the Prince de ****. He never killed anyone." [14] Not an inappropriate epitaph for a commedia dell'arte capitan.

Three years after Bendinelli's death, on 26 April 1671, Domenico Locatelli died. Tralage quotes from the *Nouvelles de Paris,* 1 May 1671: "Poor Trivelin is dead. He left a legacy of 6,000 livres." He was buried at the Augustins.[15] Locatelli was replaced briefly in the troupe by an actor who played Briguelle. He was introduced by Robinet on 13 June 1671 and is mentioned by Biancolelli in four entries: *Les jugemens du duc d'Ossone, L'hypocrite, Le collier de perle* and *Arlequin roy par hazard.* The last of these, though undated, was after *Suite du festin de pierre* in February 1673, so Briguelle probably played for two seasons. An engraving by Marinette may memorialize Locatelli's death and the debut of his replacement (fig. 9). According to Gueullette, the new actor also died; the king then asked the duke of Modena to send "Giuseppe" Cimadori, by whom he probably means Giovan Andrea Cimadori, who played First Zanni as Finocchio. Cimadori died in Lyons on the way to Paris, or so Riccoboni told Gueullette;[16] but this was another of Riccoboni's many errors, since Cimadori was in the troupe of Modena in 1675 and 1676. In fact, a letter from the duke to the abbé Riccini in Paris in September 1684 explains why Cimardori cannot be sent at that point and includes a doctor's testimony that the actor is ill with asthma and a tendency to dropsy.[17] From the date we can infer that Cimadori was being asked for to replace Giovanni Gherardi, the First Zanni who made his debut in late 1674 or early 1675 and died in 1683.

That there was a gap in 1674 can be demonstrated by two scenarios, *Addition au triomphe de la médecine* (May 1674), and *A fourbe, fourbe et demy* (October 1674), in both of which Spezzafer plays First Zanni. In the full scenario of the latter, to be found in BN Ms. 9329, Spezzafer is even listed in the cast as "man of intrigue" and enters for the first time saying that

FIG. *9*. *Domenico Locatelli, Trivelin* (right) *and an unidentified Briguelle* (left). *Engraving by Marinette.* (Bibliothèque de l'Opéra, Ms. Rés. 625; phot. Bibl. Nat. Paris)

"he has thought of a trick to get the key." [18] Robinet first mentions Gio-vanni Gherardi, Flautin, in his letter of 5 January 1675, although the play, *Arlequin berger de Lemnos,* had opened in early November 1674. Flautin is not named by Biancolelli, although it seems likely that he and Cei played the two zanni, Silvano and Flaminio. Because the play is a "heroic-comic pastoral," the comic characters use pastoral names; Diamantine, for in-stance, plays Lizette. Biancolelli also gives no indication of where, in this production, Gherardi performed the routine for which he was known and named. Robinet describes it, though: "without flute or pipe, in short with no instrument whatever, he makes come out of his throat alone a whole consort of flutes."

In *Le voyage de Scaramouche et d'Arlequin aux Indes,* Biancolelli in-cludes one of the comic routines developed to take advantage of this peculiar talent:

> In the act of the Turk, Flautin says he will give me a flute and Scar-amouche a bass by means of which we will obtain our freedom from the Sultan ... I carry the flute to my mouth, Flaminio [i.e., Flautin] behind me plays it, I imagine that I am producing the tune and I am delighted. Scaramouche plays the bass, a devil who is behind him does the same lazzi. Flautin gives me a paper and tells me to put it along side of my ear and I will sing marvelously. I open my mouth and a soprano behind me sings a song. I am so charmed I kiss myself with satisfaction and we retire. The Sultan enters, Scaramouche tells me to advance ... I say I am a virtuoso, the Sultan orders me to sit, I take his turban and make a stool of it, then I blow into the flute. A Turk behind me sounds a cow's horn. The Sultan, in a rage, orders me to be empaled. [19]

A well-known Bonnart print of Giovanni Gherardi shows him with a guitar, the typical property of First Zanni. [20]

Gherardi was a native of Spoleto. [21] His date of birth is unknown. He married Leonarda Galli and had at least one son, Evaristo Gherardi, born in Prato in 1664, who played Arlequin in Paris after the death of Domenico Biancolelli and collected and published the troupe's French repertory.

Giovanni Gherardi is the subject of one of the oddest legends of all the many that have been repeated about the members of the Paris com-pany. According to Gueullette, he was "put in prison for some dishonor-able adventure," which explains why his son, Evaristo, never mentions him in *Le théâtre italien.* [22]

The Parfaict brothers expand this tale: "Gherardi stayed for only a short time on the stage, not because he did not give pleasure as an actor, but because his depraved manners caused some unfortunate business which put him in prison. He got out, but doubtless on the condition he leave France."[23] Campardon adds a qualifying "very" to the description of his manners.[24] Rasi is sorry that the promising career of this admired and applauded actor was broken off.[25] Spada quotes Rasi.[26]

In fact, Giovanni Gherardi played in Paris from the beginning of 1675 until his death on 22 March 1683, a fact reported by Jal in 1867. He was buried at St.-André-des-Arts on 23 March.[27] On 15 May the troupe paid his widow, Leonarda Galli, 2,250 livres for six quarters of royal pension owing him.[28] His son Evaristo did not mention him either because Flautin did not play in French or because his roles had long been taken by other actors by the time the young Gherardi joined the troupe.

Although Flautin was a First Zanni whose costume was almost indistinguishable from that of Briguelle or Scapin, he did not usually play a fourbe intrigant in Paris. Biancolelli, during this period after Trivelin's death, played most of his scenes with Scaramouche as the titles of the period indicate: *Arlequin et Scaramouche juifs errans de Babilonne, Le voyage de Scaramouche et d'Arlequin aux Indes.* Flautin is mentioned in the zibaldone, but rather in the same way as Giaratoni; both names underlined as Biancolelli often did with gagistes. In the zanni pecking order of the troupe, Flautin came after both Scaramouche and Spezzafer, perhaps because he was limited as an actor, but more likely because the troupe had become accustomed to filling in for a missing First Zanni with the actors at hand. In later plays, Flautin has a more active role.

Three early plays of the new repertory call for a Pantalon. Biancolelli mentions the character twice, in a one-paragraph fragment of *Le chevallier de l'industrie* (1670) and in *Arlequin roy par hazard* (1673). In the latter piece, Pantalon is one of the two councillors of the king. Pantalon is also introduced by Robinet on 8 March 1670, in his letter describing *Arlequin esprit follet.* Dominique does not mention the character in his notes for that play, but the scenario from Ms. 9329 includes a vieillard who is also referred to as Pantalon.

The only information about this new Pantalon is Gueullette's story, probably unfounded as most of them prove to be, that Louis XIV sent to the duke of Modena around 1670 to ask for a Pantalon. According to Luigi Riccoboni, who was Gueullette's usually misinformed informant some seventy years later, the duke proposed his own Pantalone, Luigi's father Antonio, but "accompanied this proposal with such affectionate terms for Riccoboni that the actor . . . begged the duke for the favor of remaining in his service."[29] Possibly Antonio Riccoboni did play in Paris at least briefly around 1670, although the earliest record of him in Italy dates from 1674. Whoever the Pantalon, he did not stay for long, but lack of a Pantalon seems not to have been a problem for the Paris troupe, then or later, since Pantalons were always temporary. One vieillard sufficed for the neo-Plautine scenarios still in the repertory, while the pastorals and more exotic pieces often did without one at all.

For the other members of the troupe, the period was in general without incident. Brigida Fedele, who was aging, played less frequently than the Second Amoureuse, Orsola Cortesi, at least insofar as can be estimated from Biancolelli's notes. He and his wife were busy with their numerous offspring. Giovan Andrea Zanotti's first wife, Teodora Blasi, died in 1668 and he remarried a French woman, Marguerite Enguerant d'Abville. They had seven children according to Rasi: five baptised at St.-Germain and two at St.-Sauveur.[30] Jal found only one child, baptised 5 February 1677 at Ste.-Chapelle.[31] Lolli became increasingly important as the single vieillard in the company; in 1670 he devised the scenario for *Le gentilhomme campagnard,* a fairly traditional play with Arlequin in disguise as a kind of Tony Lumpkin.

The most restless member of the company remained Tiberio Fiorilli who left Paris at the end of the season in 1668. In 1669 he was in Rome, playing in a public theatre but also, from time to time, for the queen of Sweden. The same year, according to an unpublished Florentine diary, "a great storm in the Val d'Arno killed the son of an actor and buffoon named Scaramuccia."[32] This must have been Charles-Louis, canon of the Cathedral of Troyes, since Silvio was still living at the time of his father's death in 1694.

When Fiorilli returned to Paris in 1670, he definitely left his wife behind. His liaison with Marie Duval will be discussed in a later chapter, but he may have found solace in an earlier irregular union with someone named Anne Doffon. Jal found a record of the baptism at St.-Germain l'Auxerrois of "Tibère François, son of Tibère Fiorilly, Neapolitan, officer of the king, and of Mlle. Anne Doffon, his wife, rue de l'Arbre sec." Jal has copied the date as 8 November 1693,[33] but that seems most unlikely. In 1693 Fiorilli was well over eighty and thoroughly embroiled with his second wife; he was also living in the rue Tiquetonne, parish of St.-Eustache. Rasi reports the date as 1673, which seems more reasonable. Nothing more is known of Tibère François or his mother, who was certainly not Fiorilli's wife. Lorenza Elisabetta del Campo lived on in Florence until 1688.

Fiorilli, so far as is known, did not return to Italy after 1670. He was an extremely active member of the troupe. He is mentioned in all but three of the entries in Dominique's zibaldone from the time of his return, and two of those merely record speeches for Arlequin. In the third, *Arlequin roy par hazard*, Pantalon is listed, playing the sort of role Scaramouche often played. For the most part, Fiorilli played a zanni, as he had done in the 1650s in *La Rosaura imperatrice* and, probably, the first run of *Le festin de pierre*. He also played a vieillard from time to time, if more than one was needed.

Although Fiorilli did not return to Italy, he also did not remain exclusively in France. He was not only in England with the troupe in 1673 and 1675, he was there without it in 1678.

Giuseppe Giaratoni, though still a gagiste, began to introduce what was to become his role, the "valet balourd," Pierrot, whom the French adopted as their own and rechristened Gilles. The character name first appears in the zibaldone in the *Suite du festin de pierre* (1673) and reappears from time to time from then on, although sometimes Dominique merely refers to "Giaraton." Pierrot was often seen with Flautin, the two perhaps reflecting the traditional zanni roles in a company which had—for various reasons—ceased to feature them. According to Riccoboni,

> the Pierrot was born in Paris, in the troupe of the Italian actors, predecessors of those of today. It is the costume and the character of the Neapolitan Pulchinello, a little disguised.
>
> At the death of Trivelin, who was the Arlequin of the king's troupe, the famous Dominique took over the costume. Then the character of Arlequin changed on the French stage. From time immemorial Arlequin had been ignorant. Trivelin, the predecessor of Dominique, had not altered the character. When he died, Dominique, who was a man of wit and learning, recognized . . . the nature of the nation which loves wit, and decided to use the puns and sallies suitable to Arlequin.[34]

Riccoboni is wrong again. Obviously, Biancolelli did not take over the role of Arlequin when Locatelli died, and Arlequin remains witless throughout the zibaldone. His puns and sallies are mostly the typical imbroglios of earlier years, perhaps with an occasional touch of wise fool, and he continues to delight in farts and pratfalls. Yet because of the emphasis on travesty in the post-1668 repertory, and because of the importance of the pastorals and exotic plays, Arlequin gradually ceases to play patsy to First Zanni's bully. What disappears first is the function these characters served in the romance plots of the neo-Plautine comedies. Arlequin is less frequently a valet, or if a valet, usually in disguise, and the intrigues devised by the zanni on their own behalf or on behalf of their masters are excuses for extended comic routines.

Pierrot is almost always a valet, so there may be a germ of truth in Riccoboni's contention that Giaratoni, "seeing that the Italian theatre had lost the character of the ignorant valet, contrived to make him live again." But most of that transformation would take place later, when Evaristo Gherardi and French playwrights writing for the troupe in the 1690s developed the nontraditional Arlequin described by Riccoboni. Pierrot's increased importance came largely after Dominique's death in 1688, and the character, like most of the characters of the Gherardi repertory of French plays, is marked by inconsistency. Through 1680 Giaratoni remained a gagiste, with the exception of the fact that he now, unlike his fellows, played a masque.

The addition of Marc' Antonio Romagnesi was the single most important change in the composition of the Italian troupe between 1668 and 1680. Not only did he provide scenarios in the French taste, he introduced an amoureux who could participate in a variety of ways, not just as an eloquent swain, and who was later to develop the very important character of the French bourgeois vieillard. The rest of the troupe began to divide itself into those who would eventually play in French—Biancolelli, Lolli, Giaratoni—and those who would not. The actors had the advantage of adaptability; their talent for improvisation enabled them to set a new course built on old strengths.

The New Repertory

THE NEW REPERTORY the Italians introduced in 1668 is known to us largely though not exclusively from the zibaldone of Domenico Biancolelli. While the new repertory continued to employ many of the traditional elements of the commedia dell'arte, it also introduced innovations in both form and content designed to appeal specifically to the Parisian audience.

The forty-five entries in Biancolelli's zibaldone beginning with *Le régal des dames,* May 1668, include twenty-three that are complete enough to be valuable for analysis of the new repertory. The other twenty-two are fragments that record a lazzi or two or, somewhat more usefully, a harangue, or set speech. Seven of the entertainments noted by Biancolelli are attributed to Marc' Antonio Romagnesi by the gazetteer Robinet. Eleven, including two of those ascribed to Romagnesi, are allied to French scenarios included in Ms. 9329 of the Bibliothèque Nationale.[1] Several scenes, distorted versions of action and dialogue found in the zibaldone and in Ms. 9329, also appear in pirated editions of the Italian troupe's French repertory published in Brussells, Geneva, and Amsterdam.[2] None of these materials, with very minor exceptions, can be connected to any extant Italian scenarios.[3] This underscores the break with tradition that took place in France in 1668.

Although Gueullette's translation of Biancolelli's zibaldone remains the most valuable source for a reconstruction of the new repertory, the scenarios in Ms. 9329 are also important because they make it possible to accommodate the fragmentary but specific notes of the zibaldone to the complete but generalized scenarios of the manuscript. They also enable us to gauge the share which Arlequin's action—as described in Biancolelli's notes—had in the total structure. Ms. 9329 is of uncertain provenance and was apparently unknown to Gueullette and the Parfaict brothers. It is first mentioned in the catalogue of the Soleinne collection established by Paul Lacroix at the end of the nineteenth century.[4] The scenarios are, for the most part, outlines of the intrigues, generalized and lacking in detail. Although they are written in French, there is no justification for assuming that they represent material played in French. When the troupe included French dialogue in its productions, the actors worked from written texts. There was no reason for them to use scenarios in a language other than Italian.

The scenarios in Ms. 9329 are hard to date with accuracy, but cast lists suggest that they are related to performances that took place between 1675, when Flautin, who is included in the cast lists of three of the scenarios, made his debut, and 1695, when Françoise Biancolelli, Isabelle, who is featured in seventeen of them, left the troupe. Three of the plays represented by these French scenarios were performed at Versailles in the 1690s according to court financial records, but the practice of refurbishing the repertory makes it impossible to fix precise correlations between titles mentioned in passing and specific extant versions. Nevertheless, the existence of scenarios that extend our understanding of the total action of eleven of Biancolelli's entries cannot be ignored.

The question of materials from pirated editions of scenes in French from the Italian troupe's repertory will be dealt with in chapter 12 when the Gherardi collection is described in detail. These editions do include a few scenes in French that apparently are based on material played earlier in Italian, useful in establishing that the Italians retained and renovated their repertory. But the materials contained in these unauthorized printings are so obviously defective that there is little justification for using them to reconstruct and analyze the company's performances.[5]

Le régal des dames, which opened in early May 1668, was the first piece to depart from the conventional midcentury Italian repertory. Its production was an event of such magnitude that Robinet devoted 122 lines to it on 5 May. Dominique's notes for his role are unusually complete, and the Parfaict brothers' summary seems to be based not only on those notes but on other information as well, perhaps a printed synopsis like those Gueullette found for *Le collier de perle* and *Le voyage de Scaramouche et d'Arlequin aux Indes.* As a result of this unusual amount of documentation, it is possible to reconstruct *Le régal* with some precision and notice its deviations from the repertory that preceded it.[6]

The plot is traditional. Scaramouche is an old man with two wards, Aurelia and Eularia. He wants to appropriate their property and marry the younger. Their lovers, Octave and Cinthio, aided by their valets, invent various schemes to gain access to the two women, most of which feature Arlequin in disguise. In one scene he enters as a chimney sweep showing a "curiosity"; in another he comes on disguised as "an Italian gentleman native of Metz in the Lorraine." In still another he is *en marquis* and invites Scaramouche and his daughters to take the air at the foire St.-Germain, where he appears to them as the slight-of-hand artist Brioché. In the last act Arlequin disguises himself as a policeman and arrests Scaramouche for murder, then enters as the magistrate to conduct the trial. Scaramouche agrees to the marriages of the amoureux and the amoureuses in order to save his life.

It was during the scene at the fair that the troupe introduced many of the elements of spectacle that were to be characteristic of the new repertory. "In this scene," writes Dominique,

> I enter disguised as Brioché (famous puppeteer), I do the trick of the egg that I pretend to find in the sack; I say someone should bring me the table, during this time I do lazzi with Scaramouche, take him by the nose, throw him in the air, finally attach a padlock to his mouth . . . I say . . . that I have studied astrology and know how to draw up horoscopes and that I am going to show the ladies their heart's desires, but the other people must move back. I tell Aurelia to turn aside with Scaramouche, I say then that with my "powder of perlin, pin, pin" Eularia is going to see marvels. Octave appears and speaks to Eularia and kisses her hands after having assured her of his passion. I send Eularia to be with Scaramouche and have Aurelia come near and I make Cinthio appear the same way. Scaramouche is impatient and asks if I cannot give him the same satisfaction. I have him approach and I knock on the table; a pair of horns appears.

Brioché then continues with his magic tricks of the goblets, most of which are simple and require only the use of traps.[7] The combination of the "little miracles" with music, dance, and the use of a locale and personality known to the audience combine to set this scene apart from what had come before.

The first known use of French by the Italians in Paris also occurred in *Le régal* in a drinking song attributed by Robinet to "a certain author, in music past master, and . . . a man adept at beautiful words as well." The song, entitled "La chanson du ramoneur," may have been notable for its music; its lyrics are hardly the work of a master:

> Paye chopine ma voisine
> paye chopine, et moy un pot
> pour bien boire ce n'est pas trop
> chacun paye, paye, paye, paye
> pour bien boire ce n'est pas trop
> chacun paye son écot.

or, roughly,

> Pay for your pint, my neighbor,
> Pay for your pint, and pay for mine,

> It's not too much to drink good wine,
> Everyone pay, pay, pay, pay,
> It's not too much to drink good wine,
> Everyone pay his share.

Le régal also introduces a new kind of role for Biancolelli. Although the valet disguised as his master is a commonplace of the conventional commedia dell'arte, the aristocratic travesty in *Le régal des dames* is closer to Molière's Mascarille, a burlesque of the French *petit marquis* as well as a plot device.

Before *Le régal*, Dominique's gentleman travesties are simple transparent facades through which shines the true nature of Arlequin: greedy, naive, and stupid. He has trouble with his costumes, as in *Le capricieux*, when his cloak falls off and he puts his hat on backwards. He has trouble with whatever language he is meant to speak, as in *Le baron allemand*. He is easily distracted, even when in love; in *Le prisonnier vindicatif*, for instance, he enters looking for the girl he loves, but hunger overtakes him and he asks for truffles instead.

Beginning with *Le régal des dames*, however, Arlequin adopts the more specific travesty of the Parisian *petit marquis*, not only in imitation of French comic subject matter but also in order to burlesque that element of the theatre audience. He remains naive and stupid. In *Le régal* his interests are still scatological. He asks Scaramouche for permission to visit the latter's invalid wife who is about to take an enema, since he has never observed that pleasant event. When the ladies enter, he begins to engage in gallantry; he tries to give Eularia his wig when she compliments him on it, then he snatches her handkerchief from her after she has blown her nose, blows his, and neatly folds and returns the handkerchief.

Typical of Dominique's *petit marquis* is verbal imbroglio, which usually appears when he is romancing an amoureuse. In *Les trompeurs trompez*, for example, his compliment begins: "You appear so beautiful to me that one would take you for the nurse of Remus and Romulus . . . Oh, your beautiful white teeth, one would take them for rubies."[8] Besides using verbal burlesque, Biancolelli also parodies the behavior of the *petits maîtres*. In *Le gentilhomme campagnard* he attempts a gentleman's exercises—dancing, fencing, and horsemanship. When he mounts the horse (wooden), he uses a chair and ends up facing the tail.[9] In *Le monde renversé* he is escorting Eularia when they are accosted by a bravo. He says "I'll give her to you, her name is Eularia," and runs away.[10] The parody extends to costume as well. In *Le baron de Foeneste* Arlequin explains what happened to his most beautiful suit: "I told my tailor to garnish it with straw-colored ribbons according to the fashion. He so covered it with so many narrow ribbons that the fabric wasn't visible. I wore the outfit into the stable to see my horses, the coachman had not given them their hay, and my horses, who were dying of hunger, took me for a bale of straw and nearly devoured me."[11] One scene in particular in *Le régal* exemplifies the merger of conventional commedia dell'arte plotting with a more sophisticated, Moliéresque comic conception. Arlequin tells Scaramouche that, as a joke, he will introduce the amoureuses to his valet, a lunatic who thinks that every woman who sees him falls in love with him. He calls in Octave, who enters and makes violent love to Eularia. Arlequin pretends to be furious with his "valet," threatening him with death, but Scaramouche, the dupe, laughs and reminds Arlequin that this is only a joke.

Le régal includes a number of French and Parisian references and is explicitly set in Paris. This is not necessarily the case with the plays that follow in the zibaldone, although many implicitly take place there. Few of the plays are set in Italy, and although the characters remain Italian, they become more generalized, Italian but not Bolognese or Venetian. Italian dialect humor, a standby of the commedia dell'arte, is replaced by German or Swiss or Spanish dialect humor, while slighting ethnic references to Neapolitans or Genoese become Norman or Gascon jokes.

Beginning with the play that followed *Le régal* in July 1668, the Italians began to use French on stage, but in very limited ways. The principal French ornament to be found in the zibaldone is the harangue, or set speech, delivered by Arlequin in the language of his adopted nation. In Romagnesi's *Le théâtre sans comédie* Arlequin delivers a "Panégiric de Scaramouche," dead of a dose of emetic wine.[12] Octave and Cinthio order him to make the speech and a gypsy sorceress promises to help him. He "composes" his discourse with the aid of an almanac and a Cicero from which he learns the elements of rhetoric, the formula of who, what, where, by what means, why, how, and when.

When his notes are finished, he tears them into tiny pieces and makes a soup of them, cooks the soup for a moment, tastes it, and adds a few pages of Aristotle for seasoning. He then drinks the soup and with his memory thus primed launches into the panegyric, a parody of learned discourse, full of misapplied classical references and Latin tags. The panegyric was not written out in the zibaldone by Biancolelli, but—according to Gueullette—"was written in a strange hand and with good spelling not seen elsewhere in the Italian manuscript."[13] Gueullette suggests that the harangue may have been written by Fatouville, who wrote scenes with a legal flavor in French for the troupe in the 1680s. More likely, it was written either by the "anonymous gentleman" who created *Le régal,* according to Robinet, or by Marc' Antonio Romagnesi himself.

The speech is long and nonsensical. A short selection will suffice to show its qualities:

> When Hannibal wanted to force Carthage (*here Scaramouche . . . sleeps and snores*) . . . What's that, gentlemen, you sleep at the most beautiful place in my speech, Oh, please, allow me to rap the knuckles of your attention with a thought of the wise Epictetus. This great man in his *Enchiridion,* reflecting on the prerogatives of Scaramouche, let fall from his pen this wise and incomparable proverb: (E) *Enea ton pardon Scaramouchias massacrine eis de mangar alla doctorias impicandon.*
>
> I (M) could make a tumbril full of reflections on this magnificent subject, but Cicero has stopped my mouth when he says in *De oratore:* Clavus clavum pellit. That being so, let us leave, gentlemen, let us go out from this tribunal of doctrine for fear that the heat of my learning will make me fall into some learned pleurisy.
>
> I already feel my eloquence congested, I feel my memory constipated, finally I feel that my *capacità retive* wants, in spite of me, to take me home [i.e., he is as hungry as a horse].
>
> Thus to collect myself (I descend from my podium) I allege in the forms of episode and parenthesis (E) that death is frightening, that you, that I, that Paris, that nature . . . (I pretend to be unable to find the rest of my discourse) (I) I sustain thus that there is reason to protest against and declare the emetic wine imperious, unreasonable, and cruel, and that is what I conclude and without costs. Dixi.[14]

This harangue burlesques the law while most of the others, done by Arlequin disguised as a charlatan, follow Molière in parodying medicine. The first of these is the "Discours du médecin indien" in *Le remède à tous maux* (September 1668) by Romagnesi. The Indian Doctor is selling the famous "powder of perlin, pin, pin" which Brioché was hawking five months earlier in *Le régal.* Arlequin enters, "mounted on an ass decked out with plumes, leading another animal bearing a flag." He says:

> You are astonished, gentlemen, to see me in this place, mounted on this animal, and with this other that I lead by hand, but know that this one, upon which I sit, as Pliny said in his treatise on the secret of preventing head colds in frogs, is a butterfly of the North Indies and that this other is a stink bug from the West Indies that I found in the Great Mogul's shirt. I tell you I am a doctor, surgeon, apothecary, and barber, that I am perfectly acquainted with infirmities and mala-

dies, that I know how to heal wounds and other things to which the human body is subject, that I have proofs of my ability which renders all of my invalids very healthy if they were not dead already with nothing but my powder of perlin pin pin. Within the week I have cured a young man of fifteen of the mal de mere. Trivelin stops me and the Docteur says that only girls are subject to these sorts of maladies. I answer that he is wrong, that his mother hit him violently on the head with a stick, which can certainly be called a mal de mere.[15]

Although Gueullette does not specifically indicate that this discourse was delivered in French, it must have been since the pun depends on the similarity of *mer* (sea) and *mère* (mother) and does not work in Italian where "sea" is *mere* and "mother" is *madre*. The harangue continues with a list of ridiculous uses for the famous powder, "salutary for all nations imaginable, Greeks, Chaldeans, Hebrews, Milanese, and Bergamasques, and in good French it is what for more than a century has been called the unguent *miton mitaine*." The speech concludes with Arlequin saying that his powder can cure anything but illnesses under the signs of Taurus and Capricorn which "are incurable because they attack the head." The act ends after the harangue with a ballet entry of cripples who are cured by the magic powder.

Dominique remained popular as the charlatan. In *La gagure* (1677 or 1678), ten years later, the harangue is much the same. The charlatan pronounces himself well traveled; he has seen the Louvre in Madrid and the Escurial in Paris, the pyramids of Chaillot and the turnips of Vaugirard. His remedy cures everything from sciatica to hydrophobia, from plague to amputation, from damnation to worms. It also kills wolves, although catching the wolf is not the doctor's responsibility.[16]

In *Arlequin médecin d'eau douce* (1670 or 1671), the harangue—this time identified by Gueullette as having been written out in French—is a parody of an address to the Faculty of Medicine with references to Hippocrates and a pharmaceutical vocabulary reminiscent of the apothecary's bill which opens *Le malade imaginaire*. Arlequin speaks of "scammony, colocynthe, and sap to nourish, foment, and support the high and might lady Madame Fever and her retinue," and of "the Hippocratic republic which has for purpose, for aim, and for end the method of making shit, in all its dimensions, length, width, and depth."[17]

A variation of the charlatan harangue is found in *Les trompeurs trompez* when Arlequin delivers a lively mix of astrology and gastronomy:

In the heavens are the twelve signs, they are the same in the kitchen. The Ram is mutton in the kitchen, the Bull is boeuf à la mode, the

Twins are two chickens on the spit, the Crab is a bisque or a shrimp
soup. Capricorn is a venison paté, the Fish are fried sole, the Lion is
the claws of the cook who tears the meat to pieces, the Scorpion is
the hottest spices, the Scales those used in the kitchen to weigh the
meat, Saggitarius is the larding needle, Aquarius is the kitchen tap,
the Virgin is the maid who puts the pot on the fire.

Another nonmedical harangue is found in *La dot par la metempsicoʒe*
(1677 or 1678) where Arlequin elegizes his hermaphroditic ass, Margot,
the best-natured jenny in the world who, "when she meets an ass too
overloaded with hay, eats half of his burden to relieve him." The scene
that leads up to the "Eloge de la Bourique" is also interesting because it
is a mixture of Italian and French. Cinthio reads aloud a letter from Margot in Italian which Arlequin mishears and mistranslates into French. For
instance, the letter reads "Ho di morte un grand apetito, e non trovo chi
m'apra ogni vena" ("I have a great hunger to die, and can find no one
who will open a vein for me"). Arlequin hears and translates: "Elle a un
apétit à mourir, et ne trouve personne qui luy ouvre le coffre a l'avoine"
("She is dying of hunger and can find no one to open the bale of hay for
her").[18]

This lazzi is a bilingual development of a typical Italian comic routine Arlequin frequently performs. The harangue, on the other hand, continues the tradition of the set speech in French and opens with a passing
glance at the classical: "The ancient philosophers have all been of the
unanimous sentiment that death is the end of life, and, indeed, gentlemen,
there is some probability of that, but these same philosophers have said
that it is impossible for man to count the grains of sand in the sea. How
could I then, oh illustrious assembly, make the eulogy of all the remarkable qualities of my dead jenny. Oh sausage makers, lend me your
tongues." What follows is a pastiche of praises of the ash-blonde, blue-
eyed Margot by her master, who can be consoled for her loss only by the
gift of five or six suckling pigs.

The mélange of French and Italian used in *La dot* is reminiscent of
an earlier routine from *Le gentilhomme campagnard* (January 1670), a piece
devised by Angelo Agostino Lolli. In act 3 Arlequin enters "dressed one
half as a Frenchman, one-half as a Spaniard, wrapped in a long, black
cloak and with two hats on, one over the other." When the Docteur
enters, Arlequin accosts him with the French side: "Bonjour, monsieur,
are you not a M. Baloard? He answers that that is his name, I make him
a ridiculous compliment, then I reveal the other side, I speak to him in
Spanish and ask if he is the Docteur Baloard, he says yes, and me, I
continue gravely that I am Don Diego, of those Diegos as noble as the

sun, and I have come here to marry well, etc. Then I again reveal the other side and ask him in French, who is that man who was speaking to you. Do you know he had the bad manners to turn his back on me?"[19] The scene continues with a quarrel between the Frenchman and the Spaniard, with the Docteur caught in the middle.

The Docteur and Arlequin play another bilingual scene in *A fourbe, fourbe et demy* (October 1674) when the joke rests on the Docteur's supposed inability to understand French. Arlequin, disguised as a gazetteer, comes to bring a letter from the amoureux to Aurelia and Eularia, kept enclosed by their father. When the Docteur interrupts them, Arlequin begins crying "the gazette, the gazette." The Docteur wants to buy one, but Arlequin tells him that since the gazette is in French he will not understand it. The Docteur says Arlequin should read it to him and explain it in Italian. Arlequin turns first to Aurelia's window and reads:

> *From Persia, 23 August*
> Mesdames, I am sent by your lovers ... but the meeting with this old Rodrigo has constipated all my natural functions.
>   The Docteur tells me to say that in Italian. I tell him: The Great Sophy in returning from the hunt, and being warm, drank cold water which caused a terrible colic. An hour later he gave birth to a young prince who is doing very well.
> THE DOCTEUR: The Sophy gave birth to a young prince?
> ARLEQUIN: Yes, all the Sophies of Persia have this privilege.
>
> *From Milan*
> I turn to the window and pretending to read it I say: The gallants who want to marry you have sent you a note by me, but unless the Devil carries away from here that fat animal, your little papa, there is no way to give it to you.
>   The Docteur asks me for the translation of this article, I say to him in Italian: It has been heard that in the archipelago six Algerian galleys and four little Tunisian ships have defeated four squadrons of cavalry which were crossing the sea.
>   The Docteur takes the gazette from me and says, Let's see if I understand something of this French here, then he reads or pretends to read: There has arrived in this city a rascal who claims to be a gazetteer in order to carry love letters to two girls who are closely kept in their house, but the father having discovered him is going to beat him a hundred times with a stick.[20]

The audience needs to understand some Italian to get all the jokes, but the comic situation is clear without it and the punchline is in French. The

scene is both comic in itself and comic because it is self-referential, playing off the situation of the actors who both enjoyed and suffered from
bilingualism. As His Majesty's Italian actors they were expected to play
in Italian, but as residents of Paris for nearly fifteen years many were able
to act in French and were probably frustrated by restrictions that kept
them from doing so. Within seven years, French playwrights would begin
to write scenes for the troupe, which later received permission to play in
French.

Another sign in the new repertory of the Italian company's growing
adjustment to Paris is the extended parody of a French play included in
Arlequin et Scaramouche juifs errans de Babilonne (January-March 1677). Arlequin is led to the place of sacrifice in act 3, but to delay the dread
moment, tells a story that parodies the messenger's recital of the death of
Hippolytus. Gueullette is reminded of Racine's *Phèdre,* but Spada believes
the harangue more precisely burlesques Pradon's *Phèdre et Hyppolite.*[21]

Gueullette does not indicate that the harangue was in French in the
original manuscript, but it seems highly unlikely that a long, parodistic
speech should be in Italian as late as 1677 and following other long harangues we know were in French. The play was devised by the anonymous Monsieur S . . . , author of *Les trompeurs trompez.* It also features a
beloved named Margot, obviously a running gag. The speech is very
long; a selection will serve to give a taste of it.

> In this palace I served as butler to a merchant of fresh eggs who
> finding me one day speaking of love with his servant, one called
> Margot, said to me in a proud tone, take the cart and go to Babylon
> and sell four baskets of fresh eggs for me. To obey him I take the
> cart harnessed to three superb donkeys who, braying intrepidly and
> switching their tails, showed the impatience with which they suffered
> the bites of the gluttonous fleas avid for their blood. I take leave of
> Margot. I mount the cart. I give the reins to my asinine coursers who
> run full speed on the sand along the shore flying with a speed never
> equaled by the horse of bronze. This day the sea was so peaceful and
> so calm, it said not a word, and the zephyr had so lightly ruffled it
> that one would take it for whipped cream, when: Oh heaven, a hor-
> rible tempest arose . . . , a wave more violent than the others rose
> with a horrible noise, hurled against the sands, opened and gave
> birth to a frightful monster, its form appeared to be that of a pig, its
> head that of a boar, the rest of its body that of a sow. At this horrible
> sight my asses, frightened, braying with the most asinine strength
> . . . took the reins in their teeth and going off at a great trot, made
> first a half turn to the right, then a half turn to the left, in the middle

of their flight they turned over the cart, and these fragile eggs, which
by their color represent the pallor of death, in the fall of the cart, the
round baskets bouncing first on a hard pebble and then on my tender
face, left on the shore of the sea a long trace of yellow of egg, and
on my face a great, well-beaten omelet.[22]

Parody of French drama and opera became a standard of the Italian repertory in the 1680s and 1690s, but this is the earliest extant example
which shows that in the 1670s the Italians were already in direct competition with the French troupes and using French weapons.

The play first produced after 1668 that is most unlike those of the
conventional Italian repertory is *Le collier de perle* (1672) by Girardin with
music apparently by Lulli. It follows the form of a French comédie-ballet.
It includes two ballet entries, a divertissement with French songs, and an
epitaph in French. To Dominique's description of it can be joined a synopsis in French prepared so the audience could follow the plot and copied
by Gueullette into his historical notes.[23] *Le collier de perle* is an eccentric
piece, based upon a contemporary event reported in Donneau de Visé's
Le mercure galant. The plot is centered on Arlequin, who is in travesty
throughout as a *petit marquis*. He is not a disguised valet on his master's
business; he *is* a gentleman rather reminiscent of M. Jourdain. The first
act has distinct echoes of Molière's play—which had opened twenty-one
months earlier—when the tailor, the hatmaker, and the wigmaker's ap-
prentice argue over whose profession takes precedence. When Arlequin
tries to join in the fight, they "profit from his various postures" to dress
him.

Once dressed, the "Marquis de Sbroufadel" calls on Eularia, the
daughter of the Docteur, and plays a scene of the naive nobleman who
calls his lackeys in to say "God bless you" when the Docteur sneezes.
He brings along a three-volume history of the world of his own composing, one volume in verse, one in prose, one in neither verse nor prose,
thus besting M. Jourdain. When he hears that Eularia and Octave plan to
go to a costume ball, he says he will accompany them disguised as Arlequin.

The Marquis is definitely a French character, although the others
are Italian. The Docteur wants to marry his daughter to Octave because
he cannot tolerate the visits she receives from the French, "whose free
and gallant humor is not to his Italian taste." He objects to the planned
excursion to the ball and calls in Scaramouche, the apothecary, to prepare
a sleeping potion for his daughter. As she is dressing, Eularia falls asleep.
The Marquis enters disguised as Arlequin, a delightful reversal of the
usual situation. He approaches her to "steal a favor," but instead steals

her pearl necklace and swallows the pearls. Caught in the act by Eularia and Octave, he runs away, but is chased and returned by six lackeys.

Act 3 is concerned with the retrieval of the pearls by means of laxatives. The first thirty-one pearls are quickly rendered up, but the thirty-second requires an even more violent purgative. Arlequin, believing it will cause his death, composes an epitaph for himself in rhyming French.

> Arreste amy passant, le tombeau que tu vois
> Renferme Sbroufadel, un grand seigneur françois
> Il était beau, bien fait, galant, un peu follastre
> Pour la magnificence it n'eut jamais d'égal
> Et quoique l'on ait dit qu'autrefois Cléopâtre
> Fit à son Marc Antoine un trés riche régal . . .
>
> [Stop friend passing by, the tomb that you see
> Encloses Sbroufadel, a great French lord.
> He was handsome, well built, gallant, a little mad,
> For magnificence, he had no equal
> And although it's been said that once Cleopatra
> Made for her Marc Antony a very rich feast . . .][24]

The epitaph is not needed; the last pearl finally appears, the Marquis departs, Eularia and Octave are to be married at once, and Octave proposes to bring in the masquerade.

The masquerade is the third musical entry of the piece. The first entry is performed by the Docteur's scholars, who have been set a debate on the death of Lucrece. The dispute is in French verse with music underscoring each point of the argument. The second entry is the chase that ends act 2. The third entry, or the divertissement, is a pastoral. The scene changes from Eularia's room to "a solitude." Tircis, a shepherd, has been promised by a magician that he will be shown marvels. Tircis has no faith in this and explains in song to his shepherdess, Sylvie, that he will not be dazzled by magic but will discover the secrets of the illusions. The Magician enters, sings his invocation, and three devils appear with torches. He continues and five sorcerers enter, two from each side and one from the cavern at center. The devils and sorcerers do a dance "which expresses the most frightful things that can be imagined." But then the horrible figures change into burlesques, the shepherd snatches off the magician's false beard, and all the masquers reveal themselves.

So far as I have been able to discover, this was the first musical divertissement produced by the Italians. In later years, the Italians made a specialty of divertissements, and the most routine plays ended with musical spectacles that sometimes had nothing to do with the plays themselves. There is nothing especially spectacular about this first of the series, though perhaps Lulli's music made up for the lack of machines. Robinet praised the "good music" and "very beautiful dance" and mentioned especially that the lyrics were French, "which gave comfort to the ears, all coming from one who writes delicately and in an easy manner, according to our modern style." [25]

Le voyage de Scaramouche et d'Arlequin aux Indes (1676), the French synopsis for which was also copied out by Gueullette, is another example of how French songs were used by the Italian troupe.[26] The play is a fantasy, a musical spectacle that features magic and *turquerie*. It is, of all the plays included by Dominique in his zibaldone, the most extreme in its use of ornament, that is, music, magic, and machines. Because the documentation for this play is more complete than for any other, and also because it represents the fullest evolution of one genre the Italian repertory developed in the 1670s, it seems useful to give a fairly complete account of it drawn from both Dominique's notes and from the synopsis. Since the French troupe that shared the Hôtel Guénégaud with the Italians had attracted large audiences and made a great deal of money with the machine play *Circé* in 1675, it is hardly surprising to find the Italians producing their own elaborate musical spectacle a year later. Although the author is not indicated, the preface to the synopsis compares *Le voyage aux Indes* to a previous production, *Le berger de Lemnos,* definitely the work of Romagnesi: "We have added here some diverse ornaments to satisfy the curious and if those we put in *Le berger de Lemnos* contributed to attracting to us the numberless assemblies which have so many times attended its performances, we have some reason to hope that the ornaments you will find in our *Voyage aux Indes* will have no less charm for you. The orchestral music and songs are owed to the admirable genius of M. Oudot."

The prologue takes place in Hell, where Pluto sits enthroned with three infernal judges, Minos, Eacus, and Radamantes. Mercury and Music stand by. After the overture, Music sings that he has come to help celebrate the anniversary of the rape of Proserpine, when all torment ceases for the day and everyone gets what he desires.

Pluto thanks his brother Jupiter for sending Mercury to the party as well as Music. Eacus announces that the entertainment planned is not quite ready since he has just learned that an extraordinary disorder has broken out in Hell. Charon has warned him that the troubles are caused by the husbands and wives, each accusing the other of being responsible for their damnation. As a result, no one is going to enjoy the day off.

Pluto has a plan to settle the row. He will have all the spirits of all the infernal demons put in an urn and brought before him. The one who first emerges, chosen by fate, will take the body of a man and marry in the world so he can return and render judgment whether the men or women are at fault. Four monsters dance in with the urn, it is uncovered, and Belfégor pops out, the chosen demon. He complains that having to take a wife will cause him greater suffering that all the tortures imposed in Hell. Mercury and Music sing to console him as the party begins with a ballet of monsters and furies.

Act 1 takes place in the mountains "north of Rome" in a wild place with a "deep and fearsome" cave at center. Cinthio and his two valets, Scaramouche and Arlequin, have been separated escaping from a band of thieves and are lost in the mountains. The three are reunited, and Cinthio tells the others that he has come to consult the Fairy about how to evade his father's wish that he go to the Indies to marry the unknown Diamantine, the daughter of the Docteur. A monster emerges, then the cavern opens, and Melisse, the Fairy, appears. She promises to help Cinthio, then to show her power she composes a spell "accompanied by a pleasant symphony." The spell brings Belfégor from the underworld in the guise of a man. Melisse orders him to go to Peru, pretend to be Cinthio, and marry Diamantine.

Arlequin, who has fainted dead away in the sight of Melisse, is brought back to life and describes the visit he has just made to hell. This is Arlequin's harangue, but there is no indication as to whether it was spoken in French or Italian.

> I tell Cinthio I have come from Hell; he asks me the news. I say, they await you impatiently, sir. I found myself on the bank of a river where I saw Charon with a long beard in his barque. I said to him, monseigneur, will you take me across? Have you the money, he asked me. No? Well, stay where you are. . . . When he began to fall asleep, as I have always been curious to see that country, I thought of a trick, I struck the light that I always carry with me, I made a fire, I lit a candle, I got on the boat very, very quietly, I set his beard on fire. He woke up, leaned out of the boat to extinguish his beard in the river. In that moment, I took him by the feet and tipped him into the water. I took the oars and . . . crossed to the other side and found myself at the gates of Hell.

When Arlequin entered Hell he saw Pluto with his spectacles on his nose reading a gazette while Proserpine, by his side, made baby clothes. Arlequin was captured and brought before Pluto, "who ordered me put to boil in a cauldron. Proserpine said to him, my sweet, I'd like to roast this little suckling pig. I cried, Oh diabolic majesty, don't do it, Proserpine will be disgusted with me because I have the scabies. If you will let me go, I'll bring you someone much fatter than me ... Crogne [Crosnier], the candle snuffer at the Comédie."

Following Arlequin's solo, the plot continues. Melisse plans to hide Cinthio while Belfégor takes his place in Lima. She summons her chariot, drawn by two spirits in the form of dragons. The two valets, terrified by the Fairy, the cavern, the chariot, and the spirits, beg Cinthio to leave them in the mountains until he returns. He agrees, but Melisse summons Astarot (Flautin), an "esprit follet," or playful spirit, and orders him to follow the two valets, tease them with whatever tricks and illusions he pleases, and finally transport them to the Indies to rejoin their master.

The Fairy and Cinthio depart; Astarot promises Arlequin and Scaramouche that he will fulfill all their wishes. Aside, he warns the audience that the everything that happens will be illusions performed by demons and hobgoblins in disguise.

The scene shifts to the Land of Cockaigne. King Colintampon[27] receives the travelers from his triumphal chariot surrounded by his court, gives them "the privilege of the country," and has them dressed in the local fashion. An Inhabitant sings a song in honor of Bacchus and wine while the others dance the entry which ends act 1.

Act 2 begins with a magic fountain that spouts wines and liqueurs. Arlequin and Scaramouche are delighted with Cockaigne and plan to stay. Astarot, as an inhabitant, brings three bottles of wine and sings a drinking song in Italian. Another spirit, Rubican, enters and tells the valets about the virtues of the enchanted fountain which will provide them with whatever they want to drink. After a demonstration, he exits, but when Arlequin and Scaramouche try to drink again, the fountain spouts first water and then fire.

Astarot reappears in response to their screams and asks them their names, countries, and professions. They say they are Arlequin of Bergamo and Scaramouche of Naples, both married and acrobats by profession. Astarot gives each of them a magic mirror in which they can see— if they look hard enough—what their wives are doing in their absence. As they look intensely into the mirrors, an "illusion" appears on the stage; two spirits in the form of Arlequin and Scaramouche enter followed by two others disguised as their wives. The women ask for money, but the husbands refuse and retire to the rear of the stage. The women despair at first, then go out and find two soldiers who caress them and give them what they want. Two other soldiers, who also want to make love to the women, enter and fight with the first two. The vision ends, leaving Arlequin and Scaramouche in great distress.

The scene changes to Turkey. Two spirits disguised as Turks dress Arlequin and Scaramouche in Turkish costume. The Great Sultana appears, accompanied by her suite, and embraces them, but the Sultan enters, sees the Sultana being caressed by two "Turks," tries to cut off their heads, and orders them to be impaled. Astarot promises to save them with music. The Great Sultan loves music above all other things, so by means of enchantment Astarot will make perfect musicians of them. When Arlequin blows into the flute, Astarot—played by Flautin, who could imitate various instruments with his voice—stands behind him and makes the sound of a flute. The same trick persuades Scaramouche that he can play the bass. The Sultan, Sultana, and the court enter. A singer performs an Italian song, then Arlequin and Scaramouche are introduced. When Arlequin blows into the flute, a Turk behind him sounds a cowhorn, and when Scaramouche tries to play the bass, someone behind him brays like a mule. The Sultan cries "impale them," but two dragons appear just in time. Astarot forces the valets to mount, and the dragons fly off with the two valets, terrified and screaming. The act ends with another song in honor of the god of love.

Act 3 begins on the moon where Melisse has hidden Cinthio. He asks what has happened to Belfégor. The Fairy says that he has married Diamantine and is insanely jealous because he loves her but she will have nothing to do with him. She despises men. Cinthio asks what has become of his two valets and learns that they are on their way to the moon. This momentary lapse into plot is followed by a little pastoral interlude in music with Endimion in love with the Moon, Sylvie in love with Endimion, and Tircis in love with Sylvie. The songs, in French, are sung by Tircis and Sylvie.

Arlequin arrives on the moon and meets a spirit disguised as an alchemist who says he knows how to make the philosopher's stone and has the secret of restoring youth. He gives Arlequin his book of secrets. Scaramouche arrives, and the two decide to try the formula for rejuvenation. A furnace is brought in with the coals lit. Arlequin puts Scaramouche in the crucible, blows on the flames, then breaks the crucible. Out comes a small child dressed as Scaramouche. Astarot reappears and brings Scaramouche back; he has the "horses" ready for the valets to fly to the Indies. As a parting gift he gives them a magic wand; if they touch a woman with it she will fall instantly in love. They leave, just missing

Melisse and Cinthio who learn from Astarot that the valets are on their way to the Indies and that they must follow quickly to keep Belfégor from leaving his wife.

The stage changes to the shore of the *mer des Indes* with rocks and groves and the fleet at sea. Arlequin and Scaramouche enter and meet an Indian who speaks to them in his native tongue. A Knight Errant enters and informs them that any foreign knight who travels in this country is obliged to fight with a native knight who has in his power a lady of high birth of whom he is insanely jealous, believing that all who enter the country have come to seduce her. If the foreign knight wins the fight, he also wins the lady—who has 500,000 ecus. Cowards who refuse to fight are thrown into a fiery furnace. The knight enters, fights with Arlequin and Scaramouche, and falls dead. The Knight Errant calls for the girl, the most beautiful girl in the world, but when the winners try to caress her, she disappears, leaving behind a ghost. When the ghost vanishes, the valets notice Diamantine.

As she says she is the daughter of a rich merchant, Arlequin and Scaramouche—thinking their fortunes are made—touch her with the magic wand. She is instantly overcome with love for both of them and begs them to come home with her. There they encounter the jealous Belfégor. He reproaches his wife; she mocks him and says she will do as she pleases in spite of him. Belfégor speaks of the pain his wife has caused him by hiding two men in his house.

Diamantine thinks of a trick to get the two out of the house without getting herself in trouble with her father. The Docteur enters just as Scaramouche, sword in hand, rushes from the house threatening "his enemy" who is hidden there. Diamantine tells her father that she has saved the life of a man who was being chased by hiding him in her room, then Arlequin comes out and thanks her for saving his life. Belfégor detests his wife's cunning tricks.

When Melisse and Cinthio arrive, Belfégor tells the Docteur everything and announces that he is going back to Hell and tell Pluto that among humans women are much worse than men. The Docteur complains to Cinthio of the trick played on him, but having learned of his daughter's extraordinary aversion to men, accepts what has happened. He invites Cinthio to stay with him until he can return home with the fleet and promises to write to Cinthio's father explaining why the marriage is impossible. Arlequin and Scaramouche reenter and describe their adventures, then eight dancers dressed as Indians begin a ballet while another Indian sings, in French, about the trials of husbands and wives. The play ends with a combat and a triumph.

This mixture of commedia dell'arte, Italian romance derived from Machiavelli, pastoral, opera, and machine play belongs most properly to what Hannah Winter and others call the marvelous. Winter writes: "The Theatre of Marvels is the realm of the realized fantastic. It is a classically essential pure escapism . . . other worlds, supernatural or exotic inhabitants which man attempts to reproduce literally in tangible, visual form, defying time, space and natural forces . . . [where] man plays the part of supernatural powers . . . or vies with the supernatural by means of magic, legerdemain, juggling and the defiance of gravity . . . a theatre not only of the fantastic but of the impossible . . . always spectacular and popular." [28]

The elements that hold this heterogeneous entertainment together are music, spectacle, and theme. Flautin's commedia dell'arte lazzi are at war with the little pastoral of Endimion and Sylvie, but the music and lyrics provide form and continuity. As the classical commedia play had a balanced structure created by the alternation of romance plot scenes and ornamental comic scenes, so this kind of play alternates minimal plot scenes with music and with machines or scenes of spectacular action and unifies all with a theme.

Each division of the play opens and closes with music. The prologue opens with a solo, ends with a duet and ballet entry. Act 1 has no music at the beginning since it follows the prologue without intermission. It ends with the welcome to Cockaigne. Act 2 begins with Flautin's Italian drinking song and ends with the Turkish entertainment. Act 3 has the pastoral near the beginning and the ballet of the Indians followed by the combat and triumph at the end.

Machines and spectacular actions are also alternated with plot and music. Each segment has its allotted share of spectacle. Each includes an internal scene change: from Hell to the mountains at the end of the prologue, from the mountains to Cockaigne in act 1, from Cockaigne to the court of the Sultan in act 2, from the moon to the shore of the *Mer des Indes* in act 3. Act 2, at the chronological center of the play, is the most spectacular since it features both the magic fountain and the flying dragon machine. The prologue, of course, introduces Hell, act 1 has the entrance of Melisse and Belfégor's eruption from the underworld, and act 3 has the finale.

The theme of love and marriage is the most powerful formal element, carried forward in the songs and in the comic action. The delights of love followed by the trials of marriage are the subjects of most of the songs: "In life everything is boring without the charms of love"; "All our sports, all our games, without love are without allure"; "To love well is to love forever." But "At this word, spouse, you shiver in your soul"; "The devils in hell, neither in fire or irons, suffer evils as great as the evil of women." The comic action includes two long episodes on cuckoldry, the mirror scene in act 2 and Diamantine's escape plot in act 3. Belfégor, the Great Sultan, Tircis, and the jealous knight are all tormented by doubts that they are loved and fear of cuckoldry. The lover has no beloved; the woman he is meant to marry despises men. The one image of contented marriage is Arlequin's description of the domestic bliss of Pluto and Proserpine.[29]

This mélange, as Gustave Attinger chooses to call it, is not then without form, assuming with the critic Kenneth Burke that what we mean by form is the arousal and fulfilment of expectations. Interest is not held by plot to any extent, although it is hard to imagine that plot per se held the interest of many spectators of the traditional commedia dell'arte. The plot, whether Cinthio will have to marry the daughter of the Docteur, is an oddly truncated version of the standard romance plot since Cinthio has no one else in view. There is no role for an amoureuse, although presumably one of them—probably Eularia—played the Fairy Melisse. The misanthropic Diamantine enters the action late and plays a fairly standard comic routine with the zanni; her relationship with the amoureux Cinthio is not enacted.

What really acts to arouse expectations is the *organization* of the elements of music and dance, spectacle, and comic action. Music and dance appear at predetermined points in the play. Furthermore, each major comic performer, alone or in combinations, must appear a satisfying number of times and in routines that show off his most popular qualities. And the scenes, machines, and other elements of spectacle must also be utilized in a pattern that conforms to expectations. The fact that plays like this do not observe literary conventions does not mean that they are without formal satisfactions.

Although *Le voyage de Scaramouche et d'Arlequin aux Indes* differs in many obvious ways from the standard repertory, the play does include a number of traditional commedia dell'arte comic actions, their use probably linked to specific performers. Act 1 includes an echo routine between Arlequin and Scaramouche before they recognize each other. Act 2 includes the magic mirror sequence of the cuckholding of the two valets as well as the musical tricks of Flautin. Act 3 has the comic combat of Arlequin and Scaramouche with the jealous knight and Diamantine's trick to escape from her husband. A final element, traditional by this time in France—Arlequin's harangue—is introduced in the usual place, near the end of act 1.

The 1668–80 repertory includes a number of other plays that are set in exotic or imaginary places and feature magic, music, spectacle and fantasy, although none is so extreme in its use of ornaments as *Le voyage aux Indes*. The series begins with Romagnesi's *Arlequin esprit follet* (March 1670).[30] Biancolelli includes only one brief scene from this in his zibaldone, but a complete scenario is to be found in Ms. 9329.[31] Like *Le Voyage aux Indes*, it features a magician and an *esprit follet*, or mischievous familiar spirit, but the spirit is merely a variation of the fourbe intrigant, and the piece is actually more traditional than many others. It has a conventional plot of a vieillard who has promised his daughter, desperately in love with one amoureux, to the other. Arlequin, who is safe from harm because he is invisible, plays a number of tricks on the vieillard and the encroaching lover; the play includes some minor machine spectacle and one fire effect. Nothing is said of music in the scenario or the zibaldone, nor does Robinet mention it.

The *Suite du festin de pierre*, done in February 1673, was not merely a reprise of the earlier Don Juan play but a new play about Don Juan's bastard son.[32] Very little material from it is available, but we know from Robinet that it was musical and used machines. Cambert composed the music for it in the French style, but Dominique's notes give little specific information about the music and how it was introduced into the play. He does mention that "his master," that is, Don Juan, "gives the serenade" in the first scene.[33] Robinet notes that "an agreeable Sire whose voice is admirable sings two or three songs accompanied by sweet consorts." A "baladin" did a devil dance, and Scaramouche played his guitar. Aside from the music, there seems no reason to believe the play was out of the ordinary. Arlequin's routines seem conventional and include a ladder scene, a scene with a blind man, an echo scene with Scaramouche, and a scene of philosophical imbroglio. Scaramouche is part of a running gag that is interesting and adds a minor structure. He plays both a lost child named Guillaume and the child's father who in trying to catch him and beat him for running away beats Arlequin instead. The name Guillaume recurs in the echo scene and in the imbroglio scene, both times frightening Arlequin off the stage.

Probably in the same year the troupe produced Romagnesi's *Arlequin roy par hazard*, which takes place on an exotic island.[34] Arlequin is shipwrecked and, on the advise of a misunderstood oracle, crowned king. Another shipwreck and exotic locale appear in Romagnesi's *Le berger de Lemnos* (November 1674) in which Arlequin arrives on the island in the belly of a giant fish.[35] He describes his adventures to two comic peasants, Silvano and Flaminio (Spezzafer and Flautin): "I was on a ship loaded with flour and oil, there was a terrible storm, the sailors cried Save Your-selves and emptied the flour and the oil into the sea to lighten the load. The ship struck a rock, the anchor struck a spark which lit the oil which fried the fish, already covered in flour, making an excellent *friture*. I saved myself by climbing on a rock. Happily, I had a lemon in my pocket, I cut it in half and ate as much as I wanted. But then a big fish came by, saw I had eaten his nephew, and to avenge him, ate me." Flaminio asks why, with such sharp teeth, the fish did not chew Arlequin up. "I answer that with the other half of the lemon I set his teeth on edge so he could not bite."

Arlequin loves Lizette (Diamantine), whose father is marrying her off that very day to Scaramouche. The rest of the play concerns Arlequin's many efforts to prevent the wedding, including his entries disguised as a swan and a bull. The whole play has a vaguely classical flavor and in-cluded, according to Robinet, "sweet consorts and pretty songs in the Italian and French styles." Aside from the giant fish, however, and the exotic Jovian travesties, the play appears to have used little spectacle. No machines or scene changes are indicated either in Biancolelli's notes or in Robinet's appreciation.

After *Le voyage de Scaramouche et d'Arlequin aux Indes* in 1676, the next exotic piece done by the troupe was *Arlequin et Scaramouche juifs errans de Babilonne* (January–March 1677).[36] This one also begins with a ship-wreck. It features Arlequin as a fortune teller and Scaramouche as an oracle. Although set in exotic places, the play—so far as the available materials indicate—used no music, machines, or magic.

The last play with ornaments included in the zibaldone is *La magie naturelle*, the troupe's great success of 1678.[37] It is more traditional than *Le voyage aux Indes*, since its setting is not exotic and it rests on a conven-tional romance plot. It does incorporate some music along with spectacle and machines, however. Just as *Le voyage aux Indes* appears to have been produced in the hopes of cashing in on the huge success the French company enjoyed with *Circé*, so the French production in 1679 of *La devineresse*, without machines and major spectacle, but full of "little mira-cles," may have imitated the Italian's triumph with *La magie naturelle*.

Scaramouche plays the vieillard; Arlequin plays his valet. The old man has two daughters, beloved of Cinthio and Octave, but he plans to marry them to Fabrice and Cassandre, who are coming from the Indies. Spezzafer and Flautin, valets of two amoureux, set to work inventing tricks to frighten Scaramouche and steal the daughters. In the first epi-sode, Scaramouche is tormented in his bed and calls Arlequin. Spezzafer blows out the candle, moves the bed so Scaramouche and Arlequin cannot find it, raises the bed up in the air, breaks the chamber pot, and generally makes mischief. At the end of the scene the bed changes into a hellmouth. Spezzafer is inside with a squib in his mouth, spitting fire. This is followed by a love scene between Cinthio and his amoureuse, but when Scaramouche enters, the zanni quickly disguise the lover as a clockwork statue, leading to lazzi of fixing the statue and being beaten by the statue. Spezzafer enters as "a cook with a transparent belly." A table set for dinner is brought, and when Arlequin cuts into a pastry, snakes pop out. A capon on one side becomes a sirloin of beef on the other and Arlequin and Scaramouche appear on a spit as suckling pigs.

Arlequin then offers to teach the daughters their duty and does the harangue, placed as it often is near the end of act 1. This one is a mixture of classicism and cuckoldry jokes. It ends:

> You will tell me perhaps that your father is morose and churlish; that is true. That he is an animal. I do not disagree. That he is a beast. You are right. But is there anything more beastly, for example, than a snail? More uncivil? More unobliging? He greets no one, receives no one into his home, is so cross that no one has ever put him on a list of polite society. But this uncivil, this churlish snail, he is like a child. Take him by the hand, speak nicely to him, "*suspicious* little snail, show me your horns." These caresses, these engaging words, will bring out the snail's head. He will let himself be persuaded and show a regiment of horns. Now to the application, ladies. This snail is Scaramouche, your father; you are his children, caress him. I am sure that Scaramouche will poke out the head of his love from the shell of his anger, and that with great happiness he will show you the horns of his affection and good will.

Overhearing this, Scaramouche gives Arlequin a kick in the rear and chases him with his belt, ending the act in traditional style.

In act 2 Arlequin swears loyalty to his master, but a little judicious beating persuades him to help the lovers. At this point what was almost certainly a musical interlude intervenes. Scaramouche asks what has become of the figures that have been sent from Germany, and according to Ms. 9329, "The statues play and exit." Dominique begins the next scene with "when the serenade has been given and the instruments are gone." When Cinthio comes to ask how matters are progressing, Arlequin announces that he and the other zanni have invented a trick to introduce Scaramouche to the fiancés from the Indies. Cinthio sneaks inside while Spezzafer and Arlequin do a gluttony routine, discussing the wedding feast. Scaramouche discovers Cinthio and his daughter and chases them into a mill. Arlequin tries to help Scaramouche, who is being beaten by the miller, and ends up circling through the air, tied to one of the sails. This trick is achieved by the substitution of a dummy Arlequin built on a wicker frame.

In act 3, the daughters have escaped and Scaramouche is enraged. Spezzafer, doing a cripple lazzi, and Arlequin, doing a dwarf lazzi, appear as Fabrice and Cassandre. Arlequin sings, dances, and plays the castanets, but Scaramouche is not impressed. Spezzafer offers to arrange for Scaramouche to meet the devil and ask where his daughters are. The stage opens to reveal a grotto guarded by a giant who bears a mountain on his head and arms. Arlequin, disguised as a magician, rides in on a dragon (the usual dragon, no doubt), and magically shatters the giant to demonstrate his powers. He agrees to reveal the daughters if Scaramouche will let them marry Octave and Cinthio. Arlequin then sings "Descendez mère des amours" from the prologue to *Psyché*. The "figures" of the continents change into Eularia and Aurelia and the play ends with a celebration. The "figures of the continents" may have been the "German statues" of act 2, dancers as clockwork figures. Statues coming to life are a fairly common feature of the Italians' repertory in the 1680s and 1690s.

La magie naturelle is a much simpler production than its predecessor, *Le voyage aux Indes*. It is plot centered and by and large without extraneous comic actions. But like *Le voyage*, its ornaments are arranged in expectable ways with an unrelated musical interlude at roughly midpoint, with the major spectacle at the end of the second act, and with a magician to account for a spectacular finale. *La magie naturelle* is also simpler than the traditional commedia dell'arte play. It has a single romance plot without either a comic or romantic subplot. It has one vieillard, no capitan, and three zanni, all tied to the main plot. It has very little verbal action; its one major verbal routine is Arlequin's harangue, undoubtedly performed in French. It is not a mélange of disparate elements, but is perfectly coherent with all of its natural magic realistically accounted for, at least until the finale.

The repertory of the Comédie-Italienne in 1668–80 relies, finally, more on the traditional commedia dell'arte than it does on the Marvelous. Excluding the nine entertainments described above (and several of them use ornament only in passing), the plays noted by Dominique during this period were not especially spectacular, exotic, or musical. They remained linked to romance plots, to typical zanni comic action, and to the traditional staging of street and houses. They do tend to reduce the roles of the lovers, feature Arlequin and Scaramouche, and emphasize travesty. A good example of the way in which the traditional structure was modified by the Italians in France is Romagnesi's *A fourbe, fourbe et demy* (1674), which retains a semblance of Renaissance form, but holds interest largely through embellishments.[38] Colajanni pronounces the intrigue "poor," but the better word is conventional. It permits a forward movement without contributing any appeals of its own.

The amoureux are in love with the amoureuses, hardly a novelty. The young ladies are kept under the usual lock and key by their father, the Docteur. The three zanni—Arlequin, Spezzafer, and Scaramouche—devise a sequence of tricks to free the daughters. In act 1 the zanni enter disguised as moors, dance around the Docteur, and steal his key. But the scheme fails when the key turns out to be the wrong one. Arlequin confesses the error to Cinthio, who, having recently taken Arlequin into his service, asks his name. The question gives rise to Arlequin's first-act harangue, a history of his family, the Sbroufadels, and the etymology of his name. Arlequin then tries to deliver a letter from Cinthio to Eularia but is interrupted by her father. He pretends to be a gazetteer and they play the scene half in Italian half in French described earlier. For the third trick, Scaramouche enters as a Turk and offers to sell the Docteur a giant from Constantinople who will guard the house. The giant is Arlequin, who, discovering that he is too tall to go through the door, naively cuts himself in half with his Turkish sabre, and tells his lower half to meet him in an hour.

At the beginning of act 2 the women warn their lovers that the Docteur has arranged for a Spaniard named Callabasse to marry Aurelia. Scaramouche disguises himself as the pious Spaniard and enters with Arlequin in his valise. Once again, the Docteur uncovers the trick and chases the zanni away. Trick five is devised by Spezzafer, who knows that the Docteur has a good friend with a garden. Scaramouche dresses as a peasant and, saying he has been sent by Sieur Stofano, brings the Docteur an orange tree (Arlequin) and a lemon tree (Spezzafer). Light refreshments are served, and Arlequin reveals the device by stealing food from the table. In the final trick of act 2, Scaramouche enters as a peddler selling Venetian mirrors. Arlequin appears as an image in the mirror, his front half costumed as the Docteur and his rear as Diamantine. He does a mirror lazzi with the Docteur, who is suspicious and calls out the servante. Arlequin turns and does the mirror lazzi with her, almost persuading the Docteur until the latter drops his hat and Arlequin steps out of the frame to pick it up.

Spezzafer is at his wits' end at the beginning of act 3. He orders Arlequin to climb into the street light with a torch and wait there to speak to the daughters and tell them to pretend to be ill. The daughters warn him that their father has written to Count Anselme and asked for a company of infantry to guard the house. The Docteur enters and stands under the lamp while Arlequin lights bits of paper with his torch and drops them on the Docteur's head. As he exits the amoureux enter and try to shoot out the street light so that they can speak to the women. The Docteur returns and fires his pistol at the street light. The police rush in and lower the lamp with Arlequin in it, but he fights them off with his torch. setting their mustaches on fire, and escapes. The zanni then decide to take advantage of the Docteur's request for a company of soldiers. Spezzafer, disguised as a sergeant, and Arlequin, dressed as a captain, enter with a troupe of bedraggled gagistes and do a close-order drill that quickly reveals their deception.

The action finally concludes with the arrival of two physicians who say they have been told by one of the Docteur's men that his daughters are ill. He lets them go in. The physicians are Arlequin and Spezzafer wearing disguises built on willow frames. The daughters put on the disguises and escape to their lovers, leaving the zanni to thumb their noses from the window.

This play has achieved a near purity of form. In comparison to the plot complications of something like *Le dragon de Moscovie, A fourbe, fourbe et demy* has only the most elementary storyline. There is no question that the lovers will prevail; the only question is which trick will finally work. The principal comic device is amplification, piling on, which climaxes when both sides try to shoot out Arlequin's street light. The delight of the ending is that after all sorts of elaborate and even outlandish travesties fail, the old doctor disguise, probably the most predictable trick in the commedia lexicon, succeeds. The ending is almost self-parodistic; when invention reaches beyond the ridiculous, nothing is left but the traditional.

A variation combines the simplified romance plot and the emphasis on travesty with an elaborate finale. This becomes more common in the Gherardi repertory of the 1680s and 1690s, but it does exist in one example in this repertory. The evidence does not make it possible to tell if these finales were invariably musical, as was Lulli's third entry for *Le collier de perle*. In that case, the divertissement is a pastoral ballet entry sung and danced by hired artists and not by members of the troupe, and is completely isolated from the play. In *Le voyage aux Indes* the finale, a ballet of Indians followed by a combat and triumph, is somewhat allied to the play and more or less prepared for, as is the magic finale of *La magie naturelle.*

Somewhat different—more a harbinger of things to come—is the divertissement that ends *Arlequin dogue d'Angleterre et médecin du temps.*[39] The plot of this play is again conventional; the amoureux wants to marry the young lady; her father has promised her to an old merchant. Arlequin is at work both for his master and himself, since he is eager to marry the merchant's servant. After the usual travesties, including a long scene with Arlequin disguised as an English bulldog, the plot is resolved. This is followed, in Dominique's notes although not in Ms. 9329, by a combat finale:

> In this scene I enter as a doctor accompanied by Flautin. I carry a shield on my arm and a covered basket full of vials of urine and I have a sword in hand. The drums and trumpets sound, I do my lazzi of fear. Flautin mounts the hill and gives me courage, I also mount the hill as Flautin plants the flag; then Spezzafer appears on horseback followed by surgeons, apothecaries, and charlatans with their cannons, which are large syringes; they challenge me, I answer that I will defend myself to the last drop of urine. I take off my doctor's gown and make a sortie, I hit Spezzafer several times with a bladder . . . then retire into the fortress, which Spezzafer says he will set on fire.

The battle continues with bladders, syringes, and chamber pots until Arlequin raises the white flag and lowers the drawbridge. This divertissement seems to require a rather complex setting with hill, fortress, and drawbridge. It is vaguely related to the play that precedes it, but only because Arlequin continues his travesty as a doctor.

This use of a conventional play and detached spectacular finale is similar to the pattern of main play and spectacular afterpiece established in the English theatre in the early eighteenth century. The French troupes in Paris fairly often performed more than one play, if the main piece was short, but the Italians seem to have done so rarely before the 1690s. There are no other examples of isolated divertissements in the zibaldone or in Ms. 9329, but several plays end with mentions of weddings or combats, out of which divertissements may have developed.

Other elements of entertainments played in Paris in the 1670s include references to contemporary events and self-references, both commonplaces of baroque theatricality and probably, though not necessarily, of the commedia dell'arte. One always expects commedia scenarios to be more specific than they are, with a greater use of current events and local references. But of course the scenarios rarely include the specifics of the comic routines, and the peripatetic nature of the enterprise precludes the inclusion of purely local events in the highly selected written texts.

The Italian troupe in Paris was not peripatetic but established, and the material available from its repertory, though fragmentary, is highly specific. Nonetheless, there are only a few references to contemporary events to be found in it. Two criminals are mentioned by name, Devé and Dambreville. The first went to the galleys for fraudulent bankruptcy in June 1673; the second—according to Gueullette—was burned on the Grève. Devé is mentioned in passing in the *Addition à Arlequin soldat et bagage* and in *Arlequin cochon par amour.* Dambreville appears to be a travesty of Arlequin's; a short speech for the character occurs with two other brief notes appended to the zibaldone. The Italians may have introduced a play about Dambreville to compete with the French company's *La devineresse* (1679), which took advantage of the poison scandal and the execution of Voisin.

Risks were involved in using current events or common gossip. There was no institutionalization of theatrical censorship under Louis XIV, no system by which approval prior to production was gained, no office to which a manuscript had to be submitted. But although royal permission was not required to have a play performed, the monarch could of course have a run interrupted. And a privilege, or license, was required before a play could be printed. Rumor and gossip made official censorship unnecessary, and La Reynie and his men were alert to any failures in self-censorship. In later years, the Italians were in constant difficulty over indecencies and equivocations, and their plays—written by French playwrights—were full of satire and burlesque of French manners and institutions. In the 1670s no one complained of them, perhaps because they still played principally in Italian, perhaps because they took few risks.

Molière's troubles with *Tartuffe* and *Dom Juan* would have served as an object lesson. The Italians, in fact, may also have had trouble with their *Festin de pierre.* Dominique's notes (translated in full in chapter 3) for this often-repeated piece include the following: "In the last scene (it is suppressed) when the king comes on the stage, I throw myself on my knees before him and I say 'Oh, King, you know that my master is with the devils where you other great lords will go, too, some day.'"[40] This may have been too cheeky for Louis XIV.

In the repertory after 1668, although Arlequin appears as temporary ruler of an exotic island or two, the notes include nothing like the burlesque judgments in *Arlequin cru prince* that may have had some slight satiric edge. The court and the church were sacrosanct, as were the nobles—with the exception of the *petit marquis,* who were fair game for all.

Although the Italians may have restrained their references to the world outside, they did engage in self-referential and metatheatrical routines. Biancolelli's "urinalysis" of his pregnant wife has been discussed above, as has Arlequin's address to the onstage "stallions of Arcadie." Another sort of recognition of the actual nature of the theatrical event is found in *La propreté, ou Arlequin roy de Tripoli* when Eularia, who has a fetish for cleanliness, complains that Arlequin does not smell good. He admits to having eaten a dozen cloves of garlic, then climbs to the third loges with a torch and says, "Madame, you won't smell the garlic from here."[41] This display of acrobatics in the auditorium reminds the audience that, in spite of the spectacle, this is a theatrical and not an illusionistic form of theatre.

Another metatheatrical moment is to be found in Arlequin's "Panégiric de Scaramouche" in *Le théâtre sans comédie.* The eulogy recognizes that Scaramouche is an actor when Arlequin addresses "Scaramouche, the honor of our troupe." But it also is based upon the fictional events of the play. When Arlequin follows the Ciceronian formula, he confuses reality and fiction. "What? The death of Scaramouche. By what means? By the poison of the emetic wine. Why? Because he was ill. How? By swallowing the potion diabolically presented by the Docteur. When? About a quarter of an hour ago. Where? On the stage."

This kind of confusion is not uncommon, in part because the form was theatrical, in part because of the three-way split among performer, masque, and character. Although Cei had just replaced Fiorilli when *Le théâtre sans comédie* was produced, he did not play the role of the invalid; the masque Scaramouche played it. On the other hand, part of the effect of the scene was based precisely upon the fact that Cei *had* replaced Fiorilli, the real subject of the panegyric. The actor was not dead, but the character was—at least until the Paris audience accepted the new actor.

The Italians did not use self-reference as often or with as much sophistication as Molière did. But Molière used his stage as a platform and as a weapon in his wars with the *dévots* and with the actors of the Hôtel de Bourgogne. The Italians were less embattled. They were still legally foreigners, in France at the royal pleasure even after twenty years. Unlike the French, they were creatures of patronage, accustomed to servility to one duke or the other. Not only their incomes but their very professional existence rested on their ability to retain the good will of a sovereign.

The outlines of the 1668–80 repertory have emerged, although little about it can be confirmed with certainty. Dominique's notes are fragmentary and do not always coincide with the scenarios contained in Ms. 9329. The plays remained fluid, changing with the times and with the company. But certain things about them are clear. Far from following a single model, the Italians from 1668 to 1680 devised a variety of different kinds of entertainments, many of which were still rooted in the traditional repertory. The dominant developments were the simplification of plot and the addition of ornaments, the emphasis on travesties and the protean nature of Arlequin, and the introduction of the French harangue.

It is conventional to assume that the baroque period in the French theatre ended with the establishment of neoclassical norms for dramatic construction late in the first half of the seventeenth century. Machine plays like *Psyché* and *Circé* are often regarded as temporary lapses from good taste by theatrical companies that certainly knew better. Unlike their French rivals, the Italians were under no aesthetic or moral obligation to the literary establishment and could follow the prevailing winds. The combination of simplified structure and extravagant embellishment, the fascination with disguise and multiple identity, the conflation of reality and the imagined, and the delight in the exotic, the magical, and the marvelous can all be accounted for as part of that seventeenth-century pan-European tendency toward the excessive and the redundant we call the baroque. The Italian repertory of 1668–80 in Paris no longer displayed the complex and inflexible forms and patterned rhetorical embellishments of the sixteenth-century commedia dell'arte, nor was it shaped by any influence of the neoclassical categories that had been imposed on the French theatre. It was a creature of its time and place, a reflection of nothing so much as its patron monarch who adored music and dance, dressing up, spectacle, fireworks, farce, and fantasy, and who was himself the creator of a courtly world in which reality and the theatrical were indistinguishable and inextricable.

Part IV
1680-1688

CHAPTER 10

The Hôtel de Bourgogne

O N SUNDAY, 25 AUGUST 1680, the two troupes of French actors playing
in Paris—at the Hôtel de Bourgogne and the Théâtre Guénégaud—were merged by the order of Louis XIV into a single company
and began to play seven days a week at the Guénégaud. The dispossessed
Italians were granted the use of the Hôtel de Bourgogne and the French
ordered to pay them a yearly subvention of 800 livres.[1] This, along with
the 1,200-livre pension owed them by the Opéra, was meant to cover
most of the annual rental of the Hôtel de Bourgogne.

Although we know from the various registres that the French did
not miss a single performance as a result of the union, we do not know
the immediate fate of the Italians. The company had been at Fontainebleau from 15 May to 7 July, playing alternatively with the royal French
troupe.[2] The Italians returned to the Guéngaud briefly, playing their
usual days from 8 July to 22 August. In his August *Mercure galant* Donneau de Visé writes, "You will be surprised when I tell you that the two
troupes of French actors having been ordered by the king to join together,
those of the Hôtel de Bourgogne have ceded their place to the Italians,"
but he says nothing of an Italian debut. According to a legal document of
1708, the Italians did not move into the Hôtel de Bourgogne until 21
October.[3] The first mention of the troupe performing in its new home is
in the December *Mercure galant* when Donneau de Visé remarks that *Le
remède de Anglois, ou Harlequin Prince de Quinquinia* has been playing for
three weeks at the Italian theatre and has attracted large audiences in
spite of the bitter cold that has forced "the ladies to renounce public
pleasures."

His Majesty clearly had union in mind as early as 1673, when he
tried to force Molière's troupe, after its leader's death, to join the enemy
at the Hôtel de Bourgogne and succeeded in achieving a merger of the
remnants of Molière's company with most of the actors of the Théâtre du
Marais. According to La Grange, the union of 1680 was made possible
by the death on 27 July of La Thorillière, one of Molière's actors who had
decamped to the Hôtel de Bourgogne in 1673.

The king may also have been influenced by the Italians. Prevented
by the Accord of 18 February 1680 from arming themselves with spec-

tacle and entering the lists against the Opéra, the Italians apparently begged repeatedly for permission to build a new theatre in the Faubourg St.-Germain, but the king—determined not to increase the venues for theatrical production in Paris—refused them.[4] The Italians spent an unusually long time at Fontainebleau in the spring of 1680, and Biancolelli had the monarch's ear. The merger of the two French troupes may, then, have been accomplished in part to satisfy the request of the Italians for a theatre of their own.

The Hôtel de Bourgogne was the first of the Paris public theatres, built in 1548 by the Confrérie de la Passion for the performance of religious drama. It has been studied in depth by many scholars; there is no need to repeat all of its long history here.[5] In 1667 the Confrérie was dissolved by the king, and the ownership of the Hôtel de Bourgogne passed to the Hôpital des Enfants-Trouvés, one of the institutions operated by Vincent de Paul's Sisters of Charity. What the Italians rented from the Enfants-Trouvés was the oldest, smallest, and least well equipped theatre in Paris. Nonetheless, it was their own.

The Hôtel de Burgogne was located on the rue Mauconseil between the rue Françoise and the rue Montorgueil, near Les Halles and the church of St.-Eustache. After eighty years of service as the principal performance venue for touring companies, both French and Italian, playing in Paris, it became the home in 1629 of the first established Parisian troupe led by Bellerose, the troupe later known as the Comédiens du Roi. In 1647 the Confrérie de la Passion was persuaded to celebrate the centennial of the old theatre by reconstructing its interior. The competing troupe at the Théâtre du Marais enjoyed a theatre rebuilt after a fire that had destroyed its converted tennis court in 1644. The royal troupe was, thus, at a considerable disadvantage, especially when it came to attracting an upper-class audience. The new Marais was furnished with forty private loges to welcome ladies who did not wish to be jostled in the amphithéâtre; the Hôtel de Bourgogne had only twelve. Nor did it have a stage that could be adapted for changeable scenery, although this was a lesser problem for a troupe specializing in classical plays that employed single settings.

Some details of the 1647 reconstruction can be gleaned or inferred from the specifications set forth in a contract between the builders and the Confrérie,[6] although the document raises a number of unanswerable questions as well. A late eighteenth-century plan and several sixteenth-century documents establish the interior dimensions of the theatre building: 16 toises, 2 pieds (103 feet 4 inches) in length and 7 toises (44 feet 4 inches) in width.[7] These dimensions help in interpreting the contract.

In 1647 the stage of the Hôtel de Bourgogne was 7 toises, 1 pied (45 feet 5 inches) deep and 6 pieds (76 inches) high at the front. The stage stretched across the width of the building and was "higher in proportion" at the rear. No information can be derived from the document about the width of the proscenium opening after the reconstruction, but the dressing rooms were removed from the sides of the stage, with the exception of the pillars supporting the beams. This suggests that the stage was being redesigned to accommodate changeable scenery, though nothing in the document implies the installation of devices for changing scenery by these builders at this time, only two years after Torelli's splendid scenes and machines for *La finta pazza* had astonished Paris.

Another feature of the stage that can, to a limited extent, be derived from the contract is the continued existence of some sort of upper stage, or "petit théâtre"—a rear gallery or galleries used originally, one assumes, much as the upper stage of the English public playhouse was used in the sixteenth and early seventeenth centuries. Deierkauf-Holsboer argues for such a second stage based on the mention of a petit théâtre in a 1616 lease and the use of the plural, "théâtres," in several other leases, including that of 1647.[8] Other scholars agree, pointing as well to the scenic designs of Laurent Mahalot, most of which either show an upper stage or—more usually—what appears to be a means of concealing an upper stage.[9] In all but a few of the forty-eight drawings contained in Mahelot's *Mémoire,* a strong horizontal line at the rear of the acting area seems to refer to some inescapable architectural feature of the stage. Above the line are clouds, below it usually a palace or series of arches which, in some instances, frame a vista.

The contract of 1647 calls for the placement of thirteen new loges for the actors (i.e., dressing rooms) above and below the stage with two staircases by which the actors can "mount to the stage and which continue to rise to above the ceilings." From this we can deduce that there were to be seven dressing rooms at ground level and six at stage level with stairs that continued up to give access to space used for storage and, potentially, for flying machinery.[10] The contract also notes that "the two galleries ... at the back of the stage which support the ceilings should remain as they are." A likely interpretation is that one row of dressing rooms was placed under the galleries, and the other row beneath the stage.

"Two galleries" implies that the petit théâtre may have not have been a single span, but divided. Assuming that the upper row of dressing rooms was placed three and three with a space left in the middle, the stage would have been adequate to the demands of Italian scenery. The fronts of the galleries could now serve as the optique (as the "great beam" did at Palais-Royal) with the vista set into the gap left between the two sets of dressing rooms. The width at the rear of the stage—44 feet 4 inches—was adequate for two stairways, six small dressing rooms, and the vista, which—given the characteristics of forced perspective—need not have been very large.

A large percentage of the visual representations of this stage, from Mahalot's designs to the frontispieces included by Gherardi in his collection of scenes and plays in French, show an arch or series of arches with a vista behind. A few show what appears to be a stage open to the back wall, but those can very well represent painted backcloths hung in front of the optique. R. L. Erenstein points out that the arch, or "gate" as he calls it, is such a common feature of staging at the Hôtel de Bourgogne as to be an indicator for the scholar seeking to identify the theatre shown in a print or drawing.[11] While it may be true that the Hôtel de Bourgogne stage was encumbered by an upper stage that had to be incorporated into or hidden by the decor, it is also true that the use of an arch to frame a perspective vista is a cliché of baroque scenery.

The stage was relatively deep to the rear wall: 7 toises, 1 pied (or 45 feet). Assuming each dressing room was approximately 5 feet by 8 feet—a generous estimate—and including a hallway for access to them, the working depth of the stage would have been about 34 feet to the optique with a vista depth of 11 feet. This depth was more than adequate for the scenic needs of the French repertory of midcentury. The Palais-Royal stage was 32 feet to the optique with a vista depth of 10 feet.

Major renovations were also accomplished in the auditorium in 1647, the chief among them being the installation of thirty-eight loges in two rows of nineteen each along the sides and rear. The scholarly consensus now seems to be that the loges were arranged seven along each side and five at the rear.[12] The placement of the amphithéâtre remains a problem. According to the contract, "The amphithéâtre is to be made as commodious as it can be and as the place permits. . . . The floor at the gable end of the amphithéâtre to be demolished and the beam raised and the floor remade to put in place the rear loges and a staircase to mount to the galleries and paradise."[13] Deierkauf-Holsboer interprets these instructions to mean that the amphithéâtre was placed above the second loges,[14] largely, I think, because she has connected the staircase to the amphithéâtre rather than to the new floor, concluding that the amphithéâtre "is served by the same stairs which lead to the second row of loges and to the paradise." What makes infinitely more sense is to assume that the amphithéâtre was installed as usual at the rear of the parterre, while the stairs led to galleries above the side loges and a paradise above the rear ones. In any case, wherever the amphithéâtre was in 1647, it was not above the loges in 1687 when Arlequin as a fashionable wit describes taking his place in the middle of the first bench of the amphithéâtre, then jumping into the parterre to avoid paying for his lemonade.[15] Nor was it there in 1688 when the Italians charged as much for a seat in the amphithéâtre as for one on the stage.[16]

In 1656, special-effects machines and machines to change the scenery were installed in the Hôtel de Bourgogne. A contract with Denis Buret, master carpenter, for the "machines and their mechanisms and all the chariots for five changes of scene and their mechanisms" for *Le grand Astyanax* was signed on 19 July.[17] The contract calls for machines as follows:

FIRST ACT

In the first act at the opening of the stage, the great god machine which must descend to the ground in the first scene at the first wing.

SECOND SCENE

Discord leaving the stage with two furies, one flying into the air and the other sinking into the earth.

SECOND ACT

There has to be a moving sea from the optique to the back wall with a little boat for five figures who cross the stage in the last scene of the second act and in the second scene Paris and Cupid descend perpendicularly and Cupid flies off into the heavens.

THIRD ACT

In the last scene Iphigenia is carried off while kneeling in prayer and Diana appears in the glory.

FOURTH ACT

The phantom rises from below the stage and the machine of Juno, covered by a cloud, crosses the stage and the machine of Venus crosses from the other side.

FIFTH ACT

There has to be a tomb which is hollow to hold a little boy and the great machine of the gods for the end.

A second contract, signed 3 October, between the actors and the painters describes the decors for the same production:

The first decor representing a garden from the edge of the stage to the optique and from the optique to the rear of the stage a sort of countryside with a little mountain pierced through to place there a person or figure; the second decor representing cliffs with a moving sea, the sea from the optique to the rear and, the optique closing, there will appear cliffs and caverns; then a temple from the optique to the edge of the stage, some shaped wings for the temple, this will be for the third decor; then, for the fourth, will be made a camp of war tents, from the optique to the edge of the stage with some shapes of trees and rocks to accompany the tents; then, and for the fifth decor, will be made a city engulfed in flame accompanied by the borders which are necessary to the machinery and the moving sea with cliffs on both sides, and this, following and conforming to the five designs which have been made of them.[18]

Unfortunately, neither contract specifies the number of wings to be painted for each decor, but the stage depth was sufficient for the usual maximum of five wings per side in front of the optique.

No documents have come to light for the period between 1656 and 1680 that indicate any further reconstruction or reequipping of the stage of the Hôtel de Bourgogne. The repertory of the royal troupe was largely classical, with minimal dependence on scenic spectacle. That was left to the Marais, the Palais-Royal, and the Guénégaud. The scenic notes left by the décorateur Michel Laurent list the decors used for the repertory played by the French troupe in the last years of its tenure at the Hôtel de Bourgogne. Of the fifty-three plays listed, forty-three used a single setting; the other ten required two settings placed on the stage together, with the main setting in front and the second setting introduced when needed by opening or closing a shutter. The main setting is either a wood (one instance), a palace (two instances), or—most usual—an Italian-style street with houses (six instances). The secondary settings include a prison, a room, and a cabaret. For *Crispen musicien* two different rooms are required, to be changed after each act. A stage direction describes how the change was achieved: "Phélonte retiring, his six lackeys enter from the two sides of the stage and arrange themselves in a straight line and play an air to end the act. Following that, two chariots are pushed on which cover them; these wings, called the shutter, represent Dorame's room . . . in which the second act is played. The shutter must have two doors which identify two other rooms."[19] At the end of act 2, the shutter opens revealing the six lackeys still playing their air, and we are once again in Phélonte's house. The change is repeated for acts 3 and 4.

This stage direction clearly demonstrates that in the 1670s the machinery installed to change the setting in *Le grand Astyanax* was not in use. The chariots still existed, but were "pushed on." Even as late as 1683, although the Italians were gradually equipping their stage, Italianate changeable scenery was apparently not in use. In *Arlequin Protée* the Italians used precisely the same system as their predecessors; after a scene played in a "street with houses," the stage direction tells us: "The stage opens and represents a room."[20]

Limited information is available about the repertory of the Italians during the early years of their tenure at the Hôtel de Bourgogne; what is available suggests that the use of scenes and spectacle was restricted. The Italians may have had their own theatre, but it was not initially suited to the sorts of entertainments they had produced at the Guénégaud.

Although the equipment to move scenery was probably not in working order when the Italians moved into the Hôtel de Bourgogne, they may have had some sort of flying machine in operation. *Arlequin mercure galant,* which opened in January 1681, begins with a "Scène des nouvelles," included by Evaristo Gherardi in his collections of material in French played by the Italians in the 1680s and 1690s. In the scene, "Arlequin as Mercury appears in the air mounted on Jupiter's eagle." His own wings have failed because a servant emptied a chamber pot on him and got them damp. Jupiter orders him to descend and take the form of a shepherd; "the machine disappears and Arlequin is seen in his habitual costume, mounted on an ass."[21] Exactly how this was accomplished is not indicated. It would appear that the machine was not designed to raise or lower an actor and was probably rather simple. Donneau de Visé gives no specific information in the *Mercure galant* about the 1681 production, contenting himself with the note that the comedy attracted a large audience in spite of the "rigors of the season"; the possibility certainly exists that the scene described in Gherardi reflects a reprise and not the original production.

If the next plays done by the Italians included spectacle, no descriptions of it appear in the *Mercure galant,* and the texts published by Gherardi mention nothing until *Arlequin Protée,* which opened in October 1683.[22] The first stage direction reads: "The stage represents the sea. Seen there is Neptune who is chasing Arlequin and Mezzetin, one of whom is Proteus and the other Glaucus." Neptune speaks from his "chariot in the middle of the sea." Arlequin, "emerging from the sea," complains of the boredom of life in the maritime empire where everyday is a fast day, even Mardi Gras. Neptune becomes enraged and "the back of the stage closes." Some kind of wave machine was probably in use, since Arlequin refers to the sea as "these rolling mountains." This machine could not have been the "moving sea" from *Le grand Astyanax* because that was installed between the optique and the back of the stage, in the area of the forced perspective vista, whereas this "sea" was in proportion to the actors and must have been fairly close to front of the stage. This scene was almost certainly included in the original production, since a print from a Bonnart calendar almanac of 1684 illustrating it (fig. 10) includes Spezzafer as Glaucus, and Spezzafer died a few months after the play opened. Unlike the frontispiece to Gherardi's 1700 text (fig. 11), which has Neptune mounted on a chariot drawn by two magnificent horses, the Bonnart engraving realistically shows Neptune standing behind a row of waves, his boat intersecting his body at roughly knee level. Glaucus stands behind another row, while Arlequin has one foot in the sea, one on shore.[23] This is hardly spectacle of the sort that attracted audiences to plays like *Le voyage de Scaramouche et d'Arlequin aux Indes,* but the Italians appear to have been trying gradually to install some standard machines.

Arlequin Protée continues with a conventional "street with houses" until "the stage opens" revealing a hall where Arlequin as a magistrate hears complaints. The scene ends when his chair is transformed into a frightening monster with flames shooting from its mouth and nostrils, a typical Italian "little miracle." A return to the "street with houses" is followed by a parody of Racine's *Bérénice* set in the Docteur's garden. Although no stage direction indicates the means by which the setting was changed, another print from Bonnart's calendar-almanac shows a high topiary arch with trees in front and a vista behind, which appears to be upstage of the main setting. The play also contains what may be a self-referential comic routine. Arlequin, as leader of a troupe of actors, explains to Cinthio his scheme for flying twelve persons without ropes, wires, or counterweights. The scheme, which relies on barrels of gunpowder under the stage, may well reflect the lack of sophisticated machines at the Hôtel de Bourgogne.

In September 1684 the Italians opened *Arlequin Jason,* which featured their first really expensive spectacle. According to Tralage, "It had at the end a surprising machine of several cascades with forty jets of natural water at diverse heights. M. de Fatouville [author of the scenes in French] had the idea, but Sr. Angelo [Angelo Agostino Lolli] had the thing executed. It cost the troupe, which earned a great deal from it, at least five hundred pistoles [5,500 livres]."[24]

Le Comique Arlequin le plus plaisant du monde
Abandonne Neptune, la Mer, et les Poissons,
Pour venir à Paris, en diverses façons,
Montrer que son humeur peut passer sans seconde.

FIG. *10. Prologue of* Arlequin Protée *(1683) from a Bonnart calendar-almanac.* (Royal Library, Copenhagen, Department of Prints and Photographs)

FIG. *11*. *Frontispiece to* Arlequin Protée *in Gherardi's*
Le théâtre italien, *1700*. (Phot. Bibl. Nat. Paris)

Stage directions combined with six prints from a Bonnart calendar-almanac make it possible to recreate the staging of *Arlequin Jason* with some confidence.[25] The first of the scenes in French, the "Scène de l'enchantment," was played before a tapestry indicating an interior scene. In it Medea changes a heroic statue of Jason into Arlequin. The following scene between Medea and Ipsiphilia was not included in the Bonnart calendar, but it is also an interior without scenic demands. The third French scene—"Scène du triomph"—is illustrated twice in the calendar. The setting is a palace facade with a balcony. The Queen, Ipsiphilia, and a lady-in-waiting stand on the balcony as Arlequin-Jason enters in a triumphal chariot with his argonauts, Scaramouche and Spezzafer. The latter ride elaborate hobbyhorses with false legs, not real horses as H. C. Lancaster believed.[26] Nor does Arlequin "fall out" of his flying "car" as Lawrenson thinks.[27] The two following scenes are without indication of setting but appear to be interiors. The sixth—"Scène des Item"—begins as an interior played before a tapestry. Once Jason and Medea have come to an agreement about their marriage, she "strikes the earth with her wand. The stage opens and represents a garden with magnificent cascades and a number of figures on gilded pedestals." The first part of the scene must have been played well downstage, since the garden and cascades were set up in front of the optique. Following a debate between a French actor and an Italian actor, Medea strikes the earth again, freeing the statues and starting the play of the fountains. A sixth illustration shows the final setting with an exactitude almost without precedent (fig. 12).

The cascades fall from fifteen jets down three rows of eight basins. The unit has been set against the palace facade used earlier, but with the balcony removed. The fall would appear to be some seven or eight feet. At the edge of the stage another sixteen jets rise from the footlight trough, which spills in a waterfall effect into a basin set in the parterre. Three other fountains play on the top of the palace facade. Along each side are seven wings, columns with Corinthian capitals, with the pedestals set in between. The same wings were used for the scene of the triumphal entry, indicating that changeable scenery was probably still not an option. The spectacle was achieved by playing interior scenes "in one" while the more elaborate scenes were set up behind a tapestry curtain. The play and its production were inspired by the reprise eleven months earlier of Pierre Corneille's machine play *La toison d'or* at the French theatre.

Quoy que tout soit parfait, que tout soit admirable,
C'est icy ou l'Esprit, et les yeux sont charmes,
De voir tomber cette eau d'une chute agreable,
Et d'entendre parler des Corps inanimez.

Sçauez vous cher Jason, quelles sont ces Figures,
Qui font des Curieux, les plus beaux Entretiens,
Si je les ay parez de superbes dorures,
C'est pour leur faire voir, qu'ils sont Comediens.

Ces traitres m'ont déplû, dit Medée en colere,
Mais j'ay sceu les punir par mes Enchantemens:
Ils seront toûjours la, tant que je seray fiere,
Et que j'auray pouuoir sur mes ressentimens.

Des Comediens, Madame, dit Jason, Grace, Grace,
Faites que ces Corps mort, ayent les yeux ouuerts,
Et qu'ils viennent icy, montrant leur bonne-grace,
Reciter deuant nous quelques-uns de leurs vers.

Ce burlesque attirail nous fait voir que Jason,
Est un Heros d'Esprit, et d'une grande idée:
Ses Compagnons, et luy attirent la Toison,
Et benissent le sort de leur chere Medée.

FIG. *12. The cascades featured in the finale of* Arlequin Jason *in 1684. From a Bonnart calendar-almanac.* (Royal Library, Copenhagen, Department of Prints and Photographs)

The scenes in French from the next six productions included in Gherardi's collections, which opened between February 1685 and April 1687, indicate no further expenditures on machines. Stage directions in *Colombine avocat pour et contre* (June 1685) continue to imply that scenery was changed behind some screening device, in this case a shutter. The main setting is a public place; the others are interiors, revealed when "the shutter opens."[28]

The Gherardi repertory has a gap of nearly two years between *Colombine avocat* and the next entry, *Le banqueroutier* (April 1687). Donneau de Visé does not mention in the *Mercure galant* any particular production at the Comédie-Italienne during this period, although he includes the troupe in his list of "usual diversions" at Fontainebleau in November 1686. The troupe was certainly active at court; surviving records and mémoires indicate twenty-one performances at Versailles, Marly, and Fontainebleau in 1685, twenty-six in 1686.[29] The Hôtel de Bourgogne was closed during part of that time for repairs. On 19 April 1686 the actors borrowed 10,000 livres from the Bolognese doctor Domenico Amonio, an obliging royal physician who was a close friend of Domenico Biancolelli's. The purpose of the loan is clearly spelled out in the contract: the money is to be used "with other monies to pay for the construction which they must do to the Hôtel de Bourgogne, according to the agreement they have made with the directors of the Enfants-Trouvés, to whom the said Hôtel de Bourgogne belongs."[30] The loan was augmented by another 5,000 livres on 16 July 1686 and repaid a year later in June 1687.[31]

Fifteen thousand livres was not a great deal of money, considering that the cascades alone had cost 5,500. Of course, the troupe may have accumulated other funds as well. A comparison of two documents indicates that the work done was fairly substantial. In the Convention, or articles of association, drawn up by the Italian troupe on 29 April 1683, the following clause appears: "when one among them leaves the troupe that one . . . will be paid by the troupe . . . the sum of 500 livres, which they have estimated in common to be the share of each of the said actors in the costumes, properties, crystal chandeliers, decors, paintings, and other expenses which have been made . . . in common."[32] A year or so later, in the Règlement, or ordinance governing the Comédie-Italienne, drawn up by the dauphine on orders of the king, (unfortunately not dated, but not before 1684) a similar passage reads: "As to the fabric of the stage, loges, paintings, decors, machines, costumes and tools used for the performance of plays, they belong . . . to the said troupe. And when some actor dies, the rest of the troupe will pay to his heirs the sum of 1,500 livres, 1,000 livres for the share in the stage, loges, and paintings, 500 livres for the decors, lights, and tools."[33] This would seem to confirm that the Italians had reconstructed the stage and the loges and redecorated the auditorium, probably in 1686. At any rate, the troupe owned the stage and loges, which was not the case in 1683.

Several pieces of evidence imply one change that may have been made at this time: the addition of a third range of loges. In a stage direction in the prologue to *Le divorce* (March 1688), Jupiter announces that he will watch the play from the third loges; he has lost all his money but thirty sous playing *boule* with four lawyers.[34] The contract of 1647, although not precise about the arrangement of the auditorium at the Hôtel de Bourgogne, does clearly state that there will be "two rows of loges." The third loges are also mentioned in a poster, copied by Tralage, announcing the reopening of the theatre in September 1688 after the death of Domenico Biancolelli.[35]

Although "machines" are included in the dauphine's *Règlement*, the repertory after April 1687 does not immediately include machine or spectacle pieces, suggesting that the money borrowed from Dr. Amonio was not spent on new equipment for the stage. *Le banqueroutier* appears to require a single interior setting, as does *La cause des femmes* (December 1687) and its *Critique* (February 1688), while *Le divorce* (March 1688) is only slightly more spectacular. It's prologue features Mezzetin as Jupiter flying in on a turkey, and the stage directions indicate several locations, though without describing how the changes are to be achieved. The final scene is the Temple of Hymen, but the others alternate between "a public square" and various "apartments," and the traditional method of changing the setting behind a tapestry or shutter could certainly have been employed. The machines in question at the time of the dauphine's *Règlement* would, then, include the cascade, the sea from *Arlequin Protée,* and some sort of fairly primitive flying rigging.

According to Tralage, the theatre was "repaired" at the expense of the troupe.[36] Its new owners, the directors of the Enfants-Trouvés, would have been concerned with the fabric of the building and not with its equipment. But the troupe must have taken advantage of the need for repairs to make its home both more commodious and more attractive. The renovations were marked by a new motto, *Castigat ridendo mores,* over the proscenium and a new inscription over the entrance: "The only troupe of Italian actors maintained by His Majesty in their Hôtel de Bourgogne, 1686."[37] In the following year the Italian actors had a *jeton*, or token, made to be given to actors who attended company assemblies, and Donneau de Visé included a picture of it in the *Mercure galant* of February 1688 among *jetons* of the year. It shows the stage with the fountains and cascades from *Arlequin Jason* in place. Above the stage is the company's new motto; below it, *Comici Italiani del Re*. 1687.[38]

The auditorium of the Hôtel de Bourgogne in 1680 was probably smaller than that of the rival Théâtre Guénégaud. The latter had a capacity of 1,650, including stage seating, according to H. C. Lancaster.[39] Graham Barlow estimates the capacity of the Hôtel de Bourgogne at 1,176 in 1717, based on the rough sketches made by Sir James Thornhill which show the third loges in place.[40] Assuming the capacity was somewhat higher in 1686, when the auditorium contained a larger proportion of space for standing spectators, it was still lower than that of the competition. On the other hand, theatres in this period rarely if ever were filled, at least with paying customers, so there was no reason for the Italians to rebuild their theatre merely to increase its capacity. But a change from the old side galleries and paradise to a new row of loges might have been a signal that the theatre was now more suited to a "gentle" audience.

The Paris theatre audience changed between the 1660s and the 1680s. When the court withdrew to Versailles, the public theatres were left to the minor nobility, to lawyers, bureaucrats, and administrators, and to the bourgeoisie. At the Italians, especially, the parterre reigned, although the theatre did appeal to a whole range of spectators. In the prologue to *Le banqueroutier* (April 1687), Arlequin has just come from seeing *Le banqueroutier* at the Comédie-Italienne. He has nothing to say of the play itself, since his quality of fashionable wit prevents him from paying any attention to it. He has had a most successful visit, however, since he entered without paying, ate and drank at no cost, and had more money when he left than when he came. His description paints a wonderful picture of a Paris theatre and its audience in the 1680s.[41]

> Here is how I did it. This morning I met an Italian actor I had never spoken to. I greeted him very politely. I said to him: You are, sir, an illustrious actor, the most skillful man of the century. I need three tickets, so I can bring to the play two ladies who are dying to see it. Oh, of course, he said to me. He gave me three tickets and I went to the theatre alone. People were crowding around the door of the parterre buying tickets, and I took two of them aside and said: Gentlemen, I have taken two tickets for two of my friends who haven't

come. They were thirty sous each for the amphithéâtre; if you like, I will give you the two for thirty sous. They accepted the offer, gave me thirty sous, which I put in my pocket, and we went into the theatre together.

I placed myself in the middle of the first bench of the amphithéâtre. As soon as the curtain rose, I shouted: Fie, what a vile decor! What dauber daubed that? I have, without contradiction, seen better at the marionettes. There's no sense to it. Look, these darks are not light enough, and the lights are not dark enough. Absolutely, the man along side of me said. And notice that this green is not a beautiful meadow green. Apparently, sir, I replied, you are of the métier. Oh, not at all, sir, he answered. I am a dyer and I know my colors.

The play began with an actor and actress; and me as well. What a bad actor! He does everything with such bad grace! And how badly he speaks! To see him, one would think he was selling old silver lace on the street. It seems to me, however, a man said, that this actress plays rather naturally. Well, yes, I shot back, but she is too small. She does not fill the stage. But sir, he replied, if she is small, that's not her fault. Well, I added, it's certainly not mine. For my money I expect to have tall actresses.

Now you know that today the Italian actors played the first scene all in French. A bourgeois, who had never been to the Italian theatre before, turned to me and said very seriously: I am astonished. I was told that I would not be able to understand the Italian actors, but I didn't miss a word of that scene.

Finally, after having abused the actors, the play, the decor, and everything else, I took a big whistle from my pocket and began to whistle like the devil. There was a woman behind me who said, Hey, mister, I can't hear anything. I'm really sorry about that, miss, I answered. I'm whistling as hard as I can. Some other people said to me, where were you brought up, sir, that you whistle? But don't you see, I answered, that these boozers [*linottes,* "linnets" or "hard drinkers," which makes the pun on "whistle" work] need to be whistled [off the stage].

The first act ended. The lemonade seller came into the amphithéâtre, crying: Some lemonade, gentlemen, some cakes, some macaroons. And me: Hey, rascal, haven't you a better play to give us? I don't give the play, he said, I only sell the lemonade. Well, let's see if your lemonade is better than the play. I drank five or six glasses, ate as many cakes and macaroons. Then I said to him: Go get me two glasses of chocolate; your lemonade has chilled my stomach, and during his absence I pretended to recognize a man in the parterre, although I knew no one there. I shouted: Hey, chevalier, I have something important to tell you. I jumped from the amphithéâtre into the parterre, mixed into the crowd, and that is how I got in for nothing, how I played the wit, how I ate and drank well without it costing me a penny, and why I have thirty sous left over.

The "siffleur," or whistler, was not a new phenomenon in the 1680s; Boileau mentions this primitive form of criticism in 1674,[42] although it must have still been fairly rare in the Paris theatres that early. Racine gives an apocryphal history of its origins: a chronicler asks when these whistles, now so fashionable, began in Paris. One said it was Boyer's plays that were first whistled at, another said Pradon's. But no, said an actor. The parterre yawned at Boyer and threw apples at Pradon. The whistles began, I witnessed it, at Fontenelle's *Aspar*.[43] *Aspar* was played in 1680.

Whistling in the theatre was apparently the privilege of the bourgeois in the parterre and its evolution a sign of the increasing importance of that segment of society to the success of a play. The amphithéâtre was perhaps more restrained; people there wanted to know where Arlequin "had been brought up" when he pulled out his whistle and began to blow. In Regnard's *Le divorce* (1688), Jupiter promises to keep order when Arlequin complains that the new play has not been sufficiently rehearsed and will certainly be met by an outburst of whistles from the parterre. Jupiter, who is planning to sit in the third loges, has a pocketful of thunderbolts, and "the first whistler who stirs . . . I'll singe his moustache."[44]

The stage remained the province of the *petit marquis*. Seating arrangements on the stage were more formal with the addition of bancs, benches along the sides of the downstage area. The Hôtel de Bourgogne apparently did not have balcons, or stage boxes, during this period. A series of prints of Brécourt's *La noce de village*, produced at the Hôtel de Bourgogne in 1666, shows an onstage audience estimated by Mittman at some forty gentlemen, sixteen seated on bancs and fifteen standing. There is no sign of balcons.[45] Nor are balcons in view in the frontispiece for *Le divorce*, which shows, however, three rows of bancs on each side and a total onstage audience, all seated, of perhaps fifty.

In Regnard's *La coquette* (1691) Arlequin is in disguise as a restless *petit marquis* who brags that "the stage is never empty when I am on it." Colombine cannot imagine what pleasure there is in drowning out some poor actor who nearly bursts trying to make himself heard at the back of the auditorium. "Let him burst, he's paid for it," says Arlequin. "But really," answers Colombine, "do you think you should comb your wig, take tobacco, and carouse on the stage, when the Parterre has paid his fifteen sous?" "But think what an honor for him to see men of quality! ... The Parterre has become terribly proud; the Italians have spoiled him." "Go sit in the loges," says Colombine. "Me in the loges, oh, I kiss your hand, I do not hear a play from a loge like a starling, I would rather die than not be seen from head to toe."[47] Clearly, the Italians preferred to flatter the occupants of the parterre and disparage the gentry on stage.

Along with preening *petits marquis* and whistling bourgeois, the theatre still suffered from disorders caused by people who tried to get in without paying, and the king issued a number of edicts forbidding "all persons, of whatever quality and condition, even officers of the king's house, his guards, gendarmes, light horse, musketeers, and all others to enter the said theatres without paying, [or to] create any disturbance or interrupt the play in any manner whatsoever."[48] The Italians cited the edict on their posters: "It is expressly forbidden by the king to all persons to enter without paying."[49] The regularity with which such edicts were issued suggests that the problem was recurrent, although when most of the soldiers were away from Paris in the 1690s, the situation must have improved.

After 1680 the Italians no longer shared staff with a French troupe whose registres inform us of staff size and daily expenses. The Italians may have managed with a slightly smaller staff at the Hôtel de Bourgogne, at least backstage, since their staging was simplified by the shortcomings of the theatre. Court accounts for 1683 and 1685 include per diem payments to seven nonsharers, four at three livres each and three at thirty sous. Among these were the small-part actors, Soussin the décorateur, and Cadet, perhaps his junior or assistant, who received various payments for minor expenses.[50] Another may have been the company valet or dresser. Of course, the house staff would have been left behind.

In 1684 the daily expenses of the Comédie-Francaise were fifty-nine livres, two sous, more than the forty-two sous, nineteen livres at Petit-Bourbon in 1659–60, but less than the seventy-three livres, four sous, at Palais-Royal in 1661–62. The staff was larger than it had been in 1659–60, but the salaries were lower.[51] Ticket prices were also lower. Standing in the parterre continued to cost fifteen sous, as it did in all the Paris theatres from midcentury. But the first loges, the stage, and the amphithéâtre cost three livres at the Italians as opposed to the five livres, ten sous, which the French, at least, had charged at Palais-Royal in 1672–73 for the first loges and the stage. Seats in the second loges went for one livre at the Italian theatre as opposed to thirty sous at Palais-Royal; in the third loges at the Italians a seat was fifteen sous, the same price as the parterre. The French lowered their prices as well after the merger of 1680.

For the first run of a new play, ticket prices were—in this period—*au double,* not necessarily double, but increased; later the Italians bragged that they *never* increased their prices. When Jupiter pays thirty sous to see *Le divorce* from the third loges, he is, however, paying *au double.* A three-livre seat in the amphithéâtre may also have been *au double,* since Arlequin pays only thirty sous for the amphithéâtre in *Le banqueroutier.* In the 1680s theatre attendance was relatively low. Records from the Guénégaud reveal no full houses and an occasional audience of fewer than 100. The Italians probably did no better. Without increasing the prices for new plays the actors would have been less affluent than they were. In the 1690s, especially after their theatre was remodeled and equipped for machine spectacle, the Italians may have done well enough with regular prices.

The Comédie-Italienne, though now established in its own theatre, did not play seven days a week. The Italians adopted the custom of actors in their homeland and chose not to play on Fridays in honor of the passion of Christ. In 1685 they were also dark on Tuesdays, perhaps because they could not attract an audience six days a week, or perhaps because Tuesday was their day to play at Versailles during the winter season. The French proposed in 1685 to perform at the Hôtel de Bourgogne on Tuesdays and Fridays in return for the 800 livres they were contributing to its rental. The dauphine turned them down, her ears no doubt ringing with the anguished cries of the Italians protecting their theatre.[53]

The move to the Hôtel de Bourgogne was not the only change that affected the Italian troupe in the 1680s. His Majesty's decision to merge the French troupes was part of a plan to regulate theatrical activity and increase the control of the court over it. Personal patronage, which was the norm at the beginning of Louis's reign, was exchanged for a system of state subsidy in which specified kinds and numbers of performances were expected in return for subventions. One reason for the merger of the two French troupes was Louis's desire to create a troupe large enough so that one half could play in Paris while the other half played at court. This meant that the Paris audience had no grounds for complaint when the actors were summoned to Versailles or—often for weeks at a time— to Fontainebleau. They were provided with daily expenses for food and lodging when they played at court, but the royal subvention was in lieu of wages. The large gratuities of earlier years were a thing of the past.

The new system was not necessarily favorable to the Italians. Their troupe was not large enough to be divided between Paris and the court, and when the actors were called to Fontainebleau, losses must have been inevitable. Their subvention remained 15,000 livres a year, which was still larger than the subvention paid to the French. In addition, the king had arranged for 2,000 livres of the 2,400 livres which they now owed in rent each year for the Hôtel de Bourgogne to be paid, 1,200 a year by the Opéra and 800 by the French. If this arrangement broke down at times, His Majesty could hardly be held responsible.

Sometime after 1680, the king allotted his son's wife, the dauphine Marie-Christine of Bavaria, the task of drawing up official regulations for the subventioned theatres. The preface to the "Règlement que Madame la Dauphine a ordonné estre fait sous le bon plaisir du Roi pour la troupe des Comédiens italiens" makes His Majesty's purposes clear: "The king, wanting to establish good order in his troupe of Italian actors for the good of the service ... wishes that it be composed always of a fixed number of twelve actors and actresses who are agreeable to him to serve in his royal houses when it pleases him, following the orders of his First Gentlemen of the Chamber."[54] The Règlement, drawn up "in conformity to the contract in effect among the actors and actresses," has fourteen articles. The first defines the distribution of roles in the troupe: "two women to play serious roles, two other women to play the comic roles, two men to play the lovers, two others to play the comics, two others to conduct the intrigue, and two other to play the fathers and old men."

Articles 2 through 10 establish an elaborate pension system. Each retiring actor is to receive 1,000 livres a year to be paid by the person whose place he or she fills. Actors who join the troupe without filling a vacant place also must pay 1,000 livres a year for six years. Any actor who is sent away by the king or any actor who dares to act after his retirement loses his pension.

Article 11 establishes the value of the troupe's theatrical property, the stage, loges, paintings, decors, lights, machines, costumes, and tools, at 1,500 livres per share, the same amount later indicated in the actors' Règlement et Convention of 1696. Article 12 allows for a single payment of 3,000 livres to any actor willing to forego the retirement pension. Article 13 states the relationship between the actors' contract and the Règlement. Article 14 sets the chain of command:

> And if any difficulty should arise among the actors and actresses of
> the troupe by reason of the present *règlement* or for any other reason
> which they cannot adjust among themselves, they will give their

accounts to the intendant and controller of the *argenterie* [the privy purse] and the *menus* [the office which oversaw all court entertainments] to be examined in order to make a report to M. the First Gentleman of the Chamber of the year to judge and decide the thing with knowledge of cause, in order to maintain the troupe in peace and on good terms so it may better acquit itself of its duties.

This Règlement was apparently enforced. The troupe added a Pantalon, a Polichinelle, and a second servante in order to conform to Article 1. Furthermore, the king exercised his right to dismiss actors, at least in one case.

The heart of the matter was, of course, performance at court. As Louis XIV planned the move to Versailles, twenty kilometers from the center of Paris, he realized that it was essential to arrange to entertain the nobles he would keep there in self-imposed confinement. Remarks in the *Mercure galant* over the years demonstrate how those arrangements developed and solidified.

His Majesty took an annual vacation at Fontainebleau, usually in October but sometimes in the spring. These vacations were "destined to pleasures," according to Donneau de Visé in the *Mercure galant* of October 1677. Since Fontainebleau was sixty-five kilometers from Paris, it was impossible for the entertainers to commute as they did to Versailles or St.-Germain-en-Laye. It was at Fontainebleau, with two theatrical troupes and the Opéra in attendance, that a pattern of court entertainment developed. In 1677 plays alternated with operas. In 1680, when the court made its pilgrimage to Fontainebleau in the spring to recover from the marriage of the dauphin, the French and the Italians played alternately "and made up, with the Promenade, a part of the pleasures of each day."[55] In June of that year, still at Fontainebleau, the French were playing twice a week, the Italians once. Apparently the new dauphine preferred serious plays to comedies and had no taste for the naïvetés of Arlequin. In January 1681, after the merger of the French troupes, the court made its annual visit to St.-Germain. Donneau de Visé reports: "A diversion every evening, ballet, French or Italian play, dance and masquerade." The Italians were also playing in Paris in January 1681, attracting large audiences to *Arlequin mercure galant* in spite of the bad weather. In September 1681 the two troupes were at Fontainebleau, playing alternately. In January 1682 the French and Italians were playing three or four times a week at St.-Germain. In June 1682 the two troupes were playing daily at Versailles, although the king was too busy to attend. His absence underscores the change in the relationship between His Majesty and the subventioned theatres. His own interest in it waning, Louis now provided theatrical entertainment as a permanent feature of life at court.

No longer nomadic, except for the annual vacation at Fontainebleau, the king and his court—some 10,000 strong—officially settled into Versailles in 1682. Recreation was established on an official schedule. According to the January *Mercure galant,* Monday, Wednesday, and Friday were the "jours d'appartement," or days when gambling was the chief occupation. On Sunday, Tuesday, and Thursday, a dance and play were offered, on Saturday an opera. Plays were not given quite that frequently at the beginning, since court financial records, which are partially extant for 1683, indicate that the French troupe played only nine times in the first quarter of the year while the Italians played six times, on 3, 12, and 21 January, and 4, 16, and 23 February.[56] By 1685, court accounts include thirty plays performed by the French and six by the Italians at Versailles between 1 January and 6 April, an average of just over two-and-a-half a week and closer to Donneau de Visé's model.[57]

Apparently the theatrical troupes did not play regularly at court during the summer, although in 1685 both troupes played briefly at Marly and the French were also at Chambord. The regular season resumed on 29 September at Fontainebleau where the actors remained until 11 November. On the sixteenth they were back at Versailles; the Italians performed there eight times before the end of the year, the French twenty times. The pattern was now established.

By and large, the Italian troupe played an Italian repertory at court. Six performances are cited by name in the accounts for 1683. Only one of them, *Arlequin lingère,* is included in the Gherardi collection, indicating that at some point it was played partly in French. The others—*La muette, Les deux semblables, Le mariage d'Arlequin, Arlequin plaqué,* and *Le lunatique*—are not otherwise known, at least by these exact titles, although most resemble titles in the known Italian repertory: *Il lunatico* or *Le capricieux, La nopce d'Arlequin, Les deux Arlequins* or *Les deux Scaramouches, Isabelle* [or *Eularia*] *muette par amour.* Even into the 1690s the Italians continued to play their Italian repertory: *Les amours d'Arlequin et de Marinette, Arlequin valet étourdi, Les fourberies d'Arlequin et de Mezetin,* and *La folie d'Octave* in 1691 and *La folie d'Octave, Arlequin mary de trois femmes, Les disgrâces d'Arlequin roy de la Chine, Arlequin laron, prévost et juge, Aularia muette par amour ou Arlequin médecin ignorant, Le dragon de Moscovie, Arlequin toujours Arlequin,* and *Arlequin aman malheuraux* [sic] in 1695 and 1696. Only *Colombine avocat pour et contre* from the Gherardi repertory is listed in the court accounts for the 1690s, and the possibility exists that it was played there in Italian.[58]

Louis XIV permitted his Italians to play in French and to produce plays with scenes written in French by French playwrights—in Paris. At court they remained, by and large, His Majesty's Italian actors. Playing an "old-fashioned" repertory in Italian, they were unlikely to have been wildly popular with the court which—especially after the death of the old queen—was no longer Italianate. This, combined with the loss of profit entailed in being away from Paris, explains why the Italians played less frequently than the French.

The troupes were told what to play at court and given little notice. A note from Duché, the intendant of Menus Plaisirs, to the French troupe demonstrates how the actors were summoned: "5 January 1681. I beg M. de La Grange to warn the troupe this evening to be ready to go to St.-Germain tomorrow to play *Oedipe* and *Le mariage forcé*. I have just given the order to provide six carriages and a wagon. The wagon will be at the Guénégaud tomorrow morning at 7 o'clock, and the carriages at 10. I am your very humble and obedient servant."[59] The six livres in per diem expenses received for playing at court were far less than the average daily share an actor could expect to make in Paris. However, his share in the yearly pension was expected to make up for the loss. In 1685 each Italian actor lost fifty-nine days playing at court. His pension was 1,500 livres a year. Thus, for each playing day at court he received twenty-five livres, eight sous, in pension and six livres in expenses, not an extraordinary profit, but perfectly adequate so long as Louis paid his obligations.

A troupe playing at court also profited from not having to pay its daily expenses. The gagistes were paid by the court; some received three livres and some thirty sous. The court also paid for transportation, candles, firewood, costume rental, and minor expenses that could amount to a considerable sum.

Court accounts for 1683 include 531 livres in per diem payments to the Italians and 720 livres to the French for the first quarter's performances at Versailles. The other expenses rose to 4,502 livres: 1,194 livres for carriages for the actors, 285 livres for wagons for their goods, 81 livres to the woodseller for their fires, 92 livres to Baraillon, head of the wardrobe of Menus Plaisirs, for costumes, 97 livres to the Italians for "extraordinary expenses," and—the major expense—2,253 livres for candles.

Versailles had no permanent theatre in 1682 when the court was established there. Historically, temporary theatres had been set up, often in the gardens, for such productions as Molière's *Le bourgeois gentilhomme* or *Le malade imaginaire*. In the 1680s various plans were drawn up for a grand court theatre, but it was never built.[60] At some point, probably in the 1680s, it was decided to "remodel for the theatrical performances which made up part of the ordinary life of the court the vestibule on the ground floor between the Cour des Princes and the garden."[61] This temporary solution lasted for nearly a century. The theatre was small, with two rows of loges and several benches set in a semicircle around an empty parterre. A "small pit for the orchestra" was in front of the tiny stage, further reduced in size by two dressing rooms, one on each side at the rear. The king's box was a balcony, suspended on the back wall facing the stage with access from the Salle des Marchands on the floor above. The rest of the audience entered from the Escalier des Princes at ground level.

The stage was not equipped for scenes and machines. Donneau de Visé wrote in January 1683 that since there was no Grand Salle at Versailles for machines, the grandeur of the spectacle depended on the costumes. The Paris actors' costumes were apparently not grand enough, because Baraillon consistently rented costumes from the court wardrobe to the professional troupes.

The court accounts are most forthcoming on the subject of candles, which are described in 1683 in excessive detail. Each troupe was allotted, per performance, 60 pounds of white (i.e., wax) candles, 35 pounds of yellow (i.e., tallow) candles, and three pounds of tallow. More than half of the wax candles were used to light the auditorium: 80 for the ten chandeliers with eight bobeches each and 44 for the loges. The stage was entitled to 104 wax candles, 72 along the two sides, 12 at the rear, and 20 for the heavens. Four candles were for the guards. The yellow candles were for the dressing rooms and the guards' room. The troupe was also entitled to twelve torches "to lead the actors to their carriages at night." On 25 June 1685 the office of Menus Plaisirs paid out 14,576 livres for "wax for the plays at Chambord, Fontainebleau, and Versailles."

At Fontainebleau the theatre was larger and had an Italianate stage. A plan of c. 1682 shows a long, narrow room with no accommodations for spectators. The king sat in state, his family on armchairs, the others on benches, all apparently on the floor.[62] Accounts still show no expenditure for scenic spectacle, however, although 390 livres were spent for work done on the theatre, probably for the *Ballet du temple de la paix*.

Theatre at court in the 1680s was no longer an occasion or an event, although it was not necessarily unpopular. Dangeau saw the Italians perform twelve times in 1687, eight times at Versailles in January, November, and December and four times at Fontainebleau in October. His Majesty was not so faithful. Dangeau's journal does record that on 16 October

1684 the king went to the Italian play at Fontainebleau. "This was the only play that he had seen since the death of the queen: he found the play very bad and was very bored."[63]

The actors on occasion still took part in special events at court. In September 1681 the *Mercure galant* reports that the marechal de Vivonne had presented to the king a pastoral opera by Lorenzani with text by the duc de Nevers. The prologue "was done by four men who were at table, apparently at the end of their meal, for the remains of it lay on the cloth. These four men, who had been rendered a little gay by the wine, were Poisson, Rosimond, Scaramouche, and Arlequin, all fantastically dressed." Arlequin's costume was of white satin with the usual diamonds replaced by flowers, a rose for the red, a tulip for the brown, a sunflower for the yellow, and a barbel for the blue. The four began a dispute about the relative merits of French and Italian opera and were about to come to blows when La Grange and Cinthio entered and proposed to settle the matter rationally. Cinthio suggested that a little Italian opera be played.

The first interlude was played by Arlequin and Scaramouche, imitating the shepherd and shepherdess who had just appeared on the stage. After the second act, Poisson and Rosimond entered to find fault with the Italian opera and sing the praises of the French. The dispute arose again among all four after the third act. But they all agreed with La Grange when he concluded that best of all was a play with music. The king was very happy with the interludes. He "admired the costumes of the singers and actors and said that he had never seen such a . . . noble spectacle"; in fact, the king liked it so much he saw it twice.

In 1682 the Italians took part in an "impromptu" at Fontainebleau and "played very well some scenes for which they were given the subjects and most of the ideas." This was a surprise for the king which he "happened upon" on his way to the billiard room, "a serenade in the form of an opera, a mixture of French music and Italian music and comedy." The subject was the unhappiness of Fontainebleau because the king was leaving for Versailles. The Italians appeared as Apollo, Diana, and Cupid, who decided that since they were incapable of keeping His Majesty at Fontainebleau, they would go along with him.[64] A few months later at a ball given by Monsieur, Bacchus and Silenus entered followed by a goat. Arlequin played Silenus, mounted on an ass hung with vines and grapes. Bacchus was played by Spezzafer, all covered with hams, sausages, and bottles, seated on a barrel carried in by two satyrs. The scene ended in a combat between the two demigods, the ass, and the goat which "greatly diverted the assembly."[65]

In November 1684 the *Mercure galant* reported another musical impromptu at Fontainebleau expressly designed so that the ladies of the
court could dance the interludes. The king enjoyed it, according to Dangeau's journal of 13 November. His Majesty had the ballet entries danced
a second time and ordered the costumes kept so that he could see a
reprise at Versailles. The plot is reminiscent of earlier scenarios by Marc'
Antonio Romagnesi:

> Cinthio, son of King Brandimate, is kidnapped by Corsairs and
> raised at the court of King Glaucias, where he falls in love with
> Lucinde, the king's daughter. Upon discovering who he was by birth,
> he returns to his fathers court. The king expects to conclude a long
> war with a neighboring king, Adamante, by marrying his son to
> Adamante's daughter. Cinthio wants Arlequin to pass for him so he
> can remain faithful to Lucinde. He teaches Arlequin the necessary
> conduct . . . and consults some gypsies to find out what will happen.
> The gypsies (six ladies of the court) dance. Cinthio than goes to
> consult a famous sorceress. The king meets Arlequin, who is not a
> success. Cinthio returns with the sorceress who falls in love with
> him and advises him to remain incognito. She promises to make
> Lucinde appear by magic. Lucinde appears, dancing with a rival and
> looking very happy. (Another entry of the court ladies.) Act 2 begins
> with Arlequin with the ambassador of King Adamante. Cinthio
> threatens to break off with Lucinde and writes to her. The sorceress
> conjures up some spirits to deliver the letter (the third entry, three
> men and three ladies of the court). In the last act, Arlequin gets
> bored with playing the prince and tells the king all. Lucinde arrives.
> The spirits have told her what is going on; she has found another
> sorceress to transport her. The king finds her so beautiful and is so
> delighted to discover that Cinthio, not Arlequin, is his son, he con-
> sents to the marriage. The sorceress repents; all the courtiers enter
> and sing and dance for the finale.

This scenario from the November 1684 *Mercure galant* is the last long
entry in that periodical having to do with the Italians. They continued to
play at court for another ten years, but as part of the routine established
earlier. His Majesty was older, graver, and married to the devout Mme.
de Maintenon. Once Mme. Scarron, widow of a bohemian and libertine
playwright, the soon-to-be marquise de Maintenon and morganatic wife
of the king symbolized a shift at court toward piety and orthodoxy. In
1685 the revocation of the Edict of Nantes signaled the end of Henry IV's
experiment in freedom of conscience and the beginning of the reign of
Bossuet and other conservative Catholics over the conscience of the king.

The abbé de Choisy wrote in his memoirs in 1686: "There are plays every day at Fontainebleau, but the king no longer goes to them; one thought at first that it was business; then one recognized that it was scruples, and everyone admired that a prince of his age had the strength to renounce pleasures."[66]

Louis did not renounce old loyalties, however, at least not entirely. An anecdote of the period—although possibly apocryphal—demonstrates that Biancolelli was still believed to have the king's favor:

> The Italian actors ... had the idea of mixing with their Italian dialogue a few French words. The public welcomed favorably this trial, and little by little French scenes were mixed into the Italian plays. . . . The French actors, seeing in this innovation the beginning of a rivalry which could be dangerous to them ... submitted their complaints to Louis XIV. The king did not want to decide the question without having heard both parties. He had brought before him Dominique Biancolelli, the Arlequin of the Comédie Italienne, and Baron, famous actor of the Comédie Française. Baron spoke first, in the name of the French actors, but when it was the turn of Dominique: "Sire," he said to the king, "how should I speak." "Speak as you wish," said the king. "Nothing else needs to be said," answered Dominique. I have won my case." Baron wanted to object to this surprise, but the king judged it good and said that he had spoken and would not retract it.[67]

This tale is reminiscent of any number of supposed encounters between Louis and his actors and has little authority, but it does indicate that active patronage was thought to occur as late as the 1680s. The anecdotal telling of Dominique's death, supposedly the result of overexertion in an effort to please the king, also suggests that His Majesty had not totally abandoned his Italians. His financial support, in any case, lasted until the troupe was dismissed, several years after the death of Tiberio Fiorilli, the last survivor among Louis XIV's personal favorites.

The troupe that moved into the Hôtel de Bourgogne in 1680 was—like its new theatre—small and aging. It consisted of Gherardi and Biancolelli as Flautin and Arlequin, Lolli as the Docteur, Cei as Capitan Spezzefer, Fiorilli as Scaramouche, Zanotti and Romagnesi as Octave and Cinthio, Brigida Fedele and Orsola Cortesi as Aurelia and Eularia, and Patricia Adami as Diamantine. By the end of the decade, Gherardi, Biancolelli, and Cei were dead, Zanotti had retired to Italy, and Fiorilli and Brigida Fedele were no longer active performers.

New actors were recruited in Italy by a troupe member charged with that responsibility; no longer did the king merely write to some Italian monarch to send him a Pantalon or an Arlequin. Apparently the talent scout had been Zanotti. Marc' Antonio Romagnesi took over the job sometimes before 1683 and wrote to Perrault, controller of Colbert's household:

> Friday. I beg very humbly Mons. Perrault to have the kindness to put my business before Mons. Colbert. It is very necessary that I have a passport which specifies that I am going to Italy to chose actors to render the company complete and as I need to know of them to make the choice, it is necessary that I go to Rome, Venice, Genoa, Ferrara, Bologna, Padua, and other places where the troupes are in order to find out about them and to meet the ambassadors of France who are at Rome and Venice. This is why I beg very humbly Mons. Colbert to give me some little sum of money to defray my expenses, for M. Octave has always had 200 ecus and he went only to Bologna and Venice.[68]

In April 1686 the troupe consisted of fourteen actors. Brigida Fedele was almost certainly inactive by this point, while the last indicated appearance of Fiorilli was as a mute creditor in *Le banqueroutier* (April 1687). The remaining troupe perfectly met the dauphine's requirements: two old men, Lolli and a new Pantalon, Giovanni Battista Turri; two amoureux, Romagnesi and Bartolomeo Ranieri, Aurelio, in place of Zanotti; two comics, Giuseppe Tortoriti, Pasquariel, and Michelangelo Fracansani, Pulichinelle; two men "for the intrigue," Biancolelli and Angelo Costantini, Mezzetin; 2 amoureuses, Orsola Cortesi and her daughter Françoise, Isabelle; and 2 servantes, Patricia Adami and Catherine Biancolelli, Colombine.

The addition of actors to the company did not entail the addition of shares to the original ten. The Biancolelli sisters entered at part shares; so probably did the other new actors. The seven senior members of the troupe would have continued as full sharers, and the newcomers would have graduated to full shares according to their popularity and the availability of the shares.

The enlarged troupe permitted the dual repertory that emerged late in the decade. Biancolelli and his daughters, Costantini, Romagnesi, Lolli, and sometimes Tortoriti played the French repertory while the older women along with the men who did not speak French well played the Italian repertory. Eularia speaks French in the Gherardi repertory once, in *Le banqueroutier*, while Diamantine never appears in a French scene. Interestingly enough, Giuseppe Giaratoni, although still a gagiste after twenty years, began to play an important role in the French repertory where Pierrot often appears as a third zanni along with Arlequin and Mezzetin. On the other hand, Policinelle and Pantalon never appear in the Gherardi repertory, although this may be the result of editing on the part of Evaristo Gherardi.

The perfection of the dauphine's arrangements was shattered in August 1688 when Domenico Biancolelli died. In the final ten years of its tenure, the company was never to be as stable as it had been between 1668 and 1683. Furthermore, with Biancolelli dead and Fiorilli in de facto retirement, the Italians had lost their most important links with both the court and with the past of their art. The age of the actor was at an end in Paris. The age of the play was underway.

If His Majesty preferred the knockabout farce and mild ribaldry of the conventional commedia dell'arte repertory, the same was not true of the Parisian audience. With the court gone to Versailles and the theatres increasingly the domain of the middle classes, the audience looked for entertainments which were either pure fantasy or which mirrored their own lives as merchants, lawyers, financiers, and functionaries. Satires of French life and French foibles attracted audiences, as did music, machines, and the marvelous.

In the 1680s the Italian troupe made a transition. Beginning with Italian plays with French songs and harangues, they moved on to Italian plays interlaced with scenes in French and eventually to plays spoken principally in French, written down in advance and learned by heart. By 1690, although the Italian repertory was still being played both for the court and in Paris, the Italian troupe was also presenting French plays in direct competition with the French troupe.

In *Le livre sans nom,* published after Biancolelli's death, the author asks Arlequin why the company no longer does the "good old Italian plays." Arlequin answers that "we play now for certain people who only come to our theatre to laugh, and they do laugh . . . If we were to perform only our old repertory . . . our theatre would be little frequented, so I answer you as Cinthio another time answered M. St.-Evremond that good actors with excellent plays can die of hunger."[69]

A Company Rejuvenated

AFTER TWENTY YEARS of relative stability, the Comédie-Italienne in Paris began to change. By the end of the 1680s, the troupe was transformed by death, age, and the desire to go home at last, as well as by Louis XIV's decision to enlarge the company and the needs of a dual repertory.

The first changes took place in 1683. In January the Italians played three times at court, each time receiving in per diem expenses sixty-six livres for eleven actors and actresses. In February the payment rose to seventy-eight livres for thirteen actors and actresses.[1] The troupe which signed a Convention, or articles of association, on 29 April of that same year consisted, however, of only 9: Fiorilli, Biancolelli, Lolli, Zanotti, Romagnesi, Cei, Brigida Fedele, Orsola Cortesi, and Patricia Adami. Giovanni Gherardi, the tenth sharer, had died on 23 March. Who, then, was the mysterious eleventh actor who received the per diem six livres in January? Who the equally mysterious twelfth and thirteenth included in the accounts for February?

An easy solution is to assume that the eleventh actor was Angelo Costantini, Mezzetin, who according to the Parfaict brothers, arrived in Paris perhaps as early as 1681 to understudy Biancolelli. The brothers, unfortunately, seem to have no evidence for the date;[2] Gueullette merely says that Costantini was playing in Turin and came to France to "understudy" Dominique "in case of need."[3] Mezzetin is mentioned once in Dominique's zibaldone, but only in an "Addition" to *La propreté*, which could have been played at any time after the original opening date of 1677. According to Mélèse, Costantini played Arlequin in *La matrone d'Ephèse, ou Arlequin grapignan* in May 1682, but Donneau de Visé clearly refers to Biancolelli in the role in the long discussion of the play that appeared in that month's *Mercure galant*. Mezzetin is a character in Gherardi's 1700 version of *Arlequin Protée*, which opened to great applause in October 1683. However, the distribution of roles in the Gherardi texts often reflects later casting, and a print by Bonnart, from a calendar-almanac issued to celebrate the play's original production, shows Spezzafer in the role of Glaucus which Gherardi assigns to Mezzetin.[4]

Gueullette's account of Mezzetin's association with the troupe was based on a conversation he had with Costantini in 1729 at a dinner at Luigi Riccoboni's house. Time and ego made of Costantini a not very reliable witness, as we shall see, and while it is possible he came to understudy Dominique (just as Dominique is said to have come to understudy Trivelin), it is more probable that he came to replace Flautin as First Zanni in the Italian repertory sometime before 19 April 1686, when he signed a contract as a sharing member of the company.[5] Mezzetin was in origin a First Zanni, not a Second, and though Costantini claimed to have invented the role in Paris, in fact he was playing it in Parma and Venice in 1678.[6]

The Paris troupe was still searching for a new First Zanni in September 1684 when a letter from the duke of Modena explains that Giovanni Andrea Cimidori, who played the masque as Finocchio, was ill with asthma and dropsy and could not be sent to France.[7] Of course, Costantini may have been in Paris—understudying Dominique, as he said—and considered to be of insufficient merit to warrant membership in the company when the Convention of 1683 was signed. However, he apparently did not play at court, since Dangeau signals his debut at Versailles on 6 May 1686. If the eleventh actor at Versailles in January 1683 was not Costantini, perhaps it was Giaratoni, now playing Pierrot, who had risen from the ranks of the gagistes but was not yet admitted as a sharer. The court apparently recognized an intermediate category, since more actors received the six livres per diem then were legally bound to the association.

The newcomers in February 1683 are much more easily identified. They were Françoise and Catherine Biancolelli, the daughters of Domenico Biancolelli and Orsola Cortesi, who entered the troupe with half shares on 29 April 1683. The official document, an addendum to the Convention of 1683, reads as follows:

> And at the moment of the passing of the contract above, the said gentlemen and ladies composing the said troupe, in consequence of the agreement of the king obtained by Mademoiselles Françoise and Catherine Biancolelli, sisters ... to enter into the said troupe and continue to play there each of them the character which they have already begun, have willingly admitted the said ladies into their troupe to stay and play the said characters so long as it pleases them, under the good pleasure of His Majesty and share in the earnings

from the said Majesty and monies from the said box office as well as future expenses for each a half share, that is a whole share for the two, to begin today.[8]

What is especially interesting is that this document indicates that Françoise and Catherine Biancolelli had been playing the roles of Isabelle and Colombine before they were officially admitted, implying that this troupe—unlike the French troupes—restricted its number of shares.

The Biancolelli sisters entered into the share that had been held by Giovanni Gherardi, whose widow received the 500 livres they paid as an entry fee. It is assumed by the historians of the Italian troupe that the entry of the Biancolellis marked the retirement of Brigida Fedele and Patricia Adami. However, the actors' Convention of 1683 says nothing of retirement. An elaborate pension system was put into effect several years later, but few of the Italian actors took advantage of it. As a result, the evidence is contradictory. Brigida Fedele, for instance, was still a legal member of the troupe in 1686 when loan agreements were signed with Dr. Amonio. Her character appears nowhere in the Gherardi repertory, but that is hardly surprising since she was seventy and had never played in French. What suggests that she must have entered de facto retirement is a note from Père Léonard dated 1682 that gives a formula for recanting the profession, and refers to Madeleine Béjart and the "Signora Aurelia" as two actresses whose renunciations he had received.[9] But though she may have sworn not to mount the stage, she apparently did not swear to give up her share of the profits. By 1691, the date of the next surviving document related to the business of the troupe, she was no longer a legal member, although she was to live for many years more. The same confusion exists with Tiberio Fiorilli and Patricia Adami; exactly when they ceased playing cannot be determined, but we know that Fiorilli kept his share until he died, some years after his final appearance. Patricia Adami probably continued to act in the Italian repertory through the 1680s; Catherine Biancolelli did not join the troupe to replace her in the Italian repertory, but rather to play in French and to ensure that the troupe conformed to the distribution being imposed by the king and the dauphine, which required two women for the comic roles.

Presumably, Orsola Cortesi at some point became First Amoureuse and her daughter Françoise Second Amoureuse, although by this time such terms had little meaning. Orsola Cortesi did appear in the French repertory occasionally in minor roles and continued to appear in the Italian repertory into the 1690s. Françoise appeared as the "love interest" in the French repertory and also played an amoureuse in the Italian plays. Catherine played Colombine, more a French "suivante," or lady's companion, than a servante, and turned the character into a witty, active, somewhat amoral woman capable of devising plot intrigue, while Patricia Adami continued the servante in the Italian repertory.

According to Costantini, it was Louis XIV's idea to add the Biancolelli sisters to the company, "the King having said that he had heard that Dominique had some amiable daughters and that he should put them on the stage, which was a type of order for him." [10] In fact, the women of the troupe were getting old. Brigida Fedele was seventy, Orsola Cortesi fifty, Patricia Adami probably somewhere in between. But replacing women was not easy. With the exception of Cortesi, who came to France with her parents and then married a member of the troupe, and perhaps Adami (the date of whose marriage to Lolli is unknown), the women associated with the troupe had all been married to men in the troupe when they were called from Italy. The Italians were absolutely respectable and wanted to remain so. But in 1683 the Paris troupe was complete. Thus, even if one or more of the women retired, she could not be replaced from Italy unless room could be found for a husband as well. The obvious answer to the problem: the pretty, young Biancolelli sisters, born and raised in France, accomplished singers, and resident under the parental roof.

In the fall following their official entry into the troupe, Françoise and Catherine played in *Arlequin Protée,* and Donneau de Visé was ecstatic. In the *Mercure galant* of October 1683 he writes: "If Arlequin is inimitable . . . his two daughters are no less so. The different characters that they sustain are so well filled that they have attracted the applause of all Paris which cannot stop admiring them. Never has been seen such intelligence for theatre combined with such great youth. There is no point of character into which they do not enter, and they acquit themselves with such good grace that whenever they appear in whatever scene, they seem uniquely born for the characters that they play." Françoise was the older of the two by just under eleven months. She was born in Paris and baptised at St.-Germain-l'Auxerrois on 1 December 1664. Her godparents were courtiers; the king reserved himself for the first son. She was just over eighteen when she began to act with the company. Her sister Catherine, baptised on 26 October 1665, at St.-Eustache, was seventeen. Raised in France, they spoke French perfectly. Catherine was also an excellent singer and was employed in parodies of French tragedies and operas. Within two years of their debut, both Françoise and Catherine were playing title roles (in *Isabelle médecin* and *Colombine avocat pour et contre*) and Catherine at least had been granted a full share in the company.[11]

In November 1685 Catherine Biancolelli married Pierre Lenoir de la Thorillière, the son of François Lenoir, sieur de La Thorillière, who acted with the troupe of Molière from 1662 to 1673, and at the Hôtel de Bourgogne from 1673 until his death in 1680. According to La Grange, it was his death that removed the final obstacle to the union of the French troupes. His son, Pierre, made his debut at twelve in *Psyché* in 1671. He was admitted to a half share in the French troupe at the end of the 1683–84 season, replacing Verneuil. He received a full share in September 1685, just in advance of his marriage.

The marriage contract was signed at Fontainebleau, during the annual royal vacation. The witnesses included the groom's mother and sister, the French actors Baron and Dancourt, the bride's parents, her maternal grandmother, her brother Louis, her sister Françoise, the family friend Dr. Amonio, and the duc de St. Aignan, First Gentleman of the Chamber for 1685. Let us hope that the duke was present as a friend, and not because His Majesty's control of the actors had extended to approval of intercompany marriages, although the contract reads: "In the presence and with the consent of the very high and powerful lord Monseigneur the duc de Saint Aignan."[12]

The young people brought to the marriage as assets their full shares in the troupes to which they belonged. La Thorillière estimated his worth at 10,000 livres and endowed his wife-to-be with 6,670 livres 15 sous. Catherine brought "to the community of the marriage" in money and goods, both personal and professional, 20,000 livres, a more than handsome dowry. The young couple set up housekeeping with the Biancollellis, who perhaps moved into larger quarters to accommodate them. At the time of the wedding they were living on the rue Comtesse d'Artois; six months later Domenico Biancolelli, Orsola Cortesi, and Catherine Biancolelli, wife of Pierre Lenoir *dit* La Thorillière, were all living on the rue Montorgueil. This arrangement continued; in 1694 Orsola Cortesi and her daughters were "living all three together" in the rue Mauconseil and in 1696 in the rue du Regnard.[13]

According to Tralage, Catherine may have had reasons to set up housekeeping with her parents. La Thorillière the younger was a popular actor who got good roles after the death of Raisin the younger. He was "the delight of the parterre. All the others tremble before the parterre and fear the whistles. But the parterre gobbles him up and finds many things good in him that would not be suffered in another." He was not, however, the best of husbands. "Colombine," says Tralage, "is like her father and mother very thrifty; but La Thorillière spends in a day or two what his wife saves in a month. It is to be hoped that his excesses will not kill him."[14] In fact, he outlived his wife by sixteen years. They had at least two children, Jean-Baptiste and Anne Maurice, and may have had several others. Colombine was "always pregnant," according to her line in Regnard's *Les Chinois:* "The mule is a sterile animal and everyone knows that Marinette [Angela Toscana, the wife of Giuseppe Tortoriti] and Colombine have babies every nine months."[15] Another line in the same play may give an idea of how Catherine Biancolelli felt about her marriage seven years later. Colombine says: "From the point of view of self-interest, which is the only point of view in marriages today, an Italian actor always triumphs over a French actor. He pays less for his costumes; his share is larger; and it sometimes takes only one mediocre play a year to keep an Italian actor in business."[16] The audience would, of course, have known that Colombine had personal grounds for comparison.

Françoise Biancolelli had a far more unhappy personal life. On 2 April 1691, she married a young officer of the guard, Constantin de Turgis. She was twenty-six, he was twenty-one. His parents, appalled that their son had married an actress, filed suit for abduction and subornation. A year later they disinherited him. Orsola Cortesi, "ignorant of French law and following advice which dishonored her and her daughter, testified that there had been no contract or marriage ceremony." A judgment of 11 February 1695 ruled that "there had been abuse in the celebration of the marriage." The parties were forbidden to see each other (on pain of corporal punishment) or to contract a new marriage.[17]

Two children were born of the union, the first in 1692. It seems likely that the marriage, if it took place at all, was irregular since in all the documents which she signed as a member of the troupe between 1691 and 1696, Françoise Biancolelli is referred to as *fille majeure,* or an unmarried adult woman who did not need her husband's permission to sign a legal document.

Gueullette says that she left the stage and renounced her profession in 1695, yet she signed the company Règlement et Convention of 1696. The character Isabelle last appears in the Gherardi collection in the cast of *La fontaine de sapience* (July 1694). It was not, however, until 1701 that Turgis and Françoise Biancolelli were married "for the second time," their second child belatedly ceremonially baptised, and the children declared legitimate, all thanks to a dispensation from Cardinal de Noailles. Turgis refused to have the marriage entered in the church register, not wanting to hurt the feelings of his mother, but he did—from that time on—"go publicly to his wife's house and even appeared with her on the public streets."

Turgis was hardly a faithful spouse. Although he "ordinarily lived in the sight and to the knowledge of everyone in the house of Orsola Cortesi . . . received visits there and passed his days there and often his nights," he also had a house on the rue St.-Roch where he lived with his mistress and an apartment in his mother's house where he kept most of his servants and horses. In 1706 he fell ill in the house where he kept his mistress and shortly thereafter died, leaving his wife and children penniless. The court declared her his legal wife and the children legitimate, but refused to enter them in the succession to their father's family's property. The children were granted pensions of 300 livres a year each, and the widow one of 400. In 1713 the king granted her an additional pension of 300 livres a year, giving her a total income of 700 livres on which she lived for many years until her death in 1747. A year later the children received a small capital sum from a cousin, apparently left them by their father in a roundabout way to avoid legal difficulties with his family. This family tragedy seems almost designed to provide the maximum embarrassment and pain to the respectable Biancolellis, to say nothing of its economic burden on people deprived of their livelihood after 1697.

The next newcomer to the troupe after the Biancolelli sisters was Giovan Battista Turri, Pantalon, who made his debut at court on 12 December 1684, according to the Marquis Dangeau (fig. 13). He was liked by the dauphine, and presumably granted a share. He was definitely a member in April and July 1686, when he signed the loan contracts with Dr. Amonio. He was gone before November 1691, the date of the next surviving document signed by the company.

According to Gueullette and the historians who have followed him, Turri was the original Pantalon of the troupe, in Paris in 1645, 1653, and again in 1661. He is said to have been the Pantalon Bisognoza who fought with Baloardo in 1653 and the Pantalon who died in Paris in 1670.[18] Rasi points out that this last attribution is unlikely, since a letter exists from "Gio. Batt.a Turri, *detto* Pantalone," written from Venice on 30 March 1671, recommending his son for employment.[19]

Whether or not he was in Paris midcentury, Turri was certainly there in the 1680s. He is referred to only once in Gherardi's French material, in the opening monologue of Regnard's *Le divorce* (1688), when Arlequin as the troupe's orator explains why the scheduled play cannot

FIG. *13*. *Michelangelo Fracansani, Polichinelle (left) and Giovan' Battista
Turri, Pantalon (right). Engraving by Marinette.* (Bibliothèque de
l'Opéra, Ms. Rés. 625; phot. Bibl. Nat. Paris)

go on: "Gentlemen, what I am going to tell you will perhaps not please you, but truthfully I am more annoyed than you. ... We cannot perform the play today; on the one hand there is our Porter who has just now gotten sick, and Pantalon, who was supposed to play the role of Patroclus, is indisposed."[20] The scene parodies an opera, *Achille et Polixène* by Campistron and Colasse; the joke, of course, is the idea of the elderly magnifico playing the young warrior and may rest on a particular piece of casting at the Opéra. Turri may have performed for the most part in the Italian repertory, but an illustration from the 1684 Bonnart calendar-almanac of *Arlequin Protée* (fig. 14) shows Pantalon in the role of Pillardin, a French lawyer, whose long speeches equal those of Arlequin in the Gherardi text. Since Turri may well have left the troupe before Gherardi entered, Gherardi would not necessarily have known which roles had been played by Pantalon during his tenure.

Turri's presence in Paris in 1686 lends credence to an incident reported in *La vie de Scaramouche*. According to this romanticized life of Fiorilli, "The troupe [in Paris] was complete when the Pantalon fired a pistol at the old [*vieux*] Octave with whom he had quarreled. Although he missed his enemy, this did not prevent his taking flight and returning to Italy, where he became a priest."[21] This anecdote has been variously interpreted. According to Gueullette, it was Turri's son—the amoroso Virginio—who quarreled with Zanotti, returned to Italy, and joined the Carmelite order at Modena at the age of forty.[22] Riccoboni wrote that he died a few days before his profession, but was buried in his habit.[23]

Assuming something of the sort took place—Gueullette thought the pistol shot was false but the quarrel true—we might conjecture that the Turri father and son came to Paris in 1684, the father to play Pantalon, the son perhaps to try out for the role of Second Amoureux which would become vacant when Zanotti retired and Romagnesi succeeded him as First Amoureux. By 1684 Zanotti was old enough to be referred to as the "vieux" Octave, a soubriquet which would not have applied to him in the 1650s or 1660s.[24] Turri *fils*, according to his father's letter, was playing the terzo amoroso in 1671 and looking for someone to take him on as secondo.[25] If he was forty in 1684 and twenty-seven in 1671, his father's letter makes perfect sense. Assuming the younger Turri returned to Italy for whatever reason, perhaps the quarrel, perhaps the fact that he did not please, the company would then have recruited Bartolomeo Ranieri, Aurelio, as Second Amoureux in his stead, while Turri *père* remained in France, at least until 1686 and possibly 1689. A Pantalon is included in the 1689 engraving of the troupe celebrating the investiture of Mezzetin as Arlequin.

Arlequin est charmant en toute sa maniere,
Il deuient en vn jour Seigneur, Marchand Voleur,
Commissaire, filoux, Comedien, Empereur,
Amoureux, Maitre d'Arme, enfin se fait Laictiere,

Et pour finir ce jour par vn jeu delicat,
De la Cour Bazochique, il deuient aduocat;
Et l'Auditeur charme sans plaindre sa monoye,
S'en retourne remply de plaisir, et de joye.

La Cour de la Bazoche assemblée pour juger le Procez entre le chien du docteur
Balouarde, et vn clerc du Chastelet nommé Grifonnet.

Toujours Plaider *Toujours Escrire*

Pillardin qui se defend bien
fait remarquer à la Bazoche
Que rit est Aduocat le chien
Et scait aussi vuider la poche

Maistre la Ruine, qui occupe
Pour Grifonet, petit badin,
Pretend faire passer pour dupe
Le fameux maistre Pillardin,

Grifonnet.

le Docteur. *M˜ Pillardin.* 8.418 *M˜ la Ruine.*

FIG. *14. Final scene of* Arlequin Protée *from a Bonnart calendar-almanac of 1684.* (Bibliothèque Nationale; phot. Bibl. Nat. Paris)

According to the Marquis Dangeau, the court "learned of the death of Scaramouche ... a very good actor" on 17 February 1685. By this Dangeau meant to signal the death of Girolamo Cei, who played Scaramouche during Fiorilli's absence between 1668 and 1670 and then acted as Spezzafer for fifteen years until his death. La Grange noted, at the end of the 1684–85 season, "Gieronimo Cey, *dit* Spezzafer, Italian Actor and good actor, died at the beginning of April." His replacement, Giuseppe Tortoriti who played as Pasquariel, made his court debut on 15 March 1685, when Dangeau writes: "Versailles. This evening there was an Italian play, Pasquariello Trono was seen for the first time and found a good enough actor and the most nimble man in the world." The following Sunday the marquis noted: "Versailles. This evening there was an Italian play, where the new actor Pasquariello played much better than the first time. Monseigneur, Madame la dauphine and the courtiers were very happy with him." He was welcomed in Paris as well as at court. Donneau de Visé writes in the March *Mercure galant*: "The Italian troupe is augmented by a new actor who attracts the applause of all Paris and who pleases the court as much as the boneheads. He has a surprising agility of body and admirably seconds the incomparable Arlequin."

Tortoriti played a rash young capitan at first; later he did the same sort of generalized comic valets and "detached roles" that Cei had done (fig. 15). He was a very good acrobat and mime and could perform, says Gueullette, who must have seen him, "all the perilous tricks of the ladder."[26] Although he came to replace Spezzafer, he also replaced Scaramouche, although he did not officially adopt the masque until 1694, shortly before the death of Tiberio Fiorilli. Exactly when Fiorilli ceased to play is not clear. Both Pasquariel and Scaramouche appear in *Colombine avocat pour et contre* (June 1685) and in *Le banqueroutier* (April 1687), although in the latter piece Scaramouche plays a nonspeaking role, one of the creditors. On the other hand, it is not always possible to tell which of the masques was playing which character in the French repertory, and Fiorilli himself claimed to have "retired from the stage" in 1690.[27]

The new Capitan was very tall. In *Le divorce* a comic combat between the tiny Mezzetin as Madame Dorotée, a Chinese dwarf, and the tall Pasquariel, also in drag, ends the second act, its humor derived largely from the physical contrast between the two actors. Tortoriti was from Messina, according to Tralage; his date of birth is unknown. He was in the company of the duke of Modena in 1681. His extreme agility suggests that he was still young when he made his debut in Paris.

He was married to Angela Toscana, who entered the company after

FIG. *15. Guiseppe Tortoriti, Pasquariel. Engraving by
Marinette.* (Bibliothèque de l'Opéra, Ms. Rés. 625; phot. Bibl. Nat. Paris)

the retirement of Patricia Adami to play the servante Marinette. This character first appears in the Gherardi repertory in *La fille sçavante* (November 1690). Angela Toscana may have already been in Paris, married to Tortoriti, or she may have come from Italy and then married Tortoriti. They had four children born in Paris between June 1692 and August 1696,[28] leading to the remark in *Les Chinois,* quoted earlier, that Colombine and Marinette were always pregnant. In fact, Marinette *was* pregnant in December 1692, when the play was performed. The oldest child, Angélique-Catherine, married Pietro Paghetti, who played at the fairs and later in the new Italian troupe. The younger daughter, Marie-Angélique, married Pierre-François Biancolelli, the youngest child of Dominique.

Tortoriti submitted a petition to the chancellor asking for letters of naturalization in order to "die French" so that his children could inherit from him.[29] Campardon, who found letters of naturalization for Biancolelli and his wife, Lolli and his, Fiorilli and his son, and other members of the troupe, did not find them for Tortoriti, so perhaps his request was rejected. He did stay on in France after the company was disbanded, however, and received permission to organize a troupe to play in the provinces. But that troupe was apparently not successful, and he eventually returned to Italy. In 1716 he was recommended by the prince of Parma for the new company, but the regent expressed his regrets.[30]

The troupe lost another of its original members when Giovan Andrea Zanotti, Octave, returned to Italy sometime before the debut of his successor in April 1685. The father of seven children by his second wife,[31] the oldest only ten years old, Zanotti apparently wanted to educate them in Bologna. He was, besides, over sixty and perhaps a little old to be playing lovers in Paris, although evidently not in Italy. In 1688–89, he was once more in the service of the duke of Modena, replacing Giovan Battista Costantini who had gone to Paris to play the role of Octave. As late as 1693, two years before his death, Zanotti was still acting in Bologna.

Not only did he continue to act, at least from time to time, Zanotti also published Italian translations of *Héraclite* and *Le Cid* by Pierre Corneille, both in Bologna in 1691.[32] He died on 13 September and was buried on 17 September 1695. Canon Ghiselli wrote of him in his *Memorie manoscritte di Bologna:* "G. A. Zanotti *dit* Octave, celebrated actor in the role of the First Amoureux who played in the first theatres of Europe, and particularly in France where the King granted him an annual provision of 200 doubloons for life, which was always punctually disbursed."[33]

The Canon may have been as wrong about that as he was about the rest. He said Zanotti had left his profession many years before in order to save his soul, that he died in his eightieth year, and that he left three sons, one a doctor, one a lawyer, one a priest. In fact, Zanotti was seventy-three, was acting until two years before his death, and had an undetermined number of children, as many as eighteen in all according to one source. Three of his sons did become celebrated, none as actors. Ercole was a historian and poet, Francesco Maria a philosopher and famous scientist, and Gian Pietro a painter.

Zanotti was replaced as First Amoureux by Romagnesi. To play the role of Second Amoureux the troupe recruited from Italy Bartolomeo Ranieri, who played as Aurelio. Tralage identifies him as a Piedmontese from Moncenisio. According to Rasi, he was born around 1640, and was in the service of Ferdinando Carlo for seventeen years before going to France. Rasi also identifies as Ranieri an Aurelio sent by the duke of Mantua to the duke of Modena in 1676.[34] If Rasi is right, than Ranieri was 45 when he came to Paris, an experienced if slightly elderly amoureux.

He made his debut in Paris in April 1685 at the same time as Michelangelo Fracansani, Polichinelle. Donneau de Visé, thinking back to Tortoriti's successful debut in March, predicted that if the new actors pleased as much as he had, "the auditorium would be found too small for the audiences they would attract."[35] The auditorium remained adequate in size.

Ranieri appeared in the French repertory in *Le banqueroutier,* although he played only in the impromptu scenes in Italian.[36] In *Le divorce* (March 1688), he appeared as Isabelle's brother, a small role which he also played in Italian. His name appears in the cast list of *Le marchand dupé* (September 1688) as Isabelle's lover, but he actually appears in the text only in the last scene where he speaks for the first time in French— one line. His role is even smaller in *Colombine femme vengée* (January 1689), where he appears but does not speak at all. In the French repertory, at least, Ranieri does not seem to have distinguished himself.

On 23 February 1688 Seignelay wrote to La Reynie as follows: "His Majesty has ordered me to write to you to have the actor Aurelio observed to the end that if it is found that he speaks badly as is said on the business of Rome, you will have him arrested."[37] Louis XIV was then embroiled in the long and bitter Gallican controversy with Pope Innocent XI concerning the king's declared supremacy over the French clergy and church property in France. Ranieri was apparently suspected of speaking out in favor of His Holiness. On 8 September 1689 the *Nouveau journal universal* published in Amsterdam reported that "Aurelio, Italian actor, is banished from the kingdom, accused of having had intelligence with the enemies of the king."[38]

Ranieri returned to Italy where he published, in Parma in 1690, *Il favore de gli dei,* "a fantastic musical drama," and *La gloria d'amore,* a festival spectacle done for the duke of Parma. He later became a priest, according to Luigi Riccoboni, who told Gueullette he had known him and had heard him say mass.[39] Credulity is somewhat strained by Riccoboni's assertions that both Turri *fils* and Ranieri, successive amoureux in the Paris troupe, received calls to the priesthood, surely not a common experience for middle-aged actors.

Ranieri's fellow debutant Michelangelo Fracansani, who played Polichinelle, may also have appeared infrequently in the French repertory. Gherardi remarks nastily in the preface to his *Théâtre italien* that he has not included any of the scenes involving "the *Gradelins* and the *Polichinelles*" since they never pleased any one, "and if I have put them in my Preface, it is because they have always been at the door of the Italian theatre."[40] But Gherardi had private scores to settle, and his judgments are not necessarily reliable. It seems likely that Fracansani played mostly in Italian, but he probably also played some of the "detached roles" in the French repertory which are not identified by masque. In fact, there are traces of him in the Gherardi collection. In *L'opéra de campagne* (June 1692) a stage direction reads: "A hunchback comes next, carrying on each of his humps, before and behind, a reading stand with a book of music open on it."[41] The character also is visible in the frontispiece to *Le retour de la foire de Beçons* (October 1695) and perhaps, less clearly, in several others.

Fracansani was a Neapolitan, the nephew of painter Cesare Fracanzani. He was born before 1638; as witness to a quarrel between Evaristo Gherardi and Giovanni Battista Costantini in 1692 he gave his age as fifty-four "or thereabouts." All the other witnesses lied about their ages, so probably Fracansani did, too. According to Proto-Giurleo, he was born c. 1632.[42] As a young painter he married Caterina di Petruccio, a rich widow, from whom he received a good inheritance. Now able to indulge his taste for the theatre, he began to play Pulcinella, a role he learned from Ciccio Baldo, one of the best Pulcinellas of the seventeenth century, according to Perrucci. In Paris his character Polichinelle, "with a hump before and behind, kept of the original costume only the mask and the ruff . . . adding for headgear a bicorne hat decorated with ravelings."[43] In fact, there is no consistent visual image of Polichinelle. Various prints and drawings show costumes both plain and decorated and headgear varying from skullcap to beret to traditional sugarloaf hat (see fig. 13). Only the humps are invariable. The character apparently attracted Gillot, who includes him in a number of drawings. Of course, since it cannot be demonstrated conclusively that Gillot was using the Comédie-Italienne before 1697 as his model, it also cannot be certain that his Polichinelle was Fracansani.[44] One of the drawings does, however, indicate how the character was probably used in the French repertory. The scene is from *Colombine avocat pour et contre,* first performed in June 1685 but still in the repertory at least as late as 1691, when it was played at court on 7 December. The final trial scene begins with a two-line exchange between Arlequin and the Jailor, not otherwise identified. In the Gillot drawing Polichinelle stands directly behind Arlequin, the huge keys at his belt identifying his function. The Jailor is a detached role; nothing about it relies on or is identified with the masque Polichinelle. What this suggests is that as the French repertory grew in complexity, those troupe members who played the Italian repertory began to do minor roles in French that once would have been played by gagistes.

An Italian traveler, Gemelli-Careri, saw Fracansani play in Paris in 1686 and reported that the French found his Neapolitan dialect and his comic routines incomprehensible. Gueullette claims to have seen him on stage and says that "he was a very bad actor."[45] Someone must have liked him and found him useful, however, because he stayed with the troupe until its suppression in 1697. He, his second wife Clara Patro, and his son Antonio, all native of Naples, were granted letters of naturalization in August 1688.[46] Tralage included him in his list of actors who lived decent lives, along with Biancolelli and Molière. According to Campardon—who does not, however, cite a source—Fracansani put together an important collection of books, prints, and drawings.

If Dangeau is correct when he notes in his journal that Angelo Costantini was first seen at court on 6 May 1686, then he was probably a recent arrival, the product of the troupe's long search to replace Giovanni Gherardi. Costantini was the son of Constantino Costantini and the brother of Giovanni Battista Costantini, both of whom joined the company after 1688. The family was from Verona, according to Tralage. Gueullette writes that Angelo Costantini was playing Arlequin in Turin when he was called to Paris to understudy Domenico Biancolelli. "I heard him say at M. Riccoboni's house on his last trip to Paris in 1729 that he had been very well received by the public (and this is true) but that finding himself very rarely employed since Dominique played nearly every day, he adopted different detached roles which he played without mask and in which he was greatly appreciated."[47] There is no evidence that Costantini actually played Arlequin during Dominique's lifetime, although Biancolelli may have been feeling somewhat overburdened in the mid 1680s as the French repertory was added. In *Le Livre sans nom*, the author says that he went to see Arlequin to give him news of Bologna and asked him how things were going at the Italian theatre. "Not bad," Arlequin told him, "but since *La matrone d'Ephèse*, in which I was obliged to learn a French role by heart, I am overwhelmed by my character, the more so since now the authors are letting the whole weight of the play fall on me."[48] So possibly Costantini was brought in to play Arlequin in the Italian repertory from time to time while Biancolelli concentrated on the increasing amounts of new French material which had to be memorized.

On the other hand, it is not true that Costantini invented the character of Mezzetin in France; he was playing Mezzettino in Italy in 1678. The character appears in the Gherardi repertory only three times before Biancolelli's death in 1688, in *Arlequin Protée*, *Le banqueroutier*, and *Le divorce*. In the first (1683), Mezzetin's role of Glaucus is not that of a First Zanni and was originally played by Cei according to the Bonnart calendar-almanac illustration (see fig. 10). In *Le divorce* (1688) Mezzetin is a First Zanni who engages the intrigue—which is, however, of little interest. In one scene, an extended lazzi called the "Scène de la boutonmancie," Mezzetin and Arlequin do play their traditional First and Second Zanni roles. In *Le banqueroutier*, a text with many inconsistencies to be explored in chapter 12, Mezzetin appears to be a minor figure, but a few clues arouse the suspicion that he is one of the intriguers with Arlequin and Colombine. *Le banqueroutier* was played first in April 1687, and in my view should be regarded as the earliest extant piece in which Costantini appeared.

Angelo Costantini's birthdate is unknown. When he appeared at the Italian Theatre in Paris in 1729 he was described as "nearly sixty," which would have him born around 1670. But a letter of 9 April 1664 lists among a group of actors Auretta, Costantini's wife, who even if she entered the troupe when very young must have been born before 1650. Auretta and Mezzettino are both mentioned in 1678 in a letter from the duke of Parma which describes them as actors of the Farnesi and agrees to their being lent for a year to Venice.[49] She may have been older than he, but in any case, he must have been born before 1660 and was at least seventy and probably more when he made his second debut in Paris in 1729. His wife was the daughter of Angela (or Angiola) D'Orsi, celebrated midcentury as a donna. Her name was also Angiola, according to Gueullette, but unlike her mother she played the serva Auretta. Gueullette also says that she was given a trial in Paris, but did not please as she was not pretty.

The Costantini couple had at least two children. The daughter became a nun, the son Gabriel, who was still living in 1750, played Arlecchino in Italy. Auretta, according to Gueullette, left Paris to act in Germany.

In 1688, after the sudden death of Domenico Biancolelli, Angelo Costantini took over the role of Arlequin while a new Second Zanni was sought. According to Gueullette, he played with great success, but "as he had, although very dark, a handsome face and had pleased the audience infinitely without a mask, he told us, while dining at Riccoboni's house, the public had led him to understand that if he took the mask of Arlequin for good, a very varied actor, a type of Proteus, would be lost. He resolved to appear masked only until an actor could be found to fill the role of the late Dominique . . . and he had quit it only when Gherardi—who was, however, very inferior to him—was found agreeable by the public."[50] Gherardi did not like him very much either. One thing we can be sure of about Mezzetin is that he was an excellent musician with a very good voice. The Gherardi repertory is full of the stage direction "Mezzetin sings." He may or may not have written *La vie de Scaramouche*; Gherardi hints that he had it ghost-written. He was probably a troublemaker, one of the terrible Costantinis whom Riccoboni refused to allow near his new company in 1716. Gueullette goes on to say that Mezzetin played "until the closing, one should better say the rout of the theatre, to which it is claimed he contributed no little." He was certainly regarded as an enemy by Gherardi, and the troupe's history in the 1690s is clouded by quarrels involving the Costantini family.

In the mid 1680s Tiberio Fiorilli was at or near the end of his active career. He was with the company and, one presumes, still acting in October and November of 1685 at Fontainebleau, but Giuseppe Tortoriti was available to take his roles if not his famous professional name, and Scaramouche appears only once in the French repertory after 1685, as a mute creditor in *Le banqueroutier*. According to a letter he wrote in April 1692, he retired from the stage at the end of the 1689–90 season, though not from the troupe.[51] As his professional life became quiescent, however, Fiorilli's personal life became more animated. A notorious philanderer, the old Scaramouche had fathered an illegitimate child, Tibère François, in 1673. According to his son Silvio he was also one of the many famous lovers of Thérèse de Gorle, Mlle. du Parc,[52] the actress thought by some to have had affairs with Corneille, Molière, and Racine.

In his old age, Fiorilli fell passionately in love with a young woman, Marie Duval, by whom he had a daughter, Anne-Elisabeth, in 1681. Duval left him and ran away to England with a younger lover, then returned and was forgiven. In 1685 a series of letters documents a quarrel between Fiorilli and his son over the father's desire to marry Duval as soon as his wife, Lorenza Elisabetta del Campo, was dead in Florence.[53] Apparently on the complaint of Silvio, Marie Duval was taken into custody as a prostitute and kept in the Refuge. His father retaliated by throwing him out—not for the first time—and refusing to give him the money to return to Italy. The Florentine ambassador, the grand duchess of Tuscany, and Louis XIV himself were all embroiled in the business. Tiberio Fiorilli, who had given all his property to his son as part of the latter's marriage contract, now wanted to rescind the gift so he could leave at least his French estate to his young wife. The marriage finally took place on 8 May 1688, but was hardly to prove a solace to the old man.

Oddly enough, considering the state of enmity between them, the two Fiorillis, father and son, received joint letters of naturalization in February 1685.[54] Even more oddly, though now a French citizen, Tiberio Fiorilli continued to write to his Most Illustrious Signor and patron, Cosimo III de Medici, while Silvio returned to Italy to live.

Fiorilli was not the only member of the troupe to seek French citizenship. Biancolelli and his wife, Orsola Cortesi, were the first, in April 1680. Angelo Agostino Lolli and his wife, Patricia Adami, received their letters of naturalization in June 1683, and in December 1685 Marc' Antonio Romagnesi received his.[55] These Italians had been in Paris for twenty years or more, they were unlikely to return to Italy, and they had begun to accumulate substantial estates in France that would pass to the crown if they were to die. Fiorilli, however, retained property in Florence and, as a result, seems to have enjoyed a kind of dual citizenship, with both monarchs concerned with and annoyed by the behavior of "old dotard," the "old inamorato."

In the summer of 1688, then, after five years of deaths, retirements, and replacements, fourteen company members more or less precisely filled the categories ordered by the dauphine in her Règlement:

Two women to play the serious roles: Orsola Cortesi and Françoise Biancolelli

Two women for the comic roles: Patricia Adami and Catherine Biancolelli

Two men for the lovers: Marc' Antonio Romagnesi and Bartolomeo Ranieri

Two men to conduct the intrigue: Domenico Biancolelli and Angelo Costantini

Two men for the comic roles: Giuseppe Tortoriti and Michelangelo Fracansani

Two for the fathers and old men: Angelo Lolli and Giovan Battista Turri

And still receiving shares, although no longer performing: Brigida Fedele and Tiberio Fiorillo

Then, on 2 August 1688 Domenico Biancolelli died.

The story of his death is yet another tale told by Mezzetin. Although Costantini is necessarily no more reliable on this subject than on any other concerning the Italian troupe, some additional evidence supports his story. Gueullette writes:

> Here is the cause of Dominique's death as was told me by Mlle. Riccoboni who learned it from Mezzetin. Dominique was still young when he died, since he was only forty-eight [actually fifty-two]: here is what the cause of his death has been attributed to. Sieur Bauchamps [*sic*], dancing master of the king (Louis 14) and composer of his ballets, had danced before His Majesty a very unusual step, much to the taste of all the court. Dominique, who danced very well, wanted to imitate it, and in a divertissement which the Italian actors joined to one of their plays, Dominique copied it so exactly in ridiculing the sieur Bauchamps, that the king took an extreme pleasure in it. Dominique sensing the pleasure which the dance was giving to His Majesty made it last as long as possible and heated himself so much that he left the stage with his shirt soaking wet and neither the time nor the opportunity to change it at the moment; he caught a bad cold to which a congestion of the chest and a fever were joined, he was not sick more than a week and died after having renounced the theatre and received the sacraments. He was buried at St.-Eustache behind the choir opposite the chapel of the Virgin.[56]

Gueullette adds that the "Italian troupe was so stunned, it went a month without playing."

The dance in imitation of Beauchamps may have been the one indicated in act 1, scene 6 of Regnard's *Le divorce,* performed for the first time in Paris on 17 March 1688.[57] Since Biancolelli died on August 2, he must have become ill—if the story is accurate—late in July. Although surviving records indicate that the Italians generally did not play their new French repertory at court, perhaps His Majesty had requested this particular burlesque scene as light summer entertainment. Arlequin appears as a dancing master, M. de Trottenville, who enters riding a very small horse. He is accompanied by a musician who plays a very small violin while Arlequin and Colombine dance. Earlier in the piece, Arlequin describes how he escaped hanging by means of the drain pipe of a fountain, and Mezzetin wonders how that was possible, "as fat as you are." The combination of the dance, which was unusual for Biancolelli, his weight, and perhaps the heat of July makes Costantini's explanation credible.

The death was recorded in the *Registre* of the French company, in the journal of Dangeau, and in the *Mercure galant.* Dangeau included among his remarks the rumor that Biancolelli had left 100,000 ecus or 300,000 livres worth of property. If true, this would have been an enormous estate, almost eight times that of the well-to-do Molière.[58] Unfortunately, the evidence available suggests that while Biancolelli was better off than Molière, it was not to the extent suggested by Dangeau. The inventory after death of "the community"—the money and property owned by Biancolelli and his wife in which the children had an interest— reveals personal property worth 8,807 livres 18 sous and investments and other capital worth 62,400 livres for a total of 71,207 livres 18 sous.[59] The bulk of Biancolelli's estate was in funds invested in the Aides and Gabelles, 50,800 livres at 5 percent. He had loaned 6,600 livres to his son-in-law La Thorillière. He had invested 10,000 livres with a M. Bellavoine, a merchant of precious stones, and had made a profit. The estate was also expecting receipt of 3,000 livres left to Orsola Cortesi by a relative, Angelo Maria Cortezi, and paid in Italy to Biancolelli's mother, now the wife of Jacopo Paganelli, citizen of Bologna. The only debt against the estate was 8,000 livres which Orsola Cortesi had borrowed after her husband's death.

The family—Domenico Biancolelli, his wife, his five minor children, his married daughter and his son-in-law—lived in the Hôtel d'Auche, a private house, rented from M. de la Boissière for 800 livres a year. The inventory reveals that the family, excluding the young married couple, occupied five rooms with a storeroom and a shed. Their style of life was comfortable, and they were bothered with none of the petty debts found in the inventory of Giacinto Bendinelli, the First Amoureux who

died in Paris twenty years earlier. The Biancolelli household was as solidly of the bourgeoisie as Molière's, perhaps more so.

After recording a shed well-stocked with wood and coal and a
kitchen furnished with everything necessary to a *bonne cuisine,* the notary's clerk lists the furnishings of the dining room and salon: a walnut
table, 8 walnut chairs, a cabinet, a mirror, 2 paintings, and a small bed in
the former, a walnut table, 5 upholstered armchairs, 6 other chairs, an
armoire, 130 books, 2 mirrors, and a crystal chandelier in the latter. Both
rooms were hung with *tapisserie de cuir,* leather worked with silver or gold
in floral patterns. The books are identified by bindings not by title and
are categorized as works of devotion, history, and science.

The most valuable possessions were in the Great Chamber and included a matrimonial fourposter in walnut and a wool mattress, a down
comforter, and a counterpane decorated with English lace as well as a
smaller bed. In the storeroom were a set of curtains and other furnishings
for the great bed in embroidered brown silk moire, too fine for use and
the most expensive item in the inventory at 2,000 livres. The bedroom
was hung with a set of woven tapestries valued at 200 livres, much more
expensive than the gilded leather set in the salon worth a mere 60 livres.
The room was large enough for a table, six chairs and an armchair upholstered in green damask with fringe and four benches to match along
with a bureau and cabinet. It was decorated with a mirror, a crucifix,
several religious paintings, and a clock.

A second bedroom—for the girls on the second floor—contained a
fourposter and two smaller beds, an armoire, and two trunks. Where the
three sons still at home slept is not indicated. In the storeroom were
armoires and trunks where clothing and linens were kept, along with two
beds, bedding, a table, curtains, andirons, and "six large geographical
maps . . . rolled on their sticks." Orsola Cortesi's wardrobe is entered in
the inventory, but Dominique's is not. Neither his street clothes nor his
costumes are listed and presumably had been disposed of. The costumes
must have included not only Arlequin's patches but various travesty costumes, especially those for the *petits marquis.* Perhaps the costumes belonged to the company, or, more likely, were handed on to Angelo
Costantini, who took over Biancolelli's roles without having his own
wardrobe. The lack of street dress in the inventory is perhaps accounted
for by the lapse of eighteen months between the death and the inventory
and by the size of the family.

Finally, Biancolelli had 3,045 livres 10 sous worth of silver cande-
labra, candlesticks, casseroles, salt dishes, and basins as well as fifteen

spoons, seventeen forks, and twelve knives. His wife owned a modest 307 livres worth of jewelry: three bracelets, two rings, a buckle, and so forth. The picture is of a family living comfortably but, as Tralage described them, "very thrifty" as well.[60]

The loss of Arlequin was a shocking blow to the Italian troupe. Replacing him was no easy matter, since the actor had to be able to play the masque and to speak French fluently. Furthermore, the replacement, unused to memorizing, had to learn the French material by heart. The theatre was dark for a month while the company mourned and decided what to do. The reopening was announced for 1 September 1688: "We have for a long time marked our grief by our silence, and we would prolong it still if the fear of displeasing you did not outweigh our so justifiable sorrow; we will open our theatre next Wednesday, the first day of September 1688. Aware of the impossibility of making up for the loss we have sustained, we will offer you the best that our attention and our cares can give; be a little indulgent and be certain that we will omit nothing which may contribute to your pleasure."[61] No title was included in the announcement, although the troupe was opening with a new play, *Le marchand dupé,* nor was a replacement named. It was to be October 1689 before a new Arlequin was found. The death of Domenico Biancolelli hastened the course of the troupe's transformation; twenty years of gradual mutation ended in a metamorphosis when Evaristo Gherardi began to play Arlequin.

CHAPTER 12

The Transitional French Repertory

W ITH THEIR MOVE to the ill-equipped Hôtel de Bourgogne, the Italian actors ceased to perform, for a time, plays and divertissements that relied on spectacle, but continued to expand their use of French. Now playing an additional day or two a week, the Italians once again needed something new to attract a larger audience. Beginning in 1681, that something new included scenes in French offered to the troupe gratis by Monsieur D***.

Our knowledge of what the Italians performed in the 1680s is derived largely from two collections of scenes and plays in French published in 1694 and 1700 by Evaristo Gherardi, Arlequin of the troupe after 1689. Overreliance on Gherardi has led, however, to some misconceptions about the repertory of the company, chief among them being that the improvised Italian repertory was replaced in the 1680s by a new French repertory, with the scenes in French increasing until the Italians were producing French plays ornamented with improvised scenes in Italian. While it is certainly true that by 1687 the Comédie-Italienne was producing some plays largely made up of French scenes written by French playwrights, it is also true that the traditional repertory continued to be played, sometimes with new French scenes added, or perhaps with traditional scenes translated into French. It may be the case, as well, that some of the plays included in Gherardi's 1700 collection, especially those attributed to Monsieur D***, were originally improvised in Italian, with French ornaments, and that more scenes in French were added to them in later reprises.

Financial records of the court prove that the Italian company was playing an Italian repertory at court throughout the 1680s and 1690s.[1] With two exceptions, to be discussed below, the plays included by Gherardi were not performed there. Whether these court performances were spoken entirely in Italian or partly in French cannot be determined with certainty, but an allusion in the 1695 court accounts to a candle used to light the *sujet,* or scenario, of *La folie d'Octave* implies an improvised performance, and improvised performances were conducted principally in Italian.[2]

Occasional new plays in Italian were also offered to the Paris public. Tralage records the debut of Giovanni Battista Costantini on 2 November 1688 in *La folie d'Octave,* a comedy "toute italienne," while as late as April 1697 another newcomer from Italy, Maria Teresa D'Orsi, made her debut as Spinette in *Spinette lutin amoureux.*

French scenes introduced into the existing Italian repertory during this period were popular enough to be published; the document which leads us to conclude that the old repertory was reprised and periodically embellished with French scenes is the so-called *Supplément* to Gherardi, an anonymous work published first in Brussels in 1697. Among its thirty-four entries are eleven that are analogous at least by title to Biancolelli's zibaldone, many of which include one or several scenes in French based on the Italian text. (The *Supplément* also contains twelve entries related to the scenarios in Ms. 9329, and sixteen related to the second edition of Gherardi.)

The source of the material is unknown; in the preface to his 1700 edition, Gherardi writes that this *Supplément,* "which is worth less than nothing, was composed, it is said, by the author of the *Arlequiniana* [Cotelendi] or the *Vie de Scaramouche* [Angelo Costantini or his ghost writer]."[3] Obviously, Gherardi had no idea who had collected these various imperfect scenes, but he was acting on his suspicion that if mischief was afoot, a Costantini was probably implicated. He does not claim that the material included in the *Supplément* was unrepresentative of performance practices, however, something he might well have done if the *Supplément* had contained scenes that were from an archaic repertory and had never been played in French. Comparison of the *Supplément* with its predecessors shows that the French scenes published in the pirated edition include transcriptions of harangues and scenes played in French before 1680, translations of scenes originally played in Italian, and new scenes added to the plays during reprises.

In general, the material in the *Supplément* is defective. When compared with Biancolelli's or Gherardi's texts, it almost always shows signs of having been recorded by someone with no comic sense and little feel for the sounds and rhythms of language. Although it is a useful document for historical purposes, it is of questionable value for analysis of the French repertory.[4] For that, we must turn to Gherardi's own collections.

Evaristo Gherardi, the son of Flautin, joined the Italian company in October 1689 to play Arlequin. He was twenty-three, well-educated, and highly thought of, especially by himself. In the mid 1690s Gherardi apparently gained custody of the company's repertory, perhaps feloniously. The Italians, unlike the French, did not employ a prompter-copyist to look after the precious manuscripts and actors' sides. Until the mid 1680s their performances were almost totally improvised; later a member of the troupe served as "dépositaire." The troupe accused Gherardi of stealing the manuscripts from the appointed guardian. Taking advantage of his possession of the troupe's community property, however he managed it, Gherardi obtained a privilege on 24 May 1694 permitting him to have published a collection of French scenes.

His colleagues were not pleased. The troupe appealed to the king and his Council to withdraw the privilege. The actors observed that "the said Gherardi, one of them, by an act of unheard-of betrayal, had adroitly stolen from the one who was acting as dépositaire all the plays and detached scenes which had been performed for the past thirty years on the stage of the Italian actors," adding that he had gained the privilege by allowing it to be believed, "contrary to the truth," that publication was taking place with the consent of the troupe.[5] The actors pointed out that far from consenting, they regarded the plays as composing the capital of the troupe which had, after all, paid the authors for them. The actors feared that once the plays and scenes were printed, audiences would no longer come to see them.

The troupe reminded His Majesty of a similar incident that had taken place in 1683 when Domenico Biancolelli was granted a privilege to publish the final act of *La matrone d'Ephèse, ou Arlequin Grapignan.*[6] His colleagues were able to obtain the suppression of that book on the grounds of community property, and were sure Gherardi was aware of the precedent. In the meantime, the book had already been printed,[7] two thousand copies were ready to be sold, and the complainants hoped it would please His Majesty to order the privilege withdrawn and the printing plates broken up. As to the already printed books, the company requested that Gherardi and his printer be forbidden to sell them, and that they be seized and handed over to the complainants to be disposed of. The king and Council responded favorably to the petition, repealing the privilege and forbidding the sale of the book on 17 September 1694. Gherardi was fined 200 livres in costs.

On 30 October Marc' Antonio Romagnesi appeared before the magistrates in his name and in the names of Orsola Cortesi, Françoise and Catherine Biancolelli, and Tiberio Fiorilli to report that on 27 October the troupe in assembly had deliberated on the matter and decided that the books should be sold and the profit divided among the sharers. "However, in defiance of this agreement, the complainants were surprised to learn" that the Costantinis along with Tortoriti, Fracansani, and Giaratoni had decided to "burn the book, which was not as ordered by the act [of the king's Council].[8] On 5 November, Romagnesi returned to the Châtelet to complain that as he was on the way back to the Hôtel de Bourgogne on the previous occasion he met Mezzetin, who claimed that the book had been burned. That it was not burned is quite clear from the number of copies that have survived to this day.

Gherardi's own version of these events partly helps to clear up the mystery:

> The favorable welcome which the public gave to the first volume which I published in 1694 excited the envy of my comrades; they claimed that the printing of these scenes could hurt the performance of the plays from which they were taken. On this basis it pleased Monseigneur the Chancellor, in order to restore peace to the company (these are his own words), to request the return of the privilege which he had had the kindness to grant me, & which I rendered up to him in complete submission to his orders.
>
> What proves that it was only envy and not reason which motivated the suppression is that the 900 copies that were seized from me and deposited by the company with the Sieur Octave [Giovanni Battista Costantini] were sold by him at several Paris bookstores for thirty-two sous each (after he had burned two or three pages and made the rest of his comrades believe he had burned them entirely).[9]

According to Gherardi, the scenes and even entire plays "were the work of several persons of wit and merit, composed by most of them in their hours of recreation" and given not sold to the troupe. He also claims that "since none of my comrades wanted to take the trouble to make the collection, I took responsibility for the job." Given the rivalries in the Italian troupe in the 1690s, Gherardi's version is probably just as credible as Romagnesi's, although it is a little hard to envisage writers like Regnard and Dufresny giving away full-length plays. The 1694 edition of Gherardi contains scenes in French from seventeen entertainments produced by the Italians between January 1681 and May 1694. Nine of the seventeen date from before Gherardi's entry into the company, although we know that he played in a reprise of at least one of them, Regnard's *Le divorce*. In every case, the 1694 edition includes fewer scenes from each play than the 1700 edition and in some cases the scenes are shorter, but the texts are otherwise close to identical. We may infer that Gherardi either did not have access to the complete repertory when he arranged his first edition or chose to include fewer scenes in order to include representative scenes from more plays. The first edition is, after all, a single volume with 545 pages of text; the second edition contains six volumes. On the other hand, we might also conjecture that the 1694 edition is closer to the original performances, while the 1700 edition reflects reprises. Especially in the texts of the earlier pieces, performed before Gherardi entered the troupe, the 1694 edition often features materials that are similar to the French ornaments employed between 1668 and 1680: pleadings and harangues. Also included are detached comic scenes, scenes devoted to satire of French law and society, and parodies of French plays. *Le banqueroutier* (1687) is the first play in the 1694 edition with scenes in French directly connected to the plot.

In the preface to the second edition Gherardi indicates that he felt obliged to compile it because of the many counterfeit and pirated editions that had been published in provincial France and in Geneva, The Hague, and Amsterdam between 1695 and 1697. According to Gherardi, the so-called Volume 3 or *Suite du théâtre italien,* published without date or place but probably in 1696, was stolen from him in manuscript. It contains the French texts of seven plays produced between 1692 and 1695. Volume 2, the *Supplément* already referred to, appeared first in Brussels in 1697. These two were combined with pirated versions of Gherardi's original edition and published in various places as a three-volume set. It was this "multiplicity of insipid volumes" that persuaded Gherardi to augment and reissue his.[10]

Gherardi's 1700 texts may be more complete than any others, but they are not necessarily authoritative. In fact, the idea of an authoritative text is meaningless in this context. The Italian theatre in Paris remained a commedia dell'arte troupe, always ready to cut its cloth to suit the circumstances. The existence of written texts does not imply any particular consistency in the actual performances, especially over a span of years. For instance, when *Colombine avocat pour et contre* was played at court in 1691, we have no way of knowing how much that performance resembled the original performance in 1685. Nor have we any way of knowing whether the Gherardi text of 1700 was the text played in 1685 or 1691. The first edition of Gherardi contains only three French scenes from *Colombine avocat.* The second edition of Gherardi includes the full play, at least in outline, with seventeen written-out scenes in French, three written-out scenes in Italian, four written-out scenes in mixed French and Italian, and four improvised scenes, two of which may have been improvised in French. The play is Italian in style and has few points of resemblance to other works attributed to the same playwright, Monsieur D***, with the exception of the scenes included in the 1694 edition. What to conclude from this? The possibility at least exists that *Colombine avocat pour et contre* included far fewer French scenes in 1685 than as published by Gherardi in 1700, and that the 1700 text is a conflation of scenes that were written for the troupe by Monsieur D*** and scenes that are transcriptions of materials originally played in Italian and orally translated by the actors during various reprises. What tends to support such an inference are two of the four scenes from *Colombine avocat* included in the *Supplément*. One is a French version of a scene played in Italian in Gherardi, another is a rhymed "Promise of Marriage" which Arlequin makes to Colombine and which is not in Gherardi at all.

In general, then, although the 1700 edition of Gherardi remains the principal source of materials for description and analysis of the Italian's repertory after 1680, it should be used with a certain discretion, especially for the 1680s before Gherardi himself was a member of the troupe. The collection is, of course, much more complete for the years 1690–97; only thirteen of the fifty-five entries date from before Dominique's death, another four from the period when Angelo Costantini played Arlequin. The later plays are also more complete in themselves and more consistent than the "Monsieur D***" material collected in volume 1.

The first eight entries, those that precede *Colombine avocat,* include between four and seven scenes in French, while the rest of the repertory consists of increasingly complete plays. For the period preceding August 1688, when Biancolelli died, we have eight sets of fragments and five plays: *Colombine avocat pour et contre, Le banqueroutier, La cause des femmes, La critique de la cause de femmes,* and *Le divorce.* All but the last three are, according to Gherardi, by Monsieur D***, generally thought to be Anne Mauduit de Fatouville. The Fatouville repertory up to and including *Le banqueroutier* is transitional in nature and will form the subject matter of the remainder of this chapter. The rest of the material from the 1700 edition of Gherardi, beginning with Delosme de Montchenay's *La cause des femmes,* will be discussed in chapter 15.

Until the publication in 1936 of an article by Giacomo Cavallucci, historians and critics took the Fatouville in question to be a certain Nolant de Fatouville, member of the Parlement de Rouen.[11] We now know that he was, rather, Anne Mauduit, sieur de Fatouville, counselor of the Cour des Aides at Rouen, and a friend of Regnard's. He is described by the abbé Le Gendre in his *Mémoires* as follows: "M. de Fantouville [*sic*]

... a voluptuary who was overwhelmed with property and came to squander it in Paris. ... He and his patron with others of their society made the French scenes for the Comédie-Italienne."

The abbé Le Gendre thus confirms the relationship of Fatouville and the Italians, a relationship also noted by Gueullette, who adds to Biancolelli's manuscript notes for the "Panégiric de Scaramouche" in *Le théâtre sans comédie* (July 1668) his suggestion that the harangue, a rather long piece copied out in a handwriting other than Dominique's, may have been devised by "M. de Fatouville, a Norman gentleman, who frequently worked for the Italian theatre." [12]

None of this specifically connects Anne Mauduit de Fatouville to Monsieur D***. Cavallucci has, however, missed one piece of contemporary information that does so. In his discussion of the fountains for *Arlequin Jason*—the French scenes in which were the work of Monsieur D*** according to Gherardi—Tralage writes: "The play of *Jason* ... is by M. de Fatouville. There is at the end a surprising machine of several cascades and forty jets of natural water of various heights. M. de Fatouville had the idea for it, but the Sieur Angelo had the thing built." [13] Writing in the 1690s, Tralage certainly had the opportunity to know Fatouville and know that he was involved in the creation of that particular play.

Yet the incidents surrounding the publication of *Arlequin Grapignan* call the identification of Fatouville with Monsieur D*** into question. In 1683 someone named Charles Darennes received a privilege to publish a play entitled *Grapignan, ou Arlequin procureur.* This was the third act, a satirical ornament in French, of *La matrone d'Ephèse,* first performed in May 1682 and attributed to Monsieur D*** by Gherardi. The production was heavily publicized in the *Mercure galant,* where Donneau de Visé devoted six pages to it, most of them to the third-act "embellishment" played "entirely in our language."

The publication of this act in 1683 generated another long piece from Donneau de Visé in the December *Mercure galant* as well as one in April 1684 by Bayle in the *Nouvelles de la république des lettres.* [14] No author is indicated, but *Arlequin Grapignan* was published by Blageart, who also published the *Mercure galant* as well as Donneau de Visé's plays. It was included in Blageart's catalogue, published each month at the end of the *Mercure,* and placed in the listing just after Thomas Corneille and Donneau de Visé's *La devineresse.* All of this raises the possibility that this time Monsieur D*** was Donneau de Visé. However, the Act of the Privy Council of 1694 rescinding Gherardi's privilege quotes the petitioners in that action as follows: "It was not permitted to the late Dominique *dit*

Arlequin to print an act of the play under the title of *Grapignan*."¹⁵ An act
of the Council of State dated 28 February 1684 makes no mention of
Dominique, but rather rescinds the privilege of Sieur Charles Darennes.
Cavallucci argues that Darennes was a pseudonym used by Anne Mauduit de Fatouville, while Lancaster believes that Darennes was an agent
for Biancolelli who did not want his colleagues to know that he was
publishing community property. In Lancaster's view, Monsieur D*** in
this event was Dominique himself.¹⁶

It seems unlikely that Dominique wrote scenes in French for the
company, but not impossible. Someone wrote the French harangues performed before 1680, and Gueullette points out that only the "Panégiric
de Scaramouche" was not written in Biancolelli's hand in the zibaldone.
In *La critique de la cause des femmes* (February 1688), when the Marquis
complains that "I am enraged when I pay for an Italian comedy . . . and
hear nothing spoken but French," Colombine answers: "You're joking?
There's where Arlequin triumphs."¹⁷ Biancolelli, after more than twenty-
five years in France, was certainly the most adept linguist of the older
actors, and one might well argue for his having translated into French
certain scenes clearly Italian in origin. *Arlequin Grapignan,* however, is an
example of satire in the French manner, and probably was not written by
Dominique.

Its subject matter and relative lack of theatrical sophistication argue
for the authorship of Anne Mauduit de Fatouville, who was a lawyer and
could well have been responsible for the highly technical legal burlesques
featured in the Italians' repertory in the early 1680s. *Arlequin Grapignan* is
not precisely a play; it is a series of exchanges between a "procureur,"—
that is, a barrister, or lawyer entitled to plead in court,—and the clients
he cheats, wherein, according to Donneau de Visé, "all his tricks are to
be discovered, depicted in a very natural way."¹⁸ The naïveté of the structure and the dependence on legal jargon may be a reason for choosing
Fatouville over Donneau de Visé as the author of *Arlequin Grapignan.* But
why that voluptuary gentleman Fatouville needed to compound a pseudonym with anonymity to protect the fact of his authorship remains a
question—as does the extreme devotion of Donneau de Visé to the cause
of the play, both on stage and in print. Donneau de Visé also had good
reason to remain anonymous, since the French troupe for which he was
a major supplier of plays did not look kindly on French authors who
worked for the Italians. Some years later the French threatened to remove
several playwrights from the free list at the Comédie-Française unless
they would promise never again to write for the competition.

Perhaps the safest hypothesis, given all of these contradictory options and considering the lack of consistency in the materials attributed to him, is that Monsieur D*** is a generic label invented by Evaristo Gherardi who simply did not know in 1694 and 1700 who had written the French scenes performed before he entered the troupe.

The first eight sets of scenes in the Gherardi edition of 1700 have more in common with the repertory that precedes them than with the one that follows, and continue many of the developments of the previous period. This transitional repertory also demonstrates, however, some changes in comic style from traditional commedia dell'arte farce to French satire, burlesque, and parody.

The first entry is *Arlequin mercure galant* (Monsieur D***, 22 January 1681).[19] Gherardi has included one scene, two "compliments," and a *plaidoyé*, or lawyer's address to the court. The title obviously refers to Donneau de Visé's monthly gazette, which at this period was still devoted to fashion, gossip, and the theatre. The single scene in French, which is also included in a cut version in the 1694 edition of Gherardi, is entitled "Scène des nouvelles," and is almost certainly a prologue. Arlequin, disguised as Mercury, "appears in the air mounted on Jupiter's eagle." Jupiter, disguised as a shepherd, calls his messenger to earth and Arlequin disappears and reappears in his usual costume riding on an ass. Jupiter asks for news of home; Arlequin responds with various ridiculous tales of life on Olympus, half in French, half in Italian. He follows this with even more ridiculous news of the Antipodes, Barbary, Tartary, and Paris. The news items are similar in tone to those in *A fourbe, fourbe et demy* (1674), although this present scene lacks the dramatic intentionality of its predecessor. Most of the items are mildly obscene or scatological; one is self-referential, a characteristic that began before 1680 but was employed with increasing frequency in the French repertory. It seems that "a sergeant of the Châtelet has requested that the Italian actors be forbidden to make fun of his nose in their plays." Jupiter, who was played by one of the amoureux, then announces that he is in love with Rosalbe and sends Mercury to speak for him and to declare his love. Jupiter exits, Pan enters and announces that he, too, is in love with Rosalbe. Arlequin responds, in a mixture of French and Italian: "Rosalbe is beautiful, you are perfectly frightful. Rosalbe has a beautiful face, you have the face of a gallows-bird. Rosalbe has a beautiful figure, you are built like a baboon." Pan responds that he is handsome, and that he is the god Pan. "A *pane* [bread] too well baked, a *pane bruno,* better suited to make sea biscuits for the galleys than satisfy the appetites of decent people," says Arlequin. The end of the scene is improvised Italian style. Pan asks if the ass Arlequin is riding on belongs to him. Arlequin answers that it does, that it is a virtuoso ass who can keep house and play the harpsichord. Pan asks to borrow the ass and Arlequin agrees, but when Pan climbs on the ass separates in two, dumping Pan on the ground.

Nothing about this scene suggests the hand of a playwright except the news items that are in style somewhat reminiscent of the actual *Mercure galant*. The first compliment, made by Arlequin to Rosalbe in the name of Jupiter, is rather more than usually coarse, but ends with a clever local reference. According to Arlequin, "Jupiter would have come himself, but being transformed into a bull to carry off Europa, he found himself on the rue des Boucheries where the butchers took him to be a beef escaping from a slaughterhouse. . . . If I had not arrived in the nick of time and cried 'Stop! Stop! It's Jupiter,' Jupiter might have ended up a boeuf à la mode at a Gascon tavern."

The second compliment is a mixture of French and Italian, with the latter language dominant. Arlequin consoles Proserpine for the loss of her "very dear, very black, & very diabolical better half." The speech is noteworthy only for the odd mix of language: "La perdità è grande, Madama, e benche, e benche si dica: Réjouissez-vous, le Diable est mort." The compliments are not included in the 1694 edition of Gherardi.

The "Plaidoyé en faveur des petits Plutons, Orphelins par la mort de leur Père le Diable contre Proserpine leur Mère" is nearly six pages of legal parody, very different in style, rhythm, and content from the other French scenes of *Arlequin mercure galant* or, indeed, from the harangues in French of Biancolelli's zibaldone. Like most of the legal parodies in the early plays collected by Gherardi, this one rests on a close knowledge of procedures and jargon. Its comic strength—if it has one—is the reversal of expectations, the description of the careful and caring father in this case "showering on his children all the crimes of which they might be capable." Its reliance on, for instance, the differences between *procureurs* and *greffiers, notaires* and *avocats,* makes it far more specific to time and place than is usual for commedia dell'arte and of little interest except to seventeenth-century Parisians. Whether the author was Fatouville or some other Frenchman with a legal bone in his craw is not as important as the fact that this scene signals the introduction into the Italian theatre of material designed especially to interest the French bourgeoisie, which was obsessed by matters of law and finance.

Gherardi has attached to *Arlequin mercure galant* the music for six songs, four in French and two in Italian, but with no indication of where

they were introduced into the piece or by whom they were sung. Donneau de Visé mentions the play's debut in January 1681 but gives no
details. From the little we know, all that can really be concluded is that
Arlequin mercure galant was a pastoral-classical fantasy with music, local
references, plenty of indecency, and a long burlesque harangue.

During that harangue Arlequin refers to the opposing lawyer, one
Grippimini, who seems to have been a sort of tryout for Grapignan.
"Nothing is more ruinous than a procureur," claims Arlequin. "Grippimini, gentlemen, Grippimini ... his name is his portrait." *La matrone
d'Ephèse, ou Arlequin Grapignan* is the second effort attributed to Monsieur
D*** by Gherardi. It opened in May 1682 to thunderous applause from
Donneau de Visé. The first two acts of the play, only three scenes from
which are included in the 1700 edition of Gherardi, are based on the old
tale of the widow of Ephesus. According to the preface to Darennes'
published version, the first two acts were originally played entirely in
Italian; Gherardi's scenes are the usual mix.

The first, the "Scène de Margot," is between Arlequin and Pasquariel. Since Tortoriti, who played Pasquariel, was not in Paris in 1682, the
scene either represents a reprise (after March 1685) or was originally
played by Cei. Arlequin hopes to marry a one-eyed woman named Margot the fruitseller. The dialogue is unusually realistic and deserves to be
quoted:

PASQUARIEL	And who is she?
ARLEQUIN	Margot the fruitseller.
PASQUARIEL	But she has nothing.
ARLEQUIN	And what is it I have?
PASQUARIEL	She's old.
ARLEQUIN	Am I young?
PASQUARIEL	She stinks.
ARLEQUIN	Do I smell good?

And so forth. Pasquariel asks Arlequin to pretend to be a ghost, to speak
to the Matron and tell her not to cry and not to die. Arlequin agrees to
do it for 500 livres.

In the "Scène de l'ombre" Arlequin pretends to be the ghost of
Eularia's husband. Eularia speaks only Italian, Arlequin both Italian and
French. After Eularia exits, an exchange between Arlequin and Colombine (Diamantine in the original, no doubt, since Catherine Biancolelli
had not yet joined the troupe) persuades her that this is, indeed, the ghost
of her dead master whom she had tricked, and she runs away. Then Scaramouche enters with a purse he has just stolen containing 100 louis d'or.

The ghost snatches the purse away, explaining that he is the ghost of a former thief and that he deserves the purse by right of seniority. Scaramouche plays one of his famous scenes of fright and the two exit at opposite sides.

The third French scene included by Gherardi is the "Scène du compliment et de la bouteille." The compliment is full of typical imbroglios. Arlequin, "with a sword at his side and a basket on his arm containing a bottle and a cup," approaches Eularia and begins to declaim: "Oh beautiful star of the charcoal-seller . . . Alas, how sorrow has changed you. Your cheeks, which were as green as the buttocks of a newly spanked babe, are so pale and thin, they resemble nothing but two dried codfish. . . . Drink, Madame, drink, but don't drink it all, or you'll make me cry in my turn." Eularia finally responds to the pleas of Arlequin and Colombine and begins to drink. Arlequin decides to die of love for her (and because of the "matronicide" of his bottle). Eularia cannot marry this "simple soldier," but will buy for him, from her old uncle, a procureur's practice. None of these scenes were included in the 1694 edition of Gherardi or in the 1684 version published by Blageart. They contain typical routines of naïveté and gluttony, nothing that would require the hand of a French man of letters.

Act 3 begins with Arlequin, now Grapignan, learning his new trade. The name suggests *grappin,* or hook, and is reminiscent of Grippimini, the procureur in *Arlequin mercure galant.* Grapignan's mentor is Coquinière, from *coquin,* or scoundrel. The old man explains the importance of having a sergeant, a notary, and a *greffier* at one's disposal, and swears that if the new procureur follows instructions he will have ruined 100 families and acquired ten houses in Paris within four years. He will even have a carriage for his wife. "I know all the little tricks of the chambers," says Arlequin, "but I do not know these masterstrokes." "Do you love money above all things?" asks the master. "Will you do anything to get it?" And of course, Grapignan will. The scene then becomes technical: "Be hard and pitiless . . . never consent to arbitration . . . adroitly multiply the incidents and the procedures." Grapignan is promised an income of 2,000 livres a year in legal fees and 10,000 in "pickings."

The rest of act 3 consists of the various "Scènes des chambres." In the first, Grapignan complains that his clerks are writing legal documents "four words to the line." He insists on no more than two words and a comma, a reference to the fact that clients paid copyists by the line. In the next scenes the procureur interviews a highwayman, a sergeant named Maraudin, the marquis de Grimouche, a hatseller, a pastry cook, and a rich old lady. His take? Twenty-four pistoles, a diamond, a watch, and the highwayman's overcoat, four pistoles or forty-four livres for the marquis's thirty-page document, four pistoles and a beaver hat from the hat maker, sixty livres and a dish of pastries from the pastry cook, and a new eighty-year-old fiancée. But the Matron overhears his proposal to the old client, the hatmaker and the pastry cook want their money back, and the bailiff enters looking for a procureur who does more evil than all the others put together. Poor Grapignan is taken off to be hanged.

This sequence is a not-very-brilliant example of satire in the French style, and although it has been loosely attached to the plot of the first two acts, it is stylistically quite unlike them. Grapignan is not Arlequin in disguise for purposes of the plot but an entirely separate character. Only once does Arlequin shine through. In the scene with the highwayman, who has happened to ride off on a merchant's horse, Arlequin recommends putting the horse under lock and key since it was the only witness, and if the merchant were to find it, he might have it interrogated on the facts of the case. The comic inventiveness of the "Scène de la bouteille," with Eularia getting drunk and Arlequin torn between proposing to the widow and beating her up for drinking his bottle, is entirely missing in act 3, which rests solely on the variety of unscrupulous behavior demonstrated by the procureur.

According to the preface to the Blageart edition, the play was extremely popular and ran for three months. According to Bernardin, it was revived in November 1899 at a Saturday matinée at the Odéon and "still gave great pleasure."[20] According to Lancaster, "No author of the Théâtre Italien wrote better scenes than those in which are set forth Harlequin's iniquities as a lawyer."[21] In fact, the scenes are predictable, jargon-ridden, lifeless, and mean-spirited in comparison to most of the survivals from the comédie italienne.

Gherardi's next entry in the 1700 edition is *Arlequin lingère du palais,* dated 4 October 1682 after a date included in the marriage contract that ends the play. The entry includes three scenes, two of which are traditional commedia dell'arte scenes translated into French, and one of which is a parody of *Le Cid.* The entry also contains the marriage contract in French. No material from this piece is included in the 1694 edition.

Most unusually, Gherardi offers a plot synopsis, worth including since it demonstrates how a French parody is inserted into a typical Italianate plot:

> Since Scaramouche wants to marry his daughter to Pasquariel, whom she does not love, Arlequin, the valet of Cinthio, the beloved, invents several tricks to prevent the marriage. He pretends Pasquariel is a gambler and debauché, in order to disgust Scaramouche. He

substitutes the portrait of his master for that of Pasquariel, which the father is meant to present to the daughter, and this exchange gives rise to a scene of equivocation between Scaramouche and Eularia, in which the girl promises her father to marry the original of the portrait she has in her hands. During a party Scaramouche gives for his supposed son-in-law, Arlequin, hidden under a basket of fruit, drops a certain liquid in Pasquariel's glass which drives him mad and makes him believe that he is Rodrigue and, taking Arlequin for Chimène, they play together the parody. . . . The madness of Pasquariel continues, he kills a tavern keeper, whose ghost Arlequin plays in the scene where he says to Scaramouche that he is the soul of a Cabaretier who has come to take him to the devil if he does not consent to the marriage of his daughter with Cinthio.

In the end, Scaramouche—tired of all the tricks—agrees to the marriage and signs the contract.

The title scene, the "Scène de la lingère et du limonadier" is a traditional commedia dell'arte scene, here detached from the plot. Arlequin is dressed on one side as a woman who sells gentlemen's linen at the Palais de Justice. His other side is the man who tends the next boutique, a lemonade stand. Pasquariel is the client who is interested in buying a shirt. The two vendors quarrel while Pasquariel, who tries to make peace, ends up as the target. The scene is reminiscent of one in *Le gentilhomme campagnard* (c. 1670) when Arlequin is dressed on one side as a Spaniard and on the other as a Frenchman. The scene was probably not played in French in 1682, nor could it have included Pasquariel, who was not then in the troupe. The role was played originally by Cei, Capitan Spezzafer, who is shown in the engraved frontispiece included in the 1700 edition of Gherardi.

The frontispiece also shows the Docteur, who appears in the second scene in Gherardi's entry, the "Scène de la nourrice." This scene, which features Arlequin disguised as a nurse leading an ass upon which rests a cradle, forms part of the plot contrived to persuade the old man that Pasquariel is a debauché. According to Arlequin, the child in the cradle is Pasquariel's and a chip off the old block, unable to rest unless his little hands are full of cards, refusing to suckle unless the nurse rubs her nipples with wine.

The parody of *Le Cid*, written in French rhyming couplets, was, according to Gherardi, largely an opportunity for Arlequin, dressed in a black cloak that covered him from head to heels and a black veil, to mimic the French actress Mlle. Champsmeslé. The mimicry may not have been part of the original parody, but if it was then the parody must have been added to a reprise. In 1682 the role of Chimène in *Le Cid* did not belong to Mlle. Champsmeslé. She was among the members of the French troupe which left for Fontainebleau on 12 October 1682. *Le Cid* was played on 13 October in Paris. Perhaps she inherited Chimène when Mlle. Dupin retired from the French troupe at the end of the 1684–85 season.

The marriage contract is very brief and not especially funny. It does, however, mention Scaramouche *futur père,* which is presumably the source of Gherardi's casting and indicates that at some point Fiorilli played the vieillard. The date included in the contract, 4 October 1682, must be approximately accurate since *Arlequin lingère* was played at court on 4 February 1683, one of the few plays of the Gherardi repertory to be listed in the court accounts.[22]

What seems indicated is that in 1682–83 this play was part of the troupe's Italian repertory, with the marriage contract included as an ornament in French. The parody may well have been added later—it appears only as an example of the suitor's madness—and the French scenes translated from Italian at some point in the play's performance history. Although *Arlequin lingère* is not included in the first edition of Gherardi, incomplete versions of the "Scène de la nourrice" and the "Scène de la contract" are to be found in the *Supplément.* In the former, the suitor is "Spestafer," not Pasquariel. The "scènes françoises d'Arlequin homme à bonne fortune" included in the *Supplément,* in which "la nourrice" and "Spestafer" are mentioned, may also be from *Arlequin lingère.*

Arlequin Protée, which opened on 11 October 1683, marked the official introduction of Françoise and Catherine Biancolelli as Isabelle and Colombine, and is also the first piece in the Gherardi collection that might be classified as predominantly French in style. It lacks a romantic intrigue, and the French materials from the 1700 edition are not exclusively ornamental. Donneau de Visé writes, in the *Mercure galant* of October 1683, that "the Italian Comedy has never been so applauded nor so followed in France as it is presently; also, the Italian actors have never before exhibited our manners as they have done recently. They join the useful and the agreeable, and there is much to profit from in their plays, especially in the last (Arlequin protée) where one recognizes from the great number of Arlequin's lawsuits how dangerous it is to go to law."

Arlequin Protée is known to us from a prologue, three scenes in French, a parody of *Bérénice,* and the courtroom finale mentioned by Donneau de Visé. The prologue is between Proteus, played by Arlequin, and

Glaucus, played in Gherardi's version by Mezzetin. In the Bonnart calendar-almanac published in 1684 to celebrate the success of this novelty,[23] Glaucus is Spezzafer, confirming that Gherardi's version reflects a reprise. In the prologue Arlequin and Mezzetin decide to go to Paris, "the meeting place of all nations." Arlequin plans to become a cutpurse in the parterres of the Opéra and the Comédie and to teach the spectators to keep "one eye on the stage and the other on their pockets." Arlequin's long, laudatory speech about Paris suggests that the scene was spoken in French, although it was not included in the 1694 Gherardi.

In the first of the French scenes from the 1700 edition, Arlequin appears as a merchant of precious stones, dressed in a sugarloaf hat and carrying a very large sword. Two innkeepers vie for his patronage; he steals a purse from one and a watch from the other. In another illustration from the Bonnart calendar-almanac, one innkeeper is played by Pierrot, the other by a servante, probably Diamantine. The scene in dialogue is followed by an improvised scene between Arlequin and Mezzetin in which Arlequin enters the house of the Docteur and throws out various items to Mezzetin, including a little child. This scene appears in Biancolelli's zibaldone in *Les trois volleurs descouverts* (before 1668), although Trivelin as First Zanni is the inside man and Arlequin is outside holding the bag. Arlequin and Mezzetin are interrupted by the Docteur and Scaramouche from whom they steal a basket full of silver dishes. The Docteur and Scaramouche cry "Thief! Thief!" The shutter opens and Arlequin is discovered as a magistrate in nightcap and dressing gown. He dismisses their complaints, and his armchair is transformed into a frightful monster spitting flames. This scene could well have been played originally in Italian; nothing about it is untraditional or requires a playwright, nor was it included in Gherardi's first collection.

The "Scène du comédien" opens improvisationally. Arlequin tells Mezzetin that he has taken the form of a French actor, La Comète, in preference to that of an Italian actor because the latter earns very little. Mezzetin announces that he has spoken to the Docteur, who agrees that the actors may rehearse in his garden and that his daughter, Isabelle, may play a role. Arlequin is looking for someone named Colombine who, he hears, has talent for the stage. Mezzetin knows her and will find her. The scene continues in written French dialogue with the entrance of Cinthio, who recognizes La Comète. After a brief conversation, Arlequin discovers at length his secret explosive device for flying twelve people without cords, wires, or counterweights. The scene is, thus, a kind of harangue as well as a glimpse of the traditional masque whose inability to reason from cause to effect is a standard characteristic. It probably was played in French from the entry of Cinthio, since Arlequin began at that point to play a French actor. Also, of course, the harangue was traditionally spoken in French.

The harangue is followed in Gherardi's 1700 edition by the "Scène de l'incendie" between Colombine and Arlequin. Colombine speaks almost entirely in Italian, Arlequin half in Italian, half in French. He offers her a share in his troupe; she wants a good role, that of the porter who collects the money. He says they will open with *L'incendio di Troia;* he will play the Trojan horse. She wants something more elevated. He suggests the story of Titus and Berenice.

The "Parodie de Bérénice" is in five scenes in French verse and includes Isabelle, Colombine, Arlequin, Scaramouche, and an old-clothes dealer. In scene 1 Isabelle, speaking in a soliloquy, fears that her lover, Cinthio, has deserted her for a rival, her own sister. But Colombine explains that her heart belongs to Arlequin: "I hate what is serious," she says, "and I love pleasure. . . . On my faith, I only want a lover to make me laugh." One anachronism in the scene is Colombine's reference to *Arlequin Phaeton:* "Arlequin Phaeton pleases me infinitely . . . I have in my head an even greater plan, Arlequin will appear as a Roman emperor . . . He will be my Titus, I his Bérénice, and I will, if I can . . . raise up Phaeton." This would appear to refer to Palaprat's *Arlequin Phaeton,* first performed by the Italians on 4 February 1692, nearly ten years after the debut of *Arlequin Protée.* Once again, this is proof that Gherardi's version reflects a reprise, although in this case the parody—which forms the climax of the La Comète sequence—is integrated into the play's structure. The Bonnart calendar-almanac also features the parody, indicating that it was in the piece as originally performed in some form.

These early parodies differ from the later ones in the repertory in that they are based on classics of the French theatre rather than on newly opened plays and operas. Since both *Le Cid* and *Bérénice* were played periodically at the Comédie-Française, the parodies cannot be dated by the debuts of the originals. Nothing is said in *Arlequin Protée* about mimicry of specific actors or actresses; casting also does not help to solve problems of dating. Lancaster takes Arlequin's line "I am going to wipe out Floridor & Baron" to mean that those actors were being imitated in *Arlequin Protée,*[24] but Floridor had died in 1671.

When the scene between Arlequin-Titus and Colombine-Berenice finally takes place, it quickly turns into a brawl, with Colombine pushing Arlequin and tearing his sleeve. Arlequin bursts into tears over his torn costume and gives up his queen to the "lovable, young Paulin" (played by the irascible, old Scaramouche). Arlequin's tears are explained in the final scene of the parody when the Old-Clothes Man, who has rented him the tragic *habit à romain,* snatches it off his back.

In the final scene, which, like the parody, is included in both editions of Gherardi, Arlequin Proteus plays a procureur named La Ruine whose client is a law clerk, Paul Griffonnet (from *griffonneur,* scribbler). He is opposed by Pillardin (from *pillard,* plunderer), whose client is the Docteur (see fig. 15). The Docteur appears in his own person, as "Grazian Balouard, actor in the Italian troupe." Griffonnet claims that his cloak was torn by the Docteur's dog and demands 30 livres in damages and 900 in expenses. The satire is focused on the clerk, who wears a sword and wants to be a procureur and who has spent six months, night and day, preparing his case. Justice, for once, triumphs; the magistrate denies Griffonnet's claim and gives permission for this dog and all other dogs "of whatever coat, age, and quality to bark at, bite, and chase any clerks they come across wearing swords."

It seems probable that this trial was based on some sort of actual event. According to the Docteur's lawyer, Pillardin, the incident took place on the rue Guénégaud on the left bank; Angelo Agostino Lolli, who played the Docteur, was still living on the rue Guénégaud in April 1683, even though the Comédie-Italienne and most of its actors were now situated near Les Halles on the Right Bank.[25] Pillardin further points out that although the dog was a stray, he came out of the building where the Docteur lived. "The Docteur is a foreigner; this foreigner has the reputation of having money. Enough, gentlemen, to excite an avid and litigous clerk." In return, La Ruine argues: "Will you suffer a stage Docteur to triumph insolently over the Clerkature? Ah! Gentlemen, don't you see that the Italians are just laying in wait for your judgment to make another cruel and bloody joke of it? If Master Griffonnet loses his case, Arlequin and his troupe are going to enrich themselves at the expense of the clerks and of the profession." This, of course, is precisely what is happening, confirming—as does the calendar-almanac—that the trial was a feature of the piece as played in 1683.

The six scenes included in the 1700 edition of Gherardi do not make it possible to recreate the plot of *Arlequin Protée.* Of no help is the 1694 edition, which includes only the parody and the trial scene, slightly shorter, or the *Supplément,* which includes a different scene from the parody, one between Cinthio and Isabelle, following the first twenty lines of Isabelle's soliloquy. Chances are that the slender plot that held the whole thing together was the idea of Arlequin Proteus, whose ability to change identity at will makes unnecessary the use of Arlequin as a valet disguising himself for purposes of the intrigue. This is the first play in the repertory in which the character Arlequin appears to play no role, although the characteristics of the masque are still employed. It is also the first one to which the name Monsieur D*** is attached which exhibits a controlling idea not from the traditional Italian repertory. The trial scene could well be by the same writer as the last act of *La matrone d'Ephèse, ou Arlequin Grapignan,* which is mentioned in it, but the parody of Bèrènice is not related to the trial scene in theme or style. The evidence is too fragmentary to say more.

The next piece assigned by Gherardi to Monsieur D*** is *Arlequin empereur dans la lune* or *dans le monde de la lune,* first performed 5 March 1684. It was, according to Donneau de Visé, an enormous hit. "Played without interruption for fifteen days until the Easter closing, it has made here an uproar which goes beyond everything that can be imagined. All Paris ran there and at every performance the place was found to be too small." [26] Although the play's title sounds as if it were a spectacle piece, in fact the spectacle is confined primarily to verbal descriptions.

The 1700 edition of Gherardi contains eight scenes, and although it is not possible to recreate the plot exactly, it is possible to tell that its basis is once again Italianate with an old man unwilling to permit the young women in his custody to marry the men they love. The first published scene, the "Scène de la prothase," is between the Docteur and his servant, Pierrot. The stage is set as a garden with a giant telescope mounted at the rear. The Docteur is an amateur astronomer who has discovered that the moon is a world like the earth. Pierrot does not believe that something the size of an eight-egg omelet can be inhabited. This is the first time we see Pierrot as a Second Zanni, a valet balourd, a glutton, an illiterate, a wise fool. As Arlequin changes in the Gherardi repertory, Pierrot at times takes on his old characteristics, although exactly when Arlequin changes is not easily determined. The dating employed in the Gherardi collection makes it appear that changes took place before the death of Dominique; however, the likelihood that the early plays are accretions developed over several reprises means that the change in Arlequin may be attributed to the change in actors, that the new, clever, witty, and accomplished Arlequin is a creature of Gherardi and not of Biancolelli. Dominique's traditional Arlequin is by no means missing from the plays first performed before his death in 1688, but the character can be inconsistent, even within a single play.

In *Arlequin empereur* the Docteur has escaped into astronomy from his household of women: his niece Isabelle, who loves only poetry and fills his house with poets, his daughter Eularia, who always has some young fop at her heels, and the two servants who are as crazy as their mistresses.[27] He has plans to marry them all off. Arlequin overhears the Docteur's plan to give Colombine, *his* mistress, to an apothecary, a baker, or a farmer. Arlequin's unseen presence gives rise to an echo lazzi that ends with Pierrot getting beaten by his master.

The "Scène du désespoir" that follows is a solo for Arlequin, a fully developed suicide lazzi in which he fails to kill himself by holding his nose and mouth shut, "because the air gets out below," or by tickling himself so that he will die of laughter. Suicide lazzi are traditional, and several are to be found in Biancolelli's zibaldone. Having given up on death, Arlequin begins to devise strategies to recover his beloved Colombine from the Docteur. In the "Scène de la fille de chambre" Arlequin disguises himself as a chambermaid and applies for a job. Pierrot plays the Docteur's wife. The scene is largely a satiric discussion of the chambermaid's last employer, the wife of a businessman (who never goes to the water closet but "does it" in her room, who goes to the Turkish bath once a week, and who wears her gloves to bed) and other Parisian types.

Scene 4 takes place between Isabelle and Colombine. Isabelle is worried because some mysterious "devil" has been finishing her poems and Cinthio, her lover, thinks it's a rival. The ladies discuss Angélique, a very chaste girl of forty-six, leader of a salon of précieuses frequented by Isabelle. Colombine is not impressed, but Isabelle tells her that "prose is the excrement of the mind" and that "a Madrigal is worth more than thirty well-constructed sentences." "It is good, Mademoiselle, to have wit," says Colombine, "but you need something else when you're married." The character which Catherine Biancolelli was developing as Colombine begins to emerge in this scene—cynical, practical, with an eye on the main chance. Whether the invention of Monsieur D*** or of the young actress herself, Colombine is clearly not an Italian serva but a Parisian who has learned how to survive in a society where ideals and fine words butter no baguettes. She strongly advises Isabelle against marrying a poet who will earn his living "quatrain by quatrain." "Marry a good fat financier," she declares. "But how does one resolve to love an insupportable man," asks Isabelle. "Really," answers Colombine,

> who marries a rich man to love him? You marry to be well-to-do . . . and easily console yourself for the rest. . . . You will live like the women of Paris live. The four or five first years you will live high on

the hog; and then when you have used up the best part of your husband's property in furniture, clothes, carriages, jewels, you will separate and live like a great lady. ... Only the fools do otherwise. ... You have to have some legal gentleman to look after your interests and then, little by little, you make the husband angry, you insult him. In the end he loses his patience. He hits you, maybe kicks you. You file a complaint. The legal gentleman does his duty. And there you are, made for life.

In scene 5 Arlequin disguises himself as the farmer from Donfront that Colombine is meant to marry. He arrives on stage in a *soufflet,* or carriage with a hood. A clerk tries to collect a duty on it and enlists a Commissaire to help. Arlequin, in the meantime, changes himself into a baker and his carriage into a wagon. The Commissaire agrees with Arlequin that the clerk is crazy and makes him pay Arlequin six ecus for loss of time and burned bread. When the clerk turns back, the farmer and his carriage have reappeared. The clerk runs after the Commissaire, but when he returns with him, naturally the baker and the wagon are there waiting. After this lazzi Arlequin once again transforms himself into the farmer and announces to the Docteur that he has arrived to marry Colombine. The trick is discovered when a letter arrives from the real farmer.

Arlequin's next appearance is as the envoy of the Emperor of the Moon, who wants to marry Isabelle. Most of the scene is taken up with Arlequin's account of his trip to the moon, carried there by six vultures trying to steal a goose he was holding, and by descriptions of life on the moon. Pasquariel, the offstage voice of the Emperor, helps Arlequin get six louis d'or and a diamond ring from the Docteur.

In scene 7 Arlequin is carried on stage in a sedan chair that opens to reveal an apothecary's shop. Arlequin, as Colombine's third suitor, the apothecary, performs what is essentially a harangue, bragging about his excretory exploits and pressing his suit at the same time. In the final scene he appears as the Emperor of the Moon, come to earth to ask for Isabelle's hand in marriage. The Docteur, the women, and Arlequin engage in another discussion of life on the moon, the Emperor describing the manners of his subjects, the others responding: "It's just like here." On the moon and on the earth men are ruled by ambition and self-interest; the greatest virtue is property. Doctors kill their patients painfully. Husbands are accommodating. And the best minds have worked for seventy years on a dictionary which will not be finished for two centuries. The play ends with a mock combat between the Emperor of the Moon and the three Chevaliers of the Sun for the hands of Eularia, Isabelle, and

Colombine. The Chevaliers—who must include the lovers of the two Amoureuses—win, and Arlequin renounces Colombine but is given her in the end.

In the traditional plays of the Italian repertory Arlequin's pursuit of the servante is merely a subplot. *Arlequin empereur* features the comic characters. The amoureuse, Isabelle, is a straight man, or feed, for Colombine. Whether Arlequin is also Cinthio's valet is simply not established.

Unlike the material that precedes it in the 1700 edition of Gherardi, *Arlequin empereur* seems to be all of a piece. None of the scenes are detached; all are related in some fashion—however tenuous—to the plot. The only indication that Gherardi's version may be different from the original is the mention of Pasquariel as Arlequin's assistant in a play that made its debut a year before Tortoriti joined the troupe. The 1694 edition of Gherardi includes scenes 3, 4, 7, and the first part of 8 up to the entrance of the Chevaliers. This material features satire of French manners and the apothecary's harangue. The *Supplément* includes a scene between Arlequin and Colombine that may precede Gherardi's third scene, since Colombine says in it, "I would like to have found a chambermaid . . . I want to dress you as a girl."

Arlequin empereur shows little of the preoccupation with legal matters which characterizes its predecessors, although a few references to lawyers and justice are part of its satire of manners. Whether it is the work of the same Monsieur D*** responsible for *Arlequin Grapignan* or the trial scene in *Arlequin Protée* cannot be determined. If, indeed, there was a single Monsieur D***, his interests had broadened and his style had improved. Even the scenes based on traditional commedia dell'arte lazzi, like the "Scène du désespoir," no longer read like transcriptions of oral translations from the Italian. In general, the French flavor is far stronger in *Arlequin empereur* than in the plays that precede it. The form of the intrigue remains Italianate, but the details of the dialogue refer exclusively to French society and French manners. For the first time it seems possible to presume that a French playwright did more than provide a harangue or a compliment to add gallic spice to an Italian dish.

Gherardi's edition gives little information about the setting of the play, all of which seems to take place in the Docteur's garden. The spectacle is of the "little miracle" variety and consists principally of the two vehicles, the carriage that is transformed into a wagon and the sedan chair that opens into a traveling apothecary shop. Both of these scenes were drawn by Gillot. The Gherardi frontispiece shows what probably served as the backscene for the finale: a moonscape with the signs of the zodiac scattered along a road. Gherardi also attached one air by Loren-zani, sung in Italian, but the text includes no indication of who sang it or where.

Arlequin Jason, ou la toison d'or comique opened on 9 September 1684 and is the first of the parodies to burlesque a competing entertainment. The French opened a spectacular new production of Corneille's *La toison d'or* in July 1683 and played it some thirty-five times during the following season. In later years the Italians could mount a burlesque of a French play within days of the opening of the original, but in 1684 the Italians were playing in a theatre unequipped for spectacle. To parody spectacle requires the ability to create spectacle. Thus, the Italians waited while the cascades that were to be their opening gun in the new spectacle wars were prepared.[28]

So far as surviving texts indicate, *Arlequin Jason* is entirely a parody; that is, the characters have no identities other than those in the parody plot. Colombine is Medea, Arlequin is Jason—although Jason trans-formed. Medea and Ipsiphilia, probably played by Isabelle, are both in love with Jason. Medea, the sorceress, decides to create a counterfeit Ja-son, one so stupid, so ugly, that her rival will hate him. Creating a spell in the name of all the devils, procureurs, sergeants, commissaires, and clerks of the court, and suggestively "counting out" a little money, Medea changes a heroic statue of Jason into Arlequin.

In the second scene, which is in French verse like the first, Ipsiphilia and Medea discuss the manners of the local inhabitants. Colombine-Medea is once again cynical. Ipsiphilia dreams of a warrior; Medea tells her that in this country "the faith of a warrior weighs less than the plumes on his hat." Ipsiphilia begs for Jason, her hero. Medea points out that Jason is ugly, badly built, small as a dwarf, but—"if you love him, so much the better."

The third scene, "Scène du triomphe et du récit du combat," is in prose. Jason enters in triumph in his chariot followed by his Argonauts, Scaramouche and Spezzafer, wearing winged hats and riding hobby-horses. The Queen, played probably by Eularia, greets Arlequin in Ital-ian. He does a harangue describing a naval battle fought with—among other things—sea horses for cavalry. The Queen gives him Ipsiphilia, but Arlequin turns down the gift, saying to her "My heart is not for you."

Scene 4, between Jason and Medea, is again in French verse. Arle-quin agrees to kill himself to prove his love for Medea, but has trouble finding his heart. He finally shoves the sword in between his legs and pretends to be dead, actually fooling Medea for a moment. She admits that she loves him, and he "ceases to be dead." In the following scene Jason and Medea argue about the golden fleece and Ipsiphilia and Medea quarrel over Jason.

The finale is in French prose. Medea has the golden fleece and will not give it to Jason unless he agrees to marry her. Jason lists his conditions: no gold brocade, no *fontanges,* no lackeys, no drives without me, no clandestine dinners, no fricasees at the Pelerins, no fish stews at the Moulin de Javelle, nothing at those cabarets where "the friends of the husband try to become friends of the wife." Medea inquires if he means that she "dare not eat a morsel with her friends"; Arlequin insists that the only safe thing is to eat early at home. He adds that there is to be no acquaintance with the gentlemen of the robe, that is, with lawyers, administrators, and bureaucrats. And no association with businessmen. A financier, according to Arlequin, no matter how old, is more dangerous than fifteen noblemen. The satire of Parisian life in this scene is hardly subtle, and Arlequin suddenly metamorphosed into Alceste is disconcerting. The naive imbroglios of his harangue in the "Scène du triomphe" bear no resemblance to the sophisticated cynicism of exchanges like the one which follows:

> JASON I simply do not want to know men who entice women with money, who give them everything their husbands refuse them.
>
> MEDEA What? You take umbrage at a businessman? Surely you realize they are nothing but banal dupes. Women amuse themselves playing cards with them. Their only merit, their only distinction with women is how much money they lose at gambling.
>
> JASON So much the worse.
>
> MEDEA So much the better.
>
> JASON So much the worse, I tell you. What the devil, nothing is more pernicious for the peace of the household than a man with money to lose. He begins by going halves with a young woman. If she loses, he pays for her. If she wins, she pockets the whole thing. It would be a great miracle if these gentlemen went halves for long with the wife without also going halves with the husband.

Medea has conditions of her own: no jealousy "like an Italian," no pretty servant girls, no drunkenness, no taverns. If Arlequin agrees, he can have her and the golden fleece. "It's a bargain," says Arlequin. And what's more, the Queen has given Ipsiphilia to Lycurgus. At this point Medea strikes the ground with her magic wand. The stage opens revealing the garden with its magnificent cascades and twelve figures on gilded pedestals. Medea explains that the statues are all people whom she has changed to stone for offending her. The victims include a doctor with a face the color of gingerbread who ordered an emetic for her toothache, a man of mode who borrowed 50,000 francs from her and went bankrupt, an Italian actor who made her laugh herself sick, and a French actor from a provincial troupe who bored her to death.[29] Arlequin is appalled at the fate of the provincial actor, having "messed around with that" himself. He agrees that Medea can petrify the great actors, but he begs that, in honor of the marriage, she release the provincial. She does, and the Italian as well. The final scene is a contest between the two actors, the Docteur as the Italian actor and, judging by Bonnart's engraving of the final scene, either Scaramouche or Spezzafer as the French provincial actor (see fig. 12).[30]

The French actor thanks Arlequin for his life; all Arlequin wants in recompense is "five or six stately verses." The Italian offers great verses as well, but Arlequin refuses, remembering that one of the Italians, this "Artir ... Arpir ... Arquir ... fellow" dared to ridicule the Roman emperor Titus, obviously a reference to the parody of *Bérénice* in *Arlequin Protée*. After enjoying ten lines or so of pompous verse, Arlequin discovers from the French actor that even though his troupe performs nothing but new comedies, no one comes to see them. Everyone is at the Italians seeing "Protée, le banqueroutier, l'empereur dans la Lune." *Le banqueroutier* was first performed in April 1687. Once again, it is obvious that Gherardi's texts include additions made later.

Arlequin Jason ends with the animation of the statues and the playing of the cascades. The characters dance a parody of the chaconne in *Amadis* and finish with a song:

> The burlesque Jason
> Has won the golden fleece:
> He's very proud of his victory;
> The sound of his glory rings out:
> But the greatest of his exploits
> Is speaking French.

Gherardi explains that the "French actors, having complained not long before that the Italians were speaking French in their plays, were answered by the king: So you can speak Italian." The song, combined with an earlier reference to the Docteur being "punished" for speaking

French, suggests either that the troupe had just received permission to play in French when *Arlequin Jason* was first produced or that this material was added to it at the time the permission was received. The first edition of Gherardi includes all of the scenes but the "Scène du triomphe" and the musical finale; the play is not included in the *Supplément*.

We know, thanks to Tralage, that *Arlequin Jason* was the work of Fatouville. It has almost none of the legal satire that characterizes the earlier work attributed to Monsieur D***, nor does it show the internal consistency of *Arlequin empereur dans la lune*. Without the harangue, the inconsistencies would be less obvious, but the "Scène du triomphe" must have been included in the original production; the Bonnart engraving of it shows Spezzafer, and Cei died less than six months after the play opened. The French scenes included in Gherardi give no real clues as to the nature of the missing Italian scenes, but the Bonnart calendar-almanac includes one scene that is not present in the collection. In it Arlequin and the King are seated in armchairs as Arlequin hands His Majesty a piece of paper. Five gentlemen of the court stand behind. The other engravings show—along with the triumphal entry and the finale—the transformation of the statue into Arlequin, the presentation by Arlequin of a sausage to the Queen in the "Scène du triomphe," and Arlequin begging Medea for the golden fleece.[31]

Only a few pages of *Arlequin chevalier du soleil* are included in the Gherardi 1700 edition; nothing from it is to be found in the first edition. Oddly enough, however, three scenes are contained in the *Supplément,* and two of them, unlike most of the material in the *Supplément,* are identical to the edition of 1700. The play seems to be based on an Italianate intrigue. The four surviving scenes can be divided into two parts. In one part, Isabelle and Colombine are concerned with the problem of dressing really well when one has a miserly father; in the other Arlequin takes up the profession of medicine.

Although the plot cannot be reconstructed, the available material is useful, especially the scenes in which Colombine, the suivante, teaches Isabelle how to go about dressing fashionably without money. To the cynicism visible in the earlier plays, Colombine here adds cunning and guile. Isabelle is so badly dressed she is ashamed to be seen in public. Colombine promises her something new at a cost of no more than three or four winks at a certain gentleman, a marquis de Boutique—that is, a shop assistant. And Colombine has one in mind, a certain Monsieur Galonnier.

In the "Scène d'un garçon marchand" Isabelle demonstrates that she has learned her lesson:

COLOMBINE	Monsieur Galonnier, Madame is a good customer.
M. GALONNIER	I am much obliged to you, Madame.
ISABELLE	You're joking, Colombine. Monsieur is simply not made for a shop. He has such an air of good taste. His qualities simply leap to the eye.
M. GALONNIER	One hears only the most civil things from people like you.
COLOMBINE	M. Galonnier is very genteel.
ISABELLE	He appears well-born. That struck me the minute I set eyes on him. That can never be hidden, regardless of the condition one finds oneself in.
GALONNIER	Ah, Madame!
COLOMBINE	He belongs at court.
ISABELLE	Certainly.
GALONNIER	Madame . . .

There is finally no flattery too fulsome for M. Galonnier, who ends by giving Isabelle a bolt of the most expensive cloth in the shop, to be paid for "when it pleases Madame."

While this scene is satirical, it also celebrates the cleverness of the women who are able to get what they want by manipulating the men around them. Colombine is actually on the way to becoming a sort of French female First Zanni, a trickster who is, however, always successful and never gets caught. The character has no antecedents in the earlier repertory; Diamantine was a more traditional servante who, although cleverer than Arlequin, engaged in zanni play physically as well as verbally, and who never led the intrigue.

While the women's scenes are like nothing to be found in the Italian commedia dell'arte, the two scenes of Arlequin as a physician are traditional, especially the first which, according to Gherardi, should not have been printed, since it is one of those Italian scenes (though translated into French) "the merit of which is inseparable from the action." He has included it, he says, only because it has been published elsewhere "all mutilated." In it Pasquariel, originally Spezzafer, explains to Arlequin how easy it is to be a doctor. In the companion scene Arlequin does a harangue that sounds rather like the compliment Thomas Diafoirus makes in *Le malade imaginaire*.[32] The harangue is followed by an Italianate scene in which Arlequin interrupts the Docteur and overwhelms him with a list of symptoms and an anatomical recitation. The scene is very funny, but not typical of Arlequin's travesty as a doctor. It is a patter scene that requires glibness, extreme speed, and vocal flexibility and does not seem suited to Dominique's imbroglios and parrot voice.

According to Gherardi's dates, the next play, *Isabelle médecin,* was a companion piece to *Arlequin chevalier du soleil,* also first performed on 26 February 1685. If the dating is accurate, then one of these plays represents the first short piece to be found in the Gherardi repertory. *Isabelle médecin* is also represented by only a few scenes and is not to be found in the 1694 edition of Gherardi and only by title in the *Supplément.* In this instance, however, the available material is made up largely of plot scenes rather than detached scenes of farce or satire. Isabelle has been jilted by Cinthio, who has come to Paris to make a rich match with Colombine, daughter of the Docteur. Isabelle follows him and disguises herself as a physician with whom Colombine falls in love. Arlequin plays Isabelle's valet.

The piece is of interest largely because of Isabelle's unexpected role. She appears both as herself and in disguise as her brother, the physician. She plays a love scene with Colombine that is marked by an unusually high degree of sexual play and innuendo. In both the old repertory and the new, the amoureuse is normally a passive character whose fate is in the hands of a parent or husband and whose change in state is brought about by the actions of her lover and his valet or, in the French repertory, by the guile of her suivante, Colombine. In *Isabelle médecin,* however, she is the active character. Colombine's role is closer to that of the traditional amoureuse and has nothing in common with the character gradually being developed in the preceding plays.

The available scenes of *Isabelle médecin* also lack the legal burlesques typical of the earlier plays attributed to Monsieur D***. Nor are they attacks on medicine, since the point is *not* that Isabelle is a bad doctor. In one scene Arlequin also appears as a doctor, but after a speech of imbroglios—more typical of his usual medical travesty than the harangue in *Arlequin chevalier*—he turns into a sort of philosopher of health who insists that the way to cure patients is to write prescriptions against the true causes of disease. "If a woman is melancholy about her furniture, a doctor who knows his craft takes his pen and writes: one damask bed and a set of tapestries." When the jealousy of an old man distresses a young wife, "prescribe one financier and one gentleman. A financier to give money and a gentleman to spend it . . . In the thirty years I have been a doctor I have not ordered 12 livres worth of senna, but I have dispensed

300,000 in balls, collations, and serenades." This material suggests once again that the text published by Gherardi is an accretion that combines Biancolelli's Arlequin with his own. The play was probably first performed improvisationally in Italian with ornaments in French.

A play featuring Isabelle as an active agent was followed in the repertory by one featuring Colombine. *Colombine avocat pour et contre,* first performed 8 June 1685, is the first play of the Gherardi repertory that is essentially complete in the 1700 edition, although only three scenes from it are included in the 1694 edition. Attributed by Gherardi to Monsieur D***, it is Italianate in structure with a number of detached scenes of farce, and is far less French in style than some of the plays preceding it. Colombine, like Isabelle in *Isabelle médecin,* has been jilted, in this case by Arlequin, her fiancé. She arrives in Paris accompanied by her brother Pasquariel, played by Tortoriti who had recently joined the troupe. Arlequin, the son of a shoemaker who has inherited 100,000 ecus from a rich uncle, has set himself up in Paris as the Marquis de Sbrufadel. He has become engaged to Isabelle, the daughter of the Docteur, although she is in love with Cinthio.

The romance plot is slight and conducted in Italian in both improvised and written-out scenes. The central intrigue is Colombine's revenge on Arlequin. She appears in a variety of disguises, as a Spanish senora, a chambermaid, a Gascon tavern hostess, a mooress, images in a mirror and a painting, and a learned doctor of letters. Pasquariel appears as a Spaniard, a tavernkeeper, a moor, and a crippled painter. These disguises provide opportunities for many typical commedia dell' arte comic devices including ethnic jokes, misunderstandings based on language and dialect, and burlesques of various kinds. At the end of each sequence, Colombine reveals herself to Arlequin and says: "Perfidious traitor, you will have me in your eyes if not in your heart."

Colombine shows Isabelle her marriage contract. Isabelle gives it to her father, who has Arlequin arrested. At the trial Colombine appears both as a defense attorney and as herself, the advocates "for and against." Naturally, the defense attorney wins, reveals herself once again, and Arlequin accepts his fate.

The detached scenes largely involve Scaramouche, who plays Arlequin's valet. They include a lazzi of the sack with Pasquariel, the famous lazzi of taking fright (a mime scene lasting, according to Gherardi, for more than a quarter of an hour), and a scene with Scaramouche disguised as a pregnant woman. This is the only text in the Gherardi collection that includes a significant amount of Fiorilli's material, all of which is traditional. According to the *Supplément*, Scaramouche's role as Arlequin's valet in *Colombine avocat* was later played by Pierrot.

Although French comic style is not prevalent in *Colombine avocat*, where Italianate elements dominate, several scenes burlesque French manners. In act 1, scene 9, when the Marquis de Sbroufadel calls on Isabelle, the life of the *petit marquis* is satirized. For the first time in the repertory, the court is mentioned; Arlequin finds it "a strange land. A fop in this country swallows many bitter pills." As a savant, Colombine burlesques the French passion for the French language and rails against marriage, and in the final pleading shows a taste of her usual character when she says to Arlequin: "Colombine without property and without a fortune, does she not have the resources to make you wealthy? You know, scoundrel, that every fat financier in Paris wants me. How should a husband lack an occupation when a wife has such good acquaintances. If the occupation displeases you, could we not take up cards and live honorably in Paris like an infinitude of people as poor as we are?"

Colombine avocat not only served as a vehicle for Catherine Biancolelli, it also introduced Guiseppe Tortoriti to the Paris audience. As Pasquariel, derived from the capitan, Tortoriti replaced Cei, Capitan Spezzafer. He was best known as a spectacular acrobat. In *Colombine avocat* he demonstrates that he could play in Italian and French. He "rolled in a sack to Arlequin's feet" and emerged as a three-headed devil, and he played a long comic scene as a crippled painter who manages to fall onto Arlequin at every opportunity. His last scene introduces the ladder lazzi for which he was especially famous.

For several reasons, it seems likely that *Colombine avocat* was also originally part of the Italian repertory, with ornaments in French. The three scenes Gherardi includes in his 1694 edition—Arlequin disguised as a *petit marquis*, Colombine's parody of a French pedant, and the final pleadings—are all typically ornamental. The *Supplément*, in 1697, includes "French scenes omitted in the first volume": Colombine as a mooress, Colombine doing a long speech in Spanish, a scene of the dressing of Arlequin, and a burlesque promise of marriage, suggesting a later state of the text, although not all of this material is included in the 1700 Gherardi. Furthermore, the fact that *Colombine avocat*, like *Arlequin lingère*, was played at court underscores the probability that it, too, was part of the Italian repertory. Its final state, in the 1700 edition of Gherardi, may well reflect the process many of the long-lived and popular Italian scenarios underwent in the public theatre.[33]

Colombine avocat was followed by *Le banqueroutier*, a satire in the

French style, first produced 19 April 1687, two years after its immediate predecessor. The gap can be accounted for, in part, by the reconstruction of the Hôtel de Bourgogne that took place in 1686. *Le banqueroutier,* although it has a romance plot carried forward primarily in improvised scenes in Italian, cannot be classified as part of the Italian repertory. The French material available (a prologue and eleven scenes) reveals that the dominant plot of the piece concerns the financial difficulties of the financier, Persillet. He consults a notary who advises him to borrow a million francs and then claim fraudulent bankruptcy so that his creditors will accept questionable stock in lieu of repayment. This satire in the French mode is ornamented with a romance plot reminiscent of *Arlequin empereur dans la lune;* Aurelio, who is in love with Isabelle, tricks her father into agreeing to the marriage by pretending to be the Prince of Chimère.

Exactly how the two plots are related is unclear. Arlequin does not appear as himself in the French scenes. He plays the notary, M. de la Ressource (a role reminiscent of Grapignan), the Singing Master in the romance plot, and the King of Chimère. In one scene he plays M. Persillet himself courting Colombine, Persillet's servant, disguised as a "widow of quality." Mezzetin—definitely in the troupe from the beginning of the 1686 season—appears as the widow's brother, a Breton bravo, as well as an ambassador from Chimère. A few clues suggest that Arlequin, Colombine, and Mezzetin are, from the beginning, acting in the interests of the young lovers, and that Colombine's suggestion to Persillet that he consult the notary is in some way part of the plot to join Isabelle and her amoureux. But why Arlequin and Colombine appear as Persillet and the widow is unfathomable.

Once again, the text appears to be an accretion. Although the amoureux in the finale is Aurelio, in the "Scène du maistre à chanter" Arlequin comes on behalf of Cinthio. Isabelle may, of course, have had two suitors, but probably not both with Arlequin working in their cause. The reference is also puzzling because M. Persillet was surely played by Marc' Antonio Romagnesi, Cinthio, who specialized in the French repertory in bourgeois vieillards. His character names from play to play are similar without being identical—Persillet, Sotinet, Friquet, Nivelet, Trafiquet— a style of nomenclature reminiscent of Molière's Argon, Orgon, and Harpagon. A remote possibility exists that the role was originally played by Pantalon, while Cinthio played the amoureux, but this seems unlikely because the character Persillet is distinctly French. Why Cinthio is mentioned as Isabelle's suitor must remain another unsolved mystery.

Only four of the French scenes from *Le banqueroutier* were included in the 1694 edition of Gherardi, but they cannot be distinguished from the scenes added to the later edition. That is, none of them are clearly ornamental or detached. The *Supplément* includes only the prologue, a self-referential narrative by Arlequin of his experience at the Comédie-Italienne, and a distorted version of the "Scène du maistre à chanter." A safe conjecture in this case might be that romance-plot scenes in Italian were alternated with French scenes of the bankruptcy from the beginning of the play's history, with a few scenes from the romance plot—like the "Scène du maistre à chanter"—gradually shifting to French.

The early texts published by Gherardi are not easy to interpret, but one or two tentative conclusions can be drawn from them. The most important is that the repertory of the Italian troupe underwent a gradual transformation, not a sudden metamorphosis. The use of French ornaments, which began in 1668, continued into the 1680s. Exactly when French became the dominant language in some of the plays cannot be established, because Gherardi's texts are accretions and cannot be reliably dated. *Le banqueroutier* may have been the first play with a fully developed intrigue carried out in French, paralleling a romance plot played largely in Italian.

Some of the early plays show an increasing reliance on subject matter designed to be of interest to the French bourgeoisie. Legal burlesques are common, as are scenes ridiculing manners. The detached third act of *La matrone d'Ephèse* and the fraudulent bankruptcy of *Le banqueroutier* are the most obvious examples of materials meant to appeal to the increasingly middle-class audience. Another innovation of the 1680s was the parody, played in French verse.

These novelties did not, however, replace the Italian repertory. Many of the plays included in the first volume of Gherardi's 1700 edition were from the Italian repertory, with French gradually replacing Italian in certain scenes as the piece was reprised. The odds are high that the innovations introduced into the repertory—while important—were restrained until after Biancolelli's death by the popularity of his Arlequin. The changes Arlequin appears to undergo probably reflect material introduced by Gherardi in reprises.

The character that most clearly symbolizes what was beginning to happen to the repertory of the Italians is Colombine, played by Catherine Biancolelli, born and raised in France. While her father continued to build his travesties on a traditional foundation of naïveté, gluttony, cowardice, and roguery, she developed the modern, cynical, immoral, and successful young Frenchwoman, linked to the Dorines and Toinettes of Molière, but younger, smoother, and more certainly devoted to the feminine cause in the eternal war of the sexes. This character begins to take shape in *Arlequin empereur dans le lune, Arlequin chevalier du soleil,* and *Le banqueroutier,* although—once again—given the complexities of the texts, there is no way to be sure of the exact course of development.

A few titles known to us from sources other than Gherardi were played between 1680 and 1687, but the information available about them is too scanty to allow for much in the way of generalizations. *Le remède de anglois, ou Harlequin prince de Quinquina* took advantage of a fashionable remedy, a tonic made from the Peruvian bark cinchona. It is mentioned in the *Mercure galant* of December 1680 and may have been the first new entertainment offered by the Italians after their move to the Hôtel de Bourgogne. Donneau de Visé also mentions *Arlequin vendangeur* in December 1681. Although Gherardi includes no material from it, the *Supplément* devotes a few pages to it. The scenes include a long harangue very much in the style of the pre-1680 repertory where Arlequin laments the loss of his *frère de lait,* or foster brother, an ass of rare merit, a shorter harangue, a compliment, and a fantasy scene between Arlequin and Pasquariel who are dreaming of what it would be like to have a wife to kill and cook a chicken for them.[34] *Arlequin vendangeur* was played at court in December 1691, according to Moland.[35]

Lancaster includes, for 1684, a piece entitled *Amadis cuisinier,* a supposed parody of the opera *Amadis.* Either Lancaster or Mélèse, his source, has misstated the evidence, however. What Bayle wrote in the March 1684 *Nouvelles de la republique des lettres* was as follows: "We hear from Paris that the troupe of the Hôtel de Bourgogne, which is that of the Italian actors, is performing a very diverting comedy which attracts an extraordinary crowd. It is entitled *Arlequin empereur dans le monde de la lune.* It is a satire of the opera *Amadis,* according to our correspondent, who adds that there should be performed incessantly in the same theatre *Amadis cuisinier,* because the person who plays the character of Amadis in the opera was a cook."

Bayle goes on to add, however, that he doesn't believe the report, for "since it is known that the king himself gave the subject for the opera, who would dare burlesque it in public."[36] No other evidence supports the existence of *Amadis cuisinier,* which appears to have been only a slighting reference in a gossip column to the singer Dumesnil.

One final play of the period 1680–87 is known from a series of engravings by Nicolas Bonnart published in a calendar-almanac for 1688. Four scenes accompanied by legends make it possible to reconstruct the outlines of *Arlequin grand vizir,* played in 1687. The play is largely reminiscent of such earlier pieces as *Arlequin berger de Lemnos* or *Arlequin roy par hazard,* and was undoubtedly improvised in Italian. In the first scene Arlequin is washed up on shore "in the belly of his mother, the barrel." In the second engraving Arlequin is "surprised in the seraglio," dressed and veiled in an attempt to pass a message to one of the amoureuses. The third engraving is entitled "The rejoicing of the Turks after the election of Arlequin as Grand Vizir." Arlequin has saved himself by claiming to be the prophet himself and is being borne in triumph about the stage. His imposture discovered, Arlequin is about to be strangled when his life is saved by the intercession of the princess, a scene documented in the fourth engraving.[37] The introduction of *Arlequin grand vizir,* clearly a play in the Italian style, into the repertory of the Comédie Italienne in 1687 further confirms the importance of the Italian repertory through the 1680s. The Italians did not give up 150 years of improvisational flexibility simply because they now possessed a few sheets of paper with written-out scenes.

Beginning with Regnard's *Le divorce,* according to Gherardi a failure when first produced in 1688 but a great success as his debut piece in 1689, a true French repertory was introduced by the Comédie-Italienne with comedies of manners, classical romances, spectacle plays, critiques, parodies, and a new genre of musical afterpieces. These will be discussed in chapter 15.

Part V
1688-1697

CHAPTER 13

Struggle and
Expulsion

W HEN THE ITALIAN theatre reopened on 1 September 1688, a month
after the death of Domenico Biancolelli, the play was *Le marchand
dupé*, a piece without Arlequin or any Arlequin-like character. It was followed by three new plays featuring Mezzetin. Angelo Costantini performed them in the costume and mask of Arlequin but retained his own
character name of Mezzetin. His transformation is marked by a calendar-
almanac for 1689 that shows the reluctant Costantini, on the stage of the
Hôtel de Bourgogne, dressing himself as Arlequin as Colombine stands
by with the mask and bat (fig. 16). The rest of the troupe surrounds them.
At the rear, Orsola Cortesi weeps for her husband, while in the vista the
jaunty figure of Arlequin tips his hat from atop his tomb. The central
illustration is complemented by four medallions showing scenes from *Le
marchand dupé*.

The elaborate stage has twelve magnificent chandeliers and a proscenium surmounted by a mask of Arlequin set against a miniature perspective decor, the image reminiscent of the *jeton* included by Donneau
de Visé in the *Mercure galant* of February 1688. Two angels bear the arms
of France above, while below a ribbon displays the motto of the theatre:
castigat ridendo mores. The legend reads: "La Troupe Royale des Comédiens Italiennes Représentant sur le Théâtre de l'Hôtel de Bourgogne
Toutes Sortes de Piéces Tant sur les Histoires anciennes que modernes,
sérieuses ou plaisantes."

Whether the almanac gives an accurate picture of the stage of the
Hôtel de Bourgogne in the late 1680s is hard to determine. The chandeliers appear in many of the Gherardi frontispieces and in several other
visual sources, but the proscenium is not represented in any other late
seventeenth-century view. It seems likely, however, that the almanac engraving is meant to represent the state of things after the remodeling
done in 1686 by the Italians, and if the glories of the stage should be
slightly exaggerated, that would hardly be surprising in what is, after all,
an advertisement for a theatrical company that has just lost one of its main
attractions.

FIG. *16. Bonnart calendar-almanac for 1689 marking the death of
Domenico Biancolelli and the temporary transformation of Angelo
Costantini into Arlequin.* (Bibliothèque Nationale; phot. Bibl. Nat. Paris)

The year 1689 was also marked by the opening of the new Comédie-Française on the rue des Fossés-St.-Germain-des-Prés on 18 April. The French actors invested a total of 198,433 livres, 15 sous, 5 deniers in the first Parisian theatre designed for the visual accommodation of the spectator.[1] The new theatre was fully equipped and magnificently decorated.

The Hôtel de Bourgogne, whatever the magnificence of its proscenium, was old—nearly 150 years old—and still not equipped for changeable scenery and machine spectacle. *Le marchand dupé*, a bourgeois comedy of manners, requires only two simple interiors, the change achieved in the time-honored way by opening and closing a shutter. In March 1689, however, presumably to provide maximum competition for the new theatre that was about to open, the Italians produced *La descente de Mezzetin aux enfers*, certainly a spectacular title.

The play opens with the stage representing a sea; Mezzetin appears "in the belly of a whale" while Colombine enters mounted on the back of a large fish. None of these effects were new. The sea dates from *Arlequin Protée*, while Arlequin's entry in the belly of some sea creature is called for in *Arlequin berger de Lemnos*, produced at the Hôtel Guénégaud in 1674, as well as in *Arlequin grand vizir* in 1687. The other spectacular effect called for in *La descente de Mezzetin* is the Throne of Flames, featured in the frontispiece. This could well have been the transformation effect from *Arlequin Protée*, where the magistrate's chair turns into a "frightful monster shooting flames." What all of this suggests is that the Italians were still without the physical resources to compete with the new French theatre.

The late seventeenth-century audience expected a high level of artistry and sophisticated machinery when spectacle was employed. Tralage savages a production at the Opéra in the 1690s for its badly painted sea and its "whirlwind" cloud which extended itself, like a zigzag, to the stage for the descent of Hecate. "This machine was found ridiculous," writes Tralage,[2] who deeply regrets the loss of Servandoni because of Lulli's refusal to pay him 5,000 livres a year.[3]

Beginning in July 1689, evidence derived from the Gherardi texts suggests that the Italian troupe was investing in new machines. The texts collected in volumes 2–6 of the 1700 edition are less problematic than those in volume 1, but the dating of specific scenes can still not be perfectly established. The spectacle called for in *Mezzetin Grand Sophy de Perse*, produced 10 July 1689, is included in the first edition of Gherardi but is not mentioned by any of the gazetteers. We cannot be certain that it was actually produced in 1689, but the ending of the play would be flat without it. Mezzetin, disguised as the Sophy, explains how building is done in Persia: "Learn that in Persia a Palace is built by music. In this country there are no other masons but musicians; and doors open only with musical keys. Behold!" What we see is "a room furnish itself in the wink of an eye." At the end of the play, Mezzetin commands: "Let's go, furniture, under the pillars of Les Halles." And the furniture "folds up and disappears, leaving in its place a quantity of people who earlier made up the suite of the Grand Sophy."[4]

Another effect is indicated in *Esope*, first produced 24 February 1691. At the finale Esope says, "Appear, animals": "The stage opens and at the back appear caves out of which emerge some animals which stop at the entrace; and at the top of each cave are to be seen a quantity of different birds, and a monkey which leaps from the top to the stage.... As soon as the chorus has finished singing, the birds take flight and the animals advance in step."[5] Again, that this effect was employed in the first production cannot be absolutely established, but without some sort of spectacle, the play—which is a series of disconnected episodes—would come to a tame conclusion. The scene is also represented in the frontispiece joined to the play text in the 1700 edition, suggesting that it was among the production's memorable moments.

Shortly after *Esope*, the troupe began to accumulate money. On 15 March 1691, the actors borrowed 17,600 livres from Dr. Amonio, who had lent them 15,000 livres for the reconstruction done in 1686. On 14 September of the same year they borrowed another 22,000 livres from the Italian physician.[6] On 14 August 1691 Angelo Lolli and Marc' Antonio Romagnesi received for the troupe the payment of nine quarters of accrued royal pension, a total of 33,750 livres.[7] In November the actors drew 1,112 livres of interest from the Aides and Gabelles, signaling an investment of over 10,000 livres.[8] And finally, the actors went to the First Gentleman of the Chamber for permission to subtract half of the daily share from those members of the company who had not paid their entry fees.[9]

The Italians accumulated, at a minimum, 85,000 livres, a vast sum of money. The only logical purpose for such a hoard, achieved at considerable personal sacrifice, was a further reconstruction of the shabby old Hôtel de Bourgogne. Just how complete that reconstruction may have been can be estimated by comparing the money available to the Italians with what the French spent on the interior of their new theatre. According to the *Grand Registre* of the French troupe, the total cost of stage, amphithéâtre, loges, balcons, decoration, and machines was 24,622 livres, 12 sous, 6 deniers.[10] The Italians had more than three times as much money to spend.

They certainly spent some of it on machines. The plays produced in the fall of 1691 and the winter of 1692 clearly require a stage equipped for changeable scenery and machine spectacle. The first of these is *Ulisse et Circé*, performed on 20 October 1691. It opens on a scene representing "the camp of the Greeks before the city of Troy, which appears in the distance in flames." In act 2 the scene shifts to a "very agreeable island with the sea in the distance," and a shipwreck involves "the Docteur, Pasquariel, and Pierrot swimming in the sea, crying out, while a little boat carrying Arlequin and Mezzetin passes by, tossed on the waves." Act 2 ends with the inevitable transformation, given the subject matter. The Docteur is changed into an ass, Pierrot into a goat, Pasquariel into a pig, and Mezzetin into a cat. At the end, for the finale, "the stage changes into a magnificent garden. Violins and oboes surround the chariot of Ulisse and Circé, which is in the middle of the stage. On one side, Arlequin and Colombine are in a chariot that represents a household. On the other side, Mezzetin and Marinette are also in a chariot, which represents a whole kitchen. They are surrounded by grotesque objects, casseroles, and cauldrons."[11]

Although the stage direction does not say that the chariots fly out with their occupants, usually the point of chariots in Italianate staging is that they fly, and three flying at once indicates a very elaborate machine. And, indeed, the carnival play of 1692, *Arlequin Phaeton*, which opened on 4 February, confirms that the Italians now possessed a state-of-the-art flying machine. In act 2 two characters rest on clouds above the stage floor and talk to other characters on earth; at the end of the act "Phaeton reappears in the air, his chariot half upset as Jupiter strikes it with thunder, and he falls with his chariot (see fig. 19)."[12] This is an extremely sophisticated, not to say dangerous, effect.

These plays, but especially *Ulisse et Circé*, are different from their immediate predecessors in the repertory. *Ulisse et Circé* is a true spectacle piece, the first one we know of to be done by the Italians after their departure from the Hôtel Guénégaud. The spectacle cannot in this case represent something added during a later reprise, since the spectacle itself is the point. Nor would there be any point to an Arlequin Phaeton without Apollo's chariot.

The potential expenditure of 85,000 livres suggests that the Italians did far more than reequip their stage, but no contracts have come to light to specify what else might have been done. Scholars have identified various features of the theatre in the eighteenth century that could have been modifications made in 1691. Illingworth maintains that at some point the Italians bought the houses adjoining the theatre and converted them into lobby space.[13] The French had made a similar purchase in 1689, acquiring a house on the rue des Mauvais Garçons for badly needed storage and dressing rooms; perhaps the Italians followed their lead. Barlow expresses doubts about "the reliability of those who reported the theatre unaltered in 1716," pointing out that Sir James Thornhill's 1717 drawings of the Hôtel de Bourgogne show an orchestra and parquet, several rows of seats between the orchestra and the parterre, that could not have been there in 1647.[14] Barlow was unaware of the Italians' reconstructions of 1686 and 1691, when these features could have been installed. And although it seems unlikely that the Italians—whose plays overflow with fulsome flattery of the parterre—would install an orchestra pit and three or four rows of expensive seats between themselves and their favored patrons, the "Orqueste" is mentioned in *La coquette* (January 1691) and *Les chinois* (December 1692).[15]

One feature the Italians did not admire at the new French theatre was the balustrade. Two weeks before the theatre on the rue Fossés-St.-Germain-des-Prés opened, the French troupe agreed, in a formal deliberation, to install balustrades to confine the onstage audience to the benches provided for them. The balustrades were to be 5 toises (31 feet 8 inches) long on each side of the stage and made of wrought iron.[16] Colombine, disguised as a "gentleman of the robe" in *Mezzetin Grand Sophy de Perse*, which opened in July 1689, three months after the new French theatre, asserts that she is going to sue the French actors. "You know perfectly well," she says, "that three times a week I show myself to the public from the stage. But since they have planted there an impertinent balustrade ... I am like a bird in a cage. Oh, you'll be overturned, Madame la Balustrade. The Parterre has promised to join me. He has, I'll be sworn, an obvious interest."[17] No balustrade was added to the Hôtel de Bourgogne in 1691. In *Les chinois* Colombine and Arlequin debate the relative merits of the French and Italian troupes while The Parterre, played by Mezzetin, acts as judge. Arlequin, for the French, boasts of the gilded magnificence of their theatre. Colombine answers: "Your stage, surrounded by an iron grill, resembles a prison rather than a place of pleasure. Is it for the safety of the young men who come from the Cornemuse or Chez Rousseau, to keep them from throwing themselves into the parterre, that you put a madman's guard in front of them? The Italians give a free field on the stage to all."

The Italians were successful in the 1690s, whether because of their reconstructed theatre and expensive machines or their lack of restraints for the audience on stage, or perhaps their policy of no longer charging extra for new plays. They attracted larger audiences than their competitors. In scene 2 of *Les adieux des officiers* (25 April 1693) Arlequin as Vulcan is forging a new *baguette*, or magic wand, for the actors. He says, "the *baguettes* which only look for gold are counterfeit, the true ones attract it; and I know one that in three months has brought more than 20,000 ecus to the Hôtel de Bourgogne." The reference is to the very popular afterpiece *La baguette de Vulcain*, which opened on 10 January. If this figure is accurate, it indicates an average take of 1,000 livres per performance for the sixty performances between 10 January and 25 April. The French troupe, in the same period, averaged 580 livres per performance, in spite of opening three new plays.[18]

The audience for the Italians was largely drawn from the bourgeoisie. Tralage writes: "Cléante or Jourdain only amuses himself at the Italian plays where every act ends with somersaults or a beating. This is some ignorant partisan or wholesale merchant who, after having heard nothing but accounts, disputes, lawsuits, is happy, at least one day a week, to hear comic things which violate reason and verisimilitude. He laughs at the rules which bore him, and whistles at the Italian actors who want to speak their own language. He wants nothing but French scenes like those in *L'empereur dans la lune, Colombine avocat pour et contre*, etc."[19]

As the Italian theatre grew in popularity with the citizens of Paris, it lost more ground at court. Its very success in the city damned it. According to Tralage, "The courtiers, especially the women, affect to be contemptuous of whatever the bourgeois has esteemed. That has the air of quality and marks a superior intelligence."[20] His Majesty had lost interest in the theatre as well. Firmly under the thumb of his devout second wife, the marquise de Maintenon, Louis had set his once frivolous mind on higher things. The marquis Dangeau writes in 1692: "This evening there was an Italian play. The King never goes to any play now."

Throughout the 1690s the Italians played less frequently at court, since they were to the taste of neither the king nor the courtiers. Their last trip to Fontainebleau was in 1692. In 1693 and 1694 Dangeau reports that they were not brought along. In 1695 the Italians played at court only four times in January and February and once in November. In 1696 they played once each in January, February, and December. In 1697 they were not invited to Versailles at all.[21] The king's favorites no longer played; Biancolelli was dead, Fiorilli in de facto retirement until his death in 1694. The royal subvention continued, at least in theory, but the services it paid for were no longer in demand.

The company of the 1690s contained few members who had been sharers for more than ten years. Angelo Agostino Lolli and Marc' Antonio Romagnesi were still prominent on stage and in the affairs of the troupe, at least until the former retired in 1694. Orsola Cortesi continued to play in the Italian repertory. Tiberio Fiorilli and Patricia Adami, although still sharers, no longer acted. Newcomers included two more Costantinis, father and son, who played Gradelin and Octave, Angela Toscano, who replaced Adami as a servante and filled in as Second Amoureuse as well, and Evaristo Gherardi who made his debut on 1 October 1689 as the new Arlequin. The troupe was not harmonious.

Events surrounding the publication in 1694 of Gheraradi's one-volume collection of materials in French have been described in chapter 12. The split in the troupe between the Costantinis and their allies, on the one hand, and Gherardi and his, on the other, is only one example of what must have been almost continuous warfare.

In October 1694 Giovanni Battista Costantini, Angelo's brother, filed a complaint with the magistrates of the Châtelet against Marc' Antonio Romagnesi, who, he said, became angry with him over nothing and threatened him with a naked sword. The quarrel arose when Angelo Costantini asked Romagnesi, during the reading of a scenario, whether he planned to play the vieillard as Persillet or Brocantin. Romagnesi, furious, responded that he would play as seemed good to him. Warmer words were exchanged and Romagnesi ended the encounter by inviting Giovanni Battista to "step outside." When the assembly was over, Romagnesi waited for Costantini with a sword, but Costantini refused to fight, "not wanting to violate the king's orders," and came to complain instead. Romagnesi was over sixty at this point, Costantini perhaps in his forties.[22]

An earlier quarrel that also ended before a magistrate involved Giovanni Battista Costantini and Evaristo Gherardi, with testimony taken from Romagnesi, Lolli, Tortoriti, Fracansani, and Giaratoni. Gherardi appeared to file his complaint with a "contusion on the top of his nose." According to the Arlequin, the previous evening after the play Costantini had convoked an assembly to ask why it was that the troupe had played on Thursday after announcing it would not. Gherardi answered that the troupe had played because all the actors were available except Costantini, who was away hunting. Costantini asked who had announced the performance; Gherardi answered that he had. At this Costantini flew into a rage and said, "Ah, you want to encroach on me. I'm going to destroy you." And he took his stick and gave Gherardi, who was lying on a bench, resting from the labors of the performance, a blow on the head. Furthermore, he called him an unpleasant name, hit him with his fists, scratched his face, and tried to kill him. The other actors intervened, and Pasquariel "adroitly disarmed them." The enmity between the two men was apparently constant. Gherardi testified that he did not know the reason for it, but Costantini frequently insulted him, called him an ignorant ass, even made noise to bother him when he was on stage. A year earlier Costantini and his brother, Mezzetin, had both drawn on Gherardi during a reading of a new play, *Don Quichotte,* and he was saved from assassination only by the good offices of a member of the king's household. The Costantini brothers, according to Gherardi, were troublesome, "sedulous to shock and injure everyone. They devote themselves to all sorts of debauchery, even bringing debauched women into the first loges and causing the troupe great scandal." [23]

The witnesses agree with Gherardi's description of the events, but all add one exchange he ignores. Apparently after Gherardi admitted to having been the one who announced the performance, Costantini said something to the effect of "You want to be the master." And Gherardi responded, "Neither you nor your brother will ever be the master of the troupe."

What seems clear from this is that the troupe was without a leader. Whether Biancolelli had served as an official capocomico is unknown, but he was the orator, the one who announced performances and called assemblies, and he certainly was regarded by his fellows and by the public as someone with authority. After Biancolelli's death, Lolli was perhaps too old to establish himself as leader, and Romagnesi, who seems a likely heir, perhaps too embroiled in the troupe's quarrels. For whatever reason, in 1692 Giovanni Battista Costantini, only four years after his debut, was the orator at the Italian theatre, to which the Costantini family now lent its aura of violence and scandal.

Others of the actors served the troupe in various capacities. Giaratoni was treasurer in 1692; in his testimony before the Commissaire he notes that he came late to the assembly called by Costantini, having finished the accounts. In 1691 Angelo Agostino Lolli was the troupe's man of business, responsible for the reconstruction of the theatre. In November of that year his colleagues granted him a power of attorney to collect the interest owing on the money the troupe had invested in the Aides and Gabelles.[24] Tralage mentioned that it was Monsieur Ange who supervised the construction of the cascades built for *Arlequin Jason,* and he recounts a conversation he had with Lolli about some wonderful Italian inventions the latter had seen during a trip to Italy c. 1690, presumably scouting the latest in new machines.[25]

Constantino Costantini, though apparently not an actor of great value to the troupe, took responsibility for dealing with a pirated edition of songs that belonged to it; this suggests that he may have served the company—which now used a great deal of it—in some capacity concerning the music. The songs in question, by Gillier, were being peddled at the door of the Hôtel de Bourgogne in contravention of an Act of the Council of 1694 forbidding all persons to print or have printed any scene or song belonging to the Italian actors. Given the authority by La Reynie to recover the printed songs, and a sergeant to make sure the order was carried out, Costantini went to the shop of Christophe Ballard, the royal music printer, and recovered seven copies, which he left in the custody of Sergeant Desmazerets.[26]

No evidence from the 1690s implies any radical changes in the organization and management of the Italian company or in their production practices, with the exception of those few innovations designed to attract a larger audience. These include the decision not to charge extra for new plays and not to have a balustrade on the stage. The two choices may, perhaps, have been contradictory. The open stage appealed to the preening *petits marquis,* whose presence on stage was not to the taste of the bourgeois in the parterre. In Regnard's *La coquette* (January 1691) Arlequin as a marquis invites Colombine to come and see him on the stage. "*Parbleu,*" he says, "the stage is never empty when I am on it. . . . I am always to be found on the edge of the stage . . . *Ventrebleu,* I have no taste for the wings; at the orchestra, *mortbleu,* at the orchestra." But Colombine responds: "In good faith, Monsieur the Marquis, do you think it's to see you comb your wig, sniff your tobacco, and carouse on the stage that the parterre pays his fifteen sous?"[27]

The power of the parterre was twofold. Although the habitué of the stage paid four times as much as the *bonhomme* standing below, there were far more men with fifteen sous than with three livres. In a time of declining audiences, when the Comédie-Française often played to houses of less than 100, the numerical supremacy of the parterre was important.

Furthermore, the habit of whistling to express criticism had grown to enormous proportions. The Italians consistently found clever ways to remind the spectators not to do it. In the prologue to *Le divorce* (March 1688), Regnard's first play for the Italians, Jupiter expressly requests that the new play about divorce be rehearsed for him. When Arlequin demurs, sure that it will be whistled off the stage, Jupiter says he will take care of the problem with his thunderbolts.[28] In the prologue to *L'opéra de campagne* (June 1692), Arlequin and Colombine debate the question: Is man a laughing animal or a whistling animal. Colombine sustains the former, "after Aristotle." Arlequin sustains the latter, "after . . . me, & all the actors in France." "You know," he says to the Parterre, asked to judge the question, "it's very difficult to make you laugh, but nothing is easier than to make you whistle."[29]

In 1696 the French actors requested that some action be taken to prevent the disorder the whistlers caused in the theatre. Secretary of State Pontchartrain wrote to La Reynie that after a new ordinance was published on the subject, the police should begin to arrest the whistlers and make an example of them.[30] In August 1696 a poor butcher named René Caraque went to jail for whistling at the Comédie-Française. In a petition to La Reynie, he claims to have been at the play for the first time in his life. He allowed himself to become excited during an intermission and thoughtlessly made use of "an instrument with which he wakes his boys in the morning." Although his whistle did not trouble the actors, it being between the acts, he nonetheless finds himself in prison, from which he hopes La Reynie will rescue him. On 17 September, Pontchartrain advised La Reynie to free the butcher, the king having decided that three weeks in prison was punishment enough for having whistled at the theatre. Caraque became the subject of a popular ballad, suggesting that his arrest was unusual.[31] The example was not, however, sufficient to discourage habitual whistlers, and more ordinances were followed by more exchanges of letters between His Majesty's secretary of state and His Majesty's lieutenant general of police. It was not until 1712 that Palaprat could write: "The time of storms is passed; thanks to the police, calm reigns at the theatres."[32]

The Italians did more in their prologues than beg the indulgence of potential whistlers. While they were a nuisance, they were not dangerous. But danger did threaten the troupe, beginning as early as 1688 when the marquis de Dangeau writes on 29 January: "The Italians actors have been ordered to cut from their plays all the double entendres which are too free." In the climate of France after the revocation of the Edict of Nantes and with the ascendancy of the marquise de Maintenon and the Gallican faction in the church, what had seemed pleasantly provocative before now seemed scandalous.

In the prologue to *Les chinois* (December 1692), Regnard and Dufresny introduce Apollo and the Muses, lounging about Parnassus, discussing the Parisian theatres. Pierrot enters, dressed as a little girl who has run away from home because her mother will not take her to the Italian theatre. "Your mother is wrong, pretty child," answers Apollo, played by Colombine, "to deprive you of the most agreeable and innocent pleasure available today. The theatre forms the mind, elevates the heart, ennobles the feelings; it is the mirror of human life which shows vice in all its horror and represents virtue in all its glory. The stage is the school of manners, the meeting place of the wits, the pedestal of persons of quality. A little dose of theatre, taken when needed, renders the lady's wit more sprightly, her heart more loving, her eye more lively, and her manners more engaging. It is the place where the fair sex burns the brightest."[33] Apollo wants to know why the child's mother won't take her to the Italians. Pierrot responds: "She says that sometimes the language there is too free; but what makes me furious is that she goes every day." Apollo has an answer to that, too. "I don't know what this language can be that so shocks your mother. As for me, I find nothing there but language full of savor, language which does, to tell the truth, contain a double meaning sometimes. But all the most beautiful ideas in the world have two faces. So much the worse for those who always see the bad side; it's a true mark of their corrupt and vicious character."

The problem with this defense is that the scene wants to have its cake and eat it too. If only the "corrupt and vicious" see the risqué side of the Italians' language, then what are we to make of what follows:

APOLLO   But hasn't she said any of these dirty words to you?

PIERROT   Oh, well, only now and then. She just says that the Italians are rascals who call everything by its name. For example, she says that they call a married man . . . by a certain word that I dare not say.

THALIA   Cuckold, maybe?

PIERROT   You said it.

APOLLO   And your mother is scandalized by that word?

PIERROT   Absolutely. Oh, well, it's just that she says that it's an insult to my Papa.

THALIA   It's just that your mother doesn't know her native lan-

> guage. In the new Dictionary printed at Paris, the words
> are synonyms: cuckold-husband, husband-cuckold.

Apollo agrees to see to it that the Italians change their ways. "I will take you with me to the Italians," she says to Pierrot, "where I will assemble the actors and order them to cut from their plays all the words which are too lively, and especially all the cuckolds." Arlequin, however, advises against it, since "if the actors excise from their theatre all the cuckolds, they might perhaps wound the father of the young lady." In Arlequin's view, the new policy will probably drive the women away, since "for every one woman who loves reform, there are a thousand who cannot bear it."

The theatre may show "vice in all its horror" and "virtue in all its glory," but the real defense of its value as offered by Colombine-Apollo is social, not moral. The theatre was, to defenders and critics alike, a school of manners, the difference being whether those particular manners were to be applauded or attacked as licentious.

As far back as 1588, when Henri III invited the Gelosi to perform at the Etats Généraux at Blois and then in Paris, he aroused the spleen of the moralists. A book entitled *Remonstrances trè humbles au Roy de France* advised His Majesty that

> there is yet another great evil which is committed and tolerated in
> your good city of Paris, on Sunday and feast days; these are the plays
> and public spectacles which take place the said feast days and Sun-
> days, by Italian foreigners and by the French. And above all, those
> who make a sewer and house of Satan of the Hôtel de Bourgogne
> . . . where a thousand scandalous assignations take place, to the prej-
> udice of decency and modesty of women and to the ruin of
> the families of some poor artisans, of which the lower salle [i.e., the
> parterre] is full, and who for more than two hours before the play
> pass their time in . . . gambling, gluttony, and drunkenness.[34]

At the same period, according to L'Estoile, the Parlement de Paris de- clared that the Italian plays taught only lewdness and adultery, and served as a school of debauchery for the youth of both sexes of the city of Paris."[35]

Throughout the first two-thirds of the seventeenth century, how- ever, the theatre prospered under the Bourbon monarchs and their first ministers. Actors received the sacraments of the church and were pro- tected under civil law after 1641, when Louis XIII declared the profes- sion, when exercised with decency, legitimate. A new generation of

writers substituted "literary, embellished and decent" plays for the traditional coarse farces, and women could go to the theatre without fear that
their modesty would be offended.[36]

But the French church was only biding its time. In 1654 the "Ritual
of Paris," influenced by Jansenism and Gallican orthodoxy, refused com-
munion to "those whose infamy is known, as debauched women, and
those who live from any criminal commerce, the concubines, actors,
usurers, magicians, sorcerers, blasphemers, and other like sinners."[37] In
the 1670s this text established the clergy's right to refuse burial in sanctified ground to Floridor, Molière, and other actors who had not renounced their profession and thus died excommunicate. La Bruyère
underscores the hypocrisy of the situation: "The condition of actors was
infamous in Rome and honorable in Greece. What is it in France? We
think like the Romans and act like the Greeks. . . . What could be more
bizarre? A crowd of Christians comes together to applaud a troupe of
excommunicates."[38]

The Italian actors were not anathematized or excommunicated. As
members of the more moderate and indulgent Roman church, they were
born, married, and buried without harassment, in France as in Italy, and
even after they became naturalized citizens. Biancolelli and Fiorilli were
both buried with all due honors not in the sanctified cemetery but directly
behind the altar of St.-Eustache, the very church which had refused burial
to Molière. Some of the Italian actors were even admitted into the Com-
pagnie du Saint-Sacrament, that bastion of French piety.[39] While the Italians held the canopy during holy day processions, French actors fell
victim to the exaggerated classicism of the Gallican church, eager to distinguish itself by its adherence to the teachings of the Synod of Arles,
held in A.D. 314, on the subject of the theatre.

On the other hand, although the Italian actors were not subject to
church discipline, their plays were increasingly scrutinized for objectionable language and vulgar behavior. Beginning in the mid 1660s anti-
theatre treatises like Nicole's Jansenist *Traité de la comédie* and the Prince
de Conti's *Traité de la comédie et des spectacles,* which fueled the flames that
nearly consumed *Tartuffe,* poured off the Paris presses. In the 1690s, stim-
ulated by the daring of an Italian priest, Father Caffaro, who dared to
defend the theatre in a preface to the collected works of Boursault, the
conservative French clergy rose to attack. Best known of the treatises
that assaulted the poor young Italian is *Maximes et réflexions sur la comédie*
by Bossuet, former tutor of the dauphin, conscience of the court, and a
leader of the Gallican theologians.

Bossuet condemned the "infamies and impieties" in the plays of Molière, "which have filled the theatres with the coarsest equivocations which have ever infected the ears of Christians." But things had gotten worse. A sometime playwright of the 1690s, Lenoble—who wrote *Esope* and *Les deux Arlequins* for the Italians—points out that "since the death of the inimitable Elomire [Molière], license is taken that it would be good to repress. This wise corrector of our follies [i.e., the theatre] has never freed itself from these impertinent equivocations which make only those with low souls laugh."[40] The Sorbonne condemned the theatre in 1694 and complained to the archbishop that the Italians in particular were too "free" on the stage and that it would be good to repurge several of their plays.[41]

No official mechanism for censorship of plays in advance of performance was in force in 1694. La Reynie, as lieutenant general of the police, was charged with surveillance of the theatre by the Parlement de Paris to insure order and decency. The power to suspend performance of an objectionable play was vested in the Parlement as well. His Majesty could, of course, override the Parlement, as he did eventually in the matter of *Tartuffe,* and could also take matters into his own hands. After the establishment of the First Gentlemen of the Chamber as the court authority with responsibility for the subventioned theatres, they also had the power of surveillance.

In spite of the clerical rhetoric, plays were rarely censored or runs interrupted for reasons of obscenity. The king disliked allusions to current events or political personages; the Parlement was responsive to complaints of libel or what we now might call violation of copyright.[42] The actors were apparently sensitive to problematical material, and very few instances of censorship by authority can be found.

The play texts of the period, including those written for the Italians, are cynical and suggestive, but not obscene. Performances at the Italian theatre probably were obscene, however. According to legend, Mezzetin was incorrigible. The obscenity was no doubt improvised, as it always had been, and was easily excised if someone in authority was present in the audience. In January 1696 Pontchartrain wrote to La Reynie as follows:

> The king having been informed that the Italian actors are giving indecent performances and speaking obscenities in their plays, His Majesty has forbidden them, via M. de Trémoille, to do or say such things, and he has at the same time ordered me to write to you that his intention is that you have them brought before you and explain

to them again that if they happen to make some indecent posture or speak some equivocal words or something which violates decency, His Majesty will disband them and send them back to Italy. To this effect, he wants you to send someone reliable to the theatre every day to give you an account of what goes on there, and at the first contravention you must close their theatre.[43]

This warning was apparently not heeded, since the Italians were dismissed fifteen months later.

The idea of submitting plays for approval before production was in the air as early as 1695, when a commissaire of the Châtelet wrote to La Reynie, "It is to be wished for the public's sake that all the plays have your approval before being played." His ire had been aroused by the Italians introducing a comic commissaire into *Le retour de la foire de Bezons.* "What," he asks, "will become of our most serious functions in the service of the king and the public if you permit them thus to be made fools of by the French and Italian actors."[44] This was hardly the first time the Italians had burlesqued a commissaire, but perhaps the fact that this play was in French and a popular success had something to do with the complaint.

The *Gazette d'Amsterdam* reported in January 1697 that the "devout party, unable to forbid the diversion of the theatre during advent and lent, has suggested the establishment of commissaires to examine all plays before they are performed, in order to leave nothing at which the most scrupulous could murmur."[45] A board of censors acceptable to the "most scrupulous" would, of course, have meant the end of theatre in Paris, and was probably never a serious possibility, but after several other incidents and more threatening memorandums, official censorship was finally instituted in 1706, with the authority to approve plays in advance of production vested in the lieutenant general of the police. By that time the Italians, who must bear some of the responsibility for the introduction of still another restraint on the artistic freedom of the French theatre, were long gone.

The Comédie-Italienne was suppressed on 14 May 1697. Pontchartrain wrote to the new lieutenant general of police, d'Argenson, as follows: "The king has dismissed his Italian actors, and His Majesty orders me to write to you to tomorrow close their theatre forever." The next day d'Argenson, accompanied by officers and commissaires, went to the Hôtel de Bourgogne at 11:00 in the morning and placed locks on all the exterior doors and on the actors' dressing rooms.[46] The event hardly passed unnoticed. Although neither the *Mercure galant* nor the *Gazette de*

France, both published in Paris, mention it, almost all of the foreign gazettes devote considerable space to it. The dismissal is also included in the journals of Dangeau, St.-Simon, and Elisabeth-Charlotte of Bavaria, the second Madame. Unfortunately, no one then and no one now provides a convincing explanation of why it happened.

Germaine Brice, in 1713, says the Italians were expelled "for reasons of which no one deigned to inform the public."[47] According to Dangeau, writing in his journal on the day it happened, the dismissal was simply the logical outcome of what had gone before. They had been warned and they were not wise. The *Nouvelles extraordinaires* of 23 May agrees: "They did not obey what was several times reiterated to them, to present only modest plays and to correct their impure expressions and indecent postures." Later in the month, the *Gazette d'Amsterdam* writes that no one knows the true cause of the Italians' disgrace, but that His Majesty will profit by some 18,000 livres a year as a result of it.

The motive most often accepted by historians for the expulsion of the Italians surfaced as a possibility in the *Mercure historique et politique* in June. "Some say," writes the gazetteer, "they refused to excise certain impure expressions . . . others say that the court of France wants . . . to suppress all kinds of entertainments. Still others sustain that [the Italians] wanted to perform a new play by Lenoble, entitled *La fausse prude,* wherein was painted a picture disadvantageous to a lady much esteemed by the king." The writer, however, still thinks that the principal and probably unique reason for the closure was to save the king 18,000 livres a year.

The two great court gossips of the reign, St.-Simon and Madame, both confirm that *La fausse prude* was the last straw. The dour duke writes: "The king has expelled very precipitously the whole troupe of Italian actors and wants no more of them. As long as their stage overflowed with garbage and sometimes with impiety, everyone only laughed; but they decided to perform a play called *La fausse prude,* in which Mme. de Maintenon was easily recognized. Everyone ran to see it; but after three or four performances that they gave one after another, because of the profits they were making, they were ordered to close their theatre and leave the kingdom in one month."[48] Madame, whose views on Mme. de Maintenon are well known, wrote years later, in 1720, that

> there was a troupe of Italian actors who wanted to perform a play entitled *La fausse hypocrite* (in which, I was told, they wanted to make fun of Mme. de Maintenon). When I learned of what they were doing I had them brought in and I warned them not to perform that

play; that achieved nothing. They performed it and made a lot of money, but they were soon expelled. . . . They came back and asked me to intercede, but I said, "No! Why didn't you follow my advice?" They represented the old slut in the most comic fashion possible, I heard. I wanted to see the play very much, but I didn't go for fear the old woman would tell the king that the thing was my idea.[49]

There seems to be no reason why both St.-Simon and Madame would invent such a tale out of whole cloth, and their version is partly verified by what Angelo Costantini told Gueullette in 1729. According to Mezzetin, the troupe had commissioned from Fatouville a French version of an Italian play, *La finta matrigna* ("The False Mother-in-Law") which they renamed *La fausse prude* in order to take advantage of the scandal caused by a book of that same title, recently published in Amsterdam, which satirized Mme. de Maintenon. Costantini claimed, however, that the piece was advertised but never played.

Gueullette doubted Costantini's version at first, assuming that the old actor had invented it to cover up his own culpability. Gueullette had been unable to find a copy of the scurrilous book in France or in the Netherlands, and he had heard elsewhere that Mezzetin had struck the final blow to the troupe's declining popularity with the court when he kidnapped the actress Spinette from her lover, the duke of Bavaria, debauched her, brought her to Paris, and introduced her to the First Gentleman of the Chamber as his sister. Later, Gueullette discovered that Spinette was, in fact, Costantini's sister-in-law, and that her introduction to France was perfectly respectable.[50]

It seems credible that the Italians might have advertised a play called *La fausse prude,* although unlikely that either Lenoble or Fatouville was involved. Lenoble, who was not very active as a playwright, provided two plays to the Italians in 1691. One was *Esope,* distinguished by witty but nondramatic recitations of Aesop's fables. The other was *Les deux Arlqeuins,* based on a Plautine twin plot. As for Fatouville, his last play for the Italians (assuming that he was the only Monsieur D***) was written in 1692. By 1697 tastes had changed radically, and the last plays of the Gherardi repertory are characterized by imitation of French successes and use of Parisian local color. The principal writers were Dufresny and Monsieur B***, Dominique's oldest son, Louis Biancolelli.

If something was performed—and both St.-Simon and Madame seem sure something was—perhaps it was in the Italian rather than the French repertory. Spinette's debut piece, *Spinette lutin amoreux,* which took place in April, was almost certainly an improvised Italian entertainment.

The general confusion in the gazettes of the day as to whether any such play as *La fausse prude* ever existed is understandable if what was performed was actually *La finta matrigna,* subtitled to be as provocative as possible, and performed according to whatever opportunities the moment offered.

The author of the *Lettres historiques* (June 1697) probably presents the most defensible conjecture when he says that the *La fausse prude* was only a pretext for banishing the actors. "The impure expressions and indecent postures which filled their plays . . . are not in fashion now, even though the age is no less corrupt than when they were." The Italians were the darlings of the parterre, but not of the wits or the courtiers, and times were, indeed, changing. The Age of Sentiment and Sensibility was dawning.

According to Gueullette, the French troupe also worked to foster the downfall of the Italians. "The French actors, who hated the Italians extremely, took advantage of the moment and profited from the great credit which Mlle. Raisin enjoyed."[51] Mlle. Raisin was the mistress of the dauphin, who had primary authority over the theatres after the death of his wife, and she may certainly have done what she could to fan the flames. But His Majesty had a procedure in force for overseeing the actors and was unlikely to be influenced by a lady, herself an actress, who certainly had no entrée into the pious court life of the 1690s.

The French actors had good reason to want to see the end of their only competition in a decade of falling profits, and, in fact, did benefit by nearly 1,000 livres a share in the following season.[52] The French troupe may also have wanted the Italians' theatre, which it had tried and failed to get in 1694. This may be another indication of the quality of the reconstruction the Italians undertook in 1691, or it may merely reflect the fact that the Hôtel de Bourgogne had a better location than the Théâtre-Français. On 26 April 1694 Le Comte proposed to the assembly of the Comédie-Française the following combination. The French would take over the remaining lease of the Hôtel de Bourgogne from the Italians, who would then pay as rent to the French the 1,200 livres a year the Italians received from the Opéra to make up for their removal, in 1673, from Palais-Royal. The French would play in both theatres, while granting to the Italians the jours extraordinaires in the theatre of their choice. This plan gave the French ten playing days a week to the Italians' four, and once again cleverly restricted the Italians' access to spectacle. Although the assembly of French actors accepted the plan, the Italians, not unexpectedly, said no.[53]

The Italians also went to the First Gentleman of the Chamber to try to force the French to pay the six years owing of the pension of 800 livres which the French were meant to contribute annually as part of the arrangements made when the Italians were moved to the Hôtel de Bourgogne in 1680. The French argued that the order of 1680 was superseded by the order of 1687, which forced them out of the Hôtel Guénégaud, and refused to pay.[54] The Opéra was also in arrears for the 1,200 livres a year which Lulli had agreed to donate in exchange for the Italians vacating Palais-Royal. In February 1695 Giovan Battista Francini, the director of the Opéra, before the notaries of the Châtelet, agreed to pay the Italian troupe what was owed them, namely, three years of pension, or 3,600 livres. He paid 600 on the spot and obliged himself to pay the rest by 1 January 1697, while promising that the pension for the current year would be paid on time. The chances are very good that, by 1697, Francini owed the Italians 5,400 livres, and that he also cheered their going, if he was not an active participant in promoting it.[55]

The king, too, the king especially, had a financial interest in the dismissal of the Italians. He owed them 15,000 livres a year (or 18,000 according to the gazetteers), which was a bagatelle to the Sun King of the 1660s and 1670s, but a not inconsequential amount to the old man leading a bankrupt kingdom in an endless war. And the king, too, was in arrears. The subvention was paid through the 1680s, sometimes a year or two late, but it was paid. After the lump-sum payment of nine quarters of pension in August 1691, however, the accounts of the office of Menus Plaisirs, though admittedly scattered, record no further payment of the subvention. The king may, in May 1697, have owed the Italians as much as 99,000 livres. According to Dangeau, the order was given to pay the actors what was owing them, but no document confirms that payment was ever made. By the end of the reign, after more than twenty years of war, the monarchy was bankrupt, the treasury was empty, and expenditures exceeded receipts by 45 million livres a year, in spite of every effort by the king's ministers to avoid paying the royal encumbrances.[56]

Matters were very different in 1697 than they had been not quite a century before when the first Bourbon king and his Italian wife exchanged chatty letters with their "gossip," Arlequin, and laughed at his all-too-personal innuendos. The last remnant of patronage died in 1694 with Tiberio Fiorilli, who may or may not have once dandled the Sun King on his knee. And been pissed on for his pains. The bureaucracy so lovingly created by Louis XIV and his minister Colbert had put the actors in their place, and their place was no longer at the foot of the throne. The court jesters were now court "officers," functionaries like the thousands of others dependent on the monarch, with procedures to follow and chains of command to obey. No longer aware from his own experience of what the actors were doing, no longer interested in the theatre that had once given him so much pleasure, Louis sent word down from on high, from Pontchartrain to La Reynie, from the dauphin to the First Gentleman to the Intendant des Menus. The patron became a distant thunder, a god from the machine, indeed, whose decisions were not open to appeal.

The Italians did appeal, but without success. According to the foreign gazettes, various "persons of quality" tried to intercede for them, but the king was adamant. Even the dauphin is said to have tried and failed to change His Majesty's mind.[57] Louis clearly wanted the affair over and done with. The French troupe asked for use of the theatre, and was turned down.[58] An entrepreneur from the fairs named Bertrand rented it and played there for eight days, but the king had him turned out.[59] The final word comes in a letter from Pontchartrain to d'Argenson: "It is necessary . . . to efface the inscription which is on the theatre of the Italian actors and destroy what intrudes there on the public way."[60]

CHAPTER 14

The Terrible Costantinis

T HE CALENDAR-ALMANAC of 1689, which memorializes the vesting of Mezzetin in the costume of Arlequin, includes fifteen figures, sixteen if we count the now defunct Arlequin jauntily bowing from his tomb (see fig. 16). Across the front of the stage of the Hôtel de Bourgogne we see the expected cast of characters: Aurelio the amoureux, Bartolomeo Ranieri, about to be sent back to Italy for papal sympathies; Isabelle, Françoise Biancolelli; the Docteur, Angelo Agostino Lolli; Colombine, Catherine Biancolelli; Mezzetin himself, Angelo Costantini, arm raised to ward off the honor being bestowed on him; Pasquariel, Giuseppe Tortoriti; Scaramouche, Tiberio Fiorilli; Pierrot, Giuseppe Giaratoni; and as Monsieur Frequet, the bourgeois vieillard, Marc' Antonio Romagnesi. All of these characters except Scaramouche appear in *Le marchand dupé*, the play with which the troupe reopened its theatre on 1 September 1688, a month after Domenico Biancolelli's death.

Behind the first row of characters, on the left, between Colombine and the Docteur, is a female figure, tall, elderly, with an old-fashioned hair style and collar. The woman could be Brigida Fedele, Aurelia, but more probably is Patricia Adami, Diamantine, who was, I believe, still acting through the 1680s. Brigida Fedele had already renounced her profession.

Orsola Cortesi, Eularia, is seated on a stool just behind the optique, dressed in widow's weeds. Between her and the actors downstage are four figures who are awkwardly placed and stylistically different from the others. Two, who are standing, are known members of the troupe who played the Italian repertory: Polichinelle (Michelangelo Fracansani) and Pantalon (Giovan Battista Turri). Stage left of Pantalon, seated, is Capitan, recognizable by his moustachios, and stage right of Polichinelle, also seated, is an old man with an impressive white beard and a plumed hat. His costume appears to have the bars of horizontal braid associated with a First Zanni, although his hat had nothing in common with First Zanni's usual flat cap. He is probably Constantino Costantini, Gradelin.

The engraving suggests that the troupe of 1689 had fourteen members, two more than the twelve mandated by the dauphine's Règlement of mid-decade. Giaratoni, although included among the cast of *Le marchand dupé* in the front row, was not a sharer until 1691. He and the eight active sharers in that row make up the company that played the major roles in the French repertory. The more stylized figures of Polichinelle, Pantalon, Gradelin, and the Capitan, along with the two older women, represent the actors who played primarily in the Italian repertory or played in Italian in the French repertory.

We know that Polichinelle, Pantalon, and Gradelin were sharers, but the only other source that may indicate the existence of a capitan in Paris at this period is a scenario in Ms. 9329, *Le Capitan battu dans le jardin;* since it includes Isabelle and Colombine in its cast, it must date from after 1683. The troupe also may have wanted to include a capitan in its calendar as a kind of memorial to Girolamo Cei, who was not long dead himself, though the figure looks nothing like various images of Cei as Spezzafer. What might have happened is that c. 1689 Fiorilli went into de facto retirement and Tortoriti began to play the role of Scaramouche.[1] With the original character of Pasquariel thus unavailable, the troupe may have enlisted a new capitan or have planned to do so. If an actor was in Paris to play a capitan in 1689, he must have made a brief stay, because there is no further trace of him, and he was not there in 1691. Without Capitan and assuming that Scaramouche was no longer active, the company presented on the calendar-almanac more or less meets the dauphine's specifications as it begins the last decade of its existence—although without its Arlequin.

In November 1691 the troupe signed a document giving power of attorney to Angelo Agostino Lolli. The men in the company were Fiorilli, who no longer played, Romagnesi, Lolli, Angelo Costantini, Tortoriti, Fracansani, Evaristo Gherardi, Giovanni Battista Costantini, Constantino Costantini, and—finally—Giuseppe Giaratoni. The women were Orsola Cortesi, Françoise and Catherine Biancolelli, and Angela Toscano.[2] Gone were Bartolomeo Ranieri, Aurelio; Giovan Battista Turri, Pantalon, Patricia Adami, Diamantine; and the mysterious Capitan. New to the company were Gherardi, Giovanni Battista Costantini, Angela Toscano, and Giaratoni. The total was ten men and four women, two more than the *Règlement* dictated and all active but one.

If Constantino Costantini was in Paris in time for the 1689 almanac, he was the first of this new group to enter the troupe. Presumably he came with his son, Giovanni Battista, who made a debut in November

1688 but did not become a sharer until after Ranieri's departure the following year. According to Gueullette, the elder Costantini was the son of a well-to-do family in Verona that made its money through secret methods of dyeing silk fabrics. He fell in love with an actress, however, and joined a commedia dell'arte troupe.[3] His wife was Domenica Costantini, who played the serva as Corallina. Records in the Italian archives place him in Modena in 1668 and 1675, and in Vicenza and Venice in 1686. In May 1688 Constantino Costantini and his son Giovanni Battista were asked for by the duke of Modena in a letter to Count Marco Verità in Verona, and were probably in the Modena troupe before they came to Paris in the fall of that year.[4]

According to Riccoboni, who is undoubtedly wrong yet again, Costantini was forced to leave Paris shortly after his debut for having sung on stage an Italian song critical of France. But Costantini was certainly still in the troupe in 1696, when he was serving as its treasurer,[5] and was probably still there the following year when the company was dismissed. He was not a young man when he came to Paris. If his son, Angelo, was born before 1660, Costantini himself was born before 1640. His masque, Gradelin, was that of a First Zanni, a meaningless distinction in the 1690s in the French repertory of the Comédie-Italienne. Gherardi speaks of him scornfully in the introduction to the 1700 edition and excludes him with Polichinelle from the collection.

Although I have found traces of Polichinelle in Gherardi's stage directions and frontispieces, I have found nothing certain of Gradelin. The frontispiece of *Les filles errantes* includes a figure that might represent him, although it does not resemble the bearded figure of the almanac. In the finale of *Les filles errantes* all the characters enter with guitars and parody the chaconne of *Cadmus*. The frontispiece shows the Docteur, Mezzetin, Arlequin, and Scaramouche downstage, all with guitars, with Pierrot slightly behind and to stage left of Scaramouche. Behind Pierrot, separated both from the actors and from the six musicians in street dress at the rear of the stage, is a First Zanni with horizontal bands on the front of his costume and traditional flat cap, also playing a guitar. The text includes no detached roles, but it also is incomplete and must have originally been performed with Italian as well as French scenes.[6]

The First Zanni figure, shown between the actors and the musicians, may indicate the principal function of Constantino Costantini in the company. According to Gueullette, he was a good musician. In 1695 he was the company member responsible for dealing with a pirated version of some music by Gillier, composed for the Italians and being peddled at the door of the theatre.[7] The Italians began to feature music and musical afterpieces as soon as their theatre was remodeled in 1691. Gherardi's 1700 collection contains the music for 143 songs and calls for 340 musical numbers, mostly in plays performed in 1690 and later.[8] If Costantini took responsibility for the music, for having it composed and perhaps for rehearsing it, then his continuation in the troupe is understandable, even if his character was rarely used in the French repertory. According to Riccoboni, Gherardi was wrong to speak of him with contempt; he was an excellent First Zanni. He was also a Costantini and, in the view of Gherardi, an enemy.

His son, Giovanni Battista, the new Octave, was given a tryout on 2 November 1688 in *La folie d'Octave,* "a play all in Italian." Tralage describes the debut: "The one who plays Octavio is a young man who does the character of the lover. He is the son of Gradelin and brother of Mezzetin. This Octavio appeared for the first time 2 November. He was applauded by all the assembly. He played seven kinds of musical instruments, namely the flute, the theorbo, the harp, the psaltery, the cymbals, the guitar, the oboe. And the next day he added the organ. He sang not badly and danced very well. He is handsome and well built."[9] *La folie d'Octave* was played at court on 30 November 1688, according to Dangeau, and "the new actor was found excellent." The play was among those performed by the Italians at court in 1691 and 1695, and Gueullette saw Costantini perform it "years later at the Hôtel de Bourgogne," so it evidently became a standard of the Italian repertory.

Giovanni Battista Costantini played in Italy as Cintio but had to change his professional name when he came to Paris. He was in Modena in 1682 and again in 1688 with his father. He was married to Teresa Corono Sabolini, who played the donna in Italy, but not in France. She played seconda donna in the Modena company in 1681; she was requested by the duke of Mantua, along with her father-in-law, Gradelin, in 1683 and again in 1688. She did not play in Paris, and Rasi has found evidence in the financial records of Modena suggesting that she and her husband were living separately by 1686.[10] The couple were the parents of a daughter, Anne-Elisabeth, who married Charles-Virgile Romagnesi in 1708 and later was accepted into the new Italian troupe. She was a principal source of information for Gueullette.

The hot-tempered Costantini, whose quarrels with his Paris comrades have been described above,[11] was also the subject of a report made to the duke of Modena in July 1682. The actor had been arrested for drawing his sword on the police. Although he could have been fined and even whipped for the offense, he was released unpunished several days later.[12]

Giovanni Battista Costantini entered the Paris company after Ranieri was sent back to Italy in 1689. In 1694, when Lolli retired and Marc' Antonio Romagnesi took over the masque of Docteur, Costantini became First Amoureux. He also apparently served as orator.[13] The character of Octave appears in several of the Gherardi frontispieces and plays a prominent role in the French repertory. Although he was one of the "terrible Costantinis," he was too important to be excluded from the published texts.

Evaristo Gherardi made his debut in Paris on 1 October 1689 in a reprise of Regnard's *Le divorce*.[14] He was the son of Giovanni Gherardi, who played Flautin in Paris from 1675 to 1683. Born in Prato in Tuscany on 11 November 1663, the younger Gherardi was not trained for the stage but studied philosophy at the Collège de la Marche "under the wise M. Ballé."[15] Apparently he stayed on in France after his father's death; the baptismal record of Evaristo's illegitimate son, Florentin-Hyacinth, 5 February 1689, lists the father's profession as "professor of foreign languages."[16]

He married a French singer, Elisabeth Danneret, who appeared with the Italian troupe as Babet la Chanteuse. The first trace of her in the repertory is in *Le départ des comédiens* (August 1694). In this little afterpiece the actors are disbanding their company, and Arlequin asks the Chanteuse what she plans to do. She answers with a song:

> What a girl,
> Young and pretty, wants,
> She soon gets.
> I know of one,
> That fortune will raise to the heights
> In a cloud, at the Opéra.[17]

This prediction was to come true after the dismissal of the troupe, when she entered the company at the Opéra. The couple had one child, said to be lame, who acted at the fairs.

Gherardi is a less attractive figure than his predecessor Biancolelli. His Arlequin has little in common with Dominique's, although that may well be because the character was developed more by French playwrights writing for the troupe than by the actor. Biancolelli had over the years established his character as such a strong presence that no mere writer could efface it, but Gherardi brought nothing to the character except—perhaps—the memory of Dominique.

Gherardi was neither physically nor psychologically suited to the acrobatic, illiterate simpleton who continued to shine through Biancolelli's travesties. As he said himself, he was not trained for the stage. Biancolelli was a child of the profession, endowed with a comic imagination and learned in lazzi and imbroglio; Gherardi had sat at the feet of the philosophers.

He was perhaps a little too pleased with himself, a little too self-conscious, to play a naïve Arlequin. He was also apparently insecure about having replaced the famous Dominique. His account of his debut reveals rather more than he probably expected about his character and state of mind. It is printed as a postscript to *Le divorce* in the 1700 edition.

> This play did not succeed in the hands of Monsieur Dominique. It was crossed off the list of plays that were reprised from time to time, and the roles [i.e., the sides] were burned. However I (who had never in my life mounted the stage), I chose it for my debut . . . when I appeared for the first time by order of the king and Monseigneur [the dauphin]; And it had so much success in my hands that it pleased generally everyone, was extraordinarily attended, and as a consequence earned a lot of money for the actors.
>
> If I were a man who was vain of my talents for the stage, face uncovered or face masked, in principal serious or comic roles, where I have been seen to shine . . . in the eyes of the most polished and knowledgeable nation on earth, I would have here a good way to satisfy my conceit. I would say that I did more in the beginning, in my young years, than the most illustrious actors have known how to do after twenty years of practice and in the strength of their age. But I protest that far from being proud of these rare advantages, I have always regarded them as the effects of my good fortune, and not as the consequences of my merit; and if anything was known to please me in this conjuncture, it was only the pleasure of finding myself universally applauded after the inimitable Monsieur Dominique, who played so well the naïveté of the character of Arlequin.[18]

Small wonder Gherardi was at war with his comrades.

The Introduction to his *Théâtre italien* is full of similar self-puffery along with the denigration of others. Gherardi was not a "company man." "There are those called actors," he writes, "but who are useless and a charge on their companies. I compare an actor of this sort to a paralyzed arm . . . the only difference being that the dead arm receives no nourishment, but the actor receives as much as the actors who tire themselves out and are the most necessary. What can be said of these useless actors, of which all companies are full, people without talent and without art, who from some capricious patronage or extraordinary good luck get a whole share and from then on think only of the cashbox and not of the work required of them."[19] This show of spleen may not be unreasonable in a man who played a major role in every production and earned the same as the actors playing detached roles, like Fracansani and Constantino Costantini, but it is also unattractive.

Gherardi, of course, was taken to court in 1694 by the troupe for publishing, without the consent of the other actors, his first edition of scenes and plays in French. In his view, the action was the product of envy on the part of some of his colleagues, and he is quick to reveal, in the introduction to the 1700 edition, that 900 copies, supposedly burned, were sold by Giovanni Battista Costantini to several Paris bookstores for thirty-two sous a copy, a nice profit to the latter of nearly 1500 livres.[20]

Of Angelo Costantini, he says only that "he excuses" the real author of *La vie de Scaramouche* for the "baseness of his style" and the "falsity of the actions he recounts," since the poor fellow was "obliged to conform to the capacity of the one who wanted to put his name on it"— that is, Costantini.[21] Petty bickering was certainly not unknown to the commedia dell'arte in Italy; Italian archives are full of letters from actors complaining of their colleagues. But Italian troupes were not stable in the same way the Paris troupe was. In Paris in the 1690s the discord was irremediable since the troupe's membership was fixed. The friction must have influenced performance and may have been a factor in the king's declining affection for the company. Neither the caustic Gherardi nor the unreliable Costantinis could replace Dominique as the heart of the enterprise.

Gherardi's image as Arlequin is familiar to us from popular prints (fig. 17) as well as from Gillot's drawings and the engravings made from them. "La pompe funèbre d'Arlequin" ("Arlequin's Funeral"), published at the time of his death in 1700, describes him less elegantly.

> He was neither well nor badly made,
> Neither tall nor short, more fat than thin;
> He had a very agile body,
> A high forehead, weak but lively eye,
> A very prominent nose . . .

Euariste Gherardi faisant le personage d'Arlequin

A Paris chez I. Mariette rue S. Iacques aux colonnes d'Hercules.

FIG. *17. Evaristo Gherardi, Arlequin. Engraving by Marinette.* (Bibliothèque de l'Opéra, Ms. Rés. 625; phot. Bibl. Nat. Paris)

His mouth stretched to his ears,
His complexion was ruddy,
His chin a little double.[22]

The repertory he collected demonstrates that he was certainly a success as Arlequin and an important member of the company. Perhaps his most important contribution, however, was the collection itself.

The next newcomer to the troupe was Angela Toscana, who has already been mentioned in chapter 11. She was the wife of Giuseppe Tortoriti, although whether she came with him from Italy or married him after she came to France is unknown. The latter seems likely, since Tortoriti was in Paris in 1685, while their first child was not born until June, 1692. As they had four children between 1692 and 1696, it seems probable that they were not married until 1690 or 1691. They were definitely married in November 1691, when they signed a document as husband and wife.[23]

Angela Toscana played two roles at the Comédie-Italienne, Angélique and Marinette. Angélique, a Second Amoureuse, appears first in Gherardi's 1700 edition in *La fille sçavante* (November 1690); Marinette, a servante, appears first in *La coquette* (January 1691), but Tralage includes in his collection a sonnet for Marinette dated June 1690.

Angela Toscana's presence enabled the troupe to have four female characters, two amoureuses and two servantes, and still keep Orsola Cortesi as a sharing member. Although Orsola Cortesi may have been active in the 1690s, she no longer played young girls in love. Her daughter, Françoise, was the de facto First Amoureuse and Angela Toscana the de facto Second Amoureuse. The latter also played the servante in the place of Patricia Adami, whose share in the company she probably took. Angela Toscana was a member of the troupe on 26 November 1691, when the actors gave their power of attorney to Lolli, and Patricia Adami was not.

According to Gueullette, who saw her act, she was tall and pretty, but of "very ordinary merit."[24] She was, indeed, frequently pregnant, as jokes in the play texts indicate. Her role as Marinette was usually small, but as Angélique she could be quite important. After Françoise Biancolelli ceased playing in July 1694, Angélique was the sole amoureuse role.

Sometime between 9 October and 26 November 1691, Giuseppe Giaratoni finally became a sharing member of the troupe. He was the only one of the actors who came from Italy in 1661 that we can be certain was associated with the company for the full thirty-five years of its establishment. That he was not a sharer on 9 October is indicated by the company document signed on 26 November. The list of signers ends: "all the Italian actors composing the king's troupe with the exception of the sieur Geraton." The document in question authorizes Lolli to collect the interest owing on money which the company had invested in the Aides and Gabelles on 9 October. Giaratoni is excluded because he had not contributed to the invested sum, indicating he was not then a member.

The happy event came about, it seems, because Giaratoni had addressed a petition in February 1691 to the dauphin asking for a share. The petition, or *placet*, is a very odd mix of flattery and comic exaggeration. "I have only one wife," he writes, "and my half in eight children, who I fear in the end will devour me, if you do not save me from their teeth. . . . I have made you laugh several times, now make me laugh in turn. I repeat again, save your money; I ask from you only two or three words. Could you, great prince, be stingy with a word? Does a word cost so much to say? And the word is: Let a share be given to Pierrot." [25] With the dauphine dead in 1690, her widower now had authority over the troupe. Perhaps Giaratoni was hoping he would assign the share of the mysterious Capitan lurking in the corner of the 1689 almanac to the patient Pierrot. Whoever was responsible for the vacancy, the entrance of Giaratoni was long overdue.

Although still technically an amoureux, by 1692 Marc' Antonio Romagnesi was specializing in a bourgeois vieillard called variously Frequet, Trafiquet, Persillet, Goguet, Oronte, Géronte, and so forth. The troupe had only one amoureux, Octave, but it had two amoureuses, Isabelle and Angélique. In March 1692 a new amoureux, Léandre, appears in *Le précaution inutile*. The name appears both in the text and on the frontispiece. In *La fille de bon sens* (November 1692), although Léandre does not appear in the cast list or the text, he is represented in the frontispiece. Moreover, both Cinthio and the vieillard, Géronte, are in love with Angélique; thus is seems reasonable to suppose that Cinthio in this case was Léandre. A third mention is to be found in *Les mal-assortis* (May 1693), where Octave in the cast list is Léandre in the text. His first official appearance was in *Le départ des comédiens* (August 1694).

Léandre was Charles-Virgile Romagnesi, the son of Marc' Antonio. The play texts may once again reflect reprises, but there was also nothing especially unusual about the child of a company member beginning to act before he or she was admitted to the troupe. Both the Biancolelli sisters were admitted "to continue to play the characters they have already begun." In this case, Charles-Virgile Romagnesi was given an opportunity to learn his craft before his official debut, which took place on 24 August 1694. Gueullette saw the performance.[26]

Charles-Virgile Romagnesi, the third child of Marc' Antonio Romagnesi, was born in Paris on 7 May 1670. He was educated in Rome but did not complete his studies. When he was proposed for the company, the First Gentleman for 1694, the duc d'Aumont, wrote that the troupe should have him play as often as possible until the dauphin had a chance to see him.[27] It was more than a year before he was granted a share. On 12 July 1695 the duc de Gesvres wrote: "It is ordered to the Italian actors to give a whole share to the son of Sieur Cinthio, to begin the 11th day of this month and this according to the will of Monseigneur."[28] The share had been Lolli's.

The little afterpiece in which Charles-Virgile Romagnesi made his official debut marked a number of other changes in the troupe. Angelo Lolli, whose appearances in the French repertory were growing few and whose wife, Patricia Adami, died on 5 September 1693, appeared for the last time in two brief scenes in *Le bel-esprit* in March 1694. Françoise Biancolelli, although she retained her share, is last mentioned in the Gherardi collection in *La fontaine de sapience* (July 1694). And Tiberio Fiorilli, now a few months from death, passed the masque of Scaramouche officially on to Giuseppe Tortoriti.

No wonder the troupe introduced a play at this juncture entitled *Le départ des comédiens*. In it the actors are about to enter and pass in review one last time before Arlequin when he says, "The review will not be complete, for we have had many deserters." As each actor comes forward, Arlequin asks him what he would like to do, now that the company is disbanding. Young Léandre, the debutant, notes that "in our family we are all amoureux, father and son," and has plans to teach the town the proper method of making love. The Docteur, no longer Lolli but Romagnesi, will live on his income. Arlequin would like to join him, but "it is forbidden to an Italian actor to rest before the age of 120." Special permission was granted to Scaramouche "to retire at 94." The Chanteuse hopes to sing at the Opéra. Colombine and Pierrot have found jobs working for the same bourgeois lady on the rue St.-Denis, Octave will lead the life of a gentleman, an unnamed, very ugly actor (probably Polichinelle) has been hired as a countess to make mimic faces, and Mezzetin and Pasquariel are off to perform operas in the country. This was the final active troupe, which sang in the summer of 1694:

> Goodbye stage, goodbye balcons,
> Goodbye loges, goodbye parterre.
> Goodbye boys and girls,
> More faithful than fathers and mothers.
> Goodbye, good bourgeois of Paris
> Who come to see us on Sunday.
> Goodbye churchmen, great and small,
> Goodbye lawyers and financiers.
> You can sell your whistles
> At any tinsmith's shop.[29]

The last new actress associated with the troupe made her debut only a few weeks before it was dismissed in May 1697. This was Maria Teresa D'Orsi, Spinette, who was married to Vittorio D'Orsi, the brother of Angelo Costantini's wife, Angiola. Her debut in April was heralded in the *Mercure galant,* which rarely included theatrical news in the 1690s. According to Donneau de Visé's informant, Spinette played five or six characters in *Spinette lutin amoureux* to great applause. Gueullette said she was very pretty; he saw the production five or six times.[30] Spinette was granted an official tryout by order of the First Gentleman, the duc de Beauvillier, on 4 March 1697,[31] but nothing suggests that she entered the company before the dismissal.

Tiberio Fiorilli, according to his own statement, left the stage in 1690. From 1690 to 1694, Giuseppe Tortoriti played in the costume of Scaramouche, beginning with *Les filles errantes* in August 1690. The character name reappears in *Arlequin défenseur du beau sexe* in May 1694, implying that at the end of the 1693–94 season, when Lolli retired, Scaramouche probably did, too. His last signature on a document of company business is in July 1692.

Fiorilli's last years continued to be marred by problems with his young wife and quarrels with his son over his property. The wife, Marie Duval, had, he complained, become pregnant without his knowledge and then had an abortion.[32] His son Silvio continued to be an ingrate, and Fiorilli continued to scheme to get back the property he had given his son when the latter got married in 1666. He died on 7 December 1694 at the age of eighty-eight and was buried the next day at St.-Eustache behind the altar. The burial act was signed by his son Silvio and by Marc' Antonio Romagnesi.[33]

According to *La vie de Scaramouche,* Fiorilli left an estate of 300,000 livres, but either because it passed without question to his son, or because his daughter, Anne-Elisabeth, although only thirteen was married and thus not a minor child, his estate was not inventoried. If he left a large amount of money and property, it must have been in Italy. The troupe paid his funeral expenses out of the 1,500 livres owing for his share in the common property after his estate had failed to pay them. The remaining 938 livres, 14 sous, 2 deniers, minus 72 livres advanced by the troupe during Fiorilli's illness and 27 livres, 10 sous in legal expenses, were paid to Anne-Elisabeth.[34]

Brigida Fedele outlived her old colleague by nine years. She died in November 1703 at the age of ninety. Her grandson's wife told Gueullette that she remembered seeing her, unable to leave her bed, but still dressed in the latest fashions.[35]

Angelo Agostino Lolli was the only member of the troupe known to take advantage of the dauphine's elaborate pension system instituted in the *Règlement* of the mid-1680s. The order was issued on 30 June 1694: "Ange Lolli, *dit* the Docteur, having asked permission to retire from the Comédie because of his age and infirmities, Monseigneur has granted him the enjoyment of the ordinary pension of 1,000 livres to begin the 1st of June."[36] This pension was to be at the charge of the troupe, but if a new actor took over the share of the retiree, he or she was meant to pay 1,000 livres a year to the troupe for the pension. Apparently Lolli's share was taken by Charles-Virgile Romagnesi, since the company is admonished in the same memorandum that establishes Lolli's pension to make sure the young actor plays as often as possible so that the dauphin can see and approve him.

Lolli died on 4 November 1702 at about the age of eighty.[37] He was buried the next day at St.-Eustache. His pension ended with the troupe's dismissal in 1697, and there was no record of the king giving him any assistance. His wife had died in 1693, and the only record which suggests that he may have been survived by a child is the name Antoinette Lolli included on a list of persons investing money at Hôtel de Ville in 1692 via the same notary who handled investments for the troupe and its members.[38]

Orsola Cortesi, according to Gueullette, played principally in the Italian repertory, so the Gherardi texts are not a good indicator of her activity in the 1680s and 1690s. She played the Matron in *La matrone d'Ephèse* in Italian and the wife of Persillet and the mother of Isabelle in *Le banqueroutier* (April 1687) in French, assuming the text is accurate. The character Eularia is last mentioned in *La fille de bon sens* (November 1692) as "the barbarous aunt of Angélique," but Gueullette says he saw her play a mute role in the "Scène de l'empereur de Cap-Verd" in *La foire Saint-Germain,* which opened in December 1695 and played through the winter of 1696. Eularia must have played one of the Sultanas along with the Chanteuse, Colombine, and Angélique.[39] She signed the troupe's Règlement et Convention on 12 January 1696.[40] She may have retired before the dismissal of the company, but it seems likely that she was still an active member in May 1697; if so, she was the only sharer to remain active throughout the life of the troupe, and one of two—with Giaratoni—to have played in Paris for the full thirty-five years.

The troupe that was sent back in May 1697 officially consisted of Marc' Antonio Romagnesi and his son, Charles-Virgile, the three Costantinis, Gherardi, Fracansani, Giaratoni, Tortoriti and his wife, Angela Toscana, and Orsola Cortesi and her two daughters, Françoise and Catherine. Very few of them actually returned to Italy. Most were French citizens, either by birth or naturalization, or were married to French citizens. Only the Costantinis and the Tortoriti couple left Paris.

Orsola Cortesi first retired to her country house in Bièvre near Meudon, on the road between Paris and Versailles. At the beginning of June 1704 she went to live at the convent of the Visitation at Montargis where her daughter Marie-Apolline had been a nun since 1687. The superior of the convent, Soeur Geneviève Angélique du Cerceau, wrote in 1751 to Gueullette that "Mme. Dominique" had died there on 11 June 1718. She was "commonly believed" to have been eighty-six, but she had never told anyone her age, even her children.[41] Her delicacy may have arisen from the fact that she was a few years older than her husband.

Of the eight Biancolelli children who survived childhood, only three followed their parents onto the stage, although one wrote for it. Louis Biancolelli, the oldest son and a godson of Louis XIV, had a distinguished career as, among other things, director of fortifications in Provence. According to Gueullette, he was the Monsieur B*** of Gherardi's collection, responsible either alone or with Dufresny for eight plays performed between May 1694 and May 1697. He died at Toulon on 5 December 1729.

His brother, Philippe, sieur de Boismorand, was still living in Paris in 1655. Gueullette saw him on 8 March and said he was well, though "he must be eighty." According to Philippe Biancolelli, he had made a debut with the company as Arlequin after the death of his father, and had been very successful, but his sister, Françoise, because of her marital difficulties with the Turgis family, had forbidden him to go on the stage. He became a commissaire of the navy and councillor of the king, "known for his capacity in these employments and for his austere probity."[42] He never married and died in November 1761.

The youngest son, Pierre-François, who was born in 1680, made his debut in the theatre in the provincial troupe organized by Giuseppe Tortoriti after the Italians were dismissed. He returned to Paris in 1710 and played at the fair theatres. In 1717 he joined the new Italian troupe led by Luigi Riccoboni in the role of Pierrot. He later changed to the role of Trivelin and played in Paris successfully until his death in 1734. His daughter by Marie-Thérèse Lalande, also named Marie-Thérèse, acted at the Comédie-Italienne from 1738 until 1762. The family tradition ended with her.[43]

Orsola Cortesi's three younger daughters, Anne-Caietan, Marie-Apolline, and Charlotte-Marie, had no connection with the theatre. Marie-Apolline became a Visitation nun, Soeur Candide, and died in 1749. Anne-Caietan married Jean-Thomas Bucelini, an Italian gentleman living in France; Charlotte-Marie married Jacques Thurin de Bourneuf, and was still living in La Rochelle in 1750.[44]

The next senior member of the troupe when it disbanded was Marc' Antonio Romagnesi. Naturalized in 1685, he remained in Paris until his death on 28 October 1706. He was buried at St.-Laurent in the presence of his sons, Charles-Virgile and Auguste-Alexandre.[45] Gueullette received his information about the family from Romagnesi's daughter-in-law, Anne-Elisabeth Costantini, who lived until 1754.[46] According to her, Marc' Antonio Romagnesi left an estate valued at just under 75,000 livres. Each surviving child received 16,341 livres; the remaining 10,000 was in *effets douteux,* or bad debts.

The surviving children were Charles-Virgile and two brothers: Auguste-Alexandre, apparently in service to the duke of Mantua, and Hipolite, provincial of the Dominicans in Rome. A quarter share of their father's estate also went to the children of a fourth brother, Gaetan, who died in Brussels in 1700. The fifth brother, Hierôme, died insane at Charanton.

Troupe members who had entered in 1683 and later were not yet necessarily ready to retire. However, Catherine Biancolelli turned down an invitation to join the French troupe her husband was a member of and left the stage. Her son later entered the Comédie-Française in cape-and-sword roles. She died in Paris on 21 February 1716, and was buried at St.-André-des-Arts. Her sister Françoise, whose marital difficulties are described in chapter 11, lived on until 1747 at the Communauté de l'Union Chrétienne and was buried at Bonne-Nouvelle.[47]

The Costantinis left France in 1697. According to Gueullette, "After the rout of the Italians, to which ... he contributed no little," Angelo Costantini went to Saxony where the king of Poland employed him to organize a troupe to perform plays and operas in Dresden. This he did so successfully, the king awarded him a patent of nobility and made him treasurer of Menus Plaisirs. But Mezzetin made the mistake of propositioning the king's mistress. In a scene worthy of Tartuffe, the young woman hid the king in her room where he could overhear Costantini. The king leaped from his concealment, sword in hand, and would have killed poor Mezzetin, but was persuaded not to soil his hands with the blood of the traitor. Instead, the actor was arrested and imprisoned for twenty years in the castle of Konigstein.[48]

The aged actor finally was released, thanks to the good offices of another lady, and returned to Italy wearing the long white beard he had grown during his captivity. He made a second debut in Paris on the stage of the Comédie-Italienne on 5 February 1729 in a reprise of *La foire Saint-Germain*. In a prologue written for the occasion,

> Momus & Arlequin appear first. Momus complains that the theatres have been deserted for a long time. He asks the cause of Arlequin, who imputes it to the extreme French love of novelty. Momus promises to remedy the situation by a novelty which will exceed all others. At his order a venerable old man enters and explains that he is the Mezzetin of the former Italian theatre. At a new order of the god, who introduces him and takes him under his protection, he tears off his old man's dress and appears in the costume of Mezzetin. ... [He] tells of a dream he had in which he thought himself transported from Italy to France and even to the stage of the Hôtel de Bourgogne, the memory of which has always been precious to him. He adds that he saw a guitar thrust out through a hole, that he took it and played it, to capture the goodwill of the parterre ... All that he saw in his dream was now executed. He was presented with a guitar, sang, the public applauded.[49]

The story of Mezzetin's twenty-year captivity, carefully publicized as part of his return to the Parisian stage, is a little too good to be true and very similar to some of the adventures in *La vie de Scaramouche*. It also bears a certain resemblance to the tale of Mezzetin and Spinette, who Costantini is supposed to have kidnapped from her royal lover. The only piece of information I have found that may contradict Costantini's adventure story is included in the *Enciclopedia dello spettacolo* entry on the commedia dell'arte. A troupe led by A. Constantini [*sic*] is said to have played in Naples sometime between 1700 and 1734.[50]

Costantini's return to Paris was not, finally, successful. Although there was an enormous crowd to see him on opening night, by his fifth appearance the excitement had dwindled. "The poor Mezzetin, who was then very old, was not liked" (fig. 18).[51] According to the *Mercure de France,* he was seventy-five. He played in all seven times between 5 and 14 February. On the first night the receipts were 5,382 livres; on the closing night, 984. Public curiosity had been satisfied. Costantini returned to Verona with the 3,000 livres agreed upon in his contract with the troupe. He also left behind in Paris all the debts he had incurred.[52]

According to the Parfaicts, Mezzetin was mediocre, even though his age contributed to his lack of success. "He had never been regarded by the connoisseurs as anything other than a rather weak actor, even in the time of his great reputation."[53]

Costantini's niece did not know what had happened to his wife, Angiola D'Orsi, Auretta, or to his sister-in-law, Maria Teresa D'Orsi, Spinette.[54] He died in Verona, shortly after his return to Italy.

Angelo Costantini's brother, Giovanni Battista, went home to Verona in 1697 where, say the Parfaicts, "he had occasion to render important services" to the French army during the War of the Spanish Succession. As a result, the Imperial army did notable damage to his property. His daughter, Anne-Elisabeth, had a letter testifying to her father's service to France. In it the chevalier de Lislière, sent into Italy to reconnoiter the enemy posts, encampments, and marches, "certifies that the sieur Constantini [*sic*] Octave, gentleman of Verona, has given essential proofs of his zeal and attachment for France, having several times traveled under the orders of the generals, and ... been the first to give notice to the movement of the enemy in Italy, which he has done at his own expense ... and that the enemy ... being informed of his zeal for France, has ruined the properties that he had in the environs of Verona."[55] Costantini was evidently making up for the treason practiced in France by his predecessor, Bartolomeo Ranieri.

In 1708 Costantini returned to France and presented a petition to the king: "Octave represents very humbly to Your Majesty, for the important services that he has rendered in Italy & the losses he has suffered thereby ... that he will please to order M. de Chamillart to give him a job in Paris ... to be able to live with his children."[56] He was appointed a customs inspector. In 1712 he opened a theatre at the Paris fairs under the protection of Monsieur's son, the duc d'Orléans, who gave him asylum at Palais-Royal when an order was issued for his arrest.[57]

In 1716, after the death of Louis XIV, that same duc d'Orléans, now regent for the young Louis XV, made arrangements for a new troupe of

FIG. *18. The aged Angelo Costantini, Mezzetin, at the time of his second debut in Paris in 1729.* (Bibliothèque Nationale; phot. Bibl. Nat. Paris)

Italian actors to be established in Paris. The leader of the troupe was Luigi Riccoboni, Lélio, a pious and respectable actor and man of letters. Before he led his companions to France, Riccoboni made a formal request via the duke of Parma that certain conditions be met. These included that the fair theatres be forbidden to employ the Italian masques, that the Italian troupe be allowed music and dance in their divertissements, that the actors *not* face excommunication or withholding of the sacraments, and that "at no time shall there be received into the troupe any of the Constantini [*sic*] family from which, by the common consent of all the world, issued the misfortunes and the disgrace at court of the Italian actors, their predecessors."[58]

In general, the Italians did not get what they asked for; in particular, "one of the first faces they saw . . . was that of Giovanni Batista Constantini [*sic*]."[59] In April 1716, the *Mercure galant* announced that the Hôtel de Bourgogne was under repair and that "M. Octave, who is charged by the minister with all the details concerning this troupe, neglects nothing of those things which could contribute to the embellishment of the theatre and the satisfaction of the public." Furthermore, in a Règlement drawn up by the minister in question, Rouillé du Coudray, Octave is granted the key to the chests wherein are to be kept the plays, scenarios, music, *registres,* and records of the troupe's deliberations, and put in charge of repairs, care of the decors, disposition of the dances, and oversight of the orchestra and the music.[60]

Costantini was not to be "received," but he was appointed in advance *dépositaire* and technical and musical director. After merely three weeks, however, Octave was relieved of his administrative duties, perhaps because the restoration of the theatre was not finished in time for the company's opening, which had to take place at Palais-Royal. Octave remained in France and died in 1720 at La Rochelle. His wife, Teresa Corona Sablioni, from whom he was apparently separated, never came to France and is last heard of when her Company of Diana, in service to the duke of Parma, passed through Mantua in 1713.[61] Their daughter returned to France with her father in 1708 and married Charles-Virgile Romagnesi. She entered the Comédie-Italienne in 1730 and played there until 1746.

Unlike the Costantinis, Giuseppe Tortoriti and his wife, Angela Toscana, may have been naturalized French citizens; their petition exists but not the authorization. In any case, they did not return to Italy. He obtained a privilege from the king to organize an Italian troupe to play anywhere in France that was more than thirty leagues from Paris. The troupe was in Strasbourg toward the end of 1697, where on the recommendation of Madame a magnificent theatre was built for it.[62] It was in Lunéville in November 1704. Pierre-François Biancolelli made his debut with the company in Toulouse, where he married one of Tortoriti's daughters. She later went insane.[63] The other Tortoriti daughter married an actor named Pierre Paghetti, who acted at the fairs and later at the Comédie-Italienne.

At some point Tortoriti returned to Italy. The young men who had gone with him were back in Paris, Charles-Virgile Romagnesi in 1707 and Pierre-François Biancolelli in 1710. Tortoriti was still active in 1717 when the duke of Parma recommended him for the new company in France and the regent expressed his regrets.[64]

Michelangelo Fracansani, who was naturalized, probably stayed on in France, but nothing is known of his further life or his death. His son, Antonio, later played Polichinelle in the theatres of the fair.[65]

Evaristo Gherardi was not a citizen but was permitted to stay on in France, presumably because his wife, Elizabeth Danneret, was. He took possession of the troupe's play texts and set about what must have been the monumental job of preparing them for publication. The argument against publication which carried the day in 1694, that an audience would not come to see a play it could read, was no longer viable. On 31 August 1700, his work completed, he went to Versailles to present a copy to the dauphin. He had at some point previously fallen on his head during a private performance at St.-Maur with La Thorillière and Poisson, but thought nothing of it. On his return from Versailles, however, he was holding his son between his legs when he collapsed and died.[66] He was thirty-six. He was buried the following day at St.-Sauveur. His wife attempted to inherit from him, but because he was not a French citizen and died intestate, his property devolved on the Crown and was awarded by the king to a royal valet, Louis Bontemps.[67] Gherardi's wife entered the company at the Opéra.

The last actor to have entered the Italian troupe, Charles-Virgile Romagnesi, joined Tortoriti's company. He returned to Paris to marry Anne-Elisabeth Costantini on 6 January 1708. The couple played in the provinces until Romagnesi became ill in 1725. He died 7 March 1731 and was buried at St.-Sauveur.[68]

Giuseppe Giaratoni deserves the last word, because he was the only actor we can be absolutely certain was with the company from the beginning to the end. He married an old maid with an income of 1,500 livres a year, and according to his petition to the dauphin, had eight children.

After the dismissal, Giaratoni retired to his "little country property near Paris." Gueullette was unable to discover the details of his death.[69]

The troupe that was locked out of the Hôtel de Bourgogne in May 1697 had little of the brilliance that marked the Comédie-Italienne between 1668 and 1688. With the exception of Catherine Biancolelli, few of the actors in the 1690s were exceptional. The comic stalwarts, Angelo Costantini and Evaristo Gherardi, were generally mediocre according to Gueullette, who saw them act. Biancolelli and Fiorilli reveled in the power of the masque. Arlequin, small and agile, alive with multicolored diamonds, blazed against the tall, black, and silent figure of Scaramouche. The black mask and the white face grew, over the years, into two aspects of the same head, like the mask with multiple faces on the company *jeton*. In contrast, Costantini's Mezzetin and Gherardi's Arlequin were separate but indistinguishable. Neither character has any particularity in the texts. Costantini insisted on playing without a mask, because the audience liked his face. And Gherardi even tried to play Arlequin barefaced, although only twice. The actor had come to depend on the power of his own personality, his own presence as a performer, a very different kind of acting from that of the tipi fissi who had astonished Paris with the perfection of their action.

CHAPTER 15

The Gherardi Repertory

THE EXTANT REPERTORY of the Comédie-Italienne between 1688 and 1697 is made up of scenes and plays in French that were furnished to the Italians by French writers, most notably Jean-François Regnard and Charles Dufresny. Because the plays have been classified as French literature, they have been extensively studied.[1] It is not my intention to abstract the previous scholarship or to offer a complete analysis of this repertory, a project that would require another book, but rather to describe it briefly and identify the ways in which it is like and unlike what has come before. Especially after 1691, the Italians introduced entertainments that, although still recognizable as the progeny of the previous repertories, are transformed by the effects of a theatre newly adapted to spectacle, a reconstituted acting company, an increasingly bourgeois audience, and the pressures to compete with the Comédie-Française and the Opéra. Many of the changes in style and substance perceptible in the 1680s continued into the 1690s, but novelties were also required to lure the Parisian audience into the old theatre on the rue Montorgueil, novelties that were the invention of French writers.

These writers' texts, derived principally from the 1700 edition of Gherardi's *Le théâtre italien* but with variants from the one-volume edition of 1694 as well as from several furtive editions, some single editions, and some manuscripts, present many problems that also will not be solved here.[2] The extent to which the various versions represent progressive states of the text, the extent to which the editor, Gherardi, has modified texts to make his character, Arlequin, more prominent or has excised or abridged characters played by actors with whom he had quarreled—all are questions that can only be raised and left unanswered. In general, scholars and editors have accepted the 1700 Gherardi collection as close to authoritative. Alexandre Calame and Marcello Spaziani have done some good editorial work on the texts which they have published, but a great deal remains to be done. In the meantime, I will also use the 1700 edition of Gherardi as my principal source, although with the recognition that a text is not necessarily an accurate representation of what was played at any given time.[3] I have chosen not to discuss at length materials from Ms. 9329, the *Supplément,* or other manuscript or printed texts that may be drawn from the late repertory because some of the sources are problematic and the body of material is too large; I have included titles from these sources in the Appendix.

The writers who provided scenes and plays to the Italians after 1688 range from well-known to unidentified. Jean-François Regnard, born in Paris in 1655, provided the Italians with eleven entertainments, seven written alone and four in collaboration with Charles Dufresny. Dufresny, also a Parisian, was born probably between 1654 and 1657; he wrote four entertainments in collaboration with Regnard, two in collaboration with Louis Biancolelli, and six—all in one-act—alone. Both Regnard and Dufresny had substantial careers as playwrights for the Comédie-Française.[4]

Jean Palaprat, born in Toulouse around 1650, was also an important French playwright who provided the Italians with two entertainments in 1692. Two plays were furnished—in 1691—by Eustache Lenoble, a disbarred lawyer and literary hack who also wrote one play for the French troupe. Other writers who created more than one or two plays for the Italians were Delosme de Montchesnay, a Parisian lawyer and friend of Boileau, who wrote five plays or sets of French scenes between 1687 and 1693, and Louis Biancolelli, the oldest son of Domenico Biancolelli, who wrote six plays alone and two with Dufresny between 1694 and 1697.[5]

Mongin wrote one play for the Italians in 1695, as did Boisfran in 1696; nothing else is known for certain of either of these gentlemen. Gherardi claims to have written one play himself, but a legal document of 9 October 1695 identifies the author as Brugière de Barante.[6] The other playwrights are merely identified by initials, and although some efforts have been made to identify them, the efforts have not been rewarded by certainty. They include L.A.D.S.M. (one play), D.L.M. (La Motte, according to Lintilhac and others, but not accepted by Lancaster, one play), L.C.D.V. (one play), and L.A.P. (one play). Finally, four plays of the repertory after *Le banqueroutier* were assigned by Gherardi to our old friend Monsieur D***.

Six of the eleven entries in the 1700 edition of Gherardi first played between the end of 1687 and the beginning of 1691 are still labeled "Scenes in French from . . ."; the entries contain between four and eleven scenes, the average being seven. All are represented in either the first edition of Gherardi or the *Supplément,* but with fewer scenes. Beginning in 1691, with the exception of two plays by Delosme de Montchenay, all the entries are arranged as complete plays, with acts and scenes indicated in the mainpieces and scenes in the afterpieces. Texts of most of the mainpieces indicate that improvised scenes in Italian were employed through the decade, but their use became pro forma in the final years of the troupe's establishment. The last material in the Gherardi repertory to be presented as detached scenes in French is Delosme de Montchenay's *Les souhaits,* which was first produced on 30 December 1693. Gherardi includes seven scenes from it in his first edition, ten in his second.[7]

The first play of the Gherardi repertory not assigned to Monsieur D***, *La cause des femmes,* by Delosme de Montchenay, opened the day after Christmas 1687. The intrigue concerns a vieillard, Bassemine, who dislikes his daughter's suitors and wants to marry her to an elderly doctor. This traditional Italianate plot is transformed into a French comedy of manners by making the daughter, Isabelle, a précieuse and her suitors a selection of poets, gamblers, and abbés. Colombine plays the witty suivante, but Isabelle speaks the tirade, a discourse on the evils of marrying old men. The play ends, as usual, with the union of the amoureux and amoureuse.

Arlequin's travesties are conventional—a moor, a baron, a commissaire—but display little or nothing of the character's traditional nature. Furthermore, the play was followed by a critical afterpiece, which opened on 14 February 1688, six weeks after its subject. In it, a particular point is made that Arlequin "triumphs" speaking French.[8] On the other hand, *La critique* also discusses actions and scenes which are not to be found in the Gherardi text of *La cause des femmes:* an "inimitable" Scene of the Basket, a purse of 200 louis found by Arlequin, the "glou, glou, glou," all of which sound like traditional zanni play.

La critique itself is like nothing in the troupe's Italian repertory but presumably follows the French practice of extending a run by adding a critical afterpiece to a play that has stirred up a certain amount of controversy. This particular one begins with the premise that Isabelle, in spite of her denunciation of the practice, has married a vieillard who objects, as her father had done, to her fashionable way of life. Isabelle arrives home from the theatre with her friend, the Baroness (Colombine); they are joined by Arlequin, as the Chevalier, who has nothing good to say of *La cause des femmes* except that he rather liked the scene of Arlequin as a moor. Mezzetin enters as Count Constantin, speaking only Italian, and is mocked by Arlequin and told to speak the "good Italian of France." Mezzetin has also found the play detestable, especially the "scene where Mezzetino plays with his mouth the various instruments," that is, the "glou, glou, glou."[9]

La cause des femmes joins traditional Italian improvisation and zanni play to French comedy of manners and satire of social institutions in the same manner as *Le banqueroutier,* but the net is more widely cast. In the first half of the troupe's final decade, especially before their theatre was reequipped in 1691, the Italians increased their use of satire, attacking the conventional targets of the day. That *La critique* makes an issue of Arlequin's proficiency in French may reflect Italian victory in the conflict between the French and Italian troupes over the latter's use of their adopted tongue, and may also help explain why satire was expanded and French writers attracted to the Italian theatre at this point.

One of these was Regnard, whose first play for the Italians was also the last play of the Gherardi collection performed before Dominique's death. *Le divorce* (17 March 1688), is presented as a complete text with a prologue, seventeen scenes in French, and two scenes improvised in Italian. The plot is simple: Isabelle has married old Sotinet, a tax farmer, but is miserable. She begs her brother, Aurelio, to come to Paris to help her resolve her unhappy situation. He plots with Sotinet's valet, Mezzetin, to find a way for her to be separated from her husband, but not from his fortune. Arlequin, a former valet of Aurelio's, arrives in Paris and joins the plot with Mezzetin and Colombine, Isabelle's *suivante.*

The play continues with the usual extravagant activities of the zanni trying to carry out their master's and mistress's wishes. Arlequin gains entrance to Sotinet's house as a barber, assisted by Mezzetin, and the two rascals steal the old man's purse, typical zanni play. Later, however, Arlequin enters on a small horse as a dancing master, followed by Mezzetin as a singing master, and the scene proceeds in the manner of *Le bourgeois gentilhomme.*

Act 2 begins not with a further burlesque of Parisian types but with traditional First and Second Zanni play between Arlequin and Mezzetin. Mezzetin tries to explain to Arlequin the details of their plot, but Arlequin is absorbed in counting his buttons to see if Colombine will marry him or not. After the button scene, the play returns to its French antecedents, as Isabelle and Sotinet play a scene reminiscent of Molière's *George Dandin.*

By act 3 Isabelle is "nearly determined" to leave her husband. A mock trial is planned, to take place before the god Hymen in his temple. Arlequin as Maître Cornichon pleads for Isabelle, while Maître Braillardet, played by Colombine, speaks for Sotinet.[10] Isabelle wins her case, Sotinet is sent off to St.-Lazare for "certified lunacy" for having married a young girl, and the god Hymen reveals himself as Aurelio, a brother in this version, but very probably a lover in the original.[11] Arlequin proposes to Colombine, who agrees to the marriage provided they can be unmarried after one year.

There are sufficient lacunae in the plot to suggest that a number of improvised scenes are missing. According to Gherardi, the play was erased from "the catalogue of plays reprised from time to time and the sides burned" after its failure in the hands of Biancolelli. This suggests either that Regnard furnished a new manuscript in 1689, when Gherardi used the play as his debut piece, or that the play was reconstructed from memory. If Gherardi is telling the truth, *Le divorce,* as it exists, is more likely to reflect the reprise than the original.

On the other hand, the role of Arlequin is still very much Biancolelli's creation. Calame calls attention to the fact that several of the scenes of *Le divorce* feature the traditional naïvetés of Arlequin.[12] He walks on the uppers of his shoes in order to save the soles, weeps because the buttons say he will not have Colombine, and agrees to disguise himself as an *avocat* when he discovers that there's a tavern at the Palais de Justice where the lawyers "eat sausages, kidneys, and tongues and drink of the best." Arlequin is as clumsy, cowardly, and gluttonous as ever, insolent, gross in his language, a thief and a counterfeiter, and too fat to have escaped hanging through the drainpipe of a fountain. Even in the travesty scenes, although Arlequin is more glib, more French than in his own scenes, his true nature shines through, as it does when as ambassador of the king of China he says, "Let's see her teeth" to verify Isabelle's age.

This traditional persona gradually diminishes as various playwrights shape the character, not as a masque but as a role for Evaristo Gherardi. From time to time, though, Arlequin is suddenly restored to his historic persona, as a sort of memento. This technique is often used in the later repertory, especially after Louis Biancolelli begins to write for the company. The lazzi and zanni play become a historical footnote, expected and no doubt welcome as a set turn, but not innate in the behaviors of the characters.

The first two new plays following Biancolelli's death, *Le marchand dupé* (1 September 1688) and *Colombine femme vengée* (15 January 1689), both assigned by Gherardi to Monsieur D***, are also comedies of manners, but very different from their predecessors. The first features Friquet, a merchant being tricked by his son, Mezzetin, and by Isabelle, a young lady whose favors both men hope to obtain. Isabelle is cut off from her family and living on her wits in Paris. Mezzetin has his hand in his father's till and takes advantage of several opportunities in the play to rob and even beat him. He courts Isabelle as a *petit marquis,* a most unpleasant one, obsessed with class and rank. Colombine, who is even more conniving than usual, orchestrates Isabelle's liaisons and advises her not to marry "that great Dandin" Aurelio, the man she really loves, because he is not "generous." The comic centerpiece of the play is the quarrel and duel between Friquet and a second vieillard, the man in black, who is also enamored of Isabelle.[13] The text is relatively complete up to the denouement, which is simply sketched in. There is no indication of any kind of traditional zanni intrigue; the play's conclusion is of the French deus ex machina kind, with Isabelle forgiven by her father and married to Aurelio.

Le marchand dupé was followed by *Colombine femme vengée,* another comedy of manners, with the leading character a "man of the sword," not a merchant or petty official. This play contains a nearly complete action in three acts and twenty-six scenes. Mezzetin plays a philandering husband who returns from a trip accompanied by a young woman, Olivette (Isabelle), whom he has promised to marry and whose father has forced her to elope with him. Colombine, his wife, has amused herself in his absence with several suitors, although she claims to love no one but her husband. The two women make common cause against Mezzetin, beat him, and invent a scheme to appropriate 30,000 ecus from him for a dowry for Olivette. They call for a magistrate and bribe him to arrest Mezzetin. At the trial Mezzetin is accused of having gambled away 20,000 of the 30,000 ecus, which, luckily, have been won by Aurelio. The judge proclaims that the 20,000 ecus will serve as Olivette's dowry, that she will marry Aurelio, that Colombine is to be given the key to the strongbox with the other 10,000 ecus, and is permitted to "correct" her husband with a stick and to be, "like all other wives, absolute mistress in her house."

Although it included improvised scenes in Italian, this play, like the one that preceded it, has little in common with the troupe's normal repertory. Mezzetin's role, although played in the costume of Arlequin, resembles no role played by Biancolelli; the character is, if anything, a kind of bravo with his *ventrebleus* and *par le sangs.* Colombine is not a suivante but a modern young wife living the lifestyle her usual character advises the amoureuse to adopt. Neither *Le marchand dupé* nor *Colombine femme vengée* is an attractive play. The former, in particular, is a mean-spirited satire without comic vitality. In both plays Mezzetin's character lacks the physicality and extravagance that marked Dominique's Arlequin, both as himself and in his travesties. Isabelle and Colombine are more agreeable in the second play, where they are victimized, than in the first, where their ambiguous way of life makes them seem less than scrupulous. Both plays propose irregular sexual liaisons; both appeal to the prurient. In the typical Italian plot, the action is incited by young women being too carefully protected by fathers and guardians. In these plots, the young women have been disowned by their fathers or cheated by their husbands, and are at the mercy of a malevolent society. They cope by using duplicity in one case, violence and trickery in the other.

The two other plays that featured Mezzetin are *La descente de Mezzetin aux enfers* (5 March 1689) and *Mezzetin Grand Sophy de Perse* (10 July 1689). Gherardi includes four scenes from the former, written by Regnard, and seven from the latter, written by Delosme de Montchenay. Both plays introduce the exotic and feature some spectacle, whatever the Italians could muster in 1689. Mezzetin appears in *La descente* as Amphion with Colombine as his wife. Aurelio and Isabelle appear as Orpheus and Eurydice. The four extant scenes do not make it possible to reconstruct a plot. The play seems very much in the tradition of the Italian's post-1668 repertory, and Mezzetin's role is definitely allied to Biancolelli's Arlequin, with dialogue full of naïvetés, imbroglios, and equivocations. In the "Scène de Mezzetin et d'Isabelle," however, Mezzetin makes love to Isabelle while Colombine eavesdrops, an action reminiscent of the character Mezzetin played in *Colombine femme vengée*. The spectacle includes a sea with Mezzetin in the belly of a whale and Colombine and Pierrot astride a mackerel as well as a throne of flames for Pluto and Proserpine.

Mezzetin Grand Sophy is somewhat more fully developed in the extant scenes. According to a note included by Gherardi, in the first scene Mezzetin is a knight-errant, beloved of the sorceress Mélisse (Colombine) who keeps him confined in her palace. According to Lancaster, the scene is probably part of a parody of Quinault's *Armide*.[14] Spectacle is provided by monsters. The scene is partly sung, partly spoken, and takes advantage of the undoubted musical talents of both performers. The plot features a pedantic vieillard named Grognard who plans to marry his daughter to the Grand Sophy of Persia because in Persia husbands are respected. The scenes in French are conventional: the parody, a Moliéresque scene between the vieillard and Colombine, a discussion of the horrors of marriage between Colombine and Isabelle. In one scene the two valets, Pasquariel and Mezzetin, do a routine very similar to the one in *Le divorce* when Mezzetin tries to persuade Arlequin to disguise himself as a lawyer. In *Le Grand Sophy* Pasquariel persuades Mezzetin to pretend to be a captain of dragoons. The young women also appear in disguises, Colombine as a young lawyer calling on Mme. Grognard, Isabelle as a young man consulting an astrologer. In the finale, Mezzetin appears as the Grand Sophy and a new machine is introduced: "an apartment is furnished in the blink of an eye, to the sound of the symphony."

In 1689 Evaristo Gherardi joined the company. The first new play written after his debut was *L' homme à bonne fortune* (10 January 1690), a comedy of manners with French scenes by Regnard. Arlequin and Mezzetin are two apparently unattached valets. The former has adopted the identity of the vicomte de Bergamotte[15] in order to bilk women. He comes to visit Colombine, the fourteen-year-old daughter of Brocantin, a merchant of curiosities. Arlequin sets out to impress the eager Colombine; her naïveté points up the vacuity of his life as a man about town, as well as his vulgarity and insolence. But when he is arrested for forgery, Colombine gives him all her jewelry, her watch, and her patchbox. The character of the *homme à bonne fortune* is very much like Mezzetin's Friquet *fils* in *Le marchand dupé* or husband in *Colombine femme vengée,* more a bravo than a zanni. In a later scene, however, we meet the traditional Arlequin disguised as the Prince des Curieux, again examining a young woman as if she were a horse: "Head up! Walk! Trot!"

After his arrest Arlequin consults a lawyer, also Colombine in disguise, who does a tirade similar to the one she did as the pedant in *Colombine avocat pour et contre.* Meanwhile, Brocantin's older daughter, Isabelle, disguises herself as a young cavalier and tells the Docteur, who wants to marry her, that she is Isabelle's lover. The finale is reminiscent of earlier scenes of fantasy. Arlequin, as Prince Tonquin des Curieux, is carried in by four men in a sort of basket. Mezzetin accompanies him as a singing parrot. After assorted nonsense, Arlequin presents Octave as a Tonkinese merchant of curiosities, Brocantin agrees to his match with Isabelle, and the play ends with a show of "curiosities": a tableau vivant and a song by Mezzetin accompanied by a monkey playing a guitar.

Although *L'homme à bonne fortune* mixes Italian improvisation and French memorized scenes, in tone it is like the two comedies of manners that featured Mezzetin. It borrows heavily from Molière, especially from *L'école des femmes,* uses Colombine ironically as a naive young girl, and even goes so far as to have Arlequin recite four maxims of marriage.

Like *La cause des femmes, L'homme à bonne fortune* was also succeeded by a *Critique,* which opened on 1 March 1690. It is peopled, in the usual manner of critiques, by an audience cross-section gathered at a restaurant for supper to discuss the play just seen. In an unusual piece of casting, Isabelle appears as Claudine, the waitress.[16] *La Critique* gives us little in the way of new information about *L'homme à bonne fortune,* aside from stressing how incredibly popular it was.

The next three new plays in the repertory are all comedies of manners. Gherardi's 1700 edition includes nine scenes from Regnard's *Les filles errantes,* seven scenes from *La fille sçavante* by Monsieur D***, and a nearly complete *La coquette, ou l'académie des dames,* also by Regnard. *Les filles errantes* (24 August 1690) reintroduces the theme of young women abandoned, on their own in Paris.

Since most of the scenes are detached, the intrigue cannot be reconstructed; however, a scene printed first in the *Supplément* makes it possible to establish the foundation of the plot. Cinthio has been separated from his beloved, Isabelle, and Colombine from her lover, Octave. They arrive in Paris, pretending to be brother and sister, and take rooms in an inn where Isabelle, under the name Claudine, is working as a servant.[17] Mezzetin is Colombine's real brother in one scene; in another he is a young lawyer, Croquignolet, son of a merchant. Arlequin plays the innkeeper and, without his mask, Croquignolet's valet. The play includes several typical commedia dell'arte scenes, including a scene of bravura, with Arlequin as captain of a ragtag band of soldiers hired by Mezzetin to frighten Cinthio into marrying his sister, and another featuring jargon, with Mezzetin as a Dutchman with a wooden leg. In general, the French scenes of this play are not well developed and the characters—especially Arlequin—lack definition. Only the final scene with Arlequin as a commissaire has the comic energy traditionally associated with the character, although in it, too, Arlequin reveals none of his usual attributes except illiteracy. When handed Isabelle's marriage contract, he "has a rheumatism of the ear and can't make it out." The play ends with a song and dance, a parody of the chaconne in act 1 of Lulli and Quinault's *Cadmus et Hermione.*

La fille sçavante (18 November 1690) concerns a vieillard, Tortillon, with two daughters: Angélique, who loves books, and Isabelle, who loves officers. An uncle has left 50,000 ecus to Angélique if she will marry; if she refuses, the money will go to Isabelle. Both daughters renounce matrimony, and Isabelle joins the army. The rest of the French materials include a scene of Arlequin as a widow trying to keep her seventeen children from inheriting from their father, two scenes of Isabelle as a captain tricking a shopkeeper, L'Arc-en-ciel, into enlisting, and a scene of a Professor of Love teaching Angélique to be a proper Parisian coquette. Gherardi appeared as the Professor without his mask and dressed "properly à la française."[18] Angélique falls in love with the Professor, while Isabelle ends up with Octave, the son of L'Arc-en-ciel, who repudiates his middle-class father and calls himself the Baron Tricolor.

The casting is odd. L'Arc-en-ciel, although a vieillard, may have been played by Mezzetin or Arlequin, judging by the *ventrebleus* and *sangbleus* of his vocabulary, while Angélique must have originally been played by Colombine. A third female character is called for, a maid named Toinon, which seems like an appropriate role at this point for Angela Toscana, the actress who later played the amoueuse as Angélique but who also played a servante, Marinette. The play is more thematically centered than most and focuses on the plight of wealthy middle-class parents with children who no longer share their values. As Tortillon says: "The more I look at myself, the less I find that my daughters resemble me. Angélique speaks of nothing but books, Isabelle only likes officers. What the devil connection does all that have with me, who has neither heart nor learning, whose business is to live a good bourgeois life in Paris? Fate, you bitch, you have me by the short hairs!" [19]

Regnard's next play, *La coquette, ou l'académie des dames* (17 January 1691) ends the series of plays heavily influenced by the French comedy of manners which were performed in the eighteen months after Biancolelli's death. Gherardi has included twenty-one scenes, divided in three acts, and has indicated several places where Italian improvised scenes were played.

The distribution of roles is again unusual. Colombine plays the only daughter of the *bonhomme* Trafiquet; Isabelle is her cousin. Arlequin plays a provincial bailiff from Maine to whom Trafiquet wishes to marry Colombine. The Bailiff of Maine owes more to M. de Pourceaugnac and the French tradition of the comic peasant than to the naive valet from Bergamo. Colombine, as well, is a French coquette, a character much in theatrical fashion in 1690, more concerned with the fine points of trapping a husband than with planning tactics in the battle of the sexes. Isabelle fears that a coquette is like one of these sparkling wines that everyone wants to taste but no one buys for everyday. "An old wive's tale," answers Colombine, who supports her views by reading a verse satire, "Le portrait d'une coquette, ou la vraye morale d'une fille à marier." [20] The rest of the play consists largely of scenes proving Colombine's point; she is wooed by Octave, Pierrot, a lawyer Nigaudin (Mezzetin), a captain (Arlequin), and the Bailiff, who agrees to buy a title if Colombine will marry him.

In act 3 Colombine entertains Mme. Pindaret, a blue stocking probably played by Pierrot. Their scene, heavily dependent on Molière for its satirical edge, is interrupted by the Bailiff, who has completed his purchase and arrives *en marquis*. After a scene in which Colombine admits that "for a newly minted marquis you don't play your role badly," the play ends with a divertissement of sybils. Colombine will not marry the marquis unless he is received into her academy of women. He must dress as a woman and swear to be an accommodating husband.

M. Trafiquet interrupts the rites and discovers the Bailiff, who no longer knows if he is a man or a woman. Colombine says to her father, "I am, father, disposed to obey you, but I cannot believe that you want to give me as a husband a man who is capable of such extravagances." Angry and humiliated, the Bailiff returns to his province, and Colombine marries Octave.

Although *La coquette* was performed with some improvised scenes and has other elements reminiscent of the commedia dell'arte, it is in style and substance very largely a French comedy of manners devoted to satires of Parisian stereotypes. Although Mezzetin plays a sort of First Zanni, seconded by Pasquariel, Arlequin is not Arlequin but a provincial of a particularly French sort. Perhaps the Italians went too far with *La coquette;* in any case, its immediate successors in the repertory are quite different, and it was more than a year before the Italians produced another comedy of manners, nearly two years before they produced another play by Regnard.

Between January and September of 1691, presumably while the theatre was undergoing a major reconstruction, the Italians appear to have opened only one new play, *Esope,* attributed to Eustache Lenoble. A second play by him, *Les deux Arlequins,* opened the same year in September. Since both are quite unlike any other plays of the Gherardi repertory, they are of little use in constructing generalizations about the Italian troupe and their productions.

Esope (24 February 1691) was inspired by Boursault's *Aesop,* performed in 1690 by the Comédie-Française. It is in five acts and almost entirely in French verse, has no plot to speak of, and a cast of seventeen with the commedia types employed in totally unaccustomed ways. Isabelle, for instance, is Arlequin-Esope's lover, Colombine his daughter, the Docteur her suitor. The plot is an excuse for the recitation of twelve of Aesop's fables and the play ends with the most spectacular divertissement the Italians had managed since moving to the Hôtel de Bourgogne.[21] The play was published in Paris in 1691 shortly after its first production, which suggests that it was not popular. If it had been, the troupe—which normally owned the rights to its repertory—would not have permitted its publication.

On the other hand, they did produce Lenoble's second play, *Les deux*

Arlequins, seven months after the first on 26 September 1691, a month before the first machine play was introduced on their reconstructed and reequipped stage. *Les deux Arlequins* is in three acts and also in French verse. Although it has the same title as a play represented in Biancolelli's zibaldone, it has nothing in common with it except the Plautine comic device of confusion caused by identical characters. The play appears to be relatively complete in thirty-four scenes, only two of which—between Arlequin and Marinette—are said by Gherardi to have been improvised in Italian. In this play even the amoureux speaks French.[22]

The only unusual feature of the play's plot is that the vieillard gets the girl. In spite of Colombine's arguments to the contrary, Isabelle decides to marry Géronte and tells her other suitor, Octave, that he has "a shameful defect, very rare at your age; you are young, but a miser. He is old, but free and liberal." This conclusion is repeated in Palaprat's *La fille de bon sens* produced a year later.

Les deux Arlequins was probably an inexpensive filler, something new to attract audiences while the Italians prepared their first real spectacle play in nearly fifteen years. The first of a series of several romances based on classical or exotic themes, *Ulisse et Circé* was a not unremarkable choice for a troupe that had watched its rival thrive on Thomas Corneille and Donneau de Visé's *Circé* in the late 1670s. The author of the Italian's version, given by Gherardi as Monsieur L.A.D.S.M., has never been identified. The text has thirty-three scenes in three acts, largely in French prose. No improvised scenes in Italian are indicated, but Italian dialogue is interlarded with French, a fairly unusual technique this late in the repertory. Each act ends with a song, and there are other songs included within the scenes.

The big attraction of *Ulisse et Circé* was the spectacle, with three elaborate sets of scenery: "the Greek camp with the city of Troy, in flames, in the distance"; "a very agreeable island and the sea in the distance"; "a magnificent garden." Act 1 begins with a battle: "A great noise of trumpets, drums, and musket shots is heard and people shouting and crossing the stage, fleeing from the conquerer." Helen's jewels, liberated by Pasquariel, are transformed into gigantic pearls and mammoth precious stones by means of a bottomless jewel box and a handy stage trap. In the second scene of act 2, the Docteur, Pasquariel, and Pierrot are seen swimming in the sea while Arlequin and Mezzetin cross the stage in a little boat, tossed by the waves. In act 2, scene 12, the Docteur, who has been changed into an ass, with Pierrot as a goat, Pasquariel as a pig, and Mezzetin as a cat perform an Italian drinking song, with appropriate animal noises. In act 3 Marinette leads in the transformed masques accompanied by several other animals, which might include a bear, a boar, an elephant, and a camel—if the frontispiece can be trusted. The finale takes place in the magnificent garden. Musicians surround the chariot of Ulysses and Circe at center. Arlequin and Colombine are to one side in a chariot which represents a household, Mezzetin and Marinette to the other side, in a chariot surrounded by pots and cauldrons.

The play is rather charming. In this version Circe has fallen in love with Ulysses while flying over the Trojan war in her chariot. She makes a pact with the "Devil" to bring Ulysses and his companions to her island and transforms the companions into animals when he wants to leave. Adamant, she refuses to change them back to their human forms unless Ulysses agrees to stay with her. He finally consents, provided she will allow him to return home and put his affairs in order. Apparently, since they are together in the flying chariot at the end of the play, she plans to go along while he does so. One innovation is the character Marinette, rescued by the sorceress from a brutal husband, played by Pasquariel—the actress's real husband—in his capitan persona. Another unexpected moment is Mezzetin's unhappiness at having been rescued from his animal transformation. "It was," he says, "a great happiness not to be a man."

In this play Arlequin is a glutton and a coward but not otherwise traditional. Colombine is clever but not guileful. The text includes a few comic scenes from the repertory of the commedia dell'arte, including one lazzi of laughter with Colombine, Arlequin, and Mezzetin, but most of the text is either concerned with plot or with the character of Circe, who is obsessively in love with Ulysses. The play's appeals rest on spectacle and music and on the relationship between Colombine and Arlequin, which is much more fully developed than is usual in the French texts.

Ulisse et Circé was followed a month later by *Le phénix* (22 November 1691), with scenes in French by Delosme de Montchenay. The *Mercure galant* in October mentions that the Italian troupe was preparing to give it; this is one of only three titles included in the *Mercure* after Dominique's death. Although the play uses an exotic setting and refers to classical history and legend, it does not employ spectacle, perhaps because the machines for *Ulisse et Circé* still occupied the stage. The plot concerns a prince who doubts his wife's fidelity. He opens the play making love to Colombine, who agrees to disguise herself as a man and make love to the Princess as a test. Arlequin is Colombine's lover, who comes disguised as a Turk to announce to the Princess the imminent arrival of the

Bacha, Colombine. The latter declares her love for the Princess and gives her two hours to decide. The Prince goes to consult Democritus, Heraclitus, and Diogenes about his wife's "malady," while the Princess pretends madness to avoid answering the Bacha. In the final scene, Arlequin as a magistrate is charged with investigating several ladies who have intruded upon the Elysian Fields, in the quarter designated for virtuous women, "without qualifications or recommendation." The ladies include Lucrece, Artemis, Penelope, and Dido.

This play, like *Ulisse et Circé,* effectively mixes the classical with satire of contemporary Parisian manners. Democritus laughs uproariously at the Prince, who is offended. But Democritus believes that laughter is the only appropriate response to the world. "I see the vulgarian Adonis, by means of his milk-white complexion and his Russian leather carriage, insert himself among the *petit marquis* and solicit at vast expense the ambitious title of debauché who follows the court, and I shouldn't laugh? I see a detachment of young senators who leave for the siege of Mons, armed with Spanish wigs, pocket mirrors, and essence of bergamot . . . and I shouldn't laugh?"[23]

The carnival play of 1692 was *Arlequin Phaeton* (4 February 1692) by Palaprat, who had already furnished plays to the French troupe. The new play both imitated Boursault's *Phaeton,* which had opened six weeks earlier at the Comédie-Française, and parodied Quinault's opera. The classical legend, originally from Ovid, is, as usual, an excuse for spectacle, parody, and anachronism.

The scene is Egypt. Phaeton is disguised as Arlequin so no one will know he is the son of the sun god.[24] Epaphus, his rival for the hand of the nymph, Galatea, is disguised as Pierrot. The plot revolves around Phaeton's need to prove his parentage so that Galatea's father will permit him to marry her.

Act 2 is designed to show off the Italians' new flying machinery. It takes place in "the first region of the air." Momus (Mezzetin) has offered to guide Phaeton to his father's palace. They have been walking all night through the clouds; now at daybreak they are looking down on Paris, where they encounter various citizens, beginning with the brandy seller, the aqua vita man, traditionally the first vendor on the streets. Other passersby include a marquise, a financier, and a procureur who play out a little comedy under the eyes of the gods. The marquise, a bourgeoise married to an aristocrat, encounters her father, a "filthy procureur," on her way home from a night's gambling. After this satirical interlude, the stage changes and represents the twelve signs of the zodiac. Arlequin plays a traditional Second Zanni routine in which he mistakes the celestial bull for Io, asks the Gemini for some vinegar so he can eat the Crab, runs from the Lion, and begs the Archer to shoot the Scorpion.

Momus and Phaeton finally reach Apollo, who is happy to swear by the River Styx that Phaeton is his son. Phaeton asks to drive Apollo's chariot, and the sun god finally agrees, although he foresees that this will result in his son's death. As Phaeton flies through the sky in the chariot, the horses run away, descending toward the earth. Phaeton disappears as the Earth, the gods of the waters and forests, the River Po, and a saytr or two sing furiously that they are all being burned, and beg Jupiter for rain. "Phaeton reappears in the air, his chariot half tipped over; at the same time Jupiter casts his thunderbolt and [Phaeton] falls with his chariot" (fig. 19).[25]

Esculapius brings Phaeton back to life and tells him that Jupiter, the father of his rival, has turned his sisters into poplar trees. The text does not indicate the setting of act 3, but it must have featured Phaeton's tomb and a row of poplars. The newly resurrected Phaeton now considers a profession, although he wonders why he should have to work when the children of tax-collectors, procureurs, bankers, and bailiffs live in clover and do nothing. He rejects architecture, divinity, and justice, the metiers of his father, as well as music, medicine, and literature; most of the last act is taken up with satires of these professions and those who follow them. Apollo finally suggests that his son marry the nymph, become a shepherd, and follow the only happy way of life. The play ends with a pastoral divertissement.

Arlequin Phaeton is largely a collection of disconnected satires. Much of the comedy is based on the anachronistic mixture of classical characters and contemporary manners, a recipe used over and over in the years that followed. Arlequin and Mezzetin are only briefly reminiscent of commedia dell'arte zanni, while the other members of the troupe play roles that have no connection to the types they have been accustomed to play. This play with its predecessor, *Ulisse et Circé,* marks a turning point for the French repertory; the tipi fissi appear less and less frequently after it, and then largely in the few comedies of manners introduced in the last years of the company's existence.

One of these, *La précaution inutile* (5 March 1692), was the last play assigned by Gherardi to Monsieur D***. The plot, while complex, is orthodox, except for the fact that both young women, Isabelle and Colombine, are engaged to old men. Mezzetin and Arlequin are valets of the amoureux and plot the usual strategies, using various travesties to upset

FIG. *19. Frontispiece to* Arlequin Phaeton *in Gherardi's*
Le théâtre italien, *1700.* (Phot. Bibl. Nat. Paris)

the plans of old Gaufichon. Because the text is relatively complete, the twists and turns of the plot are clear, but the play is comically inert. It lacks any real zanni play, and reads, as Lancaster says, like a French comedy of fifty years earlier.[26] Although French in style, it contains little satire of contemporary manners; it does begin with a discussion of Descartes's theory that animals are machines, but that was hardly fodder for the gazetteers in 1692.

Palaprat's *La fille de bon sens* (2 November 1692) is more typical of French comic style in the 1690s and is the last of the Italians' plays that can be classified as a comedy of manners in that mode. Once again the play poses the question of marriage to an old man, and as in *Les deux Arlequins,* concludes that a sensible marriage to a wealthy older man is preferable to a marriage to a young man. Octave and Léandre are presented as a narcissistic fortune hunter and a vainglorious soldier, while the older bourgeois, Géronte (one of Marc' Antonio Romagnesi's vieillards), is truly in love. The question of his age is somewhat discounted by having a still older man, the Docteur, also in pursuit of Angélique with her aunt's blessing. Also, Angélique makes it clear that she is not marrying Géronte for his money or because of the freedom which the wives of old men often enjoy. She marries him because she loves him.

The seeds of a new genre were planted when Dufresny's first play for the Italians, *L'opéra de campagne,* opened on 4 June 1692.[27] It combines a parody of the Opéra with a plot which features—most unusually for a troupe descended from the commedia dell'arte—a shrewish wife and henpecked husband.[28] Also unusual for the Italians, the scene is set in a village, not in Paris, and the satire is of rural, not urban, stereotypes.

Mme. Prenelle, the Bailiff's wife (played by Mezzetin), dreams of putting her daughter, Thérèse, in a convent and going to Paris to the Opéra. "I'll go there day and night, I'll drink there, I'll eat there, I'll sleep there, I'll . . . Ah! the Opéra is the source of all pleasures, there's nothing so perfect in the world." Arlequin, the valet of Octave who has fallen in love with Thérèse, wants to take advantage of the arrival of a small touring opera company to foil Mme. Prenelle and get the girl for his master. The entrance of the opera troupe is the visual highlight of act 1.

> The sound of drums and trumpets is heard. . . . A cart appears full of the property of the Opéra, costumes, chests, decors, counterweights, ropes, etc. Marinette is on top of the cart with three little children, the carter walks at the side, dressed in black [Pasquariel, in the costume of Scaramouche] . . . with a feather beard and in his hand a magician's wand, which he uses as a whip. A humpback [Polichi-

nelle] comes next, bearing on each of his humps, before and behind, a music stand with an open book of music. This humpback is followed by a drummer, the drummer by a trumpeter, the trumpeter by a man who pulls a bass violin on two little wheels, he by the one who plays the violin, and he by one who has a little spinet hanging from his neck. ... They arrange themselves with the cart in the middle and between two men who each holds a gun to his shoulder. ... All of these people are dressed in the most comical opera costumes that can be imagined; and when the carter wants to go to the right, or to the left, or drive his horses forward or back, he sings ... and all the instruments accompany him, so that all the carter's commands like "gee" and "haw" and "geeup" and "whoa" are always sung by the carter and the chorus repeats them.[29]

Mme. Prenelle not only henpecks her husband, she also has a liaison with their servant, Pierrot, most unusually employed as the true "helmsman" of the family. Arlequin, as part of the plot to free Thérèse from her mother, arranges for the opera to be performed in the Bailiff's hearing room, with Mme. Prenelle and Pierrot taking part.

Mme. Prenelle takes a ballet lesson from Arlequin in order to prepare for her role in the opera. The comic strategies of the scene are French, derived from Molière, but the degree of exaggeration present reveals its other ancestor. After observing her walk, Arlequin gets to work. He begins by taking her head and pulling up on it: "We have to lengthen the neck by half a foot. Now then, shoulder down. (*He hits the shoulder.*) Knees out. (*He strikes the knees.*) Let's go, begin. (*She dances.*) Tra la la la, tra la la la. And the arse, my lord, the arse. (*He kicks Mme. Prenelle in the backside.*) Let's go, head up, a smile for the boxes, your eye doesn't speak. Imagine you see your lover in the wings. Extend the arms. No, yes ... very good, very good. Let's have your hand, turn! (*He makes her turn so fast that she falls one way, Arlequin the other.*)"[30] During the performance of the opera, a parody of *Armide,* monsters kidnap Pierrot, while Octave and Thérèse disappear through a trap together. Mme. Prenelle renounces opera. The parody is further enlivened by burlesque imitations of two stars of the Paris Opéra, Dumesnil and Mlle. Rochois.

The play alternates between a street and a room in the Bailiff's house. One act 3 street scene includes a somewhat artless scenic effect. Arlequin enters with Pasquariel as a crippled vendor of almanacs "followed by a man who puts down on the ground a sort of wing representing a corner of the street, upon which are stuck several different posters." The opera parody is performed in a setting "composed of household goods, with a fireplace at the rear within which several chickens turn on the spit." Mme. Prenelle takes advantage of the pots and pans to express her displeasure at the end of the play. The demons that descend and kidnap the hero are the only suggestion that the flying machinery was used, probably naively in keeping with the unsophisticated country opera.

The success of the piece is underscored by Dancourt's imitation of it, *L'opéra de village,* which opened at the Comédie-Française on 20 June, sixteen days after the premier of *L'opéra de campagne.* Dufresny took advantage of the French imitation to respond with *L'union des deux opéras,* which was first presented—presumably as an afterpiece to its predecessor—by the Italians on 16 August. This little piece in eight scenes, a sort of extended divertissement, marks a very important development in the repertory of the Italian troupe. It is the first of the twelve short afterpieces included in Gherardi's 1700 edition, produced between 1692 and 1697.

Afterpieces had long been a feature of performances by the French companies, but, except for the two critiques, there is no evidence that the Italians used them before 1692.[31] The French afterpiece before 1690 was normally a farce or brief comedy of manners, without spectacle and with minor use of music. It was extremely popular late in the century, and Lancaster points out that of eighty-four extant French comedies produced between April 1689 and the end of the 1700 season, forty-eight were in one act.[32] Dancourt, an actor in the French troupe, specialized in one-act afterpieces and, according to Lancaster, his *L'opéra de village* was the first "comédie-en-vaudeville," which Lancaster defines as a short comedy which ends with a musical divertissement.[33] Lancaster's argument is based on the fact that Dufresny's slightly earlier *L'opéra de campagne* for the Italians does not end with a divertissement, although it does end with a musical parody. In fact, it seems futile to try to assign responsibility for this new genre to either troupe; the rival troupes were so embroiled in imitation that it is often impossible to decide which was the leader, which the follower. In general, the Italians, who may have had some sort of special dispensation from the regulations governing the use of music on the Paris stage,[34] made much greater use of music and spectacle in their afterpieces than the French did. The French, however, made greater use of peasants and pastoral themes. Their short plays were often introduced in the summer and were set in villages outside of Paris during vacation, or the grape harvest, or during a fair. The occasion brings together various types who can be satirized, and gives cause for a celebration which adds some minimal verisimilitude to the divertissement.

The afterpieces played at the Italian theatre were sometimes similar to those played by the French, often dissimilar. The first one, Dufresny's *L'union des deux opéras,* was an occasional piece, highly self-referential, designed to extend the run of *L'opéra de campagne* and attack Dancourt's *L'opéra de village.* Octave, as L'Opéra de Campagne, accuses his rival of having no plot; Mezzetin, as L'Opéra de Village, retorts that "your opera would be better without Jeannot, Prenelle, Thérèse, Pierrot, and your songs from Armide." Arlequin wisely counsels them to stop their criticisms, since "the public might believe both of you," and suggests that they have a drink and plan a collaboration. The joint effort takes place in the final setting of *L'opéra de campagne* and is the celebration of a peasant marriage with Colombine and Octave as the bride and groom. Various peasants present their gifts, then Jupiter (Arlequin) "descends," announced by Mercury (Pasquariel), bringing as his wedding gift a rack of horns. He plans to make off with the bride, and has Mercury put all the peasants to sleep, but the groom's embrace is so tight that the two gods cannot pull the bride from it before Juno (Pierrot) intervenes, descending on a hen turkey. The play ends with a grand song and dance. The mixture of Italian spectacle with French village pastoral exemplifies the difference in the afterpieces performed by the two troupes.

Dufresny collaborated with Regnard on the next Italian afterpiece, a great success entitled *La baguette de Vulcain,* first produced on 10 January 1693. Dufresny also wrote *Les adieux des officiers* (25 April 1693), *Les mal-assortis* (30 May 1693), *Le départ des comédiens* (24 August 1694), *Attendez-moi sous l'orme* (30 January 1695), *Les momies d'Egypt,* with Regnard (19 March 1696), and *Les fées, ou les contes de ma mère l'oye,* with Louis Biancolelli (2 March 1697). Other afterpieces were written by Regnard (*La naissance d'Amadis,* 10 February 1694), Louis Biancolelli (*La fontaine de sapience,* 8 July 1694, and *Le tombeau de Maistre André,* 29 January 1695), and possibly Gherardi himself (*Le retour de la foire de Bezons,* 1 October 1695). Although they are all short and all employ music, they also vary considerably.

Some of the afterpieces feature machine spectacle. *La baguette de Vulcain* opens with a "dark grotto defended by a giant of enormous size." Arlequin as Roger battles the giant and cuts off its head and legs, which rejoin themselves to the body. The giant disappears, Roger touches the cavern with his magic wand, and the stage changes into an "agreeable garden with a quantity of enchanted figures, in the midst of which sleeps Bradamante on a bed of flowers." In *Attendez-moi sous l'orme* a tree opens and closes. In *Les momies d'Egypt* the stage changes to "a ruin, among which can be seen the pyramids of Egypt, with several tombs." One tomb opens, revealing Marc Antony and Cleopatra with a sword and a serpent. The scene changes again into a garden, Marc Antony's tomb into a table, and the mummies enter to serve the meal. *Le naissance d'Amadis* features a flaming funeral pyre, and *La fontaine de sapience* "a very agreeable fountain." The last play introduced by the troupe, *Les fées,* opens with a flying chariot and includes a cavern, ogres, a Great Ogre who is changed into stone, a magnificent palace, and a whole series of transformations.

Many of the afterpieces are based on classical legends, romances, or other exotic materials, often mixed with satire of Parisian manners and even with references to happenings of the day. *La baguette de Vulcain,* for instance, is certainly derived from *Orlando furioso,* but the *baguette* itself and its magic properties owe something to a wonderful divining rod, the *baguette de Lyon,* which filled the columns of the *Mercure galant* for several months before the opening of the play.[35] Although the Lyonnaise *baguette* was known for its ability to track murderers, Roger's *baguette* is best at finding cuckolds. Lancaster denies the connection of the play to the current cause célèbre, but the frontispiece clearly shows the *baguette* in the bent shape of a divining rod. *Les momies d'Egypt,* added to the repertory in March 1696 to ensure a longer run for the great success of the decade, *La foire Saint-Germain,* like the mainpiece it joined, plays off the baroque fondness for raree-shows. The *Mercure galant* of January 1692 reports an exhibition on the rue des Vieilles-Étuves, a mummy newly arrived from Egypt which "conserves all his flesh and his teeth which are very white." In the play the mummies of Marc Antony and Cleopatra wear costumes decorated with strips of cloth covered in hieroglyphics. Regnard's *La naissance d'Amadis* lacks magic and satire, but is, like *La baguette,* based on a popular romance. It employs some parody of the opera *Amadis,* but its principal appeal is its mock-heroic tone. Dufresny's *Les mal-assortis,* the only play of the Gherardi collection in two acts, appears to be based in part on *Don Quixote,* the episode on the Island of Barataria, although it does not follow its source in satirizing the romance genre.[36]

Dufresny's *Attendez-moi sous l'orme* is built on the conceit of an elm that opens to serve as a test of feminine virtue, releasing the innocent and smothering the guilty. This legend, like that of the Mouth of Truth featured in Regnard and Dufresny's *La foire Saint-Germain,* is romanesque, one of many brought to life in the Renaissance by Ariosto, Durfey, and others. Like the divining rod in *La baguette,* the magic tree or mouth provides the foundation for a satirical picture of the war between the sexes, a war in which, however, "the romanesque is devoured by the satire."[37]

Les fées was the product of a different kind of literary inspiration, the publication of Charles Perrault's *Contes de ma mère l'oye,* and by the fad for fairy tales that swept Paris late in the seventeenth century. It is by far the most spectacular of the afterpieces, the most connected to the marvelous. Whether it might have started a new trend will never be known, however, since the troupe was dismissed in early May, two months after the play's debut.

Although several of the afterpieces have classical characters or references, only Dufresny's *Les adieux des officiers* is entirely peopled by Olympians. The play is, however, not based on classical sources but is an allegory for the annual departure of the officers from Paris for the summer campaign during the war that stretched throughout most of the decade. A more realistic play by Dufresny, *Le départ des comédiens,* casts the actors as themselves, is set on an empty stage, and underscores the "desolation" of summer Paris with the officers away. It also serves to focus attention on changes in the troupe, and introduces Marc' Antonio Romagnesi as the Docteur, his son Charles-Virgile as Léandre, Giuseppe Tortoriti as Scaramouche, and Gherardi's French wife as Babet La Chanteuse.[38]

Le tombeau de Maistre André, one of several plays written alone or in collaboration by Louis Biancolelli, the son of Domenico Biancolelli, is another afterpiece designed to extend the run of a popular mainpiece, in this case Biancolelli's *La fausse coquette,* which opened just before Christmas in 1694. *Maistre André,* which made its debut on 29 January 1695, continues a mourning scene in *La fausse coquette* that must have been exceptionally popular. The scene is somewhat reminiscent of material from the earlier repertory, perhaps not surprising as its author had grown up in the troupe. In it, Pasquariel mourns the death of the only tavern-keeper in Paris who gives him credit, joined by Mezzetin and Arlequin. It ends with the three in black cloaks and crepe-covered hats, singing a dirge for Maistre André and their lost credit. The afterpiece, which extends the scene, is pure nonsense, with the zanni quarreling over a bottle. Scaramouche plans to marry Maistre André's widow and have Arlequin marry his daughter, Colombine. After the reading of the will, the tomb is revealed, but the mourning comes to an end when Maistre André wakes and sits up, singing: "Let's drink! Let's drink! Let's drink!" Biancolelli also wrote *La fontaine de sapience,* one scene of which serves as a critique of his full-length play *Arlequin défenseur du beau sexe. La fontaine* has no consistency. In the first three scenes, the women complain about men; in the fourth Arlequin as the pedant Crassotius approves of what Colombine has to say against women in *Le défenseur du beau sexe* and touts his own plays and operas. The characters then travel to the Isle of Repose and its wonderful fountain, the water of which enables anyone who drinks it to see things as they really are.

One last afterpiece, *Le retour de la foire de Bezons,* Gherardi assigns to himself. With typical modesty, he claims that it was the work of an evening, suggested by Dancourt's very popular *La foire de Bezons.* The play is longer than most of the others and more dependent on a love intrigue. It ends with the brief divertissement of "a quantity of masques returning from the fair on foot, on horseback, in carts, and on asses." The frontispiece suggests that most of the livestock were painted on the backscene.

Many of the mainpieces produced by the Italians during their last five seasons also feature music and spectacle. Some also tend toward an elaboration of intrigue and a reduction in satire. Plays with titles like *Le bel-esprit* (Monsieur L.A.P., 13 March 1694) or *La fausse coquette* (Louis Biancolelli, 18 December 1694) are actually comedies of intrigue elaborated with music, burlesques, and special effects. Two plays by Louis Biancolelli, however, *Arlequin défenseur du beau sexe* (28 May 1694) and *La thèse des dames* (7 May 1695) focus on satire rather than on plot. The first of these was inspired by Boileau's tenth satire, *Les femmes.* The play both refers to Boileau's work and enacts his complaints. It ends with a debate between Colombine, who attacks women, and Arlequin, who defends them. Mezzetin, the troupe's chief musician, is not employed in the play, which includes only one very brief song and no spectacle. Acts 1 and 2 do end with improvised scenes featuring elaborate lazzi, typical of Louis Biancolleli, who liked to introduce traditional commedia dell'arte routines as ornaments in his comédies-italiennes.

La thèse des dames is a companion piece to its predecessor and reprises the debate between Arlequin and Colombine, this time based on the question of whether women should be more faithful than men. A thin conventional plot is unable to hold the play together; most of the scenes are detached and feature such events as the zanni getting ready to depart for the front and Colombine as a demimondaine flirting with a teenaged Léandre in the Tuileries. The play features a song or two and several improvised scenes with lazzi, including a famous routine performed by Biancolelli's father in which Arlequin prepares for a debate by writing down his speech, tearing it to bits, boiling the bits in a pot, and drinking the broth. When it tastes too insipid, he seasons it with a sentence from Aristotle.[39]

The scene in the Tuileries in *La thèse des dames* introduces a series of plays that are marked by their use of fashionable resorts as settings for social satire, music, and spectacle. The first of these, *Les promenades de Paris* (Mongin, 6 June 1695) which opened a month after *La thèse des dames,* extended the earlier play's use of the Tuileries gardens, and added a scene in the more risqué Bois de Boulougne. The setting enhances the satire of the bourgeois Calmar (Cinthio) who is in love with Elise (Angélique). The plot is centered on Elise and her three lovers and their servants, each of whom tries to seek advantage for his master. The play appeals through its settings, songs, and satires in verse—love letters read by Mezzetin as a flower seller.

The following summer the Italians produced Boisfran's *Les bains de la porte S. Bernard* (12 July 1696) which, according to Lancaster, employs the full resources of the Comédie-Italienne with the exception of parody.[40] The Porte St.-Bernard, now an outdoor sculpture garden on the left bank of the Seine near the Jardin des Plantes, was—in the seventeenth century—the site of bathing machines and a popular summer resort. The plot is much as usual, but the play adds to the traditional intrigue and satire a very odd lot of mythological and burlesque spectacle, the sorts of thing usually found at the Comédie-Italienne on an enchanted island, not in Paris. Arlequin, for instance, emerges from a book in the Docteur's study as a "familiar spirit," changes the furniture into goblins, and conjures up a singing Salamander. Near the end of the act 2 he and Octave appear magically inside a globe, while the act finale reveals the Chanteuse on a Chinese throne inside a pagoda; as she sings an Italian ritournelle, two "little pagodas" play flutes. After this international mélange, the characters move on to the banks of the Seine where there are to be seen "several covered boats, tents for bathing, and a long string of carriages along the banks." Arlequin and Angélique step into a boat and are rowed away by a singing boatman. For the finale, Arlequin, now a triton, and Angélique enter "on the water in a chariot made of a shell," followed by nymphs and tritons, all of whom participate in a long mythological burlesque.

Promenades in public gardens and romps in bathing machines on the Seine were overshadowed by *La foire Saint-Germain,* which opened the day after Christmas 1695. This frolic by Regnard and Dufresny was probably the greatest success of the decade. The French had an imitation on the boards within three weeks, but the Italians rallied, first with an added scene, "La scène des carosses," and then with the afterpiece, *Les momies d'Egypt.* The play's plot is distinguished by some unusual events. The amoureuse Angélique runs away from her guardian, the Docteur, and is hidden in a booth at the fair by Colombine, a lemonade seller. The Docteur, searching for her, is advised to consult the Mouth of Truth, which will tell him if his destiny is to be cuckolded. When Arlequin moves the hat from the head of the Mouth to the head of the Docteur, it changes into a crescent, giving the old man his answer. When he visits the Zodiac, he sees Angélique and Octave, her lover, posed as the Gemini, and when he visits the harem of the Emperor of Cape Verde, he is chased by a cannibal. Angélique agrees to marry the cannibal, who is of course Octave, in order to save the Docteur. To this pleasant intrigue are added a number of scenes that show the life of the fair. A girl abandons the Mouth of Truth when she hears that it will bite her hand off if she is not viruous; Arlequin cheats Nigaudinet, a Norman, out of all his money at dice; brief parodies of opera and tragedy are played at a fair theatre. The play has five settings and the fair theatre, three more. Music is used throughout.

The added scene, the "Scène des carosses," was another example of the Italians taking advantage of the moment. According to Gherardi, "What gave rise to this scene was that two women, each in her carriage, met in a little Paris street too narrow for two carriages at once. Since neither would retreat, they continued to block the street until a commissaire arrived and made them back up at the same time, each in her own direction."[41] This scene was immortalized by Gillot and shows us Arlequin and Scaramouche (not Mezzetin, as indicated in the text) in their *petites vinaigrettes,* with two angry chairmen and the commissaire.[42] The comedy of the scene is heightened by business that refers once again to a traditional lazzi of the commedia dell'arte. Arlequin reveals that his *vinaigrette* is equipped with a stove and provisioned for three days. He extracts from "a larder ... plates, a lettuce, a chicken, bottles of oil and vinegar, forks, knives, napkins, etc. He eats and drinks, lifting his glass to the Lady opposite and to the parterre."

An earlier piece by Regnard and Dufresny was apparently almost as popular but lacks the consistent style and coherent structure of their later play. Entitled *Les chinois,* it opened on 13 December 1692 and probably ran until after 10 January 1693, when *La baguette de Vulcain* was added to it as an afterpiece. The most interesting parts of *Les chinois* are the prologue, in which the Olympians discuss impropriety at the Comédie-Italienne, and the last act, when the Parterre judges a debate between Arlequin as a French actor and Colombine representing the Italians. The play between has a plot line that makes some connection with the prologue and last act. Isabelle is in love with an Italian actor whose valet, Arlequin, appears as various bizarre suitors whom her father will naturally reject. While the play ends with the debate, an elaborate musical entry ends act 2.

A similar piece is *Les originaux* (Monsieur D.L.M., 13 August 1693) which also begins with a prologue in which an anxious author harries the actors, and the muse Thalia, descending in a machine, tells them not to be afraid of the audience. The play concerns the usual old father who introduces a number of unsuitable suitors to his daughter, in this case a Gascon, a musician, and a physician. The musician, of course, is responsible for some music. Octave is introduced into Colombine's room in a bookcase that changes into a village cabaret, from which sallies forth a wedding party to end act 2 with a little interlude. Act 3 resolves the plot and concludes with a masque. The only remotely original thing about *Les originaux* is that the text includes notes for twelve improvised scenes, more than are included in most of the plays after 1691.

Les souhaits (Deslome de Montchesnay, 30 December 1693), like the two plays just discussed, begins with the Olympians, in this case Jupiter and Momus, who arrive on earth in answer to mankind's prayers. Arlequin is Jupiter; Colombine, Momus. The scenes that follow are vaguely related to this conceit, although the various roles played by the two masques, combined with an absence of synopses of the improvised scenes, make it hard to perceive any continuity. Arlequin as himself courts Colombine as herself and is spurned, but then Colombine as Momus offers to grant Arlequin a wish. Later in the play Mezzetin as Mercury leads Juno, Minerva, and Venus to Arlequin for the Judgment of Paris. And so forth. The major spectacle is the Temple of Wishes, where Arlequin chooses between "bravery, good health, wit, good luck, favor with women, merit, wealth, good living, and other similar desirable things." When Arlequin chooses wealth, he falls through the earth. The text calls for little music, but a long scene on Parnassus, where Apollo has slept for three months after listening to a long poem, probably included more music than is actually indicated.

On 28 November 1693 the Italians introduced another play with classical characters entitled *Les avantures des champs elisées* (by Monsieur L.C.D.V., another playwright who has never been identified). The play is full of music and spectacle. It calls for thirty-seven characters, with no indication of who played most of them, along with a number of supernumeraries and a chorus. The conceit that more or less unifies this collection of detached scenes is that Pluto has fallen in love with the shade of Lucinde and has, in honor of this, allowed the denizens of the underworld to resume for three days their human dress and human passions. Proserpine and Agenor, Lucinde's lover, persuade Pluto to allow Lucinde and Agenor to return to earth. The rest of the play consists of a rather distasteful zanni plot in which Arlequin has raped Mezzetin's sister, several fantasy scenes, and a series of satirical vignettes that stress the futility of human choices.

Les avantures des champs elisées begins with a song and dance; act 2 also begins with a song, and all three acts end with elaborate musical confections. Act 1 also contains a specialty song for Arlequin, who had begun to rival Mezzetin as a featured singer, and act 2 a similarly placed specialty for "Maturine." Most of the play takes place in a single setting, the Elysian Fields, which in the frontispiece resemble a French allée. The scene changes for the finales of acts 1 and 2, to the Temple of Hymen (practically a standard decor for the Italiens), and to a "superb mausoleum," further changed by Proserpine into a "cave" where a drunken sacrifice is performed. Act 3 features a fantasy-farce sequence wherein Arlequin and the Docteur, laden with nets, cages, and bird traps, search for Cerberus in order to catch him and show him at the fair. Of course, Cerberus catches them and Charon changes them into a bird of prey and a goat.

Le bel-esprit (Monsieur L.A.P., 13 March 1694) continues the use of classical motifs, although to a much lesser extent. Cinthio as Cleanthus, a bourgeois wit, has promised to give his daughter Angélique to Octave, provided the oracle of Apollo reveals the secret of Octave's birth. Most of the play, however, is a conventional intrigue of a father who selects unsuitable prospective husbands for his daughter, with travesties by the zanni pretending to be the suitors. Spectacle is reserved for the divertissement, a burlesque investiture of Cinthio as a *bel esprit*. Although the scene does not change, Cinthio is mounted on "Pegasus," a sort of carousel horse filled with fireworks that "burns and turns round" at the end of the play.

La fausse coquette (Louis Biancolelli, 18 December 1694) was a Christmas spectacle play. It, too, combines a soupçon of the classical with the quotidian, flavored with the supernatural, in spite of a title that suggests that it is a comedy of manners. A more or less orthodox plot is overwhelmed by detached comic scenes and ornaments.

Biancolelli uses one improvised scene and some Italian dialogue. Pasquariel does the famous acrobatic lazzi of somersaulting with a full glass of wine without spilling a drop. The play also contains an echo scene and the zanni routine of the death of Maistre André, which was popular enough to be extended into an afterpiece. Spectacle and music are confined to a divertissement featuring the Pythia at the end of act 2, and an elaborate denouement at the end of the play. The former features a wood with a large rock that opens and closes, and an elevator trap. The denouement begins in the garden of the Polish prince who is in love with Colombine, where Arlequin defends himself against the Prince's scimitar with his magic wand. The wand also moves the mountain in the background forward, then changes it into a magnificent palace, at the window of which the prince sees his beloved with her elderly husband. Another tap of the wand changes the palace into a garden with arbors and fountains where Bacchus and his satyrs end the play with a song and dance.

Biancolelli's other Christmas spectacular, *Arlequin misantrope* (22 December 1696) is based upon Lucian and uses the retirement of the melancholy hero to the woods as an occasion for visits by various persons seeking advice. The result is like a combination of *Les souhaits* and *Les avantures des champs elisées,* with ambitions and dreams exploded by the satire of the misanthropic Arlequin. Arlequin never appears in travesty, but only as himself, a self that has nothing in common with the traditional Second Zanni. The satire marshals most of the targets commonly struck by the Comédie-Italienne; frivolous aristocrats, ambitious bourgeois, bumptious peasants, magistrates, *petits marquis,* braggart soldiers, coquettes and abbés, and singing and dancing masters are, in turn, held up to ridicule.

The play begins with a metatheatrical prologue in which Arlequin refuses to play a misanthrope "because a misanthrope is an intelligent man . . . and the whole world knows that I am only a fool." The discussion that follows between Arlequin and Colombine underscores the changes Gherardi and the playwrights had wrought in the persona of Arlequin, especially in the last years of the troupe's establishment. Although Arlequin defends the continuity of the masque, his argument actually reminds us of how much it had changed.

COLOMBINE   You say you are a fool?

ARLEQUIN   *Concedo majorem.*

COLOMBINE   But aren't there several pieces where you've played an
             intelligent man . . .

ARLEQUIN   *Nego consequentiam, & retorqueo argumentum.* You are a
             slut; there are pieces where you play the central female
             character; *ergo* you are not a slut. What beautiful rea-
             soning.

COLOMBINE   But weren't you the Apothecary in the *Emperor of the
             Moon?*

ARLEQUIN   Oh, it takes a very deep intelligence to put an enema
             in place.

COLOMBINE   Haven't you played the Advocate, the Procureur, the
             Baron, the Marquis?

ARLEQUIN   And among advocates, procureurs, barons and mar-

quises, are there no fools? Look, my dear Colombine,
let's not delude ourselves. Leaf through the Arliquin-
esque annals, reexamine all the actions and gestures of
all the Arlequins in the world, I defy you to find a Misanthrope. We are good little fellows, we do our som-
mersaults gracefully, we sigh tenderly over a pretty
little kitchen wench like you, we speak eloquently the
panegyric for a good soup and deplore energetically
the high price of wine and cheese from Milan. But
don't ask more of us.[43]

Spectacle includes the animals to which Arlequin speaks in his opening
monologue in the woods, an illuminated cabinet with "richly dressed
figures" that sing and dance, a magnificent palace built by dancing masons and destroyed in an instant, pictures that come to life, and a finale
in which the scene changes to a "very beautiful grove." Music is introduced in several places. Although there is one improvised scene in Italian,
a kind of tailisman, it does not include lazzi.

The last French mainpiece introduced before the Italians were dismissed was *Pasquin et Marforio, médecins des moeurs,* by Dufresny and Louis
Biancolelli, which opened on 3 February 1697. The title refers to two
ancient Roman statues to which satirical writings were affixed. The satires, known as pasquinades, were popular in France late in the seventeenth century and are featured in the play. Pasquin and Marforio, played
by Arlequin and Mezzetin, are reunited in Paris after a shipwreck and
agree to assist the amoureux with their love affairs. The play, like its
predecessors, is a mixture of more or less conventional intrigue with
music, spectacle, and classical and allegorical characters. It also includes
several improvised scenes, one with traditional lazzi for the zanni. Act 2
ends with the stage changing to a river bank where Truth, in a "magnificent gondola, advances to the edge of the stage to the sound of music."
After a scene between Pasquin and Truth, "the gondola changes into a
frightning den out of which comes Slander," who sings a trio with Pasquin and Marforio. The play has more music than any of the other mainpieces, partly because Julie, the second of the Docteur's daughters, never
speaks but only sings. This conceit may have arisen from necessity and
not from the imaginations of the writers, since Angélique and Colombine
were otherwise employed in the play, and Julie was probably played by
Babet La Chanteuse.[44] However, Mezzetin also sings much more than is
usual in a play of this genre.

Pasquin et Marforio is, in many ways, a kind of summary of the
changes that took place in the Italian repertory after 1691. One reminder

of its Italian roots comes in act 3 when Colombine goes mad, dresses as a physician, and delivers a harangue that her father could have performed thirty years earlier. And perhaps did.

> Listen to what Hippocrates and Galen have to say about [madness]. First, Hippocrates in his Treatise on madness, doesn't say anything about it at all. . . . As for Galen, I have never read him, but I myself sustain that madness can proceed from two opposing causes. Evaporation and obstruction. Evaporation, when the bottle is uncorked, the wine evaporates. Obstruction, when the flue of the fireplace is blocked. White madness, black madness, high madness, low madness, gay madness, melancholy madness, madness of the brain and madness of the liver.[45]

The final repertory of the Comédie-Italienne in Paris is marked by variety as the troupe—like all popular theatres—shifted with the whims of its audience. The major genres performed were the comedy of manners based on French models, the spectacle play, the comedy of intrigue—often spiced with classical and romanesque elements, music, and spectacle—and the afterpiece, the ancestor of the French opéra comique. Not every play fits happily into one of these categories, but given the necessities of generalization, a simple taxonomy is preferable to complex one.

The comedies of manners, which flourished between the end of Dominique's tenure and the reconstruction of the stage, mix conventional Italian plotting with satires based on French stereotypes. They do include an interesting development, one that reflects the growing importance of the bourgeois audience, and that is the introduction of a French bourgeois vieillard played by Marc' Antonio Romagnesi. Known variously as Friquet, Trafiquet, Sotinet, Grognard, Bassemine, Tortillon, Roquillard, and the generic Géronte, the character begins as a figure of fun, the typical commedia father in French bourgeois guise. In the later plays, however, and especially in Lenoble's *Les deux Arlequins* and Palaprat's *La fille de bon sens,* Géronte ends up happily married to the amoureuse in total violation of the norms of the commedia dell'arte. In *La fille de bon sens,* Colombine explains her mistress's preference: "You don't know Angélique very well. She is not one of those giddy bourgeois girls who imagine themselves to be ladies of quality, because they wear the same clothes, and who want no lovers but the fops and the marquises. Today their mistress, tomorrow their wife, the next day their servant. She knows herself, she knows you, she knows that you love her, she loves you. You have property, so does she. Your conditions are equal, and that's what leads to happy marriages."[46] This shift from satire of the bourgeoisie to praise of its values confirms that by 1692 the audience for the Italians was drawn in large measure from the Parisian middle class. The decline of this kind of play at about the same time further suggests that the Parisian middle classes preferred a livelier and more theatrical kind of entertainment.

Both the comedies of intrigue and the afterpieces relied on spectacle and music. The importance of spectacle has been discussed throughout, and its use traced in the repertory, but little has been said about music. Music was always a part of the commedia dell'arte in France; the zanni with his guitar is a commonplace of the iconography, and the use of a French drinking song signaled the important changes in the repertory that began in 1668. But not until after 1681 do we have any concrete information about music at the Comédie-Italienne. Thanks to Gherardi, who includes lyrics and some musical accompaniments, we can draw some conclusions about its use.[47]

The songs the Italians employed in the 1680s and 1690s were both composed for the purpose and set to "vaudevilles," simple popular tunes known to both actors and audience members. Some songs were incidental, introduced into the body of the play; others formed part of the divertissement. Donald J. Grout, who has studied the music of the Gherardi repertory, tells us that thirty-seven of the fifty-five texts call for music. Some 340 vocal and instrumental pieces are indicated, and 143 are actually appended to the plays. Others can be found in *Recueils des airs,* pamphlets printed to be sold at the theatre during a play's performance, or in various *chansonniers* of the period.

Grout, using only the music appended to the Gherardi texts, identifies ten Italian arias and one duet of "uniformly high musical quality," at least thirty-five vaudevilles, and the rest songs newly composed in the French style for the troupe. These songs can be divided into *récits,* compositions for singers in the style of Lulli, and *chansons,* compositions set to the rhythms of minuets, gavottes, and sarabandes for dancing as well as singing.

Grout argues that the Italians used vaudevilles to enhance their meager musical resources because Lulli's Opéra privilege restricted the Parisian theatres to six musicians and two singers. Vaudevilles, being simple, could be performed by the regular members of the troupe. But Grout overlooks the musical sophistication of many of the Italian performers, especially Catherine Biancolelli and Angelo Costantini, who regularly performed opera parody and burlesqued the stars of the Opéra itself. Vaudevilles save time and money, since no composer is needed, and they bring to the play a history which can be used ironically and which can add to a musical parody. In *L'opéra de campagne,* for instance, a lyric from the opera *Armide* is set to a popular tune. Arlequin sings the lyrical line "Tout m'invite au repos ... / Ce gazon, cet ombrage frais / et ce feuillage épais" to the tune of "De mon pot je vous en répons, mais de Margot non non." The *timbre,* or catchphrase, that identifies the vaudeville becomes part of the parody, along with the contrast between the operatic melody and the popular jingle. Even Regnard and Dufresny, who composed their own music, used vaudevilles as well, often for effect. The divertissement of Dufresny's *Le départ des comédiens* begins with Arlequin, quickly transformed into Bellerophon, singing "Princess, everything conspires to consumate my passion [tout conspire à couronner ma flamme]" to the tune of *Sur le pont d'Avignon.* Vaudevilles also enable an audience to sing along if the performer wants them to, although there is no actual evidence of this happening at the Comédie-Italienne.

Various composers worked for the Italians, creating the settings for the songs that were not vaudevilles. Gherardi mentions only three composers: "Monsieur Philbert," "M. de Masse," and the Italian Lorenzani. Paolo Lorenzani, whose name is attached to one aria from *Arlequin empereur dans la lune* (1684), was a well-known Roman organist and composer who lived in Paris from c. 1678 to 1695 and was a serious rival to Lulli. "Monsieur Philbert" was, according to Grout, Philbert Gassaud, known as Du Croisy, a French actor who joined Molière in 1653 and retired from the Comédie-Française in 1689. The song was not composed for the Italians, however, since Gherardi writes at the end of *La critique de la cause des femmes* that "Mezzetin sings an Italian air within which is imitated the song of the nightingale. This air is well known in Paris, and is said to be the invention of Monsieur Philbert."[48] As for "M. de Masse," Grout can offer only the most tentative identification. Other composers not mentioned by Gherardi include Regnard and Dufresny, the latter of whom claimed to have invented more than one-hundred songs for his plays at both the Comédie-Italienne and the Comédie-Française, in spite of the fact that he could not read or write music. Apparently, he would sing his tune to some more musically adept person, who would write it out for him.[49] A better-known composer who worked for the Italians was Jean-Claude Gillier. From a complaint filed by the troupe against peddlers who were selling illegal copies of his music outside the theatre, we know that Gillier, who also wrote for the French troupe and the fairs, provided the music for *La foire Saint-Germain;*[50] Grout believes he may have been the Italian troupe's principal French composer.

Grout remarks on the generally high quality of the music, which he calls charming and full of a "surprising rhythmic inventiveness."[51] The fact that the troupe went to the trouble of having the airs engraved and bound into a pamphlet for sale in the theatre suggests how important the music was to the success of a play in the 1690s. Moreau has discovered a number of these pamphlets issued to accompany productions of plays by Dufresny.[52]

Music was important in still another way, since play structures had to be devised to make the use of music other than in the divertissements somewhat verisimilar. The Italians still used the traditional device of lovers and valets disguised as music and dancing masters, but the most common occasion for music was opera parody, usually with burlesque lyrics sung to the original music, although the reverse happens as well. Grout counts thirty-one musical numbers that parody operas, all but one by Lulli, who was conveniently dead after 1687. In the early years of the period encompassed by the Gherardi collection, opera parody was often introduced clumsily into the plays, but in the 1690s, with the popularity of the "country" and "village" operas, along with the emphasis on classical and romanesque romance, a parody could be slipped in with no noticeable hitch.

Without the Opéra to satirize, the Italians would have had far fewer opportunities for both music and spectacle, but they took advantage of many other ways in which music was part of everyday life. In *La fille de bon sens* Mezzetin enters disguised as a song peddler from the Pont Neuf and sets up his little show: a stool and a painting representing a siege. He climbs on the stool and sings, accompanied by a blind fiddler, "a new song on the taking of Namur" while pointing out the features of the siege on the painting. This delightful vignette of Paris street life is followed shortly by another scene in which Angélique, as a well-brought-up young lady, appears with her books, her basket of wools for needlepoint, her books of music, her harpsichord, and her guitar. She sings and accompanies herself on the harpsichord. In *La fausse coquette* Mezzetin appears as two street vendors, an eau-de-vie seller and a wafer seller, singing their cries. *La thèse des dames* opens with an attempted serenade and includes a scene in a cabaret, another place where music could be expected, while in *Les promenades de Paris* Arlequin encounters a *chansonnier* who offers songs passionate, songs tender, songs bacchic, heroic, tragic, energetic, melancholic, or chromatic. Often, of course, characters sing and dance for no reason at all.

Although music is important throughout the Gherardi repertory and especially in the 1690s, Attinger's choice of the term *revue-operette* to describe the afterpieces and some mainpieces is misleading.[53] Music remains an ornament, albeit an important one, in every piece except perhaps *Les fées,* and even there, although there is music in nearly every scene, prose dialogue far outweighs it.

Other kinds of ornament are also prominent in the repertory of 1688–97. Half of the plays include a scene or scenes in verse. In the earlier plays in the Gherardi collection, verse normally signals parody, but in these plays it appears in a variety of different kinds of scenes. Some are parodic; many are burlesques, usually of French tragic style; others include travesty scenes, mythical and legendary scenes, satirical scenes, and scenes of the exotic and the marvelous. Occasionally, one character in a scene speaks verse, the others prose. In *La fontaine de sapience* the characters burst into verse after drinking the magic water that allows them to see things as they really are. The text does not always make it possible to tell if a scene in verse is spoken or sung, especially in finales and divertissements, but clearly verse was itself an expected and appreciated feature not only of the mainpieces but the afterpieces as well.

Some popular literary embellishments of the decade are reminiscent of the verbal ornaments of the earlier repertory; these include a "Defi," or challenge, in *Arlequin Phaeton,* harangues in *Les champs elisées* and *Les souhaits,* a burlesque will in *Maistre André,* and several burlesque marriage contracts. Much more clearly related to the times, however, are a number of satires in verse or prose, the first of which is a "Protocole d'un damoiseau ou le portrait fidele des passe-volans de la galanterie," a verse satire on the *petits abbés* read by Colombine. Satires became even more popular later in the decade. Among the plays that include one or more are *La fille de bon sens, Le bel-esprit, Arlequin défenseur du beau sexe,* and *La foire Saint-Germain.* Other plays introduce pasquinades, billets-doux, fables, and epigrams. Typically, the verse or prose passage is read by a character, sometimes because what it says is relevant to the action, sometimes as a kind of literary interlude.

A final ornamental element has been mentioned above. Especially but not exclusively in the plays of Louis Biancolelli, traditional commedia routines suddenly reappear, relics of the time of Dominique and Scaramouche. In a way, the troupe had come full circle. The ornaments introduced after 1668—music, spectacle, satire, and scenes in French—had become central to the appeal of the Comédie-Italienne while the former heart of their theatrical existence, the joyous and extravagent play of the zanni, was now merely ornamental.

This happened because the composition of the troupe changed at the same time it began to get more and more scenes and finally whole plays from French writers. Domenico Biancolelli, whose masque had been established for over twenty-five years, could imprint the stamp of that masque on a play written for him, as he did with Regnard's *Le divorce*. But Evaristo Gherardi, an untrained recruit, could not and perhaps did not want to. Although the troupe's last performance at court, 29 December 1696, was *Arlequin toujours Arlequin,* in fact Gherardi's Arlequin had no center, no set of defining characteristics. In spite of his patches and black mask, a mask he even tried on two occasions to discard, he was merely an actor—one hopes a good one—who played roles written for him by others. The pro forma First Zanni of the troupe, Angelo Costantini, played without a mask and was most useful as a musician. Only rarely in the later written repertory do the zanni engage in recognizeable zanni play, and when they do, they are interchangeable. Mezzetin, Pierrot, and Pasquariel are all protean, all without defining characteristics, except during the occasional scene from the old repertory.

Colombine, who had begun as a strong, consistent character, a clever, cynical and manipulative Parisian suivante, found herself at the mercy of scripts, events, and her own popularity. After her sister Françoise became inactive in 1693, Catherine Biancolelli played a range of characters from servant to sorceress, from peasant to princess. Marc' Antonio Romagnesi's bourgeois vieillard, which began as a French tipi fissi, ended as a plot convenience. None of the young men who played amoureux were powerful enough presences or good enough actors to elicit important roles from the writers; the male lovers of the 1690s are, in general, characterless.

The shortage of charismatic performers must have created the void the writers rushed to fill. While it is probable that the bourgeois audience no longer wanted to see an Italian repertory, it is equally probable that many of the younger actors could not play one with the energy and skill to which the audience was accustomed.[54] The commedia dell'arte, always a theatre of the actor, became for the last few years of its long stay in Paris a theatre of the playwright: still lively, but lacking its own inner life; still theatrical, but enervated by its music, its machines, its manic adaptivity to the demands of its audience.

All popular theatre has, as its principal goals, the entertainment of the audience and the support of the enterprise. The second can defeat the first, especially if choices are made only to solicit the greatest possible public favor. The commedia dell'arte, because it was in so many ways a fixed form with fewer choices available, could—for a long time—avoid the trap. The Paris troupe, although it did change its repertory, changed it slowly, retained many of its traditional characterisitics, and like all great popular theatres, relied on the power of extraordinary performers to attract an audience. Without those performers, the troupe searched for other lures, still more enticements, and ended more popular then ever, but as something other than itself.

Arlequin toujours Arlequin. No matter what the travesty, the black mask under the countess's fontange, the diamond patches peeping from the commissaire's robe, revealed the presence of the fourbe balourd of Bergamo. But then the masque slipped away, leaving only the travesty. The Comédie-Italienne, arrayed in its borrowed French finery, finished its glorious career with a spoof of Mother Goose.

The last words of Arlequin in the seventeenth century, sung not spoken, on the Paris stage were:

> Pour vous satisfaire,
> De toute manière
> Nous nous déguisons,
> En faisant tac, tac, par nos fariboles,
> Nous changeons
> En bon pistoles
> Nos gayes chansons.[55]

> To satisfy you,
> In every way
> we disguise ourselves
> With a tac tac, with our nonsense,
> We change
> Our gay songs
> Into good gold.

❖❖❖❖❖❖❖❖❖❖❖❖❖❖❖❖❖❖❖❖❖

Appendix

Notes

Bibliography

Index

❖❖❖❖❖❖❖❖❖❖❖❖❖❖❖❖❖❖❖❖❖

◇◇◇◇◇◇◇◇◇◇◇◇◇◇◇◇

Appendix

The repertory of the Comédie-Italienne is listed below by date of first known performance. When the date is in doubt, the play is marked by an asterisk and included at the beginning of the first year a performance was possible—an inference usually based on the latest debut year among those actors who played unique characters included in the cast list: Flautin, Isabelle, Colombine, Pantalon, Pasquariel and Mezzetin. Chronological order is assumed for entries derived from Biancolelli's Zibaldone after *Le régal des dames;* undated entries follow in order those for which first performance dates are available.

Each entry includes the play's title in French and, where available, in Italian; the author or person responsible for the scenario if known; the principal source of the text or information about the text; the source of information about the date of performance, if not derived from the principal text; additional texts with any variant titles; additional performances with any variant titles; notes.

I have retained the spelling of the titles from their principal sources, but I have added diacritical markings since many of the titles were originally written or printed in capitals. When variant titles exist in the principal source, I have used the correct or more correct one, thus *Le marchand dupé* from the title page of the volume rather than *Le marchand duppé* from the title page of the play itself.

This Appendix serves as an addendum and correction to the *Repertorio* published by Marcello Spaziani in his *Il* Théâtre Italien *di Gherardi* (Rome: Edizioni dell'Ateneo, 1960). It is another step toward a full, accurate chronology of the first Comédie-Italienne.

Abbreviations

CtAc: "Recettes et dépenses de la maison du roi, argenterie, menus plaisirs, et affaires de la chambre," série O1.2820-2829, Archives Nationales, Paris

Gh1:   Evaristo Gherardi, *Le théâtre italien, ou le recueil de toutes les scènes françoises qui ont esté jouées sur le théâtre italien de l'Hostel de Bourgogne,* one volume, Paris, 1694

Gh1gnv: Evaristo Gherardi, *Le théâtre italien. . . . augmenté de la comédie des Souffleurs,* one volume, Geneva, 1695

Gh2I–VI: Evaristo Gherardi, *Le théâtre Italien de Gherardi, ou le recueil général de toutes les comédies et scènes françoises jouées par les Comédiens Italiens du Roy, pendant tout le temps qu'ils ont été au service,* 6 volumes, Paris, 1700

Gueullette: "Histoire du théâtre italien establi en France depuis l'année 1577 jusqu'en l'année 1750 et les années suivantes," Ms. Rés. 625, Bibliothèque de l'Opéra, Paris

Mayolas: *Lettres en vers et en prose,* Paris, 1668–69 and 1671

M.G.:   *Le mercure galant*

Moland: Louis Moland: *Molière et la comédie italienne,* Paris, 1867

Ms. 9329:   "Sujets de plusieurs comédies italiennes," fonds français Ms. 9329, Bibliothèque Nationale, Paris

MsOp: Thomas-Simon Gueullette, "Traduction du scenario de Joseph Dominique Biancolelli, dit Arlequin," Ms. Rés. 625, Bibliothèque de l'Opéra, Paris

Robinet: *Lettres en vers,* Paris, 1665–78

Suite: *Suite du théâtre italien, ou nouveau recueil de plusieurs comédies françoises, qui ont été jouées sur le théâtre italien de l'Hôtel de Bourgogne,* n.p., 1697

Sup: *Supplément du théâtre italien, ou recueil des scènes françoises qui ont été representées sur le théâtre italien de l'hostel de Bourgogne,* tome 2 [*sic*], Brussels, 1697

Repertory of the Comédie-Italienne, Paris, 1645–1697

1645

14 December

> *La folle supposée (La finta pazza);* text by Giulio Strozzi, music (lost) by Francesco Sacrati; *Explication des décorations . . . et les argumens de la pièce* (Paris, 1645); first performed Venice, 1641, and Florence, 1645

1658

> *La Rosaure impératrice de Constantinople (La Rosaura imperatrice di Constantinopoli); Argument de la grand pièce . . .* (Paris, 1658)
> *Le festin de pierre (Il convitato di pietra);* MsOp; Villiers, preface to *Le festin de pierre, ou le fils criminel* (Paris, 1659); known reprises: 1668, 1669 (Robinet, 11 Feb. 1668, 27 Nov. 1669)

1662

> **La double jalouzie (Le dopie gielosie);* MsOp
> **Les morts vivans (I morti vivi);* MsOp
> **L'hospital des foux, ou le deuil d'Arlequin (L'ospital de pazzi);* MsOp; see June 21 1680 *Le deuil de Scarmouche et d'Arlequin* and 21 June 1682 *Le deuil d'Arlequin*

Le dragon de Moscovie (Il basilisco di Bernagasso); MsOp; Ms. 9329;
    performed at Versailles 5 Jan. 1696 (CtAc)
Les trois volleurs descouverts (Tre ladri scoperti); MsOp
Le triumvirat de l'amitiez (Il triumvirato dell'amicizia); MsOp
Le capricieux (Il lunatico); MsOp; see 23 Feb. 1683 *Le lunatique*
Le coeur me fait mal (Ohime il cuore); MsOp
Le baron allemand (Baron tedesco); MsOp
Les quatre Arlequins (Li quatro Arlechini); MsOp
La hotte (La zerla); MsOp
Le médecin vollant (Medico volante); MsOp
Le portrait amoureux (Ritrato amoroso); MsOp
Les trois faux turcs (Tre finti turchi); MsOp
La pauvreté de Renaut de Montauban (Povertà di Rinaldo); MsOp
L'amour ne veut point de rivaux (Non vol rivali amore); MsOp
Les dédains, ou le dépit amoureux (Li sdegni); MsOp
Les deux Arlequins (Li dui Arlechini); MsOp; no connection with Le-
    noble's *Les deux Arlequins, 1691*
L'innocence persécutée (L'inocente travagliata); MsOp
Les tapis (Li tapeti); MsOp; *Sup.* (under heading "Scènes françoises
    dans *Isabelle médecin*")
Les maisons dévalizées (Le case svaligiate); MsOp
Arlequin cru prince (Arlechino creduto principe); MsOp
La cruauté du Docteur (La barbaria del Dottore); MsOp
Dans le vallet d'opérateur (Nel servitore da palco); MsOp; also known
    as *Les levantins et la chèvre de calicut*
La vieille grotte (Grotta vecchia); MsOp
Les ateliers (Le fabriche); MsOp
La grotte nouvelle (Grotta nuova); MsOp
Arlequin laron, prévost et juge (Arlechino ladro, sbiro, et giudice); MsOp;
    performed at Versailles 28 Feb. 1695 (CtAc)
Le prisonnier vindicatif (Prigionier vindicativo); MsOp
Les engagemens du hazard (L'impegno d'un acaso); MsOp
Le maistre vallet (Servo padrone); MsOp
Ma maîtresse est préférable à tout autre chose (Antes che todo mi damma);
    MsOp

1664

Scaramouche ermite; not extant; preface to *Tartuffe*

1665

November
    La cabaretière; not extant; Mayolas, 15 Nov. 1665

December
  La bonne-femme et le mary méchant; not extant; Mayolas, 20 Dec.
  1665

1666

Il maritaggion d'una statua; not extant; Philip Skippon, *An Account of a
  Journey Through . . . France* (London, 1732).
Quattre Scaramuccie; Skippon; see 11 June 1680 *Les quatre Scara-
  mouches*

1667

29 October
  La fille désobéissante (*La figlia disubidiente*); MsOp; Robinet, 5 Nov.
  1667

1668

2 May
  Le régal des dames (*Il regallo delle damme*); anonymous gentleman;
  MsOp; Robinet, 5 May 1668
  Addition à la comédie d'Arlequin soldat et bagage; MsOp; probably mis-
  titled since the material for the most part amplifies travesty
  routines in *Le régal des dames*

July
  Le théâtre sans comédie et les comédiens juges et parties (*Il teatro senza
  comedie*); Romagnesi; MsOp; Robinet, 11, 14 July 1668

September
  Le remède à tous maux (*Il rimedio a tutti malli*); Romagnesi; MsOp;
  Robinet, 9, 15 Aug. 1668; see Feb. 1669 *La nopce d'Arlequin*

  ———

  Le pont neuf (*Il ponte nuovo*); MsOp

1669

February
  La nopce d'Arlequin; Ms. 9329, *Sup.;* Robinet, 9 Feb. 1669; Ms. 9329
  proves this is the same as Sep. 1668 *Le remède à tous maux;*
  Sup. includes under this title one scene from *Le remède,* one
  unrelated to MsOp or Ms. 9329

March
  Les métamorphoses d'Arlequin (*Metamorphosi d'Arlechino*); Romagnesi;
  MsOp; Robinet, 23 Mar. 1669; *Sup.*

May

>*Le soldat par vengeance, ou Arlequin soldat en Candie* (*Il soldato per vendetta o Arlechino soldato in Candia*); Romagnesi; MsOp; Robinet, 1 June 1669; also known as *La femme guerrière*
>
>*Addition au soldat en Candie* (*Agiunta al soldato in Candia*); MsOp; addendum to the previous entry

July

>*Scaramouche pédant et Arlequin écolier;* not extant; Robinet, 6 July 1669
>
>———
>
>*Ne prêtte ny ta femme ny ton epée à personne* (*Ne la damma, ne la spada non si fida al amico*); MsOp
>
>———
>
>*Le monde renversé, ou Arlequin jouet de la fortune* (*Il mondo a la roversa*); MsOp; Ms. 9329 (*Le monde à la renverse*)

1670

January

>*Le gentilhomme campagnard, ou les débauches d'Arlequin* (*Il gentilhommo campagnard*); Lolli; MsOp; Robinet, 4 Jan. 1670; see 1686 *La débauche de Mezetin*
>
>———
>
>*Le chevallier de l'industrie* (*Il cabalista, o il cavalier del industria*); MsOp

March

>*Arlequin esprit follet* (*Arlechino spirito folletto*); Romagnesi; MsOp; Robinet, 8 Mar. 1670; Ms. 9329
>
>———
>
>*Arlequin poète et petit enfant* (*Arlechino poeta e putino*); MsOp

September

>*La folie d'Eularia* (*La pazzia d'Eularia*); MsOp; Robinet, 6 Sep. 1670
>
>———
>
>*Arlequin soury* (*Arlechino suri*); MsOp
>
>———
>
>*Arlequin médecin d'eau douce* (*Arlechino medico d'acqua dolce*); MsOp
>
>———
>
>*Arlequin vallet enchanté, singe et Margot la pie* (*Arlechino servo incantato &*); MsOp

1671

June

>*Les jugemens du duc d'Ossone* (*I giudici del duca d'Ossuna*); Romagnesi; MsOp; Robinet, 13 June 1671

———

Le mari (*Il marito*); MsOp

———

L'hypocrite (*L'ipocrita*); MsOp

1672

July
> *Le collier de perle;* Girardin; MsOp, Gueullette; Robinet, 30 July, 13
> Aug. 1672.

September
> *Les fripiers;* MsOp; Robinet, 24 Sep. 1672; *Sup.*, Ms. 9329 (*Arlequin*
> *embarrassé parmi les fripiers*)

1673

February
> *La suite du festin de pierre* (*Agiunta al convitato di pietra*); MsOp; Robi-
> net, 4 Feb. 1673; not a reprise but a new play about the bas-
> tard son of Don Juan; MsOp includes it twice, once following
> *Le festin de pierre,* once in chronological order

———

Arlequin roy par hazard (*Arlechino creato re per ventura*); MsOp

1674

*Arlequin et Scaramouche usuriers; Ms. 9329; cast includes Flautin

January
> *Le baron de Foeneste;* MsOp; Robinet, 6 Jan. 1674

May
> *Addition au triomphe de la médecine;* MsOp; Robinet, 12, 19 May 1674;
> although an "addition" by title, the entry is substantial

August
> *Addition au baron de Foeneste;* MsOp; Robinet, 7 Aug. 1674; reprise of
> Jan. 1674

October
> *A fourbe, fourbe et demy;* Romagnesi; MsOp; Robinet, 20 Oct. 1674;
> Ms. 9329; *Sup.* (*Arlequin fourbe fourbe et demy*)

November
> *Arlequin berger de Lemnos;* Romagnesi; MsOp; Robinet, 10, 24 Nov.
> 1674; *Sup.* (*Le berger de Lemnos*)

1676

Le voyage de Scaramouche et d'Arlequin aux Indes (Il viaggio di Scara-muccia e Arlechino alle Indie); MsOp, Gueullette (*Le voyage d'Arlequin et de Scaramouche aux Indes*)

Arlequin cochon par amour (Arlechino porco per amore); MsOp; Ms. 9329

Les trompeurs trompez; Monsieur S.; MsOp; Ms. 9329, *Sup.*

La maladie de Scaramouche (La maladia di Scaramuza); MsOp; possibly the same as 1 May 1682 *La maladie de Spezzafer,* performed at St.-Germain (Moland)

1677

January

Arlequin et Scaramouche juifs errans de Babilonne (Arlechino e Scaramuza hebrei erranti di Babilonia); Monsieur S., MsOp; *M.G.* Jan. 1677; performed at Fontainebleau (*Les juifs de Babylone*) 1 July 1680 (Moland)

July

La propreté, ou Arlequin roy de Tripoli (La proprietà o Arlequin roy de Tripoli); MsOp; *M.G.* July 1677; Ms. 9329, *Sup.* (*La propreté ridicule*); performed at court July 1678 (Moland)

La gageure; MsOp; Ms. 9329 (*La gageure d'Arlequin*)

La dot par la métempsicoze (Dotte per la metempsicose); MsOp

1678

December

La magie naturelle (La maggia naturalle); MsOp; *M.G.* Dec. 1678; Ms. 9329, *Sup.;* performed at court Dec. 1678 (Moland)

Arlequin hotte et masson (Arlequino, hotte et masson); MsOp

1679

June

Arlequin dogue d'Angleterre et médecin du temps; MsOp; *M.G.* June 1679; Ms. 9329, *Sup.;* performed at court 7 Apr. 1682 (Moland); *Le médecin du temps* performed at Fontainebleau 31 Aug. 1679 (*M.G.,* Sep. 1679)

—————

"Scène pour l'avocat juge et partie"; MsOp; a scene belonging to
the following entry

—————

L'auberge d'Arlequin juge partie avocat et temoin (*L'albergo d'Arlechino
giudice, parte, avvocato, e testimonio*); MsOp

—————

"Dambreville"; MsOp; fragment of a harangue, perhaps from a
play designed to compete with *La devineresse* at the Guénégaud in 1679

1680

18 May
 Le combat à cheval; not extant; Moland; performed at Fontainebleau

29 May
 Eularia muette par amour; Moland, performed at Fontainebleau; CtAc
 (*Aularia muette par amour, ou Arlequin médecin ignorant*), performed at Versailles 25 Nov. 1695; see 1686 *Isabelle muette par
 amour*

11 June
 Les quatre Scaramouches; not extant; Moland; performed at Fontainebleau, see 1666, *Quattre Scaramuccie*

21 June
 Le deuil de Scaramouche et d'Arlequin; Moland; performed at Fontainebleau; possibly a reprise of 1662 *L'hospital des foux, ou le deuil
 d'Arlequin*

26 June
 La jalousie de Scaramouche et d'Arlequin; not extant; Moland; performed at Fontainebleau

20 July
 Arlequin soldat déserteur; not extant; Moland; performed at Fontainebleau

December
 Le remède de Anglois, ou Harlequin prince du Quinquina; MsOp; *M.G.*
 Dec. 1680; not Dominique's notes, merely a copy of the no-
 tice in *M.G.*

1681

22 January
 Arlequin mercure galant; Monsieur D***; Gh2I; *M.G.,* Jan. 1681; Gh1

December

> *Arlequin vendangeur; M.G.,* Dec. 1681; Ms. 9329 (*Arlequin et Scara-mouche vendangeurs*); *Sup.* (*Les vendangeurs*); performed at court Dec. 1681 (Moland)

1682

2 April

> *Arlequin valet étourdi;* Moland; performed at St.-Germain; performed at Versailles 26 Nov. 1691 (CtAc); probably the same as 1683 *L'étourdi*

1 May

> *La maladie de Spezzafer;* Moland; performed at Fontainebleau; possibly a reprise of 1676 *La maladie de Scaramouche*

12 May

> *La matrone d'Ephèse, ou Arlequin Grapignan;* Monsieur D***; Gh2I; Gh1

15 June

> *Arlequin tombé dans le puits;* not extant; Moland; performed at St.-Germain

21 June

> *Le deuil d'Arlequin;* Moland; performed at St.-Germain; possibly a reprise of 1662 *L'hospital des foux, ou le deuil d'Arlequin*

24 June

> *Arlequin juif, peintre et tailleur;* not extant; Moland; performed at St.-Germain

30 June

> *Arlequin cabaretier, turc et capitaine espagnol;* not extant; Moland; performed at St.-Germain

4 October

> *Arlequin lingère du palais; Monsieur D***;* Gh2I; *Sup.* under its own title and probably as "scènes françoises d'*Arlequin homme à bonne fortune*"; performed 4 Feb. 1683 at Versailles (CtAc)

1683

*L'étourdi; Ms. 9329; cast includes Isabelle, Colombine
*Les amours du bonhomme Ballouard; Ms. 9329; cast includes Isabelle, Colombine; use of vaudevilles and presence in cast of two "dames ragondes" suggest a later text, perhaps from a fair theatre

Arlequin dupé par sa femme; Ms. 9329; cast includes Isabelle, Colombine

12 January

Les deux semblables; not extant; CtAc; performed at Versailles

21 January

Le mariage d'Arlequin; CtAc; performed at Versailles; probably a version of Feb. 1669 *La nopce d'Arlequin*

16 February

Arlequin plaqué; not extant; CtAc; performed at Versailles

23 February

Le lunatique; CtAc; performed at Versailles; see 1662 *Le capricieux*

11 October

Arlequin Protée; Monsieur D***; Gh2I; Gh1, Sup.

1684

Arlequin mule et médecin ignorant; Ms. 9329; cast includes Pantalon

5 March

Arlequin empereur dans la lune; Monsieur D***; Gh2I; Gh1, Sup.

9 September

Arlequin Jason, ou la toison d'or comique; Monsieur D*** (Anne Mauduit de Fatouville); Gh2I; Gh1

1685

26 February

Arlequin chevalier du soleil; Monsieur D***; Gh2I; Sup., under its own title and as *Isabelle médecin,* Ms. 9329 (*Les marchands de la rue aux Fers et des Bourdonnais*)

26 February

Isabelle médecin; Monsieur D***; Gh2I; Sup. includes title, but scenes are from *Arlequin chevalier du soleil*

8 June

Colombine avocat pour et contre; Monsieur D***; Gh2I; Gh1, Sup.; performed at Versailles, 7 Dec. 1691 (CtAc)

1686

La dame diablesse; Ms. 9329; cast includes Mezzetin.
Octave et Arlequin soldats enrollés par force; Ms. 9329; cast includes

Mezzetin; *Sup.* has first nine scenes in French dialogue (*Arlequin et Octave soldats enrollés par force*)

Isabelle muette par amour; Ms. 9329; cast includes Mezzetin; probably the same as *La muette* performed at Versailles 3 Jan. 1683 (CtAc), and see 29 May 1680 *Eularia muette par amour*

Arlequin embarrassé parmi les fripiers; Ms. 9329; cast includes Mezzetin; MsOp, *Sup.* (*Les fripiers*), and see Sep. 1672

Les médecins raillés; Ms. 9329; *Sup.* (*Les faux médecins raillez*); cast of *Sup.* includes Mezzetin.

La débauche de Mezetin; Sup.; cast includes Mezzetin; possibly a reprise of Jan. 1670 *Le gentilhomme campagnard, ou les débauches d'Arlequin*

Arlequin soldat et bagage, ou hôte et hôtellerie; Sup.; cast includes Mezzetin; hand copied in Gueullette from an edition published in the Hague in 1698 by Jacques Xuaur

1687

19 April

Le banqueroutier; Monsieur D***; Gh2I; Gh1, *Sup.*

26 December

La cause des femmes; Delosme de Montchenay; Gh2II; Gh1

1688

14 February

La critique de la cause des femmes; Delosme de Montchenay; Gh2II

17 March

Le divorce; Regnard; Gh2II; Gh1, *Sup.* includes one scene under its own title, one under *Les deux zany,* one under *Le banqueroutier*

1 September

Le marchand dupé; Monsieur D***; Gh2II

2 November

La folie d'Octave; not extant; Tralage; performed at Versailles 30 Nov. 1688 (Dangeau), reprised 27 Dec. 1691, 5 Jan. 1695 (CtAc).

1689

15 January

Colombine femme vengée; Monsieur D***; Gh2II

5 March

La descente de Mezzetin aux enfers; Regnard; Gh2II; Ms. 9329, *Sup.* (*La descente d'Arlequin aux enfers*)

10 July
> *Mezzetin Grand Sophy de Perse;* Deslome de Montchenay; Gh2II;
> Gh1, *Sup.* (*Le Grand Sophy de Perse*)

1690

10 January
> *L'homme à bonne fortune;* Regnard; Gh2II; Gh1; scenes in *Sup.* under
> title *Arlequin homme à bonne fortune* are probably from *Arlequin
> lingère du palais*

1 March
> *La critique de l'homme à bonne fortune;* Regnard; Gh2II

24 August
> *Les filles errantes;* Regnard; Gh2III; *Sup.* under title *Les intrigues des
> hôteliers*

18 November
> *La fille sçavante;* Monsieur D***: GH2III; Gh1

1691

> **Le docteur amoureux;* BN Ms. fonds français 12.545; cast list includes
> Marinette; published by Lancaster from Ms. altered for per-
> formance by the new Comédie-Italienne after 1716, a near lit-
> eral transcription of a story by Mlle. Desjardins

17 January
> *La coquette, ou l'académie des dames;* Regnard; Gh2III

24 February
> *Esope;* Lenoble; Gh2III

26 September
> *Les deux Arlequins;* Lenoble; Gh2III

20 October
> *Ulisse et Circé;* Monsieur L.A.D.S.M.; Gh2III

17 November
> *Les amours d'Arlequin et de Marinette;* not extant; CtAc; performed at
> Versailles

22 November
> *Le phénix;* Delosme de Montchenay; Gh2III; Gh1

17 December
> *Les fourberies d'Arlequin et de Mezetin;* not extant; CtAc; performed at
> Versailles

1692

4 February
   Arlequin Phaeton; Palaprat; Gh2III; *Sup.*

5 March
   La précaution inutile; Monsieur D***; Gh2I

7 June
   L'opéra de campagne Dufresny; Gh2IV

16 August
   L'union des deux opéras; Dufresny; Gh2IV; *Suite*

2 November
   La fille de bon sens; Palaprat; Gh2IV

13 December
   Les chinois; Regnard and Dufresny; Gh2IV

1693

   **Les souffleurs;* Gh1gnv; dated from internal evidence, a mention of
      La baguette de Vulcain

10 January
   La baguette de Vulcain; Regnard and Dufresny; GH2IV; Gh1 (Act 3
      of *Les Chinois*)

25 April
   Les adieux des officiers; Dufresny; Gh2IV

30 May
   Les mal-assortis; Dufresny; Gh2IV

13 August
   Les originaux, ou l'italien; Monsieur D.L.M.; Gh2IV

28 November
   Les avantures des champs elisées; Monsieur L.C.D.V.; Gh2IV; Gh1

30 December
   Les souhaits; Delosme de Montchenay; Gh2V; Gh1

1694

10 February
   La naissance d'Amadis; Regnard; Gh2V; *Suite*

13 March
   Le bel-esprit; Monsieur L.A.P.; Gh2V

28 May
> *Arlequin défenseur du beau sexe;* Monsieur de B**** (Louis Biancolelli); Gh2V; Gh1

8 July
> *La fontaine de sapience;* Monsieur de B**** (Louis Biancolelli); Gh2V; *Suite*

24 August
> *Le départ des comédiens;* Dufresny; Gh2V

18 December
> *La fausse coquete;* Monsieur B**** (Louis Biancolelli); Gh2V; *Suite*

1695

21 January
> *Arlequin mary de trois femmes;* not extant; CtAc; performed at Versailles

29 January
> *Le tombeau de Maistre André;* Monsieur B**** (Louis Biancolelli); Gh2V; *Sup., Suite*

30 January
> *Attendez-mois sous l'orme;* Dufresny; Gh2V; *Suite*

10 February
> *Les disgrâces d'Arlequin roy de la Chine;* CtAc; performed at Versailles; possibly *Les chinois*

7 May
> *La thèse des dames, ou le triomphe de Colombine;* Monsieur B**** (Louis Biancolelli); Gh2VI

6 June
> *Les promenades de Paris;* Mongin; Gh2V

1 October
> *Le retour de la foire de Bezons;* Gherardi (Brugière de Barante); Gh2VI; *Suite*

25 November
> *Arlequin médecin ignorant;* CtAc; performed at Versailles; another title for 1683 *Aularia muette par amour*

26 December
> *La foire Saint-Germain;* Regnard and Dufresny; Gh2VI; *Sup.*

1696

21 February
Arlequin aman malheuraux [sic]; not extant; CtAc; peformed at Versailles.

19 March
Les momies d'Egypte; Regnard and Dufresny; Gh2VI

21 July
Les bains de la porte S. Bernard; Boisfran; Gh2VI

22 December
Arlequin misantrope; Monsieur de B**** (Louis Biancolelli); Gh2VI

29 December
Arlequin toujours Arlequin; not extant; CtAc; performed at Versailles

1697

3 February
Pasquin et Marforio, médecins des moeurs; Dufresny and Monsieur B**** (Louis Biancolelli); Gh2VI

2 March
Les fées, ou les contes de ma mere l'oye; Dufresny and Monsieur B**** (Louis Biancolelli); Gh2VI

April
Spinette lutin amoureuse; Gueullette, *M.G.,* Apr. 1697

Undatable

Le Capitan battu dans le jardin; Ms. 9329; cast includes the Capitan who could be Pasquariel or the Capitan of the calendar-almanac of 1689
La belle soliciteuse; Ms. 9329, *Sup.;* a French comedy of manners without commedia dell'arte character names
Percée & Andromède par enchantement; Sup.; a tirade in French verse for Arlequin; Spaziani dates to 1683; no source
Peintre par amour; Sup.
Tarquin et Lucrece; Sup.; a parody in French verse
Le carousel des dames; Sup.; song from a play by this title, possibly *Le régal des dames*
Les deux jumeaux; Sup.; song from a play by this title, possibly *Les deux Arlequins*

◇◇◇◇◇◇◇◇◇◇◇◇◇◇◇

Notes

Chapter 1: Debuts in Paris

1. *Journal d'Olivier d'Ormesson*, 1:190, cited by Emile Campardon, *Les comédiens du roi de la troupe italienne* (1880; reprint, Geneva: Slatkine, 1970), 1:xiii–xiv. All translations, unless otherwise indicated, are my own.

2. Armand Baschet, *Les comédiens italiens à la cour de France* (Paris: Plon, 1882), pp. 20–24, and S. Wilma Deierkauf-Holsboer, *Le théâtre de l'Hôtel de Bourgogne* (Paris: Nizet, 1968), 1:25–26. The livre was the standard currency. In the mid-17th century, workers at the Comédie-Italienne were paid between 1 and 3 livres a day; a 10-livre fine 80 years earlier was a substantial, though not outrageous, sum. Other denominations of coinage in use during the ancien régime were the denier, one-twelfth of a sou; the sou, one-twentieth of a livre; the ecu, worth 3 livres, the ecu d'or 6 livres, the louis d'or 15 livres and the pistole 10 livres. A reform of the currency in 1689 made the louis d'or worth 11 livres, 5 sous, and the ecu d'or worth 5 livres, 16 sous.

3. Deierkauf-Holsboer, *Hôtel de Bourgogne*, 1:24.

4. Baschet, p. 74.

5. Ibid., p. 102.

6. Ibid., p. 106.

7. Ibid., pp. 137–38.

8. Deierkauf-Holsboer, *Hôtel de Bourgogne*, 1:95–96.

9. Ibid., pp. 96–97.

10. Baschet, pp. 248–49.

11. Jean Héroard, *Journal de Jean Héroard sur l'enfance et la jeunesse de Louix XIII, 1601–1628*, ed. Eudore Soulié and Edouard de Barthélemy (Paris: Didot, 1868), 2:253–85. Baschet has combed the entire manuscript and counted the number of times the doctor reports that his young charge has been to the Comédie-Italienne. See pp. 282 and 303n.

12. Baschet, pp. 332–33.

13. Margaret McGowan, *L'art du ballet de cour en France (1581–1643)* (Paris: Editions du Centre national de la recherche scientifique, 1964), p. 286. For the date of the *Ballet de la Reine* see Héroard, entry for 2 March 1621, 2:255.

14. Héroard, 2:269. The king, who was staying at the Louvre, went to the "room above" to see the play.

15. Ibid., 2:284.

16. Henry Prunières, *L'opéra italien en France avant Lulli* (1913; reprint, Paris: Honoré Champion, 1975), p. 69, cites a letter in the Archives of Naples, Carte Farnesiane, 190, 4.

17. Thomas-Simon Gueullette, "Histoire du théâtre italien establi en France depuis l'année 1577 jusqu'en l'année 1750 et les anneés suivantes," Bibliothèque de l'Opéra, Ms. Réserve 625, fol. 61v. Gueullette's notes on the history of the Comédie-Italienne are attached to his translation of the zibaldone of Domenico Biancolelli.

18. Archives Nationales (AN), Minutier Central (MC), Etude LXXIII, file 441. Also cited in Madeleine Jurgens and Marie-Antoinette Fleury, *Documents du Minutier Central concernant l'histoire littéraire, 1650–1700* (Paris: Presses Universitaires de France, 1960), 28 June 1659.

19. Pierre-Louis Duchartre, *Les compositions de rhétorique de M. Don Arlequin* (Paris: Duchartre et Van Duggenhoult, 1928).

20. Baschet, pp. 193–94.

21. Gueullette, "Histoire," Ms. Rés. 625, fol. 62r&v.

22. Auguste Jal, *Dictionnaire critique de biographie et d'histoire* (Paris: Plon, 1867), s.v. "Biancolelli-Cortesi" and "Fiorilli."

23. This actress is generally known as Brigida Bianchi. See chap. 2 for the evidence that justifies the change of name.

24. The play, *L'inganno fortunato o vero l'amata aborrita,* was published by Cramoisi in Paris in 1659. Loret wrote about it in his *Muze historique* of 31 May and 7 and 28 June 1659. Unless otherwise indicated, quotations from and references to *La muze historique* will be cited by date in the text.

25. Prunières, p. 66.

26. *Gazette de France,* 4 March 1645.

27. Agne Beijer, "Une maquette de décor récemment retrouvée pour le *Ballet de la prospérité des armes de France* dansé à Paris, le 7 février 1641," in *Le lieu théâtral à la renaissance,* ed. Jean Jacquot (Paris: Editions du Centre national de la recherche scientifique, 1964), p. 377.

28. Charles Varlet de La Grange, *Registre,* ed. Edouard Thierry (Paris: par la Comédie-Française, 1876), entry following 11 October 1660. Unless otherwise indicated, this source will be cited by date in the text.

29. Prunières, p. 375.

30. McGowan, p. 88n.

31. According to Henri Sauval (*Histoire et recherches des antiquités de la ville de Paris* [Paris: Moette, 1724], 2:209) the room was as high as St.-Eustache or St.-Germain l'Auxerrois.

32. *Explication des décorations du théâtre, et les argumens de la pièce* (Paris: René Baudry, 1645). A surviving copy is included in Bib. de l'Opéra Ms. Rés. 625, fols. 66r–73r.

33. Sauval (2:209) paced out the remains of the building and concluded that the room was 35 toises, or 221 feet long, a dimension that makes Torelli's remark about "such a little stage" seem totally irrational. If the room had been 221 feet long, Torelli could have built a stage with whatever depth he wanted.

34. Campardon, *Comédiens du roi,* 1:xv.

35. Charles Sorel, *La vrai histoire comique de Francion,* ed. E. Colombey (Paris: Garnier, 1877), pp. 184–90.

36. Adolphe Berty, *Topographie historique du vieux Paris: région du Louvre et des Tuileries,* 2d ed. (Paris: Imprimerie Nationale, 1885), 1:facing p. 138. Although Berty has redrawn the ancient maps, he has not distorted them, and the convenience of being able to compare several views on a single page is great.

37. M. Horn-Monval, "Le Théâtre du Petit-Bourbon," *Revue d'histoire du théâtre* 1 (1949):46–48.

38. Berty, 1:facing p. 32.

39. See chap. 2 for information about the actors.

40. Prunières, p. 82n.

41. Gueullette, "Histoire," Ms. Rés. 625, fol. 42v. Foreigners who died intestate in France forfeited their property to the crown.

42. They signed a contract with a young French woman to serve as their maid on the trip, See AN, MC CXXI, 2. This and a number of other documents from the Minutier Central have been transcribed by Anna Migliori ("Contributo all storia dell'ancien théâtre italien," *Biblioteca teatrale*, no. 8 [1973], pp. 78–137). When a transcription is available in Migliori, it will be cited along with the original document for the convenience of the reader.

43. La Grange, entry for 1658.

44. Samuel Chappuzeau, *Le théâtre français* (1674; reprint, Editions d'Aujourd'hui, n.p., n.d.), p. 60.

45. La Grange, entry for the end of the season of 1659.

46. Eugène Despois, *Le théâtre français sous Louis XIV* (Paris: Hachette, 1874), pp. 144–45.

47. Gueullette, "Histoire," Ms. Rés. 625, fol. 65r.

Chapter 2: Actors of the 1640s and 1650s

1. Gueullette, "Histoire," Ms. Rés. 625, fol. 60v; fol. 83v says 6 November 1608.

2. Angelo Costantini, *The Birth, Life and Death of Scaramouch*, trans. Cyril W. Beaumont (London: C. W. Beaumont, 1924), p. 1. The original, *La vie de Scaramouche*, was published in Paris by Barbin in 1695, a year after Fiorilli's death.

3. Jal, s.v. "Fiorilli."

4. Campardon, *Comédiens du roi*, 1:233–34.

5. Ibid., p. 226; Jal, s.v. "Fiorilli."

6. Luigi Rasi, *I comici italiani* (Florence: Bocca, 1897), 1:894–95.

7. *Enciclopedia dello spettacolo*, s.v. "Fiorillo, Silvio."

8. Costantini, pp. 1–2.

9. Gueullette, "Histoire," Ms. Rés. 625, fols. 58 ff.

10. Campardon, *Comédiens du roi*, 1:222.

11. Jal, s.v. "Fiorilli."

12. Rasi, 1:921–22. Rasi also accepts the opinion of Evaristo Gherardi, Arlequin of the Paris troupe after 1689, that the Costantini book is worthless. Gherardi writes, in the "Avertissement" to *Le théâtre italien*, a six-volume collection of French scenes and plays written for the Italian troupe (Paris: Cusson et Witte, 1700) that Costantini was possibly the scoundrel responsible for the *Supplément* (a pirated addition to the 1694 one-volume *Théâtre italien*), "composed, so it's said, by the author of the *Arlequiniana* [Cotolendi] or *La vie de Scaramouche*. It is true that these authors are so similar in the baseness of their style and in the falseness of the actions they recount, that one can easily be mistaken and take one for the other without much difficulty. They are two equally bad writers, and equally false historians, each of them attributing to their heroes things that Arlequin and Scaramouche have never done nor said. I excuse, however, the author of *La vie de Scaramouche*, because he recognizes that his book is detestable, but he was obliged to make it so to conform to the capacity of the one who wanted to put his name on it." Thus, according to Gherardi, the biography of Scaramouche was written by a ghost writer, forced to conform to Costantini's "capacity" and write a book distinguished by error and poverty of style.

It should come as no surprise that Gherardi despised the Costantinis: Angelo, his brother Giovanni Battista, and their father, Constantino. He quarreled with them openly even before the dismissal of the company from Paris in 1697, an event for which the Costantinis may have been more than slightly responsible. Gherardi is, thus, hardly a disinterested critic.

Nino Borsellino argues in "Percorsi della commedia dell'arte: Scaramuccia de Napoli a Parigi" (*Le théâtre italien en l'Europe XVe–XVIIe siècles,* ed. Christian Bec and Irène Mamczarz [Paris: Presses Universitaires de France, 1983], p. 114) that if Costantini had lied about Fiorilli's parentage, Gherardi certainly would have specifically cited such an astonishing lie as proof of the fraudulence of the book.

13. Ulisse Prota-Giurleo, *I teatri di Napoli nel '600: la commedia e le maschere.* (Naples: Fausto Fiorentino, 1962), p. 170.

14. Rasi, 1:925.

15. Vito Pandolfi, *La commedia dell'arte: storia e testi* (Florence: Sansoni Antiquariato, 1957–61), 5:398.

16. Rasi, 1:925.

17. Jal, s.v. "Fiorilli."

18. AN, MC XC, 259 (Migliori, pp. 97–101. Migliori has inaccurately cited the docment to AN, MC XV, 259).

19. AN, MC VI, 368 (Migliori, p. 101).

20. AN, MC XV, 292.

21. AN, MC VI, 578 (Migliori, p. 106).

22. AN, MC CXIII, 129 (Migliori, p. 112).

23. AN, MC XV, 327, 331 (Migliori, pp. 127, 129).

24. Prota-Giurleo, p. 20. Silvio Fiorillo published a play in Naples in 1608.

25. *Enciclopedia dello spettacolo,* s.v. "Fiorillo, Silvio."

26. See *I balli di sfessania,* c. 1622, in Gerald Kahan, *Jacques Callot, Artist of the The-atre* (Athens: Univ. of Georgia Press, 1976), pp. 12–15.

27. *Enciclopedia dello spettacolo,* s.v. "Fiorillo, Silvio."

28. Kathleen M. Lea, *Italian Popular Comedy* (1934; reprint New York: Russell and Russell, 1962), 1:284. Silvio Fiorillo's character name did cross the mountains. A painting, *French and Italian Farceurs,* which hangs at the Comédie-Française, shows Captain Matamore, though the figure does not wear Silvio Fiorillo's costume. Another version of the same painting has a legend that divides the figures into French and Italian. Matamore is on the French list (see Cesare Molinari, *Theatre through the Ages* [New York: McGraw-Hill, 1975], p. 178). The figure is taken from a popular print of the period, impossible to date with accuracy, but probably after 1630. Thus, it seems reasonable to assume that Matamore was the nom de guerre of the French actor who played capitan roles at the Hôtel de Bourgogne in the middle of the 17th century, probably the actor identified by Deierkauf-Holsboer as Louis Galien, in 1631 part of the troupe that included the other French farceurs shown in the painting. The character Matamore appears, of course, in Corneille's *L'illusion comique* (1636) and also in Scarron's *Les boutades du capitan Matamore* (1646).

29. See chap. 1.

30. Jal, s.v. "Fiorilli."

31. Campardon, *Comédiens du roi,* 1:226.

32. Prunières, pp. 375–76.

33. AN, MC CXXI, 2 (Migliori, pp. 80–81).

34. *La muze historique,* 16 August 1653.

35. Rasi, 1:895.

36. *La muze historique,* 5 February 1656.

37. Ibid., 31 May 1659.

38. AN, MC LXXIII, 441.

39. Rasi, 1:422. The spelling *Fedeli* of a name usually spelled in signature *Fedele* is consistent with the French habit of changing the endings of all Italian names to *i* or *y*. The French notaries who drew up the various legal documents for the Italians almost invariably spelled their names differently than they did themselves.

40. Gueullette, "Histoire," Ms. Rés. 625, fol. 52v.

41. AN, MC XV, 292 (Migliori, p. 103).

42. AN, MC LXXIII, 441.

43. AN, MC VII, 104 (Migliori, p. 103n).

44. *La muze historique*, 31 May 1659.

45. *Lettres en vers*, 14 July 1668.

46. Gueullette, "Histoire," Ms. Rés. 625, fol. 53v.

47. Pandolfi, 5:400.

48. Rasi, 2:393.

49. Gueullette, "Histoire," Ms. Rés. 625, fol. 94v.

50. Rasi (1:422) suggests that *Aurelia Fedeli* should be interpreted as meaning "the actress Aurelia who is a member of the Fedeli company," but there is absolutely no evidence linking this actress with Giovan Battista Andreini and the troupe that played in Paris in the 1620s, nor is there any reason for her to signal in 1666 something she might have done in 1636. In any case, in France there seems to have been little or no consciousness of troupe names; they were all known as "His Majesty's Italian Actors"; furthermore, the companies that came to France were usually gathered from various sources.

51. Ibid., 1:415–19.

52. Prunières, p. 47n.

53. Angus Heriot, *The Castrati in Opera* (London: Da Capo Press, 1956), pp. 58–59.

54. Prunières, p. 63n. Benedetti's use of *Capitando* suggests a way in which Rasi may have given birth to Giuseppe Bianchi, Capitan Spezzafer. First of all, Rasi— citing the Parfaict brothers—assumes that Giuseppe Bianchi was the actor who was referred to as the "New Scaramouche" in Paris in 1668–70 while Tiberio Fiorilli was in Italy, and who later played the role of Capitan Spezzafer. But that actor was Girolamo Cei. Rasi goes on to say that we know from a reference in H. A. Soleirol (*Molière et sa troupe* [Paris: H. A. Soleirol, 1863]) that this was the same actor who played the Capitan in 1645. Rasi quotes Soleirol as follows: "In 1645 the duc de Guise, leaving for Italy, made a gift of his wardrobe to the principal actors of Paris: it was divided among Beauchâteau of the Hôtel de Bourgogne, Floridor of the Théâtre du Marais, *il capitano* (Giuseppe Bianchi, director?) of the Comédie-Italienne [parenthetical insertion by Soleirol], La Béjart, Carlo Beys, and Molière of the Illustre Théâtre."

The source of this anecdote is to be found in Eudore Soulié (*Recherches sur Molière et sur sa famille* [Paris: Hachette, 1863] pp. 34–35): "M. Paulin Paris has found in a *Recueil de diverses poésies* printed in 1646, and sent to M. Bazin some verses addressed to the duc de Guise about the gifts he made of his clothing to the actors of all the troupes: Floridor of the Marais, the Capitaine of the Petit-Bourbon, Beauchâteau of the Hôtel de Bourgogne." There are four possibilities for this Capitaine, which is, incidentally, the French word for *captain* and not the word normally used to indicate the theatrical character. One is the castrato "Capitando" Giuseppe. One is Tiberio Fiorilli, whose Scaramouche is, in part, a capitan, and who also may have been serving as head, or capo, of the troupe. The letter from Carlo Cantù accusing him of blocking Cantù's wife's trip to France suggests that. A third possibility is a yet unidentified actor who played the role of capitan, but was not necessarily head of the troupe—Beauchâteau was not the leader of the troupe at the Hôtel de Bourgogne—and the final possibility is an actor serving as capo of the troupe, but playing a different role. Capitan was a masque, and the actor playing him normally wore a significatory costume, not the fashionable clothing of the day. Scaramouche also certainly had no need for the duc de Guise's cast-off finery. Thus, assuming this anecdote to be true—and to assume that is already to stretch probability—the most likely interpretation is that the clothing was given either to the castrato, who was singing as a concert performer as well as in opera, or to an actor playing the role of an amoureux and perhaps serving as capocomico.

55. Prota-Giurleo, pp. 13–26.

56. Lea, 2:495.

57. Rasi, 2:184.

58. Ibid., 1:593.

59. Ibid., 1:594–95.

60. Ibid., 1:882.

61. Prunières, p. 66.

62. Ibid., p. 67n.

63. *New Grove Dictionary of Music* (London: Macmillan, 1980), s.v. "Bianchi, Giulio Cesare."

64. *La muze historique,* 31 May 1659.

65. Enrico Bevilaqua, "Giambattista Andreini e la compagnia dei Fedeli," *Giornale storico della letteratura italiana* 23 (1894): 140.

66. Thomas-Simon Gueullette, "Traduction du scenario de Joseph Dominique

Biancolelli," Bibliothèque de l'Opéra, Ms. Rés 625, pp. 244–47. Two sets of numbers appear on the manuscript of the "Traduction," one set continuing the folio enumeration of the "Histoire du théâtre italien" through vol. 1 of the Ms., the other beginning page enumeration with the first translated scenario in vol. 1 and continuing through vol. 2. I will cite page numbers rather than folio numbers. For the convenience of the reader I will also cite the transcription of the "Traduction" published by Stefania Spada in *Domenico Biancolelli ou l'art d'improviser* (Naples: Institut Universitaire, 1969).

67. Gueullette, "Traduction," Ms. Rés. 625, p. 62 (Spada, p. 33).

68. Ibid., p. 87 (Spada, p. 48).

69. François and Claude Parfaict, *Histoire de l'ancien théâtre italien* (Paris: Lambert, 1753), p. 25. An actor known to have died at about this time was Leoni. Perhaps he was confused with Horace.

70. La Grange, entry following 7 July 1659.

71. Rasi, 1:419.

72. Ibid., 1:960.

73. Gueullette, "Histoire," Ms. Rés. 625, fol. 62r&v.

74. *La muze historique,* 28 June 1659.

75. Lea, 1:136.

76. Rasi, 1:960.

77. Jal, s.v. "Locatelli."

78. See chap. 1, n. 41.

79. Rasi, 2:27–28.

80. *La muze historique,* 16 August 1653.

81. The assertion that Fiorilli played Don Juan's valet in *Il convitato di pietra* is supported in chap. 3.

82. Campardon, *Les comédiens du roi,* 1:295.

83. Jal, s.v. "Lolli."

84. Campardon, *Les comédiens du roi,* 1:245.

85. AN, série O1, Maison du roi, 848, Comédie-Italienne.

86. AN, MC XV, 327.

87. Rasi, 2:30–32.

88. Parfaict and Parfaict, *Histoire de l'ancien théâtre italien,* pp. 32–34.

89. Lea, 2:497; Rasi 2:854–55.

90. *Enciclopedia dello spettacolo,* s.v. "Lolli, Angelo Agostino."

91. But see chap. 14 for a possible surviving child.

92. Rasi, 2:742–43.

93. Gueullette, "Histoire," Ms. Rés. 625, fols. 60v&61r; Rasi, 2:605.

94. AN, MC CXIII, 129, 131 (Migliori, pp. 110–13).

95. Prunières, p. 69.

96. Ibid., p. 82n.

97. AN, MC LXXIII, 441.

98. Gueullette, "Histoire," Ms. Rés. 625, fol. 65r.

99. Rasi, 2:174–76.

100. *La muze historique,* 16 August 1653.

101. Rasi, 1:929–30.

102. Ibid., 1:930.

103. Gueullette, "Histoire," Ms. Rés. 625, fol. 65r.

Chapter 3: The Magician of Fano

1. Lea, 1:129–220.

2. R. L. Weaver and N. W. Weaver, *A Chronology of Music in the Florentine Theatre, 1590–1750* (Detroit: Detroit Studies in Music Bibliography, 1978), p. 116.

3. Cochin's engravings are included in an Italian version of the *Explication* dedicated to the queen mother. A copy may be consulted at the Bibliothèque de l'Arsenal, Rés. Ra E 89. Balbi's *Balletti d'invenzione nella Finta pazza* with plates by Spada is also at the Bibliothèque de l'Arsenal, Ra E 55. Marie-Françoise Christout, *Le Ballet de cour de Louis XIV, 1643–1672* (Paris: Picard, 1967) includes one plate by Cochin and nine by Spada.

4. See chap. 2.

5. Prunières, p. 67.

6. Ibid., p. 69.

7. Ibid., pp. 69–70, 372–73.

8. Ibid., pp. 375–76.

9. See chap. 1 for a history of the Petit-Bourbon. The theatre had been out of use for 20 years and required a general refitting.

10. Prunières, p. 375,

11. *Gazette de France,* 1645, p. 1180.

12. *Journal d'Olivier d'Ormesson,* quoted by Prunières, pp. 75–76. See chap. 1 for a discussion of the "four-foot stage."

13. Prunières, p. 74.

14. Christout, *Ballet de cour,* pp. 25–26 and pl. 7.

15. See fig. 3.

16. Prunières, p. 75n.

17. Christout, *Ballet de cour,* p. 46.

18. A clear reproduction of this print can be found in Rasi, 1:576.

19. Christout, *Ballet de cour,* p. 195.

20. Agne Beijer, "*La naissance de la paix:* ballet de cour de René Descartes," in *Le Lieu théâtral à la renaissance,* ed. Jean Jacquot (Paris: Editions du Centre national

de la recherche scientifique, 1968), pp. 412–13.

21. *La muze historique,* 23 March 1658.

22. *Argument de la grand pièce intitulée la Rosaure imperatrice de Constantinople* (Paris: René Baudry, 1658). A copy is included in Bib. de l'Opéra, Ms. Rés. 625, fols. 76r–79v.

23. Evaristo Gherardi, *Le théâtre italien,* 1700 ed., 1:377–78.

24. La Grange, entry following 10 October 1660.

25. Lea, 1:200.

26. Cicognini, *Il convitato di pietra* (Rome, 1671), reprint. in G. Gendarme de Bévotte, *Le festin de pierre avant Molière* (Paris: Cornély, 1907), pp. 369–424. But see also Oscar Mandel, *The Theatre of Don Juan* (Lincoln: Univ. of Nebraska Press, 1963), p. 100, who calls this version the pseudo-Cicognini.

27. The story of Queen Joan is hardly amusing. Its mention here may be related to the production in 1654 of Magnon's *Jeanne de Naples.* The Parfaicts point out, in their *Histoire du théâtre français* (Paris:

Morin et Flahaut, 1734), 8:108, that the queen's sexual habits were well known, which by implication ties her story to the conversation between the King and Arlequin.

28. The lazzi seems out of place, and may belong with the Addenda. No other version of the play has two eating scenes.

29. In Cicognini, Pantalon appears as a cuckolded husband with Brunetta and the Docteur. Their plot line seems to be based on the Aminta-Batricio-Gaceno plot in Tirso.

30. Gueullette, "Traduction," Ms. Rés. 625, pp. 192–210 (Spada, pp. 102–8).

31. Sieur de Villiers, *Le festin de pierre, ou le fils criminel* (Paris: N.p., 1660), au lecteur.

32. Costantini, p. 9.

33. Jean Donneau de Visé, *Nouvelles nouvelles,* cited by Parfaict and Parfaict, *Histoire du théâtre français,* 8:318.

34. John Lough, *Paris Theatre Audiences in the Seventeenth and Eighteenth Centuries* (London: Oxford Univ. Press, 1957), pp. 47–55.

Chapter 4: Establishment at Palais-Royal

1. Jal, s.v. "Locatelli."

2. Rasi, 2:68. The actor is referred to in the French legal documents surrounding his death as François Mansac. Rasi's entry for Francesco Manzani cites Bartoli: "actor who flourished around 1655" and played the role of Capitano under the name Capitan Terremoto. The probability seems high that Mansac was Manzani.

3. AN, série KK, Monuments historiques, 213–14, comptes des menus plaisirs.

4. Deierkauf-Holsboer, *Hôtel de Bourgogne,* 2:95–96.

5. AN, MC VI, 578 (Migliori, p. 106).

6. Campardon, *Comédiens du roi,* 1:34.

7. Subligny, *Lettres en vers,* 18 November 1666.

8. In general, however, the French and Italian companies were probably called to court at the same time. In the 1660s the court was still based in Paris, but Louis, who disliked his capital, removed for long periods to St. Germain-en-Laye, Fontainebleau, and Versailles and invited the actors to come along. Once the court was established at Versailles the pattern changed, and the theatrical troupes made

day trips that interfered less with their Paris performance schedule.

9. Gueullette, "Traduction," Ms. Rés. 625, p. 499 (Spada, p. 331).

10. AN, KK.213-14.

11. Jal, s.v. "Fiorilli."

12. Sebastiano Locatelli, *Voyage en France,* trans. Adolphe Vautier (Paris: Picard, 1905), p. 65. Locatelli also tells (pp. 183-84) a long story about Eularia, who supposedly found herself in compromising circumstances with an Italian prince who was forcing his favors on her. She is supposed to have told him that she had vowed to the Virgin, during an illness nine years earlier, that she would "forever preserve her chastity in this perilous profession of actress." The prince excused her and rewarded her virtue with a diamond ring, but he warned her that the ring was meant to remind her that she was to grant to no one else what she had refused to him, or "you will die without warning, victim of my fury." Her Majesty is said to have asked to see the ring, and then to have decided that Eularia had best marry, since she risked losing in Paris what she had preserved elsewhere.

13. Campardon, *Comédiens du roi,* 2:3.

14. AN, MC LIII, 54 (Migliori, pp. 85-92). Bendinelli owed 56 livres, 5 sous, for a quarter's rent. The Biancolellis must have lived in somewhat greater comfort. According to Sebastiano Locatelli, Eularia and her husband paid 250 ecus a year in rent, or 187 livres, 10 sous a quarter in 1665. "Rents are very high in Paris," she told her fellow Bolognese, "because of the great number of inhabitants" (*Voyage en France,* p. 182). The Biancolelli household did include Orsola Cortesi's parents and sister, as well as the couple and two children. She also told Locatelli that the couple had 3,000 livres a year in spendable income after their

professional expenses, including her costumes.

15. La Grange, 8 January 1662.

16. Beijer, "Une maquette," p. 377.

17. Sauval, 2:162.

18. Beijer, "Une maquette," p. 381 and pl. 3 (see fig. 5). The grisaille is in the collection of the Musée des Arts Decoratifs, Paris.

19. Ibid., pp. 379-80. Beijer argues convincingly that this production represents the true introduction of Italianate spectacle into the French theatre four years before Torelli arrived and produced *La finta pazza.*

20. Mme. de Motteville, *Mémoires,* in *Nouvelle collection des mémoires pour servir à l'histoire de France,* ser. 2, vol. 2, ed. Joseph F. Michaud (Paris: L'Editeur du commentaire analytique du code civil, 1836-39), p. 113.

21. Sauval, 2:163.

22. AN, MC LIII, 35, transcribed in Madeleine Jurgens and Elizabeth Maxfield-Miller, *Cent ans de recherches sur Molière* (Paris: Imprimerie Nationale, 1963), pp. 351-55.

23. Beijer, "Une maquette," p. 394 and pl. 4 (see figs. 7, 8).

24. La Grange, 19 July 1671.

25. AN, MC XLII, 156, transcribed in Jurgens and Maxfield-Miller, pp. 399-401.

26. AN, série Y, Châtelet de Paris, 13,858, transcribed in Jurgens and Maxfield-Miller, pp. 370-74.

27. Lough, p. 93.

28. La Grange, 25 February 1660.

29. Sylvie Chevalley, ed. "Le *Registre* d'Hubert," *Revue d'histoire du théâtre* 26 (1973):166.

30. Jean Nicolas de Tralage, "Receuil," Bibliothèque de l'Arsenal, Ms. 6544, fol. 177r. Although his name is often printed Du Tralage, I follow his bookplate in his copy of the first edition of Gherardi's *Le théâtre italien*, in the collection of the Bibliothèque Nationale, Paris.

31. Lough, p. 108.

32. Ibid., pp. 55–162. A very thorough and fair discussion of the available evidence bearing on the composition of the Paris theatre audience in the two middle quarters of the 17th century. Lough's ten-tative conclusion is that although some shopkeepers, artisans, and valets were found at times in the theatres, the audience was largely drawn from the bourgeoisie, the functionaries, and the aristocracy.

33. Sandro D'Amico, "Le théâtre italien," *Encyclopédie de la Pléiade*, vol. 19, *Histoire du Spectacle*, (Paris: NRF, 1965), p. 638.

34. Luigi Riccoboni, *Histoire du théâtre italien* (Paris: Delormel, 1728), p. 61.

35. Locatelli, pp. 184–85.

Chapter 5: The Second Arlequin

1. See below for a discussion of her last name.

2. Rasi, 2:876.

3. Spada, p. xxv.

4. Rasi, 1:430.

5. Florence, 1646, reprinted in Pandolfi, 4:118–56.

6. Jal, s.v. "Biancolelli-Cortesi."

7. Spada, p. xxviiin.

8. Jal, s.v. "Biancolelli-Cortesi."

9. AN, MC XCVI, 82 (Migliori, pp. 81–83).

10. Tralage, "Recueil," Ms. 6544, fol. 215.

11. Gueullette, "Histoire," Ms. Rés. 625, fols. 119v–120r.

12. Gueullette, "Traduction," Ms. Rés. 625, p. 516 (Spada, p. 343).

13. Abbé Michel de Pure, *Idée des spectacles anciens et nouveaux* (Paris: Brunet, 1668), p. 170.

14. Jal, s.v. "Biancolelli-Cortesi." Spada (p. xxix) found the records of the deaths of Elisabeth-Charlotte and Louis in the Archives de la Seine.

15. Jal, s.v. "Biancolelli-Cortesi," and Gueullette, "Histoire," Ms.Rés. 625, fo. 97r.

16. Campardon, *Comédiens du roi*, 1:65–66.

17. Xavier de Courville, *Un apôtre de l'art du théâtre au XVIIIe siècle: Luigi Riccoboni dit Lélio: L'expérience française* (Paris: Droz 1945), p. 26.

18. State Archives, Bologna, Ms. of the Malvezzi family, quoted by Spada, p. xxxn.

19. Gueullette, "Histoire," Ms. Rés. 625, fol. 93v.

20. Gueullette, "Traduction," Ms. Rés. 625, p. 411 (Spada, p. 269).

21. Gueullette, "Traduction," Ms. Rés. 625, pp. 507–8 (Spada, pp. 338–39).

22. Robert L. Erenstein, *De Geschiedenis van de Commedia dell'Arte* (Amsterdam: International Theatre Bookshop, 1985), p. 97.

23. Spada (p. xxxiii) describes the "splendid" portrait at length: "The features show a remarkable mobility and subtlety. Under the thick and regular brows, the eyes ... alive, sincere,

deep. . . . The mouth sketches an ironic smile. . . . In the face one feels clearly the presence of life, truly felt and lived." The director of the Museo La Scala, Dr. Tintorri, was kind enough to communicate to me—through the much-appreciated offices of my colleague Dr. Richard Trousdell who interviewed him on 11 June 1987—his own feeling that the subject of the portrait may not be Biancolelli. The portrait formed part of the *raccolta* Sambon, the museum's founding collection, acquired in 1911. Many attributions of materials in that collection, made by the first director of the Museo La Scala, have proved to be inaccurate.

24. Christout, *Ballet de cour,* pp. 133 n. 185 and 134 n. 205.

25. Gueullette, "Histoire," Ms. Rés. 625, fols. 92v–93v.

26. Campardon, *Comédiens du roi,* 2:152.

27. Gueullette, "Traduction," Ms. Rés. 625, p. 267 (Spada, p. 150).

28. Gherardi, "Avertissement," *Le théâtre italien,* 1700 ed., n.p.

29. [Charles Cotolendi], Introduction, *Arlequiniana* (Paris: Florentin et Pierre Delaulne, 1694), n.p.

30. Campardon, *Comédiens du roi,* 1:62–63.

31. Gueullette, "Histoire," Ms. Rés. 625, fols. 89v–90v.

32. AN, MC XCVI, 82 (Migliori 81–82).

33. Rasi, 1:701.

34. Cited by Jal, s.v. "Biancolelli-Cortesi."

35. Gueullette, "Histoire," Ms. Rés. 625, fol. 87r.

36. Jal, s.v. "Biancolelli-Cortesi."

37. AN MC I, 183 (Migliori, p. 110).

38. Jal, s.v. "Biancolelli-Cortesi."

39. Auguste Vitu, "Molière et les Italiens," *Le Moliériste,* 1 (November 1879): 234–35.

40. Gueullette, "Histoire," Ms. Rés. 625, fol. 94v.

41. Spada, p. xxvn.

42. Rasi, 1:696–99.

43. Ibid., 1:701.

44. Ibid.

45. Lea, 1:257n.

46. Allardyce Nicoll, *The World of Harlequin* (Cambridge: Cambridge Univ. Press, 1963), p. 169.

47. Gueullette, "Histoire," Ms. Rés. 625, fol. 87r.

48. Ibid., fol. 87v.

49. Ibid., fol. 88r. The original letter is included in the Ms., p. 959.

50. AN, MC XV, 346 (Migliori, pp. 132–33).

51. Campardon, *Comédiens du roi,* 1:68–69.

52. Gueullette, "Histoire," Ms. Rés. 625, fol. 88r.

53. Jal, s.v. "Bendinelli"; AN, MC LIII, 54 (Migliori, pp. 87–92).

54. Rasi, 1:342.

55. Campardon, *Comédiens du roi,* 1:33–34, cites AN, série Y, Châtelet de Paris, 13,868.

56. AN MC LIII, 54 (Migliori, p. 87).

57. Bert Edward Young and Grace Philpott Young, *Le Registre de La Grange,* vol. 2, *Notice sur La Grange et son oeuvre* (Paris: Droz, 1947), p. 84.

58. Jurgens and Maxfield-Miller, pp. 566–70; AN, MC XLV, 266. Molière's professional wardrobe was valued at 656 livres. The most expensive set was the wardrobe for *Bourgeois Gentilhomme* valued at 70 livres. One of the coats was

trimmed with "false" silver lace, perhaps accounting for its relatively minimal value.

59. Campardon, *Comédiens du roi,* 2:2–5, cites AN, série Y, Châtelet de Paris, 13,858. I have translated this somewhat loosely, trying to avoid the tortured legalisms of the original and to clarify the event.

60. Although Molière later lived—and died—on the rue de Richelieu, in 1662 he was living in a house owned by the physician Louis Henri Daquin situated across from the corps de garde of Palais-Royal at the entry of the rue St.-Thomas-du-Louvre (Jurgens and Maxfield-Miller, pp. 136–37). The resident of the rue de Richelieu before whose lodging Manzani died was Louis de Mollier, the dancer, then living at no. 36 (Vitu, p. 231n).

61. Rasi, 2:68.

62. Campardon, *Comédiens du roi,* 1:295–96, cites AN, série Z, Juridictions spéciales et ordinaires, 6013.

63. Gueullette, "Histoire," Ms. Rés. 625, fo. 96v.

64. AN, MC XV, 292 and CXIII, 129, 131 (Migliori, pp. 103–5, 110–13).

65. Jal, s.v. "Fiorilli"; AN, KK.213.

66. Campardon, *Comédiens du roi,* 1:226–30. I have been unable to discover anything more about Fiorilli's claim to ownership of a theatre in Florence. From what I know, it seems unlikely.

67. Rasi, 1:900.

68. Jal, s.v. "Locatelli."

69. Ibid.

70. Tralage, "Recueil," Ms. 6544, fol. 196v.

71. Rasi, 1:1021–22.

72. Gueullette, "Histoire," Ms. Rés 625, fol. 113v.

73. Campardon, *Comédiens du roi,* 2:3n.

74. Rasi, 1:881.

Chapter 6: The Old Italian Repertory

1. Cesare Molinari, *La commedia dell'arte* (Milan: Mondadori, 1985), p. 15.

2. Ibid., p. 13.

3. Lea, 1:131–33.

4. Cited by Lea, 1:133n.

5. Molinari, *Commedia dell'arte,* p. 26.

6. Lea, 1:137. The Locatelli manuscript is held in the Biblioteca Casanatense in Rome.

7. Ibid., 1:145.

8. Ibid., 1:146–47. This manuscript is also held in the Biblioteca Casanatense.

9. See especially Nicoll, pp. 175–84, and Gustave Attinger, *L'esprit de la commedia dell'arte dans le théâtre français* (Paris: Librairie Théatrale, 1950), pp. 167–83.

10. Gueullette, "Histoire," Ms. Rés. 625, fols. 8v–9.

11. Gueullette, "Traduction," Ms. Rés. 625, note following p. 6 (Spada, pp. 6–7).

12. See Spada's notes for each entry and Appendix I, pp. 361–526.

13. Parfaict and Parfaict, *Histoire de l'ancien théâtre italien.* Gueullette gave or lent his translation of Biancolelli's manuscript to the Parfaicts, who "edited" and printed thirty-eight of the seventy-nine entries. The Parfaicts put these "scenarios" into the third person and did what they could to make them less "boring" by casting them into narrative form. See pp. vii–xiv.

14. Gueullette, "Traduction," Ms. Rés. 625, p. 76 (Spada, p. 40).

15. Gueullette, "Histoire," Ms. Rés. 625, fol. 104r.

16. Biblioteca Comunale "Augusta," Perugia. A late collection of 22 scenarios featuring Pulcinella. See Suzanne Thérault, *La commedia dell'arte vue à travers le zibaldone de Pérouse* (Paris: Editions du Centre national de la recherche scientifique, 1965).

17. Giuliana Colajanni, ed., *Les scenarios franco-italiens du Ms. 9329 de la B.N.* (Rome: Edizioni di storia et letteratura, 1970). Ms. 9329 at the Bibliothèque Nationale is a document of unknown provenance which will be discussed more fully in chap. 9. According to Colajanni, this collection of 26 scenarios and scenes in French represents a part of the repertory played by the Italians between 1662 and 1697. Casts of characters suggest that these versions were played in 1683 and later. Although nine, possibly ten, of the scenarios correspond to entries in Biancolelli's zibaldone, only one is analogous to the pre-1668 repertory and that one is *Le dragon de Moscovie*. The presence in the cast list of Flautin implies a production date for this version of 1683 at the latest, although some version of the comedy was still being played as late as 1696 according to court financial records.

18. *Il basalisco del Bernagasso,* Biblioteca Nationale, Naples, Ms. XI.AA.41. Included in Spada, pp. 460–66. See also the second Naples version, same title, same Ms., included in Spada, pp. 467–74.

19. Gueullette, "Traduction," Ms. Rés. 625, pp. 39–41 (Spada, pp. 24–25).

Sources of further quotations from the various versions are indicated in the text.

20. Molière, *Tartuffe,* 1.5.293–95.

21. Gueullette, "Traduction," Ms. Rés. 625, pp. 64–79 (Spada, pp. 35–41). See also Bib. Nat. Naples Ms. XI.AA.41, included in Spada, pp. 443–50.

22. Gueullette, "Traduction," Ms. Rés. 625, pp. 79–87 (Spada, pp. 42–44).

23. Ibid., pp. 156–59 (Spada, pp. 83–84).

24. Ibid., pp. 87–96 (Spada, pp. 45–49).

25. Ibid., pp. 111–24 (Spada, pp. 58–62).

26. Ibid., pp. 124–36 (Spada, pp. 63–70).

27. Ibid., pp. 147–56 (Spada, pp. 79–82).

28. Ibid., pp. 215–25 (Spada, pp. 116–22). See also Bib. Nat. Naples Ms. XI.AA.41, included in Spada, pp. 484–90.

29. Spada, pp. 137n, 140n, 144n.

30. Gueullette, "Traduction," Ms. Rés. 625, p. 1 (Spada, pp. 1–2).

31. Ibid., pp. 126–29 (Spada, pp. 65–68).

32. Ibid., pp. 94–96 (Spada, p. 48).

33. Ibid., pp. 90–94 (Spada, pp. 47–48).

34. Constant Mic, *La commedia dell'arte* (1924; reprint Paris: Librairie Théatrale, 1980), pp. 124–63.

35. Gueullette, "Traduction," Ms. Rés. 625, p. 4 (Spada, p. 3).

36. Ibid., pp. 50–51 (Spada, p. 29).

37. Ibid., pp. 111, 118 (Spada, pp. 58, 61).

38. Mic, p. 125.

39. Ibid., p. 124n.

Chapter 7: From Palais-Royal to the Guénégaud

1. *Mercure galant,* July 1694, p. 340.

2. Gueullette, "Traduction," Ms. Rés. 625, pp. 257–72 (Spada, pp. 146–62).

But see also Parfaict and Parfaict, *Histoire de l'ancien théâtre italien,* pp. 313–25. The plot synopsis here suggests that the Parfaict brothers had access to material in addition to Dominique's notes.

3. Gueullette, "Histoire," Ms. Rés. 625, fol. 102v–103r. But see chap. 10. This is another of Riccoboni's many errors, since Cimadori was still alive in 1684 (Rasi, 1:664).

4. Eleanor Boswell, *The Restoration Court Stage: 1660–1702* (Cambridge: Harvard Univ. Press, 1932), p. 118.

5. *The London Stage*, vol. 1, *1660–1700*, ed. William Van Lennap (Carbondale: Southern Illinois Univ. Press, 1965), p. cxli.

6. Boswell, pp. 118–19.

7. *London Stage*, 1:207.

8. La Grange, order of June 1673.

9. Boswell, pp. 60, 121.

10. *London Stage*, 1:234.

11. Boswell, pp. 49, 121.

12. *London Stage*, 1:239.

13. *The Prologues and Epilogues of John Dryden*, ed. W. B. Gardner (New York: Columbia Univ. Press, 1951), p . 58.

14. Gueullete, "Traduction," Ms. Rés. 625, pp. 344–45 (Spada, pp. 218–19).

15. Boswell, p. 124.

16. Gueullette, "Traduction," Ms. Rés. 625, p. 532 (Spada, p. 353).

17. Boswell, p. 124.

18. Jurgens and Maxfield-Miller, pp. 496–502.

19. The Italians gave a different version of these events in the Accord et Transaction of 1680. According to their statement, "after the death of Molière . . . they were obliged to address themselves to His Majesty to ask him for a theatre in which to perform. It pleased him to send them to the Sieur Lulli, whom His Majesty enjoined to give them the freedom of his theatre. The Sieur Lulli made an agreement with the French troupe of the Hôtel de Guénégaud on the condition that the sum of 1,200 livres be paid each year" (AN, MC XC, 259 [Migliori, p. 99¹).

20. Charles Nuitter and Ernest Thoinan, *Les origines de l'opéra français* (Paris: E. Plon, 1886), p. 106.

21. Ibid., pp. 143–44.

22. *Lettres en vers*, 18 April 1674.

23. Nuitter and Thoinan, pp. 147–48.

24. H. C. Lancaster, *A History of French Dramatic Literature in the Seventeenth Century, Part 4, The Period of Racine, 1673–1700* (Baltimore: Johns Hopkins Univ. Press, 1940), 1:42.

25. Chevalley, *"Registre* d'Hubert," p. 168.

26. Barbara Mittman, *Spectators on the Paris Stage in the Seventeenth and Eighteenth Centuries* (Ann Arbor: UMI Research Press, 1984), p. 3.

27. Chevalley, *"Registre* d'Hubert," p. 166.

28. Trans. Mittman, p. 7.

29. Mittman, p. 36.

30. Gueullette, "Traduction," Ms. Rés. 625, p. 404 (Spada, pp. 262–63).

31. Nuitter and Thoinan, pp. 211–13.

32. Ibid., pp. 247–48.

33. Jean Nicolas du [*sic*] Tralage, *Notes et documents sur l'histoire des théâtres de Paris au XVIIe Siècle*, ed. Le Bibliophile Jacob [Paul La Croix] (Paris: Librairie des Bibliophiles, 1880), p. 24.

34. Anatole de Montaiglon, "Depenses des menus plaisirs et affaires de la chambre du roi pendant l'année 1677," *Journal général de l'instruction publique*, no. 17 (Paris: Dumoulin, 1857), p. 13. The

ms. is in the Bibliothèque de Rouen; the *Mercure galant*, October 1686, identifies M. Girardin as ambassador to the Great Mufti.

35. The original is not extant. Gueullette copied it by hand and included it in Ms. Rés. 625, pp. 546–67.

36. Nuitter and Thoinan, pp. 234–35.

37. AN, O1.16, cited by Nuitter and Thoinan, pp. 237–40.

38. Ibid.

39. Courville, *Lélio: L'expérience française*, p. 26.

40. *Lettres en vers*, 4 February 1673.

41. Ibid., 10 November 1674.

42. Gueullette, "Traduction," Ms. Rés. 625, pp. 339–41 (Spada, pp. 215–16).

43. Ibid., pp. 532–37 (Spada, pp. 353–55).

44. Ibid., pp. 411–18, 568–606 (Spada, pp. 269–73).

45. Ibid., p. 444 (Spada, p. 292).

46. Ibid., pp. 488–500 (Spada, pp. 321–31).

47. See, for instance, Attinger, pp. 167–72, and Nicoll, pp. 175–84.

48. Chappuzeau, pp. 113–22.

49. François de Dainville, "Lieux d'affichage en 1753," *Revue d'histoire du théâtre* 3 (1951):248–53. Only six posters are extant from the 17th century, none from the Italians.

50. Gherardi, *Le théâtre italien*, 1700 ed., 2:109–10.

51. *Grands Registres*, Troupe du roy du Hôtel Guénégaud, 1673–74, cited by Young and Young, 2:119–20.

52. Abbé de Pure, 2:169–76.

53. *Lettres en vers*, 6 July 1669.

54. Georges Monval, "M. Loyal, un signification," *Le Moliériste* 7 (May 1886): 45–46.

55. Gueullette, "Traduction," Ms. Rés. 625, p. 537 (Spada, p. 356).

56. AN Y.7179, in Migliori, p. 96.

57. AN, MC XC, 259 (Migliori, pp. 97–101).

58. AN Z1j.347, in Migliori, p. 97.

59. AN, MC XC, 259 (Migliori, 97–101).

Chapter 8: The Stable Company

1. Campardon, *Les comédiens du roi*, 1:244; Rasi, 2:394.

2. Pandolfi, 5:400.

3. Rasi, 2:394.

4. Gueullette, "Histoire," Ms. Rés. 625, fol. 99r.

5. Rasi, 2:394.

6. Jal, s.v. "Romagnesi."

7. Gueullette, "Histoire," Ms. Rés. 625, fols. 99v–100r.

8. Charles Cotelendi, *Le livre sans nom* (Paris: Michel Brunet, 1695), p. 424.

9. Riccoboni, p. 73.

10. See chap. 9, n. 3.

11. *Lettres en vers*, 1 June 1669.

12. La Grange, end of season 1685.

13. *Lettres en vers*, 21 April 1668.

14. Cotelendi, *Livre sans nom*, p. 272.

15. Tralage, "Recueil," Ms. 6543, fol. 203.

16. Gueullette, "Histoire," Ms. Rés. 625, fols. 102v–103r.

17. Rasi, 1:664.

18. Colajanni, pp. 353–63.

19. Gueullette, "Traduction," Ms. Rés. 625, pp. 415–16 (Spada, pp. 271–72).

20. See in Pierre-Louis Duchartre, *La commedia dell'arte et ses enfants,* 2d ed. (Paris: Librairie Théatrale, 1978), p. 146.

21. Rasi, 1:1006.

22. Gueullette, "Histoire," Ms. Rés. 625, fol. 103v.

23. Parfaict and Parfaict, *Histoire de l'ancien théâtre italien,* pp. 81–82.

24. Compardon, *Les comédiens du roi,* 1:240n.

25. Rasi, 1:1008.

26. Spada, p. 261n.

27. Jal, s.v. "Gherardi."

28. AN, MC VI, 578 (Migliori, p. 106).

29. Gueullette, "Histoire," Ms. Rés. 625, fol. 60v.

30. Rasi, 2:744.

31. Jal, s.v. "Zanotti."

32. Rasi, 1:900.

33. Jal, s.v. "Fiorilli."

34. Abbé Pierre François Guyot Desfontaines, *Le nouvelliste du Parnasse* (Paris: Chaubert, 1731–32), 2:265.

Chapter 9: The New Repertory

1. A recent discussion of the dating and provenance of Ms. 9329 by Philip Koch ("Nature et signification des 'Sujets de plusieurs comédies italiennes,'" *Revue d'histoire du théâtre,* 38 [1986]:67–87) bases some of its conclusions on questionable assumptions. Koch is unaware, for instance, of Turri's tenure as Pantalon after 1684, and finds the joint presence of Isabelle, Colombine, and Pantalon in a single scenario to be "historically impossible." He builds a tenuous case for the Ms. having been translated for a French commedia dell'arte troupe improvising the repertory of the Comédie-Italienne at Sceaux in the early eighteenth century. The case rests on an allusion in one scenario to two "dames Ragondes," which Koch assumes to be a reference to *Les amours de Ragonde* played in 1714 at Sceaux as *Le mariage de Ragonde et de Colin.* "Dame Ragonde," was, however, a characteristic name for the old peasant woman in French farce. Louis Nivellon, a French pantomimist and fair entrepreneur, appeared at Drury Lane in London in 1702 in "Dame Ragonde and her eight children" (*London Stage, Part 2,* 20 August 1702).

2. See especially *Supplément du théâtre italien, ou recueil des scènes françoises qui n'ont point encore été imprimées,* tome 2 [*sic*] (Brussels: chez M. *****), *1697.* A copy of this very rare edition may be found in the Rondel Collection, Bibliothèque de l'Arsenal, Paris.

3. Although four plays of the post-1668 repertory have titles similar to scenarios in the extant Italian repertory, two are too fragmentary to admit comparison and one, although similar in title, is unlike in action. The fourth, *Arlequin soldat par vengeance,* has no specific actions in common with the Italian *Il soldato per vendetta,* but the plot premises are the same.

4. [Paul Lacroix] Le Bibliophile Jacob, *Catalogue de la bibliothèque dramatique de M. de Solienne* (Paris: Administration de l'Alliance des Arts, 1843).

5. Frédéric Deloffre ("Aspects inconnus de l'ancien théâtre italien," *Cahiers de l'association internationale des études françaises* 15 [1963]:177–88) argues that the *Supplément* represents an uncensored version of the Italian company's repertory and is marked by political and social satire. He

admits, however, that he has not compared it to Ms. Rés. 625. He does not even mention Ms. 9329. His conclusions are based largely on materials which are exclusive to the *Supplément* and without provenance.

6. Gueullette, "Traduction," Ms. Rés. 625, pp. 257–71 (Spada, pp. 146–52).

7. See chap. 7 for a discussion of the spectacle.

8. Gueullette, "Traduction," Ms. Rés. 625, p. 429 (Spada, p. 280).

9. Ibid, p. 327 (Spada, p. 202).

10. Ibid., pp. 322–33 (Spada, p. 199).

11. Ibid., p. 381 (Spada, p. 244).

12. Ibid., pp. 285–91 (Spada, p. 170–73).

13. Ibid., p. 284 (Spada, pp. 175–76); Gueullette's note.

14. According to Gueullette, "M" signifies "mutation of the voice," "E" means "speak energetically," and "I" indicates an "imbroglio."

15. Gueullette, "Traduction," Ms. Rés. 625, pp. 294–95 (Spada, pp. 178–79).

16. Ibid., pp. 479–81 (Spada, p. 315).

17. Ibid., pp. 337–39 (Spada, pp. 213–14).

18. Ibid., pp. 481–88 (Spada, pp. 316–20).

19. Ibid., pp. 329–31 (Spada, pp. 203–4).

20. Ibid., pp. 393–95 (Spada, pp. 254–55).

21. Spada, p. 299n.

22. Gueullette, "Traduction," Ms. Rés. 625, pp. 456–60 (Spada, pp. 298–301).

23. Ibid., pp. 348–62 (Spada, pp. 224–30). The scenario in French, copied by hand, is to be found in Ms. Rès. 625, pp. 546–67.

24. Although it is possible that Gueullette may have translated this from Italian into French verse, it seems unlikely, especially given the relative complexity of the meter and rhyme scheme.

25. *Lettres en vers,* 13 August 1672.

26. Gueullette, "Traduction," Ms. Rés. 625, pp. 411–18 (Spada, 269–72). The complete scenario in French, copied by hand, is to be found in Ms. Rés. 625, pp. 568–606.

27. A drumbeat, something worthless. Equivalent to "not worth a straw."

28. Marian Hannah Winter, *The Theatre of Marvels* (New York: Benjamin Blom, 1964), p. 11. See also Marie-Françoise Christout, *Le merveilleux et le théâtre du silence* (Paris: Mouton, 1965).

29. Delia Gambelli ("'Quasi un racamo di concertate pezzette': le composizioni sul comico dell'Arlecchino Biancolelli," *Biblioteca teatrale,* no. 1 (1971), pp. 47–95) suggests we revise our notion that the "Commedia dell'Arte in France shows the characteristics of a spectacle fragmented by isolated lazzi based on the skills of the individual actors." She proposes that "the fragmentation and use of parallel elements could be in reality the superficial aspect of a much more complex organization by 'themes.'" She takes the term *theme* from the vocabulary of music, not literary criticism.

30. Gueullette, "Traduction," Ms. Rés. 625, pp. 331–32 (Spada, p. 206–7).

31. Colajanni, pp. 109–18.

32. *Lettres en vers,* 4 February 1673.

33. Gueullette, "Traduction," Ms. Rés. 625, p. 210 (Spada, p. 113).

34. Ibid., pp. 363–69 (Spada, pp. 231–34).

35. Ibid., pp. 403–11 (Spada, pp. 261–68).

36. Ibid., pp. 444–61 (Spada, pp. 292–302).

37. Ibid., pp. 488–99 (Spada, pp. 321–31); Colajanni, pp. 279–89.

38. Ibid., pp. 390–402 (Spada, pp. 251–

60); Colajanni, pp. 353–63.

39. Ibid., pp. 507–22 (Spada, pp. 338–46); Colajanni, pp. 149–59.

40. Ibid., p. 207 (Spada, p. 108).

41. Ibid., p. 463 (Spada, p. 304).

Chapter 10: The Hôtel de Bourgogne

1. La Grange, *Registre*, end of 1680 season.

2. *Mercure galant*, June 1680; La Grange, *Registre*.

3. Pierre Mélèse, *Le Théâtre et le public à Paris sous Louis XIV, 1659–1715* (1934; reprint: Geneva, Slatkine, 1976), p. 44n, cites "Mémoire pour les Comédiens du Roy contre Charles Dolet," AN, AD VIII 10, théâtres.

4. Mélèse, *Théâtre et public*, p. 44n.

5. See, for instance, Deierkauf-Holsboer, *Hôtel de Bourgogne;* D. H. Roy, "La Scène de l'Hôtel de Bourgogne," *Revue d'histoire du théâtre*, 13 (1963):227–35; David V. Illingworth, "Documents inédits et nouvelles précisions sur le théâtre de l'Hôtel de Bourgogne," *Revue d'histoire du théâtre*, 22 (1970):125–33; Graham Barlow, "The Hôtel de Bourgogne according to Sir James Thornhill," *Theatre Research International*, 1 (1976):86–98.

6. AN, MC XCIX, 172, cited by Deierkauf-Holsboer, *Hôtel de Bourgogne*, 2:183–86.

7. Barlow, p. 88.

8. Deierkauf-Holsboer, *Hôtel de Bourgogne*, 1:18.

9. H. C. Lancaster, *Le Mémoire de Mahelot, Laurent et d'autres décorateurs* (Paris: Honoré Champion, 1920); See also Roy, p. 234.

10. The height of the building is unknown, but even at the Palais-Royal, so low it required a trompe l'oeil gallery

painted on the ceiling to extend its apparent height, there was enough room above the ceiling for the rooms which brought down the beams. See chap. 4.

11. Robert L. Erenstein, paper on Gillot delivered at a Symposium on Theatre Iconography, Amsterdam, 1983. Privately communicated. See also Robert L. Erenstein, "Claude Gillot e il Théâtre Italien," *Biblioteca teatrale*, n.s. no. 2 (1986), pp. 23–43.

12. Roy, p. 231.

13. AN, MC XCIX, 172, cited by Deierkauf-Holsboer, *Hôtel de Bourgogne*, 2:184.

14. Deierkauf-Holsboer, *Hôtel de Bourgogne*, 2:57.

15. *Le banqueroutier*, Gherardi, *Théâtre italien*, 1700 ed., 1:425–27.

16. Tralage, "Recueil," Ms. 6544, fol. 178.

17. AN, MC IX, 421, cited by Jurgens and Maxfield-Miller, pp. 401–3.

18. Jurgens and Maxfield-Miller, pp. 403–4.

19. T. E. Lawrenson, *The French Stage in the XVIIth Century* (Manchester: Manchester Univ. Press, 1957), pp. 112–13.

20. Gherardi, *Théâtre italien*, 1700 ed., 1:98.

21. Ibid., 1:1–2.

22. Ibid., 1:83–134.

23. For a view of the complete almanac see Günter Schöne, "Almanache als

Zeugnisse für die Comédie Italienne, *Maske und Kothurn* 18 (1972):fig. 5. This set of prints, as well as the set for *Arlequin Jason* (see Erenstein, *De Geschiedenis,* pp. 171–73) are probably more reliable images of staging than the frontispieces done for the Gherardi collection of 1700. Created for the large calendar-almanacs so popular in the 1680s, these sets, along with the set of four from the almanac that featured *Arlequin grand visir* (See C. D. Rouillard, "A Forgotten *Arlequin Grand Visir* of 1687," *Theatre Annual* [1977], pp. 87–112) are in accord with other information about these performances.

24. Tralage, "Recueil," Ms. 6544, fol. 182.

25. Erenstein, *De Geschiedenis,* pp. 171–73.

26. Lancaster, *History, Part 4,* 2:618.

27. Lawrenson, p. 116.

28. Gherardi, *Théâtre italien,* 1700 ed., 1:331.

29. AN, O1.2821–22, and marquis de Dangeau, *Journal de la cour de Louis XIV,* ed. Eudore Soulié (Paris: Firmin-Didot, 1854–60). This source will be cited by date.

30. AN, MC CXIII, 129 (Migliori, pp. 111–12).

31. AN, MC CXIII, rep. 3., Jurgens and Fleury, p. 130. The actual documents are missing from the archives of this notary's chambers for the year. Dr. Amonio was a personal friend of Biancolelli's; the three young Bolognese noblemen whom he entertained met the doctor at Biancolelli's house (see Spada, p. xxxin).

32. AN, MC XV, 292 (Migliori, p. 103).

33. AN, O1.848; transcribed in Campardon, *Comédiens du roi,* 2:225–30.

34. Gherardi, *Théâtre italien,* 1700 ed., 2:111–12.

35. Tralage, "Recueil," Ms. 6544, fol. 178.

36. Tralage, *Notes et documents,* p. 62.

37. Ibid.

38. These *jetons* were struck by the troupes and given out to the actors who attended company meetings or assemblies. The French *jeton* was struck in 1682 and featured Louis XIV on one side and, on the other, a beehive with the motto *simul et singulis* above and *comédiens du roy* below. Each silver *jeton* had a value of 30 sous. Absentees forfeited their *jetons.* See La Grange, *Registre,* 31 August 1682.

39. Lancaster, *History, Part 4,* 1:42.

40. Barlow, p. 94.

41. Gherardi, *Théâtre italien,* 1700 ed., 1:424–27.

42. *L'Art poétique,* 3:146–47, cited by Mélèse, *Théâtre et public,* p. 217n.

43. Mélèse, *Théâtre et public,* p. 216.

44. Gherardi, *Théâtre italien,* 1700 ed., 2:111.

45. Mittman, pp. 42–43.

46. Gherardi, *Théâtre italien,* 1700 ed., 2:facing p. 109.

47. Ibid., 3:211–13.

48. Quoted by Lough, p. 96.

49. Tralage, "Recueil," Ms. 6544, fol. 178.

50. AN, O1.2820–21.

51. H. C. Lancaster, *The Comédie-Française, 1680–1701* (Baltimore: Johns Hopkins Univ. Press, 1941), p. 14; La Grange, end of season 1683–84.

52. Tralage, "Recueil," Ms. 6544, fol. 178.

53. Lancaster, *History, Part 4,* 1:19.

54. AN, O1.848, transcribed in Campardon, *Comédiens du roi*, 2:225–30.

55. *Mercure galant,* May 1680.

56. AN, O1.2820.

57. AN, O1.2821.

58. AN, O1.2826–28.

59. Charles Montjean, "La troupe de Molière à Saint-Germain-en-Laye au XVIIe siécle," *Revue de l'histoire de Versailles* 38 (1936):146–61.

60. Alfred Marie, "Les théâtres du château de Versailles," *Revue d'histoire du théâtre,* 3 (1951):136–41.

61. Ibid., p. 141.

62. Alfred Marie, "La salle du théâtre du château de Fontainebleau," *Revue d'histoire du théâtre,* 3 (1951):237–47.

63. Dangeau, 16 October 1684.

64. *Mercure galant,* November 1682, pp. 343–50.

65. *Mercure galant,* March 1683, p. 329.

66. Pierre Mélèse, *Répertoire analytique des documents contemporains d'information concernant le théâtre à Paris sous Louis XIV* (Paris: Droz, 1934), p. 31.

67. Campardon, *Comédiens du roi,* 1:xx–xxi.

68. Jal, s.v. "Romagnesi."

69. Cotolendi, *Livre sans non,* pp. 4–5.

Chapter 11: A Company Rejuvenated

1. AN, O1.2820.

2. Parfaict and Parfaict, *Histoire de l'ancien théâtre italien,* p. 83.

3. Gueullette, "Histoire," Ms. Rés. 625, fol. 104r.

4. See fig. 11.

5. AN, MC CXIII, 129 (Migliori, pp. 111–12).

6. Rasi, 1:714.

7. Ibid., 1:663–4.

8. AN, MC XV, 292 (Migliori, pp. 104–5).

9. The formula: "I, the undersigned, promise to renounce and do henceforth renounce the profession of actress." See Jurgens and Maxfield-Miller, p. 504n, who only refer to and do not reproduce the original document, AN, M.792, 43, a note made by Père Léonard in 1682. The original has been removed from the file and is in the possession of Mme. Jurgens, head of the Minutier Central section of the Archives Nationales. Although I asked repeatedly that it be retrieved, it never was.

10. Gueullette, "Histoire," Ms. Rés. 625, fol. 106r.

11. Marriage contract, AN, MC I, 183 (Migliori, pp. 107–10).

12. Ibid.

13. AN, MC XV, 339, 346 (Migliori, pp. 130, 132).

14. Tralage, "Recueil," Ms. 6544, p. 220.

15. Gherardi, *Théâtre italien,* 1700 ed., 4:273.

16. Ibid., p. 270.

17. Gueullette, "Histoire," Ms. Rés. 625, fols. 114r–120v, copied from the Mémoire de Maître Mars, avocat au Parlement, pour le sieur Charles-Dominique de Turgis et la dame Anne-Marie Reine de Turgis, etc.

18. Parfaict and Parfaict, *Histoire de l'ancien théâtre italien,* pp. 30–31.

19. Rasi, 2:605.

20. Gherardi, *Théâtre italien*, 1700 ed., 2:109–10.

21. Costantini, p. 59.

22. Gueullette, "Histoire," Ms. Rés. 625, fol. 84r&v.

23. *Lettres italiennes*, 2:15, fol. 966, quoted by Gueullette, "Histoire," Ms. Rés. 625, fol. 61r.

24. I take the *vieux* in this case to mean that Zanotti was an old man, and not that it was used as a means of distinguishing him from the new Octave, Giovanni Battista Costantini, who made his debut in 1688 after Aurelio was deported. The term normally employed to avoid confusion between two actors who played the same role or used the same name in art is *ancien*, as in *le Scaramouche ancien*. There is no need to assert, as Spaziani does, that Zanotti must have returned to Paris and played simultaneously with Costantini. See Marcello Spaziani, ed., *Il* Théâtre Italien *di Gherardi* (Rome: Ateneo, 1966), p. 609.

25. Rasi, 2:605.

26. Gueullette, "Histoire," Ms. Rés 625, fol. 125r.

27. Rasi, 1:907.

28. Jal, s.v. "Tortoriti."

29. *Revue d'histoire du théâtre* 1 (1949): 161. The original document is in the Bibliothèque Mazarine, Ms. 3951, and is not dated.

30. Courville, *Lélio: L'expérience française*, p. 12.

31. Rasi, 2:744.

32. Ibid., 2:747.

33. Ibid., 2:746–77.

34. Ibid., 2:323.

35. *Mercure galant*, April 1685.

36. Gherardi, *Théâtre italien*, 1700 ed., 1:518–19.

37. Despois, p. 68.

38. Mélèse, *Répertoire*, p. 16.

39. Gueullette, "Histoire," Ms. Rés. 625, fol. 123r.

40. Gherardi, "Avertissement," *Théâtre italien*, 1700 ed., 1:n.p.

41. Gherardi, *Théâtre italien*, 1700 ed., 4:15. Polichinelle is a character in a play entitled *Les souffleurs* added to the 1694 edition of Gherardi's *Le théâtre italien* when it was reprinted the following year by Jacques Dentand in Geneva. In the play Cinthio and the Docteur are searching for the philosopher's stone. Polichinelle enters, hoping to join the assembly of philosophers. They examine him, ask him who he is and what his secrets are. He answers: "Who am I? What a question, ha, ha. I am the true Polichinel of Rome, prime mover, great administrator of the marionettes and director of the machines that accompany them. I am a famous astrologer, clever mathematician, engineer, sorcerer and magician. That's what I am. I know how to make inanimate bodies speak and move. I know how to compose almanacs, make talismens, bring hidden treasures to light, conjure up spirits, and make myself invisible." When asked what he knows of projection, the great elixir, perpetual motion, and other alchemical matters, he answers: "The great elixir is good wine, perpetual motion is the movement of the jaws, the fixed point is the table." The Doctor sends him away, saying in Italian: "I don't like an ugly face. Like yours. Go away." Polichinelle answers, "I going to reduce you to a cinder." At which, "he sets off a rocket and a rain of fire falls."

42. For a brief biography of Fracansani, see Proto-Giurleo, pp. 243–47.

43. Ibid.

44. Gillot was not born until 1673 and was only twenty-four when the Italian troupe was expelled from Paris. According to Emile Dacier, the drawings are too skillful to have been done by such a young man, and must represent either imagined scenes based on a later reading of the texts published by Gherardi or performances by the fair theatres or the new Italian troupe which came in 1716. Yet the extant and available drawings all represent scenes from the pre-1697 repertory, and the characters represented in them are all characters played by the Italian troupe in the 1690s. The drawings do not necessarily match exactly the Gherardi texts, but that is hardly surprising since the Gherardi texts do not necessarily reflect what actually happened on the Italian stage. Robert L. Erenstein's "Claude Gillot e il Théâtre Italien" is an excellent analysis of the problems the historian encounters in using as evidence Gillot's drawings and the engravings later made from them.

45. Gueullette, "Histoire," Ms. Rés. 625, fol. 109r.

46. Campardon, *Comédiens du roi,* 1:236.

47. Gueullette, "Histoire," Ms. Rés. 625, fol. 104r.

48. Cotelendi, *Livre sans nom,* p. 1.

49. Rasi, 1:793–94. Her mother was also in the troupe.

50. Gueullette, "Histoire," Ms. Rés. 625, fols. 106v–107r.

51. Rasi, 1:907.

52. Ibid., 1:903.

53. Ibid., 1:902–8.

54. Campardon, *Comédiens du roi,* 1:233–34.

55. See variously in Campardon under the actors' names.

56. Gueullette, "Histoire," Ms. Rés. 625, fol. 93r&v.

57. Gherardi, *Théâtre italien,* 1700 ed., 2:142–43.

58. Eudore Soulié, p. 97, estimates Molière's worth at 40,000 livres.

59. AN, MC XXIII, 364 (Migliori, pp. 115–24).

60. According to Gueullette ("Histoire," Ms. Rés. 625, fol. 117r.) Biancolelli also owned a country house at Bièvre near Meudon. It is referred to in the lawyer's memorandum concerning the marriage of Françoise Biancolelli—"The widow Biancolelli had a country house at Bièvre"—but does not appear in the inventory. When Molière's inventory was done, the notaries accompanied Armande Béjart to Auteuil, where Molière "occupied an apartment" and listed the property found there along with the Paris property. Perhaps the house at Bièvre was bought by Orsola Cortesi after her husband's death.

61. Tralage, "Recueil," Ms. 6544, fol. 177.

Chapter 12: The Transitional French Repertory

1. See chap. 10. Louis Moland (*Molière et la comédie italienne* [Paris: Didier, 1867], pp. 371–72) lists a number of other productions at court which he claims to have derived from court accounts.He gives no specific sources, however, and I have been unable to find the accounts for these years in either the Archives Nationales or the Fonds Colbert at the Bibliothèque Nationale. I have thus decided to make limited use of Moland's list, but will reproduce it here and include it in the Ap-

pendix: *La propreté ridicule* (July 1678), *La magie naturelle* (December 1678), *Le combat à cheval* (May 1680), *Eularia muette par amour* (May 1680), *Les quatre Scaramouches* (June 1680), *Le deuil de Scaramouche et d'Arlequin* (June 1680), *La jalousie de Scaramouche et d'Arlequin* (June 1680), *Les juifs de Babylone* (July 1680), *Arlequin soldat déserteur* (July 1680), *Arlequin vendangeur* (December 1681), *Arlequin valet étourdie* (April 1682), *La maladie de Spezzafer* (May 1682), *Arlequin tombé dans le puits* (June 1682), *Le deuil d'Arlequin* (June 1682), *Arlequin juif, peintre et tailleur* (June 1682), *Arlequin cabaretier, turc, et capitaine espagnol* (June 1682). Several of these entertainments appear to be the same as or similar to entries in Biancolelli's zibaldone; several others may be related to materials in Ms. 9329 and the *Supplément;* none are included in Gherardi's collection. The pattern of performance is as one might expect from other information.

2. AN, O1.2827.

3. Gherardi, "Avertissement," *Théâtre italien,* 1700 ed., 1:n.p.

4. But see Deloffre, who argues that this irregular publication contains satirical material which was played by the Italians but could not be published under royal license. He calls particular attention to the attack on the military in *Arlequin soldat enrolé par force.*

5. Campardon, *Comédiens du roi,* 2:110–12, cites AN, Y.11, 123.

6. See below for details of this incident.

7. Evaristo Gherardi, *Le théâtre italien, ou le recueil de toutes les scènes françoise qui ont esté jouée sur le théâtre italien de l'Hostel de Bourgogne* (Paris: Guillaume de Luynes, 1694).

8. Campardon, *Comédiens du roi,* 2:109–10.

9. Gherardi, "Avertissement," *Théâtre italien,* 1700 ed., 1:n.p.

10. An excellent bibliography of counterfeit and pirated editions can be found in the *Enciclopedia dello spettacolo,* s.v. "Gherardi, Evaristo."

11. Giacomo Cavallucci, "Fatouville, auteur dramatique," *Revue d'histoire litteraire de la France,* 43 (1936):481–572.

12. Gueullette, "Traduction," Ms. Rés. 625 (Spada, p. 176).

13. Tralage, "Recueil," Ms. 6544, fol. 182.

14. Pierre Bayle, *Nouvelles de la republique de lettres,* March 1684, Amsterdam, pp. 199–210.

15. Campardon, *Comédiens du roi,* 2:111, cites AN, Y 11,123.

16. Lancanster, *History, Part 4,* 2:607.

17. Gherardi, *Théâtre italien,* 1700 ed., 2:99.

18. *Mercure galant,* December 1683, p. 321.

19. Gherardi, *Théâtre italien,* 1700 ed., 1:1–16. All the references to play texts which follow in this chapter, unless otherwise cited, are to be found in vol. 1 of the 1700 edition of Gherardi.

20. N.-M. Bernardin, *La Comédie-Italienne en France et les théâtres de la foire et du boulevard, 1570–1791* (Paris: Editions de la Revue Bleue, 1902), p. 56n.

21. Lancanster, *History, Part 4,* 2:610–11.

22. AN, O1.2820.

23. See fig. 10.

24. Lancanster, *History, Part 4,* 2:614.

25. AN, MC XV, 292 (Migliori, p. 103).

26. *Mercure galant,* March 1684.

27. The second *servante* must originally have been Diamantine.

28. See chap. 10 for a discussion of the cascade.

29. Arlequin also wants to know if the Italian actor is being punished for speaking French, which suggests that the use of French by the Italian troupe was an issue at the time *Arlequin Jason* appeared.

30. In the Gherardi frontispiece (1700 ed.) the French actor appears to be an amoureux.

31. Robert L. Erenstein, "Unbekannte Illustrationen des Théâtre Italien," *Maske und Kothurn* 31 (1985):fig. 13.

32. Although it is entered in the *Supplément* as a scene from *Isabelle médecin*, the scene in question is actually the tirade from *Arlequin chevalier du soleil*. The possibility certainly exists that the *Supplément* has the attribution right and Gherardi has it wrong, since the material is unlike Arlequin's usual medical burlesques.

33. For a more detailed discussion of *Colombine avocat pour et contre*, see my article, "The *Jeu* and the *Rôle*," in *Western Popular Theatre*, ed. David Mayer and Kenneth Richards (London: Methuen, 1977), pp. 1–27.

34. *Supplément*, pp. 1–5, 278–80.

35. See n. 1 above.

36. Lancaster (*History, Part 4*, 2:617) relies on Mélèse (*Répertoire*, p. 178), but Mélèse has misdated and slightly misrepresented Bayle, who writes: "On écrit de Paris que la Troupe de l'Hôtel de Bourgogne, qui est celle des Comédiens Italiens représente une comédie très divertissante, & qui attire une foule extraordinaire. Elle s'intitule Arlequin Empereur dans le Monde de la Lune. C'est, dit-on, une Satyre de l'opera d'Amadis, & on ajoûte qu'on doit répresenter incessamment dans le même Hôtel, Amadis Cuisinier, parce que ce lui qui fait le personnage d'Amadis dans l'opera a été Cuisinier. Ces nouvelles ne sont pas trop apparentes, car comme on sçait que le Roy lui-même a donné le sujet de l'opera d'Amadis, qui oseroit en faire des railleries si publique." By separating this into three notes, one announcing a satire of *Amadis*, one on *Arleqin empereur*, and one on *Amadis cuisinier*, and by attributing part of it to March 1684 and part of it to April, Mélèse has managed to lose the sense of the whole.

37. For an excellent account of this illustrated calendar see Rouillard, pp. 87–112.

Chapter 13: Struggle and Expulsion

1. Parfaict and Parfaict, *Histoire du théâtre français*, 13:121–22.

2. Tralage, *Notes et Documents*, p. 99.

3. Ibid., p. 6.

4. Gherardi, *Théâtre italien*, 1700 ed., 2:453, 458.

5. Ibid., 3:309.

6. AN, MC CXIII, rép. 4. The contracts are missing; only the index remains. As a result, there is no record of how the money is to be spent.

7. AN, O1.2824.

8. AN, MC XV, 327 (Migliori, p. 126).

9. AN, O1.848.

10. Parfaict and Parfaict, *Histoire du théâtre français*, 13:121.

11. Gherardi, *Théâtre italien*, 1700 ed., 3:613.

12. Ibid., 3:504.

13. David V. Illingworth, "L'Hôtel de Bourgogne: une salle de théâtre à l'italienne à Paris en 1647," *Revue d'histoire du théâtre*, 23 (1971):43.

14. Barlow, p. 89.

15. Gherardi, *Théâtre italien,* 1700 ed., 4:271; 3:211.

16. Mittman, p. 59.

17. Gherardi, *Théâtre italien,* 1700 ed., 2:436–37.

18. Ibid., 4:324. The Italians played five days a week, with three weeks off for the annual Easter break. During the same period the French, who played seven days a week, gave 81 performances and made 46,967 livres, 8 sous. See Lancaster, *Comédie-Française,* pp. 127–30.

19. Tralage, "Recueil," Ms. 6544, fol. 205v.

20. Tralage, *Notes et documents,* p. 30.

21. AN, O1.2827–29; Dangeau, 21 September 1693 and 21 September 1694.

22. Campardon, *Comédiens du roi,* 1:141–42.

23. Ibid., 1:242–43.

24. AN, MC XV, 327 (Migliori, p. 127).

25. Tralage, "Recueil," Ms. 6544, fols. 181–82.

26. Campardon, *Comédiens du roi,* 1:137–39.

27. Gherardi, *Théâtre italien,* 1700 ed., 3:211–12.

28. Ibid., 2:109–12.

29. Ibid., 4:4.

30. Mélèse, *Théâtre et public,* pp. 219–20.

31. Tralage, "Receuil," Ms. 6544, fol. 171.

32. Mélèse, *Théâtre et public,* pp. 219–20.

33. Gherardi, *Théâtre italien,* 1700 ed., 4:218.

34. Parfaict and Parfaict, *Histoire du théâtre français,* 3:237–38n.

35. Raymond Lebègue, "Premières infiltrations de la commedia dell'arte dans le théâtre français," *Cahiers de l'association internationale des études français* 15 (1963):167.

36. Georges Mongrédien, "La querelle du théâtre à la fin du règne de Louis XIV," *Revue d'histoire du théâtre,* 30 (1978):103.

37. Gaston Maugras, *Les comédiens hors la loi* (Paris: Calmann Lévy, 1887), p. 108.

38. Ibid., p. 142.

39. Ibid., p. 158.

40. *L'école du monde,* cited by Tralage, *Notes et documents,* pp. 34–35.

41. *Relations véritables,* 31 December 1694.

42. Mélèse, *Théâtre et public,* pp. 76–77.

43. Campardon, *Comédiens du roi,* 1:xxii–xxiii.

44. Ibid., 1:248.

45. 21 January 1697, quoted in Mélèse, *Théâtre et public,* p. 79.

46. Jal, s.v. "Comédie Italienne"; Campardon, *Comédiens du roi,* 1:xxiv.

47. Germaine Brice, *Description de la ville de Paris,* 6th ed. (Paris: Fr. Fournier, 1713), 1:317.

48. Mélèse, *Théâtre et public,* p. 54 n. 3.

49. Ibid, p. 54.

50. Gueullette, "Histoire," Ms. Rés. 625, fol. 127r.

51. Ibid., fol. 126v.

52. Lancaster, *Comédie-Française,* pp. 156–72.

53. Jules Bonnassies, *La Comédie-Française: histoire administrative, 1658–1757* (Paris: Didier, 1874), p. 51.

54. Ibid., p. 52.

55. AN, MC XV, 341 (Migliori, p. 131).

56. Pierre Goubert, *Louis XIV and Twenty Million Frenchmen*, trans. Anne Carter (New York: Vintage, 1972), p. 281.

57. *Relations véritables*, 21 March 1699.

58. Bonnassies, p. 52.

59. Claude Parfaict and Godin d'Abguerbe, *Dictionnaire des théâtres de Paris* (Paris: Lambert, 1755) 1:434.

60. Jal, s.v. "Comédie Italienne."

Chapter 14: The Terrible Costantinis

1. Beginning with *Le marchand dupé*, the Gherardi frontispieces show a Scaramouche, while the texts indicate Pasquariel.

2. AN, MC XV, 327 (Migliori, p. 127).

3. Gueullette, "Histoire," Ms. Rés. 625, fol. 102r&v.

4. Rasi, 1:708–9.

5. AN, MC XV, 346 (Migliori, p. 134).

6. Gherardi, *Théâtre italien*, 1700 ed., 3:1–50.

7. Campardon, *Comédiens du roi*, 1:137–38.

8. Donald J. Grout, "The Music of the Italian Theatre at Paris, 1682–97," *Papers of the American Musicological Society* (1941), p. 162.

9. Tralage, *Notes et documents*, pp. 64–65.

10. Rasi, 1:723–24. The couple played together in London in the 1670s along with Constantino Costantini and Giuseppe Tortoriti. See Ifan Kyrle Fletcher, "Italian Comedians in England in the 17th Century," *Theatre Notebook* 8 (1953–54):86–91.

11. See chaps. 12 and 13.

12. Rasi, 1:722.

13. Campardon, *Comédiens du roi*, 1:242–43. This document, from AN, Y. 14,500, implies that Costantini was the orator of the troupe in 1692. An excellent portrait of Octave can be seen in an anonymous painting, reproduced in color by Molinari, *La commedia dell'arte*, p. 214. Left of center, in a red coat decorated with gold,

Octave, as orator, accepts the order closing the theatre. The original painting is in the Musée de la ville de Le Havre.

14. Gherardi, *Théâtre italien*, 1700 ed., 2:201.

15. Ibid.

16. Jal, s.v. "Gherardi."

17. Gherardi, *Théâtre italien*, 1700 ed., 5:345.

18. Ibid., 2:201–2.

19. Ibid., "Avertissement," n.p.

20. Ibid.

21. Ibid.

22. Parfaict and Parfaict, *Histoire de l'ancien théâtre italien*, p. 125.

23. AN, MC XV, 327 (Migliori, p. 127).

24. Gueullette, "Histoire," Ms. Rés. 625, fol. 125r.

25. Tralage, "Recueil," Ms. 6541, fol. 256.

26. Gueullette, "Histoire," Ms. Rés. 625, fols. 100r, 82v.

27. AN, O1.848; Campardon, *Comédiens du roi*, 1:296.

28. AN, O1.848; Campardon, *Comédiens du roi*, 1:116.

29. Gherardi, *Théâtre italien*, 1700 ed., 5:359–60.

30. Gueullette, "Histoire," Ms. Rés. 625, fol. 125v.

31. AN, O1.848; Campardon, *Comédiens du roi*, 2:144.

32. Campardon, *Comédiens du roi,* 1:234.

33. Jal, s.v. "Fiorilli."

34. AN, MC XV, 346 (Migliori, pp. 134–35).

35. Gueullette, "Histoire," Ms. Rés. 625, fol. 53v.

36. AN, O1.848; Campardon, *Comédiens du roi,* 1:296.

37. Jal, s.v. "Lolli."

38. AN, MC XV, *Répertoire des minutes des contractes de l'hot. de ville de paris passez par . . . Jean Desgranges, 1692.*

39. Gherardi, *Théâtre italien,* 1700 ed., 6:300–321.

40. AN, MC XV, 346 (Migliori, pp. 132–33).

41. Letter to T.-S. Gueullette, Ms. Rés. 625, pp. 516–517.

42. Gueullette, "Histoire," Ms. Rés. 625, fol. 120v.

43. Campardon, *Comédiens du roi,* 1:65–68.

44. Gueullette, "Histoire," Ms. Rés. 625, fol. 97r.

45. Jal, s.v. "Romagnesi."

46. Gueullette, "Histoire," Ms. Rés. 625, fols. 99r–101r.

47. Jal, s.v. "Biancolelli."

48. Gueullette, "Histoire," Ms. Rés. 625, fol. 107v; Parfaict and Parfaict, *Histoire de l'ancien théâtre italien,* pp. 85–87.

49. *Mercure de France,* February 1729.

50. *Enciclopedia dello spettacolo,* s.v. "Commedia dell'arte."

51. Gueullette, "Histoire," Ms. Rés. 625, fol. 104v.

52. Thomas-Simon Gueullette, *Notes et souvenirs sur le théâtre italien au XVIIIe siècle,* ed. J.-E. Gueullette (Paris: Droz, 1938), p. 113; Courville, *Lélio: L'expérience française,* 314n.

53. Parfaict and Parfaict, *Histoire de l'ancien théâtre italien,* p. 92.

54. Letter to T.-S. Gueullette from Anne-Elisabeth Costantini, Ms. Rés. 625, p. 515.

55. Parfaict and Parfaict, *Histoire de l'ancien théâtre italien,* p. 117.

56. Ibid.

57. Michèle Venard, *La foire entre en scène* (Paris: Librairie Théatrale, 1985), p. 87.

58. Courville, *Lélio: L'expérience française,* p. 26.

59. Ibid., p. 28.

60. AN, O1.848; Courville, *Lélio: L'expérience française,* pp. 29–30.

61. Courville, *Lélio: L'expérience française,* p. 44.

62. Mélèse, *Théâtre et public,* p. 56 n. 4.

63. Courville, *Lélio: l'expérience française,* p. 101.

64. Ibid., p. 12n.

65. Campardon, *Comédiens du roi,* 1:236.

66. Guellette, "Histoire," Ms. Res. 625, fol. 124v.

67. Campardon, *Comédiens du roi,* 1:242.

68. Parfaict and Parfaict, *Histoire de l'ancien théâtre italien,* pp. 126–27.

69. Gueullette, "Histoire," Ms. Rés. 625, fol. 113v.

Chapter 15: The Gherardi Repertory

1. Lancaster (*History, Part 4*) reconstructs plots and speculates about antecedents from the French repertory; Attinger analyzes the influence of the Gherardi plays on the French comic theatre of the late 17th century; Alexandre

Calame has written an excellent literary biography of Regnard (*Regnard: sa vie et son ouevre* [Paris: Presses Universitaires de France, 1960]) and has published a critical edition of the eleven plays he wrote alone and with Dufresny (*Jean-François Regnard: comédies du théâtre italien* [Geneva: Droz, 1981]); François Moureau has published an equally excellent biography of Dufresny, with particular attention paid to the theatricality of his work (*Dufresny, auteur dramatique, 1657–1724* [Paris: Klincksieck, 1979]); Marcello Spaziani's anthology of pieces from Gherardi's collection has a useful introduction and notes.

2. See Moureau's bibliography in *Dufresny, auteur dramatique,* pp. 478–79, 482–83, for a listing of some manuscripts and single editions.

3. There are often differences, even in Gherardi's final edition, between the texts, the cast lists, and the frontispieces. The text may indicate Cinthio, the cast list Octave, the frontispiece Léandre. Many of these plays were in the repertory over a period of time and changed as the company changed. I assume that the late texts are the most accurate, since there are fewer discrepancies, the texts are more complete, and they were produced closer to the date of publication.

4. See bibliographies in Calame, *Regnard: sa vie,* and Moureau, *Dufresny, auteur dramatique.*

5. Some questions have been raised about his authorship, but Gueullette, who interviewed his brother, writes: "He gave to the Italian theatre *La fausse coquette,* played the 18th of December, 1694, and (I have been assured of this) he worked with Dufresny on the comedy of *Pasquin and Marforio, médecines des moeurs* given to the public the 3rd of February 1697" (*Histoire,* Ms. Res. 625, fo. 95v).

6. Campardon, *Comédiens du roi,* 1:248. Gherardi, in a note crammed into the last page of the text (*Théâtre italien,* 1700 ed., 6:212), admits that one scene was given to him by "one illustrious in the Republic of Letters."

7. The possibility continues to exist that the first edition of Gherardi contains earlier states of the texts. In *La cause des femmes,* for instance, the 1694 Gherardi includes only detached scenes and ornaments, while the later edition includes plot scenes as well.

8. Gherardi, *Théâtre italien,* 1700 ed., 2:99. All references to the texts and all quotations from them are from this edition, although only substantial quotations have been cited.

9. This comic routine was introduced to Paris in 1674 by Evaristo Gherardi's father, Giovanni Gherardi, who played Flautin.

10. Although the actor playing the role is not identified, Arlequin's line "That man there's a woman . . ." gives the travesty away.

11. Assuming that in the original text, played in 1688, Aurelio was Isabelle's lover, why should the published text be different? One possible answer is that Isabelle is a married woman and the more prudish world of 1700 would not tolerate a married woman seeking a divorce in order to be with her lover.

12. Calame, *Regnard: sa vie,* pp. 149–50.

13. A typical textual problem. In the text the "man in black" is the Docteur, but in the cast of characters the Docteur is Isabelle's uncle. The frontispiece shows Scaramouche, which is far better casting. The discrepancies probably arise from the fact that Fiorilli, an old man, was replaced by Tortoriti, a young man, mean-

ing that the Docteur had to take over the role.

14. Lancaster, *History, Part 4,* 2:634.

15. After the bergamot orange, and a scent much used in the period, but also with overtones of Bergamask, resident of Bergamo, Arlequin's home town.

16. The frontispiece, however, shows Isabelle at the table and Claudine behind. Gherardi may have confused this with Isabelle's role in *Les filles errantes.*

17. The plot is reminiscent of *Le dragon de Moscovie* and *Colombine avocat pour et contre.*

18. This is the second time Gherardi notes playing without a mask. Perhaps Gherardi was envious of Costantini, who had discarded his mask so his handsome face could be seen. Playing without masks suggests that neither the actors nor the playwrights really understood the way in which the tipi fissi functioned in a play.

19. Gherardi, *Théâtre italien,* 1700 ed., 3:54.

20. Ibid., p. 132. For a discussion of the use of satires and other literary ornaments, see below.

21. See chap. 13.

22. For various reasons—convention, frequent replacement—the amoureux were the last characters to consistently speak Italian.

23. Gherardi, *Théâtre italien,* 1700 ed., 3:414–15.

24. This is only the second time in the entire extant repertory that the masque of Arlequin is used as a disguise. See chap. 9 for a discussion of *Le collier de perle.* In *Arlequin Jason* Medea changes Jason into Arlequin, which is slightly different.

25. One of the most spectacular effects performed on a Paris public stage in the century. Gherardi, *Théâtre italien,* 1700 ed., 3:504.

26. Lancaster, *History, Part 4,* 2:630.

27. There is some question about the date. Gherardi has 4 June, Gueullette has 4 February. Since that was the opening day of *Arlequin Phaeton,* it seems likely Gueullette is in error. A summer date is also supported by Arlequin's line in the Prologue: "We don't earn very much in the summer."

28. While a standard feature of farce, the henpecked husband is not usual in the commedia dell'arte, perhaps because the role of the shrew did not appeal to the women. When an older woman was included in the cast of characters, the role was normally played by a man, although Orsola Cortesi did play several at the Comédie-Italienne. In the Gherardi repertory, beginning probably with the Nurse in *Colombine femme vengée,* older women's roles were played by Pierrot and Mezzetin.

29. Gherardi, *Théâtre italien,* 1700 ed., 4:15–16.

30. Ibid., 4:59.

31. *Isabelle medicin* and *Arlequin chevalier de la soleil* opened on the same day, according to Gherardi, so one may have been an afterpiece. However, both are too fragmentary to infer which one it might have been.

32. Lancaster, *History, Part 4,* 2:820.

33. Ibid., 2:782. For the Italians' plays, the label *comédie-en-vaudeville* is a misnomer. Although they used vaudevilles, no single play uses only vaudevilles. See below for a discussion of the use of music by the Italians.

34. Riccoboni requested, in 1716, that the new troupe be granted "dances and music in the divertissements of their

plays as their predecessors had enjoyed" (Courville, *Lélio: L'expérience française,* p. 26).

35. *Mercure galant,* November 1692, January 1693, etc.

36. Lancaster, *History, Part 4,* 2:669.

37. Moureau, *Dufresny, auteur dramatique,* p. 185.

38. These were official changes in the composition of the troupe. De facto changes had taken place earlier in the cases of Léandre and Scaramouche.

39. In *Le théâtre sans comédie,* Gueullette, "Traduction," Ms. Rés. 625, fols 274–291 (Spada, pp. 166–73).

40. Lancaster, *History, Part 4,* 2:693.

41. Gherardi, *Théâtre italien,* 1700 ed., 6:321.

42. A print based on Gillot's drawings is included in Duchartre, *La commedia dell'arte et ses enfants,* facing p. 256. The French director, Ariane Mnouchkine, used a similar scene in her recent film on the life of Molière.

43. Gherardi, *Théâtre italien,* 1700 ed., 6:486–88.

44. Spinette, Maria Teresa D'Orsi, is also a possibility, but she was Italian and a recent arrival, and the songs are in French.

45. Gherardi, *Théâtre italien,* 1700 ed., 6:646–47.

46. Ibid., 4:170.

47. The music of the *Théâtre Italien* has been studied by Grout, and by Maurice Barthélémy, "La Critique et l'actualité musicales dans le 'Théâtre Italien' de Gherardi," *Revue d'histoire littéraire de la France* 59 (1959):481–90.

48. Gherardi, *Théâtre italien,* 1700 ed., 2:105.

49. Moureau, *Dufresny, auteur dramatique,* p. 47.

50. Campardon, *Comédiens du roi,* 1:137. The complaint was filed by Constantino Costantini. The date, 5 February 1696, is slightly more than a month after the 26 December 1695 opening of *La Foire St. Germain.*

51. Grout, p. 167.

52. Moureau, *Dufresny, auteur dramatique,* pp. 470–72.

53. Attinger, p. 200.

54. An Italian repertory was played, certainly at court through 1696, probably in Paris, but nothing is known of it other than a few titles and dates, so it cannot be described or analyzed. The titles suggest typical commedia dell'arte entertainments, but it would not be surprising if they had been affected by developments in the French repertory. For titles and dates, see the Appendix.

55. *Les fées,* Gherardi, *Théâtre italien,* 1700 ed., 6:682.

◇◇◇◇◇◇◇◇◇◇◇◇◇◇◇◇

Bibliography

Manuscripts

Archives Nationales

Série KK. Monuments historiques.
213–214, Comptes des menus plaisirs.
Série O1. Maison du roi.
848–854, Comédie-Italienne.
2815–2829, Recettes et dépenses de la maison du roi, argenterie, menus plaisirs, et affaires de la chambre.
Minutier Central.

Etude I	File 183.
Etude VI	Files 368, 578.
Etude VII	File 104.
Etude IX	File 421.
Etude XIII	File 121.
Etude XV	Files 292, 327, 331, 339, 341, 346.
Etude XXIII	File 364.
Etude XLII	File 156.
Etude XLV	File 266.
Etude LIII	Files 35, 54.
Etude LXXIII	File 441.
Etude XC	File 259.
Etude XCVI	File 82.
Etude XCIX	File 172.
Etude CXIII	Files 129, 131.
Etude CXXI	File 2.

Bibliothèque de l'Arsenal
Tralage, Jean Nicolas de. "Recueil." Ms. 6541–45.

Bibliothèque de l'Opéra
Gueullette, Thomas-Simon. "Traduction du scenario de Joseph
Dominique Biancolelli, dit Arlequin" et "Histoire du théâtre
italien establie en France depuis l'année 1577 jusqu'en l'année
1750 et les anneés suivantes." Ms. Réserve 625.

Bibliothèque Nationale
  "Copie de la traduction du scenario de Joseph Dominique Bianco-
    lelli." Ms. fonds français 9328.
  "Etats de la dépense et recette du trésor royal, 1662–1681." Ms.
    fonds Colbert 264–310.
  "Sujets de plusieurs comédies italiennes non imprimées dans le re-
    cueil de Gherardi." Ms. fonds français 9329.

Periodicals

La gazette. 1631 et seq.
La muze dauphine. Subligny. 1666–67.
*La muze historique, ou recueil des lettres en vers contenant les nouvelles du
  temps.* Jean Loret. 1650–1665. Edited in five volumes by J.
  Ravenal and V. De La Pelouze. Paris: Jamet, 1859–78.
Le mercure galant. Donneau de Visé. 1672–74; 1677 et seq.
Lettres en vers à Madame. Robinet. May 1665–June 1670; *Lettres en
  vers à l'ombre de Madame.* July 1670; *Lettres en vers à Monsieur.*
  August 1670–September 1673; *Lettres en vers à LL. AA. RR.
  Monsieur et Madame.* April–December 1674. Robinet's gazettes
  through 1667, along with those by Mayolas and Subligny, are
  collected in *Les continuateurs de Loret.* Edited in three volumes
  by James de Rothschild. Paris: Morgand et Fatou, 1881–89.
Lettres en vers et en prose. Mayolas. 1668–69, 1671.
Nouvelles de la république des lettres. Amsterdam, 1684–89, 1699–1710.
Relations véritables. Brussels, 1659–1715.

Books and Articles

Adam, Antoine. *Histoire de la littérature française au XVIIe siècle.* 4 vols.
  Paris: Domat, 1948–54.
Apollonio, Mario. *Storia della commedia dell'arte.* 1930. Reprint. Flor-
  ence: Sansoni, 1982.
*Argument de la grande pièce intitulée la Rosaure imperatrice de Constanti-
  nople.* Paris: René Baudry, 1658. A surviving copy is bound
  into Bibliothèque de l'Opéra Ms. Res. 625, fols. 76r–79v.
Attinger, Gustave. *L'esprit de la commedia dell'arte dans le théâtre fran-
  çais.* Paris: Librairie Théatrale, 1950.
Barlow, Graham. "The Hôtel de Bourgogne according to Sir James
  Thornhill." *Theatre Research International* 1 (1976):86–98.
Barthélémy, Maurice. "La critique et l'actualité musicale dans le
  'Théâtre Italian' de Gherardi." *Revue d'histoire littéraire de la
  France* 59 (1959):481–90.
Baschet, Armand. *Les comédiens italiens à la cour de France.* Paris:
  Plon, 1882.

Beauchamps, Pierre-François. *Recherches sur les théâtres*. Paris: Prault, 1735.

Beijer, Agne. "*La naissance de la paix:* ballet de cour de René Descartes." In *Le lieu théâtral à la renaissance*. Edited by Jean Jacquot. Paris: Editions du Centre national de la recherche scientifique, 1968.

————. "Une maquette de décor récemment retrouvée pour le *Ballet de la prosperité des armes de France* dansé à Paris, le 7 février 1641." In *Le lieu théâtral à la renaissance*. Edited by Jean Jacquot. Paris. Editions du Centre national de la recherche scientifique, 1968.

Bernardin, N.-M. *La Comédie-Italienne en France et les théâtres de la foire et du boulevard, 1570–1791*. Paris: Editions de la Revue Bleue, 1902.

Berty, Adolphe. *Topographie historique du vieux Paris: région du Louvre et des Tuileries*. 2d ed. 2 vols. Paris: Imprimerie Nationale, 1885.

Bevilacqua, Enrico. "Giambattista Andreini e la compagnia dei Fedeli." *Giornale storico della letteratura italiana* 23 (1894):76–155; 24 (1895):82–165.

Blondel, Jacques-François. *L'architecture française*. 4 vols. Paris: C. A. Jombert, 1752–56.

Body, Jacques. "Le personnage d'Arlequin." Doctoral thesis, Université de Paris III, n.d.

Bonnassies, Jules. *La Comédie-Française: histoire administrative, 1658–1757*. Paris: Didier, 1874.

Borsellino, Nino. "Percorsi della commedia dell'arte: Scaramuccia di Napoli a Parigi." In *Le théâtre italien et l'Europe XVe–XVIIe siècles*. Edited by Christian Bec and Irène Mamczarz. Paris: Presses Universitaires de France, 1983.

Boswell, Eleanor. *The Restoration Court Stage: 1660–1702*. Cambridge: Harvard Univ. Press, 1932.

Bouquet, Guy. "La comédie italienne en France, au début du règne de Louis XV. Etude culturelle." Doctoral thesis, Université de Paris X—Nanterre, 1973.

————. "Les comédiens italiens à Paris au temps de Louix XIV." *Revue d'histoire moderne et contemporaine* 24 (1979):422–38.

Bourdel, Nicole. "L'établissement et la construction de l'Hôtel des comédiens français rue des Fossés-Saint-Germain-des-Prés (Ancienne Comédie) 1687–1690." *Revue d'histoire du théâtre* 7 (1955):145–72.

Brice, Germain. *Description de la ville de Paris*. 6th ed. 3 vols. Paris: Fr. Fournier, 1713.

Bucciolini, Giuleo. *Cronache del teatro fiorentino*. Florence: Olschki, 1982.

Calame, Alexandre. *Jean-François Regnard: comédies du théâtre italien.* Geneva: Droz, 1981.

——. *Regnard: sa vie et son oeuvre.* Paris: Presses Universitaires de France, 1960.

Campardon, Emile. *Les comédiens du roi de la troupe italienne.* 2 vols. 1880. Reprint. Geneva: Slatkine, 1970.

——. *Documents inédits sur J.B. Poquelin Molière.* Paris: Plon, 1871.

Cavallucci, Giacomo. "Fatouville, auteur dramatique." *Revue d'histoire littéraire de la France* 43 (1936):481–572.

Chappuzeau, Samuel. *Le théâtre français.* 1674. Reprint. Editions d'Aujourd'hui. N.P., n.d.

Chevalley, Sylvie. "Le *Registre* d'Hubert." *Revue d'histoire du théâtre* 26 (1973):1–195.

——, ed. *Le Registre de La Grange, 1659–1685.* Geneva: Minkoff, 1972.

Christout, Marie-Françoise. *Le ballet de cour de Louis XIV, 1643–1672.* Paris: Picard, 1967.

——. *Le merveilleux et le théâtre du silence.* Paris: Mouton, 1965.

Colajanni, Giuliana, ed. *Les scenarios franco-italiens du Ms. 9329 de la B.N.* Rome: Edizioni di storia e letteratura, 1970.

Costantini, Angelo. *The Birth, Life and Death of Scaramouch.* Translated by Cyril W. Beaumont. London: C. W. Beaumont, 1924.

[Cotelendi, Charles.] *Arlequiniana.* Paris: Florentin et Pierre Delaulne, 1694.

——. *Le livre sans nom.* Paris: Michel Brunet, 1695.

Courville, Xavier de. *Un apôtre de l'art du théâtre au XVIIIe siècle: Luigi Riccoboni dit Lélio: Chef de troupe en Italie.* 2d ed. Paris: L'Arche, 1967.

——. *Un apôtre de l'art du théâtre au XVIIIe siècle: Luigi Riccoboni dit Lélio: L'expérience française.* Paris: Droz, 1945.

Dacier, Emile. "Les scènes et figures théâtral de Claude Gillot." *La revue de l'art ancien et moderne* 49 (1926):280–94.

Dainville, François de. "Lieux d'affichage en 1753." *Revue d'histoire du théâtre* 3 (1951):248–53.

D'Amico, Sandro. "Le théâtre italien." *Encyclopédie de la Pléiade,* vol. 19, *Histoire du spectacle.* Paris: NRF, 1965.

Dangeau, Phillipe de Courcillon, marquis de. *Journal de la cour de Louix XIV.* Edited by Eudore Soulié. 19 vols. Paris: Firmin-Didot, 1854–60.

Deierkauf-Holsboer, S. Wilma. *Histoire de la mise en scène dans le théâtre français.* Paris: Droz, 1933.

——. *Le théâtre de l'Hôtel de Bourgogne.* 2 vols. Paris: Nizet, 1968–70.

————. *Le théâtre du Marais.* 2 vols. Paris: Nizet, 1954–58.

Deloffre, Frédéric. "Aspects inconnus de l'ancien théâtre italien." *Cahiers de l'association internationale des études françaises* 15 (1963):177–88.

Depping, G. B., ed. *Correspondance administrative sous la règne de Louis XIV.* 4 vols. Paris: Imprimerie Nationale, 1954.

Desboulmiers [Jean-Auguste Julien]. *Histoire anecdotique et raisonnée du Théâtre Italien depuis son rétablissement en France jusqu'à l'année 1769.* 7 vols. Paris: Lacombe, 1769.

Descotes, Maurice. *Le public du théâtre et son histoire.* Paris: Presses Universitaires de France, 1964.

Des Essarts [Nicolas-Toussaint Le Moyne]. *Les trois théâtres de Paris, ou abrégé historique de l'établissement de la Comédie-Française, de la Comédie-Italienne et de l'Opéra.* Paris: Lacombe, 1777.

Desfontaines, abbé Pierre François Guyot. *Le nouvelliste du Parnasse.* 4 vols. Paris, Chaubert, 1731–32.

Despois, Eugène. *Le théâtre français sous Louis XIV.* Paris: Hachette, 1874.

Dieckmann, M. H. "Claude Gillot, interprète de la commedia dell'-arte." *Cahiers de l'association internationale des études français* 15 (1963):201–24.

D'Origny, Antoine. *Annales du théâtre italien depuis son origine jusqu'à ce jour.* 3 vols. Paris: Veuve Duchesne, 1788.

Dorimond [Nicolas Drouin]. *La comédie de la comédie.* Paris: Ribou, 1662.

Duchartre, Pierre-Louis. *La commedia dell'arte et ses enfants.* 2d ed. Paris: Librairie Théatrale, 1978.

————, ed. *Les compositions de rhétorique de M. Don Arlequin.* Paris: Duchartre et Van Duggenhoult, 1928.

Du Gérard, N. B. *Tables alphabétique et chronologique des pièces representées sur l'ancien théâtre italien.* 1750. Reprint. Geneva: Slatkine, 1970.

Dumont, Gabriel-Martin. *Parallèle des plans des plus belles salles de spectacles d'Italie et de France.* 1774. Reprint. New York: Benjamin Blom, 1968.

Enciclopedia dello spettacolo. Edited by G. C. Sansoni. Rome: Casa Editrice le Maschere, 1954–62.

Erenstein, R. L. "Claude Gillot e il Théâtre Italien." *Biblioteca teatrale,* nuova serie, no. 2 (1986), pp. 23–43.

————. *De Geschiedenis van de Commedia dell'arte.* Amsterdam: International Theatre Bookshop, 1985.

————. "Satire and the *Commedia dell'arte.*" In *Western Popular The-*

atre, edited by David Mayer and Kenneth Richards. London: Methuen, 1977, pp. 29–47.

———. "Unbekannte Illustrationen des Théâtre Italien." *Maske und Kothurn* 31 (1985):263–79.

Explication des décorations du théâtre, et les argumens de la pièce, qui a pour tiltre, La folle supposée, ouvrage du Seigneur Giulio Strozzi. Paris: René Baudry, 1645. A surviving copy is bound into Bibliothèque de l'Opéra Ms. Res. 625. A version in Italian with engravings by Cochin is in the Bibliothèque de l'Arsenal.

Gambelli, Delia. "Arlecchino dalla preistoria a Biancolelli." *Biblioteca teatrale,* no. 5 (1973), pp. 17–78.

———. " 'Quasi un racamo di concertate pezzette': le composizioni sul comico dell'Arlecchino Biancolelli." *Biblioteca teatrale,* no. 1 (1971), pp. 47–95.

Gendarme de Bevotte, G. *La légende de Don Juan: son évolution dans la littérature des origines au romantisme.* Paris: Hachette, 1906.

———. *Le festin de pierre avant Molière.* Paris: Cornély, 1907.

Gherardi, Evaristo. *Le théâtre italien, ou le recueil de toutes les scènes françoises qui ont esté jouée sur le théâtre italien de l'Hostel de Bourgogne.* Paris: Guillaume de Luynes, 1694.

———. *Le Théâtre italien, ou le recueil général de toutes les comédies et scènes françoises jouées par les comédiens du roy, pendant tout le temps qu'ils ont été au service.* 6 vols. Paris: Cusson et Witte, 1700.

Golder, John. *"L'hypocondriaque* de Rotrou: un essai de reconstitution d'un première mise en scène à l'Hôtel de Bourgogne." *Revue d'histoire du théâtre* 31 (1979):247–70.

Goubert, Pierre. *Louis XIV and Twenty Million Frenchmen.* Translated by Anne Carter. New York: Vintage, 1972.

Grivel, Marianne. *Le commerce de l'estampe à Paris au XVIIe siècle.* Geneva: Droz, 1986.

Grout, Donald Jay. "The Music of the Italian Theatre at Paris, 1682–97." *Papers of the American Musicological Society* (1941), pp. 158–70.

Gueullette, J.-E. *Un magistrate du XVIIIe siècle, Thomas-Simon Gueullette.* Paris: Droz, 1938.

Gueullette, Thomas-Simon. *Notes et souvenirs sur le théâtre italien au XVIIIe siècle.* Edited by J.-E. Gueullette. Paris: Droz, 1938.

Heck, Thomas F. *Commedia dell'arte: A Guide to the Primary and Secondary Literature.* New York: Garland, 1988.

Héroard, Jean. *Journal de Jean Héroard sur l'enfance et la jeunesse de Louis XIII, 1601–28.* 2 vols. Edited by Eudore Soulié and Edouard de Barthélemy. Paris: Didot, 1868.

Herzel, Roger. "The Scenery for the Original Production of *Dom Juan.*" *The Age of Theatre in France*. Edited by David Trott and Nicole Boursier. Edmonton: Academic Printing and Publishing, 1988.

Hilgar, Marie-France. "La parodie et le théâtre italien au XVIIe siècle." *Maske und Kothurn* 17 (1981):312–21.

Horn-Monval, M. "Le théâtre du Petit-Bourbon." *Revue d'histoire du théâtre* 1 (1949):46–48.

Illingworth, David V. "Documents inédits et nouvelles précisions sur le théâtre de l'Hôtel de Bourgogne." *Revue d'histoire du théâtre* 22 (1970):125–33.

———. "L'Hôtel de Bourgogne: une salle de théâtre à l'italienne à Paris en 1647." *Revue d'histoire du théâtre* 23 (1971):39–49.

Jal, Auguste. *Dictionnaire critique de biographie et d'histoire*. Paris: Plon, 1867.

Jurgens, Madeleine, and Marie-Antoinette Fleury. *Documents du Minutier Central concernant l'histoire littéraire*. Paris: Presses Universitaires de France, 1960.

——— and Elizabeth Maxfield-Miller. "Cent ans de recherche sur Molière. Paris: Imprimerie Nationale, 1963.

Kahan, Gerald. *Jacques Callot, Artist of the Theatre*. Athens: Univ. of Georgia Press, 1976.

Kirkness, W. John. *Le français du théâtre italien d'après le recueil de Gherardi, 1681–1697*. Geneva: Droz, 1971.

Koch, Philip. "Nature et signification des 'Sujets de plusieurs comédies italiennes.'" *Revue d'histoire du théâtre* 38 (1986):67–87.

Krogh, Torben. "Den italienske Komedie i Frankrig." *Musik og Teater*. Copenhagen: Munksgaard, 1955.

[Lacroix, Paul] Le Bibliophile Jacob. *Catalogue de la bibliothèque dramatique de M. de Solienne*. Paris: Administration de l'Alliance des Arts, 1843.

La Grange, Charles Varlet de. *Registre*. Edited by Edouard Thierry. Paris: par la Comédie-Française, 1876.

Lagrave, Henri. *Le théâtre et le public à Paris de 1715 à 1750*. Paris, Klincksiek, 1972.

Lancaster, H. C. *A History of French Dramatic Literature in the Seventeenth Century. Part 4, The Period of Racine, 1673–1700*. 2 vols. Baltimore: Johns Hopkins Univ. Press, 1940.

———. *Le mémoire de Mahelot, Laurent et d'autres décorateurs de l'Hôtel de Bourgogne et de la Comédie-Française au XVIIe siècle*. Paris: Honoré Champion, 1920.

———. *The Comédie-Française, 1680–1701*. Baltimore: Johns Hopkins Univ. Press, 1941.

Lawrenson, T. E. *The French Stage in the XVIIth Century.* Manchester: Manchester Univ. Press, 1957.

Lea, Kathleen M. *Italian Popular Comedy.* 2 vols. 1934. Reprint. New York: Russell and Russell, 1962.

Lebègue, Raymond. "La comédie italienne en France au XVIe siè-cle." *Revue de littérature comparée* 24 (1950):5–24.

———. "Premières infiltrations de la commedia dell'arte dans le théâtre français." *Cahiers de l'association internationale des études françaises* 15 (1963):165–76.

Léris, Antoine de. *Dictionnaire portatif historique et littéraire des théâtres.* Paris: Jombert, 1763.

Lintilhac, Eugène. *Histoire générale du théâtre en France.* Paris: Flam-marion, 1908–9.

Locatelli, Sebastiano. *Voyage en France.* Translated by Adolphe Vau-tier. Paris: Picard, 1905.

London Stage, The. Volume 1, *1660–1700.* Edited by William Van Lennap. Carbondale: Southern Illinois Univ. Press, 1965.

Lough, John. *Paris Theatre Audiences in the Seventeenth and Eighteenth Centuries.* London: Oxford Univ. Press, 1959.

McGowan, Margaret. *L'art du ballet de cour en France (1581–1643).* Paris: Editions du Centre national de la recherche scientifique, 1964.

Mandel, Oscar. *The Theatre of Don Juan.* Lincoln: Nebraska Univ. Press, 1963.

Marie, Alfred. "La salle du théâtre du château de Fontainebleau." *Revue d'histoire du théâtre* 3 (1951):237–47.

———. "Les théâtres du château de Versailles." *Revue d'histoire du théâtre* 3 (1951):133–52.

Maugras, Gaston. *Les comédiens hors la loi.* Paris: Calmann Lévy, 1887.

Mélèse, Pierre. *Le théâtre et le public à Paris sous Louis XIV, 1659–1715.* 1934. Reprint. Geneva: Slatkine, 1976.

———. *Répertoire analytique des documents contemporains d'information concernant le théâtre à Paris sous Louis XIV.* Paris, Droz, 1934.

Mic, Constant. *La commedia dell'arte.* 1924. Reprint. Paris: Librairie Théatrale, 1980.

Migliori, Anna. "Contributo all storia dell'ancien théâtre italien." *Biblioteca teatrale,* no. 8 (1973), pp. 78–137.

Mittman, Barbara. *Spectators on the Paris Stage in the Seventeenth Cen-tury.* Ann Arbor: UMI Research Press, 1984.

Moland, Louis. *Molière et la comédie italienne.* Paris: Didier, 1867.

Molinari, Cesare. *La commedia dell'arte.* Milan: Mondadori, 1985.

———. *Theatre through the Ages.* Translated by Colin Hamer. New York: McGraw-Hill, 1975.

Mongrédien, Georges. "La querelle du théâtre à la fin du règne de Louis XIV." *Revue d'histoire du théâtre* 30 (1978):103–19.

Montaiglon, Anatole de. "Dépenses des menus plaisirs et affaires de la chambre du roi pendant l'année 1677." *Journal général de l'instruction publique,* no. 17. Paris: Dumoulin, 1857.

Montjean, Charles. "La troupe de Molière à Saint-Germain-en-Laye au XVIIe siècle." *Revue de l'histoire de Versailles* 38 (1936):146–61.

Motteville, Mme de. *Mémoires.* In *Nouvelle collection des mémoires pour servir à l'histoire de France.* Ser. 2, vol. 2. Edited by Joseph F. Michaud. Paris: L'Editeur du commentaire analytique du code civil, 1836–39.

Moureau, François. "Décor et mise en scène chez les italiens de Paris avant 1697, ou Arlequin architecte." *The Age of Theatre in France.* Edited by David Trott and Nicole Boursier. Edmonton: Academic Printing and Publishing, 1988.

———. *Dufresny, auteur dramatique, 1657–1724.* Paris: Klincksieck, 1969.

———. "Les comédiens-italiens et la cour de France, 1664–1697." *XVII Siècle* 33 (1981):63–81.

New Grove Dictionary of Music. 20 vols. London: Macmillan, 1980.

Nicoll, Allardyce. *The World of Harlequin.* Cambridge: Cambridge Univ. Press, 1963.

Nuitter, Charles, and Ernest Thoinan. *Les origines de l'opéra français.* Paris: E. Plon, 1886.

Pandolfi, Vito. *La commedia dell'arte: storia e testi.* 6 vols. Florence: Sansoni Antiquariato, 1957–61.

Parfaict, Claude, and Godin d'Abguerbe. *Dictionnaire des théâtres de Paris.* 7 vols. Paris: Lambert, 1755.

Parfaict, François, and Claude Parfaict. *Histoire de l'ancien théâtre italien depuis son origine en France jusqu'à sa suppression en l'année 1697.* Paris: Lambert, 1753.

———. *Histoire du théâtre français depuis son origine jusqu'à présent.* 15 vols. Paris: Morin et Flahaut, 1734.

Perman, R. C. D. "The Influence of the Commedia dell'arte on the French Theatre before 1640." *French Studies* 9 (1955):293–303.

Prota-Giurleo, Ulisse. *I teatri di Napoli nel '600: la commedia e le maschere.* Naples: Fausto Fiorentino, 1962.

Prunières, Henry. *L'opéra italien en France avant Lulli.* 1913. Reprint. Paris: Honoré Champion, 1975.

Pure, abbé Michel de. *Idée des spectacles anciens et nouveaux.* Paris: Brunet, 1668.

Rasi, Luigi. *I comici italiani.* 2 vols. in 3. Florence: Bocca, 1897.

Riccoboni, Luigi. *Histoire du théâtre italien.* Paris: Delormel, 1728.

Rouillard, C. D. "A Forgotten *Arlequin Grand Visir* of 1687 and Its
    Echoes in the Théâtre de la Foire." *Theatre Annual* (1977), pp.
    87–112.
Roy, D. H. "La scène de l'Hôtel de Bourgogne." *Revue d'histoire du
    théâtre* 15 (1963):227–35.
Sanesi, Ireneo. *La commedia.* 2d ed. Milan: Vallardi, 1954.
Sauval, Henri. *Histoire et recherches des antiquités de la ville de Paris.* 3
    vols. Paris, Moette, 1724.
Schöne, Günter. "Almanache als Zeugnisse für die Comédie Ital-
    ienne." *Maske und Kothurn* 18 (1972):207–18.
Scott, Virginia. "The *Jeu* and the *Rôle:* Analysis of the Appeals of the
    Italian Comedy in France in the time of Arlequin Domi-
    nique." In *Western Popular Theatre.* Edited by David Mayer and
    Kenneth Richards. London: Methuen, 1977.
Soleirol, H. A. *Molière et sa troupe.* Paris: H. A. Soleirol, 1858.
Soulié, Eudore. *Recherches sur Molière et sur sa famille.* Paris: Hachette,
    1863.
Spada, Stefania. *Domenico Biancolelli ou l'art d'improviser.* Naples: In-
    stitut Universitaire, 1969. Transcription of Gueullette's "Trad-
    uction du scenario de Joseph Dominique Biancolelli," Ms.
    Rés. 625, Bibliiothèque de l'Opéra, with added transcriptions
    of scenarios from Mss. XI.AA.40–41, Biblioteca Nationale,
    Naples, and Ms. 9329, Bibliothèque Nationale, Paris.
Spaziani, Marcello. *Il* Théâtre Italien *di Gherardi.* Rome: Ateneo,
    1966.
*Suite du théâtre italien, ou nouveau recueil de plusieurs comédies françoises,
    qui ont été jouée sur the théâtre italien de l'Hôtel de Bourgogne.* N.p.,
    n.p., 1697.
*Supplément du théâtre italien, ou recueil des scènes françoises qui n'ont point
    encore été imprimées.* Tome 2 [*sic*]. Brussels: N.p., 1697
Taviani, Ferdinando, and Mirella Schino. *Le secret de la commedia dell'-
    arte.* Translated by Yves Liebert. Carcassone: Contrastes
    Bouffonneries, 1984.
Tessari, Roberto. *Commedia dell'arte: la maschere e l'ombra.* Milan:
    Mursia, 1981.
———. *La commedia dell'arte nel seicento: "industria" e "arte giocoso"
    della civiltà barocca.* Florence: Olschki, 1969.
Thérault, Suzanne. *La commedia dell'arte vue à travers le zibaldone de
    Pérouse.* Paris: Editions du Centre national de la recherche
    scientifique, 1965.
Tralage, Jean Nicolas du [*sic*]. *Notes et documents sur l'histoire des thé-
    âtres de Paris au XVIIe siècle.* Edited by Le Bibliophile Jacob
    [Paul La Croix]. Paris: Librairie des Bibliophiles, 1880.

Valabrègue, Antony. *Un maître fantaisiste du XVIIIe siècle, Claude Gillot, 1673–1722*. Paris: Librairie de l'Artiste, 1883.

Venard, Michèle. *La foire entre en scène*. Paris: Librairie Théatrale, 1985.

Villiers, sieur de. *Le festin de pierre, ou le fils criminel*. Paris: N.p., 1659.

Vitu, Auguste. "Molière et les italiens à propos du tableau des farceurs." *Le Moliériste* 1 (1879):234–35.

Weaver, R. L., and N. W. Weaver. *A Chronology of Music in the Florentine Theatre, 1590–1750*. Detroit Studies in Music Bibliography no. 38. Detroit, 1978.

Wiley, W. L. *The Early Public Theatre in France*. Cambridge: Harvard Univ. Press, 1960.

———. "Another Look at France's First Public Theatre." *Studies in Philology* 70 (1973):1–114.

Winter, Marian Hannah. *The Theatre of Marvels*. New York: Benjamin Blom, 1964.

Young, Bert Edward, and Grace Philpott Young, eds. *Le Registre de La Grange*. 2 vols. Paris: Droz, 1947.

Index

Actors: anathematized, 323–24; excommunication of, 104–5; finances, 84; life-style, 85–86

Actors, Italian, recruited from Italy, 249–50

Actresses, legal names of, 40

Adami, Patricia [Diamantine], 47, 82, 116–17, 250, 332; death, 342; debut, 116–17; marriage, 117; naturalization, 117, 270; physical description, 117; see also Lolli, Angelo Agostino

Addition à la comédie d'Arlequin soldat et bagage, 394; contemporary event in, 218

Addition au baron de Foeneste, 396

Addition au soldat en Candie, 395

Addition au triomphe de la médecine, 396

Adieux des officiers, Les, 317, 372, 374, 403; see also Dufresny, Charles

A fourbe, fourbe et demy, 214–16, 283, 396; bilingual lazzi, 200–201

Afterpieces, 371–75

Amadis cuisinier, 307

Amonio, Dr., 235, 314, 425 n. 31

Amours d'Arlequin et de Marinette, Les, 244, 402

Amours du bonhomme Ballouard, Les, 399

Andreini, Francesco, 34

Andreini, Giovan Battista, 57

Andreini, Isabella, 17

Anne of Austria (the queen mother), 19, 21, 42, 53–55, 65

Arcadie the ass, 171–72

"Arlequin": as fashionable wit, 237–39; as petit marquis, 195–96, 202, 239–40; as played by Biancolelli, 146–51, 357; as played by Gherardi, 387; travesties by, 140, 155, 170, 193–94, 215–16

Arlequin aman malheuraux [sic], 244, 405

Arlequin berger de Lemnos, 166, 169–70, 172, 313, 396

Arlequin cabaretier, turc et capitaine espagnol, 399

Arlequin chevalier du soleil, 300–302, 400; see also Monsier D***

Arlequin cochon par amour, 397; contemporary event in, 218

Arlequin cru prince, 143–45, 219, 393

Arlequin défenseur du beau sexe, 375, 404; see also Biancolelli, Louis

Arlequin dogue d'Angleterre et médecin du temps, 103, 107, 397; divertissement of, 217

Arlequin dupé par sa femme, 400

Arlequin embarrassé parmi les fripiers, 401

Arlequin empereur dans la lune, 293–97, 400; see also Monsieur D***

Arlequin esprit follet, 156, 171, 211, 395

Arlequin et Scaramouche juifs errans de Babilonne, 169–70, 212, 397; parody in, 201–2

Arlequin et Scaramouche usuriers, 396

Arlequin grand vizir, 308, 313

Arlequin hotte et masson, 397

Arlequin Jason, 297–300, 400; calendar-almanac of, 233; parody in, 297; staging, 232–33; use of French in, 299–300; use of spectacle, 230; see also Fatouville, Anne Mauduit de

Arlequin juif, peintre et tailleur, 399

Arlequin laron, prévost et juge, 244, 393

Arlequin lingère du palais, 244, 287–89, 399; see also Monsieur D***

Arlequin mary de trois femmes, 244, 404

Arlequin médecin d'eau douce, 395; French harangue in, 198

Arlequin médecin ignorant, 404

Arlequin mercure galant, 229, 283–85, 398; music in, 284–85; see also Monsieur D***

Arlequin misantrope, 380–81, 405; see also Biancolelli, Louis

Arlequin mule et médecin ignorant, 400

Arlequin Phaeton, 366–67, 403; *see also* Palaprat, Jean

Arlequin plaqué, 244, 400

Arlequin poète et petit enfant, 395

Arlequin Protée, 289–93; self-referential routine, 230; use of machines, 229–30; *see also* Monsieur D***

Arlequin roy par hazard, 156, 169, 211, 396

Arlequin soldat déserteur, 398

Arlequin soldat et bagage, ou hôte et hôtel-lerie, 401

Arlequin soury, 395

Arlequin tombé dans le puits, 399

Arlequin toujours Arlequin, 244, 387, 405

Arlequin valet étourdi, 244, 399

Arlequin vallet enchanté et Margot la pie, 170–71, 395

Arlequin vandangeur, 307, 399

Ateliers, Les, 393

Attendez-moi sous l'orme, 372–73, 404

Attinger, Gustave, 6, 9

L'auberge d'Arlequin juge partie avocat et te-moin, 160, 170, 177, 398

Audiences, 98; changes, after 1680, 237, 317; described in *Le banqueroutier,* 237–39; onstage, 165–66, 239–40, 320; power of parterre in, 320–21; whistlers, 239, 321

Aularia muette par amour, see *Eularia muette par amour*

Aurelia, *see* Fedele, Brigida

Avantures des champs elisées, Les, 378–79, 403; *see also* L.C.D.V.

Baguette de Vulcain, La, 372–73, 403; prof-its, 317; *see also* Dufresny, Charles, *and* Regnard, Jean-François

Bains de la porte S. Bernard, Les, 376, 405; *see also* Boisfran

Balbi, Giovan Battista, 43, 53, 60

Banqueroutier, Le, 235–36, 304–6, 401; prologue of, 237–39; *see also* Mon-sieur D***

Barbieri, Annibal, 120

Baron allemand, Le, 149–51, 393

Baron de Foeneste, Le, 107, 195–96, 396

Baroque stage: conventions of, 75–76, 220; spectators on, 165

Bel-esprit, Le, 375, 379, 403; *see also* L.A.P.

Belle soliciteuse, La, 405

Bendinelli, Giacinto [Valerio], 82, 111–14; complaint for alienation of affections, 112–13; death, 113; in-ventory, 113–14; finances, 85–86; marriage, 112; in Modena troupe, 101

Berger de Lemnos, Le, 211–12

Bertalotti, Marguerita, 26, 48, 57, 63

Bianchi, Brigida, *see* Fedele, Brigida

Bianchi, Giulio Cesare, 42–43

Bianchi, Giuseppe, 40–41, 43, 411 n. 54

Bianchi, Marc' Antonio [Horace], 26, 39, 44, 50–51

Biancolelli, Anne-Caietan, 103, 346

Biancolelli, Catherine, 250, 253–56, 332; birth, 103–4; marriage, 256–57; re-tirement and death, 346; serenade to, 105

Biancolelli, Charles, 104

Biancolelli, Charlotte-Marie, 103–4, 346

Biancolelli, Domenico [Arlequin], 82–83, 101–8, 250; as Arlequin, 146–51; author of *Arlequin Grapignan,* 277, 281–82; birth, 101; called to France, 81–82, 102; children, 103–4; death, 271–73; family life, 105; "honesty," 103; inventory, 272–74; as man of learning, 108; marriage, 102; natu-ralization, 111; orator of Comédie-Italienne, 174; physical description, 105–7; supposed portrait, 107, 416 n. 23; in Vienna, 102; vocal defect, 107; zibaldone, 9–10, 125–29, 192; *see also* Cortesi, Orsola

Biancolelli, Elisabeth-Charlotte, 103–4

Biancolelli, Françoise, 250, 253–56, 332; birth, 103–4; death, 346; marriage, 257–58

Biancolelli, Louis, 103–4, 345; as play-wright, 354, 434 n. 5

Biancolelli, Louis, II, 103–4

Biancolelli, Marie Apolline, 103–4, 346

Biancolelli, Marie-Thérèse, 104, 346

Biancolelli, Orsola Cortesi, *see* Cortesi, Orsola

Biancolelli, Pierre-François, 104, 346

Biancolelli, Philippe, 104, 345–46

Bilingual lazzi, 199–200, 283

Blasi, Teodora, *see* Zanotti, Giovan An-drea

Boisfran (playwright), 354
Bonnart, Nicolas, *see* Calendar-almanacs
Bonne-femme et le mary méchant, La, 394
Bossuet, Jacques, 324–25
"Briguelle," 26, 157, 185
Brugière de Barante, 354
Bulstrode, Richard, 159

Cabaretière, La, 393
Calendar-almanacs, 233, 307, 311, 332
Camperon, Laurent Bersac, sieur de,
    163–64
Campo, Lorenza Elisabetta [Isabella] del
    [Marinette], 26, 63, 76; in Paris,
    1664, 116–18; son's marriage, 118;
    wife of Tiberio Fiorilli, 37, 50–51
Cantù, Carlo [Buffetto], 19, 26, 43, 48,
    50, 61, 101–2; letter to Gaufredi,
    54–55; role in *La finta pazza,* 61–63
"Capitan," 121, 332–33
Capitan battu dans le jardin, Le, 333, 405
Capocomico, 46
Capricieux, Le, 137–43, 244, 393
Caraque, René, 321
Carousel des dames, Les, 405
Carpiano, Orazio ["il carpiano"], 42, 44;
    as Pantalon, 120–21; *see also* Bian-
    chi, Marc' Antonio
Casamarciano manuscripts (Biblioteca
    Nazionale, Naples), 126, 129
Cause des femmes, La, 236, 355–56, 401;
    see also Delosme de Montchenay
Cei, Girolamo [Capitan Spezzafer, Scara-
    mouche], 121, 156, 183–85; death,
    262
Censorship, 218, 325–26
Chappuzeau, Samuel, 172–75
Charles II (king of England), 160
Chevallier de l'industrie, Le, 395
Chiesa, Elisabetta Giulia della, 180–81;
    see also Romagnesi, Marc' Antonio
Children, use of, in flying effects, 64
Chinois, Les, 377, 403; obscenity in, 322–
    23; *see also* Dufresny, Charles, *and*
    Regnard, Jean-François
Church, the French, and censure of the-
    atre, 324–25
Cicognini, Jacinto Andrea, 71, 76
Cimadori, Giovan Andrea, 157, 185, 253
Circé, 171
Coeur me fait mal, Le, 393

Collier de perle, Le, 167, 193, 202–4, 396
"Colombine," as Parisian suivante, 294–
    95, 300–301, 306–7; *see also* Bianco-
    lelli, Catherine
Colombine avocat pour et contre, 235, 244,
    303–4, 400; versions of, 279–80; *see
    also* Monsieur D***
Colombine femme vengée, 358–59, 401; *see
    also* Monsieur D***
Combat à cheval, Le, 398
Comédie-Française: established, 176,
    223; new theatre of, 313–15; role in
    suppression of Italians, 329–30;
    stage balustrade at, 316–17
Comédie-Italienne (troupe): acting style
    in France, 99; censure of, 321–26;
    consequences of establishment, 6,
    127; debut, 1644, 15; debut, 1661,
    81–82; dissension in, 277–78, 318–
    19; early troupes, 26–27; in En-
    gland, 157–60; French authors
    writing for, 77; Italian repertory
    played at court, 244–45, 275–76;
    loss of popularity at court, 317–18;
    officers, 320–21; profits, 83–84,
    171, 317; relations with French
    troupe, 162–63, 176–79; reopening,
    after death of Biancolelli, 311; re-
    turn to Italy c. 1648, 27; return to
    Italy, 1659, 30, 77–78; 1668 troupe,
    156–57; 1662 troupe, 82; 1680s
    troupe, 249–51, 271; 1690s troupe,
    318, 332–33; subventions of, 82;
    suppression of, 326–31
Comédie italienne (genre): contempo-
    rary events in, 218, 373; formal ele-
    ments in, 209–10; French repertory
    of, 251, 275, 306–7, 382–83; meta-
    theatricality in, 219; new repertory,
    155–56; obscenity, 321–23, 329; ro-
    mance, 373; satire, 144, 218; 1662–
    68 repertory, 99–100; traditional
    commedia dell'arte elements, 210,
    214–15
Comedy of manners, 356, 361, 367, 382
Commedia dell'arte: acting style, 98–99;
    balanced structure, 123–24; cos-
    tumes, 4; establishment in France,
    6; extant scenarios, 123; farce, 124;
    improvisation, 5, 122; "masques"
    of, 4; and normative definitions, 6–

Commedia dell'arte (*cont.*)
    8, 122–24; origins, 5; ornamental
    scenes, 123–24; pastoral, 70, 124;
    repertory, 52; tipi fissi, 5, 122; tragi-
    comedy, 124; use of machines, 23
Confrérie de la Passion, theatrical privi-
    lege of, 16–17
Convitato di pietra, Il, 30, 392; distribution
    of roles, 76–77; reprises, 70–71;
    scenario, 70–75; settings, 75–76;
    statue in, 76; see also *Festin de pierre,
    Le*
Coquette, La, 362–63, 402; see also Reg-
    nard, Jean-François
Coris, Alessandra, 109
Coris, Barbara Minuti, 102, 109, 162–63
Coris, Bernardo, 101, 109
Coris, Orsola, *see* Cortesi, Orsola
Cortesi, Antonio, 109
Cortesi, Orsola [Eularia], 82, 108–11,
    189, 250, 254, 332; author of *La
    bella Bruta,* 108; death, 345; in
    French repertory, 111; in *Madda-
    lena,* 110; naturalization, 111; par-
    entage, 109–10; physical
    description, 110–11; pregnancies,
    103; retirement, 344; signatures,
    109; in troupe of Mantua, 110; vow
    of chastity, 415 n. 12; see also Bian-
    colelli, Domenico
Costantini, Angelo [Mezzetin], 250, 267–
    69, 332; as Arlequin, 269; at court
    of Saxony, 347; possible arrival,
    1681, 252–53; possible author of
    Supplément du théâtre italien, 276;
    probable author of *La vie de Scara-
    mouche,* 32; probable debut, 1686,
    267; second debut, Paris, 346–47
Costantini, Constantino [Gradelin], 332–
    35; responsible for music, 320
Costantini, Elisabeth, 181
Costantini, Giovanni Battista [Octave],
    333, 335–36, 348; connection to
    new Comédie-Italienne, 348–49; as
    fair entrepreneur, 348; as orator,
    319; portrait, 432 n. 13; quarrels
    with Romagnesi and Gherardi,
    318–19
Costumes: commedia dell'arte charac-
    ters, 4; "jeune premier," 113–14; of
    Molière, 417 n. 58

Court, English, Comédie-Italienne at,
    157–60
Court, French: attends *La Rosaura,* 65;
    entertainments, 29–30, 247–48;
    performances at, 83, 235, 241–47,
    317–18, 387, 428 n. 1
Crispen musicien, use of shutter in, 228
Critique de la cause des femmes, La, 355–56,
    401; *see also* Delosme de Montch-
    enay
Critique de l'homme à bonne fortune, La,
    360, 402; *see also* Regnard, Jean-
    François
Cruauté du Docteur, La, 393

"Dambreville" (tirade), 177, 398
Dame diablesse, La, 400
Dance: *Le collier de perle,* 203–4; *Le régal
    des dames,* 156; *La Rosaura,* 67; *Le
    voyage d'Arlequin et Scaramouche aux
    Indes,* 209
Dangeau, marquis de: and dismissal of
    Italians, 327
Danneret, Elisabeth [Babet le Chan-
    teuse], 336; *see also* Gherardi, Evar-
    isto
Dans le vallet d'opérateur, 393
Darennes, Charles, 281; see also *Matrone
    d'Ephèse, La*
D'Argenson, 326, 331
D'Aumele, duc, letter to, 29
Débauche de Mezetin, La, 401
Décorateurs, 29
Dédains, Les, 393
Delosme de Montchesnay, 354
Départ des comédiens, Le, 372, 374, 404; *see
    also* Dufresny, Charles
Descente de Mazzetin aux enfers, La, 313,
    359, 401; *see also* Regnard, Jean-
    François
Deuil d'Arlequin, Le, 399
Deuil de Scaramouche et d'Arlequin, Le, 398
Deux Arlequins, Les, 363–64, 402; *see also*
    Lenoble, Eustache
Deux Arlequins, Les, scenario, 244, 393
Deux jumeaux, Les, 405
Deux semblables, Les, 244, 400
Devineresse, La, 177
Disgrâces d'Arlequin roy de la Chine, Les,
    244, 404
Divertissements, 60–61, 203–4, 216–17

Divorce, Le, 174, 236, 239, 308, 356–57, 401; Gherardi's debut, 337; *see also* Regnard, Jean-François

D.L.M. [La Motte?], 354

"Docteur," trial of, 292; *see also* Lolli, Angelo Agostino

Docteur amoureux, Le, 402

Doffon, Anne, 189; *see also* Fiorilli, Tiberio

Dominique, *see* Biancolelli, Domenico

Donneau de Visé, 77, 167; editor of *Le mercure galant,* 202; possible author of *Arlequin Grapignan,* 281–82

D'Ormesson, Olivier, 15, 55–56

D'Orsi, Maria Teresa [Spinette], 343, 348

*Dot par la metempsico*ze*, La,* 172, 397; French harangue in, 199

*Double jalou*zie*, La,* 147, 392

Dragon de Moscovie, Le, 129–37, 244, 393; cast, 129–30; property list, 130

Dryden, John, as critic of Comédie-Italienne, 159

Du Croisy, Philbert Gassaud, 92, 97; as composer, 384

Dufresny, Charles, 353–54

Duval, Marie, 189, 343; *see also* Fiorilli, Tiberio

Elisabeth-Charlotte of Bavaria (Madame), and dismissal of Italians, 327–28

Enfants-Trouvés, Hôpital des, 236

*Engagemens du ha*zard*, Les,* 393

Esope, 314, 363, 402; *see also* Lenoble, Eustache

L'étourdi, 399

Eularia muette par amour, 398

Evelyn, John, 159

Exotic locales, use of in comédie italienne, 211–12

Expenses: at court, 245–46; ordinary, 1684, 240; ordinary, 1659–60, 28; ordinary, 1672–73, 172; ordinary, 1661–62, 96

Fatouville, Anne Mauduit de, 280–83, 328; *see also* Monsieur D***

Fatouville, Nolant de, 280

Fausse coquette, La, 375, 379–80, 404; *see also* Biancolelli, Louis

Fausse prude, La, 327–28

Fedele, Brigida [Aurelia], 20, 26, 39–45, 50, 76, 82, 189; author of *L'inganno fortunato* and *Rifuti di pindo,* 40, 119; death, 344; death of husband, 44; in Italy, 44; marriages, 39–40; name, 39–40; parentage, 40–42; in Paris, 20–21, 44; recantation and retirement, 254

Fedele, Flaminio, 41

Fedele, Lutio, 41

Fedeli, Aurelio, 42

Fedeli, I (troupe), 17–18

Fées, Les, 372–74, 405; *see also* Biancolelli, Louis, *and* Dufresny, Charles

Festin de pierre, Le, 392; suppression of scene in, 218; see also *Convitato di pietra, Il*

Fiala, Giuseppe Antonio, 116

Fille de bon sens, La, 369, 403; *see also* Palaprat, Jean

Fille désobéissante, La, 394

Fille sçavante, La, 361–62, 402; *see also* Monsieur D***

Filles errantes, Les, 361, 402; *see also* Regnard, Jean-François

*Finta pa*zza*, La* [*La folle supposée*], 27, 37, 53, 56–64, 392; distribution of roles, 61–64; expenses, 64; extras, 63–64; opening in Paris, 55–56; scenes and machines, 25, 56–61

Fiorilli, Anne-Elisabeth, 344

Fiorilli, Charles-Louis, 118, 189

Fiorilli, Silvio Bernardo, 118

Fiorilli, Tibère François, 189

Fiorilli, Tiberio, 20, 26, 31–39, 50–51, 82, 156, 189–90, 250, 332; birth, 32; children, 37, 189; death, 343–44; death of son, 119, 189; debut, Paris, 32; de facto retirement, 269–70; in England, 160; false report of death, 38; lazzi of taking fright, 303; marriage of son, 118; naturalization, 270; parentage, 32–36; parodied by Beauchamps, 38; presence in Paris, 20–21, 37–38; property, in Italy, 118; return to Italy, 1668, 182, 189; role in *Il convitato di pietra,* 77; royal gifts to, 85, 117; as Scaramouche, 68–69; second marriage, 270; signatures, 35; "table de Scara-

Fiorilli, Tiberio (*cont.*)
    mouche" as played by, 67–68; *see also* Campo, Lorenza Elisabetta del
Fiorillo, Giovan Battista, 34
Fiorillo, Silvio, 33–36, 410 n. 28
"Flamine," 48–49
Foire Saint-Germain, La, 111, 376–77, 404; *see also* Dufresny, Charles, *and* Regnard, Jean-François
Folie d'Eularia, La, 171, 395
Folie d'Octave, La, 244, 401; at court, 11; in Paris, 276
Fontainebleau, theatre at, 246
Fontaine de sapience, La, 372, 374–75, 404; *see also* Biancolelli, Louis
Fourberies d'Arlequin et de Mezetin, Les, 244, 402
Fracansani, Michelangelo [Polichinelle], 250, 266–67, 332
Franchini, Isabella, 101
Fredi, Carlo, *see* Fedele, Lutio
French, use of, by Comédie-Italienne, 156, 172, 194–95; bilingual lazzi, 199–201; harangues, 196–99; rhyming epitaph, 203; permission to use by king, 249
Fripiers, Les, 396

Gabrielli, Giulia [Diana], 19, 26, 43, 48, 50, 63, 69, 76; *see also* Leoni, Pietro Paolo
Gabrielli, Luisa [Lucille], 26, 45, 48, 50, 51, 63; death, 119; *see also* Locatelli, Domenico
Gagure, La, 397; French harangue in, 198
Galli, Leonardo, 187; *see also* Gherardi, Giovanni
Gazetteers, 174–75, 326–27
Gazotti, Dom Pierre, 112–13
Gelosi, I. (troupe), 16
Gentilhomme campagnard, Le, 195, 395; bilingual lazzi, 199–200
Gherardi, Evaristo [Arlequin], 187, 336–40; as Arlequin, 387; author of *Le retour de la foire de Bezons,* 375; death, 351; debut, 337; editor, *Le théâtre italien,* 8, 19, 276–80, 353–54; physical description, 338–40; quarrels with colleagues, 277–78, 318–19; *see also* Danneret, Elisabeth; *Suite du théâtre italien; Supplément du théâtre italien*

Gherardi, Giovanni [Flautin], 82, 187–88, 207
Giaratoni, Giuseppe [Pierrot], 119–20, 250–51, 332; acceptance into troupe, 340–41; development of Pierrot, 190–91; retirement, 351–52; testimony in death of Manzani, 115–16; treasurer, 319
Gillier, Jean-Claude, composer for Comédie-Italienne, 384
Gillot, Claude, 428 n. 44
Girardin, Joseph, 167, 202; *see also Collier de perle, Le*
Grand Astyanax, Le, scenes and machines, 227–29
Grotte nouvelle, La, 393
Gueullette, Thomas-Simon, 19; translation of Biancolelli's zibaldone, 125

Henri IV, 16–17, 19–20
L'homme à bonne fortune, 360; *see also* Regnard, Jean-François
"Horatio," in Biancolelli's zibaldone, 44, 145–46
L'hospital des foux, ou le deuil d'Arlequin, 392
Hôtel de Bourgogne, 16: amphithéâtre, 226–27; capacity, 237; Comédie-Italienne use of, 223–24; installation of machines, 227–28; reconstruction, 1686, 235–37; reconstruction, 1647, 224–27; reconstruction, 1691, 314–17; stage of, 1688, 311
Hôtel Guénégaud, [Théâtre de]; capacity, 164, 237; move of Comédie-Italienne to, 162; as opera house, 166; origins, 163–64; physical description, 164
Hotte, La, 393
L'hypocrite, 396

Improvisation: in Biancolelli's zibaldone, 151–52; in commedia dell'arte, 5; in *La Rosaura,* 65
L'innocence persécutée, 393
Institutionalization of theatre in France, 84, 157, 176, 241–47
"Isabella," 180–81
Isabelle médecin, 302–3, 400; *see also* Monsieur D***

Isabelle muette par amour, 401

Italian actors: finances, 85–86; recruitment, 249–50

Italian troupes in Paris, 15, 19; absence of, 18; objections to, 15; *see also* Comédie-Italienne

Jalousie de Scaramouche et d'Arlequin, 398

Jargon, in comédie italienne, 150–51

Jeton of 1687, 237, 425 n. 38

"Jours ordinaires et extraordinaires," *see* Playing days

Jugemens du duc d'Ossone, Les, 159–60, 395

L. A. D. S. M., 354

La Grange, Charles Varlet de, 82, 179; chronicler of troupe of Molière, 81; costumes of, 113–14

L. A. P., 354

La Reynie, Nicolas de, 265, 325–26

La Thorillière, Pierre Lenoir de, *see* Biancolelli, Catherine

Laurent, Michel, scenic designs of, 228

L. C. V. D., 354

Lenoble, Eustache, 328, 354

Leoni, Pietro Paolo, 19, 26, 43, 48–49, 50–51, 69; *see also* Gabrielli, Giulia

Local color, in comédie italienne, 376–77

Locatelli, Domenico [Trivelin], 45–46, 50–51, 82; death, 185; illness, 1661, 81; in Modena troupe, 101; as orator, 174; pension, 119; privilege for *La Rosaura,* 65; role in *Il convitato di pietra,* 77; second marriage, 119; *see also* Gabrielli, Luisa

Locatelli, Sebastiano, 99, 102

Lolli, Angelo Agostino [The Docteur], 46–47, 51, 82, 119, 189, 250, 292, 332; death, 344; as man of business, 319–20; naturalization, 270; retirement, 342

Lorenzani, Paolo, 384

Louis XIII, 17–19

Louis XIV: bored at Italian play, 246–47; and bureaucratic ordering of theatres, 84, 241–43; decline of interest in theatre, 157, 243–44, 317; personal relationships, with Italian actors, 20–21, 85, 249; suggests Biancolelli sisters for troupe, 255;

and suppression of Comédie-Italienne, 330–31; *see also* Institutionalization of theatre in France *and* Patronage

Louvre, Salle des Gardes of the, 22

Lulli, Jean Baptiste, 158, 162, 166–67; composer of *Le collier de perle,* 167–68, 202–4; quarrel with Molière, 168

Lunatique, Le, 244, 400

Machines, 170–71; afterpieces, 372–73; *Arlequin Phaeton,* 366–67; *Arlequin Protée,* 229–30; *La finta pazza,* 25; intalled in Hôtel de Bourgogne, 227–29, 236, 315; installed in Palais-Royal, 87, 162; at the Opéra, 313; *La Rosaura,* 67; *Suite de festin de pierre,* 211; *Le voyage d'Arlequin et Scaramouche aux Indes,* 209

Magic, use of in comédie italienne, 204, 211, 373

Magie naturelle, La, 170–71, 212–14, 397; profits of, 83–84

Maintenon, marquise de, 248, 327–28

Maisons dévalizées, Les, 393

Maistre vallet, Le, 393

Ma maîtresse est préferable à tout autre chose, 393

Maladie de Scaramouche, La, 172, 397

Maladie de Spezzafer, La, 399

Mal-assortis, Les, 372–73, 403; *see also* Dufresny, Charles

Manzani, Francesco [Capitan Terremoto], 82; finances, 86; murder of, 97, 114–16

Marais, Théâtre du, 224

Marchand dupé, Le, 311, 357–59, 401

Mari, Le, 396

Mariage d'Arlequin, Le, 244, 400

Marie-Christine of Bavaria (dauphine), authority over actors, 242–43

Marie de Medici, 17, 19–20

Marie-Thérèse (queen of France), 102

Maritaggion d'una statua, Il, 394

Martinelli, Tristano, 17, 19–20

Marvelous, the, *Le voyage d'Arlequin et Scaramouche aux Indes* as example of, 209

Matrone d'Ephèse, La, ou Arlequin Grapignan, 285–87, 399; authorship, 281–

Matrone d'Ephèse, La (cont.)
    82; publication suppressed, 277; *see
    also* Monsieur D***
Mazarin, Cardinal, 19
Médecin vollant, Le, 147–49, 393
Médecins raillés, Les, 401
Métamorphoses d'Arlequin, Les, 170, 394
Metatheatricality, in the baroque theatre,
    219–20
Mezzetin Grand Sophy de Perse, 313–14,
    359–60; *see also* Delosme de
    Montchenay
Mic, Constant, 7
Mirame, 87
"Mlle. Beatrix," *see* Vitelli, Beatrice
Modena, troupe of, 1651, 101
Molière [Jean-Baptiste Poquelin], 97,
    158, 168, 219; *L'avare,* 129; *Le bour-
    geois gentilhomme,* 202; *Dom Juan,*
    161, 218; *L'école des femmes,* 129,
    360; *Le malade imaginaire,* 157, 198;
    Les précieuses ridicules, 77; *Psyché,*
    161–62, 167; *Tartuffe,* 100, 129, 135,
    218
Molière, troupe of: 86–87; agreement,
    with Comédie-Italienne, 162–63;
    quarrel, with Comédie-Italienne,
    176–79; shares Guénégaud with
    Comédie-Italienne, 158; shares
    Palais-Royal with Comédie-
    Italienne, 83, 86–87; shares Petit-
    Bourbon with Comédie-Italienne,
    27; subvention of, 84
Molinari, Cesare, 7, 122
Mollier, Louis de, 418 n. 60
Momies d'Egypt, Les, 372–73, 405; *see also*
    Dufresny, Charles, *and* Regnard,
    Jean-François
Monde renversé, Le, 195, 395
Mongin (playwright), 354
Monsieur D***, 280–83, 354; *see also* Fa-
    touville, Anne Mauduit de
Monsieur S (playwright), 182
Morts vivans, Les, 147, 392
Motto, new (1686), for Comédie-
    Italienne, 236–37
Ms. 9329 (Bibliothèque Nationale,
    Paris), 129, 192–93, 419 n. 17, 422
    n. 1
Muette, La, 244; *see also Isabelle Muette
    par amour*

Music: *Arlequin mercure galant,* 284–85; *Le
    collier de perle,* 203–4; in comedy of
    intrigue, 375; *La magie naturelle,*
    213; opportunities for, 385; *La Ro-
    saura,* 67; *Suite de festin de pierre,* 211;
    Le théâtre italien, 383–86; *Le voyage
    d'Arlequin et Scaramouche aux Indes,*
    209; use by Comédie-Italienne, 166

Naissance d'Amadis, La, 372–73, 403; *see
    also* Regnard, Jean-François
Naïveté in comédie italienne, 147
Napolioni, Marco [Flaminio], 49
Naseli, Alberto [Zan Ganassa], 15
Ne prête ny ta femme ny ton epée à personne,
    395
Nicoll, Allardyce, 6
Noce de village, La, 239
Nopce d'arlequin, La, 244, 394

Obscenity in comédie italienne, 147–48,
    321–23, 325–26, 329
Octave et Arlequin soldats enrollés par force,
    400
Opéra, privilege of, 166
L'opéra de compagne, 369–71, 403; *see also*
    Dufresny, Charles
Orator, function of, 173–74
Originaux, Les, 377–78, 403; *see also*
    D. L. M.

Palais-Royal, Grande Salle of, 22, 87–89;
    changeable scenery, 87, 94–95; di-
    mensions, 89–91; "great beam" in,
    94; raked parterre in, 91–93; recon-
    struction, 1671, 173–74; reconstruc-
    tion, 1660, 89–95; shared by
    Italians, 96
Palaprat, Jean, 354
"Pantalon," 120–21, 156, 188–89
Paris: in stage settings, 57–59; fashion-
    able resorts of, 376
Parlement de Paris, 15–16
Parody: of *Bérénice,* 291–92; of *Le Cid,*
    288–89; of French tragedy, 201–2;
    legal, 284, 286–87; musical, 384; of
    the Opéra, 369–72, 385; of *La toison
    d'or,* 297
Pasquin et Marforio, médecins des moeurs,
    381–82, 405; *see also* Biancolelli,
    Louis, *and* Dufresny, Charles

Pastoral, *La Rosaura* as, 70
Patro, Clara, 267; *see also* Fracansani, Michelangelo
Patronage: by Anne of Austria and Cardinal Mazarin, 19–21; by the French monarchy, 15; by Henri IV, 17, 19–20; by Louis XIII, 17; by Louis XIV, 21, 82; by Marie de Medici, 17, 19–20; end of, 241
Pauvreté de Renaut de Montauban, La, 393
Peintre par amour, 405
Pension system, 242
Percée & Andromède par enchantement, 405
Performance times, 29
Petit-Bourbon, Grande Salle of, 22–25; access, 25–26; demolition, 86; dimensions, 23; location, 26; loges, 28
Petits marquis, burlesques of, 195–96, 202, 239–40
Phénix, Le, 365–66, 402; *see also* Delosme de Montchenay
"Pierrot," *see* Giaratoni, Giuseppe
Playing days, 27–28, 83, 241
"Polichinelle," 427 n. 41; *see also* Fracansani, Michelangelo
Pontchartrain, comte de, 325–26, 331
Pont neuf, Le, 394
Portrait amoureux, Le, 393
Posters, 173–74
Poulain, Jeanne Marie, 112; *see also* Bendinelli, Giacinto
Précaution inutile, La, 367–69, 403; *see also* Monsieur D***
Prisonnier vindicatif, Le, 393
Promenades de Paris, Les, 376, 404; *see also* Mongin
Propreté, ou Arlequin roy de Tripoli, La, 169, 397; self-referential elements, 219
Prosperité des armes de France, La, 87
Public theatre, typical 17th-century, 25
Publicity, *see* gazetteers
Pure, abbé de, 77, 165, 175–76

Quatre Arlequins, Les, 393
Quatre Scaramouches, Les, 398
Quattre Scaramuccie, 394

Ranieri, Bartolomeo [Aurelio], 250, 265, 332; banished to Italy, 266

Régal des dames, Le, 107, 155–56, 183, 193–96, 394
Règlement of Madame la Dauphine, 235–36, 242–43
Regnard, Jean-François, 353–54
Remède de anglois, Le, 223, 307, 398
Remède à tous maux, Le, 171, 394; French harangue in, 197–98
Retirement, 254
Retour de la foire de Bezons, Le, 326, 372, 375, 404; *see also* Brugière de Barante, *and* Gherardi, Evaristo
Riccoboni, Antonio, 188–89
Riccoboni, Luigi, 7, 98, 105, 123, 185, 188–91, 350
Richelieu, Armand-Jean du Plessis, duc de, 18–19, 157; and Palais-Royal, 22, 87–89
Romagnesi, Auguste-Alexandre, 181, 346
Romagnesi, Charles-Virgile [Léandre], 181, 341–42, 346, 351
Romagnesi, Gaetan, 181, 346
Romagnesi, Hierôme-Alexandre, 181, 346
Romagnesi, Hipolite, 181, 346
Romagnesi, Marc' Antonio [Cinthio, Docteur], 39, 156, 180–82, 250, 277–78, 332; author of *Poésies héroiques et amoureuses, sacrées et morales,* 182; children, 181, 346; death, 346; as French vieillard, 382; marriage, 180; naturalization, 270; quarrel with Costantini, 318; scenarios by, 182; son of Brigida Fedele, 39
Romagnesi, N. [Christian name unknown], 39
Rosaura imperatrice di Constantinopli, La [*La Rosaure impératrice de Constantinople*], 30, 65–70, 392, distribution of roles, 68–69; expenses, 69; improvisation, 66; music, 67; opening, 65; settings, 65–66; special effects, 67–68

Sacrati, Francesco, 53
St.-Simon, duc de, 327
Satire: in early repertory, 144; French style, 287; legal, 292
Satires, as literary ornaments, 386

Scala, Flaminio, 6; author of *Il teatro delle favole rappresentative*, 123–24
"Scaramouche," *see* Cei, Giralomo; Fiorilli, Tiberio; Tortoriti, Giuseppe
Scaramouche ermite, 393
Scaramouche pédant et Arlequin écolier, 395
"Scaramouche, table de," 57–68
"Scène pour l'avocat juge et partie," 398
Scenic spectacle, 56–61, 65–66, 169–71; *Arlequin Protée*, 229–30; *Il convitato di pietra*, 75–76; *Dom Juan*, 94; at Hôtel de Bourgogne in 1680, 229; at Hôtel de Bourgogne in 1688–89, 313–14; in pre-1668 repertory, 94–95, 145; *Psyché*, 161; *Le régal des dames*, 156, 194; as source of quarrel with French, 176–79; *Le voyage d'Arlequin et Scaramouche aux Indes*, 209; *Ulisse et Circé*, 364–65; *see also* Machines
Self-reference in comédie italienne, 283, 292
Sexual innuendo in comédie italienne, 147
Shares, 27, 242
Sincerita triomfante, La, 58
Soldat par vengeance, Le, ou Arlequin soldat en Candie, 395
Souffleurs, Les, 403
Souhaits, Les, 378, 403; *see also* Delosme de Montchenay
Sourdéac, marquis de, 163–64
Spanish sources, 145–46
Special effects: *La magie naturelle*, 212–14; *Le régal des dames*, 194; *La Rosaura*, 67
Spinette lutin amoureux, 276, 405
Strozzi, Giulio, see *Finta pazza, La*
Subventions, 82–84, 156, 241–42; *see also* Patronage
Suite du festin de pierre, 169, 211, 396
Suite du théâtre italien, 279
Supplément du théâtre italien, 276, 422 n. 5

Tapis, Les, 393
Tarquin et Lucrece, 405
Théâtre italien, pirated editions, 192–93, 276, 279; *see also* Gherardi, Evaristo
Théâtre sans comédie, Le, 172, 394; French harangue in, 196–97; self-referential elements, 219
Theatre staff: 1680s, 240; 1659–60, 28; 1674, 172–74; 1661–62, 96

Thèse des dames, La, 375, 404; *see also* Biancolelli, Louis
Ticket prices, 97–98, 240–41
Time of performance, 175
Tipi fissi, 4
Tipping, 172
Tirso de Molina, *El burlador de Sevilla*, 70, 75
Toison d'or, La, 233
Tombeau de Maistre André, Le, 372, 374, 404; *see also* Biancolelli, Louis
Torelli, Giacomo, 23–25, 53; "author" of *Explication des décorations du théâtre et les Argumens de la pièce*, 53; loss of favor at court, 69–70; quarrel with Italian troupe, 53–55; settings for *La finta pazza*, 53, 55–61; settings for *La Rosaura*, 66
Tortoriti, Giuseppe [Pasquariel, Scaramouche], 104, 250, 332; debut, 262, 304; inherits role of Scaramouche, 342; marriage, 262–64; provincial troupe of, 350–51; request for naturalization, 264; *see also* Toscana, Angela
Toscana, Angela [Marinette, Angélique], 262–64, 333, 340; *see also* Tortoriti, Giuseppe
Travesties, 143, 155, 170, 193–94, 215–16
Triumvirat de l'amitiez, Le, 393
Trois faux turcs, Les, 393
Trois volleurs decouverts, Les, 393
Trompeurs trompez, Les, 397; French harangue in, 198–99
Turgis, Constantin de, *see* Biancolelli, Françoise
Turri, Giovan Battista [Pantalon], 48, 250, 258–60, 332
Turri *fils* [Virginio], 48, 260

Ulisse et Circé, 364–65, 402; *see also* L.A.D.S.M.
L'union des deux opéras, 372, 403; *see also* Dufresny, Charles

Versailles, theatre built at, 245–46
Verse, use of in comédie italienne, 386
Vie de Scaramouche, La, 32–35; value of, 409 n. 12; *see also* Costantini, Angelo
Vieille grotte, La, 393

Vigarani, Carlo, 70, 89–90
Villiers, sieur de, 76
Violence: in comédie italienne, 149; at Palais-Royal, 96–97; in the theatre, 175–76, 240
Vitelli, Beatrice [Mlle. Beatrix], 49, 51
Voyage de Scaramouche et d'Arlequin aux Indes, Le, 105, 168–70, 187, 193, 204–8, 397; authorship, 204; French synopsis, 204

Zan Ganassa, *see* Naseli, Alberto
Zanni, comic routines of, in *Il convitato di pietra,* 71–75
Zanotti, Giovan Andrea [Octave], 47–48, 51, 82, 119, 260; death, 264; "the excellent Zanotti," 99, 112; in Modena troupe, 101; retirement to Italy, 264–265; second marriage, 189
Zibaldone di Perugia, 129